The Democrats' Dilemma: Walter F. Mondale and the Liberal Legacy

The Contemporary American History Series
William E. Leuchtenburg, General Editor

Contemporary American History Series
William E. Leuchtenberg, General Editor

Lawrence S. Wittner, *Rebels Against War: The American Peace Movement, 1941–1960* 1969

Davis R. B. Ross, *Preparing for Ulysses: Politics and Veterans During World War II* 1969

John Lewis Gaddis, *The United States and the Origins of the Cold War, 1941–1947* 1972

George C. Herring, Jr., *Aid to Russia, 1941–1946: Strategy, Diplomacy, the Origins of the Cold War* 1973

Alonzo L. Hamby, *Beyond the New Deal: Harry S. Truman and American Liberalism* 1973

Richard M. Fried, *Men Against McCarthy* 1976

Steven F. Lawson, *Black Ballots: Voting Rights in the South, 1944–1969* 1976

Carl M. Brauer, *John F. Kennedy and the Second Reconstruction* 1977

Maeva Marcus, *Truman and the Steel Seizure Case: The Limits of Presidential Power* 1977

Morton Sosna, *In Search of the Silent South: Southern Liberals and the Race Issue* 1977

Robert M. Collins, *The Business Response to Keynes, 1929–1964* 1981

Robert M. Hathaway, *Ambiguous Partnership: Britain and America, 1944–1947* 1981

Leonard Dinnerstein, *America and the Survivors of the Holocaust* 1982

Lawrence S. Wittner, *American Intervention in Greece, 1943–1949* 1982

Nancy Bernkopf Tucker, *Patterns in the Dust: Chinese-American Relations and the Recognition Controversy, 1940–1950* 1983

Catherine A. Barnes, *Journey from Jim Crow: The Desegregation of Southern Transit* 1983

Steven F. Lawson, *In Pursuit of Power: Southern Blacks and Electoral Politics, 1965–1982* 1985

David R. Colburn, *Racial Change and Community Crisis: St. Augustine, Florida, 1877–1980* 1985

Henry William Brands, *Cold Warriors: Eisenhower's Generation and the Making of American Foreign Policy* 1988

Marc S. Gallicchio, *The Cold War Begins in Asia: American East Asian Policy and the Fall of the Japanese Empire* 1988

Melanie Billings-Yun, *Decision Against War: Eisenhower and Dien Bien Phu* 1988

Walter L. Hixson, *George F. Kennan: Cold War Iconoclast* 1989

Mitchell G. Hall, *Because of Their Faith: CALCAV and Religious Opposition to the Vietnam War* 1990

Robert D. Schulzinger, *Henry Kissinger: Doctor of Diplomacy* 1990

Henry William Brands, *The Specter of Neutralism: The United States and the Emergence of the Third World, 1947–1960* 1990

David Anderson, *Trapped By Success: The Eisenhower Administration and Vietnam* 1990

The Democrats' Dilemma:
Walter F. Mondale and the
Liberal Legacy

Steven M. Gillon

Columbia University Press
New York

This book was published with the assistance of the Frederick W. Hilles Publications
Fund of Yale University

Columbia University Press
New York   Oxford

Library of Congress Cataloging-in-Publication Data.
Gillon, Steven M.
    The Democrats' dilemma : Walter F. Mondale and the liberal
legalist / Steven M. Gillon.
        p.   c.m. — (The Contemporary American history series)
    Includes bibliographical references and index.
    ISBN 0–231–07630-4 (acid-free paper)
        1. Mondale, Walter F., 1928- .   2. Presidential candidates—
United States—Biography.   3. Legislators—United States—
Biography.   4. United States. Congress. Senate—Biography.
    5. United States—Politics and government—1945–1989.
    6. Liberalism—United States—History—20th century.   I. Title.
    II. Series.
    E840.8.M66G55   1992
    973.926'092—dc20
        [B]   92-8339
                                                                                     CIP

Casebound editions of Columbia University Press
books are Smyth-sewn and printed on permanent
and durable acid-free paper.

Book design by Teresa Bonner
Printed in the United States of America
c 10 9 8 7 6 5 4 3 2

This book is dedicated with love
to
Catherine and Benjamin Waldov
and to
the memory of
Alice and Francis Gillon

Contents

Preface

I met Walter Mondale for the first time in November 1986, two years after his crushing defeat in the 1984 presidential campaign. He sat in the comfortable confines of his Washington, D.C law office, playfully toying with a large Cuban cigar. Deep, heavy pockets shadowed his blue eyes, the expression on his pale face seemed lifeless. "Who would want to read a book about me?" he asked while fidgeting in his chair. I responded that his career served as a prism for viewing recent American politics. He remained unconvinced. "OK," he said, cutting short my rambling discourse. "So maybe Lane Kirkland will buy a copy."

After more thought he changed his mind. Over the next few years, in a series of thoughtful discussions, Mondale shared with me his private reflections about his career, liberalism, and the Democratic Party. Along with giving generously of his own time, he granted me unrestricted access to his rich collection of private papers at the Minnesota Historical Society. He encouraged friends and former associates to do the same, even when he knew the material provided was not always flattering. Stu Eizenstat, for one, gave me notes he had recorded while serving as President Carter's domestic policy advisor. These notes provided unique access to Mondale's private frustration as Vice President and were an indispensable resource for this study. Mondale also convinced the National Security Council to issue me a security clearance to examine briefing notes for his weekly meetings with the President, and for his Friday foreign policy discussions with Carter, Vance, Brzezinski and Turner.

Although he granted unrestricted access, Mondale exercised no editorial control over the manuscript. He read, with great care and precision, three drafts of the manuscript. Each reading was followed by long, sometimes heated, discussions about the book. These sessions proved enormously valuable. Not only did they provide an opportunity to correct factual mistakes, to elicit information, and to sharpen my perspective, but they also revealed to me the different dimensions of this complex figure. In some ways he is a man of striking contrasts. Though renowned for his compassion and decency, he can be indifferent and imperious to those around him. In public he frequently appeared reserved, dispassionate, and sometimes stodgy; but in private encounters he could be witty, stimulating, and fervent. For a man who has spent most of his adult life in the rough-and-tumble world of national politics, he remains surprisingly sensitive to criticism.

Though he played a major part in the book's development, Mondale does not endorse any of its conclusions. He believes that, especially in the years after 1974, I have presented an unfair portrait. "Its like a goddamn lead ball drops on my head in 1974," he fulminated. He thinks I have exaggerated his differences with President Carter, overplayed his flirtation with resignation as vice president during the spring of 1979, and placed too much emphasis on his personal limitations in my discussion of the 1984 campaign. Yet much to his credit, even after reading the drafts and expressing his displeasure, Mondale continued to provide interviews and valuable manuscript material.

Those who pick up the book for the first time may also harbor doubts. The obvious question that comes to mind is why a book about Walter Mondale? After 1984 he seemed destined to become a trivia question for some future television game show. The political analyst Kevin Phillips dismissed him—along with George McGovern, Jimmy Carter and Michael Dukakis—as one of "the four faces on the Mount Losemore of American Politics." I believe it would be a mistake, however, to allow Mondale's defeat in the 1984 presidential campaign to blind us to the insight his career can provide. In many ways, his experience serves as a metaphor for the plight of the modern Democratic Party. He journeyed to Washington in 1964, filling the seat vacated by Vice President Hubert Humphrey. That year, the Johnson–Humphrey ticket scored a massive landslide, winning 44 states, 486 electoral votes, and 61 percent of the popular vote. Over the next two decades, Mondale had a hand in crafting or passing almost every major piece of Democratic social legislation, served four years as Vice President, and ran in three national elections—more than any other Democrat since Roosevelt. Yet, twenty years after Johnson's electoral landslide, Mondale, running as the Democratic nominee for President, won only his home state of Minnesota and the District of Columbia.

Mondale was a transitional figure between two generations of Democrats. On one side of the divide stood those whose historical memory was rooted in the economic emergency of the depression and the tragedy of Munich. These liberals hoped to sustain the New Deal coalition through appeals to economic self-interest and vigilant anticommunism. On the other side stood younger Democrats whose perceptions were shaped by postwar affluence and the "lessons of Vietnam." "We were the children of Vietnam, not children of World War II," declared Colorado Senator Tim Wirth in defining his differences with many older Democrats. "We were products of television, not of print. We were products of computer politics, not courthouse politics. And we were reflections of JFK as president, not FDR." The competition between these groups created deep generational and ideological divisions within the party.[1]

In the years after 1972—as a Senator, Vice President, and presidential candidate—Mondale played the central role in building consensus among the party's competing factions. Self-consciously trying to fill the void left by Robert Kennedy's death, Mondale hoped to convince all Democrats—liberal and conservative, black and white—that they shared a common agenda. Since the Democrats lost four of the next five presidential campaigns, it is obvious that Mondale's ambitious goal went unfulfilled. In many ways, he was not the ideal person to play the role of party healer. A product of the unique Minnesota political environment in which he had been raised, Mondale hoped to forge a national community of Democrats through personal contact with the leaders of representative groups. Although deeply rooted in tradition, Mondale's political vision was increasingly irrelevant to national Democratic politics.

The problems confronting the Democratic party, however, transcend the personal limitations of any one man. Perhaps no individual could have united the party in the years after 1968. The emergence of controversial social issues such as school prayer, abortion, crime, and homosexual rights, have eroded support for traditional Democratic appeals to economic self-interest and altered the battle lines in American politics. Since 1968, Republicans successfully defined the debate over these issues as a clash between the insurgent values of a liberal elite and the traditional values of middle-class Americans. This new conservative populism has replaced contempt for greedy businessmen with a disdain for lenient judges, unresponsive bureaucrats, and arrogant minorities. "Just as the Civil War dominated American political life for decades after it ended," observed the journalist E.J. Dionne, "so is the cultural civil war of the 1960s, with all its tensions and contradictions, shaping our politics today."[2]

Perhaps no issue has been more explosive than race. As the national Democratic Party became identified with the civil rights struggles, the white South as well as many urban ethnics in the Northeast and Midwest moved comfortably into Republican hands. Many of these voters no longer viewed the Democratic Party as a vehicle for advancing the economic well-being of all Americans, but as a hostage of its black constituents. The party's support for controversial policies such as affirmative action and busing, the growing visibility of "threatening" leaders such as Jesse Jackson, and fears about the emergence of a "black underclass," have fed old racial stereotypes and further divided the races. Race is the prism through which many of the new social issues are filtered. As the journalist Thomas Edsall concluded: "Race helps define liberal and conservative ideologies, shapes the presidential coalitions of the Democratic and Republican parties, provides a harsh new dimension to concern over taxes and crime, drives a wedge through alliances of the working classes and the poor, and gives momentum and vitality to the drive to establish a national majority inclined by income and demography to support policies benefiting the affluent and the upper-middle class."[3]

Part of the problem was that Democrats scorned ideology at a time when technology increased the importance of ideological appeals in American politics. The 1960s left deep emotional scars on the conscience of American liberals. Many believed their blind acceptance of Cold War assumptions prevented them from foreseeing the tragic consequences of Vietnam, while their unquestioning faith that social progress at home could be achieved through gradual, piecemeal reform left them unprepared for the rise of black militancy and the resulting white backlash. They emerged from the decade uncomfortable with simplistic and painless suggestions that a growing economy could solve social problems, removing legal barriers could end racial discrimination, or fighting communism would secure America's position in the world. Convinced that problems of poverty and racial justice were far too complex and the patience of most Americans far too brief to allow for significant change, liberals have pursued a more circumscribed agenda. "Afraid to run on ideology, the Democrats ran as technicians," Robert Kuttner wrote, "and they were beaten by better technicians who were clearer about their own ideology and thus better able to manipulate powerful symbols."[4]

The party's rejection of its populist heritage stands as the most striking example of its abandonment of ideology. In the years after 1932, Democrats translated public resentment against the wealthy and powerful into a governing coalition. The party united its diverse coalition by championing the cause of the "common man" and identifying the Republicans as the defenders of special privilege. As the journalists Thomas Edsall and Robert Kuttner have shown, a series of social and institutional changes tilted the party away from the concerns of the working and lower-middle classes and toward the middle and upper-middle class. By 1984, as many of the poor and lower-class voters gradually withdrew from political participation, they were replaced by more established groups. Prosperity which weakened labor's influence, expensive television campaigns which required constant fundraising, electoral reform which increased the influence of more affluent voters, and campaign financing reform which strengthened the power of political action committees, had narrowed the class divisions between the Democratic and Republican parties. Like Republican candidates, Democrats had to rely upon big business—real estate magnates, insurance agents, investment bankers—to fund their campaigns.[5]

Finally, Democrats were unable to develop a style of campaigning appropriate for an age of mass media. Television forced candidates to speak to general audiences and to articulate themes that could appeal to a broad spectrum of the electorate. This proved difficult to a generation nurtured on union halls, interest-group conventions, and political rallies where the message was geared to the specific audience.

These problems haunted Mondale's 1984 presidential campaign and help account for his devastating defeat. Though Mondale's weaknesses and Reagan's extraordinary popularity helped shape the election's outcome, the dimensions of the Republican triumph indicated that voters were rejecting more than one particular nominee. "What was defeated in 1984 was not some fringe candidate, not someone demonstrably unfit to govern the nation," commented the political scientist William Galston. "It was the Democratic party itself, as it had come to be perceived by a strong majority of Americans."[6]

As they confront the last decade of the twentieth century, Democrats are undergoing a painful redefinition. The liberal legacy, which had sustained Democrats for thirty years and had helped the party achieve its greatest electoral victories, had become a burden. The declining liberal fortunes have forced Democrats to confront a painful dilemma: How does the party of Franklin Roosevelt and Harry Truman attract more conservative and independent voters without alienating its loyal supporters? In order to escape its predicament, Democrats must retain the allegiance of blacks while winning back southern whites and working class ethnics. The party must continue to arouse the enthusiasm of liberal activists at the same time that it courts more conservative voters. Finally, Democrats must articulate a single compelling vision that energizes middle-class America without abandoning the concerns of its marginalized constituencies.

Along with providing insight into the modern Democratic Party, a study of Mondale's career suggests that historians need to develop a better framework for understanding political change in twentieth-century America. For decades, liberal historians have used the success of major reform movements—progressivism, New Deal, and the Great Society—and the achievements of "great" leaders—Woodrow Wilson, Franklin Roosevelt, Harry Truman, and John F. Kennedy—to chart the steady triumph of liberal values in America. Charting the extraordinary growth in the size and scope of the national government, and celebrating the achievements of successful presidents, does not fully explain the dynamics of American politics in the twentieth-century. As the years after 1968 indicate, enacting legislation does not always alter public attitudes. Despite three major civil rights laws, racial attitudes have changed little; despite a dramatic increase in spending for social welfare, public perceptions of the poor have remained remarkably constant. I believe that American politics has been characterized by a tension between the haphazard growth in the size of the federal government and the persistence of conservative attitudes about race, limited government, self-help, and individualism. This tension defines the nature of the problem against which Walter Mondale and the Democratic Party had to struggle in the years after 1968.

Acknowledgments

I have incurred many debts during the four years that I worked on this book. A Morse junior faculty fellowship allowed me to devote the 1987–88 academic year to the project. Grants from the Griswold Fund and the Enders Foundation helped defray some of the expenses I incurred traveling to Washington and Minneapolis. During the summer of 1987, I shared a small two-bedroom house in Georgetown with seven students. The generosity of my roommates, and the friendships that were cemented during those months, compensated for the cramped living quarters and the oppressive Washington heat. My thanks to the friends who made that summer so memorable: Greg Weinberger, Dennis Jones, Jim Ryan, Roger Wynne, David Hoffman, Tracy Mehr, and Nanette Ferrell.

During that sultry summer, I talked with many close Mondale friends and associates. None was more able and accessible than Jim Johnson. I relied heavily on his nearly photographic memory and keen insight. Mike Berman, whose relationship with Mondale spans three decades, offered perceptive comments about his former bosses' personality and temperament. Richard Moe, who from 1977 to 1980 served on the President's senior staff and as Mondale's chief-of-staff, provided the most acute analysis of the Carter-Mondale relationship. Finally, Stuart Eisenstat, the soft-spoken former domestic policy advisor, allowed me to view the private notes of his conversations with Mondale, and gave generously of his time and thoughts. All read drafts of the manuscript and offered useful criticism.

Over the next three years, many people took time from their busy schedules to talk with me. The bibliography lists my debt to all of these people, but a few deserve special mention. Marty Kaplan allowed me to examine dozens of boxes of speech material from the 1984 presidential campaign. In exchange, I cleaned and organized the storage room on the grounds of his elegant Hollywood Hills home. I spent two enlightening hours with Bill Galston, a sharp critic and perceptive observer of the modern Democratic party. The numerous references to Finlay Lewis only begin to suggest the extent of my debt to him. Bob Schulzinger, my "anonymous" reader, offered a thoughtful critique of the manuscript.

Many librarians, secretaries, and office assistants, facilitated my research. At the Minnesota Historical Society, Steve Nielsen and Ruby Shields shuttled hundreds of manuscript boxes to my desk, photocopied thousands of pages of material, and answered dozens of stupid questions. A special thanks to Ruth Brauer who frequently cut through bureaucratic red tape to get the information I needed. Lynda "pronto pup" Pedersen, Mondale's perpetually cheerful and efficient secretary, Ross Corson, and Amy Klobuchar helped make my trips to Minneapolis more enjoyable. Frank Wright and Sylvia Frisch of the Minneapolis *Star-Tribune,* allowed me to rummage through the *Tribune*'s newspaper clippings. Rick Boyland, Secretary of the Democratic Party, granted access to the DNC Papers in the National Archives, and answered numerous questions as I fumbled through the collection. Judy Koucky, Nancy Smith, and Doug Thurmond guided me through the National Archives maze. My thanks to the unknown person at the National Security Council who granted me a security clearance. Diania Walker, *Time*'s brilliant photojournalist, gave permission to use a number of her photographs in the book. Also, Mark Solomon made available photographs from the Time/ Life, collection. At Columbia University Press I am grateful to Kate Wittenberg, who guided this project to completion, and to Leslie Bialler, who edited the manuscript with skill and patience.

I have also benefited from the advice of a number of friends and colleagues. Gary Ginsberg, a talented lawyer and a good friend; Jim

Ryan, a Yale graduate and aspiring lawyer; and Jonathan Cedarbaum, a promising historian in his own right, read early chapters and made useful comments. I have profited in many ways from the wise counsel of my mentor, James T. Patterson. On this occasion, his penetrating criticisms of an early draft led me to cancel a summer vacation in California and instead spend the time rewriting in New Haven. I hope that some day I can return the favor! Alan Brinkley, who has been a good friend and a constant source of support and encouragement, read the manuscript and made many helpful suggestions. As always, I benefited from the wisdom of John Blum, who retired from Yale in 1991 after a brilliant career as a teacher and scholar. A number of other colleagues—Jon Butler, Bill Cronin, Gaddis Smith, John Boswell, Ramsey McMullen, and Howard Lamar—have made my Yale experience more enjoyable and rewarding.

The Mondale family has patiently endured my numerous requests for information. Though not always satisfied with my conclusions, Walter Mondale never waivered in his commitment to the project. He blocked out whole days for our meetings; he made phone calls and wrote letters on my behalf; and he read three drafts of the manuscript. Joan, who also gave generously of her time, spoke candidly about the joys and frustrations of being married to a public man. Clarence shared family letters and old photographs. Lester, the family historian, offered valuable insight into the family's early years.

I am grateful for having the opportunity to work so closely with Bill Leuchtenburg on this book. Until recently, I had known of him only by his reputation as a brilliant historian and editor, a tough critic, and a warm and gracious man. Over the past few months I have had the opportunity to experience first-hand each of these qualities. Despite his busy schedule, Bill spent countless hours reading the manuscript, exorcising weak verbs, pruning repetitive words, clarifying turgid prose, and simplifying tortured logic. But understanding that young scholars have delicate egos, he always mixed gentle words of encouragement with his criticism. He has strengthened this book, and he has inspired me to become a better historian.

The Democrats' Dilemma: Walter F. Mondale
and the Liberal Legacy

A Father's Faith

By the middle of the nineteenth century wrenching economic changes were undermining the community life which the Mundal family had known for generations on the western coast of Norway. For centuries steep mountains had separated the fertile rural communities from the distant cities. Life's essentials were produced and consumed within a closely knit community. But now a combination of overpopulation and mechanization were disrupting the tranquil life in the villages on Norway's beautiful fjords. As steamships and railroads introduced trade to the rural areas, self-supporting villages became threatened by the values of an emergent commercial urban society. "In the face of such conditions," wrote Theodore Blegen, "came reports of boundless fertile lands available for settlers in the [American] West."[1]

Frederick and Brita Mundal, who owned 60 acres of farmland on the shores of Fjäerland Fjord, shared these fears of encroaching urban life. Like many of their neighbors, the Mundals also wondered if their small farm could produce enough crops to feed their family of two sons, Ole and Hans, and daughter, Ingeborg. Many of the Mundal's neighbors and friends had already made the journey to America in hopes of finding fertile open lands. By 1850, nearly 20,000 Norwegians had emigrated, and over the next ten years 36,000 would follow.

In 1856, Frederick and Brita decided to join the sea of emigrants fleeing to America. They sold the farm and, with their three children, boarded a sailing ship in Bergen for the long trip to America. It was a difficult journey through temperamental winds and raging storms which forced the passengers to sit in the dark infested air below the ship's deck. Resting on straw between the decks, they huddled around a large barrel packed with food and supplies for the eight-week journey. The first phase of their voyage ended in New York, where they caught their first frightening glimpse of America. Abrupt immigration officials hurried them through the casual procedures at Castle Garden at the tip of Manhattan. When an immigration official suggested that adding a vowel to his surname would help him to "blend in," Frederick registered as Mundale.

From New York they boarded a train with a specially equipped immigrant car. "The modern ship of the Plains," as *Harper's* Magazine called it, was as barren as the ship on which they had crossed the Atlantic. And the trip across the continent was no less treacherous than that across the seas. For days they traveled in packed uncomfortable quarters until arriving in their temporary residence in Fox River, Illinois. After a brief stay they continued on to Wisconsin, a common resting point for Norwegians planning to settle in the Midwest. After spending five years in Wisconsin, the Mundales were lured across the Mississippi by word of abundant land in the Minnesota territory.

On July 4, 1864, Frederick purchased three acres and "twenty-eight rods" of land in Faribault County for seventy dollars. Described as a pioneer of the county, Frederick built a two-story log cabin. "Neighbors came from all around to see the structure when it was first completed," recalled a family member. "All neighborhood meetings and entertainments of any size were held there." Like the courageous protagonists in Ole Rolvaag's epic saga of Norwegian immigrants, *Giants in the Earth*, Frederick and Brita Mundale "threw themselves blindly into the Impossible, and accomplished the Unbelievable." Engulfed in the vast solitude of the prairie, they mastered the vicissitudes of pioneer life. Through resourcefulness, ingenuity, and abounding courage, they dealt with the monotonous but momentous events that daily threatened their livelihood: raising a patch of potatoes, snaring wild ducks for food, plastering a sod hut, protecting newly sown wheat from an early snow, capturing straying cows, huddling against the frigid cold.

In 1869, Frederick and Brita's son Ole, obtained land under the Homestead Act, which gave any person twenty-one years old who was a citizen, or had applied for citizenship, the right to claim for 160 acres. When the title papers came back from Washington they had misspelled Ole's name as Mondale. Fearing the discrepancy would cost him his land, Ole accepted his new name. Over the years, through hard work and considerable shrewdness, he transformed a small farm into a successful business. Unlike his father, who was known for his serious bouts with alcoholism, Ole was "the soul of temperance," rarely partaking of either drink or smoke. Trained in Norwegian and self-taught in English, he took pride in his accomplishments and set similar standards of success for his children.

Two of Ole's three sons inherited his personality and temperament. Hardy and resourceful, both Frederick and Edward were physical marvels, gifted with thick chests and powerful grips. Frederick, as legend has it, enjoyed entertaining bystanders by bending nails in his hands. Both were confident and poised, possessing their father's talent for quick talking and smooth business. The second-born son, Theodore, was different. Physically awkward, he lacked the strength and dexterity of his brothers. A severe stutter compounded his problems. Constantly ridiculed by friends and sometimes physically abused by his older brother, Theodore appeared the castaway of this rugged pioneer family. His father, clearly disappointed that young Theodore would not live up to his high standards, rarely spoke publicly about his son. Bragging endlessly about Frederick and Edward's exploits, he conveniently ignored the less talented Theodore. "He's slow," he explained to friends while a dejected Theodore stood by his side.[2]

When his father provided him with a fertile plot in Cottonwood County, Theodore resigned himself to continuing the family occupation of independent farming. To everyone's surprise he met modest success and in 1902 married Jesse Alice Larson of Redwood County. While his brothers struggled and eventually failed in business, Theodore and Jesse began raising a small family. In 1904 they gave birth to their first son, Lester. A second son, Clifford, followed two years later. In 1910, after losing an infant to meningitis, they adopted a daughter, Eleanor, whose deranged father had committed suicide. Demonstrating the compassion that would characterize his life, Theodore defied the customs of a society that shunned those who died in sin, and attended the funeral. "Dad was the only one with him when he was buried," recalled Lester. In January 1916, they had their last son.[3]

Despite his modest success, Theodore disliked farming and entertained hopes of entering the ministry. Although raised as a Lutheran, Theodore had bitter memories of the time when the strict Norwegian Lutheran Church expelled his father because of his heretical support of free will and rejection of predestination. Afterwards, Theodore was raised in the more pietistic Hauge Lutheran Church. By 1909, however, Theodore had converted to Methodism. He found his new faith more practical: less concerned with abstract theological questions and more involved in the everyday lives of common people. Once converted, he found greater satisfaction in his faith than ever before. For the first time, he became an active participant in the church. That same year, aided by a "mystical experience" while working in the fields, Theodore decided to quit farming and begin a career as a minister. In 1911, after completing a two-year home correspondence course, he graduated from Red Wing Seminary. With degree in hand, Theodore traveled to the Black Hills of South Dakota where he spent six weeks working among the silver and lead miners as a Methodist missionary before returning to Minnesota.

For the first few years, Theodore enjoyed remarkable success. Although physically and verbally awkward, he had a gift for caring— giving solace to the sick and helpless. This gift enabled him to overcome his handicaps and rise within the church hierarchy. For a brief time he revealed a talent for investment as well. As the demand for food created soaring property values during World War I, Theodore began purchasing small tracts in southern Minnesota. The prosperity was short-lived. At the end of the war, as government subsidies ceased and revitalized European farms flooded American markets, bankruptcies and foreclosures multiplied. Nationally, half a million farmers lost their farms. "When the depression came, the land all came back on my father," said Lester. "He could not pay the mortgage or the interest charges. So he lost all the land and suddenly was poor."[4]

It was the first of a series of calamities that befell Mondale. In February 1921, his wife began experiencing paralysis, first in her lower limbs then in her upper body. The pain increased and the paralysis spread until she lost her ability to speak clearly, to walk, or to tend to normal body functions. After more than two years of suffering, she died of encephalitis on June 1, 1923. While mourning the death of his wife, Theodore confronted his own deadly disease: lockjaw. Living on the brink of starvation for months, he eventually learned to open his mouth by manipulating a wooden cone-shaped instrument. "He lived on soup for a long while," said Lester.[5]

For months Theodore languished in depression. Nearing fifty, he had no money and his children were without a mother. Demonstrating a resiliency that would have impressed his immigrant grandparents, Theodore rebuilt his life. He acted on Jesse's death-bed suggestion that he contact Claribel Cowan, a woman fifteen years his junior, who had been a member of his church in Jeffers. After a brief correspondence, Theodore proposed. Claribel accepted Theodore's offer because of her fear of growing old alone and her desire to have children. "She was single and she thought she'd be single all her life," reflected a family member. "And that was a terrible fate for a woman in those days." In March 1925, just two years after his wife's death, Theodore and Claribel married in a small, private service.

It was not a match made in heaven. She had been raised in a prosperous family of Scottish descent, studied music at Northwestern, and developed an appreciation for the arts. He had struggled for most of his adult life, received minimal formal education, and possessed little interest in the arts. Claribel was tall and angular, with a warm, outgoing personality; Theodore was broad and stocky, and frequently stern and dour. Claribel had also grown accustomed to the independent lifestyle of a single professional woman and was more interested in giving music lessons or participating in the local choir than in performing many traditional household chores. These differences did not prevent them from transforming a marriage of convenience into a deep and loving relationship.[6]

Theodore's ordeal was not over. In December 1925, he was awakened by the sound of fire bells. As he ran to the window he confronted a horrible sight: flames shooting from the roof of his church. Reinvigorated by his marriage, Theodore erected a new church on the ashes of the old. Impressed by Mondale's resiliency, a church official noted that he "looked into a rather impossible future with a hope and a faith that would cheer the angels of heaven." Despite his accomplishments, the church frowned on twice-married ministers, and soon banished Mondale to Ceylon, a little town in southern Minnesota. Gradually reconciling himself to the status of a poor backwoods preacher, Theodore devoted more attention to raising a family. In 1926 Claribel gave birth to their first son, Clarence. Walter, nicknamed Fritz at birth, followed two years later in January 1928. A third son, Morton, was born in 1934.[7]

By the time of young Fritz's second birthday, his family, and thousands of other families across the nation, were gripped by fear and despair. The farm areas of the Midwest had been in a depression for most of the decade. The rest of the nation soon joined them. Capitalism had failed, the Reverend Mondale believed, and democracy would soon follow. More than a fourth of the labor force was unemployed. The newspapers carried stories of long bread lines and Hoovervilles—clusters of ramshackle huts made of tin and paper. In Minneapolis, the twenty thousand jobless exhausted the city's relief funds. A series of violent strikes between angry workers protesting against low wages, and unyielding businessmen eager to preserve their profits, raised fears that the social fabric was disintegrating. In 1932–33 farm-mortgage foreclosures became commonplace in a state where one-third of the population lived on farms or in villages dependent on farm income. Heaviest hit were the wheat counties in western Minnesota where the relief rolls swelled to 60 percent.[8]

The depression experience, combined with his own suffering, transformed the Reverend Mondale's political allegiance. Like most other Norwegians, he had always supported the Republican Party. "His first vote was for McKinley," recalled a family member. For the last few decades of the nineteenth century and first two of the twentieth, Lincoln's party proposed a more positive view of government than its Democratic rival. In response to pressure from numerous third-party movements, Republicans in Minnesota had enacted regulation of railroad and freight charges, a child labor law, and a workman's compensation act. Religious and ethnic rivalry had reinforced Mondale's identification with the Republicans. Mondale had identified the Democrats, the party of "rum, romanism, and rebellion," with cities, the Irish, and urban vice.[9]

The depression forced him to reconsider many of these ideas. Although he had never finished the eighth grade, Mondale read extensively about political issues and subscribed to both *The New Republic* and *The Nation*. His social philosophy mixed depression-bred economic populism with a traditional Scandinavian concern for community, and like many Norwegians, he rejected the American emphasis on self-interest and rugged individualism. Norwegians "hoped instead to retain the important features of the old-country community, its organic qualities, neighborly relationships, and co-operative spirit," commented one scholar.

Mondale believed the depression occurred because greed had undermined community values. The distant and impersonal forces of industry were destroying local institutions and eroding the independent, personalized way of life his grandparents had hoped to find in America. "I believe the greatest danger confronting capitalism is the ever increasing concentration of wealth in the hands of a few," he wrote in a local newspaper during the depression's early years. "The concentration of wealth gives an undue power to a well organized group for economical and political control and for further concentration of wealth and more complete control. Thus building up a plutocracy at the expense of democracy and of a just, and a stable economic order." Individual interest, in his view, should be subject to the test of community need. Government, which represented the collective will of its citizens and served as the best vehicle for expressing the public interest, had the right to regulate private power. The greatest threat to America's democratic promise, he believed, came not from eternal threats or collective government, but from the excesses of greed and exploitation by individuals.[10]

When the Republicans responded to the new economic realities of the 1930s with outworn nineteenth-century slogans about rugged individualism, Mondale turned to the Farmer-Labor Party, the most recent manifestation of Minnesota's long history of protest politics. Like the Grange of the 1860s, the Farmer's Alliance of the 1880s, and the Populists of the 1890s, the Farmer-Labor Party was nurtured by the bad times that fell upon the farmers. In 1930, with wheat prices plummeting and 70 percent of iron miners unemployed, agitated farmers and laborers turned to the charismatic Farmer-Labor candidate for governor, Floyd Olson. A handsome man of soaring oratory—"I am not a liberal," he said, "I am a radical"—Olson forged a broad coalition of farmers, workers, socialists and progressives behind his calls for a "cooperative commonwealth" of public ownership of industry, banks, and public utilities. "In the lore of this party of protest," wrote one observer, "he stands as the all-time champion of the underprivileged."[11]

First elected in 1930, Olson hoped to avoid confrontation with the conservative legislature by proposing a moderate program of reform. As the depression deepened, however, he took radical steps. With city streets overflowing with the unemployed, factories at a standstill and farm prices dropping, Olson moved dramatically to the left. "Just beyond the horizon is rampant lawlessness and possible revolution," he warned the legislature in 1933. "Only remedial social legislation . . . can prevent its appearance." At his party's 1934 convention, he reaffirmed his concern with "human welfare rather than with selfish privilege." As his rhetoric became more fiery, his measures grew more bold. He asked for a mortgage moratorium bill, higher taxes on corporations, unemployment insurance, and an end to labor injunctions.[12]

In 1932, Theodore refused to support Franklin Roosevelt—the "wet" Democratic candidate—and instead voted for Norman Thomas, the Socialist candidate for President. But over the next few years, as he witnessed the tangible benefits of many New Deal policies, he emerged as an ardent Roosevelt supporter. Theodore never received direct relief from the New Deal, but he knew of farmers whose income had increased because of the Agricultural Adjustment Act, heard stories of people who received life-saving relief from the Federal Emergency Relief Act, and saw the results of Works Progress Administration (WPA) spending in nearby towns. If any doubts remained, they dissipated in 1937 when Roosevelt made his impassioned attacks on "economic royalists," and his pledge to help "one-third of the nation" which remained "ill-housed, ill-clad, and ill-fed."[13]

Roosevelt and Olson emerged as the twin political icons in Theodore Mondale's vision of secular reform. By placing society's needs above individual rights they touched on a critical nerve; by asserting the government's responsibility to address social wrongs they established a mechanism for reform. They spoke the language of social bonding and placed blame where Mondale thought it belonged—on the shoulders of big business. Both leaders, he thought, made the critical adjustment that he had made in his personal philosophy. The old nineteenth-century of rugged individualism was no longer applicable to an emerging industrial order. Some form of regulation and control was necessary. Mondale believed these programs relieved suffering, preserved local democracy, and helped small towns and communities resist the growing influence of business greed.

In 1937, the Church reassigned Mondale to Elmore, Minnesota, less than a mile from the Iowa border. It was here, in a modest two-story frame house that sat halfway between Main Street and Elmore High School, that Fritz spent most of his childhood years. Built in the

1880s by a wealthy department store owner, the Mondale home was one of the largest in town. Just before the turn of the century the Methodist Church had purchased the house for its parsonage. Over time it had fallen into disrepair. "My mother broke down and cried when she saw it," recalled Clarence. "It was a ramshackle affair, the roof leaked and there was no insulation. We used to try and keep the furnace going with corncobs, but the breeze kept coming through."[14]

Elmore was a poor parish, even by rural depression-ridden Minnesota standards, and the Mondales were among the town's poorest residents. The family rarely earned more than $1,500 a year, including the few dollars Claribel made from music lessons. Because of the Mondales' frugal ways, the family always had a car, food on the table, and gifts under the tree at Christmas. The family kept food bills low by maintaining a large garden planted with tomatoes, sweet corn, cantaloupes, and green beans. During the summer, Fritz and his brothers took a small wagon through the streets and sold the produce, while Claribel canned vegetables for storage. Theodore also raised chickens which he slaughtered for food.

All the Mondale children were expected to supplement the family's meager income. After school and during summer vacations, Fritz worked long hours at odd jobs—grocer's clerk, newspaper delivery boy, and canning factory laborer. The canning factory employed him in the lowly chore of checking plants for pea lice— small green bugs that could destroy entire fields. During another summer, while picking corn side-by-side with migrant workers, Fritz participated in a strike for better working conditions.

The Mondales established demanding standards of conduct for their children. A strong sense of religiosity permeated the household. The children were required to attend regular church services and say prayers before meals. More important, Claribel and Theodore insisted that all thoughts and actions be in accordance with Christian values. "Was it the Christian thing to do?" Claribel asked repeatedly of her children. While the Mondales provided some latitude in allowing the children to decide for themselves what Christian behavior allowed, on some issues they were inflexible. Neither Claribel nor Theodore tolerated alcohol or gambling of any kind. Theodore once dragged Morton to the bedside of a man dying of cirrhosis of the liver to demonstrate the evils of drinking. "They could be the most strict, most fundamentalist kind of parents you were ever going to find," recalled Morton.[15]

A Scandinavian influence was also apparent in Fritz's upbringing.

"There is a restraint against feeling in general," one writer observed about Norwegians. "There is a restraint against enthusiasm . . . there is restraint in grief, and always, always restraint in showing your feelings." While strongly devoted to each other, Theodore and Claribel rarely displayed that affection in public. Emotional demonstrations, lying, or self-aggrandizement of any kind were considered un-Christian and expressly forbidden. They believed that passion in pursuit of a larger cause was acceptable, but demonstrations of emotions for personal reasons were self-indulgent and unnecessary. "In my family, the two things you were sure to get spanked for were lying or bragging about yourself," Fritz recalled. "Both were equally unacceptable."[16]

Any violations of the rigid code of conduct brought about a quick response. Minor infractions such as smoking, missing curfew, or performing poorly in school usually led to stern lectures. But when Fritz was caught stealing pennies from the Sunday collection, Mondale removed his son's pants and whipped his bottom until blood appeared. Theodore's punishment was swift and certain, but in some ways Claribel's was more painful. After a serious violation by one of her children, she sulked for days, making clear that she was personally offended by the transgression. "My mother was a great purveyor of guilt," recalled Morton.[17]

The Mondales were not all fire and brimstone though. Both Theodore and Claribel tried to provide a healthy, nurturing environment for their children. "There was always somebody in the house," recalled a childhood friend. "Mrs. Mondale would be giving music lessons in one room; Reverend Theodore would be advising somebody in another room. It was always noisy." During the summer, neighbors could hear music coming from the open windows as Claribel gave music lessons to local children. Many people had "Mondale" weddings or funerals where Mondale preached, Claribel played the piano, and Walter sang.[18]

As a teenager, Fritz rebelled against his parent's intense religiosity and discipline. Although his parents forbade gambling of any kind, Fritz could often be found playing pool at the local hall, his hat pulled down over his eyes to avoid detection. In an effort to avoid his regular music lessons, he once kicked the back out of a cello. He was also a renowned prankster. "A minister's son," Fritz recalled, "has to fight against the danger of being taken for a dandy." One of his favorite pranks was to expose the local bootlegger by hanging a sign on Main Street that read: "Bootlegger > this way." Halloween was always the most exciting night of the year for Fritz and his friends. An undated police report listed Fritz's offenses during one evening of mischief:

1. Tipped over toilets at Art Mosses, Collison's, Millers, Wells, and one east of Lange's.
2. Pushed down sign at Olson filling station.
3. Moved trailer off the road that others had put on the road down by the park.
4. Tipped over the flower pot east of frerichs.
5. Put ladder in road southwest of park.
6. Pushed flower pot over south of Lowery's.
7. Tipped over top of chimney at park.[19]

While religion was always an important matter in the Mondale household, young Fritz showed little interest. He frequently appeared restless during Sunday services, and on a few occasions had to be scolded for talking during his father's sermon. Despite his parents' emphasis on education, Fritz did not take school work seriously. In a curriculum limited to basic courses and functional skills, Fritz earned half of his high school credits in shorthand, typing, and bookkeeping. Even with this unchallenging course load, he ranked only thirteenth in a graduating class of twenty and scored in the fifty-sixth percentile on his college entrance exams. Fritz's casual attitude toward his studies frequently frustrated his father. "That Fritz," he once said to his son's Sunday school teacher, "he'll never amount to anything."[20]

Siblings and peers observed a certain restlessness in Fritz. Though they described him as "intense" and "headstrong," he rarely channeled his energy into constructive paths. For a brief time he focused his attention on sports. In high school, Fritz ran track, played basketball, and earned the name "Crazy Legs" as the left halfback on the football team. What people remember most about his sports days, however, was that while running the 220-yard dash during the final track meet of his high school career, he abruptly quit without finishing the race. "What the hell, there's no point in this—I'm not interested in this," he said to himself.

Like many other young men growing up in small rural towns, Fritz appreciated the warmth and comfort his community provided, but yearned to prove himself on a larger stage. "There was a sense of envy of the larger world," reflected Clarence. "A feeling that if you had any reason you should try for it." The automobile, by shrinking the distance between cities, fed this instinctive curiosity about life outside of Elmore. In 1938, the first paved road was built between

Blue Earth and Elmore. Bus service began shortly thereafter. At one time, local residents had depended on the community for all their needs. Now they could travel to outside towns which provided a greater variety of goods.

The radio and newspapers carried news from far-off places while the local movie theater reminded residents of the possibilities that lay outside the community. In 1936, the entire family gathered around the radio to hear FDR's vibrant speech at Madison Square Garden: "I should like to have it said of my first administration that in it these forces of selfishness and lust for power met their match. I should like to have it said of my second administration that in it these forces met their master." Later, Fritz lay in bed listening to the CBS radio as it brought word of the oncoming European war. He listened in suspenseful anticipation as Edward R. Murrow, Charles Collingwood, Howard K. Smith, and other pioneers of modern broadcasting described the onward march of German soldiers through Denmark, Holland, Belgium, and finally France. The resonant voice of Edward R. Murrow—"This is London"—projected across thousands of miles captured the howling of sirens and the pounding of antiaircraft guns in a distant city.[21]

The Mondales encouraged their children to explore the world outside Elmore. "I was fortunate to have a literate mother and a father who insisted we read, listen to the news, and discuss issues over the dining room table," Fritz recalled. Hoping to avoid becoming victims of what Sinclair Lewis called the "Village Virus," which infected "ambitious people who stay too long in the provinces," the Mondales frequently invited traveling ministers to entertain the family with stories about their travels to exotic places. Among Fritz's favorites were ministers who had traveled to China. When singing groups from black colleges passed through town on fund-raising tours, the Mondales provided shelter. The gesture, not always appreciated by the community, reflected the Mondales openness to all kinds of people.

Despite his meager resources, the Reverend Mondale took his family to Yellowstone Park in 1938, and in 1941 he loaded his wife and children into the family Ford for a trip to the nation's capital. Their green 1935 Ford pulled a dilapidated house trailer that he had built and stocked with canned goods, a stove, and beds so the family would not have to buy food or lodging along the way. "I don't know how he did it," said Lester. "He was not a great man with his hands."

But the Reverend Mondale got the dresser out of the bedroom and the oil stove out of the kitchen and he crowded them on the trailer and headed east. After four weeks they finally arrived in Washington. They spent the night camped out on the banks of the Potomac after driving more than 1,200 miles from their home in Elmore. The next day, the Reverend Mondale called on Henrik Shipstead, Minnesota's Farmer-Labor Senator, to talk over some of his ideas. "I was roaming through there barefoot," Fritz recalled, "and they must have thought we were starving because old Henry Shipstead took us right down to the dining room and bought us all the spaghetti we could eat." Fritz sat down with his feet tucked under the tablecloth so that nobody could see them.[22]

After their meeting, the family took in the various tourist attractions. As they walked through the Capitol, the Reverend Mondale spied a statue of the Wisconsin reformer, Robert La Follette. "He was a great man, a man of the people," Mondale said. Outside the National Gallery of Art, Mondale read from a small plaque indicating the building had been constructed in part by the powerful Mellon family. Unable to hold his populist rage, he shouted: "Do you see that? That was built out of the sweat of working men." Visiting Ford's Theater, Mondale took special note of President Lincoln's Bible on display. "Don't ever forget—that is what Lincoln lived by and [what] made him great," he said.[23]

Fritz may have rebelled against his parents oppressive religiosity, but he absorbed most of his father's politics. "I didn't know just how, but I knew all the time back then that my life was somehow going to be involved in politics. Deep down, I guess you'd say I wanted Dad to be proud of me," he reflected nearly a half-century later. Cautious about expressing his deeply partisan feelings from the pulpit, the Reverend Mondale let them out over the dinner table. From an early age, young Fritz sat attentively listening to his father's lectures about the excesses of corporate greed, the dangers of individualism, and the need for liberal government. Combined with the biting critique of excessive wealth was an emphasis on compassion and social service. Stewardship was the central precept of his political philosophy. "We are here on earth to serve God's purpose, and help others who are less fortunate," the minister said many times. "He was a devout Christian, a believer in the social gospel, a Farmer-Laborite. He believed Christ taught a sense of social mission and this was heavily given to me throughout my childhood," Fritz recalled. "The notion that there are things that impose a social responsibility on us, to be concerned about the problems of others, to help them in any way we can, was drilled into me from my first days."[24]

Nurtured on his father's populist preachings, Fritz developed deep, visceral political values that endured for a lifetime. His family's behavior reinforced these values. The Mondales assisted the needy in their community, welcoming into their home anyone who was temporarily homeless, passing through town, or had fallen on hard times. "They were always concerned with people who had problems," recalled a childhood friend. "No one was ever beneath them." Mondale's responsibilities as a minister gave him a direct role in providing for the community welfare, but Claribel also contributed to the family occupation of caring by participating in local groups and various civic functions.[25]

Fritz made no secret of his political ambitions. "We knew he was going to be a politician because he said he was," recalled a high school friend. "He said he was going to be an attorney and get into politics." In high school he ran for political office and was elected president of his junior class. Though he lost the election for senior class president, the high school yearbook recorded his political ambitions: "His ambition is to be a member of the state legislature, preferably a senator, although he says every politician wants to be president eventually."[26]

He impressed people with his ability to organize his friends for social events, his interest in current issues, and his unbounded energy. "He was a clear thinker. He was an organizer," said Clarence. "He was sort of the ring-leader," his Sunday school teacher recalled. "If he decided it was time to have some fun in class, the others would follow along. Fritz didn't think that life was supposed to be all hard work." Most of all, Fritz loved to talk. "He was a natural," remembered his Sunday school teacher. "He would talk with anyone who would listen." "He was raised to argue," said an old football coach. "He'd always take the other side just to get an argument going." "He was a live wire," said a former social studies teacher. "He kept the discussions going and always had a view on the important subjects of the day." A supervisor at a poultry factory once scolded Fritz for constantly picking arguments with the other workers. "I'm sorry, George, I didn't mean any harm," Fritz said. "But I'm planning on going into politics someday, and I've gotta learn how to get people's hackles up."[27]

During Fritz's senior year in high school, his father suffered a heart attack from which he never fully recovered. While his father had instilled in Fritz a deep compassion for the underprivileged and a strong populist disdain for wealth and power, he had given him little instruction in translating abstract principles into a practical political philosophy. As he graduated high school and prepared to move to the Twin Cities for college, Fritz was a young man torn by two emotions—intense ambition to make his own imprint and extreme uncertainty about whether he was capable of competing and surviving in the outside world.

2

Political Baptism

The small stately campus of Macalester College, with its Gothic ivy-clad buildings, covered 40 acres in a residential neighborhood in Saint Paul. Founded in 1885 by Presbyterian ministers, Macalester had cultivated a staid atmosphere, in keeping with its founders' desire to train young men for a career in the ministry. That closely defined mission, however, was under assault in the fall of 1946 when Fritz Mondale arrived on campus for the first time. Dr. Charles Turck, the College's dynamic new president, planned to transform Macalester from a small provincial college into a major center of international learning. Putting his new approach into practice, he ordered the United Nations flag flown over campus, required students to attend chapel service once a week, and to listen to lectures given by important public figures invited to campus. He attracted—usually against the protests of the college trustees—young, energetic faculty members like the outspokenly liberal Hubert Humphrey.

By aggressively recruiting veterans, Turck doubled to 1,202 the number of students at Macalester. In 1946, veterans made up 70 percent of the 600 men at Macalester. Fritz's entering class of 470 was nearly double the size of any previous freshman class. The veterans, older and more experienced, had a profound impact on the campus. Since many were married and concerned about making a living, they were usually more serious about their work than most eighteen-year-old freshman. They challenged professors, forcing them to examine their own ideas and engage students in discussion.

To accommodate the flood of new students, the administration pressed all available space into service. The faculty lounge, various administration buildings, and library study rooms were converted into classrooms. The real crunch came in housing. For the first few weeks of the semester, Fritz was forced to sleep on a cot in Shaw gymnasium until additional housing could be found. In October, he moved into the cramped quarters of Bigelow Hall, a converted women's dormitory.

The Mondales—like many Scandinavians—placed considerable emphasis on education. "It was always assumed that we would go to college," recalled Clarence. "There was never any question about it." In many ways, however, Macalester was an odd choice for Fritz. There were colleges closer to home, but his parents encouraged Fritz to leave Elmore and live in "the city." There were cheaper alternatives in the Twin Cities, notably the University of Minnesota, but the Mondales believed a good Christian education was worth the extra money. Macalester was expensive: for the 1946–47 academic year tuition and board totalled $385, and the following year it jumped to $475. Fritz had to use all of his summer savings and take out a small loan with the college to pay the bill.

Fritz entered college full of doubts about his academic ability. Because of his mediocre high school grades, the college had accepted him on probation, warning that he would be asked to leave if he performed poorly. Could he compete against more worldly students from better high schools? Was he attending college because his parents expected him to, or because he really had a desire to learn? Many of his doubts and fears dissipated when he walked into Theodore Mitau's introductory class in political science. Like many liberal intellectuals of the day, Mitau suggested that political divisions in America should be thought of not as lying along a line with left and right extremes, but as forming a circle where left and right would meet. Influenced by Reinhold Niebuhr, Mitau believed that only a delicate balance of conflicting interests could preserve democracy against the "moral cynicism" of the "children of darkness" and the utopian idealism of the "children of light." "The tactic of the extreme right and the extreme left was to undermine the center and force people to make extreme choices," he told students. Mitau suggested a similar change in thinking was necessary on foreign policy. American isolationism was dead, he preached, and liberals needed to recognize that "American military and economic security is intimately tied into the stability of world affairs." Liberals needed to create a political climate where differences could be settled "without recourse to either fascism or communism."[1]

Mitau had an immediate and profound impact on young Fritz. "I don't think he had a clear sense of what direction to go before his political science classes with Mitau," recalled a roommate. "I believe that Mitau was probably the biggest influence on his life at that time." A Mondale classmate recalled that Mitau "provided the antidote" to the mistaken view that "politics was dirty, something that you stayed away from as much as possible." Mitau's teaching, a friend reflected, "found fertile ground among a few of his students. Fritz was one."[2]

That interest was reflected in Fritz's grades. He performed well enough in his first year—seven "B" grades and one "C"—to be removed from the probation list in March 1947. His highest grades at Macalester came in classes dealing with politics, government, contemporary issues, and debate. He showed little interest in traditional subjects, or in discussions about issues that had little practical relevance. His extracurricular activities, too, reflected his fascination with politics. In high school, sports had been his principal preoccupation, but now he joined the debate team, the international relations club, and was active in various political clubs on campus. To appease his mother, he also sang in the college choir.[3]

College photographs reveal a handsome young man with a trim, athletic build, short brown hair, blue eyes, and a slightly beaked nose. Although popular with women on campus, Fritz rarely showed interest. Classmates described him as "friendly, and easy-going, with a quick smile and a hearty laugh." He enjoyed amicable teasing among friends, and frequently surprised people with his dry wit and self-depreciating humor. "He enjoyed laughing at himself," commented a classmate. At times he could be light-hearted and somewhat mischievous, but he was deadly serious about politics. He talked incessantly about issues and accepted all challenges to debate. His roommates complained that because of his preoccupation with politics Fritz could sometimes be inconsiderate and sloppy. "He would come back at night and just step out of his clothes," recalled a roommate. "He was too busy for the mundane things of life." On one occasion Fritz borrowed a pair of socks from a friend, wore them for a week, and then returned them unwashed. "They should have been buried," the friend recalled.[4]

Mondale's interest in politics developed at a pivotal time in the evolution of postwar American liberalism. The central question over which liberals agonized was the appropriateness of forming associations with communists. During the war communists had opposed strikes, abandoned their status as a political party, and made important gains in local Democratic party organizations and in the trade union movement. Minnesota had one of the most active branches of the Communist Party in the country. Many liberals welcomed the communists into an alliance against fascism and allowed them into ward clubs and county associations.[5]

The uneasy wartime alliance showed strains as the prospects of peace forced liberals to consider the shape of the postwar world. Soviet domination of Eastern Europe had challenged liberal hopes for world order and stability based on international cooperation. Abroad, Roosevelt had maintained the fragile alliance with a careful mixing of realpolitik and idealism; at home, his enormous stature prevented an open rupture in his coalition. All of that changed in April 1945, when Roosevelt died suddenly. His successor, an inexperienced Harry S Truman, was unskilled in the art of international diplomacy and lacked the stature to sustain Roosevelt's broad coalition. As evidence mounted, Truman became convinced that Soviet actions represented naked aggression that needed to be challenged. Acting on his new policy, he abruptly canceled lend-lease shipments to the Soviets, refused to allow the Soviets a major role in the occupation of Japan, and publicly criticized Stalin for breaking his word at Yalta to allow "free and unfettered elections" in Poland.

These Cold War tensions added to liberal anxiety about the wartime alliance with communists. Many liberals had already grown suspicious of communist behavior which, because of its fidelity to the international movement, appeared more interested in domination than in cooperation. Now Soviet aggression seemed to confirm that liberalism and communism were irreconcilable. These liberals who gravitated toward the Union for Democratic Action, and later Americans for Democratic Action (ADA), wanted liberals to banish communists from their political organizations. Others, however, arguing that the continuing threat of fascism posed the chief danger to American democracy, urged liberals to form a common bond with reform-minded communists and work toward perpetuating the Popular Front. Rallying around former Vice President Henry Wallace and the Progressive Citizens of America, they threatened the Democrats with the possibility of a third party challenge.

This national schism among liberals produced serious divisions within the newly created Minnesota Democratic Farmer-Labor Party. This uneasy alliance had emerged from a common desire to assure a Roosevelt victory in 1944. By 1946, however, Cold War pressures were dividing the party into opposing camps. One group, led by former Governor Elmer Benson and supported by a large communist contingent, hoped to retain the Popular Front and encouraged Wallace to seek the presidency on a third-party ticket. Another faction, headed by Mayor Hubert Humphrey of Minneapolis and closely aligned with the ADA, feared the "soft on communism" issue would spell doom for the Democratic party in 1948, and, though not enamored of Truman, opposed any attempt to align the DFL with a third party candidate.

All of these recriminations swirled around the campus in the fall of 1946. Should the DFL oppose Truman and support Wallace's postwar plans? Or did the communists, as Humphrey argued, present a challenge to the party's future? These were complex issues, especially for a small town, eighteen-year-old freshman hearing of these intramural debates among liberals for the first time. Uncommitted to either side but eager to decide for himself, Fritz immersed himself in the debate. Whether reading the papers, listening to the radio or attending local events and rallies, Fritz studied each perspective and weighed the conflicting evidence. In October 1946, he walked to the Shaw Field House at Macalester to hear Henry Wallace explain that "Stalin and Molotov have many of the same ideas that I have but that does not make me a communist." In December, he heard Humphrey speak for the first time. The Minneapolis Mayor declared his support for minimum wage and fair housing legislation but also made clear his opposition to working with communists and the importance of standing firm against Soviet aggression abroad.[6]

The Reverend Mondale had instilled in Fritz basic liberal values, but this debate was not between liberals and conservatives but among different factions of liberals. On foreign policy issues his father had been a pacifist, and young Fritz was originally sympathetic to Wallace's critique of American foreign policy. While Truman and the anticommunist liberals spoke about balance of power and military containment, Mondale believed that poverty, not communism, posed the greatest threat to American interests abroad. Humphrey was by far the more attractive personality, but Fritz was troubled by his strong anticommunist rhetoric and heavy emphasis on military containment. His father had always spoken highly of Wallace, and Fritz too found him inspirational. But he felt a nagging doubt about the progressives that kept him undecided. What if Mitau and Humphrey were right? What if Wallace's communist followers, despite their moving rhetoric about peace and jobs, were antidemocratic? If their loyalty to the Soviet Union outweighed their commitment to American principles of democracy, then Fritz could never support them.

As Cold War tensions mounted, the middle ground rapidly eroded. In February 1947 the British announced they would no longer provide economic and military aid to Greece and Turkey. Fearful that the Soviets would take advantage of the situation, Truman decided to have the United States assume responsibility for the aid. In an address to the nation on March 12, 1947, the President placed his proposal for assistance to Greece and Turkey in the context of a worldwide ideological struggle between communism and democracy. Wallace attacked the policy, claiming Truman's support for reactionary regimes in Greece and Turkey made him "the best spokesman Communism had." Humphrey, and most anticommunist liberals, supported the Doctrine and castigated Wallace for his position. "We're not going to let the political philosophy of the DFL be dictated from the Kremlin," Humphrey declared.[7]

On this critical issue Fritz agreed with Wallace. "The first thing to remember about the Administration's proposed loan to Greece is that it is attempting to prop up the reactionary Greek monarchy by force, as a supposed defense against communism in the area," Fritz wrote in the school newspaper. It would not be in America's interest to allow Greece to fall to the Communists, Mondale agreed, but he charged that the administration's anticommunist zeal blinded it to the real problems facing the Greek nation. "To the Greek people it is not an issue of communism versus capitalism, but starvation versus subsistence," he argued. "They don't want communism, but they would rather be eating and communistic, than starving and capitalistic." America, he suggested, should encourage a more liberal Greek government, not prop up a reactionary regime. "Our policy in Greece, and in the world, should be to make democracy so overwhelmingly superior to communism that the people will adopt democracy by their own free will."[8]

Realizing that it needed to provide both a carrot and stick for its new policy of global containment, the administration announced a bold new program of economic aid to Europe. In June, Secretary of State George Marshall explained that his program was "directed not against any country or doctrine, but against hunger, poverty, desperation, and chaos." Fritz, home for a summer of intensive labor, read about the plan in the local papers. He welcomed a proposal that he felt properly deemphasized military containment in favor of economic assistance. All liberals, he thought, could applaud the initiative. But Wallace's reaction surprised him. While Humphrey and the anticommunists enthusiastically supported the initiative, Wallace called the plan just another attempt to divide East from West and to impose "reactionary governments and influence the economic system of Western Europe to the benefit of Wall Street."

When Fritz returned to campus in the fall, Humphrey was planning to purge the party of communist control as the first step in his effort to win a Senate seat in 1948. It was Humphrey's personality, and his strong support of New Deal domestic legislation, not his position on divisive foreign policy issues, that attracted Fritz to his cause. Though uncomfortable with his strident anticommunism, Fritz was fascinated by Humphrey's boundless energy and infectious optimism.

To help the Humphrey cause, Mondale joined a small group of students from Macalester and the University of Minnesota to outorganize the communists in the upcoming party caucuses. At Macalester Mondale became the chief organizer of the Students for Democratic Action (SDA), the college arm of the ADA. He and a small army of supporters passed out literature, rang doorbells, and made phone calls to local leaders. "I remember him as a political animal," recalled one former roommate. "He was out politicking all the time," said another. His intense involvement in DFL politics left him little time for other activities. "He was not a regular participant in student life," recalled a friend, "because he was so busy campaigning for DFL politics."[9]

Friends and associates remembered Fritz as a hard-working, dedicated volunteer with a consuming passion for politics. One friend described him as "a natural leader. He was the person we would gather around." Another recalled that most campus leaders were veterans who were older, and in most cases, more serious than other undergraduates. "Fritz was the exception." Despite his relative youth, Mondale impressed many of the older students. "I did not have the sense that he was young and brash," reflected a former GI. "I viewed him as a peer. He had a certain maturity about him. He fit in with the older guys." He also impressed seasoned DFL politicians. "He wasn't even old enough to vote, but Mondale just kind of came to the front as being particularly well organized, particularly able," reflected Humphrey's campaign manager, Orville Freeman.[10]

The first critical battle for the Humphrey forces came in their attempts to gain control of the Young DFL caucus held in November 1947. Having carefully cultivated support ahead of time, Humphrey's talented group of young organizers elected their entire slate of candidates. While rebuffing every Progressive attempt to place their members on the executive committee, Mondale and the other Humphrey proteges passed resolutions calling for repeal of the Taft-Hartley Act, and in favor of universal military training, minimum wage legislation, federal aid to education, public housing, and farm price supports. They endorsed Truman's program and called for his reelection. The victory was the first in a series for Humphrey that culminated in June when the DFL nominated him for the Senate. When Progressives complained afterwards of Mondale's "Goebbels-like tactics" at the YDFL meeting, Fritz drafted a statement defending his actions. "The Macalester chapter of SDA stands fully behind the actions that occurred at the Young Democratic-Farmer Labor Convention," he declared.[11]

Although he was gradually drawn into the Humphrey circle, Mondale was not committed to Truman on the national level. He found much that was inspiring about Wallace until late February 1948, when the communists staged a coup in democratic Czechoslovakia. The Czech leader Jan Masaryk, who died mysteriously in the overthrow, had been a symbol of democratic nationalism. A few days later Mondale heard Henry Wallace speak at the Armory in Minneapolis defending the Soviet action. "I'm not going to be a part of this," he recalled thinking at the time. It represented his final break from Wallace. But he had still not reconciled himself to Truman.[12]

That summer, though he was working ten-to-twelve hour days, six days a week at a canning factory to raise money for next year's tuition, Mondale searched for ways to stay politically active. He still devoured newspapers to see what Humphrey and the Democrats were doing, and listened intensely on the radio to coverage of Humphrey's eloquent speech at the Democratic national convention in Philadelphia. Humphrey electrified the hall with his call for the party to enact a "new emancipation proclamation." The young Minneapolis mayor declared: "To those who say that we are rushing this issue of civil rights, I say to them, we are 172 years too late. To those who say that this civil rights program is an infringement of states rights, the time has arrived in America for the Democratic party to get out of the shadow of states rights and walk forthrightly into the sunshine of human rights."

Aroused by the speech, Mondale decided he had to get involved. "I just couldn't stand working in that canning factory when that campaign was going on," he remembered. He called fellow Humphrey partisan Don Fraser to ask if he could help organize the Second Congressional District—an area almost the size of New Jersey with 318,000 citizens who were scattered across a prairie that stretched from the center of the state south to Iowa and west from the Mississippi River nearly to the South Dakota border. Fraser told Fritz he would be glad to have his help in the district but could not pay him. Undeterred, Mondale accepted the challenge. He quit his job, hitchhiked to Mankato, and found a Democratic car dealer in town. "We're trying to do something for Humphrey and I got to have a car," Fritz told the dealer, who quickly offered him any car on the lot. Setting up an office in town, Mondale sold Humphrey buttons for a dollar. "We'd make a hundred and fifty bucks, two hundred a month on that, to kind of keep the whole thing going," he recalled later.[13]

Mondale continued working in the area even after classes resumed in the fall. During September and early October, Fritz spent weekdays on campus and commuted home for long weekends. As election day approached, he frequently slipped away from campus at midweek. Since he did not own a car, Fritz discovered that it was not easy to find dependable transportation for the three-and-a-half-hour trip between St. Paul and the second district. Most of the time he borrowed cars from friends. Occasionally he rounded up a small group of interested students, and their cars, and had them accompany him for the weekend. In return, he said, they would get to see Humphrey in action. They were rarely disappointed.

Humphrey proved himself a tireless campaigner, traveling night and day, addressing crowds from the back of a flatbed truck. Through September and October, he visited all eighty-seven counties at least twice, attended almost every county fair, and went to most other civic festivals. By Freeman's estimate, he made 700 speeches and traveled 31,000 miles. For the first time, labor and farm groups played an active role in the campaign. The passage of the Taft-Hartley Act, as well as signs of anti-union activity on the state level, convinced previously dormant organizations of their urgent stake in the election's outcome. As a consequence, the Minnesota State Federation of Labor initiated an active voter registration drive, established phone banks, and organized political rallies. The farm cooperatives experienced a similar conversion to political activism. Fearing that Republican attempts to apply corporate income taxes to their patronage funds would destroy their businesses, many cooperatives organized behind the Minnesota Association of Cooperatives to produce literature and provide Humphrey with lists of farmers willing to volunteer for his campaign.[14]

Humphrey sought to reach the struggling middle class with a strong populist message. "We have tried to slant the campaign so that the so-called middle class will be led to realize where their interests lie," Freeman commented later. Humphrey convinced his audiences that he understood the plight of the "little man" by constantly reminding them of his work as a clerk in a small Dakota drugstore. After establishing a common bond with the crowd, he launched into a strident, and usually long-winded, assault against big business. "I want to break up these monopolies," he shouted in a raspy voice, "because monopoly is the socialism of the big corporations."[15]

For Fritz one of the most moving moments of the campaign occurred during a Humphrey trip through his district. His father, a strong Humphrey supporter, decided to venture into the bitter cold to hear him speak. Wrapped in thick wool blankets to keep the frigid air away from his fragile body, the Reverend Mondale sat in the family car as Humphrey's rapid-fire voice boomed through his bullhorn. Like the hundreds of others who had waited hours for Humphrey's arrival, Mondale applauded as the young mayor launched his attack against the forces of special interest. After the speech, a solicitous Fritz escorted Humphrey to the car where his nervous parents were waiting. The elder Mondale, too weak to stand, reached for Humphrey's hand. The symbolism of the moment was striking. In the car, old and frail, sat a poor, tongue-tied preacher who had instilled in his son deep values of social justice but had left for him to decide how to fulfill those ideals. Standing beside him was the young and ambitious mayor who would teach Fritz that politics would be the best means of fulfilling his father's hopes. As young Fritz looked on, his past and his future embraced.

While Humphrey traveled the state denouncing the defenders of special interest, Truman crisscrossed the nation disseminating a similarly potent populist message. Following the advice of political advisors Jim Rowe and Clark Clifford, the president made specific appeals to each of the party's major constituencies—labor, blacks, Jews, and liberals. Truman traversed the country by train with "whistle stop" appearances from the rear platform. In September he began in Michigan, crossed the continent from Pennsylvania to California, and returned to Washington through Texas and Oklahoma. During October he concentrated on the Middle West and the East with speeches always tailored to his local audiences. Some pundits criticized Truman for sounding more like a local ward leader than a president, but few of the tens-of-thousands who listened to his folksy style had any complaints. Like Humphrey, Truman spoke of his love of the "common man" and his disdain for wealth and power. Depicting politics as a struggle between the people and the special interests, he attacked the Republican-led 80th Congress as "the worst in history," assailed the "gluttons of privilege" dominating the GOP, and called Republicans "bloodsuckers with offices in Wall Street."[16]

In October, Truman's train made a swing through Minnesota. An excited Fritz stood in the cold morning air in the Mankato train station listening to the President launch into a strong partisan attack on the Republicans. "The big power trusts are trying to choke off the REA," he declared, adding that the GOP is "always on the side of special interests." He asserted: "When you vote Democratic you are voting for yourself and your welfare." After the speech, Fritz climbed aboard the train where he met Truman for the first time. He remained on the train as it wound its way through central Minnesota, where he observed the thousands who turned out to get a glimpse of the President.[17]

Despite the large crowds that greeted the presidential caravan, Truman was the decided underdog. Plagued by the constant unfavorable comparison to Roosevelt, besieged from the right by the "Dixiecrat" challenge of South Carolina Governor J. Strom Thurmond and from the left by Henry Wallace's candidacy, and burdened with high inflation, labor unrest and revelations of corruption in Washington, Truman had his work cut out for him. His opponent, New York Governor Thomas Dewey, convinced of his own invulnerability, radiated confidence. Still Mondale was confident of a Truman victory. "Fritz was steadfast in his belief that Truman would ultimately win," recalled Harry Char, a former college roommate. In October, when, on learning that Dewey would be speaking in St. Paul, Char told Mondale he was going "to see the next President of the United States," Mondale laughed. "You're wasting your time," he said.[18]

Fritz rooted for Truman, but his first concern was securing a

Humphrey victory. "A vote for Humphrey is a vote for true liberalism," Mondale wrote in the school newspaper, "which means government for the great majority and not a privileged few." When the vote was tallied, Truman had stunned the nation by winning with 304 electoral votes to Dewey's 189. Of more immediate concern, Humphrey scored a major victory over incumbent Republican Joseph Ball, winning the state by 243,000 votes and carrying eighty-five of eighty-seven counties. Mondale had reason to believe he had played a role in the Humphrey triumph. The new Senator carried the normally Republican second district, which included Mondale's home town, by 8,500 votes.[19]

The 1948 campaign shaped the style as well as the substance of postwar Democratic politics. A successful campaign required staging events that allowed for close interaction between the candidate and voters. Mondale referred to this approach as "family politics." It consisted of employing intense personal activity and effective organization to develop a "relationship" with the people. Over time, voters would develop a "reservoir of trust" which would provide their elected leaders with the support needed to tackle difficult issues. Mondale's vision of "family politics" was perfectly suited to this pre-television style of campaigning. Candidates made effective use of newspapers and radio to disseminate their message, but they spent the bulk of their time traveling the state, meeting with voters in small groups and at large rallies. Democratic candidates used these local settings to highlight how the party of Roosevelt had improved the average American's quality of life and to promise continued benefits in the future. When appearing before an audience of working people, Humphrey spoke of the gains made under Roosevelt and promised to champion the fight for higher wages and better working conditions. To farm groups, Humphrey called for continued government price supports; to liberals he reaffirmed his commitment to education, civil rights, and an activist foreign policy. In all of these cases, the message was focused and the benefits tangible.

The second important dimension to building public support consisted of negotiating with the key constituency blocs. Humphrey and his close advisors believed in the power of opinion-makers. They were convinced that individuals viewed the political process through the prism of established groups and respected leaders. Their faith in pluralism convinced them that political information should be mediated by responsible groups. As a result, the campaign went to great lengths to win the endorsement of prominent local politicians and established interest groups.

"It was not my victory, but a victory of the Democratic party for the people," a triumphant Truman announced after the election. Democratic success in Senate and House races suggested the 1948 election did represent a victory of party. Democratic congressional candidates won a sizable majority of the popular vote. In Senate races, Democrats won 56 percent of the vote; in House races they outscored Republicans by a 52–46 margin. The large popular vote translated into a party gain of nine seats in the Senate and 75 in the House. "Mr. Truman's own victory, the Democratic majorities in both houses of Congress, the Democratic victories in so many states, attest to the enormous vitality of the Democratic party as Roosevelt led it and developed it from 1932 to 1944," observed Walter Lippmann. "[T]he party that Roosevelt formed has survived his death, and is without question the dominant force in American politics."[20]

Like Roosevelt, Truman drew most of his strength from the cities, where he convinced working-class voters that he would best protect their interests. "The higher the socioeconomic status, the more Republican the vote," concluded one study: "put crudely, richer people vote Republican more than poorer people." As the journalist Samuel Lubell argued, the coalition that had elected Roosevelt and Truman had its roots in an expanding urban population. The economic and social realities of a new urban America, he argued, rendered obsolete the Republican philosophy of "leaving things alone" and provided a social context for more active government. Unlike past political realignments, the "Revolt of the City" depended on a sense of class-consciousness that transcended "not only regional distinctions but equally strong cultural differences." By 1948, the Democrats had controlled the twelve largest cities in the country through six presidential elections. More important, those cities were strategically located in states that accounted for 231 electoral votes. In many elections, overwhelming Democratic victories in the cities compensated for weak performances in suburban and rural areas and provided the margin of victory in the state.[21]

Truman also scored well with farmers in the Midwest who had defected from the party because of foreign policy issues. The President convinced farmers, who were suffering from a decline in prices and a shortage of storage facilities, that he would serve their economic interests. "I talked about voting for Dewey all summer," a farmer told Lubell, "but when voting time came, I just couldn't do it. I remember the depression and all the good things that have come to me under the Democrats."[22]

Truman's successful campaign institutionalized the New Deal political philosophy. By 1948, most liberals shared a common set of assumptions. At the heart of the new liberal creed was a belief that economic growth would eliminate class divisions, guarantee social harmony, and provide a constant source of revenue for necessary social programs. During the depression, liberals had experimented with plans for managing the limited potential of a mature economy; now they focused on employing fiscal and monetary policy to fine-tune a vibrant economy of abundance. Prominent liberal intellectuals now argued that a mixed economy, which included limited government planning and restrained welfare programs, could guarantee a constantly growing economy and a stable society. "Keynes, not Marx is the prophet of the new radicalism," Schlesinger commented.[23]

Liberals also emerged from the experience of depression and war with a clearer sense of the role government could play in promoting the national interest. In the early years, Roosevelt had believed the public welfare could best be served through cooperation and community. After 1935, he abandoned the rhetoric of social solidarity and focused on political conflict. By 1948, liberals had merged both strains of thought into a pluralistic vision of democracy. Believing that the experience of Nazi Germany and Stalinist Russia revealed the excesses of a messianic ideology, "Vital Center" liberals were committed to piecemeal reform working through the established institutions of government. The new liberalism, rejecting the totalitarianism of both the right and left, believed "in the integrity of the individual, in the limited state, in due process of law, in empiricism and gradualism." Liberals believed government could neither play its traditional role as neutral arbiter nor assume the responsibility for planning and managing the economy. Instead, government should empower groups— labor, farmers, Blacks, Jews, senior citizens—that could provide a "countervailing" influence to big business and create a balanced and fair society.[24]

The 1948 election set the tone for an entire generation of Democratic politicians. Throughout the campaign, Truman and other leading liberals articulated a new public philosophy that distinguished itself from the New Deal. These "Vital Center" liberals remained faithful to the key ingredients of Roosevelt's vision: a sense of economic injustice, the commitment to federal activism, and respect for the political influence of the party's interest groups. Yet they grafted onto the old philosophy a new reverence for the healing power of economic growth and a belief in the need for a strong anticommunist foreign policy. For the next twenty years, the "Vital Center" philosophy would define the liberal impulse and shape the nature of the two-party competition.

By the early 1970s, however, liberals would be struggling to apply these ideas to changed circumstances. How could a generation nurtured on the beneficence of economic growth justify increased social spending during a time of limited growth? Did the emergence of a multipolar world undermine the liberal commitment to global anticommunism? How could liberals preserve a sense of class struggle in the face of aroused racial and regional tensions? Could a political philosophy that celebrated pragmatism and preached the gospel of pluralism sustain its ideological integrity while responding to the morally ambiguous problems of the 1970s and 1980s? In 1948, as a twenty-year-old college student working on his first political campaign, Mondale had little reason to worry about these questions. Little did he know that he would spend most of his years in public life searching for the answers.

3

Organizing for a New Generation

By December the euphoria of Humphrey's victory had begun to fade. Finals were approaching and, since he had spent much of his time campaigning, Fritz had fallen far behind in his classes. Borrowing notes from classmates, staying up late at night to read old assignments, Fritz struggled to earn passing grades. Immersed in his studies, he was struck by the contrast between his love of politics and his indifference to course work. Why, he thought, should he be wasting his time sitting in classes learning meaningless information when he could be making a difference in politics? He was too restless, too eager to be involved, to play the passive role of student. Humphrey's victory, he thought, could open new opportunities for him in Washington, the mecca of aspiring young politicians. Perhaps, he thought he could accompany Humphrey to Washington and earn a staff job.[1]

Normally before making such a critical decision Fritz would have sought his father's advice. This decision, however, would have to be made alone. In December, the elder Mondale had suffered a massive heart attack and died at the age of seventy-four. Fritz had known this day would come, and probably soon. His father had never fully recovered from a previous heart attack he had suffered two years earlier, and his health had taken a turn for the worse in recent months. But the awareness of impending death did little to ease Fritz's pain.

The most pressing decision was what to do about school. The winter semester would start shortly after the new year. He was already in debt and would need to borrow money to complete the year. With his father's death, his mother's future uncertain, and his own ability to repay his debts in doubt, Fritz questioned whether he should return for another semester. But what else could he do? There were no offers from Humphrey for a staff position and he could not afford to go to Washington without some assurances of earning money. A fellow Humphrey campaign worker, Bill Shore, solved this problem. He told Fritz of a position available in Washington as the secretary of SDA. Fritz leaped at the opportunity.

In January, Fritz traveled to Washington with high hopes. Invigorated by the ADA's successful campaign in Minnesota, Fritz believed he would be part of a powerful new political group that had already helped restore Democratic control of Congress and revitalize American liberals. "I was going to organize the nation," he recalled. He hoped to add another 150 chapters to the organization, establish a speaker program, and initiate an aggressive public education schedule. More important, the position would allow him to make contacts with influential political figures who might someday help further his own career. "I am in an excellent position to meet and know national figures in the liberal movement," he wrote his mother shortly after arriving in Washington, "and am exploiting this advantage to its fullest." Finally, being in Washington and working for the SDA allowed him to be close to Humphrey. He was fascinated by the new Senator. In one of his first letters home he told his mother about his desire to go to the Senate chamber and watch Humphrey perform. "They really like that guy down here, and I personally want to see him in action," he explained. Occasionally on weekends he would drive by Humphrey's home, which he described as "modest and middleclassish," in hopes of catching a glimpse of his mentor.[2]

Mondale and Shore rented a $50-a-month basement apartment in an old townhouse in Washington Circle, just a few blocks from the White House. At first, Fritz felt he could not afford anything better so he tolerated the cockroaches and mice. But when he discovered a mouse had been electrocuted by an exposed wire, Fritz decided it was time to move. He and Shore joined a few other young students in a large, refurbished house in Georgetown. Over the course of the year, Shore and the other roommates lost interest in politics. But not Fritz. "I realized I just couldn't be totally absorbed by politics from morning till night—totally committed to it," Shore told Finlay Lewis. "That was the big difference between Fritz and the rest of us." [3]

It was not long, however, before reality crushed Fritz's idealistic hopes. Consumed by his new Senate duties and protected by an overzealous staff, Humphrey had little time to listen to former campaign workers. When Fritz tried to telephone Humphrey directly with some advice, an aide scolded him. From then on, the aide told Fritz, all of his messages needed to be channeled through a staff member. Mondale complained to a friend that Humphrey's Washington advisors had secluded the senator from many of the people who had helped elect him. "That hurt me," Mondale recalled. "I worked my damn heart out for the guy." [4]

It was the first of many blows he would experience that year. The SDA job proved a big disappointment. Poor morale, a weak staff, no money and little assistance from the larger organization doomed his goals from the beginning. The organization languished as union contributions, critical to any liberal movement, dried up, and an uncertain relationship with the Truman Administration muted the ADA's independent voice. With a crippling debt, small staff, and limited membership, the ADA was in no position to provide relief to a fledgling student organization. Despite working long hours, Mondale complained to his mother that he felt "so little sense of accomplishment" that it was "easy to get down-hearted." Mondale spent most of his time performing clerical duties and pleading for more money and staff support. "I can't recall writing you a letter in which money wasn't mentioned," he wrote the organization's secretary in December 1949. [5]

His hopes of being part of a new liberal vanguard were also dashed by developments in national politics. The 1948 election did not provide a mandate for liberalism. "Any illusion that the liberal Democrats dominate either the House or the Senate has been completely blasted," Humphrey said. The 1948 election was "not so much a victory as a reprieve." A devoted Mondale listened as Harry Truman outlined his Fair Deal legislation and called on Congress to support new foreign policy initiatives. But most of Truman's proposals for civil rights, health insurance, repeal of Taft-Hartley, increases in the minimum wage and federal aid to education were stymied by a conservative coalition of Republicans and Southern Democrats. In foreign policy, as questions of subversion and espionage dominated national affairs, the President's uplifting calls for aid to underdeveloped nations were engulfed by suspicion and hostility. In 1949, Washington was also shaken by a fear of subversion which, according to the historian Eric Goldman, "loosed within American life a vast impatience, a turbulent bitterness, a rancor akin to revolt." Loyalty programs, the trial of former State Department official Alger Hiss, and the fall of China distracted public attention from the Fair Deal agenda and eroded congressional support for new social programs.[6]

During these lonely days away from home, Fritz met and fell in love with Norma Dinnerstein, a young SDA organizer. During their stormy two-year relationship, which saw him make and later rescind an offer of marriage, Fritz shared his private thoughts and doubts. He told her of his desire for "freedom" and "greatness" in the larger world outside of Elmore. Dinnerstein believed that in trying to achieve fame, Fritz idealized Humphrey, the ADA, and the "Palace Guard"— a small group of Humphrey supporters in the Minnesota DFL. "Then like all of us who try to rise out of what we consider mediocrity and 'blandness,' " Dinnerstein observed in a long, thoughtful letter, "you were quick to be disillusioned with each new and supposedly glorious experience. Often you achieved something real and worthy of confidence, sometimes you bit off too much—but because you were moving so very fast and seeking so very much, you found corruption and a certain defeat in every victory. And worst of all, you figured out that 'Crazy Legs' from Elmore wasn't worth so very much in the big wide world."[7]

Dinnerstein's letter highlighted an important dimension of Fritz's personality. Mondale was driven by a deep-seated desire to succeed. By proving himself in the larger world he hoped to escape being drawn back into the obscurity of Elmore. Yet he was also plagued by nagging uncertainties about his ability. Fritz viewed the world through the lens of his small-town, midwestern upbringing. For him, the world of politics was the providence of a more skilled and cosmopolitan elite. This insecurity was at the core of Fritz's personality and provides insight into his future political persona. In later years, unable to shed his small-town perspective, Mondale frequently questioned his self-worth, required constant encouragement from staff and friends, and was subject to long periods of brooding self-reflection. Often he compensated for the insecurity by pushing himself and those around him to extraordinary degrees. Over time, a combination of maturity and success dulled but never eliminated the sharp edges of Mondale's self-doubt.

During the summer of 1949, Mondale joined forty other young liberals on an SDA trip to Britain. The SDA coordinated the trip with the British Labour party to introduce future American leaders to the new proposals sponsored by the Labour Prime Minister, Clement Atlee. Upon replacing Winston Churchill's Conservative Party in July 1945, the Labour Party launched an ambitious program of social reform that included national health insurance, nationalization of many basic industries, and a dramatic increase in the size of the welfare state. The SDA tour consisted of three weeks of lectures in London and Oxford followed by carefully choreographed tours of factories and coal mines. On one occasion, Mondale crawled on his stomach down a dark narrow tunnel where coal miners risked their lives everyday. "This trip," Fritz wrote his brother Clarence, "is a good thing for me, providing new perspective, which I need." The trip reinforced the strong sense of class politics which had infused his father's populism and been so much a part of the Humphrey and Truman campaigns in 1948. "To the workers, the capitalist is unprincipled and an exploiter," he observed. "To the capitalist the worker is weak minded [and] lazy."

The tour obviously had its desired effect; Mondale came away impressed by and supportive of the Labour Party program. "The Labour Party has wonderful leadership and is doing a wonderful job in educating the worker," he said. He predicted the Party would stay in power "with a much reduced, but yet working majority."[8]

After completing the four-week stay in England, Fritz spent a few weeks traveling around Europe with friends. Returning to Washington, he began planning for the national Young Democrats convention meeting in Chattanooga. The first meeting of national Democrats since the Dixiecrat walkout at the 1948 convention, the gathering provided an indication of the depth of party division on civil rights. Southern conservatives, who controlled the presidency and all key committees, hoped to avoid a bitter fight over civil rights by pushing for a motion forbidding resolutions from the floor. Fritz, who attended the convention as one of six Minnesota delegates, complained to a local reporter that it was a "greased" affair and predicted a fight between opponents and supporters of Truman's Fair Deal. During the two days of sometimes emotional debates, southerners argued against support of Truman's civil rights policies, while many moderates fought for a compromise that expressed appreciation for the President's domestic program but stopped short of a specific endorsement of his civil rights policies. Mondale, who the Chattanooga *Daily Times* claimed "quarterbacked" the liberal forces, argued for specific and enthusiastic support of the entire Fair Deal. "We understand that this thing has to be done by evolution," he told a reporter, "but we have learned that we should never compromise in stating our goals." His skill and persistence paid off. On the closing day, the convention voted 297–173 in support of the liberal resolution.[9]

In January 1950 Fritz returned to school after a two-year hiatus. Rather than finishing at Macalester, Fritz chose the less expensive University of Minnesota. He had gained a greater appreciation for the value of a college education, but the old doubts about his academic ability persisted. In the hopes of identifying his weaknesses, Fritz completed a battery of tests, conducted by the University psychology department, designed to evaluate basic analytical and reasoning skills. The results were not encouraging, especially to a student who already harbored doubts about his intelligence. Fritz performed so poorly that the final evaluation concluded that he was incapable of doing successful graduate work. He was "shattered" by the results, he confessed, because "I've always assumed that I could more or less choose the field I wanted to go into. . . . "[10]

Despite the poor test results, the private doubts about his own political future, and the need to prove that he could earn good grades, Fritz found himself spending much of his time talking politics and planning campaigns. Mondale and other young liberals hoped to use Humphrey's 1948 success to transform the DFL party. Humphrey had scored a major victory, but the party remained in the hands of a much older leadership that resisted the youthful energy of its newer members. After the 1944 fusion, many older Farmer-Labor members had remained in the party. Largely from rural areas where they had little political opposition, they established a strong base among the craft unions that opposed racial integration and the successful farmer cooperatives that resisted government regulation. Humphrey's combative style and militant anticommunism built a broad coalition of older, conservative Farmer-Labor leaders and the younger, university-educated ADA liberals. It was, however, a defensive coalition, dependent on the mobilization of trade unions and farm co-ops against the threat of a Republican victory in 1948. With the Popular Front shattered and Humphrey's election secured, tension within the anticommunist faction emerged. In 1950, Humphrey wrote a friend that it had been easier when they ganged up "for the purpose of licking the Commies, but now are only too willing to charge off in different directions when they find no common enemy to shoot at."[11]

Important class differences separated these two groups. Labor and its working-class supporters resented the university-educated, ADA liberals with whom Mondale was closely identified. Both groups supported an expanded welfare state and both voted for Humphrey. But in style and temperament middle-class liberals had little in common with most union leaders. Labor publications were full of scornful remarks about the arrogant attitude of the "university highbrows." The *Union Advocate,* a popular labor publication, said liberals were "inclined to be quite self-conscious over the fact that they are college men." The ADA, it declared, was composed "largely of campus rah rahs, college professors, flippant talkers and visionaries who evidently thought the time had come to Save Minnesota from the Communists." Younger liberals, on the other hand, perceived many of these established labor figures as self-serving influence peddlers who were more concerned with staying in power than they were with fighting for liberal ideas. "These people are never going to be friends or supporters of ours and unless we stop them it will be a serious mess," Freeman wrote Humphrey in August 1949.[12]

These class differences accompanied a basic disagreement about the extent and pace of desirable change. The ADA liberals were more aggressive in their calls for government activism in a whole range of areas. Labor's agenda was more circumscribed and focused on issues directly concerning working people. The differences, however, did not always revolve around specific issues. "This was a real transition of generations," remembered Arvonne Fraser. The older generation was closely tied to the memory of Franklin Roosevelt and Floyd Olson, the fiery Farmer-Labor governor of the 1930s, depended heavily on labor and political bosses for its support, and used patronage to cement its alliance. Having witnessed their own fall from grace, they recognized the public's limited capacity for change and were more reserved in their calls for reform. The younger liberals identified more with the Fair Deal than the New Deal and accepted Humphrey, not Roosevelt, as their leader. They supported the economic reforms of the older generation but believed that new issues, especially civil rights, needed to be part of the agenda. The younger generation was also more impatient, less willing to "wait their turn" to assume power. "The older folks saw people like Mondale and Freeman as upstarts, usurpers," reflected Arthur Naftalin. "They were too pushy, too aggressive and maybe even too radical." Ironically, Mondale, who began his career championing an assault against the "old politics," was one day to find himself on the opposite side of the generational divide.[13]

The younger generation turned to Orville Freeman to fill the void created by Humphrey's departure from state politics. After graduating from the University of Minnesota in 1940, Freeman served as a Marine Corps Captain during World War II. In 1943, while leading a patrol in the Solomon Islands, Freeman had his left jaw shattered by a Japanese bullet. Months of painful rehabilitation helped him to regain his speaking ability, but it did little to mend the fragmented bones that left his face permanently scarred. In 1944, he had enrolled in the University of Minnesota Law School. After completing his studies in 1947, Freeman immersed himself in DFL politics where he had proven himself an effective leader of the Humphrey forces.

By 1950, Freeman, at the age of 32, was a bright light of the party. Considered an idealist, he was, according to the *Progressive*, "serious almost to the point of grimness." Intense and ambitious, Freeman lacked Humphrey's ability to appeal across the party's generational divide. Where Humphrey succeeded by co-opting the older leaders, Freeman waged a frontal assault on his adversaries. To help fight his battle, Freeman enlisted a small group of left-over Humphrey campaign workers. They called themselves the "Palace Guard," but many party members, contemptuous of the group's youth and inexperience, referred to them as the Diaper Brigade. Along with Mondale, the key players included Don Fraser of the American Veterans Committee, a liberal organization that emerged out of World War II as an alternative to the American Legion, and three other recent Minnesota graduates: Tom Hughes, Dale MacIver, and Bill Waters.[14]

This small cadre sought to transform Minnesota into a reliably liberal Democratic state. "We were a pathetic minority," Mondale recalled. "We had a Humphrey victory and that was it," he added. "In order to really change Minnesota we needed to encourage a whole generation to start out at the bottom—in the legislature, the city councils." To increase their visibility, Mondale and the other "Palace Guard" members set up a DFL booth at the state fair, began registration drives, and provided a sample ballot to identify DFL-endorsed candidates. They pulled professors off campus to give community conferences on important issues. When not studying for tests or writing papers, Fritz traveled around the state talking to other aspiring young politicians, encouraging them to seek office and to challenge conservative incumbents. "We saw this as a movement which could pull together disparate groups and through institutional and personal relationships create a community that could go somewhere," he reflected.[15]

While helping recruit candidates for local office, Mondale encouraged Freeman to seek the state's highest position. Freeman, though, understood better than Mondale the political difficulty of winning a nomination for governor. For one thing, the older party members would not step aside and allow a young upstart to capture the party apparatus. Party stalwarts and most of organized labor had already endorsed Harry Peterson, a retired state Supreme Court justice. One of the few remaining links with the old Farmer-Labor party, Peterson had served as Attorney General under Floyd Olson before joining the court. Mondale, and other younger DFL members, were not impressed by Peterson's credentials. "This Peterson is a first class dud in my humble estimation," Mondale wrote a friend. He was, Mondale recalled, "a voice out of the past. A last gasp of the old farmer-labor group."[16]

The opposition of entrenched party interests did not dampen Freeman's political ambitions, however. Even if he did not win, he thought that he could shake up the party, get his name before the public, and encourage others to do the same on the local level. In the process, he would be establishing a foundation for a future campaign. Freeman also feared that a Peterson candidacy would add prestige and power to the older DFL leaders and demoralize the new generation. Peterson's candidacy, he reasoned, would give "all the malcontents" in the party "a tremendous stimulus and a strong power position" while "our strongest forces, mainly the people who have an idealistic affiliation in politics, will be discouraged . . . [and] drift away." Much to Mondale's delight, Freeman, believing that continuing the Humphrey revolution was worth the risk of personal embarrassment, announced his candidacy for governor.[17]

Freeman's diminished expectations proved well-founded as he was overwhelmed by Peterson's reputation and organization at the party's convention in June. Although Freeman lost in his bid for governor, he won endorsement as the party's candidate for attorney general. In November, the DFL slate lost but Freeman made a respectable showing, thus ensuring himself a bright future in the party.

The defeat taught Mondale a valuable lesson: the battle to wrestle control from the older party leaders would be long and fierce. The resistance to Freeman's candidacy from entrenched interests disabused Mondale of the notion that the Palace Guard could singlehandedly restructure Minnesota politics. But it did not lessen his enthusiasm for regaining control of the party. Mondale believed the campaign revealed that supporting a youthful candidate in Humphrey's image would not alone guarantee victory. Liberals had to transform the party from the bottom up by out organizing the opposition on the local level. Shortly after the election, he expanded on his new strategy in a long, prescient letter to his former friends in the ADA.

> The heroic era of Minnesota liberal and DFL efforts has ended. . . . The 'practical' boys are slowly seeping back into party control. . . . The hope for the long run lies in the growing realization among young convinced liberals that they must build themselves up the hard way by election to the state legislature or municipal offices. . . . The thing the Oldtimers don't understand is that this is the Roosevelt, and increasingly, the Humphrey generation that has grown up to plague the normal and traditional way of doing things. . . . If I were to point up one thing which I consider crucial to a building of liberal strength in Minnesota, that would be the slow careful nurturing of this generation. We have to be careful not to be too fast, to adopt unrealizable plans calling for the winning of all major offices presently, lest, in the failing of them, we kill off the enthusiasm and idealism of this group by the consequent disillusionment. Presently we should concentrate on (1) keeping strong college chapters and making a conscious effort to tie the more promising liberals into the movement in some tangible way, (2) urging those ready to run for some office to aspire for a lesser office, preferably the legislature, where there is a chance of winning and building up their name, and (3) keeping contact with as many of this generation as possible by periodic issue conferences and action programs to keep their interest fresh.[18]

Before remaking Minnesota politics, however, Fritz needed to tend to more practical needs. Most pressing, he needed to decide what to do following his graduation from the University after completing his requirements in the 1951 summer session. Despite his campaign involvement, Fritz had graduated *cum laude* with a degree in political science. He thought briefly about pursuing a graduate degree in political science but decided he needed a break from the classroom.[19]

His decision had to be made in the shadow of a bloody war. In June 1950, North Korean forces had crossed the thirty-eighth parallel in an invasion of South Korea, and within twelve months U.S. casualties had reached over 62,000 with more than 11,000 dead, and a lot more dying still to be expected. Fritz was not attracted to the idea of spending a few months risking his life on the front lines in Korea, but the military did offer one attractive incentive: the GI Bill. Two years in the military, he thought, would not only give him time to muster the courage to attend law school, but would also provide the funds to pay for it. On September 27, 1951 Fritz strolled down to the local draft board and volunteered for the army.[20]

A few days later, his mother sent him a short note. "I cannot understand why, when we are given such a beautiful world, all our grand boys must get caught in this militaristic machine and have their lives interrupted in such a ghastly way," she wrote. "Dad always said that the only way to fight Communism is to bring it right out into the sunlight and not try to run it underground, and then fight the Communistic ideas with Christian Ideas, and that the better is bound to win, just has happened over and over in history."[21]

Mondale's induction papers listed him as standing five-feet-ten-inches tall, weighing 154 pounds with brown hair and blue eyes. He reported no unusual medical problems, although he had been treated in 1946 for a sinus infection. In October, after a brief stint at Fort Sheridan, Illinois, he completed his training at Fort Knox, Kentucky—a small city 35 miles south of Louisville. His basic training set the tone for the rest of his military service. While the other trainees were doing calisthenics, Mondale managed to get a position assisting the Company Clerk as a typist. "I hit 70 words on a typing test and have been banging away since that time, getting very little of the training," he wrote his brother in September.[22]

After completing his basic training, Mondale applied for a position in the prestigious Counter Intelligence Corps (CIC). Mondale remembered scoring well on the factual part of the test, which questioned knowledge of political personalities and events, but flunking the section on political loyalty. He told the interviewer "a person shouldn't be canned from a job until substantial evidence of disloyalty was proven," and that "accusation is not tantamount to proof, despite McCarthy." He also registered his disagreement with loyalty oaths, which he called "silly and completely off the point if one were concerned with countering Communism with effective measures." The Army never told him why it rejected him, but Mondale was certain it was because they considered him "an unsafe security risk."[23]

After his rejection by CIC, Mondale remained at Fort Knox working as an information officer in basic training.[24] With little supervision and few demands for his services, Mondale spent most of his two years trying to improve his social life.[25] "You might say my Army career has been colorless, in the sense that I am a mediocre GI who learns nothing except that class time provides a good opportunity to sleep," he acknowledged. Meeting women, not battling invading armies, proved the most difficult problem he faced. Mondale was not attracted to the hardened women who gravitated toward young men at the camp. He searched elsewhere and found "a small, but yet desirable, supply of unmarried, unattached, slightly attractive, and quite intelligent girls," at a local Unitarian Church. Although a Methodist, Mondale was willing to try any religion that offered attractive companionship. "There are some 400 churches in Louisville," he said. "Certainly my true religion can be found amongst them!"[26]

Mondale's letters to friends at home revealed his irrepressible humor. He frequently poked fun at the monotony of Army routine. "I couldn't get off this weekend," he wrote Don and Arvonne Fraser, "because I am one of 202 persons picked out of a possible 202 persons to stand Fireguard for the weekend. It is our duty, in case of fire, to assault the flames with a fully loaded canteen." During their time off, Mondale and Minnesota friend Tom Hughes went into town with hoĵes of meeting women. Complaining that his uniform limited his appeal, Fritz begged the Frasers to send him civilian clothes. "It is the sincere hope of Thomas R. Hughes and Walter Frederick Mondale, respective protectors of our freedoms, that the latter's civilian clothes, including three white button-down collar shirts, be sent to Fort Knox in sufficient time to make them available for wear for a weekend pass this coming weekend. There is uncontestable proof that a trainee's uniform i[s] woman-proof and is therefore a detestable garment to be wearing on pass."[sic] Fritz also had fun with word that his brother Clarence—whom he called Pete—and his wife Ginny were expecting a child. "I think my brother Pete, and wife, are having a baby," Fritz wrote Don Fraser. "Pete is pretty sure he did it and is quite proud over the whole affair." When the Frasers informed him they, too, were about to have a child, Fritz responded: "Oh, yes, I almost forgot, how many children do you have now? (In round numbers, please)." He contrived some political wit as well. "Best of luck to you, and may all our days be filled with the Divine grace of Democratic Rule," he concluded a letter to Pete. "Do not sin, and forget not thy precinct."[27]

His years in the military also provided Fritz with an opportunity for reflection about himself, his political ideas, and his future. Fritz

Frederick Mondale, who
emigrated to America
with his wife, Brita,
in 1856.   (MHS)

Ole Mondale, Fritz's
grandfather.   (MHS)

Frederick Mondale's original home, years after it had fallen
into disrepair.   (MHS)

Fritz's parents, Claribel and Theodore Mondale.
(Clarence Mondale collection)

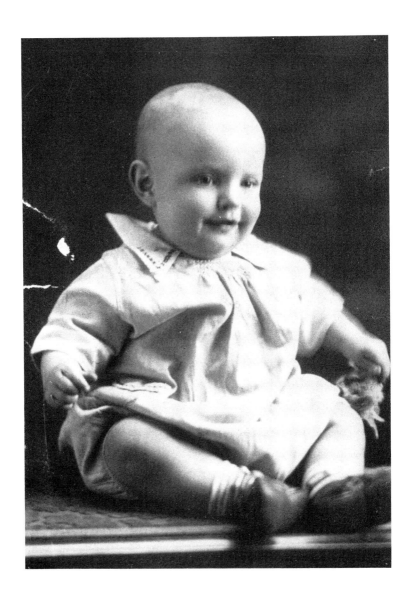

Fritz as a baby, and as a student at Macalester College.   (MHS)

In high school, Fritz channeled much of his energy into sports. Here he is pictured with the Elmore track team. (MHS)

"Crazylegs" Mondale as a star running back for the Elmore High School football team. (MHS)

Joan and Fritz on their wedding day, December 27, 1955.　(MHS)

was thoughtful and intelligent, but rarely introspective. Since he knew from an early age that he wanted to be involved in politics, he avoided the anxiety about choice of career that many ambitious young adults experience. He was uncomfortable with abstract thinking and reluctant to question basic instincts. He expressed some of these thoughts in a letter to Clarence in the fall of 1951.

> When I was younger, say 18 through 20, I assumed that the questions I had would gradually erase as I gained more experience and rounded out my education but I am now quite convinced that I will reach my grave without having any idea as to the basic Why's of mankind's status and meaning. This feeling makes me lazy and defensive to any issue which deals with the basic Why's, because I don't even want to discuss it or have my mind bothered by the question. Truthfully I am afraid to discuss it. Instead I seek a tentative satisfaction for the human-itarian drives Dad instilled in us by taking some publicly obstinate stand on such things as economic and racial equality. . . . [sic].

Despite occasional doubts, Mondale refused to consider a change in his career path. Three reasons, he said, accounted for his desire to go into politics. First, his training had "progressed so far in this field so I am better there than in any other;" second, "the people I know, loved ones as well as business acquaintances, are in the political field;" finally, "[My] ferver takes on a momentum which maintains itself through the periods of indecision." [sic].[28]

Even though he was hundreds of miles away, Mondale badgered friends for political intelligence from "back home." "By God, peo-ple," he wrote the Frasers, "I certainly would like to hear some political news. Everyone I hear from tells me someone else will shortly inform me on politics, but it never happens." What he did learn from afar was that Freeman had made another run for Governor in 1952. This time he secured the DFL endorsement without opposi-tion but, confronting a popular incumbent and facing an Eisenhower landslide, he had lost the general election. Freeman's defeat did not deter Mondale in his hopes of gaining control of Minnesota politics for the Humphrey liberals. He was looking forward to returning home and helping Freeman win in 1954. "[W]e should begin imme-diately," he wrote Freeman shortly after his unsuccessful campaign, "to rebuild your organization for the big push in '54 which will be aided by HHH." He insisted that effective organization and a strong party program were the keys to success. "Perhaps no single person has the power to take this reality of party weakness and enervation out of the talking stage and kick a strong party program into being other than you. If you get mean about it, there could be adequate improvement."[29]

During these years of quiet reflection in the army, Mondale roused the courage to attend law school. The day after his discharge in 1953 as a corporal, Mondale enrolled at the University of Minnesota. Law, he believed, would provide him with professional independence. "I could see that just working in politics—with no profession of your own—put[s] you in the position of being entirely too dependent on the political structure," he said. "I think you have to be in a position where, if something offends you deeply enough in politics you can walk out without starving. You have to be able to be independent." But his doubts persisted. "I went there wondering whether I could do it," he remembered. "He wasn't sure of his ability," Clarence recalled.[30]

To save money and avoid political distractions, he moved in with his mother. At the age of sixty-one, Claribel had moved to a small house in St. Paul and accepted a position teaching Sunday school at Hamline Methodist Church. The law school work did not come easily to Fritz. He spent long days in the library only to return home late at night and finish reviewing cases. When he finally went to bed his mother could hear him tossing and turning, his head occasionally thumping against the wall.[31]

In a first year curriculum that included classes in torts, contracts, criminal law, and property, Mondale earned mostly "B" grades. Though his marks were not outstanding, he ranked highly enough to be selected to law review. Many of his classmates viewed him as a hard-working, bright, and engaged student who had little interest in abstract debates. "Mondale impressed me as a quick study," a member of Mondale's law school study group has said. "He could go in knowing nothing about a subject, be told about it and pick it up very quickly and retain it. But he was also careful. He always wanted to know the facts before moving ahead. . . . He had a lawyer's way." Another classmate told Finlay Lewis: "Law review was never particularly attractive to Mondale. I think that was a little too scholastic in the intellectual sense—too many people playing Aquinas and splitting legal hairs about how many angels could stand on the head of a pin. He was more practical. None of us had the feeling Fritz was going to become a legal scholar or a courtroom giant. That just did not seem to be his bent. He was going to be in politics."[32]

While in law school, Mondale joined a study group with three other students, two of whom were staunch Republicans, who engaged in frequent late-night bull sessions that often turned heated. There was much to talk about. In April 1954 Wisconsin Senator Joseph McCarthy clashed with Army Counsel Joseph Welch on national television, and the following month the Supreme Court ruled against segregation in the nation's public schools. In all of these debates and discussions, Mondale reflected his father's populism. One member of the group commented that he sensed in Mondale a powerful and instinctive distrust "for the possession of power gained by wealth." He never hid his own ambition to enter politics and contribute to the debate. "He said he wanted to be the George Norris of the Senate," said Douglas Head. "When asked why, he said it was because Norris was a great liberal, and that he had influenced the United States in a liberal direction." A figure worthy of admiration, Norris, a Nebraska Republican (later an Independent) first elected in 1902, had emerged as a champion of the "common man," an insurgent who lead a revolt against his own party, and later became a leading supporter of the New Deal. Another participant in the discussions observed a similar commitment: "There was a core of beliefs. You could strip away some of his peripheral beliefs and he might even agree with you. Reasonable minds can agree on a lot of things, but when you got down to the core, I felt he was immovable."[33]

As usual, Mondale displayed tremendous energy. During the week he spent twelve-to-fifteen hours a day sitting in classes, reading legal briefs and participating in study groups. He spent weekends working as a paid DFL field organizer traveling the state recruiting liberal candidates for office. He devoted summers to working full time for the DFL, traveling in the heavily Republican first and second congressional districts and in the southern half of the seventh. While ostensibly working for the DFL, Mondale recruited liberal candidates to oppose conservative members of his own party. He kept in close contact with promising candidates, while discouraging weaker people from running. "I am absolutely convinced that the liberal [state] Senators must have an organizer in the field before the senatorial elections," he wrote, stressing again the importance he placed on effective organization. The state party, he argued, needed to coerce local committees to find liberal challengers to run for office. Unresponsive committees "should be blasted from every end."[34]

These years of tedious travel reinforced the style of politics Mondale had learned during the 1948 campaign and practiced for the rest of his career. It was based on painstaking attention to organizational detail, careful cultivation of opinion leaders, and direct and regular personal contact with key constituencies. Mondale's style was well suited to Minnesota politics in the 1950s. Television was still in its infancy, so most campaigning centered on public rallies and events. The parties were still effective vehicles for building broad coalitions, attracting voters to the polls, and dispensing patronage. Every year the state DFL organized county fairs and farmers' picnics, as well as a bean feed that filled the Minneapolis auditorium. Geographically, the state was manageable. Its population was relatively small and clustered around major cities—Minneapolis and St. Paul, Duluth, and Rochester.

It was not organization alone that inspired Mondale, for he also shared the dissatisfaction of liberal intellectuals with Eisenhower's bland leadership. Mondale believed that, though Republicans controlled the White House, liberal intellectuals were dominating the public dialogue, and these fertile years for liberal thought impressed upon him the important role that ideas played in politics. Confident that the surplus generated by an expanding economy could pay for an arms race with the Soviets and provide for social needs at home, many liberals criticized Eisenhower for his restraint abroad and his timidity at home. Leon Keyserling, who had served as chairman of the Council of Economic Advisors under Truman, advocated a "national prosperity budget" which included among its provisions full employment, higher-minimum-wage law, a massive housing program, and a tax cut for the middle class. Others complained that the President's commitment to low taxes and limited spending gave the Soviets a decided edge in the superpower competition. "In this age of nuclear weapons and unbridled Soviet aggression the American people have far more at stake in peace and security than in lower taxes," wrote Robert Nathan.[35]

Mondale lacked the patience to read the books and articles written by the constellation of liberal academic stars who helped articulate the postwar liberal tradition. But he had frequent discussions with many of the chief proponents of the "new liberalism" in Minnesota. Included in this group were two Macalester College political science professors, Theodore Mitau and Dorothy Jacobson; Arthur Naftalin, an astute student of Minnesota politics, Mayor of Minneapolis, and close Humphrey associate; and a young University economist named Walter Heller. For a number of reasons Minnesota proved especially receptive to the new liberal faith. A rich Scandinavian heritage that valued education and a strict civil-service law that limited political patronage had created a unique form of "programmatic" politics in the state. The political parties in Minnesota, one observer noted, "were issue-oriented rather than primarily job-oriented," and most politicians in the state "wanted to win elections in order to translate certain political programs into public policy." Polls also showed that liberal ideas were popular with most of the state's voters. A 1954 poll indicated that 76 percent supported higher pensions for older people; 67 percent wanted the government to spend more money on public works; 63 percent favored economic assistance to underdeveloped countries; and 52 percent endorsed some form of national health program.[36]

In 1954 the young generation of liberals who had been pressing for power broke through the resistance to their ideas and ambitions. Campaigning on a liberal platform that promised to "bring jobs, markets, profits and new wealth" to the state, the DFL scored a dramatic victory. Humphrey easily won a second term in the Senate and Freeman finally won election as governor. He became only the fifth Democrat in the state's history to assume that post. Along with winning the governorship, the DFL gained control of the statehouse and elected seven of eight candidates to statewide office. For Mondale, the results confirmed his belief that his efforts at rebuilding the party's grassroots would eventually pay off.

Freeman wasted little time enacting his progressive platform into law by increasing workman's compensation and unemployment benefits, signing a strong Fair Employment Practices Act, boosting old age insurance, and expanding services for the mentally ill. Many of the "Palace Guard" accepted positions in the new Freeman administration. "None of us have yet become used to the idea that it's our friends who will be running things in Minnesota come Jan. 5," Arvonne Fraser wrote her parents. "Out of the five boys who lived in this house in academic '49–50 Tom Hughes is the governor's secretary, Dale MacIver is assistant attorney general and Don is a senator." Mondale, who had his hands full with law school, continued working as a DFL field organizer on weekends and during the summer.[37]

In the summer of 1955, during a weekend at home, Mondale was introduced to Joan Adams, an attractive twenty-five-year-old art student from Macalester. Fritz had been a junior at Macalester when Joan started her freshman year. Although they had not met before their blind date, she knew of Fritz because of his work in the Humphrey campaign. "He was well known on campus," she recalled.

"Everybody knew who Fritz Mondale was." After majoring in history with a minor in art and French, Joan was graduated in 1952 and, hoping to pursue a career in art, went to Boston where she worked in the slide library at the Boston Museum of Fine Art. The following year, when the Minneapolis Institute of Arts offered her a job in its education office, she returned home. Like Fritz, Joan was the child of a sometimes itinerant Minister who stressed moral character over financial gain. Born in Eugene, Oregon in 1930, she had migrated with her parents to Ohio, Pennsylvania, and finally, in 1947, to St. Paul. Her father, who served as chaplain at Macalester College, was a man with strong convictions. A pacifist who opposed American entry into World War II, he also was committed to social justice and especially to civil rights. But unlike Fritz, Joan was raised in a genteel family that traced its roots to colonial days and included doctors, college professors, and ministers. The Adamses lived comfortably, and sent all of their children—Joan was the oldest of three sisters—to St. Paul's most exclusive girl's college-preparatory school.

Over the weekends, after their first date, as they canoed down the St. Croix river or listened to Dixieland music in Mendota, they talked about politics. Joan tried to expose Fritz to the world of art. They attended an exhibit at the Walker Art Center and looked at rare portraits at the Minneapolis Institute of Arts, where Joan worked; but Fritz never evinced much interest. She had better luck convincing Fritz he should learn to ski. Over the years, it became his principal form of recreation. It did not take Joan long to realize that Fritz was most inspired by politics. He told her of his plans to run for office. "There was no doubt about it," she recalled. "It was very clear he knew who he was. He knew what he wanted and he knew how to get there." Joan found the prospect of being in politics exciting, although she had no idea what the pressures of public life would be.[38]

After a whirlwind eight-week romance, they married on December 27 at the Macalester Student Union. The families made for an odd mix. Although the Adamses were liberal Democrats, they lived in a wealthy old-line Republican neighborhood in St. Paul. For the most part, the Adamses avoided discussing political issues with their conservative neighbors. Much to their dismay, Mondale invited to the service the entire state Democratic leadership—including Governor Freeman. As the Governor walked down the aisle to his seat, there was a distinct grumbling from the Adams side of the congregation. Finally, a perturbed Republican whispered just loud enough for the entire assemblage to hear: "That man is here."[39]

The demands of married life did not distract Fritz from his course work. In January, 1956 Joan and Fritz moved into a small apartment in southeast Minneapolis while Fritz completed his last semester of law school. Joan continued working at the museum and paid the bills with her $100-a-week salary. In May, Fritz finished classes and the following month he received his law degree. Driven by insecurity and intense ambition, he had finally achieved a level of academic success that had long eluded him. Along with earning a position on law review, he graduated near the top of his class, and won a competitive clerkship with a Minnesota State Supreme Court judge during his senior year. As an undergraduate he had excelled in classes dealing with politics, government, and labor. That pattern did not continue in law school. He scored his highest grades in banking and family law, while his grades in public and constitutional law were undistinguished.[40]

After passing the bar examination that summer, Fritz joined a Minneapolis law firm that already included a number of prominent political figures, including Freeman. At the same time, he and Joan moved in with her parents in their spacious St. Paul home. The Adams house included a private, fully furnished apartment with one undersized bedroom and a cramped living room. The apartment was free and allowed the Mondales to save enough money to buy a house eventually.

Although he was trained as a lawyer, Fritz's real interest remained politics. He had joined Freeman's law firm because it had a reputation of encouraging its lawyers to get involved in politics. But things did not work out as he had hoped. At its annual Christmas party in December 1957, the firm handed Fritz a set of chattering teeth in honor of his penchant for incessant talking. Mondale laughed at the present, but he also understood its meaning. "It was clear to me that the firm had had enough politicians and there was a lot of resentment at the junior level toward the reputation that the firm had gotten of being primarily political," Mondale reflected. "When I came in they had just about had enough of it and didn't want any more, and I could sense that: They didn't want another politician in that shop."[41]

Unwilling to abandon his political pursuits, Mondale quit the firm after eighteen months. He set up a private practice with his law school classmate Harry MacLaughlin in a tiny two-room office with a used typewriter and no secretary. It was not an easy decision. In 1957, Joan quit her job at the museum. The following year she gave birth to their first child, Teddy. Her income had provided a financial cushion, but now Fritz was the family's sole wage-earner. Mondale did not have to worry about rent, but there were bills to be paid and a family to support. Private practice provided the freedom to pursue his political interests, but it did not guarantee a regular paycheck. Fortunately, both Fritz and MacLaughlin had enough contacts in the city to stay busy with small projects. "We handled anything that came in the door," Mondale recalled.[42]

Even while struggling to establish a private law practice, the two men had a tacit understanding: either could leave at any time to run for office or to accept a political appointment. Mondale had good reason to expect that the party might reward him. His work during Humphrey's 1948 Senate campaign and Freeman's unsuccessful 1950 bid for lieutenant governor, combined with his extensive efforts as a DFL organizer, made him one of the most experienced young liberals in the party. Within the Humphrey faction of the party he had established a solid reputation as an energetic and articulate spokesman of liberal values. He had also proven himself as a successful organizer. Perhaps just as important, Mondale seemed the ideal party man. Personally nonabrasive, he rarely polarized factions. While strongly committed to issues, he understood that practical considerations sometimes required negotiation and compromise. He had also demonstrated a willingness to drudge in the shadows while others received the attention.

The opportunity Mondale hoped for emerged in 1958 when Freeman asked him to manage his reelection campaign for governor. "I had confidence in Mondale," Freeman said. "I was out most of the time, meetin', greetin', speakin', and handshakin'—and being governor. Doing that and campaigning was one helluva burden, so I let Mondale run things with a free hand." Leading nearly two-to-one in the polls, Freeman's reelection seemed almost certain. Mondale's biggest challenge was to prevent the hot-tempered Freeman from responding to the provocative charges of his Republican opponent, former congressman George MacKinnon, who tried linking the Governor to organized crime. Apparently the strategy was successful, because on election day Freeman won with an impressive 56.8 percent of the vote.[43]

Mondale spent most of the rest of the decade helping other candidates win election. In late 1958, the party recognized his efforts by appointing him state DFL finance director. In addition, Attorney General Miles Lord hired Mondale as a special-assistant working part-time on interstate trade issues. But by 1959, Mondale wanted to be more than just a good party man. He decided it was time to become a candidate for public office. He planned to start small, perhaps by seeking a state senate seat. After a few years of toiling on the local level, establishing a solid reputation and a base of support, he could run for Congress. It looked as though his time had come when in 1959 the Minnesota legislature created a new legislative district in south Minneapolis. In November, Mondale made a down-payment of $250, moved into a modest three-bedroom home on Park Avenue in Minneapolis, and began laying the groundwork for a 1962 campaign for the new state senate position.

The move aroused press speculation about Mondale's intentions. The Minneapolis *Star* noted that Mondale now resided in the fifth congressional district, making him a possible challenger for the congressional seat held by Republican Walter Judd. Another report more accurately predicted Mondale's interest in the new state legislature seat. Calling him "one of the bright young men of his party," the Minneapolis *Tribune* observed that his "move to this side of the river may be the first in preparation for the election campaign of 1962."[44]

While establishing roots in his new neighborhood, Mondale learned that a far more prestigious position would soon be available: the mercurial Miles Lord announced he was planning to retire as attorney general. Governor Freeman, facing a formidable challenge himself in 1960, had to find someone to fill the slot before the November election. Freeman considered Mondale one of the most promising young leaders in the state, someone who could be a force in state politics for many years. He also recognized that Mondale's youth and inexperience as a practicing attorney was a serious liability. The other leading contender, George Scott, a powerful Hennepin County attorney whose years of party service had earned him the support of many top party officials, had no such liabilities. But Freeman, who took seriously the generational battles of the 1950s, wanted to give a chance to one of the party's younger lights.[45]

Hoping to avoid a split in the party over the appointment, Freeman called a special session of the DFL executive committee. In a long, sometimes acrimonious meeting, party leaders debated which candidate would best serve the party's interest. Many older members favored Scott, charging that Mondale's inexperience as a practicing lawyer disqualified him. "Fritz was perceived as a young party hack" by many of the older members, Arvonne Fraser, a close Mondale friend and former "Palace Guard" member recalled. After listening to the older leaders snipe at Fritz for his inexperience, she rushed to his defense. He had a solid reputation, excellent political instincts, distinguished service to the party, and perhaps most of all, could sustain the party for years to come, she asserted. He was, she concluded, worth the gamble. Many party members agreed, and the committee voted to support Mondale's nomination, an endorsement that confirmed Freeman in his instinct that Mondale should be the state's next attorney general.[46]

On May 5, 1960, in the presence of friends, relatives and state officials, Mondale took the oath of office as Minnesota's twenty-third attorney general. At the age of thirty-two, he was the youngest attorney general in the nation. "Appointment to the office of the attorney general of the state of Minnesota is indeed a high honor," a nervous Mondale said at a press conference. "I promise the people of Minnesota I will dedicate all of the talents and energy I have to the duties of my new office." Declaring himself, "by training and instincts," a strong advocate of civil liberties and rights for all citizens, Mondale promised that he would "scrupulously protect" the right of Minnesotans to know the facts of government and to "criticize the conduct of government."[47]

He spent most of his first six months in office campaigning for election the following November. For the previous ten years, Mondale had been a campaign "background" man advising DFL candidates. In 1960, he needed to run his own campaign. He quickly learned it was different to be on the firing line. "I'm finding I'm a little stiff in meeting people," he confessed. "And in speaking, I'm a bit too factual, I don't have a fund of stories for a change of pace, for instance." But, he added, "I'm going to try to project the image of a hard-working young attorney general." In keeping with the style he had developed as Freeman's campaign manager, Mondale made himself available to all the county and district political gatherings and attended DFL meetings anywhere in the state. He spoke before civic groups, labor organizations, farmers, and anyone else from whom he could get an invitation. Though he purchased some radio time, he could not afford television ads and most of his expenses went for travel or for printing brochures which were handed out when he spoke.[48]

Press revelations of a shocking consumer fraud case provided Mondale with the issue he needed. In June, the Minneapolis *Star* recounted the details of a four-month government investigation into the financial dealings of the Sister Elizabeth Kenny Foundation, a private group supposedly devoted to helping the handicapped. Much of the background work was actually done by Mondale's predecessor. But no one remembered that when the headlines appeared. The investigation uncovered widespread irregularities, deception, and fraud amounting to millions of dollars. Mondale joined the Foundation in filing a $3 million lawsuit against Marvin Kline, a former executive director of the foundation, and Fred Fadell, a Minneapolis public relations expert. The complaint charged that the two men had "wasted" or "unlawfully diverted" millions of dollars in public donations. Between 1952 and 1959, Mondale charged, only half of the $30 million contributed to the foundation actually provided for hospitalization, treatment and research facilities. In one year, only 1.5 percent of public contributions supported medical activities.[49]

The Sister Kenny scandal virtually guaranteed Mondale's election. The press placed Mondale at the center of the biggest story of the year. Mondale's report inspired a federal investigation into charitable fund-raising and led to successful convictions on criminal charges and a reorganization of the Foundation's Board. "It was a major source of strength to me," Mondale reflected. "You know, it was my first big public issue and I was scared to death, because even though I was trained as a lawyer and had been in politics for some time, it was sort of awesome to take this on. And so I was very apprehensive. But, in fact, what happened was that I went into office in May unknown, untested, and very young and inexperienced, and within a month or two I was a very well-known state figure."[50]

Joan, who in January 1960 had given birth to their second child, Eleanor Jane, also played an active role in the campaign. "I had a choice of staying home with the children and feeling sorry for myself," she recalled, "or joining him in a sense by being active in the DFL." Along with participating in the neighborhood DFL group, she helped organize fundraising events, attended voter registration drives, and toured the state with other political wives. Though she had grown accustomed to Fritz's absence, Joan hoped that as a candidate her husband would not be as absent as he had been when he managed Freeman's 1958 campaign. "I saw Fritz for dinner one night a week— Saturday night—during the last six weeks or so of that campaign," she said. "Now, at least, we'll be able to exchange household problems at the banquet table."[51]

Gaylord Saetre, the Republican candidate for attorney general, attacked Mondale for politicizing the office. Pledging to cut up to $100,000 from the present payroll and return the office "to its former status as a nonpolitical balance wheel," Saetre suggested that Mondale's attorneys spent more time on DFL politics than state legal business. The attorney general's office, Saetre complained, was "loaded with people who don't have to be there. These boys make politics pay," he said. He charged that, at the age of thirty-two and just four years out of law school, Mondale lacked the experience and wisdom to serve effectively as attorney general.[52]

The charges had little impact on the voters. On election day Mondale won by a margin of 246,000 votes; at the same time, Freeman, who had appointed Mondale to office, was losing by a 23,000-vote margin to Republican state senator Elmer L. Andersen. Mondale's rise to prominence was sudden and dramatic. In just six months, he had established himself as a statewide political figure. Along with Lieutenant Governor Karl Rolvaag, Mondale had emerged as one of the DFL's most powerful state leaders. After surveying the election results, the Brainard *Daily Dispatch* advised its readers: "Keep an eye on Walter F. Mondale."[53]

4

The People's Lawyer

Like millions of Americans, the young attorney general sat enthralled in front of his television. It was noon on January 20, 1961 and John F. Kennedy, the new president, was standing on the Capitol steps giving a powerful inaugural address. Mondale had not always thought well of Kennedy. For most of the previous year the Massachusetts Senator had stood as the only Democrat between Hubert Humphrey and the White House. Mondale believed that Kennedy lacked Humphrey's passion for social justice, his knowledge of government, and his record of service. During the primaries, however, Kennedy's wealth and charm proved to be greater assets. While Humphrey campaigned by bus, Kennedy traveled on his private plane; while Humphrey scrambled for radio and print interviews, Kennedy purchased nightly television time. After Kennedy's decisive victory in West Virginia, Humphrey withdrew from the race.

Mondale endorsed Kennedy's candidacy shortly after his mentor's withdrawal from the race. As a loyal party man, there was never any doubt that Mondale would support the Democratic nominee. But it was not political calculation alone that pushed Mondale into the Kennedy camp. He was impressed by Kennedy's vigorous style, his emphasis on youth and vitality, his call for national community, and his acceptance of positive government. "We will need in the sixties a President who is willing and able to summon his national constituency to its finest hour," Kennedy told the nation, "to alert the people to our dangers and our opportunities—to demand of them the sacrifices that will be necessary." Consumed by his own campaign for office, Mondale had little time to help Kennedy in his battle against former Vice President Richard Nixon, but he observed the Massachusetts Senator with growing admiration.

One powerful person blocked Mondale's plans for emulating Kennedy's activism on the state level: the new Republican Governor, Elmer Andersen. Freeman had used the attorney general's office extensively, having Mondale screen bills before he signed them into law and asking Mondale's opinion on a whole range of legislative matters. Andersen, on the other hand, constantly sniped at Mondale. In particular, the Governor tried to fluster Mondale by uncovering embarrassing incidents, buried deep in the bowels of various state agencies, that would cast doubt on the competence of his office.

When these efforts failed, Andersen requested that the Attorney General voice an opinion on controversial issues. In one case, the Governor asked Mondale to rule on the financing practices of Dayton's—a large and successful Minneapolis-based department store. For years the store had charged a one-percent-a-month finance fee at a time when the state had an annual 8 percent usury ceiling. The finance fee clearly violated the statute, but if found guilty under Minnesota law, Dayton's would lose both the interest and principal on all outstanding debts. A negative ruling would cost Dayton's millions of dollars, possibly destroy the business, and have a profound impact on the Minneapolis economy. Seeing the trap, Mondale sidestepped the issue. He told the governor that "revolving charge credit plans" involved private contract disputes and did not involve the state.[1]

Occasional skirmishes with the Governor did not deter Mondale from putting into effect his notions about active government. The attorney general traditionally had performed such functions as handling highway condemnations, representing the state in court, appearing before administrative agencies, and providing state and local officials with legal opinions. Mondale was not content with such routine assignments. Conceiving of himself as "the people's lawyer," he aggressively expanded the role of the Attorney General. Recruiting his own "best and brightest" from the top national law schools, he established separate departments for consumer protection, antitrust, and civil rights/civil liberties, each headed by an assistant attorney general.

Always at the center of the action was the young, energetic Mondale. He wanted to establish a reputation for honesty and effectiveness that would enhance his political stature. As a result he worked long, hard days and pushed himself and his staff to the end of their endurance. "He was very intense about it and would get jumpy in the office," said one attorney. "His intensity made people uncomfortable. . . . I don't think he liked people who were relaxed. We all worked like slaves." Mondale, though, never asked his staff to push themselves any harder than he pushed himself. "Brutal but not unethical" was the way many former staff members characterized his style.[2]

"Politics was completely consuming for him," Joan Mondale said, reflecting on these early years in public office. "He didn't have time for anything else." Despite having a young family, he rarely spent more than two evenings a month at home. The other nights, even weekends, he was out politicking—giving speeches, talking with party leaders, attending fundraising gatherings. Neither Fritz nor Joan had anticipated what a dramatic impact public life would have on their personal lives. "The change from private to public life when Fritz was appointed Attorney General was the greatest change in our family life," Joan reflected. "Once you are in public life everything is different." Joan, always playing an active part in her husband's political career, spent many of her evenings attending civic and women's political groups. In the spare moments that remained, she pursued her lifelong interest in the arts. "I've always claimed," Joan recalled, "that my children turned out successfully because they were raised by a series of good baby sitters."[3]

Every day, seven days a week, Fritz devoted to his work. Two weeks a year he took a vacation. During the winter he skied in Colorado; and during the summer he fished in the pristine north Minnesota woods. He never watched television, except perhaps to see how the local news covered one of his press conferences or some other important political event. He rarely played sports and never developed a hobby that would help take his mind off the daily grind of politics. "He never had an avocation," Joan said. Even at family events, rather than engage in small banter, he discussed the issues of the day. He refused to do household chores. Usually Joan cut the grass, changed the storm windows, and performed minor repair work around the house. "When you are in public life every weekend, every evening, every moment of your working time is consumed by politics," Joan said. "There is nothing else." "He is always on the move, making countless speeches to party groups and rallies throughout the state," commented Minneapolis *Tribune* reporter Frank Wright. "When he is not practicing politics or government, he is reading about them—usually after midnight at home while uncoiling from long hours in the office and on the road." He occasionally watched football games, "but baseball takes so long that it tends to make him squirm." He also attended Minneapolis Symphony concerts, Wright observed, "mainly out of a desire to see personal friends who have nearby seats rather than out of a burning interest in the music."[4]

Mondale worried that his age and inexperience would enable critics to brand him as a political appointee lacking the maturity to handle the job. That perception, if allowed to persist, could be fatal to any future political ambitions. Believing a severe countenance would convey maturity, Mondale adopted a dour public demeanor. "He thought looking stern and serious would make him more dignified and older," reflected a former aide. "You just watch," Mondale told a friend shortly after assuming office, "I'm not going to smile for a year." Many who knew him claimed he was faithful to the promise. In public he always appeared spotlessly neat, with shoes highly shined and hair carefully combed. Those who worked with him found him cold and impersonal. He rarely socialized with staff members, had difficulty making small talk and never showed a personal interest in people who devoted most of their waking hours to furthering his career. Staff members who accompanied him on long campaign trips hoping to spend a few hours engaged in thoughtful conversation were usually disappointed. Mondale busied himself reading newspapers and magazines, taking short naps and staring out the window.

Mondale was clearly a man in a hurry and everyone knew it. Even his closest friends, while admiring his talents and respecting his values, often remarked about his ambition. One acquaintance coined a phrase that captured the sentiment: "How would you like to get caught between Walter Mondale and anything in which he is even slightly interested?" People who stood in his way felt his wrath. On one occasion at a state DFL meeting, Conrad Hammer, a party leader, harshly criticized the young Attorney General's performance in office. Enraged by the verbal assault, Mondale pursued Hammer into a public lobby where he challenged him to a fist fight. Bystanders looked on in shock as the medium-sized Mondale confronted his large, barrel-chested critic. Mondale, shouting at his adversary, threw his coat to the floor before thrusting himself in front of his opponent. Hammer, clearly surprised by the display of anger, backed off as party officials intervened to haul away their incensed Attorney General.

Such behavior shocked observers who had known Mondale only as the composed and imperturbable party operative who had helped mastermind Freeman's rise to governor. Not so those who knew him well. His temper tantrums were legendary among those who worked for him. When performance did not live up to his perfectionist standards, he exploded in awkward demonstrations of rage. His face would grow beet red; veins would protrude from his neck as he berated a terrified young attorney. Sometimes he would slam books—or any other object within his reach—to the ground and stomp his feet for added effect. Despite the harsh treatment, staff attrition was minimal. Throughout his years in public life, Mondale attracted and retained a first-rate staff because they admired his ability, respected his values, and saw him as someone who could advance their own careers. It was, however, always a relationship of shared commitment, not affection. "He gets people because they believe in what he stands for, because he allows for responsibility and because he provides an exciting place to work," commented a former aide.

Mondale impressed even the most seasoned lawyers as a smart and effective attorney. His extraordinary success demonstrated how a sharp legal mind, shrewd political instincts, and intense commitment could bring rewards. The abuses uncovered in the Sister Kenny Foundation case convinced Mondale that other groups might also have taken advantage of the public trust by using charitable donations for improper purposes. After a brief investigation, he discovered that Minnesota Boys Town, which raised money promising to provide a safe shelter for troubled teenagers, had for years been stealing from Minnesota residents—and especially senior citizens. Mondale's suit against the group claimed that over a ten-year period it had raised more than $250,000 in private donations but had never spent a penny on troubled teens. In some cases, Boys Town had extracted as much as $12,000 from elderly donors with the promise that the amount given would be returned with interest.[5]

Mondale also pursued a well-publicized consumer protection case against the Holland Furnace Company of Michigan. The problem started in December 1959 when aggressive Holland representatives used the pretense of a "furnace inspection" to gain entrance to the home of an unsuspecting housewife. After conducting phony tests to "prove" the furnace was a "death trap," the salesmen convinced her to purchase a new model for an exorbitant fee. After a few days the woman became suspicious and wisely contacted a lawyer, who happened to be a former Mondale law school classmate. When informed about the incident, the attorney general launched an investigation into the company and soon found other cases of suspected fraud. Mondale wanted to take action against the company, but the absence of an effective consumer fraud statute restricted his efforts. Undaunted, Mondale searched for other ways to force the company into court. Sitting around a large conference table, Mondale and his staff debated how to proceed. One attorney suggested they prosecute using a public-nuisance law originally intended to silence barking dogs. Most of the lawyers were skeptical, but Mondale expressed interest. After listening to arguments about why it would never work, Mondale exploded: "You mean we can shut up barking dogs but we can't put these crooks out of business? To hell with it! Let's go to court and find out!"[6]

Mondale tried his unorthodox strategy in a state courthouse. Alleging that Holland employees often posed as public officials to gain entry to private homes and then coerced people into purchasing expensive furnaces, Mondale asked the court to revoke the company's operating license in Minnesota. The action was drastic, he admitted, but the company had been warned repeatedly in the past by local and federal law enforcement agencies and Better Business Bureaus. Mondale's strategy worked. The judge came to the "inescapable conclusion" that Holland "lied to the people of Minnesota in attempting to sell its products." For the first time since 1911 an out-of-state corporation had its authority to do business in Minnesota canceled.

The Attorney General's highly publicized courtroom successes gave him added leverage in his dealings with other potential adversaries. Fearing expensive and public trials, many businesses agreed to make voluntary changes in order to avoid prosecution. Mondale successfully forced Family Publications Service, for example, one of the nation's largest sellers of magazine subscriptions, to change its sales methods. The company, he argued, in its telephone solicitations for new orders, falsely claimed to be giving away free publications. Company representatives told prospective customers that if they purchased either *Life* or *Look* at the regular newsstand price of 39 cents per week, they would receive a second magazine subscription for free. Mondale discovered the regular *Life* and *Look* weekly newsstand price was actually 19 cents, not the 39 cents the company claimed. Rather than getting a second magazine for free, customers were paying an exaggerated price for one. Confronted with the charges and the possibility of litigation, Family Publications quickly agreed to change its sales methods.[7]

To redress other potential consumer problems, Mondale appointed a Consumer Protection Advisory Council. Comprised of business, labor, and government representatives, the Council proposed legislation designed to address a whole range of consumer complaints. In recognition of his pioneering efforts in consumer legislation, President Kennedy appointed Mondale to a new National Consumers' Advisory Council. Mondale joined the Council with an ambitious agenda. He hoped to create a national clearing house for information on state attempts to control racketeering and to oversee the expansion of the Federal Trade Commission. Among the specific pieces of legislation he wanted to propose were a simple interest bill, federal regulation of deceptive packaging, a federal truth-in-lending statute, and a full disclosure measure. Despite Kennedy's verbal commitment to a "Consumer's Bill of Rights," Mondale was disappointed with the council's work. He believed that by denying the council cabinet rank, the administration prevented it from enjoying the level of presidential attention it needed to be effective.[8]

During his stint as attorney general, Mondale took on other controversial issues. He intervened, for example, on behalf of Clarence Gideon, a poor Florida convict who asked the United States Supreme Court to extend the right to free counsel to indigents charged with felonies in state courts. In 1932, the Supreme Court had established that the Fourteenth Amendment required the right to counsel in capital cases, but ten years later, in *Betts v. Brady,* it had denied that right to criminal defendants. When Florida's Attorney General wrote the attorneys general of the forty-nine other states, asking them to join in a friend-of-the-court brief opposing the Gideon argument, Mondale rejected the invitation. He believed that requiring counsel would not infringe on states' rights. "I believe in federalism and states' rights too. But I also believe in the Bill of Rights." Mondale called the proposal to provide counsel "fair and feasible" and charged that one of the responsibilities of an attorney general was "to see that the defendant has a fair trial." He proposed a brief asking the Court to impose this requirement on the states. Mondale stated that "arrest without a warrant or on mere suspicion, unreasonable detention without arraignment, and interrogation without benefit of counsel are practices which have no place in the judicial system of a democratic society." Mondale did not stop with writing the letter. He sent copies of his correspondence to several friends, including Massachusetts Attorney General Edward McCormack, who decided to write an *amicus curiae* brief in favor of Gideon. Mondale agreed to join the cause and helped enlist others to sign. In the end twenty-three state attorneys general signed McCormack's brief.[9]

By 1962, Mondale had established himself as a fresh face on the Minnesota political scene. His vigorous defense of consumer protection, his forceful advocacy of sometimes controversial positions, and his youthful energy made even his detractors recognize that he was a political force to be reckoned with. "He was the rising star of the party," reflected a DFL leader. "There was no question about that." "He was at the center of where things were happening in the state," recalled a young attorney on the attorney general's staff. When visiting politicians came by the state house, they made the obligatory visit to the governor's office, but it was Mondale they wanted to meet. "Everybody knew Mondale was headed for higher office," one of his aides recalled.[10]

He became a favorite of the Minnesota press. "Personable, able, young, politically astute, he is making himself available—and gradually is assuming leadership—filling the void caused by the mass [DFL] exodus to Washington," commented the Catholic *Bulletin*. The New Ulm *Daily Journal* called Mondale "a dedicated young man" who prosecuted "malefactors, big and little, without regard to politics." The Fairmont *Daily Sentinel* declared: "His service to date has been tops, rendered without fear or favor; without the slightest trace of partisan prejudice." The St. Paul *Dispatch* stated: "In our governmental system it is also important that new and highly promising political personages be continually found in the interests of the future progress and welfare of the state. Walter F. Mondale is one such personage."

Nor did Mondale's success escape the purview of the national press. "The Attorney General of Minnesota, Walter F. Mondale, has the attitude of a law-enforcement officer who gauges victory not by the number of convictions he 'obtains' but by the advancement of justice," observed the Washington *Post*. "This is the course not alone of prudence but of elementary justice as well."[11]

Mondale's achievement was no accident. As in the past, hard work and boundless energy were at the heart of his success. During regular work hours he played the role of nonpartisan Attorney General. After work he shifted into political gear. He carefully cultivated his relations with the media, meeting frequently with local reporters in order to forge relationships with those he considered loyal. He mastered the art of the press release. Almost daily his office announced some bold new Mondale proposal or statement. "As Attorney General, everything good Mondale did, he merchandised so you knew about it," reflected an associate. Staff members wrote columns under his name for publication in local newspapers. He rarely turned down an opportunity to appear on radio or to shake hands at the state and county fairs. "He made himself available to all the county and district political meetings who needed a speaker," said a lawyer in Mondale's office. "If there was a DFL meeting going on anywhere in the state, he was available to go and talk." [12]

In the process he transformed the Attorney General's office from a remote and secluded bureaucratic post into a high-profile hub of legal and political activity. "The word was clearly out that this guy Mondale was a comer," reflected another attorney. As a consequence, "the office became the center of aspiring young politicians in the state." Republicans repeatedly criticized Mondale for politicizing the office, charging him with "empire building in the state capitol," and accusing him of producing headlines, not service. "Publicity and glory are the only things that count there," charged a Republican leader. One small-town newspaper accused Mondale of "building his own private legal WPA project." [13]

These charges revealed more about the frustrations of Republicans who were unable to counter Mondale's growing popularity than they did about the actual operations of the attorney general's office. Mondale maintained a well-defined sense of propriety about the office. During the day he and the other attorneys in the office focused on legal work. He confined his political activities to evenings and weekends and he never bent a legal opinion for personal gain. "He tried to keep a straight ship as far as the legal work was concerned," recalled an assistant.

There was only one dimension of his new position that Mondale had difficulty mastering: public speaking. "The first time I met Walter Mondale was at a press conference in 1960," recalled Mike Berman who would become one of Mondale's closest political advisors and friends. "I thought he was a real turkey." His high-pitched nasal voice lacked the range of emotion which the ebullient Humphrey conveyed from the podium. Lacking confidence, he insisted on having a fully prepared text for every speech, no matter how brief. When forced to speak extemporaneously, Mondale could captivate audiences with his intelligence and sincerity. But on most occasions he lulled listeners to sleep reading from a script in a monotone. Staff members pleaded with him to be more spontaneous, but Mondale refused.[14]

His ineffective speaking style did not prevent him from becoming, in just two years, the most promising young figure in Minnesota politics. He had become so popular in fact that many Democrats urged him to run for governor. Democrats were determined to regain control of the state house in 1962, and since the two-year term of office had been increased to four by constitutional amendment, the 1962 race was especially important. Freeman, who had been appointed Kennedy's Secretary of Agriculture, was no longer a candidate. The two leading possibilities were Mondale and Karl Rolvaag, who as Lieutenant Governor was the highest ranking party official and, according to unwritten party rules, the next in line to challenge for the job. Believing winning more important than adhering to party hierarchy, many younger party leaders thought Mondale would be a more attractive candidate. Apparently the public agreed. The Minneapolis *Tribune* published a poll showing both Rolvaag and Mondale defeating the incumbent Republican Andersen: Mondale by eight points, Rolvaag by only two.

Mondale was not eager to run for governor. In public office little more than two years, he wanted more time to establish his base of support. "I'm young," Mondale told people who suggested he run. "I'm not in a hurry—I've got lots of time." A battle for the nomination could split the DFL, he feared, causing people to blame him if the party failed in November. Mondale was also a firm believer in what one observer called "the politics of loyal progression." Rolvaag, he reasoned, had done his time in the trenches. It was his turn to run for governor. Mondale would support him now, just as he would expect other party leaders to put aside personal ambition and rally around his candidacy when the time came. Ambition, however, prevented him from completely dismissing the idea. He decided he would run if a groundswell of support within the party appeared for his nomination. Then it would not look as though he were pushing aside his more senior colleague. When that groundswell did not occur, he issued a firm declaration of support for Rolvaag. "I have stated my position several times in the past," he told the St. Paul

Dispatch. "I support Rolvaag for governor and . . . I am a candidate for reelection, and that position never changed."[15]

Mondale faced only token opposition in his reelection campaign. After a number of leading Republicans refused to challenge Mondale, the party recruited Robert Kunzig, a Minneapolis business executive who had been chief counsel to the U.S. House of Representatives Committee on Unamerican Activities in 1953–54. "He's been elected once," Kunzig said of Mondale. "He's 34 years old. Yet, they say he's unbeatable. The time to cut off Mondale is right now." Kunzig was eager for battle, but with few weapons in his arsenal, never presented Mondale with a serious threat. In 1960, Mondale had campaigned very little, relying instead on the news generated from the Sister Kenny case to keep his name in the public eye. In 1962, however, he campaigned extensively telling voters about his efforts on behalf of consumer protection, antitrust, and enforcement of civil rights.[16]

In the governor's race, the DFL's early optimism faded as polls showed the contest tied with only two weeks left. Desperate for an issue that would swing support to their side, a number of DFL officials falsely accused Governor Anderson of having endangered lives by hurrying construction of a stretch of highway in the northeastern part of the state so he could claim credit at a public ceremony a few days before the election. A partisan Mondale joined Humphrey and Congressman John Blatnik in a press conference aimed at keeping the issue before the public. As the campaign moved into its final days, the charges, which appeared every day in the evening newspapers, embarrassed the Governor and helped the Democratic challenger. Even with the assistance of the fraudulent accusations, the results were so close that it took three-and-a-half months to determine a winner. Finally, on March 25, 1963, Rolvaag was declared the new governor by ninety-one votes.

As expected, Mondale scored a decisive victory over his lackluster opponent. He received 730,783 votes, more than any other state official. Observers could not remember a time when an attorney general, previously an obscure state official, led all state candidates in the number of votes received in an election. Also, his 236,162 victory margin was the highest ever received by a candidate for state office in Minnesota. "Minnesota has a new champion," wrote the *Fargo Forum*, "A vote getter who in the November 6 election took a big step toward the governor's chair or the United States Senate."[17]

Exhilarated by his victory, Mondale became more outspoken on national political issues, especially the emotionally charged issue of civil rights, which anyone seeking higher office in Minnesota or anywhere in the nation had to confront. By 1963, no national question aroused more public attention. In the fall of 1962, Kennedy had reluctantly called in federal troops to protect James Meredith's attempt to enroll at the all-white University of Mississippi. The first major confrontation of 1963 occurred in Birmingham, Alabama when Martin Luther King targeted the city to end discrimination in department stores and at lunch counters. In response, the police commissioner unleashed dogs and water cannons. Shortly after the events in Birmingham, Governor George Wallace blocked the doorway at the University of Alabama in a futile effort to prevent two black students from registering. In response to a growing national demand for action, Kennedy presented legislation to Congress banning segregation in public facilities. Mondale declared: "I believe the civil rights bill is a reasonable proposal, certainly a moderate proposal and perhaps our last chance to avoid a major social upheaval which will make our past racial disturbances look like tea parties."[18]

In August 1963, to coincide with a March on Washington at which Martin Luther King described his dream of a just society, civil rights leaders organized a large rally on the Capitol steps in St. Paul where Mondale was the main speaker. Although he could not match King in eloquence or passion, Mondale drew repeated applause as he outlined both the moral and legal case against discrimination. The voice was more refined, the delivery more polished, but the inspiration came directly from his father's dinner table preachings. "Beyond bare tolerance lies acceptance—acceptance of every fellow citizen as a man with heart and mind, body and soul, and every child as a child of God—acceptance of every man as a fellow American," he sermonized. The problem of discrimination, he declared with naive confidence, could, with effective leadership, be solved in a generation. The enthusiastic crowd of eight hundred responded warmly to Mondale's message. "As principal speaker the youthful state official," reported the Minneapolis *Spokesman* "made a distinct hit with the people who stood in the bright sun to hear the program."[19]

Mondale used the momentum created by the national civil rights movement to write an ambitious civil rights bill for submission to the legislature. While the national legislation addressed only discrimination in public facilities, the state bill Mondale advocated included provisions for fair housing—a cause Mondale would later champion in the Senate. It also dramatically increased Minnesota's power to prosecute civil rights violators. Yet at the same time that he pushed for new legislation, Mondale recognized that laws by themselves would not be enough. "We need a major reassessment of our individual religious values, and a recommitment to the ideals expressed in the Declaration of Independence. We cannot, and must not, point a sanctimonious finger at Birmingham [Alabama] and Albany [Georgia] unless we act to put our own house in order," he declared. Making effective use of religious imagery, he asked Americans to listen to a higher voice. "In our individual lives, as well as in our actions as public officials and as citizens, it is well for us to recall the words of God: 'first cast out the beam of thine own eye; and then thou shalt see clearly to cast out the mote of thy brother's eye.' "[20]

The two issues Mondale chose to champion as attorney general provide insight into his approach to politics. Because both consumer protection and civil rights enjoyed widespread support in the state, Mondale could champion causes that were both morally correct and politically shrewd. Even the potentially divisive question of racial equality failed to polarize voters. Since Minnesota had a minuscule black population and little history of racial strife, there was limited political risk to supporting civil rights. "It was a non-issue," recalled Berman. Mondale's consensus politics were perfectly suited to the times. During these early years, he could support meaningful reforms while also enhancing his own political stature.[21]

By the fall of 1963, Mondale was getting restless. After just three years as attorney general, and at the age of thirty-five, he wanted to move to a higher office, but there were few political openings on the horizon. The DFL controlled both U.S. Senate seats and the governorship. He could challenge for a Republican congressional position but that would require moving into a new district.

On November 22, Mondale sat at his desk thinking about his plans for President Kennedy's Minnesota reelection committee, of which he was chairman, when an aide crashed through his door screaming "the President's been shot." Like most of the nation, Mondale sat motionless listening to radio reports of the President's condition. Stunned by the news, Mondale canceled his speaking engagements for the evening and went home to be with his family. The next week he released a public statement. "I came to know President Kennedy in several ways. He was warm, very brilliant, humane and brave. I feel that I and all Americans have lost a true friend." Calling him a "great man" and "courageous leader," Mondale said Kennedy "died a martyr to the cause of freedom."[22]

Mondale's grief for Kennedy was genuine, but he also realized that the assassination could change the political situation in Minnesota. Lyndon Johnson, he reasoned, would need a midwestern liberal to balance the ticket in 1964, and both of the state's senators—Eugene McCarthy and Humphrey—would be leading contenders. "In his last year he started thinking about the Senate and he became a little more political as attorney general," recalled his close friend Warren Spannaus. If Johnson chose McCarthy, Mondale planned to run for his seat, which was up in 1964. If Johnson chose Humphrey, then the Governor would have responsibility for choosing his successor. Mondale, hoping he might get the nod, became especially deferential toward Rolvaag. "He made doubly certain nothing happened to get the governor's office mad at the attorney general's office," recalled Spannaus.[23]

The greatest test Mondale faced in proving himself a good candidate for the Senate came in a confrontation over the Mississippi Freedom Democratic Party, a small group of dissidents who challenging the right of the regular, all-white delegation to represent their state at the Democratic National Convention. The white Democratic organization in Mississippi, which excluded blacks from participation and opposed most of Johnson's domestic program, still exercised considerable political power within the party. Johnson, who wanted to avoid an embarrassing Southern walkout that would jeopardize his electoral mandate, had no plans to oppose the regular delegation. "If you seat those black buggers," Governor John Connally of Texas told him, "the whole South will walk out." Mississippi State Senator F. K. Collins made a similar threat, warning that seating the Freedom Party "could mean the destruction of the Democratic Party in the South." Unwilling to offend his native South, Johnson offered the dissidents only two symbolic seats without voting privileges. The Freedom Democrats, and their talented lawyer Joseph Rauh, were in no mood for compromise. "We will accept nothing but equal representation with the regular Democrats," Rauh declared.[24]

Rauh realized that success depended on getting his motion out of the Credentials Committee and on to the convention floor where liberals exercised greater power. On August 22, he brought his case to the Credentials Committee in search of the eleven votes needed for a floor challenge. As he scanned the Committee room, he spied the face of a young delegate from Minnesota—Walter Mondale. One of the one hundred committee members, Mondale was in a delicate position. Johnson had been dangling the vice presidency in front of Humphrey for weeks. He had also made it clear that his final decision might rest on whether Humphrey could manage a compromise with the Freedom Party. "That was always in the background," recalled Geri Joseph, the other Minnesota representative on the committee. Mondale, knowing how eagerly Humphrey sought the office, wanted to prevent a Southern walkout. "He felt that in a sense he was representing Humphrey and he did not want to let him down," Joseph reflected. But Mondale shared his father's passion for racial equality and instinctive concern for society's outcasts.[25]

Like most committee members, Mondale hoped for a compromise that would allow the Freedom Party the respect it deserved and Johnson the support he desired. As he sat in the steamy committee room listening to the moving testimony of Freedom Party delegates describing the injustices inflicted upon them, Mondale came to appreciate the emotional nature of the challenge. "I have only one hour," Rauh told the committee, "to tell you a story of moral agony that could take years." Fannie Lou Hamer, a sharecropper who had been brutally beaten for attempting to register to vote, told the committee of her "woesome times." "Is this America," she asked rhetorically, "the land of the free and the home of the brave, where we are threatened daily because we want to live as decent human beings?" "We have shed our blood," pleaded Reverend Edwin King. "All we ask is your help." They closed their presentation with the eloquent testimony of Martin Luther King who just a year earlier had stirred the nation with his call for racial equality at the Lincoln Memorial. King implored the predominantly white committee to support the movement for true democracy in the South. "You, who must sit here judging their validity as delegates to this convention, cannot image the anguish and suffering they have undergone to get to this point. They come not to complain of their suffering. They come seeking the actual fulfillment of their dream for democracy in Mississippi."[26]

The nationally televised testimony polarized a committee already seriously divided along regional lines. While many southern and western representatives persisted in suggesting only symbolic recognition to the Freedom Party, many northern liberals, impressed by the Freedom Party's moving affirmation of democratic values, insisted on seating them no matter what the political cost. Governor

David Lawrence of Pennsylvania, the aging committee chairman, overwhelmed by the intense political pressure from both sides, searched for a way out.

Mondale believed that the large, unwieldy committee, with its strong personalities, was not the proper place to discuss such a difficult issue. On Sunday, August 23, he suggested creating a subcommittee to study the problem. Grasping at the opportunity to relieve himself of the issue, Lawrence quickly agreed and appointed Mondale its chairman. Mondale convened a meeting that night at 8:00 in his room at the Shelbourne Hotel. The subcommittee appeared just as divided as the full committee and made little headway. Charles Diggs, a black representative from Michigan, fiercely defended the Freedom Party's right to be seated. Sherwin Markman, an Iowa lawyer, expressed sympathy for the blacks' plight, but made clear his ultimate concern that Johnson not be embarrassed. Price Daniel, a former Texas Governor, and Irving Kaler, a Georgia businessman, defended the regular party. In the middle sat Mondale, hoping to find a fair compromise that would prevent an awkward floor fight and save Humphrey's vice presidential candidacy. As the hours wore on, he became increasing pessimistic that any such compromise existed. Frustrated and exhausted, he stopped the meeting at 3 A.M. and asked dembers to reconvene only a few hours later, at 8:30 A.M..[27]

With the opening of the convention only hours away, both sides escalated the pressure. Johnson enlisted the support of United Auto Workers head Walter Reuther and civil rights leader Bayard Rustin to bring pressure on the Freedom Party to accepted his token gestures. Prominent Southern politicians warned that any solution which seated the Freedom Party as Mississippi delegates would result in a united Southern walkout and a divided party. At the same time, Freedom Party supporters paraded before television cameras to condemn the party regulars and express their moral outrage at Johnson's offer.

As he listened to the debate, Mondale saw emerging the faint possibility of an eventual compromise. Partisans on both sides, he believed, had painted the issue in stark shades: Would the national Democratic party follow its conscience and repudiate the South by seating the dissidents, or would it accept political reality and continue its historic relationship with the South? Mondale believed common ground existed. The national party, he suggested, had a moral responsibility to atone for its transgressions against blacks by giving real power to the dissidents. It also had to recognize the regulars' legal right to represent the state and accept that change in the South would be a slow process.

Although Mondale headed the subcommittee created to solve the Freedom Party issue, the power to make decisions rested with the President. After a series of tense negotiating sessions with two Johnson aides, Walter Jenkins and Thomas Finney, Humphrey proposed a compromise. He suggested that, after signing a loyalty oath, the regular delegation be seated. Two Freedom Democrats would then be given seats as at-large delegates, not as delegates from Mississippi. The party would also establish a civil rights commission to bar from future conventions any state delegations that practiced discrimination.

After securing White House approval of the plan, Humphrey called Mondale to see if he could sell it to his committee. Mondale believed the compromise addressed both problems: it gave the dissidents real voting power and provided proof that the national party took their grievances seriously. Also, by establishing a commission to prevent discrimination in the future, the national party shared the blame for past injustices and offered a solution.

After gaining the support of his subcommittee, Mondale needed to sell his plan to the full Credentials Committee. Time was of the essence. Administration supporters hoped to pass the resolution before the Freedom Party, which was sure to reject any effort at compromise, could mobilize support against the plan. Joseph Rauh, the Freedom Party's attorney, learned of the details just as the Credentials Committee was filing into the room for the vote. He pleaded with Mondale to hold off his presentation until he had time to brief his clients. Personally Mondale thought it only fair and agreed to wait twenty minutes. The President had different ideas and ordered his supporters on the committee to accept the compromise without delay.[28]

Mondale opened the meeting by laying out the terms of his compromise. While admitting a "clear pattern of discrimination and intimidation" existed in Mississippi, he argued that the Freedom Party was "a protest movement not a political party" and therefore "their claim under the call of the Convention is not so clear." Anticipating attacks from partisans on both sides, Mondale defended the effort at compromise. "I can say and I think everyone knows we did not go as far as the Freedom Democratic Party wanted us to go, nor did we go as far as many of the Southern delegations wanted us to go. It would have been impossible to meet those extremes." After only brief debate, the committee roared its approval of the plan.[29]

As Mondale had foreseen, neither side was satisfied with his offer. The regular Mississippi delegation, except for three loyalists, announced, "We did not leave the Democratic Party, it left us," then promptly bolted the convention. Mississippi Governor Paul Johnson appeared on television statewide to announce his support of the delegation's decision to leave the convention. On the other hand, many Freedom Party leaders, who heard of the compromise only after it had been accepted, drew a bitter lesson from their experience: white liberals could not be trusted. They felt betrayed—not by the white racists in Mississippi but by liberal allies who presumed to speak for them. In one sense the compromise, by finally achieving some representation for blacks in a racist state, signified a major triumph. But to many blacks it revealed the white hypocrisy they had long suspected: liberals who spoke so passionately about civil rights refused to suffer the political consequences of doing what was morally right. "The MFDP was the duly chosen representative of the powerless of Mississippi," commented one critic, "and Walter Mondale was the hatchet man who executed the orders to deny them power."[30]

Despite the criticism, both then and later, Mondale never wavered in his belief in the compromise. "The committee members felt that they wanted to open up the regular party for full participation," he told a packed press conference shortly after the vote. "Giving separate status to the Freedom Democrats could have delayed the establishment of an integrated party for many, many years. We have recommended changing the laws so that never again can such an unfair situation occur in Mississippi or elsewhere in the future. Never before in history has such a small group of protesters brought about such widespread advances."

More than twenty years later he still referred to the compromise as a human rights "victory," claiming that "This was not a fight to seat blacks at the exclusion of whites, or the other way around." He reflected, "This was a fight to open up the party to prohibit discrimination so that those who tried to walk through the door could do so without discrimination and come with an integrated delegation from an integrated state." Though the decision may have alienated a few radicals, overall it made for a better Democratic Party. "That decision was the beginning of a healthy black-and-white party in the South. We developed an integrated, non-discriminatory southern Democratic party."[31]

The final compromise did have a profound impact on the Southern Democratic Party. Rule changes that resulted from the plan brought new groups into the party and led to the unseating of two southern delegations at the 1968 convention. As Southern whites had warned, however, the party did pay a heavy price. Mondale may have devised the only compromise possible in 1964, but he and many other liberals did not appreciate the depth of racial division in America or understand the extent to which racial antagonism would transform politics over the next ten years. The tension between blacks and whites that marked the 1964 convention soon exploded. The ensuing social disorder antagonized many middle- and working-class whites who had supported the party since the era of Roosevelt. The black-white schism introduced new social issues into the political debate, as a result of which traditionally Democratic voters flocked to the Republicans. For Mondale and other Democrats raised in the New Deal tradition, it created a far different political environment, one to which they could never fully adjust.

In the short run, Mondale's work at the convention dramatically enhanced his stature within the party. The compromise not only secured Humphrey's position on the Democratic ticket, but also increased Mondale's chances of being selected to fill the vacant seat. "He was certainly recognized as a comer by everyone at the convention," recalled Geri Josephs. "[T]here seemed little question," wrote Charles Withers in the Rochester *Post-Bulletin*, "that Fritz Mondale had achieved an important step up on Minnesota's political ladder for his role in this national matter." Mondale, in a letter to relatives, described the compromise as "a major break for me." His family agreed. His sister-in-law wrote him: "We were very proud of your magnificent handling of the Dixie question at the national Convention. The Mondale stock definitely soared to a new high. I am only sorry that your politically minded father did not live long enough to watch his 'Fritz' on television."[32]

As he thought about the possibility of ascending to Humphrey's Senate seat, Mondale began to articulate the basic principles of his politics. Over the next few months, in speeches and talks given across the state, he revealed the social philosophy that guided his public career. A harmonious society required a careful balancing of groups and interests, he believed. His father's populist preachings had convinced him that for many years big business and powerful monied interests had exercised inordinate power. But Roosevelt had limited corporate influence by asserting the government's right to regulate business and protect the interests of the "common man"—the small businessman, farmer, laborer, minorities, and intellectuals. It was government's responsibility to provide for those long excluded from the system. That perennial tension between selfish big business and the common man, although mellowed by postwar prosperity, persisted and was reflected in the cleavage between the two parties. Republicans represented the interests of big business, the wealthy, and those who had attained a degree of social status. The Democratic party defended the rights of the struggling workers, small farmers, and minorities who had been excluded from exercising political and economic power. Acknowledging the basic division between the "haves" and the "have nots" was for Mondale the first principle of politics.[33]

This populist strain competed with a belief in social solidarity and the importance of community. Mondale believed it was government's responsibility to continue integrating marginal groups into the national mainstream. In a democratic community, he argued, all people deserved an equal chance to pursue the American dream, and only government could remove the barriers to equal opportunity. In the early 1960s the two most obvious barriers to equal opportunity were poverty and racism. The poor, Mondale asserted, "trapped in a vicious circle of poverty, misery and depression," were "detached from the surging tide of plenty." At the same time the scourge of racism that denied blacks basic voting rights prevented millions from participating in society as full and equal members. "The American dream will always remain a dream for some," he told audiences. "But as a liberal I am committed to the proposition that we must search constantly for ways to make that dream come true for as many of our citizens as we can."

Government was a moral force that had the responsibility to act in the common good. "To the extent that government acts to carry out the common aspirations of the people, it succeeds," he repeated on many occasions to union leaders and civic groups. "[T]o the extent that it allows itself to be hobbled and sidetracked by selfish interests or immorality, it will fail." Speaking the language of the social gospel he had learned so well from his father, he told an audience in 1962: "I want to point out what I feel is a simple truth that underlies all politics. This is that government—any government—is the moral agent of the citizenry. It is the strong right arm through which they do those things together which they cannot do separately. It is, if you will, one of the corporate bodies, along with the family and the church, through which men work out their salvation and assist in the salvation of others." Though private charity may have worked in a more simple era, in the complex, interdependent world of the 1960s only government could provide for the common good.

Like many other liberals of his generation, Mondale possessed unbridled confidence that America could address problems like racism and poverty without changing the institutions of government or redistributing power and wealth. "We in America have now all the wealth, the sociological and political know-how to root out poverty and its causes," he declared. "We simply have not gotten around to taking care of it." Erasing poverty, he argued, would not involve a redistribution of wealth or cause serious strains on society. Reflecting his own experience, Mondale argued that what the poor needed was not money, but skills. "What we must seek to do," he said in April 1964, "is to restore human dignity to the poor by educating them and by giving them the skills to rise above their substandard way of life by their own efforts." Mondale opposed any suggestions of income redistribution, calling efforts at direct relief "as useless as giving aspirin to a man with a brain tumor." Dramatic structural changes were also not necessary to address the problems of blacks. The first line of assault against racism involved statutory changes—voting rights, public accommodations, fair housing. For the poor and minorities Mondale suggested increased educational opportunity, equal access to employment, and economic growth.

While recognizing that integration of the poor and minorities into the national community would produce real economic benefit through increased productivity and lower social spending, Mondale argued that ethical principle and not economic calculation should compel the nation to act. "Our moral obligation to be concerned about our brothers' welfare is a far better reason," he stated. Government did not have to justify all action on behalf of its citizens "on the ground that reform will improve our image with the underdeveloped nations in Africa, or the war on Communism demands it." Political leaders should be guided by pure religious principle. "Our mutual religious heritage makes our obligation clear: We are our brothers' keeper." He admonished his listeners to heed the words of the Book of Proverbs: "Do not withhold him from doing good, who is able; if thou are able, do good thyself also. Say not to thy friend: Go, and come again, and tomorrow I will give to thee; when thou canst give at present."

Mondale pictured America as a fluid, open society where only minor adjustments in the machinery of government could create a vibrant national community of shared values and purpose where all citizens could participate as equals. The poor could be helped by providing opportunity, not relief. Blacks could be assisted through legislation and strict enforcement. It was a vision compelling in its simplicity. He envisioned no need for large government intervention and anticipated little hostile reaction outside narrow Republican circles. Beneath his secular view lay a pietistic faith rooted in the Social Gospel. He frequently spoke the moral vocabulary of Protestant evangelicalism.

By 1964, Mondale's faith in American society had dampened much of his populist anger. He believed that moderation and pragmatism were the keys to successful public policy. Individuals and groups, no matter how just their cause, needed to avoid a "messianic complex" which would lead them to pursue their own cause at the expense of all others. Meaningful reform could best be achieved by working through established institutions. Change might be slow, but it would come. Mondale's liberalism was at heart a process not an ideology. It was a commitment to gradual reform which depended on established institutions and representative groups using their legislative expertise to achieve socially desirable ends. He declared: "I am a liberal. I understand by this that I am committed to a political approach based on a study of all alternative solutions to a problem, followed by a choice of that alternative which seems most likely to solve the problem, without regard to political dogma."

Mondale's experience in public life over the next twenty years would chasten his social vision. Poverty programs fell short of his expectations, the civil rights struggles of the decade succeeded in removing legal barriers, but did not much alter popular attitudes or attack underlying economic inequities. Heightened racial tensions and the emergence of politically potent social issues ended his hope of creating a progressive community of shared economic interest. Vietnam and Watergate were to diminish Mondale's faith in government beneficence. Experience taught him to appreciate the limits of change and the resiliency of conservative values in American society. The unbounded optimism and grand vision of his early years gave way to lower expectations and limited goals. An older Mondale would be wiser, but his tempered liberalism would fail to rally public support.

Johnson and Humphrey waltzed to the finish line in November, and with Humphrey secure in the vice presidency, Governor Rolvaag began the process of choosing someone to fill his vacant Senate seat. A Minneapolis *Star* poll indicated that Mondale led the list of possible appointees. From a list of ten prospects, one person in five chose Mondale. Orville Freeman finished second with 13 percent and Congressman John Blatnik third with 12 percent. Actually Rolvaag's first choice to fill the vacancy did not even register on opinion polls. Tired of state politics and eager for a new challenge, the Governor seriously entertained the idea of announcing his own appointment to the position. His friends and advisors soon disabused him of that notion. Such a move, they suggested, would be unpopular and probably give both seats to the Republicans in the next election. Although Freeman was a familiar face in Minnesota, Rolvaag feared that he was out of touch with local politics. The other leading candidate, Iron Range congressman John Blatnik, had years of distinguished service to the party and had been an effective spokesman for constituent interests in Washington. Older than Mondale, he would have less opportunity to accumulate seniority. Since he was little known around the state, Rolvaag wondered if he could win a statewide election against a tough opponent.

The evidence weighed in Mondale's favor. He had shown remarkable popularity for a two-term attorney general. He had a solidly liberal record and had demonstrated his strength in statewide elections. Perhaps of greatest importance, Rolvaag shared a strong sense of loyalty to other members of the generational vanguard that had helped elect Humphrey in 1948 and recapture the party during the 1950s, and he felt a responsibility to assist their advance. In 1964, Walter Mondale, the candidate who twenty years later would be branded as old and outdated by a younger breed of Democrats, came to national prominence because he spoke for a new generation of leadership.

On November 17, at a crowded reception, Rolvaag announced the appointment. Mondale, who had kept himself out of the public eye in the days leading up to the announcement, said it was "hard to find words" to express his gratitude to Rolvaag. Noting both the "opportunity for service and grave responsibility" his new position held, he promised "not only to work as a member of the Johnson-Humphrey team for the peace and prosperity of the nation, but to work with equal effort for the economic, social and cultural well being of our great state." Later that evening he wrote an effusive personal note thanking the Governor for the appointment. "You have given me the opportunity to fulfill every dream that I've ever had, and you have entrusted me with a responsibility as great as any that I could imagine. My respect for you and my desire to reflect honor upon your choice knows no bounds."[34]

The appointment received widespread public approval. Humphrey called Mondale "an excellent choice," and Orville Freeman said he would be "an excellent successor." According to the Minneapolis *Tribune,* 72 percent of those polled believed that Mondale would be a good senator. "Mondale is a brainy, industrious man, well qualified for success as a senator," the Duluth *Herald* commented. The Minneapolis *Statesman* editorialized: "Those Minnesotans who believe in justice and equality of opportunity for all people will applaud the appointment by Governor Karl Rolvaag of Attorney General Walter F. Mondale as U.S. Senator from Minnesota." The Rochester *Post-Bulletin* declared: "The 36-year-old attorney general appears to be an extremely capable, energetic young figure who could become an outstanding senator in the years to come." Perhaps the St. Louis *Post-Dispatch* captured the feeling of many people when it asked: "How does Minnesota produce so much first-class political talent?"[35]

Learning the Ropes

Senator Mondale sat in boyish wonder in the back row of the crowded House chamber. In the moments before President Johnson arrived to deliver his State of the Union Address, he gazed around the ornate room. In front of him was the three-tiered rostrum from which the President would speak. Behind the rostrum a huge American flag was draped from an impressive, grey-white marble facade. Above the flag, and carved into the marble, was the country's motto: In God We Trust. The Chamber walls—a stately mix of dark oak and walnut—reflected the serious business of government. Symbols of history and government abounded. On one side of the center rostrum hung a portrait of George Washington, on the other a painting of General Lafayette. Above the gallery doors were marble portraits of twenty-one law-givers from Hammurabi and Moses to Jefferson and Napoleon. The seals of all the states and territories bordered the edge of the ceiling, which opened up to reveal a glass eagle grasping a banner which read *E Pluribus Unum*.

The symbols of history covered the walls and the spirit of America's past permeated the air. The podium from which Johnson would speak was the same used by Woodrow Wilson to outline his Fourteen Points and by Franklin Roosevelt to express his outrage over Pearl Harbor. Now it was Johnson's turn, and to a lesser degree, Walter Mondale's turn as well. Glancing at the faces of his fellow Senators, most of them unfamiliar to him, Mondale might have recalled that shoeless teenager who had been an awestruck visitor to the nation's capitol. Much had changed in his life since that time, but he still felt like a stranger in that august company. After just a few moments, the doorman's voice jarred Mondale's quiet reflection. "Misteh-Speakeh Mis-teh Speak-ah! The President of the United States of America." Mondale rose to his feet as Johnson's hulking figure strode down the center aisle.

It was an exciting time for Mondale. At the age of thirty-seven, he was young to occupy a Senate seat. Before him lay the prospect of a long career in national politics. The Democratic Party had just scored an electoral landslide, providing it with control of the White House, overwhelming majorities in both houses of Congress, and a popular mandate for reform. Strongly committed to the Great Society agenda, Mondale applauded enthusiastically as Johnson promised legislation for Medicare and aid to education. "It was thrilling," Joan Mondale recalled, "because we thought that government could do something to make life better. We really believed in Humphrey and Johnson and the possibilities of improving society."[1]

The excitement of the moment did not blind Mondale to the obstacles he would have to overcome. "When I went to the Senate in 1964 I was young, still green and had a lot to learn," Mondale recalled years later. "I had to learn all of these federal issues. I was tested in a different way than when I was Attorney General." Ironically, he also had to adjust to a decline in his personal status. Accustomed to front-page headlines and constant political attention, the junior Senator was just one member of a large, impersonal institution. Unfamiliar with Senate procedures and overwhelmed by the maze of the federal bureaucracy, Mondale struggled to master his new environment. "The thing that surprised me when I first met him was how insecure he was," recalled Mondale's administrative assistant Dwayne Scribner. "He did not trust himself. He thought he did not know the issues."[2]

Along with mastering the federal bureaucracy, Mondale had to adjust to life in Washington. The Mondales rented a modest home in suburban Chevy Chase. Arriving in Washington on New Years Eve, they found the house in disrepair—the dishwasher was broken, the shower did not drain properly, and a thick layer of dust and dirt covered the furniture. As usual, Joan tended to the household chores while Fritz took care of political business. Even after a rigorous cleaning, neither Joan nor Fritz could develop much enthusiasm for the house or the neighborhood. With Teddy already seven years old, Eleanor approaching her fifth birthday and William his second, the Mondales also wanted to find a neighborhood with a better school system. Perhaps more important, with the 1966 campaign approaching, both Fritz and Joan planned to spend more time in Minnesota than Washington. During the summer of 1966, after just six months in the house, the Mondales terminated their lease. Joan, hoping to get an early start on the campaign, returned with the children to the Minneapolis home the family had been renting. While Joan begin speaking at local DFL and civic meetings, Fritz rented a small room in the Congressional Hotel in Washington and commuted regularly to Minnesota.[3]

The transition to Washington life was much easier for Fritz than it was for Joan. The nation's capital, which one writer referred to as "the most complicated political machine on earth," provided Mondale with almost everything he had spent the past twenty years working for: power, recognition, the influence to shape public policy, and a concentration of people who shared similar interests. It did not take him long to realize he loved the town and wanted to stay. One of his proudest moments occurred on his thirty-seventh birthday—January 5, 1965—when his ailing mother, who would die the following year of cancer, traveled to Washington to witness his swearing-in ceremony in the Capitol gallery. In the beginning, Joan did not share her husband's enthusiasm for Washington. "Oh, it was very difficult at first. In Minnesota there had been a great deal of camaraderie among all the political wives," she told Doris Kearns Goodwin. "In contrast, in the Senate, I found 100 wives going 100 different directions." Joan's unaffected and sometimes demure manner seemed out of place in a fashion and image-conscious city. According to Finlay Lewis, she "seemed so self-effacing, so proper, so wifely" that many Minnesota reporters dubbed her "Phony Joanie."[4]

As always, Mondale resolved to surmount the political obstacles with painstaking persistence. He maintained the same fourteen-hours-a-day, seven-days-a-week work schedule, and continued to expect similar efforts from his staff. "He was go, go, go all the time," said a young attorney who followed his boss from the attorney general's office to the Senate. "I think he drove himself and everybody for those two years after his appointment probably as hard as he had ever pushed anyone in his whole life." A stern and rigid taskmaster, Mondale was not above rousing an aide from a sickbed, forcing him into the office. "A lot of people found him difficult to work for," recalled one staff member. "He was very demanding. He expected things to be done and done well. He was very critical when they were not and [he] let people know about it. Mondale did not suffer fools gladly." Despite the torturous hours and oppressive atmosphere, he showed his assistants little appreciation for their toil. "It is very difficult for Mondale to extend himself in gratitude," remarked a long time friend. "Saying thank you is not a natural reaction."[5]

His new stature did nothing to improve his interpersonal skills. If anything, his insecurity seemed to make him more aloof and unfeeling. "We had to literally drag him into the other offices to say hello to his staff," a disgruntled former aide recalled. "He had kids working there for two months who never even saw him." After months of prodding, Mondale reluctantly agreed to spend more time mingling with staff, trying to get to know them on a personal basis. The experiment failed. "It was a disaster," a former employee told Finlay Lewis. "The idea was to stop by people's desks and make small talk. He just wasn't good at it. But to make matters worse, he would paw through their papers, and if he came across a letter that should have gone out days earlier, he would end up chewing the person out. So instead of being happy to see their boss up close and informal, the staff was terrified he'd come through again."[6]

An irrepressible sense of humor competed with Mondale's sometimes cold exterior. In early 1966, when the Washington Press Club held its annual congressional banquet, Mondale delighted guests with his discourse on the subject: "Resolved: It's easier to be appointed than elected to the U.S. Senate." When Georgia's powerful conservative Senator Herman Talmadge offered his liberal colleague a Cuban cigar, Mondale stepped back and feigned anger. "Herman," he said mocking Talmadge's strong anti-communist views, "I'm shocked a good, patriotic American like you would deal with Communist merchandise." On another occasion, during a long Senate debate, Mondale occupied himself by signing pictures for constituents. Robert Kennedy of New York, who sat next to him, reached over and grabbed several prints. "You're a fine group and I'm with you all the way," Kennedy wrote before signing his name. "That's great; I appreciate that," Mondale said. "You'll go over big with Planned Parenthood of Minnesota."[7]

Although Mondale came to Washington as Hubert Humphrey's protégé, observers noted the important differences of style and temperament that separated the two men. People respected Mondale for his positions on issues and his decency; people loved Humphrey for his passion and conviction. Humphrey was impetuous and instinctive, frequently acting on impulse. Mondale was deliberate and controlled, always calculating consequences before acting. Humphrey was a fighter who challenged problems head on; Mondale carefully examined situations, probed for points of compromise, and worked toward common ground. "You could not know, see, or hear Humphrey without having a strong visceral reaction to him," recalled a former Mondale staff member. "Mondale never had that affect on people."

In both private and public, Humphrey was an unrepentant idealist, who overwhelmed those around him with his warmth and energy. There was no tension between the public and the private persona. The opposite was true of Mondale. Privately, Mondale's fatalistic wit revealed a skeptical and cynical mind that rarely showed itself in public statements. He impressed those who knew him as a shrewd and extraordinarily ambitious man, yet he conveyed a public impression of political naïveté and personal innocence. In personal dealings, especially with his staff, he was frequently abrupt, impatient, and hot-headed; yet he presented a public image of reserved dignity and patience. In his early years, the gap between the private and public Mondale was, on balance, a political asset. His excessive ambition, emotional outbursts, and general insensitivity would have clashed with his public image and made him a much less attractive figure. In later years, however, Mondale closed that gap. The confidence that accrued from continued success tempered his emotions while the recognition of his own weaknesses would make him more understanding of human error.

Mondale had the fortune to participate in one of the most extraordinary sessions of Congress in two hundred years. During Mondale's first year in the Senate, the President proposed and the Congress approved major programs that had been part of the Democratic agenda for twenty years. Most notable were aid to elementary and secondary education, medical care for the aged, an expansion of the anti-poverty program, federal aid for housing and urban development, the Voting Rights Act, as well as legislation designed to protect the environment. House Majority Leader Carl Albert declared that the 89th Congress was "the most significant in all our history." Most conservatives, however, agreed with Indiana Representative Richard Roudebush, who warned: "For those who believe in limited government and preservation of personal liberties, this Congress has been a disaster." Though they did not agree on the results, both liberals and conservatives were impressed by Johnson's legislative skill. "He's done," observed Walter Lippmann, "what President Kennedy could not have done had he lived."[8]

As a freshman Senator, Mondale did not play a major role in articulating Great Society ideals or in legislating its various programs. While confining his few speeches from the Senate floor to flattering tributes to Johnson or effusive praise of Great Society initiatives, he focused his energy on his committee assignments. He had hoped for a high-visibility assignment on the Appropriations Committee, but settled for positions on three less prestigious committees: Agriculture, Banking, and Space. In hearings, both private and public, Mondale focused attention on issues related to Minnesota. "Mondale has not been an innovator but has successfully pushed proposals originated by other Minnesotans and midwesterners," observed the Minneapolis *Tribune*. On the Agriculture Committee he sponsored an amendment allowing farmers to receive payment for establishing wildlife habitats and opening them to the public for hunting, fishing, and camping. Like other midwestern Senators, he fought unsuccessfully for removal of restrictions on selling wheat to the Soviet Union and Eastern Europe and spoke out for an increase in food aid and agricultural assistance to developing countries. On the Banking Committee he helped amend the Economic Development Act to allow areas to remain eligible for aid despite temporary dips in the unemployment rate—a popular measure in the state's depressed Iron Range.[9]

Despite his concentration on Minnesota issues, Mondale pledged his fidelity to the broad aims of the Great Society. "Government must help many people who are in need of help if we are to have a decent society," he declared. "We must work to alleviate conditions which cause social and cultural deprivation." The impulse for government activism and social compassion that inspired Mondale's support of the Great Society traced to his father's dinner-table sermons. In his mind, the barriers liberals faced in the 1960s were similar to the problems his father had inveighed against in the 1930s: poor education, maldistribution of income, and racial segregation. "His politics were an extension of our father's preaching," recalled Clarence Mondale. At the heart of his philosophy was the belief that government had the primary responsibility to guarantee every citizen an equal chance at success. Like most liberals, Mondale believed only modest government action was necessary to remove the barriers of racial segregation and create economic opportunity for the underprivileged. His was an optimistic outlook, one that celebrated the essential goodness of American society and refused to accept the existence of deeply rooted class and racial differences. "The greatest promise of America," he said on the Senate floor in 1965, "has always been the unqualified assurances of equal opportunity for all people regardless of their background or circumstances. We have made it a fundamental principle that every American be offered the chance to build a full life for himself and his family. Today in America there are a wide range of programs and projects to guarantee that no one is denied this chance because of race, because of a lack of education, or because of the poverty of birth."[10]

Mondale also continued his strong interest in consumer rights, which he had championed as Attorney General. In April 1966, working closely with consumer advocate Ralph Nader, he successfully proposed legislation forcing auto makers to notify owners of safety defects in their products. Calling his bill the Fair Warning Act, Mondale told his Senate colleagues: "It's not enough to simply correct the defect in next year's model or that the industry should merely notify the dealer. We cannot continue to let people drive time bombs which can cause fatal or crippling injuries." Two years later, charging the auto industry with exaggerating the cost of safety equipment, Mondale supported a bill requiring manufacturers to disclose the real cost of the equipment. Auto manufacturers sidetracked the legislation by proposing a voluntary plan to disclose prices. The Senator was more successful in other efforts to increase consumer protection. In 1967, he sponsored legislation which provided federal aid to states for improving meat inspection and gave the national government broad authority to examine meat plants.[11]

While committed to all Great Society programs, Mondale believed that the fight against racial injustice was the most important problem facing the nation. He entered the Senate at a critical juncture in this long struggle, with the current battle being waged over voting rights. The President had already expressed his commitment to eliminating "every remaining obstacle to the right and the opportunity to vote." The real question, then, was tactical: when and how were these obstacles to be removed? In March, the President and the liberals received an unexpected boost when blacks decided to protest segregation in Selma, Alabama by leading a peaceful march to the state capital in Montgomery, 52 miles away. Tensions had been running high in Selma since January, when Martin Luther King had begun organizing nonviolent protests. During the march, these tensions erupted into violence. An orgy of police brutality greeted marchers as they tried crossing the Pettus Bridge. Like much of the nation, Mondale watched the horrifying television pictures of 60 club-swinging policemen wading into a group of 650 protesters.[12]

Mondale hoped the incident would provide Johnson with the opportunity he needed to rally public support behind the voting rights bill which authorized federal examiners to register voters and banned literacy tests. In the meantime, Mondale did what he could to muster the enthusiasm of his own constituents. At a large rally at the Capitol building in St. Paul, where he had once urged enactment of the 1964 civil rights bill, Mondale spoke eloquently in favor of voting rights. He told the crowd: "The basis of brutality in Selma is clear. The white power structure, sustaining itself by denying political power to half the people they presume to govern, has seen that violence is their last desperate defense. We now know that correction by federal law is essential to the political health and tranquility of the South and of the Nation." He warned that "we must not, seeing hatred, give way to hating." Those supporting the civil rights struggle, he told the crowd, must follow the example of the Selma marchers "who met brutality with prayer, violence with love, and injustice with dignity."[13]

For Mondale the protests were successful because on March 15, Johnson went before a joint session of Congress to ask for guarantees for the voting rights of all Americans. It was an inspiring and emotionally powerful performance. "I speak tonight for the dignity of man and the destiny of democracy," the President declared. Mondale applauded as Johnson demanded that Congress enact legislation placing federal registrars in every county with unrepresentative black turnout. An eerie silence then swept through the chamber as the President prepared for his dramatic finish. "What happened in Selma is part of a far larger movement . . . the effort of American Negroes to secure for themselves the full blessings of American life," he declared. In a forceful tone, he concluded: "And-we-shall-over-come!" Mondale jumped to his feet, leading his colleagues in a long, sustained ovation. "Listening to Johnson say those words," Mondale recalled, "represented the five most dramatic seconds in my public life." Five months later, on August 6, Johnson signed the Voting Rights Act of 1965.[14]

In just two years, the administration had outlawed official discrimination, fulfilling, in spirit, much of the liberal agenda to which Mondale ascribed. "We're entering a new phase of American history," Mondale told reporters in October 1965. "We've enacted the charter of many new measures and now we're entering into a period where we've got to make certain these measures are administratively sound and wisely funded." If individual blacks had the right to vote, to attend desegregated schools, and to pursue jobs free of legal restrictions based on race, Mondale had argued, they would join other Americans as equals in the search for prosperity and success.[15]

Unfortunately, the reality of change lagged behind the promises of reform. Enacting laws could not change deeply held racial animosity, alter the emotional damage caused by years of neglect, or redress pressing economic inequities. As many blacks lost faith in America's capacity for change, their support for liberal reform gave way to bitter alienation from white institutions. Rejecting King's vision that "the Negro's dream is rooted in the American dream," blacks began asserting their independence. No longer content to work within the system, many blacks also spurned King's conciliatory methods and attitudes, and became insistent on controlling their own destiny. At just the time when liberals were passing far-reaching civil rights legislation, blacks were revolting in the streets. In the summer of 1965, race riots laid waste the Watts area of Los Angeles, leaving thirty-four dead, four thousand arrested, and more than $35 million in property damage. During the summer of 1966, racial disturbances were occurring almost daily, with thirty-eight separate confrontations taking place in cities like Cleveland, San Francisco, Milwaukee, and Chicago.

Mondale believed the riots occurred because liberals had promised more than they could deliver. "We exaggerated the scope of what we were doing by rhetoric that did not relate to the reality of the programs. The substance never matched the commitments," he reflected. Government, he argued after the Watts riot in 1965, "must attack the seeds of poverty and discrimination which cause such tragedies." Painfully, he was coming to the realization that poverty was more tenacious and the level of government assistance needed was more massive than he had ever imagined. "It is not enough to set up programs," he concluded after Watts. "We have to appropriate funds for them."[16]

Convincing parsimonious conservatives to fund new social programs was hard enough in itself, but the Great Society also had to compete for funds with a growing military involvement in Vietnam. The escalation began early in 1965 after Vietcong rebels killed seven Americans and wounded 109 at Pleiku, a town 200 miles north of Saigon. Having anticipated such an attack, the White House organized retaliatory air strikes in response to "provocations ordered and directed by the Hanoi regime." Three days later Johnson authorized regular bombings, again on targets chosen in 1964. Johnson, who interpreted the events in Vietnam as part of a larger communist conspiracy, explained that America's defeat in South Vietnam "would encourage and spur on those who seek to conquer all free nations within their reach." Johnson justified his actions claiming that he was following the policy initiated by his predecessor. "My first major decision on Vietnam," he said, "had been to reaffirm President Kennedy's policies."[17]

Refusing to open his policies to congressional criticism, Johnson concealed both the direction of his strategy and its possible consequences. While insisting that he was not leading the United States into a "ground war" in Southeast Asia, Johnson simultaneously increased the ground forces there. By the end of the year, there were more than 180,000 American combat troops in Vietnam; in 1966, that number doubled. Sorties against North Vietnam increased from 25,000 in 1965 to 79,000 in 1966. Despite the increased American presence, the military situation continued to deteriorate, and American casualties continued to mount. In 1961, fourteen Americans had died in Vietnam; by 1963, the toll was 489. By the spring of 1966, more than 4000 Americans had been killed.[18]

Like most other leading politicians of his generation, Mondale instinctively viewed the Vietnam conflict as a superpower confrontation. He came to Washington with no experience in foreign policy. His only foreign travel had been a six-week trip to Europe in 1950, when superpower tensions and fear of Soviet aggression pervaded Western Europe. His experience purging communists from the DFL had added a strong anti-communist perspective to his world view. With little knowledge of or interest in foreign policy issues, Mondale simply repeated the conventional liberal wisdom. The young idealist who, like his father, once suggested the United States could defeat communism by demonstrating the economic and political advantages of democratic capitalism, now accepted the necessity of military containment. In the early 1960s, the liberal approach rested on the lessons of Munich: any attempt to appease aggression would require further sacrifice in the future. Mondale placed his trust in the presidency and the team of foreign policy experts who filled the bureaucracy and determined the direction of American policy in the postwar era. Initially, his trust kept him from seriously questioning either the government's intentions or the military results in Vietnam. He listened with relief as Defense and State Department officials, flaunting body-count statistics, claimed continued progress in the war.

There was no shortage of credible information to contradict these dubious statistics. Enterprising young reporters, such as David Halberstam of the New York *Times,* had been casting doubt on Administration optimism about American success in the field. At the same time, the phrase "credibility gap" found its way into the American vocabulary as journalists began questioning the truthfulness of Johnson's statements on a whole range of issues, including the war. Mondale listened to the private grumbling of many of his colleagues. Senator Gaylord Nelson, a friend from neighboring Wisconsin, frequently shared the plane ride back to Washington with Mondale after long weekends at home. An early critic of the war, Nelson tried repeatedly to convince Mondale that—despite all the Defense Department statistics—the war could not be won.[19]

Mondale heard these dissenting reports but, at first, dismissed them. Confident in the power of government, and uncertain about his knowledge of Southeast Asia, Mondale placed inordinate faith in the wisdom of experts. These were, after all, the "best and the brightest" lured from the finest universities in the country, deeply committed to the public welfare. "He felt very constrained by the whole situation in Vietnam," recalled Michael Berman. "I think he was part of a group of young Senators who were taken in by the Johnson cabinet types who were all famous men." A staunch partisan, he instinctively trusted that a Democratic president would not deceive his own party.[20]

At heart, Mondale wanted to believe reports that the war would soon end. Primarily interested in domestic issues, he worried that a costly war would drain resources from domestic programs, divide the Democratic coalition, and lead to an early death of the Great Society. The Democratic moment of opportunity, he feared, would be lost. "I was mindful that this would open up a big dispute in the Democratic party and hurt us badly," Mondale recalled later. "I hoped it would be resolved and we would not have to go through the pain."[21]

Mondale's public statements on the issue simply repeated the Administration's rationale for fighting. In March 1965, he told reporters that "to withdraw from South Vietnam and permit what would obviously be a takeover of that area by Communist forces is intolerable." Removal of American forces, he declared, "would not only constitute a breach of our commitments given by three presidents, but would whet the Communist appetite for more territory and the subjugation of more people." A few months later, he placed in the *Congressional Record* results of a Minnesota poll showing that 58 percent of the public supported the administration's policy and 77 percent accepted the President's explanation of America's commitment. "I am proud," he concluded, "that the people of my State are so clearly in support of President Johnson's policies in Vietnam." A few critics raised questions about Johnson's ability to handle complex foreign policy issues, but Mondale had no such reservations. "I have never been more impressed by a man," Mondale told reporters after a special White House briefing. "I have great confidence in his handling of this matter."[22]

In January 1966, Mondale took a well-publicized tour of Vietnam as part of his responsibilities on the Agriculture Committee. He spent five days traveling throughout South Vietnam and meeting with General William Westmoreland, Ambassador Henry Cabot Lodge, and many servicemen. Designed more as a State Department booster tour than a fact-finding trip, it provided Mondale with positive information about America's involvement and good pictures for the voters at home. After returning to the states, Mondale told members of the Twin Cities Air Force Reserve that Vietnam was a "testing ground" for the communist strategy of gaining territory through "wars of national liberation." Praising the Air Force's role in the war, he warned that the "whole credibility of American promises" would be in doubt if the United States pulled out of South Vietnam without a military victory. Like most liberals, he supported Johnson's "moderate strategy" of applying firm but limited pressure in Vietnam. If the peace overtures failed, Mondale called for expanded "military pressures," including adding 75,000 troops, blockading the North Vietnamese port of Haiphong, increasing the number of air strikes, and possibly interdicting Laotian supply trails.[23]

Despite his wish, the war would not go away. As it continued, the number of protesters swelled and the vehemence of their dissent intensified. Johnson's escalation of the conflict coincided with the completion of the integrationist phase of the civil rights movement. Many young whites, some militant, who had been working in the South now began returning North in search of a new cause to champion. At first they organized teach-ins, believing that they could change policy through a reasonable discussion of issues. As the escalation continued, however, students took more active measures. By late 1965, students had already planned mass demonstrations, burned draft cards, and chanted slogans like "Hey, Hey, LBJ, how many kids did you kill today?"

Many establishment figures also began raising disturbing questions about American involvement in Vietnam. In January 1966, Senator J. William Fulbright, chairman of the Senate Foreign Relations Committee, held a series of nationally televised hearings which subjected Vietnam policy to a penetrating, sometimes caustic, analysis. Fulbright followed the hearings with a series of lectures at the Johns Hopkins University, where he declared that the United States was "in danger of losing its perspective on what exactly is within the realm of its power and what is beyond it." Martin Luther King, who had muted his criticism for fear of dividing the civil rights movement, now complained that "the promises of the Great Society top the casualty lists of the conflict." Freshman Senator Robert Kennedy criticized the President for resuming the bombing of North Vietnam after a brief Christmas pause.[24]

Just as Mondale had feared, the Vietnam war divided Democrats and aided the Republicans. As voter dissatisfaction with the war grew, Johnson's popularity declined. Republicans, while proposing no solutions of their own, worked desperately to translate the public's dissatisfaction into political gain. A rejuvenated Richard Nixon traveled the country in preparation for the 1966 congressional elections carrying the Republican banner. "The administration's current policy resigns America and the free Asian nations to a war which could last five years and cost more casualties than Korea," he warned. If the war were not enough of a burden, polls also showed massive "resistance of whites" against black power activism. In one survey, over half the American public believed the administration was pushing integration "too fast." Pollster Lou Harris warned that "the white backlash could . . . tear the Democratic Party apart at the seams in the North."[25]

This volatile national climate concerned Mondale, who in 1966 was running for his first full term in the Senate. In reality, Mondale had little reason to worry. Polls showed him with an approval rating of almost 60 percent, and nearly certain of victory. After a three day, eight-hundred-mile tour of the state, his chief-of-staff confirmed what the polls indicated, reporting Mondale to be "remarkably strong" and without any concentrated opposition. Simply winning, however, was not enough for Mondale. He was determined to prove that he deserved Humphrey's seat by winning with the widest possible margin. Despite his strong standing in the state and weak opposition from the Republican challenger, Robert Forsythe, a former state party chairman, Mondale waged a relentless campaign. "One of the problems we had was that Fritz wanted everything—teletypes, private plane to go 30 miles—the pressure he put on people was just tremendous," the Senator's administrative assistant complained. "He went balls out, despite the fact that Forsythe was his opponent. His goal was to be the state's political leader."[26]

Mondale still refused to master the art of communicating on television. Raised in a political environment where positions on the issues and personal contact were paramount for a politician's success, Mondale relied upon radio, newspapers, and personal contact to reach his constituency. Despite growing evidence that television would transform the way politicians communicate with the public, Mondale refused to adapt. "I never thought Mondale was very good on television," Berman said. "He refused to learn technique. He wanted to rely more on substance. He never wanted to come to grips with it." When he did appear on television, his unease was obvious. "I always had the feeling with Fritz that when he goes before an audience, he puts on this mask," recalled press secretary Dick Conlon. "He puts on this wooden suit and goes out and presents a wooden image."[27]

Mondale's strict decorum, which often made him appear unapproachable and impersonal, exacerbated this problem. He always wore a coat and tie in public, even at informal picnics and barbecues. At social functions, Mondale would drink only beer, afraid that someone would mistake soda for a potent mixed drink. He refused to allow himself to be photographed with either a cigar or a drink in hand. "I can't count the number of lit cigars I have stuffed in my pocket over the years," Berman recalled. His staff urged him to loosen up by allowing himself to be photographed in more informal settings. "We got one picture of him in a convertible with his hair blown loose and we wet our pants," recalled the Senator's press secretary. Mondale always vetoed use of the pictures.[28]

During the last six weeks of the campaign Mondale traversed the state in a small plane. He began each morning before sunrise with a breakfast meeting or hand-shaking session at a factory gate. During the afternoon and evening, he made numerous appearances, grasped hundreds of hands, and gave dozens of speeches before ending his grueling schedule at midnight. Aides who traveled with Mondale had difficulty keeping up with the schedule. Frequently, they would accompany him for a week at a time and rotate, because no one could maintain his pace for all six weeks. Mondale never seemed to rest. In some of the small towns along the campaign trail, the local motel offered only two rooms. When Mondale went to check in, he was asked: "Do you want the room with the bathroom or the room with the phone?" Without hesitating, Mondale took the room with the telephone. While his exhausted staff member slept in the other room dreading another long day, Mondale stayed up until early morning making phone calls.

Neither Vietnam nor urban unrest became major issues in the campaign. The dependable *Minnesota Poll* showed declining support for Johnson and growing anxiety about Vietnam, but little racial hostility. The President's approval rating, which in May 1965 had climbed to 71 percent, dropped to 53 percent by October 1966. Like much of the nation, the state was divided on the war. In the spring of 1966, 73 percent called American policy in Vietnam "wise," 56 percent felt U.S. troops should remain in Southeast Asia, and 78 percent approved of raids on Hanoi oil depots. Yet less than half of those interviewed expressed overall support for the war and many people were pessimistic about the possibility of an American victory. While polls showed growing concern about urban violence, most Minnesota voters did not consider racial riots a major issue in 1966. A number of unique circumstances provided the state with a temporary reprieve from the emerging political backlash. Blacks made up only 1 percent of the population and did not appear threatening to the state's white population. Minnesota's political culture, which was shaped by a Scandinavian faith in positive government and a tradition of civic responsibility, rejected hostile anti-statist rhetoric.[29]

The election was never close. Campaigning against the New Deal in a state with a long history of support for activist government, Forsythe made little impact. When that effort failed, he tried discrediting Mondale's reputation for honesty by accusing him of having accepted an illegal corporate campaign contribution during his term as Attorney General. The accusation concerned an illegal $2,000 contribution to Mondale's campaign from a subsidiary of American Allied Insurance Company—a high-risk insurer whose questionable business practices had resulted in bankruptcy and indictment of a number of state officials. The evidence revealed the contribution had been solicited by a Rolvaag fund-raiser. Mondale and his campaign staff never saw the check and had returned the money when alerted to its source.[30]

Mondale argued that the main issue of the campaign was whether the country would "continue the progress made under the [last] session of Congress or return to Republican negativism." He pointed to the economic policies which had resulted in "68 straight months of economic growth and the lowest unemployment rate in Minnesota in 13 years." He supported Johnson's course in Vietnam, arguing that every avenue to a peaceful settlement had been explored. Irritated by his opponent's attempt to impeach his integrity, Mondale heatedly charged Forsythe with "conducting a disgusting smear campaign" against him. In its endorsement, the St. Paul Pioneer *Press* called Mondale "not just a gifted collector of votes," but "a bright, talented and forceful man whose brief service in the Senate has been marked by an unusual amount of accomplishment."[31]

On election day, Mondale won the state with a respectable 110,000 vote margin and 53.9 percent of the vote. Although his margin of victory was smaller than expected, it was impressive when compared to other Democrats, both locally and nationally. The election decimated the DFL which Mondale had worked so painstakingly to nurture. Stung by the American Allied scandal and divided by a bitter primary fight, the party lost the governorship, a congressional seat, and most state offices, and was reduced to an impotent minority in the state legislature. Nationally, the election results were equally discouraging for liberals. Republicans gained forty-seven seats in the House, three in the Senate, and eight governorships.[32]

Election statistics suggested that Mondale maintained traditional New Deal loyalties. Like Humphrey, Mondale performed impressively in the heavily unionized Iron Range, won by smaller margins in the Twin Cities, and lost narrowly in the rural western and southern parts of the state. He scored well with minorities, union members, and urban voters. Lower income people were most likely to have voted for Mondale. He won 78.6 percent of voters with an annual income of less than $7,000; 56.5 percent of those who earned between $11,000 and $12,000; but only 41.1 percent of those earning over $13,000.[33]

Mondale had reason to feel good about his election victory, but there seemed little for liberals to celebrate in the fall of 1966. During Mondale's first two years in Washington, a popular president and a united party had produced a spectacular harvest of legislation. The war eclipsed many of these accomplishments. Witnessing the unraveling of the liberal consensus proved a bitter lesson for many idealistic young liberals. "I recall the joyous exuberance of 1964 and early 1965, when we were going to have a Great Society, and a growing, stable economy with more and more people at work and assets being poured into human development," a mournful Mondale reflected more than twenty years later. "Then slowly came Vietnam, which like a dark cloud over the horizon, began to gather and corner and shape itself, and twist that whole dream into a nightmare."[34]

The New Politics and the Old

The Senate to which Mondale returned after his successful campaign had changed in both tone and character. The threat of increasing involvement in Vietnam provided Republicans and conservative Democrats with a strong incentive to cut back on domestic programs. Mondale's fears about Vietnam's effect on the Great Society were proving disturbingly accurate. "We've got a war on our hands," said Senate GOP leader Everett Dirksen of Illinois, "and I think some of these domestic programs can be scaled down." Arkansas Democrat John McClellan, member of the powerful Appropriations Committee, agreed: "We are going to have to retrench and hold down new programs until the budget is under better control."[1]

If he needed any further evidence that the national mood had changed, Mondale received it when he sat in the House chamber and listened to Johnson's fourth State of the Union Address in January 1967. The contrast with the first address Mondale had heard was striking. Missing were the evangelical language, the reminiscences of childhood poverty, the promise of change. Johnson's tone was modest and restrained. The conservative climate on Capitol Hill and the economic realities imposed by the war tempered his legislative goals. He admitted that the Great Society "required trial and error, and it had produced both." On Vietnam, he was somber, urging patience and restraint and dampening hopes that the war would end soon. "I wish I could report to you that the conflict is almost over. This I cannot do. We face more cost, more loss and more agony."[2]

Agony indeed captured the feeling of many liberals at the unfolding events. The President increased American troop strength beyond the level of the Korean War. U.S. casualties climbed over the 100,000 mark, including 13,000 dead. At the same time, the monetary cost of the conflict reached a staggering $25 billion for the year. The bombing of North Vietnam, which the United States had undertaken with such optimism in 1965 and now insisted so vehemently was necessary, had neither prevented North Vietnam from increasing its military effort in the South nor forced North Vietnam to the negotiating table. Costly in both men and planes, it strained belief in American good will around the world. Politically the Great Society was the war's greatest casualty. Increasingly, people blamed Johnson for the debacle. The president's popularity, which once had stood at 80 percent, plummeted to a low of 38 percent by October 1967.[3]

As the war escalated in Vietnam, with no end in sight, so too did the racial war at home. In the summer of 1967 flames swept through thirty cities. In one week in August, forty-five were killed, thousands injured, and billions of dollars lost in property damage. Congress, reflecting a widespread fear among white Americans, passed stiff antiriot legislation. Having raised expectations far beyond reason, liberals watched helplessly as critics on the right and left raised profound questions about the very foundation of postwar liberal reform.

For the first time in his public life, Mondale found that championing civil rights and poverty programs could be potentially harmful to the Democratic Party. Such support, he discovered, was alienating many white, middle-class voters, whose allegiance was essential for the party's health. State polls revealed declining enthusiasm for Great Society initiatives, overwhelming approval of harsher penalties for rioters, and growing disdain of antiwar demonstrations. Almost half of all Minnesotans believed winning the Vietnam war was more important than victory in the war against poverty. At the same time more than 70 percent of those polled expressed dissatisfaction with progress in Vietnam. As public disillusion with events at home and abroad increased, Johnson's approval rating in the state dipped below the 50 percent mark.[4]

Johnson retreated and many liberals equivocated in the wake of declining public support for the Great Society, but Mondale embraced increased funding for existing social programs. Testifying before a Senate subcommittee on urban affairs, Mondale urged Congress to pass a fair housing bill, to expand the antipoverty effort by spending more on education and job training, and to provide "decent housing" for the poor by restoring funds for the model-cities and rent-supplement programs. "The violence which erupted in city after city in recent months has exposed a massive failure on the part of our affluent society," Mondale said in October 1967. "And it is now abundantly clear that a total national commitment is required to assure both order and social justice in American cities—and justice is not cheap."[5]

While Mondale demonstrated political courage by supporting increased spending for controversial social programs, he showed less interest in addressing the conceptual confusion and administrative disarray that also limited the effectiveness of many Great Society programs. Poor funding prevented the administration's main initiative, the war on poverty, from receiving a fair trial. But other problems, including disagreement within the administration about the nature of poverty and fighting between elected officials and reformers within the community action program, made doubtful the suggestion that additional funding alone would have solved the problem. "The program," commented one scholar, "was carried out in such a way as to produce a minimum of the social change its sponsors desired, and to bring about a maximum increase in the opposition to such change."[6]

Only once did Mondale publicly recognize that issues other than funding plagued the war on poverty. In 1967, he introduced the Full Opportunity and Social Accounting Act. Modeled after the Employment Act of 1946, the legislation would have established a President's Council of Social Advisors, required the President to submit an annual Social Report to Congress, and created a joint committee of Congress to examine the report and propose legislation. Despite the pervasive mood of disenchantment and skepticism, Mondale suggested that minor tinkering with the system—in this case bringing social scientists into the inner councils of government—would have "a revolutionary impact on government." Not surprisingly, few others shared his optimism, and the legislation died in committee.[7]

Vietnam remained the most painful issue facing Mondale and the nation. By 1967, Mondale began expressing private doubts about the wisdom of America's involvement. Reading widely about the war, he learned that the conflict had a long history that predated American interest or involvement. Most of all, as he came to realize that the European analogy that had been guiding his thought was not relevant to the situation in Southeast Asia, he became increasingly skeptical of State Department pronouncements. "I think it was a torturous period for him," reflected aide Phil Byrne. "While trying to learn the facts, he was slowly coming to the realization that the whole machinery of government, all of the information systems . . . were skewed toward giving a different slant to the facts."[8]

As he became increasingly skeptical about the possibility of a military solution and critical of the corrupt South Vietnamese government, Mondale privately began discussing proposals to reduce America's commitment in Vietnam. His list of grievances would grow, but he refused to voice a general condemnation of administration policy. By late 1967 Mondale had publicly distanced himself from the administration on a number of points. In contrast to the official position, he called for including the National Liberation Front (NLF) in the peace negotiations and allowing the United Nations, or any other responsible third party, to help mediate negotiations; complained about bombing raids that caused civilian casualties, endangered Russian shipping or antagonized the Chinese; advocated more funds for rural pacification; and criticized the corruption and inefficiency in the Saigon government. For the most part, these differences eschewed the real issue dividing the party. On the question of bombing—the litmus test of dissent—Mondale continued to support the administration's claims that a unilateral pause would endanger American troops in the field.[9]

In October 1967, hoping to clarify his own position and diffuse the growing schism within the party, Mondale returned to Macalester College to give a major speech on the war. As he walked to the podium, the hostile student crowd waved signs reading: "Sen. Mondale, People are Dying while you Decide;" "Sen. Mondale, Your Fence is Moving;" "Are you a Dove, Hawk, or Flying Squirrel?" The speech was designed to minimize the differences among Democrats on the war and to emphasize their common stake in fighting poverty and racism. Applying the same formula he had used to mediate the dispute at the 1964 Democratic convention, Mondale split the difference between irreconcilable positions. "I fear the passion which assigns broad significance to narrow distinctions," he said. Resorting to ideological strawmen he argued he could support neither a policy of "unlimited military attacks" or "unilateral withdrawal."

For all the emotionalism on both sides, he pointed out, differences between doves and hawks within the Democratic party were actually very small. Neither wanted to see South Vietnam fall to the communists, and both believed that an American presence would be necessary for years to come. After emphasizing the area of common agreement, Mondale spoke of the other issues that required liberal attention—closing the gap between rich and poor nations; establishing international organizations to preserve the peace; addressing pressing urban problems; and renewing the nation's commitment to education. At issue, he declared, was not limited resources, but "a basic problem of will" which threatened to divide the party and prevent further progress.[10]

Events, however, conspired against compromise. In March 1967, Allard Lowenstein, a 38-year-old peripatetic liberal who was convinced Johnson would not alter his war strategy and confident in the political power of young voters, had organized a "Dump Johnson" movement. Over the next few months as he traveled across the country in search of support and a candidate, Lowenstein found a deep reservoir of discontent with Johnson and the established Democratic party. He, and other self-identified advocates of the "new politics," charged that the older liberalism was bureaucratic and manipulative, rooted in forging consensus among established power structures. The new politics, which borrowed tactics from the early civil rights struggle, was activist and spontaneous, depending on drama and demonstration to arouse public sentiment. Television was their new weapon of guerrilla warfare.[11]

The new and the old appealed to different constituencies. Older liberals tried to build a broad coalition among the ethnic working classes, minorities, and intellectuals. Supporters of the new politics, having witnessed the white working class's resistance to racial change and strong support for the war, suggested building a new coalition—an alliance, in journalist Jack Newfield's words, of "campus, ghetto, and suburb." For leaders of the new politics protest against the war was part of a larger revolt against old structures of authority—big bosses, union leaders, and the ethnic working class. As American society became richer and better educated, the old coalition based on economic self-interest was giving way to a younger coalition.[12]

Age established Mondale's ties to the "new politics," but style placed him in the realm of the old. Mondale was only one year older than Lowenstein, but years building the DFL had taught him the importance of organization and the need for building coalitions.

Mondale believed that both the old and the new, despite their differences, possessed a common interest in social reform. Compromises would have to be made: the old needed to appreciate the healthy impatience of the young, while the new needed to accept the political clout of the old. Only a broad-based coalition that included the working class and the young would have any chance of staying in power.

The gap between the old and new widened when, in November 1967, Eugene McCarthy announced he would challenge the Johnson-Humphrey ticket in the upcoming Democratic primaries. Self-consciously exploiting the growing divisions within the party, McCarthy appealed directly to the younger, educated faction that opposed the war. Mondale had been disappointed but not surprised by McCarthy's announcement. They had never been very close. "We basically tried to avoid embarrassing each other," Mondale recalled. McCarthy, who resented Mondale's close relationship with Humphrey, complained that Mondale, like Humphrey, lacked both the courage and the political independence to speak his mind. Mondale found McCarthy arrogant and aloof. Self-absorbed and egotistical, McCarthy, he charged, selfishly pursued his own interests while refusing to accept the hard sacrifices imposed by party politics.[13]

Mondale's loyalties lay with Humphrey, not Johnson. The President seemed oblivious to the rumblings within his own party and incapable of winning the confidence of the young. On the biggest issue of the day, Johnson refused to show the flexibility necessary to prevent an insurrection. With the rest of the country, Mondale was jolted when on January 31, 1968, Communist troops launched an offensive on the first day of the lunar new year called Tet. The Vietcong invaded the U.S. embassy compound in Saigon and waged bloody battles in the capitals of most South Vietnam provinces.

Tet confirmed Mondale's doubts about administration policy. Convinced that Johnson had misled his own party and the American people about the war's progress, Mondale, like other dissident Democrats, believed all possible peace alternatives needed to be explored—including a unilateral bombing pause. Yet Mondale continued to express public support for the administration. He felt that loyalty to Humphrey bound him to the administration. Mondale feared that a public break with Johnson on the critical issue of a bombing pause would further undermine Humphrey's credibility and limit his ability to influence policy. In reality, Mondale overestimated the potential impact of his break with the administration. By 1968, Humphrey's position on the war differed little from Johnson's and he had already lost what little influence he had once exercised. In retrospect, Mondale admitted the miscalculation, calling his support for the war "the greatest mistake" of his political career. He would pay a high price for his caution.[14]

As Mondale became more critical of the war effort, the gap between his private thoughts and his public statements widened. "No issue concerns me more than Vietnam—I think of little else," he told an antiwar group during a heated exchange in Washington on February 6. "Tragic and disheartening as this problem is, critical as I am of certain aspects and desirous as I am for meaningful negotiations, I still think our policy is better than any of the alternatives." He said he was "painfully aware" that much of the money spent in Vietnam could be used for housing and other needs. But, he asked: "What would be the consequence of our withdrawal now? If we break our word, there would be a real question of who will believe us next time." He also refused to accept any relationship between urban unrest and the war in Vietnam. "I don't think American policy can be predicated on the fact that somebody is going to resort to violence," he retorted.[15]

On March 12, McCarthy and his youthful supporters successfully translated dissatisfaction with Vietnam from both the right and left into a dramatic symbolic victory in the New Hampshire primary, winning 42 percent of the popular vote compared to Johnson's 49 percent. McCarthy's strong showing did not convince Mondale that his colleague could win the Democratic nomination. Not only did the President still control the party apparatus, which elected most delegates, but also McCarthy's constituency was too narrow, unable to reach into the ranks of labor, blacks, and the poor. The candidate who could end the divisions within the party, he felt, would have the best chance of securing the nomination and winning in November. Besides Humphrey, the only other figure with such broad appeal was Robert Kennedy.

Before New Hampshire, Kennedy had refused to run. He feared the public would view his candidacy as a personal vendetta against Johnson, split the party, and ruin his chances in 1972. Now he found the possibility hard to refuse. Four days after McCarthy's New Hampshire victory, Robert Kennedy entered the race.[16]

Mondale's feelings toward his popular colleague oscillated between resentment and respect. Like many Humphrey protégés, Mondale thought that Jack Kennedy's money and looks, rather than his talent and accomplishments, had enabled him to trounce Humphrey for the Democratic nomination in 1960. He resented the Kennedys' star status that attracted constant media attention and intense public interest. The wealth and glamour, the sometimes extravagant lifestyle, clashed with Mondale's small-town midwestern values. Sharply contrasting public personalities added to the distance. Where Kennedy was passionate and brooding, Mondale was reflective and reserved. Mondale sometimes found Kennedy difficult to work with or understand. "Bobby was a strange character, a little spooky," he recalled. "He was alternately happy and glum, introverted and extroverted."[17]

The two men also managed, however, to develop a close working relationship born of mutual respect. Mondale was impressed by Kennedy's passion and conviction. He observed a visceral bond between Kennedy and the poor, whether it be Chicano farm workers in California, Native Americans on reservations in Oklahoma, or urban blacks in Harlem. Kennedy, for his part, admired Mondale's intelligence and dedication. They shared the same concern for the poor and outcast, hoped to expand the Great Society, and had nearly identical voting records. Even on Vietnam, both criticized the slow pacification program, denounced the corrupt South Vietnamese government, advocated including the NLF in negotiations, and hoped for a peaceful noncommunist South Vietnam. They disagreed on one issue: whether the administration should initiate a unilateral bombing halt.

While substantively compatible, stylistically they could not have been more different. Kennedy was the crown prince of the new politics. A masterful media presence, he understood the power of television and used it to his advantage. "Robert Kennedy always understood Guthman's Law," a new politics supporter explained: "three minutes on the six-o'clock news is worth all the rest of the publicity you can get." Compounding the differences, Mondale, despite his populist antipathy toward wealth and privilege, always seemed comfortable in power, at ease with the establishment. Kennedy, despite his life-long proximity to power, always appeared uncomfortable with the establishment. He radiated a nervous energy that conveyed a disdain for the very institutions he helped to perpetuate.[18]

The rhythm of legislative politics temporarily removed Mondale from the partisan bickering that followed Kennedy's announcement. In January, Johnson asked Congress to enact the five measures still pending from his 1967 civil rights proposals. Mondale decided to take a bold initiative by sponsoring the most controversial part of the administration's civil rights bill: fair housing. Since Johnson had first introduced the measure in 1966, it had gained little congressional support. In 1966, liberals had fallen ten votes short of imposing cloture, a motion which required two-thirds of the Senate to end a filibuster. Johnson gave only verbal approval to the measure, and civil rights leaders were unable to lobby effectively. In 1967, Senate liberals had suffered defeat by a similar margin.[19]

When Mondale introduced the legislation, Roger Mudd, a correspondent with CBS, laughed. "You don't really think this is going anywhere do you?" he asked. Mondale realized the chances for passage in 1968 were slim. Attorney General Ramsey Clark, a strong supporter of open housing, privately pleaded with Mondale not to push the legislation. Citing polls showing a serious white backlash against the previous summer's rioting, Clark feared the entire civil rights package would be jeopardized. Even Democratic Senators like Philip Hart of Michigan, one of the Senate's strongest civil rights advocates, told Mondale it was a hopeless cause. Their reservations were well founded. In order to build the necessary coalition of northern Democrats and liberal Republicans, Mondale would need the support of Senate Minority Leader Everett Dirksen, who strongly opposed open housing legislation. The nation's attitude toward civil rights had hardened in response to the rash of riots that plagued many cities. Many legislators believed the rioters should not be "rewarded" for their behavior with new programs for the poor. Also, while earlier civil rights legislation focused primarily on injustice in the South, this legislation affected northern homeowners and labor unionists.[20]

Mondale believed that the fair housing issue would serve as a useful antidote to the pervasive rancor and perhaps remind Democrats of their common interests. He spoke eloquently about the purpose of the legislation: "The barriers of housing discrimination stifle hope and achievement, and promote rage and despair; they tell the Negro citizen trapped in an urban slum there is no escape, that even were he able to get a decent education and a good job, he would still not have the freedom other Americans enjoy to choose where he and his family will live." The failure to act, Mondale argued, "lends a powerful argument to the black separatists and black racists, and can only speed the process of separation and alienation." Mondale believed that Congress needed to strengthen the hand of the moderate civil rights leaders by demonstrating its commitment to racial justice. "There is no longer any economic, political, moral, or other justification for segregated housing. On this one issue alone, liberals and conservatives alike can be condemned, and we all know that justice, morality and the national interest demand that the Congress act"[21]

Conservatives were just as passionate in opposition. "Unless the United States Senate has lost its collective mind," thundered the conservative columnist James Kilpatrick, "the Mondale 'open housing' amendment to the pending civil rights bill will be decisively rejected." Southern Democrats led the Congressional opposition. Senator Allen Ellender of Louisiana, who had organized dissent against the 1964 Civil Rights Act, declared that the bill represented "the ultimate in social extravagance in the United States." In melodramatic overtones he charged "every cherished liberty purchased at a high cost in Anglo-American history" would be "trampled under foot" if the legislation became law. Robert Byrd, a West Virginia moderate, argued that "Decent housing does not necessarily have to be integrated housing." Congress needed to recognize the rights of those who "wish to be selective in the management, use, and disposition of the property which is the product of their own sweat and industry." North Carolina's Sam Ervin, a bible-quoting constitutional conservative, claimed that the open housing amendment was a proposal "to bring about equality by robbing all Americans of their basic rights of private property."[22]

Mondale knew that the battle would be won or lost on cloture—a filibuster-killing motion that would enable the bill itself to be voted on. If all members voted on the open-housing cloture motion, Mondale would need sixty-seven of the one hundred senators to silence the opposition. He realized history was not on his side. Of the fifty-eight cloture votes in fifty-one years, only seven had been successful. Cloture had been attempted thirteen times on civil rights issues, in particular, and had carried only twice.

On February 20, after five weeks of debate, the Senate showed unexpected support for the open housing amendment, but the vote fell short of the two-thirds majority required for adoption and was not enough to convince Majority Leader Mike Mansfield to continue the battle. Fearing that the open-housing amendment would kill a promising civil rights bill, he moved "with regret" to quash Mondale's amendment. Surprisingly, proponents defeated Mansfield's motion, 55–37, thus guaranteeing another cloture vote. Although twelve votes short of the required number, the tally demonstrated that support for cloture was greater in 1968 than in either of the two cloture votes on the 1966 civil rights bill which had also included an open housing provision.

Mondale believed the vote demonstrated that a clear majority favored "the strongest possible fair housing measure." A number of events seemed to be moving in his direction. The President declared that he supported the Mondale amendment. More important, Minority Leader Everett Dirksen, under pressure from moderate Republicans, indicated he was ready to work on a compromise bill that would include open housing. On the twenty-fifth day of the civil rights debate, Dirksen told the Senate that "at long last we seem to be approaching a common denominator." A few days later, Dirksen presented his own proposal. He insisted on only one exemption—affecting 10 percent of housing units. Mondale described the compromise as "a miracle" and said it was much more than he could have anticipated "just a week ago." Mondale cleared the way for the compromise version by moving to kill his pending amendment. But under pressure from conservatives, Dirksen insisted on added revisions exempting owner-occupied, single-family dwellings sold or rented privately without the assistance of a broker. The new exemptions meant only 80 percent of housing—rather than 91 percent in the original Mondale proposal—would be covered by fair housing standards. Mondale admitted that he accepted the compromise "reluctantly," but that he was trying "to make an accommodation in light of the realities of the current legislative situation." Dirksen's last minute revisions, however, divided civil rights supporters and reduced support for the compromise measure.[23]

Mondale's efforts received a further boost when the President's Commission on Civil Disorders released its long-awaited report on February 29. Urging vast efforts to address the problem of racism in this country, the report warned: "Our nation is moving toward two societies, one black, one white—separate and unequal." Unless drastic action was taken, the commission warned, there would be a "continuing polarization of the American community and, ultimately, the destruction of basic democratic values." Mondale hoped the report's stark descriptions of the racial problem and strong prescriptions would add weight to his case that fair housing was imperative.[24]

On March 1, Mondale and the liberals failed for the third time to win a cloture vote. Dirksen had managed to switch only two other Republicans. Open housing was in grave danger and possibly doomed. Mansfield, his patience at an end, made it clear that he would allow only one more vote. There seemed little hope the measure could pass. The day before the final vote, supporters of the bill gathered for a strategy session in Mondale's office. No matter how they added things up, they came out short. Abruptly, and without notice, Mondale left the meeting. He called on Humphrey to seek his advice. The Vice President told him to call the President who was traveling on Air Force One. Reaching the President by phone, Mondale quickly explained the status of the bill: "Mr. President, we have a cloture vote for tomorrow afternoon and we need a few more votes." Democrat Edward Bartlett of Alaska had promised to vote for the bill, but only if he was given $18 million for public housing. Johnson listened intently but hung up without making any promises. The next day, as the voting began, Mondale was uncertain whether Johnson had ever called Bartlett or if he had won him over. As the vote came to a close, Mondale realized he was one vote shy. He searched the chamber for Bartlett. "I looked around the chamber and Bartlett wasn't in the room," Mondale recalled. "I knew we had it." Just before the gavel fell, Bartlett came out of the cloak room and said "AYE." "It cost us $18 million but it was worth it," Mondale recalled. With the filibuster broken, the Senate passed the open housing bill by a vote of 70 to 20. The New York *Times* called the vote "a stunning victory for the tiny band of scrappy liberals that guided the bill through more than seven weeks of stormy debate." [25]

The scene shifted to the House, where the legislation faced an uncertain fate; but as had happened before in the violent history of civil rights, a tragic death breathed new life into the struggle. That tragedy was the assassination of Martin Luther King in Memphis. Within minutes of hearing the news, angry blacks swarmed into the streets. More than one hundred cities witnessed violence. In Chicago alone, riots destroyed twenty blocks, while in Washington D.C. machine guns were emplaced to protect the halls of Congress. More than 5,500 troops were needed to quiet the disturbances.

Mondale believed King's assassination made House passage of the bill even more urgent. "The foremost proponent of a non-violent confrontation between the races is dead," he told the Senate. "We can pray today that the death of the non-violent leader will not bring violence to life. In the days ahead we must act to fulfill King's dream." Apparently many congressman agreed. On April 10 the House voted 250 to 171 to approve the open housing bill. The President termed the House action "a victory for every American. It has been a long, tortuous and difficult road," he said. "There have been days of sunshine and sorrow. But it is now a reality." [26]

Mondale's victory earned him the respect of his colleagues. Just an hour after Johnson signed the bill into law, Phil Hart, who had counseled against the amendment, scribbled: "You were magnificent—your energy, your counsel, your courage, and your leadership combined to move the Senate 'to do right.' Everyone of us associated together over the months in this venture have said this many times. You may not have heard us, but it is now in writing." Another Senator suggested the victory marked Mondale's emergence as an important legislative player. "I think it could safely be said that Mondale has 'arrived' in the Senate, that he's now a first class citizen," commented a fellow Senator.[27]

For Mondale, championing a major piece of civil rights legislation represented an important personal accomplishment as well. In a sense, he was finally putting his father's preachings into practice. "[I]f you were to visit the grave site, in St. James Minnesota, of one Theodore S. Mondale," wrote his half-brother Lester. "I feel certain that you'd be amazed at the greenness of the grass about his burial plot: a result of a powerful radiance emanating from those old bones in response to your truly great and history-making championship of the Civil Rights Bill." His sister-in-law Ruth concurred. Referring to a picture of Mondale in her local paper, she wrote: "I could almost see Clarabel and Dad catching sight of the pictures and the 'Amens' that would have issued forth."[28]

Although an important victory for the civil rights movement, the fair housing fight did nothing to heal the divisions within the party. Indeed, after a two-month hiatus, Mondale found himself thrust back into the party divisions. On March 31, the President, torn between the military's request for more troops and the opposition of newly appointed Defense Secretary Clark Clifford, had informed a national television audience that he was ordering a temporary pause in the bombing. Then the embattled President, looking directly into the camera, uttered words few had anticipated: "I shall not seek, and I will not accept the nomination of my party, for another term as your president."

After some initial hesitation, Humphrey planned to fill the vacuum created by Johnson's withdrawal. Realizing he needed to make inroads with younger voters, Humphrey asked Mondale to manage his campaign. Mondale accepted, but only after forcing Humphrey to agree not to choose conservative John Connally as his running mate. Concerned about public impressions of an all-Minnesota effort, Mondale convinced Humphrey to appoint Oklahoma Senator Fred Harris as co-chairman. Commenting on the appointment, the journalists Rowland Evans and Robert Novak referred to Mondale and Harris as "Humphrey's Establishment Radicals" because they represented "the future of the Democratic party and its hope for revitalization, both in the Senate and the nation, more accurately than any other party leaders." Both men, Evans and Novak observed, were "totally un-afraid of radical currents in the politics of the Black and young," and "accepted by the regulars in a way that 'unwashed' radicals such as Allard Lowenstein are not and never will be."[29]

Humphrey's promise to give the two Senators complete control of the campaign did not ease Mondale's doubts. "I'm giving you carte blanche," Humphrey said. "I'll meddle as little as possible," but added, "and as much as necessary." Mondale knew the Vice President and his ambitious staff well enough to realize there would be constant internal bickering. "It was typical Humphrey," Mondale recalled. "He had about 800 informal campaign managers," and few of them could agree. A competing organization, Citizens for Humphrey, and a shadow campaign run by two senior staff people, William Connell and Max Kampelman, began immediately challenging Mondale's au-thority. Kampelman complained privately to Humphrey that neither Mondale nor Harris had any national political experience. The differ-ences were both tactical and ideological. Mondale and Harris encour-aged Humphrey to solidify his liberal base by emphasizing his com-mitment to social justice and distancing himself from Johnson on the war. The other advisors, more concerned about losing the white middle class than pacifying liberals, suggested the Vice President stress his commitment to law and order and campaign as the Presi-dent's candidate. Occasionally, Mondale would protest and Hum-phrey would warn Kampelman and others not to interfere. "I am bringing this to an abrupt end—I do not want you, Maguire, Kam-pelman or anyone else bypassing the two senators," Humphrey blus-tered. Days later, his staff, usually at his instruction, was running its shadow campaign as though nothing had happened.[30]

Humphrey had asked Mondale to run his campaign to demonstrate his concern for the new politics, but Mondale emerged a master practitioner of the old politics. While the public focused its attention on Kennedy and McCarthy's primary battles, Mondale gathered del-egates in nonprimary states. The state conventions, although lacking the glamour and publicity of the primaries, chose the majority of delegates for the convention. Behind closed doors Mondale bargained with labor leaders, party bosses and elected officials, working out deals to keep the delegations in firm control. Mondale scored his greatest personal victory in Pennsylvania, where he convinced the party leadership to reschedule an unprecedented preference poll from June 4 to May 28—the day before the Oregon primary. Confident Humphrey would score well in the Pennsylvania poll, Mondale hoped to divert attention from Kennedy's anticipated Oregon victory.[31]

That evening, Mondale sat down with other Humphrey aides to watch the results from Oregon. The expected Kennedy triumph, Mondale believed, combined with his previous wins in Nebraska and Indiana, would make him a serious threat. To everyone's surprise, the election results revealed an upset: McCarthy would carry the state. Mondale believed the Kennedy loss, the first family defeat after twenty-two years of victories, ended his chances of overtaking Humphrey. Only by sweeping the primaries could Kennedy claim that popular will dictated a choice other than Humphrey. After McCarthy's defeats in Indiana and Nebraska, and Kennedy's loss in Oregon, neither candidate could overmatch Humphrey's convention strength.

But Mondale had dismissed Kennedy too soon. A few days later, Kennedy won a decisive 52 percent of the vote in California, more than anyone had predicted. He also scored an upset victory in Humphrey's native South Dakota. Confident that his victories had eliminated McCarthy and established him as Humphrey's sole competitor for the nomination, Kennedy challenged the Vice President to debate. The stage seemed set for a convention showdown: Kennedy's popular support versus Humphrey's institutional strength. Tragically, the confrontation would never be. Shortly after giving his victory speech, Kennedy was assassinated.[32]

Kennedy's death left Mondale depressed and disillusioned. "People feel the recent tragedy to varying degrees. You obviously feel it quite deeply," Berman wrote Mondale. "As much as you may not have the stomach for it right now," he wrote, the campaign must continue. On June 6, Mondale stood on the floor of the Senate and delivered a moving eulogy to his slain colleague. "Senator Kennedy was a magnificent leader," he said in a voice quivering with emotion. "There are never enough men like Robert Kennedy in our nation. The violence and senselessness of his death are a deep shock to the very structure of the American system of government."[33]

Mondale's heartfelt grief did not stop him from wooing Kennedy delegates and resuming the strong-arm methods of winning state delegations. McCarthy supporters continued screaming foul at the procedures Mondale used to secure Humphrey the nomination. In Minnesota DFL regulars captured most delegates at the state convention after antiwar forces had carried the big-city caucuses. In New York, McCarthy swept the primary with a slight majority of the 125 elected delegates but received only 15 of the 65 appointed delegates. The Humphrey regulars beat down insurgencies in Montana, Utah, Delaware, and Connecticut. In some states, McCarthy delegates walked out of state conventions when Humphrey forces refused to provide them adequate representation. In district conventions Humphrey supporters refused to recognize McCarthy delegates.[34]

Politically, the assassination, by denying voters an alternative and making Humphrey's nomination appear inevitable, built public resentment against the Vice President. The press focused more on Humphrey's dependence on the President. *Esquire* pictured Humphrey on its cover as a ventriloquist's dummy in the President's lap. Tom Wicker made the same point, though more gracefully. Humphrey's "politically painful identification with the administration and the war," he wrote, "is the primary reason the Vice President's campaign is not catching fire with the public." On the few occasions when Humphrey did appear at rallies, his crowds were, in the words of the Washington *Post,* "thin, apathetic and ominously hostile."[35]

With the campaign in disarray and Humphrey under assault from every direction, Mondale pleaded for changes. First of all, he suggested the Vice President place a single person in charge of the campaign. In response, Humphrey asked former party chairman Larry O'Brien to become "convention coordinator." But Mondale believed Humphrey needed to make some dramatic unifying gesture to the McCarthy and Kennedy forces. If he was to be the candidate of unity, Mondale argued, he needed to distance himself from Johnson. Mondale believed that politically and militarily, the President's Vietnam policy was flawed. Unless the Vice President supported a unilateral bombing halt the party's nomination would be worthless. On the other hand, William Connell and Max Kampelman, both fervent believers in the old politics who opposed any gestures to the peace forces, insisted that Humphrey stand as the administration's candidate. For his part, Humphrey rejected Mondale's advice, refusing to take any steps that would incur Johnson's wrath.[36]

Mondale understood Humphrey's dilemma: The Vice President needed to divorce himself from Johnson but without appearing disloyal or opportunistic. Pragmatic political considerations reinforced Humphrey's desire to stay on good terms with the President. Many of the southern delegations warned they would place Johnson's name in nomination if Humphrey "sold out" to the liberals. In Mondale's mind, the predicament required a Vietnam platform position which appeased both hawks and doves. "I worked for a better part of a year to get compromise language for the platform," Mondale recalled. Mondale asked David Ginsburg, a prominent Washington lawyer, to try to write the draft. Ginsburg spent two months talking to representatives from both sides and finally wrote a draft acceptable to both. "So we thought we had something that could help the party unite, yet would make it possible for Humphrey to start winding down the war," Mondale told Al Eisele. The draft read: "Stop the bombing of North Vietnam. The action and its timing shall take into account the security of our troops and the likelihood of a response from Hanoi."

The language pleased Kennedy and McCarthy delegates. "There's not ten cents worth of difference from the Vice President's policy," Ginsburg said after reading Ted Kennedy's speech before the platform committee. Humphrey also had the language cleared through secretary of state Dean Rusk and national security advisor Walt Rostow. "We can live with it, Hubert," Rostow said. At the last minute, however, Johnson withdrew support. "That plank undercuts our whole policy," he said, "and, by God, the Democratic Party ought not to be doing this to me, and you ought not to be doing it—you've been part of this policy." Mondale urged Humphrey to assert his independence and support the compromise position. Once again, Humphrey refused. "I did not come here to repudiate the President of the United States. I want that made quite clear," he said in response to a question.[37]

When he arrived in Chicago for the Democratic convention on August 25, Mondale found a city prepared for war. Militant antiwar groups had announced in the spring that they would organize mass demonstrations against the war and the Democratic candidate who supported it. A few weeks before the convention opening, Mondale appealed to Richard Daley, the crusty 66-year-old mayor, to use restraint against the protesters. But Daley emphatically made clear his intention to use force to crush the first signs of rebellion. To emphasize the point, he mobilized 12,000 police and alerted 7,500 national guardsmen. The convention hall, itself a fortress, was surrounded by chain-link fences with barbed wire. Mondale was forced to navigate police barriers to gain entrance to the hotel lobby. The putrid smell of limburger cheese, which protesters had rubbed into the carpet,

pervaded the hotel lobby. To make matter worse, the city was virtually paralyzed by a telephone and cab strike.[38]

On Tuesday evening, August 27, the night before the critical
Vietnam debate, Mondale looked out his hotel window and saw the
demonstrations in Grant Park. In the background he could hear the
faint shouts of protesters shouting "Stop the War, Stop the War, Stop
the War." He shook his head in despair. "Democrats fighting Democrats," he muttered. They misunderstood Humphrey, he believed.
Humphrey wanted to end the war, but Johnson had tied his hands. "I
always thought that if Humphrey were elected president, he would
get that war over with," Mondale later reflected. "That was an act of
faith. You couldn't prove it on the record. . . . But I always thought,
knowing Humphrey, that he'd want that war over. I also knew he
couldn't do a hell of a lot on his own when he was serving under
President Johnson, as vice president, and before he was nominated."[39]

On Wednesday, Mondale stood expressionless on the floor while
an emotional convention debated its Vietnam plank. With his compromise effort sunk, he watched as the party fought bitterly over
majority and minority resolutions. The differences between the two
planks were minor. Both planks, with varying emphasis, advocated
withdrawal of American and North Vietnamese troops from South
Vietnam, the holding of free and open elections when the fighting
stopped, and a scaling down of search-and-destroy missions in the
interim. The majority Vietnam plank supported a bombing halt "when
this action would not endanger the lives of our troops in the field;
this action should take into account the response from Hanoi." The
dovish position called for a unilateral bombing halt. Despite his work
on the compromise position and his private support for the peace
plank, in the end, Mondale voted for the administration's position.
For almost three hours, many of the party's most distinguished leaders went to the microphone. At the end the majority plank won by a
roll call vote of 1,567 to 1,041. As the afternoon session adjourned,
supporters of the minority plank on the convention floor and in the
gallery donned black arm bands and remained in their seats, singing
"We Shall Overcome."

While the convention debated the Vietnam plank, a major battle
broke out between police and demonstrators near the bandstand at
Grant Park after one of the youths hauled down an American flag.
Four hours later, as the night session of nominations was beginning,
there was another and more serious clash on the street in front of the

Conrad Hilton. Television crews filmed the battle as it occurred, and scenes of the violence were shown during the nomination speeches. Veteran campaign chronicler Teddy White, observing the scene, recorded in his notebook: "The Democrats are finished."[40]

On nationwide television the violence replaced the speech of Carl Stokes, the black mayor of Cleveland, placing Humphrey's name in nomination. Allard Lowenstein leaped to his feet demanding the convention adjourn; no business should be transacted, he shouted, while "people's rights are being abused on the streets, maced and beaten unconscious." Senator Abraham Ribicoff of Connecticut, making the nominating speech for South Dakota Senator George McGovern, departed from his text to say, "With George McGovern, we wouldn't have Gestapo tactics on the streets of Chicago." The theatrics were just enough to spoil Humphrey's nomination, not to stop it. Just before midnight, when Pennsylvania cast its votes, Humphrey was nominated by the world's oldest political party.

For Mondale it was a bittersweet moment. He witnessed the culmination of twenty years of hard labor in the political trenches. As the states cast their votes, Mondale may have thought of those cold days in 1948 when he had walked door-to-door canvassing for the young Senate candidate. He may have remembered the smile on his father's face after shaking Humphrey's hand. All the days, all the hard work, and now, their day: Hubert Humphrey was the Democratic nominee for President of the United States. But the public mood was so hostile. Middle-class anger about government indifference to their concerns was matched by black bitterness at a political system which ignored their demands. A united civil rights movement which had aroused the moral indignation of the nation was now divided in the face of more subtle forces of discrimination. A nation once possessed of unbridled confidence now expressed a growing fear of social decay.

Humphrey spent most of his time huddled in his room at the Hilton debating his vice presidential choice. Johnson pushed hard for him to choose a southerner, especially North Carolina Governor Terry Sanford or Georgia's Carl Sanders. Humphrey leaned toward New Jersey Governor Hughes, or one of two Senators: his campaign co-chairman Fred Harris or Maine's Edmund Muskie. Mondale remained on the fringes of the decision, occasionally checking to make sure Humphrey did not give in to pressure and choose a conservative. He preferred either Muskie or Harris. Both had strong liberal records. After hours of agonizing, Humphrey announced his pick. "When it came down to making a choice between Harris and Muskie, I went for the quiet man," Humphrey told Mondale. "I know I talk too much, and I wanted someone who makes for a contrast in styles. Two Hubert Humphreys might be one too many."[41]

On Thursday night, Humphrey came before the public on the night of his acceptance speech as the standard-bearer of a party wracked by internal controversy. His "moment of triumph" was stunning in its irony. Twenty years earlier, Humphrey had led a minority challenge against the Democratic establishment and won a famous victory a the civil rights plank. Young and combative, he had been the self-proclaimed leader of the "new" liberalism. Now, older and cautious, Humphrey was the establishment, and could not muster the courage to challenge the President. Although his philosophy had changed little in the intervening years, to many younger liberals he symbolized the last hurrah of the old order.

As a member of the Minnesota delegation, Mondale listened to the speech from the convention floor. After a moving recital of the prayer of St. Francis of Assisi, Humphrey recited the list of Democratic ghosts—Roosevelt, Truman, John Kennedy, and Johnson. He did his best to heal the party, reaching out to McCarthy and Robert Kennedy supporters. "And I appeal to those thousands, yea millions of young Americans to put aside recrimination and dissension [and] join us. . . . Believe, believe in what America can do, and believe what America can be." It was, Mondale thought, classic Humphrey—emotional, his face flushed, his voice rising and falling. But the President had denied him the one gift he needed: a compromise plank on Vietnam. Humphrey, said Teddy White, gave the convention "a standard political oration of the kind of prose which . . . had been rendered archaic by the events of the previous twenty-four hours."[42]

Events in Chicago shattered all pretense of party unity. McCarthy, who had spent the night of the nominations comforting wounded demonstrators brought into the hotel for medical treatment, flatly refused to appear with Humphrey at the traditional reconciliation scene of winners and losers. Anti-Humphrey delegations went home angry and unappeased. The convention had been a disaster. "I didn't leave Chicago," Mondale said, "I escaped it." The violence in Chicago exacerbated the public's sense that the nation was unraveling and that the Democratic party was incapable of stopping it. "All the forms of civility appeared to be disappearing," Mondale reflected. "There was a sense of anarchy in the land.[43]

After Chicago, Mondale devoted his efforts to reuniting the Minnesota Democratic party, which had been severely divided during the McCarthy-Humphrey fight. State leaders believed he was the only politician in the state who could reconcile competing interests in the party. "Now 40 and a rising star in the Senate, Mondale is the only DFL figure who has the youth and stature even to contemplate becoming a bridge between the factions, the generations and the interests," one observer commented.[44]

Mondale did not see himself as the great healer in the party. "The stories about me going home and putting Humpty Dumpty together again sound fine," he said. "But there's not really much I can do. Nothing cute or contrived is going to work. There's nothing magic I can bring to the problem." There was little he could do until Humphrey escaped Johnson's shadow and developed a less hawkish position on Vietnam. Also significant, he suggested, was the outcome of the fourth-party effort to put McCarthy on the Minnesota ballot. Polls were showing that in a four-way race, 39 percent of the state's voters favored Nixon, 29 percent Humphrey, 22 percent McCarthy, and 7 percent George Wallace.[45]

Mondale remained out of public view until September 16 when he was scheduled to speak to students—McCarthy's base of support—on the University of Minnesota campus. In that speech Mondale expressed publicly what he had felt privately for months: the United States should cease all bombing of North Vietnam. "We should halt the bombing and see what Hanoi does, without requiring any guarantees in advance," he told reporters. "I would expect that they would not take advantage of the bombing pause and that they would reciprocate. But after we stop the bombing, we can see what they do and then take another look." Humphrey responded graciously to word of his protégé's public break with his Vietnam position. "Senator Mondale is, of course, a good friend of mine and an outstanding United States Senator," he told reporters while campaigning in Buffalo. "As a Senator, he has a right and responsibility to speak out, and I welcome his views."[46]

Years later, observers suggested that Mondale's loyalty to Humphrey prevented him from expressing his "true" private feelings against the war. Many former staff members, who shared distinct memories of the Senator's expressing strong views against the war in private, were convinced his affection for Humphrey forced him to remain silent in public. "He really let himself be immobilized by Humphrey and his being veep in terms of the war issue," reflected a former administrative assistant. "That's the thing that kept him from acting sooner. He'd turned sour on it long before he went public." Another close Mondale aide concurred. "We all knew that his position on the war personally was different from his public position on the war for as long as Hubert Humphrey was in office he thought he had to be loyal," Dwane Scribner recalled. Mondale's press secretary, who was responsible for translating private thoughts into public pronouncements, shared the consensus. "The one criticism I have," Dick Conlon said in reference to Mondale's position on Vietnam, "is that he shows a lack of courage of his own convictions sometimes."[47]

Critics, believing they had discovered a chink in the Mondale armor, took full political advantage of the situation. In 1967, when Mondale underwent an emergency appendectomy, an antiwar Minnesota Democrat grumbled: "I hope they stuffed him with some guts before sewing him up." "How could Mondale in honesty support the candidacy of Hubert Humphrey, knowing the Vice President's need to back Johnson's bombing policy?" asked George Thiss, the Minnesota Republican state chairman. "Surely Mondale must have compromised his own convictions when he urged the Democratic party to nominate Humphrey, yet feeling all the while that the party's Vietnam position was wrong." Mondale's silence on this issue raised serious questions about his capacity for bold and independent political action—questions which would haunt him for the rest of his career. Years later, critics would wonder if Mondale could exercise his independence from the powerful interest groups of the Democratic party.[48]

As the general election campaign commenced, Humphrey still had not solved the one problem that lay at the heart of his political difficulties—the public's perception that he was an administration mouthpiece. Campaign crowds were small and frequently hostile, often greeting him with unmerciful heckling. Young blacks yelling "Honky, go home" drove him out of a hall in Watts. Five thousand antiwar protesters ringed his Los Angeles hotel for an entire day, waving "Dump the Hump" signs, and pouring blood into the hotel fountain. In California, he was greeted by 5,000 demonstrators waving cards: "Hitler, Hubert, Hirohito" and "Help Hubert Hibernate."

Richard Nixon, the perennial anticommunist crusader, pounced on the helpless Democrats. By avoiding discussion of his Vietnam strategy, Nixon effectively focused public attention and scorn on the divided Democrats. His top priority at home, he said, was "the restoration of law and order." Pledging to transform the Supreme Court, which he claimed had given the "green light" to American criminals, Nixon made a ringing appeal to the constituency he most coveted—middle-class whites who were growing daily more alienated. "If you want your president to continue the do-nothing policy toward crime, vote Humphrey," he said. "If you want to fight crime, vote Nixon."[49]

A third-party challenge from Alabama Governor George Wallace threatened to tear needed votes from the Democratic candidate. Wallace's appeal transcended geographic boundaries and offered a grave threat to the Democrats. Campaigning hard in the north, he pitched his appeal to working-class whites angry with rioting blacks and protesting students. "The stereotypical Wallace voter," the historian Allen Matusow has observed, "was a bullet-headed third-generation Polish steelworker in Gary, Indiana, fearful of Negroes trying to marry his daughter and driving a pickup truck with a bumper sticker reading, 'America, love it or leave it.' " Espousing a message that included both cultural populism and economic liberalism, Wallace offered relief to many Americans who felt disdain for the cultural sophisticates who challenged deeply held racial and moral values. By focusing working class anger on the arrogance of the liberal establishment, he added moral legitimacy to the white backlash. "Wallace performed for the Republican party a critically important function," the journalist Thomas Edsall observed, "pioneering the specter of a new, hated liberal establishment to compete with the reviled corporate upper-class conservative establishment traditionally targeted by American populist politics."[50]

Trailing by fifteen percentage points in late September, Humphrey decided to make the break Mondale had urged for so long. Appearing on nationwide television from Salt Lake City, he announced that if elected, he would temporarily cease the bombing of North Vietnam. Although not a radical departure from the administration's position, it was a move in the right direction politically. Suddenly the campaign picked up, the heckling quieted, and the old Humphrey exuberance returned. Mondale, who had long advocated the change, was thrilled. Humphrey, he said, "has shown himself to be what I have always believed him to be—but what so many have come to doubt— a candidate of peace." Yet some students still harbored deep resentment toward Humphrey. On October 26, when hostile students called Humphrey a "warmonger" and an obstacle to peace, Mondale snapped: "How can you say that Hubert Humphrey is no longer interested in the causes to which he has devoted his life? It's one thing to be partisan; it's another to be atrociously unfair." Of Humphrey's recent record he said: "No man is ever at his best in the vice presidency. No man has ever done well there. You must judge Humphrey on his entire record, not just the years in the vice-presidency."[51]

By October 21, Humphrey had cut Nixon's lead to only eight points and was gaining, but his surge came too late. His defeat was agonizingly narrow: 43.4 percent of the vote for Nixon compared to 42.7 percent for Humphrey and 13.5 percent for Wallace. "We ran out of time," Mondale said. "What we needed was two more days." The following morning, with Mondale at his side, the "Happy Warrior" told his faithful followers: "I have done my best. I have lost. Mr. Nixon won. The democratic process has worked its will, so now let's get on with the urgent task of uniting our country."[52]

The Mondale who stood next to Humphrey that November morning was different from the man who had campaigned for his own election just two years earlier. The war had transformed Mondale, forcing him to reconsider his strong faith in government and optimistic hopes for reform. "The agony of Vietnam and of the country closed in on me like a casket," he reflected, "and perhaps accounts for the evaporation of many of my optimistic hopes for social progress. . . ." The war represented Mondale's rite of passage. He came to recognize how the presidency could be used to deceive people, how experts could fool themselves, and how the bureaucracy could perpetuate its own errors. He had learned a new, but valuable feeling— skepticism. "I just couldn't believe that they could be that wrong," he reflected years later. "It slowly dawned on me," he said, "that there are limits to American power; limits to how we can influence what are essentially indigenous problems of another country."[53]

7
Questioning Liberalism

Hours before the scheduled speech, students began filtering into the small field house on the Macalester College campus. It was October 1969, and the Republican president's promise of "peace with honor" had translated into the same quixotic hope of a noncommunist South Vietnam. While no more successful in winning the war, Nixon's combination of troop withdrawals and appeals for an international cease-fire did briefly deflate the antiwar movement. Hoping to resuscitate the cause, activists from across the nation organized a massive peaceful mobilization. The Minneapolis organizers asked Mondale to be their speaker. Two years earlier when Mondale spoke on that campus he had pleaded for patience and expressed his support of Johnson's Vietnam policy. Since that time, he had inched away from the war without ever renouncing it. As he prepared his remarks for the moratorium, he hoped to break cautiously with the war without admitting his mistake. "When I first started writing that speech at Macalester I tried to say I hadn't changed my position," he reflected. "I tried to be artistic. I realized I could not write the speech. So I said to myself either you say you are wrong and make a break and take a new position with integrity or you are done in public life."[1]

When he arrived for the 8 P.M. address, Mondale found an auditorium packed with students. He could sense both the anticipation and the anger. Applause mixed with shouts of protests greeted his introduction. Students heckled as he launched into a partisan critique of Nixon's policy. As he moved from partisanship into a personal reflection on the war the crowd fell silent. "Surely tonight it is clear that it is not enough to hope for peace, we must seek it, we must demand it," he said. "It is not enough to say that we have failed in our objective, we must openly and frankly admit that our objectives were in error." The crowd burst into long and sustained applause. The war, he went on, was "a military, a political and a moral disaster" that threatened to take from an entire generation "all confidence in the ability of a democracy to respond with justice, reason and humanity." Mondale called for the government to confess its error. "The United States," he declared, "cannot impose its solution upon an essentially internal conflict in a far-off land."[2]

There were a number of reasons for Mondale's conversion. Partisanship and political calculation certainly played a role. With Johnson removed from office he no longer felt constrained from expressing his views. Opinion polls now showed that a majority of Americans opposed the war and wanted to see it brought to an end. Perhaps most important, he watched as the new Republican administration attempted to slash important social programs at the same time that it spent an inordinate amount on the war. The nation, he told students that night at Macalester, spent $21,000 for every soldier in Vietnam but only $44 for every student in an American school. For one billion dollars, "enough to run the Vietnam war for 10 days," the nation could pay for 625,000 headstart children, fund jobs for 500,000 welfare recipients, and expand by five-fold the money spent on cancer research.

Many applauded Mondale for his candor. "It is asking a lot of a political leader to confess he had made a mistake on Vietnam," editorialized the Minneapolis *Tribune*. "Whether this was political folly or wisdom, the future will determine. We believe it was political courage by this former supporter of the war." The scope of the change in Mondale's position on the war also raised questions about his understanding of foreign policy issues. In less than eighteen months, Mondale had moved from support of Johnson's escalation of the conflict to endorsement of a limited bombing halt to condemnation of the war as "a military, a political and a moral disaster." Although the nature of the war had changed little during that time, Mondale's public position had moved from nearly blind acceptance of the need for American involvement to strident condemnation of the entire war effort. Before 1968, he had mirrored the mainstream party position on the war with only minor variations; after 1969 he shared the disaffection of the liberal wing of the Democratic party.[3]

Once in opposition, Mondale endorsed a number of unsuccessful efforts to bring the war to a speedy conclusion. In 1970, he supported the Church-Cooper Amendment which called for cutting off all funding for American forces in Cambodia after the promised withdrawal date of July 1. In 1971, he voted for the McGovern-Hatfield Amendment which would have ended American military operations in Cambodia and required the withdrawal of all American forces from Vietnam by the end of 1971. "I am not talking about Nixon's war or Johnson's war," he said on the Senate floor. "This war belongs at the doorstep of every public official—including myself—who stood by and let it happen. We quibbled. We gave the benefit of the doubt. We were never more wrong." Later, in 1973, he successfully co-sponsored the War Powers Act, which he called "a bipartisan, nonideological attempt to restore the constitutional balance of power between Congress and the President." The act required the President to notify Congress within forty-eight hours of American troop deployment to combat areas, and forced him to withdraw the soldiers after sixty days unless Congress specifically authorized them to stay.[4]

Like the administration, Mondale refused to admit publicly that the United States should allow South Vietnam to fall to the communists. He spoke instead of a "political settlement," which would accommodate "some of the aspirations which have made the other side one of the most tenacious foes in the history of warfare." Privately, Mondale realized an American withdrawal would result in a communist victory. Although he criticized the Saigon regime for violating human rights, he believed a communist victory would produce an orgy of violence. In his mind, this was the painful Vietnam reality: only a massive infusion of American aid could save South Vietnam from a brutal communist takeover, but continued American involvement strained resources and fed social tensions at home. For Mondale, however tragic the possible consequences of withdrawal, the nation could not continue to pay the price of involvement.

Along with the lives lost in battle, perhaps the greatest price was the diversion of funds from needed social programs at home. After

1968, Mondale sought and gained membership on committees that focused attention on the problems of the disadvantaged. He told friends that he planned to follow in Robert Kennedy's footsteps. Acting on his strategy, Mondale took Kennedy's seat on the Labor and Public Welfare Committee and he earned a spot on the new Select Committee on Nutrition and Human Needs. These new assignments intensified his liberal instincts by providing first-hand exposure to the problems of the disadvantaged. "We can look at a statistic and two minutes later have forgotten it," he said. "But one cannot forget the loneliness of a 5-year-old Navajo boy—a boy who barely came up to my knee—who must live in a boarding school, far away from his parents, far away from his home. . . . Those are the things one remembers, not the statistics."[5]

No longer satisfied with government reports or budgets, Mondale decided to search for answers himself. "He is a liberal who is moving further to the left, far enough that it almost can be said there is a new Mondale," observed the Minneapolis *Tribune's* Frank Wright. Mondale traveled to the Mexican border and watched early one morning as migrant workers crossed into the United States unchecked by customs officials. From there they would be bussed to southern California farms where they served as part of the steady supply of cheap and exploited labor. He traveled to Alaska to see how Eskimos survived. He and his wife went on a "welfare diet," eating only what the poor could afford. He marched with California's United Farm Workers to protest the hiring of Mexican labor to break Cesar Chavez's strike. He did all this to gain an understanding that only first-hand knowledge could afford. As he said years later, "I went on that diet and I went to the border to see, to feel, to be there, to experience what is going on rather than read about it."[6]

Although he remained committed to the idea of an "equal opportunity society," he came to recognize the existence of real barriers—especially of race and class—that excluded individuals from taking equal part in society's opportunities. The challenge of the liberal in the 1970s, he argued, was to extend to minorities the privileges enjoyed by most other Americans. In order to create those opportunities, however, Mondale realized Americans needed to reassess their priorities. "Unless we begin spending our money on the people of this country, we won't be a society worthy of the ideals we profess," he said. Mondale told an affluent Minneapolis church group in 1970 that the United States "is not as compassionate, as understanding, as sensitive as we think we are. Our priorities are screwy; our priorities are pretty close to being obscene."[7]

Over the next two years, Mondale raised troubling questions about liberal willingness to address difficult social problems. Freed from self-imposed political restraints and exposed to a wide variety of pressing troubles through his committee assignments, Mondale tried to find solutions to problems that had confounded most liberals. His foray into the problems of "powerlessness" produced little legislation. Despite his sometimes strident criticisms of liberal complacency, he articulated no new conceptual framework. "He questioned the conventional solutions, but I don't think he came up with anything better," asserted staff member Bill Smith. Not only were the issues he addressed enormously complex, but Mondale remained a conventional politician wedded to the established institutions of government and the key constituency groups of the Democratic party. There existed during these years a gap between Mondale's ambitious agenda and his conventional tactics. In the end, he learned that the established groups which served as the backbone of the Democratic Party had little interest in extending privileges to new groups. When the coalition balked, he backed away. Mondale, wrote former staff member Roger Morris, "represents a haunting paradox for Democrats: the limits and fatigue of conventional liberalism along with its best qualities of competence and compassion."[8]

Meeting intermittently between May and September of 1969, Mondale's Subcommittee on Migratory Labor held hearings that documented the horrible conditions which plagued migrant workers. Mondale tried to bring hired farm workers under the protection of the federal labor, health, and welfare laws which covered workers in non-farm areas. In 1935, farm laborers had been excluded from the National Labor Relations Act, which guaranteed workers the right to organize unions. As a result, large farm corporations continued shipping massive numbers of Mexican workers across the border to avoid paying higher wages to American workers.[9]

Describing conditions among migrants in counties in Florida, Texas, and Michigan, doctors told the committee about large, undernourished families, crowded together in housing projects, without heat, water, or sanitary facilities. Most of the children examined were infected with intestinal parasites; most had skin infections, and an "amazing number" had chronically infected ears that resulted in partial deafness. "The children we saw that day have no future in our society," said one doctor. "Every effort is directed toward isolating the farm worker from the rest of society, maintaining him at the lowest level of subsistence that he will tolerate—then making certain that he has no means of escape from a system that holds him in virtual peonage." The moving testimony came as no surprise to Mondale, who had once tried to organize a strike among migrant workers in Minnesota. "The capacity of our society to mangle people is virtually limitless," he concluded bitterly.[10]

The hearings dramatized an important issue, but they did not result in major legislation. As Mondale expected, conservatives opposed the reforms. But he had not anticipated the apathy with which most liberals greeted his efforts. The coalition, he concluded, was more concerned with protecting its prerogatives than it was with redressing a pressing national wrong. When his attempts at enacting legislation to address migrant problems failed, Mondale proposed strengthening existing laws and extending their coverage to include migrants. Congress frustrated even these plans. It defeated his attempts to extend unemployment compensation and Social Security coverage to migrants, and to obtain increased funding for migrant health, education, and legal-service programs. Despite all of his efforts, he succeeded only in extending occupational hazards coverage to farm workers.[11]

This limited success did not deter Mondale. On the contrary, it sparked his interest in another powerless group—children. The "fundamental question" facing children, he told the Senate in December 1970, was "power and powerlessness. The basic underlying reason, more important than any other, why millions of American children are victimized, is powerlessness." The victims, he argued, were a diverse and tragic group: children of migrant workers trapped in a feudal arrangement with powerful landowners; black children in the rural South still victims of segregation and poor education; American Indian infants whose mortality was almost twice the national average; poor urban children afflicted by all the problems of urban life—drug addiction, venereal disease, lack of space, poor housing. "I am unable to express the profound frustration that I feel at knowing that we are such a powerful and wealthy society and at the same time seem to so tragically fail thousands and millions of our children," he told a subcommittee in 1970.[12]

The social welfare programs which he and other liberals had supported during the 1960s, he charged, did little to address these problems. "It is time for us, as liberals, to face the fact that our approach has too often been self-satisfied, Washington-centered, insensitive, and conformist," he concluded. As an alternative, Mondale proposed an ambitious $3-billion program providing a broad range of day care, nutritional, educational, and health services for preschool children. Children of poor families would be eligible for free services and children of middle-income families would be charged a fee based on annual income. Together with Wisconsin's Gaylord Nelson, Mondale carefully orchestrated the floor debate over the legislation. He believed his legislation acknowledged that changing economic conditions had forced mothers into the workforce in massive numbers.[13]

In December 1971, the Senate and House engaged in a highly charged debate over what House Speaker Carl Albert called the "paramount moral vote of the session." Senate conservatives called the program "radical and socialistic." "Communist Russia and socialist nations have long had such programs," cried Alabama's James Allen. Despite these objections, Mondale successfully maneuvered the legislation through the Senate, defeating conservative attempts to weaken the bills key provisions. On December 9, after a conference committee ironed out minor differences between House and Senate versions of the bill, the Congress sent the legislation to the President. On December 10, Nixon vetoed the program because of its "fiscal irresponsibility, administrative unworkability, and family-wrecking implications." The following day, Mondale's efforts to override the veto fell short by seven votes as thirteen Republicans reversed their original support for the legislation and backed the President. Disappointed but not surprised by the veto, Mondale compared Nixon's opposition to child support with his approval of an expensive space shuttle to dramatize the nation's "obscene" priorities. "Typically," he said, "this administration can squander $6.5 billion to fly four people in orbit, while it refuses to invest less than one-third that amount to provide desperately needed day care and development programs for millions of pre-school children."[14]

When not using his committee assignments to address the long-ignored problems of the poor and disadvantaged, Mondale voiced his outspoken views from the Senate floor. In 1969 he fought Nixon Administration attempts to give governors the power to veto legal services projects in their states. Mondale said that prior to the establishment of the legal services program, the poor of the nation had been denied access to the country's courts. With the help of the program, he said, grievances could be redressed "in the institutions used by the rich, not on the ghetto streets of the poor." In response to the administration's effort, Mondale sponsored legislation to create a National Legal Services Corporation. The bill placed no restrictions on legal-services attorneys, permitting them to bring action against government agencies at all levels and to file class-action suits. Strong bipartisan support for Mondale's legislation convinced the Nixon administration to present a similar bill. In July 1974, Nixon quietly signed into law legislation transferring the legal services program from the Office of Economic Opportunity to an independent corporation. An eleven-member board of directors, appointed by the President, was established to run the new corporation.[15]

Mondale also fought, and lost, repeated battles to shelve the space-shuttle project, calling it "another example of perverse priorities and colossal waste in government spending." Mondale's opposition was risky since Honeywell, one of the shuttle's major contractors, was a big employer in Minnesota. Despite the political risks, Mondale would not ignore what he saw as a waste of money. The shuttle, he charged, had a proposed budget greater than the combined federal expenditure on education of the handicapped, the Emergency Food Program, and air pollution programs. "For the $13 billion cost of the shuttle alone, we could quadruple the Federal government's combined annual outlays to fight crime, pollution, and cancer," he declared. "Is a space shuttle 4 times more important than safe streets, clean air and water, and freedom from deadly diseases?"[16]

Mondale and other liberals also rallied against Nixon's attempt at welfare reform. In August 1969 Nixon proposed a Family Assistance Plan which would have guaranteed all families with children a minimum of $500 per adult and $300 per child a year, or $1,600 for a two-parent family of four. The bill included a workfare provision requiring adult recipients to work for their subsidy. Mondale was especially critical of the workfare provisions which, despite the exaggerated cost-cutting claims of proponents, would affect only 80,000 of the 9.5 million people on welfare. He believed too, that the proposal fell short of need, complaining that the level of support promised would leave "millions of people in destitute circumstances." He insisted that a four billion dollar program was "only a start" for beginning to tackle the poverty problem. "The real question returns to how much substance we are willing to give to these programs," he concluded bitterly. "We authorize dreams around here and we continue to appropriate peanuts."[17]

After his election, Nixon moved shrewdly and aggressively to mobilize a "silent" majority around the social issues of patriotism, concern about crime, and traditional values. Nixon's civil rights policy played a central role in his attempts to attract Middle American support. Responding to public concern over court activism on a whole range of issues in the 1960s, Nixon appointed conservative judges to the Supreme Court. In June 1969, he replaced Chief Justice Earl Warren with the more conservative Warren Burger. Unsuccessfully, he tried to appoint two conservative southern judges to fill court vacancies. In August, 1969 Nixon announced the nomination of Clement F. Haynsworth of the Fourth Circuit Court of Appeals in South Carolina. His announcement immediately aroused the indignation of liberal groups who claimed the nominee was insensitive on civil rights and labor issues. On November 21, Mondale joined other liberals in voting 55–45 to defeat Haynsworth's nomination.[18]

Nixon, eager to assert the presidential prerogative, immediately announced a new, even more controversial, nominee, Judge Harrold Carswell of the Fifth Circuit Court of Appeals in Florida. Possessed of a mediocre judicial record, Carswell had also espoused white supremacy and had participated in a scheme to maintain segregation in a Tallahassee golf club. "What is unique about Judge Carswell's nomination," Mondale declared in a blistering attack from the Senate floor, "is that it raises the question of whether a person who has a lifetime record . . . of antagonism and hostility to human rights and civil rights, and to the enforcement of the law of the land, and specifically to orders of the circuit court under which he operated, should be permitted to serve on the highest court of the land." On April 8, 1970, the Senate rejected the nomination 51–45.[19]

The busing issue lay at the heart of Nixon's middle American strategy. Busing had been mainly a southern problem until early in the 1970s, when courts ordered northern cities to use busing to achieve racial balance. Boycotts and violence ensued among many working-class whites. Emboldened southerners relished watching the north confront its own civil rights problems. Georgia's Governor Lester Maddox flaunted his racism in the restaurant of the House of Representatives by passing out replicas of the ax handles he had used to bar blacks from his Pickrick Chicken House in Atlanta. Alabama's George Wallace announced that he was once more running for governor "to get our schools back from the federal Government."[20]

In the Senate the battle lines formed when Mississippi's John Stennis submitted the Elementary and Secondary Education Amendments of 1970. Stennis's bill aimed to ensure that federal desegregation pressure would "be applied uniformly in all regions of the United States." A powerful Southern Senate baron, Stennis had first won election in 1947 following the death of the legendary race-baiting demagogue Theodore Bilbo. Never a demagogue on racial matters, Stennis nonetheless promised to "preserve the Southern way of life" and voted against every civil rights bill to come through Congress. He and other conservatives planned to undermine support for busing by attacking the federal courts and the Department of Health, Education and Welfare for distinguishing between *de jure* and *de facto* school segregation. Only the former was subject to federal attack, and it was in the South, where schools were once separated by law, that deliberate segregation was easiest to prove. Stennis covered pages of the *Congressional Record* with HEW statistics showing that there was as much racial isolation in the North and West as in the South. Stennis realized that if the government applied the same pressure toward integration in regions outside the South, citizens would force Congress to change the law. "If you don't believe sentiment in your part of the country is against this," he warned, "you'd better get your ear a little closer to the ground." [21]

Mondale led the opposition to the Stennis Amendment. Seeing it as a veiled attempt to legalize freedom-of-choice plans everywhere, Mondale urged liberals and moderates to vote against the amendment. "I do not know what the politics of human rights is today," Mondale said during the debate. "I sense that it's less popular than it's been for a number of years. But unless we sustain it, the cause of our country will be lost." The amendment, he charged, "is designed principally to stall elimination of dual school systems in the South. That is why it has been introduced. That is why, if it is agreed to, the national program to eliminate the disgrace of separated school systems will be imperiled." [22]

Stennis received unexpected support from liberal Abraham Ribicoff of Connecticut who accused the North of "monumental hypocrisy" for refusing to face its own problems of discrimination. "If Senator Stennis wants to make honest men of us Northern liberals," Ribicoff said, "I think we should help him." Conservatives from both parties hailed the address, one of the strongest denunciations of Northern segregation delivered by a Northern Democrat. Russell Long said the speech marked the first time "a so-called Northern liberal has arisen who has not treated the South as a conquered province." Mondale agreed that the North had failed to integrate but questioned whether the Stennis Amendment would improve the situation. He feared that eliminating the distinction between *de jure* and *de facto* segregation would make it more difficult to achieve a racial balance in the South rather than making it easier to do so in the North.[23]

On February 18, the Senate voted by a decisive 56 to 36 margin to approve the Stennis Amendment. Adoption of the bill represented a major triumph for the South made possible by support from outside the region. Only twenty-six of the votes for the proposal came from Southern or border states. Stennis hailed the victory as "a landmark . . . a new gateway . . . a turning point." The amendment's success, Mondale said, had raised the question "whether this nation any longer believes in an integrated society." The victory proved to be largely symbolic. The amendment required HEW to act against school segregation in the North with the same intensity as in the South. But the heaviest desegregation pressure on the South came not from HEW but from the federal courts. Moreover, two months later, a House-Senate conference committee stacked with liberals diluted the controversial Stennis language.[24]

For Mondale, the defeat in the Senate confirmed national doubts about measures such as busing to achieve desegregation. In response, he and New York's Jacob Javits established a new Select Committee on Equal Educational Opportunity to look into all aspects of school segregation. The fifteen-member committee included nine Democrats and six Republicans, with four Senators from border or southern states. "I tried to find some answers that could pull the community back together again. That is why I set that committee up," he reflected. "I wanted to probe and ponder the question to see if we could reassure Americans that some of this made sense." As chairman, Mondale promised that the Committee would "reargue the case for integration."[25]

Mondale's new committee began its hearings on April 20, 1970. Over the next three years, the Select Committee heard more than three-hundred witnesses and compiled more than 11,000 pages of testimony and documents before writing its 440-page final report. Experts who appeared before the committee outlined a problem growing more pressing as time passed. Two-thirds of all black first-graders in public schools and one-half of all black 12th graders were in segregated schools. Four-fifths of both white first-graders and 12th-graders in public schools were in schools that were between 90 and 100 percent white. "There is more racial segregation in public education today than there was in May 1954 at the time of the U.S. Supreme Court ruling against *de jure* school segregation," testified Harvard's Thomas Pettigrew. The growing racial and class divisions between city where most blacks lived, and suburbs, where most whites lived, was compounding the problem.[26]

In July 1970, as part of his attempt to understand conditions in the South, Mondale made an unannounced visit to segregated school districts in Alabama, Louisiana, and Texas. "You need a visit like that," Mondale told reporters after the trip, "to sense the deep frustration, the anger—and the potential violence." The Senator said he experienced "a feeling of absolute hopelessness towards us whites and Anglos—a feeling that we're basically racist and will not deal from a standpoint of reason." The point struck home when a Mexican-American from San Antonio warned Mondale: "You better do something—or never come back here again!" In Homer, Louisiana, Mondale saw what official segregation meant: Entire classes of black grade-school students kept separate and relegated to a crowded basement and an abandoned industrial arts building. "The teachers told us how hard it was to teach an overcrowded class, separated from others only by a plywood partition, so they could hear everything in the next class," Mondale reported. At the same time there was a new private academy across town with a gymnasium and playground. Mondale suspected that these private academies were being built with a considerable amount of public money. "There is no question in my mind but that tax money will flow into those segregated academies."[27]

On the Senate floor, Mondale successfully fought all attempts to prohibit busing either by law or constitutional amendment. In February 1972, the House had added three strong antibusing amendments to a general education bill. When the bill came to the Senate, Mondale made an impassioned thirty-minute speech on the floor outlining his position on busing. "School desegregation is a fact of American educational life," he said. "The law of the land is clear, and it will not change. Officially imposed school segregation—whether the result of state law or covert policy—must be overcome." Citing Supreme Court positions that busing was a legitimate desegregation tool, Mondale said, "Nothing we do here next week will reverse eighteen years of unanimous rulings by the Supreme Court or alter the 14th Amendment requirements" concerning equal education. There were some limits to his support. He opposed both "unnecessary transportation to achieve an arbitrary racial balance," and busing small numbers of advantaged students into predominantly disadvantaged schools. "But," he concluded, "if we bar the use of reasonable transportation as one tool for achieving desegregation, we will set in concrete much school segregation which is the clear and direct product of intentional government policy, segregation which would not exist if racially neutral policies had been followed." Busing "is unpopular," he admitted, "but in many areas sensible transportation of children is the only way for this generation to achieve some school integration."[28]

Liberals praised Mondale for his forthright defense of busing. "For sheer guts we hand it to him," declared the columnist TRB. "He's up for reelection this fall and he's put his political life on the line." Even the New York *Times* complimented Mondale on his mettle. "We think he is right. We wish more of his colleagues in official and political life had the guts to speak out as he has."[29]

Despite hundreds of hours of hearings and research, however, Mondale never found a direct relationship between busing and better education. "When we got all done we could find nothing but commitment and resources made for a better education. We could never make a case that busing helped, or that it didn't cause white flight," Mondale reflected. "We could not find conclusive evidence to move the debate on busing." What he learned, recalled the Committee's chief-of-staff Bill Smith, "was that the problem of educating school kids was a hell of a lot more complicated and harder to solve than would be represented by putting kids on a bus."[30]

Not only did he fail to find the answers he was looking for, but also political realities were making the search more risky. A 1971 Gallup Poll found 77 percent of the public opposed busing. In 1972, a federal district court added to the uproar by requiring busing across city and county lines to desegregate schools. Although later reversed, the decision unnerved many white suburban parents who feared sending their children to predominantly black inner-city schools. White boycotts, antibusing marches and demonstrations, and increased incidents of racial violence greeted many attempts at court-ordered integration across the country.[31]

By 1972, Mondale confronted a painful question: How much could you expand the rights of minorities without arousing the antagonism of the American working-class? Many Minnesota Democratic Farmer-Labor leaders did not appreciate his closer ties with the peace movement and the young. A working-class threatened by inflation had little sympathy for "the powerless" who demanded their tax money. Berman noted Mondale had been able to champion liberal programs because "some harm could be absorbed because there was a substantial reservoir of support." By 1972, that reservoir was running dry.[32]

Polls revealed that Minnesota was experiencing a belated but vengeful white backlash. A large majorities of whites in the state believed that blacks were too aggressive in their demands for equality. Many whites expressed concern about violence and opposition to the "militant" tactics employed by some blacks. In 1969, Charles Stenvig, a former police officer turned politician, tapped into this growing sentiment to win election as mayor of Minneapolis on a tough law and order platform. Running without financial support and with few endorsements, Stenvig defeated the DFL candidate by promising "to take the handcuffs off the police . . . [and] . . . to protect law-abiding citizens from hoodlums." In 1970, Humphrey, making a successful bid for the Senate seat left vacant by Eugene McCarthy, sensed the changing political tide. Hoping to neutralize the conservative backlash on social issues, Humphrey warned that liberals "must let the hardhats, Mr. and Mrs. Middle America, know that they understand what is bugging them, that they too condemn crime and riots and violence and extreme turbulence, that they scorn extremists of the left as well as extremists of the right."[33]

A confidential political survey completed in preparation for Mondale's reelection campaign showed that racial tensions were creating strains in Mondale's coalition. "We are surprised . . . to find so much anti-black sentiment in a state like Minnesota, which has a miniscule [sic] black population," observed the pollster Oliver Quayle. "In part, we feel this stems from the feeling held by so many voters that they are being taxed to death. Lashing out in anger, many pick on one tax expenditure that they see no benefit in to themselves—blacks on welfare." The survey warned that many voters felt that Mondale "cares more for minorities (blacks in particular) than he does for the average voter and his family."[34]

Mondale took the warnings to heart. The 1972 election resulted in what friends referred to as the "homogenization of Walter Mondale"—a conscious attempt to make him more acceptable to the middle class by downplaying his recent past. Mondale's disillusion with the Vietnam War, combined with the limited success of his work on behalf of the "powerless," revealed to him the limits of change. "It made me realize how begrudging progress is," he reflected. "You had to be modest in your expectations about what government intervention could do to fundamentally affect the life opportunities of millions of children." He realized he had overestimated the capacity of the old coalition to expand to accept new ideas. He could have continued to champion the cause of the outcasts, but Mondale was not temperamentally suited to leading unpopular causes over a long period of time. He conceived of politics as the art of the possible. "I don't like wasting my time slaying windmills," he repeated on many occasions.[35]

The "homogenization" program took on an added urgency as Mondale tried to distance himself from his party's presidential candidate, South Dakota Senator George McGovern. The 1972 election became a battle for the "silent Americans." For Nixon, they were people like Richard Rogin's mythical Joe Kelly—white, middle-class, and socially conservative. "The time has come," Nixon declared in 1972, "to draw the line, . . . for the Great Silent Majority . . . to stand up and be counted against the appeasement of the rock-throwers and the obscenity shouters in America."

For the Democrats, the "silent majority" were the poor and minorities excluded from the system, and the educated, socially liberal middle class. Committed to the "new politics" agenda, McGovern believed he could build a new Democratic majority without the support of the working-class. Recent passage of the twenty-sixth amendment, granting 18-year-olds the right to vote, he hoped, would provide a vast source of support for his candidacy. Unfortunately for McGovern, his assumptions proved wrong.[36]

Mondale had rejected McGovern's strategy from the beginning. Convinced that working-class support formed the basis of a successful Democratic campaign, Mondale felt McGovern had lost touch with his own party. "I was mystified by George's theory," Mondale later recalled. "He tried to ride the youth vote into the White House and found there was no constituency out there." Mondale appreciated better than McGovern that the party's future depended on a coalition of both the old and the new. "I didn't think they were sufficiently sensitive to how traditional Democrats felt," Mondale reflected. "Many of the people surrounding the McGovern campaign scared traditional Democrats. There was a lot of national guilt built into their rhetoric. There was no rhetoric that was familiar to the average farmer or worker or traditional family. Instead, their rhetoric was excessive."[37]

Mondale refused McGovern's suggestions that he allow himself to be considered for the vice presidency. Early in the summer, McGovern sent his campaign manager Gary Hart and actor Warren Beatty to visit Mondale in Washington. They spent three hours at the posh Four Seasons Hotel in Georgetown trying to convince Mondale to accept McGovern's overtures. But Mondale would not budge. His political differences with McGovern were part of the problem. Perhaps more important was the widely accepted assumption that the

Democrats did not have a chance of winning in 1972. Mondale was not about to give up his Senate seat for such a risky proposition. He knew that if he won reelection to the Senate by a wide-enough margin, he would have other opportunities to run for national office—and not necessarily in the number two spot.

While McGovern intentionally steered further from the political center, Mondale tried to keep his own DFL coalition within the mainstream. Like many Democratic organizations, the DFL was deeply divided. At the 1972 state convention, one journalist wrote, "every faction was a minority most of the time, and every DFL delegate a minority of one." New groups which had never participated in party politics before disrupted the convention with strident demands. Homosexual delegates, wearing purple shirts marked "gay rights caucus," danced in the aisles demonstrating their independence. There was a youth caucus, a radical caucus, a women's caucus, as well as a liberal caucus. The convention became bogged down in procedural questions and unable to agree on platform resolutions. The DFL's powerful labor contingent watched helplessly as the new activists passed a radical platform which endorsed gay rights, amnesty for draft evaders, legalization of marijuana, and an "immediate end to military intervention in Southeast Asia."[38]

The divisions did not prevent the DFL convention from unanimously endorsing Mondale for a second term in the Senate. He won the support of many of the radical groups even though he cautiously distanced himself from their agenda. Mondale's personal conservatism made him uncomfortable with many expressions of cultural liberalism—gay rights, legalization of marijuana, and later, abortion. He also believed these issues usually divided Democrats and helped Republicans. Understanding the explosive nature of social issues, Mondale chose to rally the faithful with a traditional partisan speech. "I believe history will most harshly judge this administration for the damage it has done to the spirit of America," he shouted. "Instead of calling upon and responding to the basic American instinct, which respects the humanity of all men, we have an administration that pursues the policies of opportunism and cynicism." The delegates, perhaps exhausted from the internal wrangling and eager for a unifying message, responded enthusiastically. "The ovation given Mondale indicates he has the ability to unite both sides in the DFL," observed a local reporter.[39]

His Republican opponent, Philip Hansen, director of an alcohol and drug dependency center, tried to exploit the Democratic divisions by casting Mondale as a "McGovern liberal." "I think this year as perhaps seldom," he said in one of a series of debates with Mondale, "we see a clear-cut decision to be made between what I consider to be the extreme point of view politically and philosophically between the McGovern/Mondale ticket, and the middle-of-the-road, common sense Nixon/Hansen ticket." Hansen also ran a series of radio adds that attempted to link Mondale with McGovern.[40]

In October, just one month before the election, Mondale's Select Committee on Equal Educational Opportunity planned to release its final report. Labeled as a "McGovern liberal" in a year of a white backlash, Mondale had second thoughts about maintaining such a high profile on the busing issue. His staff divided on what role he should play. "I do not believe that the Select Committee's Report is worth seriously jeopardizing the Minnesota campaign," wrote Bert Carp. Berman, in a cryptic note, complained that the report would hurt Mondale's attempts to reach out to the middle class. "Select Committee not helping politically. . . . Whatever hearings the Select Committee holds should be of low profile—do whatever necessary to get report out . . . area where need most emphasis now is middle America . . . high cost of living, etc." Another staff member expressed shock that a suggestion was made that Mondale not give a strong statement. "Education is not the most exciting issue, but it is one issue where WFM has institutional leverage. Can not sell out on education and the committee."[41]

In the end, Mondale decided to have it both ways. He drafted a strong report but withheld release until January 1973, two months after the election. Calling for national support of "quality integrated education," it recommended spending $1 billion a year to assist emergency school desegregation, including money for "reasonable transportation." It also recommended a new, separate $1.5 billion yearly program of compensatory education aid and a $5 billion-a-year federal program aimed at encouraging and supplementing reforms in local and state financing.[42]

Delaying his controversial report did not prevent a big disappointment on election day. As expected, Nixon won reelection with 60 percent of the popular vote and 520 electoral votes. Almost ten million Democrats, nearly one-third of all registered Democrats, voted for Nixon. Surprisingly, although he won by a comfortable 57 to 43 percent margin, Mondale's performance fell short of his expectations. Early in the campaign, Mondale had decided that to become a major player in the party as well as an important national figure he needed to win with at least 60 percent of the vote. He campaigned hard, and until the final weeks of the contest, internal polls, which showed him garnering almost 70 percent of the electorate, fed his optimism. Friends described him as "depressed" by the results. He questioned why the polls had been so wrong, and why, even in the wake of a Republican landslide, so many voters had apparently abandoned him.

A comparison of his 1966 and 1972 campaigns showed that Mondale continued to draw most of his support from larger cities, minorities and union workers. Income remained the most important indicator of voting preferences. Votes for Mondale decreased as income increased. He polled 78.3 percent of voters with an annual income of less than $7,000. Of those earning between $11,000 and $12,000 a year, 58.5 percent voted for Mondale. But only 46.8 percent of voters earning more than $13,000 a year supported him. There were, however, a few troubling signs. His percentage of the vote dropped in heavy union areas and among those making under $10,000. While he gained support in some college towns, there was noticeable slippage in the growing suburban areas around Minneapolis and St. Paul.[43]

The campaign taught Mondale a clear lesson: he had paid a political price for his advocacy of liberal ideas. "I think it is fair to say certain of your initiatives and actions during the last six years, which would be described as 'liberal' did have an adverse impact upon the campaign in certain quarters," Berman noted in his election analysis. "You are," he reported, "too liberal" and "tied in with busing in a much stronger way" than was politically acceptable. Berman argued that most voters saw Mondale "as being very much like McGovern." There was noticeable "resentment among HHH loyalists" who felt "you let him down and that you should have done more." Although broadly based, Mondale's support lacked the depth and passion of Humphrey's following. Mondale, Berman concluded, could not claim "the basic reservoir of support" Humphrey enjoyed. Mondale agreed that Hansen had successfully exploited middle class resentment over the party's turn to the left. "Hansen media campaign did help [him]," Mondale scribbled in the margins of a election analysis. "Radio spots were effective," because they tapped "anti-McGovern" feelings.[44]

The election results demonstrated the fragile nature of the Democratic party. Nixon's shrewd appeals to the "silent majority" touched a responsive chord with many working-class Democrats who felt their party had abandoned them in pursuit of more liberal voters. The resentment Nixon harnessed had many sources, but race remained the most significant. As the national Democratic party became more identified with the civil rights struggles of the previous twenty years, the white South moved comfortably into Republican hands. The basic reason, in the words of former Johnson advisor Harry Mc-Pherson, lay "in the white man's view that the Democrats had cast their lot with black Americans, to the ultimate disadvantage of the whites." The thirteen southern states that gave FDR all their electoral votes in 1944 gave Humphrey only Texas' twenty-five in 1968, and none to McGovern. At the same time, massive black migration from the south combined with white flight to the suburbs divided the Democratic base in the north. From 1950 to 1970, urban population increased by only 9.2 million and most of that came from migrating blacks. While blacks were occupying increasingly decaying cities, 35 million people—all but 1.5 million of them white—were migrating to the more conservative suburbs.[45]

The decade began with Mondale challenging Americans to confront new and difficult issues. Finding few legislative victories and considerable political opposition, he returned to his party's mainstream. The challenge now, he decided, was to heal party divisions and win back the White House for the Democrats.

8

Searching for Common Ground

The hot television lights glared down from above while chants of "We Want Fritz" filled the air. By Mondale's side on the crowded podium stood Hubert Humphrey, who two years earlier had captured the Senate seat vacated by Eugene McCarthy. As the national television stations flashed to the Minneapolis ballroom, Humphrey could not resist giving a speech. With typical exuberance he congratulated Mondale on his great victory. Mondale, feeling disappointed that his margin had not been as great as he had hoped, graciously accepted his mentor's kind wishes. But the former presidential nominee was not finished. "We are seeing the beginning of a truly great national career that can take Mondale to the office which I long sought," Humphrey announced. Looking startled by the proclamation, Mondale stood silently while Humphrey continued his oration. "I have always thought we ought to have a Minnesotan in the White House. If it isn't being too sacrilegious, I don't mind being John the Baptist to Walter Mondale."[1]

Humphrey was not the only one who viewed Mondale as a potential presidential candidate. The Wall Street *Journal* praised him, and columnists as diverse as George Will and Anthony Lewis suggested that Mondale was the man for the Democrats in 1976. A news story in the New York *Times* cited his reputation as "a voracious worker with a sharp mind for details and an outstanding staff." The *New Republic* said that Mondale "evokes memories of John Kennedy's enthusiasm and ambition, if not his patrician style." James Reston, referring to Mondale's "moral authority and quiet determination," called him "one of the most promising of the rising generation of Democratic politicians." His strongest asset, a columnist wrote, "may be the general air of intelligence, solidity and fairness he projects." Another wrote: "He's conscientious—a characteristic which earns one the esteem of Senate colleagues, but not much fame." Harvard psychiatrist Robert Coles, who worked closely with Mondale on migrant labor issues, called him "an active, outgoing, attractive, and unusually intelligent man, who does not need legislative aides and administrative assistants to tell him what to say, what to do, or how to vote."[2]

Unlike most members of the Senate, Mondale possessed little wealth and frequently had trouble making ends meet. His 1975 financial statement listed his net worth at a modest $77,361. Most of his income came from a Senate salary of $44,500, which he supplemented with speaking fees. He owned no stocks or any other investments and refused to accept speaking fees from profit-making organizations. The family lived in a comfortable three-story house on Lowell Street in the Cleveland Park section of Washington. Although tastefully decorated, the house remained partially unfurnished because of a lack of money. His children had been enrolled in the District of Columbia public school system; but when it became obvious they were receiving little education and sometimes faced the threat of violence, Joan and Fritz reluctantly decided to send them to private schools. Ted and Eleanor attended Georgetown Day School and William went to St. Albans. The private schools were expensive, totaling nearly $8,000 a year in tuition. The switch was also politically embarrassing to Mondale, who had spearheaded the desegregation fight on the Senate floor.

Balancing personal and political responsibilities was not always easy. Although not active in the Washington social scene, Mondale occasionally attended evening political receptions and fundraisers. On weekends he returned alone to Minnesota for more political events. As always, Joan accepted that Fritz needed to spend time away from home. "I didn't think it was so hard because I didn't know anything else," she reflected. "I didn't really resent it." The children also seemed to take his absence in stride. "They don't expect him at home," Joan said. "If he's around on a weekend, they'll ask 'What are you doing home this weekend?'" Once, after returning from a weekend trip, Fritz asked Eleanor if she missed him. "Were you gone?" she responded nonchalantly.[3]

Unable to spend lots of time at home with the family, he tried to make the most of his limited opportunities. Occasionally he put on an old pair of sneakers and played basketball with Teddy and William at the local playground. Every year, the family took two vacations. In the winter they went skiing in Colorado and every August they returned to Minnesota for a week of fishing. The vacations were expensive, and sometimes Mondale had to borrow money for the trips. But they were rare moments when the family could be together with few distractions.

During these years Joan also began spending more time away from home pursuing her lifelong interest in art. Overcoming her original distaste for Washington, she joined a number of local civic organizations, and, with a small group of Cleveland Park residents, created a successful food cooperative. Along with performing traditional household chores—sewing, cleaning, cooking, and grocery shopping—Joan found the time to attend weekly pottery classes, serve as a tour guide at the National Gallery, and write a children's book entitled *Politics in Art*. Published in 1972, the book showed how many artists had used their work to express concern about political figures and issues. "Artists can reveal the truth about ourselves in powerful and compelling ways," she wrote. "And when they do this, they can spur us into action."[4]

Revealing a traditional Scandinavian concern for privacy, self-discipline, and emotional containment, Mondale enjoyed being in the public eye, but was careful not to reveal too much about himself. "Mondale has a wall of reserve around him that's very hard to penetrate," his biographer Finlay Lewis observed. "Of course, there's a charming side, but it's not the same as real openness. There's a guarded quality, a line which very few people are allowed to cross." He could sit alone for hours staring out a window. He actively resisted questions about his childhood, his family, or other aspects of his life he considered private. "Where I grew up, bragging and immodesty were equal crimes with lying," he reflected years later. "Your honesty, your involvement in your faith, your ability and your values—those things were intended to speak for themselves. If you started telling people about them, it was a sign that you weren't too sure of them—or of yourself."[5]

He remained a modest man, with an irreverent sense of humor and an appealing sense of proportion. Once, when informed that Mc-George Bundy, scion of the Harvard establishment, was calling to ask for his help, Mondale could not let the moment escape. "George Bundy calling me, a little kid from Elmore, Minnesota," he told staff members gathered in the office. "Put U Thant on hold." Mondale had also matured as a public figure. Tested under fire, he was more confident in his knowledge of issues, less trusting of "experts" and more willing to follow his own instincts.[6]

In the Senate, Mondale's low-key, cautious style earned him the respect of his colleagues. "The thing that is most evident about Mondale," Humphrey said, "is that he's nonabrasive. He is not a polarizer." Even when leading controversial causes, Mondale searched for areas of compromise and agreement and tried to avoid making enemies. "He was not a contentious flame thrower," remarked Missouri's Thomas Eagleton. "Some senators would rather stake out a position—and lose—just to have staked out the position. Mondale would rather stake out a position and see how much of that position he could translate into a finite result." Unlike many liberals, Mondale developed friendships with conservative senators and was not afraid to be seen socializing with the political opposition. "I regard him as one of the few senators I get along with best," said Alabama's conservative James Allen. "We have opposing views, but we joke back and forth quite a bit. I see him as a friendly opponent on the Senate floor." Mondale participated in an informal group of senators who met most evenings at 6 P.M. to discuss the day's business. Bound by personal interest rather than ideological similarity, the group included liberals Gaylord Nelson, Tom Eagleton, and Iowa's John Culver, as well as conservatives such as Mississippi's James Eastland and South Carolina's Fritz Hollings.[7]

The same skills that made Mondale a respected Senator and appealing personality did not translate into broad public acceptance. Despite his liberal voting record, Mondale's reserved manner led many party activists to question his commitment to their agenda. "I'm never sure how strongly he feels about any issue, but I like the stands he takes," commented one Democratic leader. The biggest question was whether someone with Mondale's natural reserve could arouse public passion. "Mondale lacks pizzaz," a prominent Democrat told George Will.

"Sure he is earnest, conscientious. But he is a painfully plain midwesterner, just not the sort of chap who causes the party's pulse to pound with excitement." Poking fun at his own lack of charisma, Mondale often remarked that he could walk "through any airport in the country and not a head will turn." There was also the problem of Mondale's discomfort with television. He rarely watched it, refused to participate in practice sessions before appearances, and disliked the way he appeared on the screen. Though years of practice had made him a more effective speaker, he still insisted on reading from a prepared text. Without a good speechwriter, his speeches were not only uninspiring, but also lacked the eloquence many people expected of a presidential aspirant.[8]

Lingering doubts about his political fortitude also tarnished Mondale's image. Journalists, political professionals, and even close friends asked whether a man who had led such a charmed public life, had never suffered defeat, and had always campaigned as an incumbent, could endure the rigors of a presidential contest. "Fritz Mondale's biggest weakness is that political success has come too easy for him and that he's never been tested in a really tough campaign," an associate charged. Even Humphrey wondered publicly whether his protégé had the "fire in the belly" to run for president. Other observers, who inevitably mentioned Mondale's reluctance to break with Humphrey on the war, offered more trenchant criticism. "I think he lacks the self-confidence or the guts to stand up and fight when things really get rough," declared one Minnesota congressman. The basic question, a journalist suggested, was "what's he going to do when the chips are down?"[9]

Although bothered by these nagging doubts, Mondale had, by 1973, turned his attention to a more pressing concern: helping the Democrats win the White House in the next election. A number of events fed his hopes. A stagnant economy assisted efforts to lure the working class back into the Democratic fold. In 1970, real GNP had declined for the first time since 1958. Unemployment, at a low 3.3 percent when Nixon took office, had climbed to 6 percent by the end of 1970. Despite the slowdown, prices continued their upward spiral. The cost of living rose nearly 15 percent during Nixon's first two and a half years in office. In 1971, the United States recorded its first balance-of-trade deficit in eighty years. At first Nixon employed erratic fiscal and monetary policies. Later he converted to economic controls. Neither prevented both prices and unemployment from rising through 1974.[10]

Revelations of a growing Watergate scandal weakened the Republican hold on middle-class voters. On the night of June 17, 1972 police arrested four men who had broken into the Democratic National Committee headquarters in Washington. Industrious reporters at the Washington *Post* revealed that the burglars were former employees of the Committee for the Re-Election of the President. The issue received little public attention until early 1973 when one of the burglars, James W. McCord, agreed to cooperate with a grand jury. Over the next few months a flood of allegations and confessions about illegal White House activities emerged. These developments were very damaging, but a central question remained: Nixon's role. "What did the President know and when did he know it?" asked Senator Howard Baker. While defending himself against all charges— "I am not a crook"—Nixon fired many of his closest aides associated with the scandal. In July 1974, the Supreme Court ordered Nixon to release tapes of his private conversations in the White House. Days later, the House Judiciary Committee recommended impeachment. Early in August Nixon relinquished the "smoking gun" tape which proved his involvement in a cover-up of the burglary. A few days later, he announced his resignation—the first President ever to do so. He was succeeded by Vice President Gerald Ford, who had earlier replaced the discredited Spiro Agnew. One month later, the new president announced a pardon of Nixon.[11]

The sluggish economy combined with the Watergate crisis provided the Democrats with good short-term issues to win back the presidency in 1976, but in the long run they presented the Party with serious new obstacles. The level of trust in public institutions, which had been declining since the 1950s, dropped precipitously after Vietnam and Watergate. By eroding trust in government, Watergate would undermine public support for new Democratic initiatives in the future. Just as ominous, a struggling middle class watched as inflation consumed much of its purchasing power. By the early 1970s, postwar prosperity along with many successful Democratic programs had created a growing middle-class, which now fought to protect its hard-earned status. Many middle-class voters were eager to express their frustration with Republican economic mismanagement and their outrage at the Watergate scandal, but they had little sympathy for old-style Democratic social programs. Aroused by the threat of rising prices they would play a prominent role in the political debate. Fiscally more conservative and politically more independent than traditional Democrats, middle-class voters would limit the range of debate within the Party.

For now, however, the Republicans were vulnerable and Mondale hoped to take advantage of their difficulties. In January 1974, while still undecided about whether he was ready to make the sacrifices necessary, Mondale authorized the creation of a committee to finance an exploratory bid for the 1976 nomination. As part of his exploration, he asked Peter Edelman, a former aide to Robert Kennedy, to assess his chances. Edelman concluded that Mondale had a number of assets. Along with a distinguished Senate record, Mondale had solid liberal credentials to attract young volunteers, but was not identified as a liberal by most voters. Edelman also identified enormous liabilities. Most voters could not identify him and did not associate him with a particular issue. His strong advocacy of busing was likely to hurt him "in many Northern states where he has to have solid support if he is to be nominated." But the most serious threat came from Senator Edward Kennedy. "Mondale's ship floats in a Kennedy pond," Edelman concluded, "and Teddy can pull the plug whenever he likes." [12]

Mondale did not share Edelman's concerns about a possible Kennedy candidacy. His respect for John and Robert did not extend to the youngest of the Kennedy children. He believed that Ted, lacking Robert's visceral commitment and John's native intelligence, had advanced by virtue of his family's name. Mondale always felt that Ted's flower would wilt if forced to stand alone in a presidential race. "I thought that I could handle Kennedy," he recalled. "He always had a brilliant staff but I thought I could show a depth that Kennedy lacked. He had an impressive drive and was a good speaker, but he was also erratic and inconsistent." Mondale was more concerned about his own low standing in the polls. [13]

Interest in the presidency forced Mondale to give foreign policy and defense issues serious attention. Though he had worked on specific defense issues, he lacked a comprehensive framework for analyzing international events. "He had not given foreign policy much thought," reflected his former chief-of-staff. "He held orthodox liberal views on defense policy." With the exception of his efforts to open trade with Eastern Europe—a popular position in the agricultural Midwest, which was eager for new markets—he showed little or no initiative on foreign policy questions. He focused most of his attention on domestic issues to which he had both an intellectual and emotional commitment. Mondale realized he had to broaden his interests to include foreign policy if he were going to be a serious presidential contender. In 1974, he added to his Senate staff David Aaron, a former Kissinger aide who had recently left the National Security Council to accept a Council on Foreign Relations Fellowship. Over the next ten years Aaron educated Mondale about international relations. Like Kissinger, Aaron understood the importance of power in diplomacy and recognized the need to establish a strategic framework for analyzing international events. A "power idealist" rather than a "power realist," Aaron did not share Kissinger's pessimism about human nature, his fear of disorder, or his anxiety about the indecisiveness of most democracies. By developing a consensus at home, establishing clear priorities abroad, and using power to provide incentives to allies and potential adversaries, Aaron believed America could continue to play the role of a major world power.[14]

Over the next few months, Aaron and Mondale engaged in a series of philosophical discussions about American diplomacy in the post-Vietnam era. Like many other liberals whose faith in American power had been shattered by Vietnam, Mondale was searching for a new conceptual structure for understanding America's role in the world. Aaron advised a position in the responsible center of the Party. "You want to keep [Henry] Jackson on your right and McGovern and even Kennedy on your left," he said. To educate himself about foreign policy, Mondale traveled to Jerusalem, Bonn, Brussels, London, and Paris, and spent a week in the Soviet Union meeting with high-level Russian officials. Walking an ideological tightrope between hawks and doves in his own party, Mondale skillfully warned the Soviets against future aggression while appealing for mutual cooperation and trust.[15]

Under Aaron's close tutelage, Mondale developed a previously unseen sophistication in his foreign policy views. Like his mentor Hubert Humphrey, Mondale continued to be a strong supporter of Israel. He frequently joined other liberals in increasing Administration requests for military and economic assistance to the Middle East. Unlike more dovish liberals, he spoke frequently about maintaining strong military relations with allies in Western Europe. Yet by immersing himself in the complicated details of modern nuclear weapons systems he emerged as a leading Democratic spokesman for arms control. He argued against the development of destabilizing first-strike weapons and instead suggested that the United States develop less threatening mobile land and sea-based ballistic missiles and long-range cruise missiles. These weapons systems, he argued on the Senate floor, "would continue the traditional U.S. policy of producing an assured deterrent" but would not "threaten the Soviets with a first strike."[16]

When not visiting foreign capitals, Mondale traveled around the country campaigning for congressional candidates. The same Senator who just a few years earlier had challenged the fundamental tenets of liberalism and argued for a "restructuring of American society" to address the problems of the powerless now campaigned by repeating the orthodox Democratic position about helping the struggling working-class. "The Democratic Party," he told audiences in small towns and large cities across the country, "has only succeeded when the average worker and his family, the average farmer, the average citizen, identified with us, and felt we had their best interests at heart." To labor audiences he stressed job security, to businessmen he called unemployment "a poison," to senior citizens he spoke of increases in social security. He denounced Watergate ethics, attacked the imperial presidency, and criticized Ford's economic program and his pardon of Nixon. Mondale's own program consisted of higher taxes for oil companies and the rich and lower taxes for middle and lower income families. He ignored the difficult social issues which divided the party and made no mention of his earlier concerns about "obscene priorities."[17]

Mondale's first national political campaign revealed that he possessed an outdated view of the national electorate. "I can remember the first time [during the 1974 campaign] he was forced to confront that in New York, Connecticut, and New Jersey, the Italians were the backbone of the Republican Party," recalled Jim Johnson. "His socio-demographic understanding was Italian, Catholic, lower-middle-class had to be Democratic. He was always saying 'How could a guy named Ciaconi from Jersey City be a Republican.' " As Johnson observed, Mondale "missed a generation of change as former Democrats moved out of the city into the suburbs, into the middle class and developed an anti-black, anti-welfare state orientation. In his world, Republicans were bankers, rich people, the farm bureau, and people who talked through their teeth."[18]

Mondale imposed on the national electorate the framework of politics he had learned during his Democratic Farmer-Labor days in Minnesota. The Democrats stood on the side of working men and women, minorities, farmers, and all others who identified with the New Deal and who harbored mutual antipathy to big business. He continued to believe that the common concerns of most Democrats found expression in the large interest groups—labor, farmer, teachers, civil rights, and environmentalist. "When talking to a teacher's convention, Mondale believed he was addressing all people concerned with education," recalled Johnson. "When addressing a labor convention, he thought he was speaking to all people concerned with jobs, wages and a better workplace." This perception may have accurately described the peculiar political and social setting in Minnesota during Mondale's formative years, but it was rarely duplicated on the national scene. The emergence of volatile social issues combined with declining public trust in established institutions limited the political effectiveness of many interest groups. Especially in recent years, the leadership of these groups did not always express the concerns of its members.

In October 1974, after ten-months of campaigning, Mondale told reporters in Duluth he was "99-percent sure" he would be a presidential candidate. In November, campaign manager Mike Berman traveled to Washington to rent space for a campaign headquarters, while other staff members made plans for his formal announcement in the Minnesota state house in January. But he could not purge his doubts. Travel removed him from his family for long periods and he saw no movement in the polls. "He would go from 3 to 2 in the Gallup Poll and then go into a funk for a week," recalled an aide. In July, Mondale had called in his staff and announced, "This isn't working. I want to stop." They had convinced him to stay in the running until the congressional election in November. Reluctantly, the Senator agreed and never raised the subject again. But deep down he had the feeling he was not ready to make the sacrifices necessary to become President.[19]

On November 21, at a hastily called Washington press conference, Mondale announced his decision to a surprised audience: he would not be a candidate for president. After joking that he did not want to spend the rest of his life living in Holiday Inns, Mondale confessed that he "did not have the overwhelming desire to be President which is essential for the kind of campaign that is required. I don't think anyone should be President who is not willing to go through the fire." The brief exposure to national politics, however, did provide Mondale with valuable insight into the problems of running for president in an age of mass media. A presidential candidate, he complained, was forced to spend too much time asking for money from wealthy donors and not enough talking about the problems that affected the lives of most Americans. "There's a feeling that there are a lot of unemployed people, marginal workers and middle-income Americans who are entitled to similar time for a discussion of their problems," he said. He found the process superficial, more concerned with appearances than with issues. "There's the pressure to perform, to impress that I found very uncomfortable," he told reporters. "Maybe I'm not very good at it. The suggestion always was: You're a fine man but you really need to comb your hair differently, you need different kinds of suits, what you need is a speech instructor—I probably do—what you need is two hours in a Hollywood studio. It is a form of remake I don't like." Mondale suggested that important questions about character and competence were frequently subordinated in national campaigns to shallow concerns about appearances and style.[20]

A few weeks before Mondale's announcement that he would not pursue·the presidential nomination, voters went to the polls in the 1974 mid-term elections. Fortunately for the Democrats, voters were more concerned about the faltering economy and the Watergate scandal than about the social issues which had damaged the party in the previous two presidential races. Sixty percent of the voters chose Democratic congressional candidates. Political pundits argued that the old coalition had reemerged while Democrats declared the party cured of its recent schism. The rejoicing proved premature. Polls showed the party's foundation no longer rested exclusively on the venerable New Deal coalition. A large percentage of those who voted Democratic in 1974 were educated business and professional people of high income who lived in small cities. "Can anyone seriously describe a contest in which Democrats secured the support of two-thirds of young college-trained, professional and managerial white voters as a 'New Deal type' election?" asked the political scientist Everett Carll Ladd.[21]

Many Democratic gains in the 1974 congressional elections came from previously Republican suburban areas with little taste for new social programs. They promised to make government more efficient and responsive, not to address economic grievances or class interests. Gary Hart, George McGovern's 1972 campaign manager, won a Colorado senate seat campaigning against the "bankruptcy" of New Deal liberalism. "We are not a bunch of little Hubert Humphreys,"

Hart declared after his election. Like other Democrats who won election that year, Hart ran a decidedly nonideological campaign promising a balanced federal budget and better fiscal management.

The new Democrats made an astonishing net gain of forty-nine seats in the House. Seventy-five freshman Democrats entered the House in 1975; almost two-thirds had won seats previously held by Republicans. Taking control of the House Democratic Caucus, they required that committee chairmen be elected by secret ballot, gave party leaders the power to make committee assignments, and democratized the subcommittee system. They shared a similar generational experience. "We were a generation that was much more questioning, because of Vietnam," Congressman Tim Wirth told *Congressional Quarterly* in 1984. They shared a common vocabulary and style of politics. Media conscious and independent, they were anti-establishment and pragmatic political entrepreneurs who hoped to exorcise passion and social division from political debate and replace it with reasoned agreement among consenting groups. "Their approach to politics was not rooted in party loyalty or interest-group advocacy," wrote William Schneider. "They were Kennedy's children, and, like him, they were committed to a new kind of politics—a politics of ideas."[22]

Exactly what new ideas the "Class of '74" had to offer remained unclear, but their victory certainly intensified the generational challenge of the "new politics." The Party was increasingly divided between traditional Democrats who were anti-communist and rooted in the hard social struggle of the New Deal, and a New Class of younger, independent, economically conservative and socially liberal Democrats. Older Democrats had built a powerful base of support among the Democratic Party interest groups which were committed to fulfilling the New Deal agenda. Though liberal on many social welfare issues, they were also anti-communist and culturally conservative. The younger, white-collar Democrats, nurtured on postwar affluence, tended to oppose higher taxes and expanded social programs but were more liberal on controversial social issues. Polls showed gaping differences between these groups on issues such as welfare, union rights, extramarital sex, homosexuality, abortion, divorce, and discrimination in the sale of housing.

While the younger Democrats gained power, the traditional wing watched its base of support erode. A decline in the percentage of workers who were unionized robbed it of a traditional source of money and organization. Union membership, which had stood at

34.7 percent of the workforce in 1954, fell steadily to 27.3 percent in 1970. Volatile social issues divided union membership from its leadership, forcing Democrats to compete against Republicans for a constituency they once had taken for granted. Busing and affirmative action weakened the party's ties to two major groups: Jews and the white working-class. Finally, the political universe was shrinking from the bottom up. As poor lower and lower-middle class Americans dropped out of the system, Democrats needed to reach out to more traditionally Republican, economically conservative voters. Only senior citizens and blacks voted consistently Democratic.[23]

In the past traditional Democrats and their constituencies exercised considerable influence within the national party. But by the mid-1970s, the party had become an ineffective tool for mediating differences between and among competing factions. Rule changes opened up participation; new financing methods provided candidates with checks from the federal treasury, not from the party; the proliferation of presidential primaries meant that party leaders could no longer control the awarding of the presidential nomination; and television bypassed the traditional party structure as broker of political information. A new atomized politics emerged in which special interest groups filled the role previously played by party leaders. Interest groups did not work for common goals under a party umbrella: they were concerned with gaining specific benefits for their membership regardless of party affiliation. These structural changes forced politicians to alter the way they campaigned and passed legislation. "Rather than build coalitions," commented Nelson Polsby, "they must mobilize factions."[24]

The generational divisions, compounded by the weakening of party influence, the proliferation of special interest groups, and the emergence of mass-media campaigns, made broad consensus within the party nearly impossible to sustain. Mondale was one of the few figures in the party with the stature and ability to help the Democrats maintain a governing coalition. His background in the Minnesota Democratic-Farmer-Labor Party, his close ties with Humphrey, his long years of struggle for basic Democratic issues of social and economic justice, and his early support of the Vietnam War established his credibility with veterans of the New Deal era. After 1968, his outspoken support of busing and his conversion on the war made him acceptable to younger Democrats. While recognizing the differences between the two groups, Mondale searched for points upon which they could agree.

He realized it would be a difficult task. Politically, the party needed to remain rooted in its traditional constituencies and always mindful of their interests. Yet it also had to make necessary adjustments to new fiscal realities. Promises of ever-expanding social programs were never realistic, he believed, and now stagflation made them even less feasible. Like many of the younger liberals he saw politics as the art of the possible, recognized the limits of government power, understood the need for procedural change, and appreciated how a mindless commitment to an ideology, even one as necessary as anti-communism, could have tragic consequences.

The search for common ground between the party's competing factions shaped the rest of Mondale's political career. As he identified areas of agreement, Mondale moved away from many of his more liberal positions on social welfare and economic policy. For most of his career, Mondale's liberalism had provided a secular outlet for his moral passion. Confidently, he had believed problems of poverty and racial hatred would bend easily to the will of government. By 1974, those hopes had lessened. Limited resources, a conservative public backlash, and the unfulfilled promise of many Great Society programs severed the connection between morality and politics that had sustained his liberalism.

The years after 1974 marked an important evolution in Mondale's thinking—a process that culminated in his campaign for president in 1984. Demonstrating a capacity for self-education, he emerged as a mature, sophisticated politician who had abandoned his hopes for quick and painless reform. He would succeed in refining and refurbishing the liberal agenda by developing thoughtful proposals on a wide range of issues. By the time he did seek the presidency in 1984, Mondale possessed a knowledge of issues and command of the complexity of public policy that were unmatched by his peers. Skilled in debate, knowledgeable on issues, persistent in pursuit of his goals, he learned to use his influence to achieve his more circumscribed agenda. A few years earlier, Mondale had used his committee assignments as public forums to admonish liberals for their complacency, lash out at America's "obscene priorities," and champion the cause of the underprivileged. After 1974, Mondale played the role of Washington insider, using his influence to fight for incremental increases in important social programs. Earlier, Mondale had challenged the fundamental precepts upon which the welfare state rested. Now, without questioning its assumptions or objectives, he simply defended its prerogatives by promising a constant source of revenue.

As part of his centrist strategy, Mondale lobbied for new commit-tee assignments which would permit him to deal with middle-class issues. With the unexpected assistance of the powerful Mississippi Senator James Eastland, Mondale earned a coveted position on the Finance Committee. He also gained a seat on the new Budget Com-mittee—created by the 1974 Congressional Budget and Impound-ment Control Act which required Congress to abandon its piecemeal approach toward fiscal policy and to map out a budget strategy before considering individual spending and revenue bills. While adding two new substantive committee assignments, Mondale shrewdly switched the critical focus of his work on children away from the theme of "powerlessness" and toward the more traditional concerns of the American family.[25]

He joined the Finance Committee as it was beginning deliberations on the 1976 tax reform act. Initiated in the House Ways and Means Committee, the reform measure attempted to simplify the tax code by eliminating costly loopholes. It trimmed shelters in real estate, cattle raising and oil and gas drilling, increased the minimum tax, and reduced the generous provisions for international business firms. The Senate Budget Committee supported the reform efforts by insisting that whatever bill emerged from the Senate should eliminate two billion dollars in tax preferences. As the bill made its way to the Senate Finance Committee, supporters realized their efforts lay in the hands of the intractable Russell Long.

Long, son of Huey Long and powerful satrap of the Senate Finance Committee, was the undisputed expert on tax issues in Congress. He had mastered the intricacies of the tax code well enough to intimidate most Senators who tried to challenge him. Part corporate defender, part populist, the Louisiana Democrat was always an aggressive, knowledgeable, and formidable opponent. Reformers begged Mon-dale to use his joint positions on the Finance and Budget Committees to champion the tax reform cause. "The staff always wanted him to take on tax reform as his issue because there was a great need for reform," recalled chief of staff Dick Moe. Mondale refused. "My influence was more apparent than real," he reflected. "Russell had no intention of paying anything more than diplomatic recognition of my role." Long, he claimed, "was unreachable and incorrigible," and the committee stacked with conservatives. "There was no hope in the committee. The numbers just were not there."[26]

Despite the disclaimers, his staff persisted in arguing that he should be more combative. "This laying back in the weeds isn't you and it doesn't come off very well in my judgment," Berman commented. Resisting the pressure of his staff, Mondale pursued a two-track approach. On the one hand, he played by the rules to get concessions for the groups he cared about the most. For the most part, Long supported Mondale's request for certain child care and education tax benefits. In return, Mondale rejected suggestions that he assume the role of liberal antagonist. On the other hand, Mondale kept careful mental notes of questionable tax breaks which he later challenged on the Senate floor.

The cautious approach satisfied Mondale but it did little to promote effective tax reform. Rather than simplifying the tax code, the Finance Committee added seventy-three amendments that provided benefits to a handful of corporations. Mondale did not escape blame. Critics pointed out that he authored two major provisions designed to help Minneapolis-based industry: one on behalf of Honeywell, Inc., the other for Investors Diversified Services, (IDS). Under one amendment, IDS would have saved $100,000 in taxes in 1976, $150,000 in 1977 and an estimated $500,000 a year by 1979. The other would have provided an indirect benefit for Honeywell by making one of their products eligible for a tax credit.[27]

Mondale pursued a similar strategy on the Budget Committee where he fought for modest increases in existing programs. Stagflation helped his cause. By February 1975, the unemployment rate had surged to 8.2 percent, confirming fears that the nation was in the midst of the worst recession since World War II. Ford, however, remained committed to his tight fiscal approach, warning that added spending would increase the already ballooning $52 billion deficit and exacerbate inflation. The President's austere budget proposed $17 billion in spending cuts, including a cap of 5 percent on increases in federal pay, Social Security benefits, and other programs linked to the inflation rate.

The Budget Committee's membership was decidedly hostile to the type of social spending Mondale championed. The three southern Democrats serving on the committee—South Carolina's Ernest Hollings, Florida's Lawton Chiles, and Georgia's Sam Nunn—often voted with the Republicans. The only certified liberals on the committee were California's Alan Cranston, the chairman, Edmund Muskie, and the temperamental Joseph Biden who, having won election in 1972 at the age of thirty, occasionally tried distinguishing himself from older liberals like Mondale.

Rather than addressing all the issues the committee confronted,

Mondale focused his attention on selected programs—education, public works, and jobs—about which he cared most deeply. Instead of leading assaults against basic ideas and championing the cause of the "powerless," Mondale lobbied for additional funds for existing programs. In April 1975, he complained about the small sum Ford had allocated for social spending. "Of all the budgets, the one that took the toughest cut in the president's budget was this," he told the committee. "[T]here was no adjustment for inflation, but in many cases there were real cuts in dollar amounts over previous years." Republicans disagreed, moving quickly to slice Ford's already meager recommendations. Mondale exploded at the suggestion that inflation pressures required a much lower appropriation. "Before we vote, let's understand it first," he shouted. "This means that there will be utterly no increase in public service, even though the unemployment figures are now at 9 percent. Every tenth worker is unemployed." When conservatives moved to combine temporary anti-recession spending for jobs with other social programs without significantly raising the spending ceiling, Mondale warned the money for jobs would have to come from needed social programs that served the poor. "We are in a situation, and we might as well be candid, when we are pitting unemployed Americans off against handicapped children." In the end, by constantly proposing spending limits on social programs that were a few billion dollars higher than those which the Republicans were advocating, Mondale forced compromise at a point higher than many conservatives would have liked.[28]

In 1975, Mondale also led a successful floor fight to alter the filibuster rule. Civil rights foes had used the filibuster against legislation in the 1960s and then again in 1972 against a bill giving the Equal Employment Opportunity Commission the power to issue cease and desist orders. Ever since a filibuster had almost frustrated his attempts to pass Fair Housing legislation, Mondale had targeted the cloture vote. For the previous seven years he had been too busy with busing, child care, and his presidential campaign to muster the time for battle. Now the filibuster battle seemed to be among the few issues that all liberals could agree on fighting. "This is a time of severe economic crisis, and the 94th Congress is going to be faced with some tough choices in the coming months," Mondale declared. "With a reformed Rule XXII, the Senate will be able to deal with the pressing problems of America in 1975. This reform will make the Senate more efficient, more democratic and more effective."[29]

In January, he joined Kansas Republican James Pearson in filing a resolution that lowered the cloture vote necessary to end a filibuster from two-thirds of voting Senators to three-fifths. If all hundred Senators were present, Mondale's plan would require that only sixty Senators, instead of the current sixty-seven, would be needed to impose cloture. For the next six weeks, Mondale battled with Alabama's James Allen, a George Wallace protégé and master of parliamentary debate. Allen and other conservatives argued that changing the two-thirds rule would remove the constitutional protection of the minority to disagree with the majority. The rule change, one conservative blustered, "would be a fundamental and far-reaching and radical change, at a time when the people of the United States demand some kind of stability in Government, not radicalism." While opponents bellowed from the Senate floor, Mondale assiduously lobbied for support behind the scenes. Realizing he had been outflanked, Allen tried to sink the resolution through skillful parliamentary maneuver. Anticipating the move, Mondale had spent weeks studying the Senate's complex procedural rules to prevent an inadvertent mistake. Allen used every legislative trick possible to force Mondale into a fatal miscue. Surprising Senate veterans who had seen many skilled debaters fall prey to Allen's traps, Mondale held his ground.[30]

In late February, with tempers flaring and no end in sight, Russell Long proposed a compromise which required a 'constitutional' three-fifths of the Senate's 100 members instead of the Mondale proposal of three-fifths of those present and voting to invoke cloture. The Senate leadership rallied around the compromise but many liberals wanted Mondale to refuse the offer and stick with his original bill. But despite the grumblings of a few on the left, Mondale accepted the Long compromise and thus ensured passage of the bill. Though the compromise did not give him all he wanted, it represented a significant triumph for liberals at a time when victories were rare. The vote marked the first time in twenty years that Senate liberals had successfully challenged the filibuster procedure.[31]

Mondale's circumscribed agenda and his increased emphasis on procedural reform reflected his assessment of political realities. It also resulted from his growing skepticism about the use of government power. Beginning in January 1975, his work on the Senate Select Committee on Intelligence only confirmed his worst suspicions about the potential abuses of unrestrained power. Headed by Idaho's Frank Church, the committee planned a comprehensive investigation of CIA and FBI spying on civilians. Since Church spent most of his time campaigning for president, Mondale provided direction to the investigation. The committee divided the inquiry into two parts and assigned Mondale to scrutinize domestic abuses. "Mondale," recalled a staff member, "involved himself in the staff work with uncommon attention and commitment." More than any other Senator, he mastered the details of the investigation and emerged as the most knowledgeable and effective member. Along the way he upstaged the committee's egotistical chairman, who feared Mondale would steal the press exposure he so desperately wanted for his fledgling presidential campaign. As "Mondale stole the show," a staff member wrote, "I watched the chairman's reaction; his facial expressions alternated between mild annoyance and acute irritation."[32]

For fifteen months, the committee listened to the testimony of eight hundred witnesses and examined more than 110,000 pages of classified information. The evidence provided a stunning indictment of the United States intelligence agencies and six American presidents. The FBI's COINTELPRO operation had spent twenty-five years searching in vain for communist influence in the NAACP, had launched an infiltration of the women's liberation movement, and had drawn list after list of political critics to be detained in case of a national emergency. There was nothing partisan about the abuses; every president from Roosevelt to Nixon had used the FBI for political purposes. Most shocking for Mondale were revelations that FBI head J. Edgar Hoover had made numerous attempts to undermine Martin Luther King. The FBI had maintained a total of eight wiretaps and sixteen bugs on King, producing thousands of hours of tapes including motel-room romances. Mondale found that even his efforts at the 1964 Democratic National Convention had been closely monitored by the FBI. "No meeting was too small, no group too insignificant to escape the FBI's attention," Mondale said. While some of the FBI's misdeeds took place with the knowledge and support of the president, Mondale noted that most were "kept from the Congress and the Justice Department" and all were "kept from the American people."

These revelations struck another blow to Mondale's confidence in the powers of government. An incredulous Senator tried to fathom why the government would go to such extraordinary lengths to suppress dissent. "What was the threat that the FBI believed that Martin Luther King posed to this country?" he asked during the hearing. "Was there any evidence at any time that they were suspicious that he was about to or had committed a crime?" "No," answered Fred Schwartz, the committee's expert on domestic intelligence. "Was he ever charged with fomenting violence? Did he ever participate in violence? Was it ever alleged that he was about to be violent?" "No," Schwartz responded. Though King had never participated in a crime, the FBI, Mondale said used every weapon short of violence to intimidate him. "Well," Mondale concluded in disgust, "apart from direct physical violence and apart from illegal incarceration, there is nothing in this case that distinguishes that particular action much from what the KGB does with dissenters in that country. I think it is a road map to the destruction of American democracy." It was essential, he declared, that "this kind of unrestrained, illegal, secret intimidation and harassment of the essential ability of Americans to participate freely in the American political life shall never happen again."[33]

In hopes of preventing future abuses, Mondale helped convince his colleagues to establish a permanent oversight committee with broad authority over the intelligence agencies. He had argued for more stringent regulations, which would have stripped the CIA of its authority to spy on Americans traveling abroad, and turned over the CIA's "dirty tricks" section "to a politically responsible official of the executive branch." "Those bastards," he complained, "have got to figure out that there are some rules in this society that they're going to have to live with, along with everyone else."

By 1976, Mondale was a different politician from when he first entered the institution eleven years earlier. He had gained considerable stature and influence in a relatively short period. His handling of fair housing and filibuster reform had earned him praise as a skillful legislator while his careful attention to his committee assignments enhanced his reputation for thoughtfulness and dedication. Like the liberalism he espoused, he was more circumspect, less optimistic, more likely to focus attention on the limited issues upon which all liberals could agree. The coalition that had confidently launched the Great Society now defensively protected the prerogatives of existing programs. Only the Republicans' more evident problems with the Watergate crisis and a stagnant economy obscured the Democratic divisions. As they looked to the upcoming presidential campaign, Democrats searched for a ticket that could reinvigorate the party, articulate a new vision, and heal the divisions. It did not take a great leap of imagination to realize that Walter Mondale would play an important role in that effort.

9

Fritz and Grits

It was a cold December morning and the sun had not yet peeked over the horizon of this old industrial New Hampshire town. Ice glazed the trees and a howling wind magnified the biting cold. Standing alone before the gates of a large factory stood a medium size man with silver hair and sun-freckled skin. He waited in quiet anticipation until the blare of the shift whistle brought hundreds of workers pouring from the rusted plant gates. In a soft unassuming voice he greeted the tired and indifferent workers. "I'm Jimmy Carter," he said flashing his toothy grin, "and I'm running for president." The scene, repeated dozens of times each day, revealed the enormous self-confidence and intense discipline which characterized this little known former Georgia governor. "He'll shake hands with three-fourths of the voters in New Hampshire," one man remarked.[1]

Only days after the 1972 elections, Carter and his top aides had mapped out their strategy for gaining the Democratic nomination. Using election law changes that allowed for proportional representation, Carter planned a grass-roots approach which ignored traditional

Democratic power brokers. Over the next few years Carter fueled his campaign by tapping into the vast reservoir of public cynicism that followed in the wake of Vietnam and Watergate. Realizing that most voters were more interested in moral leadership than in specific programs, Carter remained vague on issues and instead preached the politics of moral uplift. The main issues of the campaign, he argued, could be summed up in two questions: "Can government work? And can government be decent, honest, truthful, fair, compassionate, and as filled with love as our people are?"[2]

Rather than responding to the specific legislative demands of powerful interest groups, Carter spoke of competence and trust. When he did make promises, they were couched in artfully vague language which allowed everyone to hear what they wanted to hear. He promised to overhaul the tax system but did not say how; to institute welfare reform and national health insurance but did not give details; to cut the number of government agencies from 1,900 to "no more than 200" but avoided specifics; to curtail defense spending but not to weaken American defenses; to reduce unemployment without aggravating inflation. Comic Pat Paulsen, noting Carter's contradictory statements, remarked: "They wanted to put Carter on Mount Rushmore—but they didn't have room for two more faces."[3]

Many Democratic party regulars found Carter puzzling because he did not fit traditional liberal-conservative stereotypes. They were bothered by his anti-Washington rhetoric and by his vagueness on most issues. Most were disturbed by the heavily religious overtones of his message of political salvation. "With this man Jimmy Carter I don't know whether the country is having a presidential election or a religious revival," grumbled the liberal *New Republic* columnist TRB. There were specific grievances as well. Labor wondered about how committed he was to its agenda. Jews were disturbed by his vagueness on the question of Israel's precise borders, the status of Jerusalem, and the resolution of the Palestinian issue.[4]

These fears did not prevent Carter from wooing voters in key primary contests. In January 1976 Carter transformed 27.6 percent of the vote in the Iowa caucus into a symbolic victory, even though he finished second to "uncommitted." Carter's sudden rise to prominence caught liberals off-guard. After an all-out stop-Carter movement failed in Pennsylvania and Hubert Humphrey reluctantly decided not to join the race, liberals hoped that Idaho Senator Frank Church, Arizona Congressman Mo Udall, and California Governor Jerry Brown could deny him the votes needed for a first-ballot victory at the Convention. The strategy failed. In June, Carter's victory in the Ohio primary guaranteed his nomination on the first ballot. Afterward, driven by the necessity of party unity rather than by personal enthusiasm, many party stalwarts endorsed Carter. "It is more resignation than enthusiasm," commented one disgruntled liberal. "They've stopped resisting."[5]

Carter realized that his choice of a running mate would shape public perceptions of his leadership ability. Campaign chief Hamilton Jordan wrote the Governor that the selection would be the first "of presidential magnitude that you will make," observing "in 1976 the best politics is to select a person who is accurately perceived by the American people as being qualified and able to serve as President if that became necessary." Hoping to avoid repeating McGovern's mistake of 1972, Carter planned a long, thoughtful process of interviewing candidates personally and carefully examining their backgrounds. Although his original working list included congressmen, mayors, and governors, Carter realized he needed to select someone from the Senate who understood Washington and could compensate for his inexperience in national politics. With that thought in mind, Carter narrowed a long list of candidates to just a few serious contenders—Ohio Senator John Glenn, Edmund Muskie of Maine, Henry Jackson of Washington, Frank Church, Adlai Stevenson IV of Illinois, and Mondale.[6]

Mondale knew he was a leading candidate for the office. "I had some doubts about pursuing the opportunity," Mondale recalled. After eleven years in the Senate he was finally emerging as a major player. He loved the institution and had finally mastered its ways. He had painful memories of Humphrey's years as vice president and had no desire to relive them. On the other hand, the vice presidency would satisfy—at least temporarily—his large ambition and provide him with the opportunity to have a greater impact on those issues he cared about the most. As a loyal Democrat, he knew he would complement the ticket and provide it with a chance of victory.

Mondale was also more forgiving of Carter's native conservatism than were many of his liberal friends. Though Carter may have appeared conservative on fiscal issues, on the critical question of civil rights he had built an impressive record. "He had a solid, unequivocal civil rights record and had established that record in what Andy Young referred to as the meanest county in Georgia," Mondale recalled. Mondale saw Carter "as someone who could end the vestiges of the Civil War and put race behind us." The vice president's office, he believed, would also enhance his own chance of seeking the presidency at some future date. Uncertain what to do, he asked Humphrey for advice. "Go for it," Mondale later quoted Humphrey as saying. "My vice presidential years were tough years but I am a better man for it and I would have made a better President. I learned more about the world and the presidency than I could have ever learned in the Senate."[7]

Carter had a number of reservations about Mondale—that he was too liberal for the South, that he was too concerned with "peripheral issues," and that he lacked the heart for a long, grueling campaign. Some aides supported Muskie, because he provided a better religious and ethnic balancing. A Polish Catholic, Muskie could appeal to the middle-class urban ethnics who were so suspicious of a born-again Southerner. Also, as a member of the Washington establishment and a liberal, he could appeal to traditional elements in the Party who were distrustful of Carter. Others pulled for Glenn, who had high name recognition and hailed from a crucial state.[8]

On July 5, less than two weeks before the convention, Carter began interviews in Plains. Muskie was first, followed by Mondale and Glenn. Church, Jackson, and Stevenson were to meet Carter in New York. Mondale guaranteed that the interview would be successful. His staff worked tirelessly in the days preceding the interview, researching and comparing their respective positions on every conceivable political issue from acid rain to arms control. The process served to emphasize points of agreement and obscure conflict. Rather than identifying real political differences, Mondale struggled to convince Carter that on all issues the two men were completely compatible. Mondale pored over the thick black book for hours before traveling to Plains. If that preparation were not enough to guarantee success, he also read the Governor's autobiography, talked to people who knew Carter, learned the names of all the family members, and called Muskie to get his impressions.[9]

Mondale's homework impressed Carter. "When he came to Plains, I didn't know him well," Carter recalled later. "But when he came he was extremely well prepared." Throughout the meeting, Mondale assured Carter of their compatibility on key issues and of his willingness to engage in a tough campaign. Responding to the persistent rumors that he lacked the "stomach" for a tough national campaign, the Senator convinced Carter that he had made a serious run for the presidency in 1974 and dropped out only after he was convinced he could not win. Most of all, he emphasized that he was proud of his achievements in the Senate and "would not trade them for a ceremonial office. I would only be interested in the office if it could become a useful instrument of government," he said. There emerged, along with the forced ideological compatibility, a genuine personal chemistry between the two men that was to endure through four painful years. Both had grown up in small towns and had strong religious influences in their lives. "We hit it off right away," Mondale recalled.[10]

Over the next few weeks Carter's reservations about Mondale gradually disappeared. The nominee checked and found that Mondale had waged very aggressive, hard-working campaigns in Minnesota for attorney general and the Senate. Similarly, he learned Mondale held seats on both the powerful Senate Finance and Budget Committees, and he was one of the few people who could get along with both their chairmen, Russell Long and Edmund Muskie. Senate leaders told Carter that Mondale was a valuable "go-between" and that his most important Senate work came on vital fiscal matters. Even Mondale's liberalism did not seem too offensive. Not only were they intellectually compatible, but Carter also liked Mondale's style: rational, un-dogmatic. "Mondale has got one unique quality that stands out," said a Carter advisor. "He'd probably be the easiest man in the group for the president to live with in a very difficult role."[11]

Mondale left Plains after the interview and returned to Washington confident that he had made a good impression. He joked when reporters reminded him of his remark in 1974 about not wanting to spend the rest of his life in Holiday Inns. "I've checked and found they've all been redecorated," Mondale quipped. "They're marvelous places to stay and I've thought it over and that's where I'd like to be."

Four days later he left for New York where the Democrats were about to hold their national convention. This convention promised to be different from its immediate predecessors. No great issues, like civil rights in 1964 or the Vietnam War in 1968 and 1972, dominated the discussions. Carter was going to be nominated on the first ballot and there was a desire to avoid the kind of fighting that had marred previous conventions. Watergate provided them with a real chance for victory. "Nothing so concentrates the minds of Democrats of whatever persuasion as the prospect of installing themselves in office," observed the New York *Times*. "For the first time in more than a decade," *Time* commented, "it seemed possible that the old coalition of labor, the South and the Blacks could be reconstituted."[12]

With the party's platform decided and even "spontaneous" floor demonstrations carefully orchestrated, the selection of a vice presidential nominee remained the only unanswered question. As tension mounted the speculation centered on Muskie and Mondale. Carter recalled that it was "a difficult decision. Both were good men, experienced legislators, knowledgeable about the nation, popular in their own states, and respected by their colleagues." On Wednesday night, July 14, after Ohio's votes provided him the first ballot nomination, Carter had still not made public his choice. He informed the finalists he would call each individually the next morning to inform them of his decision. Then he went to bed.[13]

There was nothing Mondale could do but wait. On Wednesday, less than twenty-four hours before Carter planned to announce his nominee, Mondale abruptly canceled a scheduled appearance on a morning talk show to avoid appearing to be pressuring Carter into a favorable decision. Instead, he went into seclusion at his friend Herb Allen's penthouse suite at the Carlyle Hotel. During the day Mondale found that many people who tried to call him were having trouble reaching him. "Our standard joke was that Carter would call and get a recording, 'Sorry, this number is temporarily disconnected,' " recalled Dick Moe. To deal with the problem, Mondale installed a separate phone line. On Thursday morning, Mondale rose early and was soon joined by a small group of friends and Senate staffers. At 8:26 A.M. the button flashed on the phone indicating an incoming call. Before the first ring, Mondale picked up the receiver and heard Carter's familiar southern accent. After a few seconds, Mondale flashed the thumbs up to the others gathered in the room. Carter recalled that when he said "Senator, I called to ask if you will run with me," he "received one of the quickest agreements" of his life.[14]

Carter made the decision public at a morning press conference. "I've asked to serve as my running mate Senator Walter Mondale of Minnesota," the Georgia Governor told the packed hall. While television cameras broke away to show Mondale pushing his way through a crowd of reporters on his way to the press conference, Carter explained he had chosen the Minnesota Senator because he was widely respected by Democrats and personally compatible. Mondale, he said, had a "great feeling of understanding and compassion for people who need government help," had earned the "trust of a wide range of Democrats," and possessed a "clear concept of what the vice presidency should be." A few minutes later Mondale entered the room to the sustained applause of partisans. Appearing tense, he praised Carter as a remarkable man "who has brought so much hope and unity to this country." His would be, Mondale predicted, "one of the greatest presidencies in American history."[15]

Most pundits applauded both the process and Mondale's selection. "Jimmy Carter has shown a disposition to be a consensus President, and equally—by the selection of Fritz Mondale as his running mate—to make bold decisions," commented the columnist Joseph Kraft. Most, but not all, liberals were reassured by Carter's selection. House Majority Leader Tip O'Neill, who would become Speaker of the House the following January, said that "all of a sudden, people are talking about rolling up their sleeves and going to work." Civil rights leader Joseph Rauh revealed the deep suspicion many traditional Democrats still harbored for their presidential nominee. "The question in my mind is whether the choice of Mondale means a turn to the left or is simply a sop to liberals," he said. Southern Democrats were undecided whether Carter's selection represented a move away from his more conservative rhetoric in the primaries. George Wallace said his reaction was "sorta mixed—like a father seeing his daughter come home at 4 o'clock in the morning with a Gideon Bible tucked under her arm." Wall Street reacted warily. The New York *Times* reported that Mondale's reputation "as a reform-minded populist" caused a "mood of caution among investors" and a sag in stock prices. When shown the story, Mondale smiled. "My father would have been proud of me," he said.[16]

It is not uncommon for the presidential nominee to choose a running mate with different political roots. That was certainly the case for the Democrats in 1976. A product of the "New South," Carter had shared in the region's transformation from a rural–small town economy dependent on agriculture to a more urban and industrialized society. Like many members of the new middle class, Carter shared the entrepreneurial vision that required government to create a climate conducive to business growth through low tax rates, minimal regulation, and a limited welfare state. A Democrat who thought like a Republican, Carter had a passion for efficiency. Mondale, despite his recent move to the middle, had a visceral identification with the outcasts in society and a deep faith in government's responsibility to promote the general welfare.[17]

Carter's training as an engineer had a dramatic impact on his leadership style. He hoped to lead through example and mastery of the mechanism of government, not through passion and eloquence. Carter possessed an engineer's fascination with definitive answers to complex problems. Mondale's attempts to address difficult national issues, on the other hand, left him skeptical about the existence of definitive answers. Raised in the Humphrey tradition, he understood the role eloquence and passion could play in establishing an emotional bond with the public. Symbolic gestures, he believed, could not permanently replace substantive achievement, but they could sustain hope during difficult times.

Carter's religious beliefs infused every aspect of his personality. His Christianity combined with his deep-seated populism created a mystical relationship with "the people." For Carter, "the people" were his flock and he was the shepherd elected to protect them from the narrow interest groups scheming to corrupt their democratic institutions. Since he communed directly with the people, he felt little need to broker among interest groups in his deliberations. Those who interfered with this mandate—Congress or interest groups—were dismissed as trying to thwart the people's will. Mondale's political topography revealed a landscape deeply divided by partisan clusters which represented distinct class and racial groupings. Successful governing, he argued, required careful cultivation of, and service to, Democratic interest groups.

Other important differences emerged over the next four years. Carter did not enjoy the process of legislating. He disliked politicians, and shunned ideological distinctions. He tried to build coalitions around particular issues. Mondale was a strong partisan who appreciated the company of other politicians, and believed in the art of compromise and negotiation. Like most Norwegians, Mondale possessed a reserved manner. He avoided public expressions of feelings. Carter, on the other hand, was more free in expressing his private emotions. "There is no problem with the Southerner saying what he feels about you," a Mondale friend observed. "He kind of told me that he liked that. He kind of told me that he wished he could do it. And he can't."

Though both were critical of the Kissinger-era style of diplomacy, neither had developed an alternative framework. Both suggested in general terms that a sound foreign policy required first addressing problems at home; that any policy needed to reflect American ideals and values; that moral authority, not military might, was the cornerstone of an effective policy; and that Congress and the American people needed to be better informed about important policy decisions. On specific issues there were differences in emphasis. Carter suggested playing down the importance of U.S.–Soviet relations and focusing more attention on the Third World. While recognizing the

importance of other issues, Mondale believed the Soviet Union remained America's chief adversary and that progress on other matters
would be impossible without Soviet cooperation. Another potential
area of conflict concerned the Middle East. Aaron observed that
Carter accepted that Israeli security was more important than Arab
oil, but he also seemed to support the possibility of a Palestinian
homeland. Mondale realized that any attempt to voice interest in
securing Palestinian rights would have severe political repercussions
at home.[18]

What they shared was a common faith in the Democratic Party
and a deep personal commitment to civil rights. Both believed their
ticket would heal racial divisions within the party. They also shared a
populist disdain for wealth and a feel for the common man. Even
here, however, they defined the "common man" in different ways.
For Carter the average citizen was rural, Protestant, politically independent, financially secure, and fiscally conservative; for Mondale
that person was a struggling, urban, blue-collar, union member concerned about a secure job, decent wages, and education for his children. While Carter hoped to commune directly with the "common
man's" sense of alienation and frustration, Mondale believed the
party's large interest groups represented the average citizen's welfare
and could serve as liaisons between the administration and its constituents.

Mondale spent most of the convention in his hotel room preparing
his speech for the final night. Gathered around a small table with his
aides, he read aloud from the numerous drafts, cutting paragraphs,
substituting words, searching for the right phrase. His convention
speech would be his first opportunity to show himself off to millions
of Americans, and he wanted to make sure he made a good impression. It was only fitting that his mentor, Hubert Humphrey, place his
name in nomination. In 1946, as an impressionable freshman at
Macalester, Mondale had heard Humphrey's staccato voice for the
first time. Now, thirty years later, he heard the same voice, projected
over television sets across the country, nominate him for the nation's
second highest elected office.

Never known for restraint, Humphrey described Mondale as
"brilliant of mind and sensitive of heart—a man who has translated
his concern for others into political action." While a delegate from
Minnesota waved a placard proclaiming "The Civil War ends,"
Humphrey declared that the Carter-Mondale ticket marked a "significant turning point" in the nation's history. "This ticket" he declared,

"represents a final reunification of North and South. This represents an end of an epoch which all too often has set one region against another." A few hours later, Nebraska's fifteen votes pushed Mondale over the 1,505 threshold needed for the nomination.[19]

On the convention's closing night, Carter and Mondale hoped to unite the party for the fall campaign. Mondale continued the theme of unification in his acceptance speech. "For well over a century, our nation has been divided North against South and South against North," he said. "But tonight we stand together. . . . Our days of discontent are over." In a partisan speech designed to reassure liberals and party regulars that a Carter administration would be sensitive to their agenda, Mondale attacked his Republican opponents. The Republicans, he charged, have "paralyzed the momentum for human justice in America. They have used the power and influence of the White House to try to persuade us to abandon one of our most cherished objectives: the special American notion of fairness and compassion." His partisan juices flowing, Mondale could not resist the temptation to mention Watergate. "We have just lived through the worst political scandal in American history and are now led by a president who pardoned the person who did it," he shouted as the crowd responded with a loud and sustained ovation.[20]

Following Mondale to the platform, Carter attacked the "political and economic elite," the "big-shot crooks," who never go to jail and the "wholly, self-perpetuating alliances [that] have been formed between money and politics." As usual, his rhetoric was general, populist, and preachy. As he had throughout the campaign, Carter emphasized the theme of alienation from government. "It is time for the people to run the Government and not the other way around," he said. "The tragedy of Vietnam and Cambodia, the disgrace of Watergate, and the embarrassment of the CIA revelations could have been avoided if our government had reflected the sound judgment, good common sense and high moral character of the American people." The crowd responded with a long ovation for the Democratic ticket. With arms raised triumphantly in the air, balloons falling from the roof, and the crowd singing "Happy Days Are Here Again," Carter and Mondale had reason to feel confident about the fall campaign.[21]

Despite the high hopes the convention engendered, the Democratic ticket faced serious problems. Liberals who had voted for Eugene McCarthy in 1968 and George McGovern in 1972 were still uneasy about Carter's commitment to their agenda. McCarthy promised to make matters worse by running for president on an independent ticket. Carter's problems with ethnic voters and liberals required him to draw better than previous Democratic nominees had from traditionally Republican areas. "We barely carry urban Democratic areas such as Pittsburgh, Cleveland, Toledo, and the Bay Area of California," his pollster Patrick Caddell wrote in September, "The only reason we carry most of these states is because of our showing in normally Republican areas." A successful campaign required a delicate balancing act. While appealing to the conservative concerns of traditionally Republican constituencies, Carter needed to convince liberals and ethnics to support him. The answer was to keep the focus on his opponent, highlight nonpartisan issues such as integrity in government, and avoid specific commitments. Though a convincing campaign strategy, it was not a recipe for effective governing.[22]

Little known around the country, Mondale got a taste of his new prominence when he boarded a commercial jet in Washington for the trip to Minnesota following the convention. Passengers cheered when he stepped onto the plane. Touched by the gesture, he walked the length of the plane, shaking hands, posing for pictures and signing autographs. After serving as guest of honor at the annual Aquatennial ceremony in downtown Minneapolis, Mondale retreated to a remote cottage in the small town of Hibbing in northern Minnesota for a few days of rest with his wife and a few friends. When in need of inspiration, privacy, or just time to relax, Mondale always sought refuge in the quiet of Minnesota's northern lakes. This time the entire national press corps, all three major television networks, and numerous local reporters accompanied him and dozens of Secret Service agents watched his every move. Despite the distractions, he still found time to sit alone for long hours thinking about the upcoming campaign.[23]

Mondale was confident of victory. Gallup polls taken after the Democratic convention showed President Ford trailing Carter by more than thirty-five percentage points. Ford found himself burdened by the legacy of Watergate, which had soiled the entire Republican Party with the muck of corruption, and overwhelming public disapproval of his pardon of Nixon. He also had to endure a long primary campaign which saw his chief opponent, conservative former California Governor Ronald Reagan, ask tough and effective questions about his leadership ability. Although Ford won the nomination, many of the questions Reagan asked resonated in the public mind.

Assuming the offensive, Republicans tried portraying Carter as a big spender whose policies would result in bigger government, higher taxes, and increased inflation. With the memory of McGovern in voters' minds, Republicans charged that while Carter campaigned on anti-Washington rhetoric, he would govern as an establishment liberal. "No matter how many statements to the contrary that Mr. Carter makes, he is firmly attached to a contract with you to vastly increase the powers of government. Is bigger government in Washington really what you want?" asked the Republican platform. Ford's running mate, conservative Kansas Senator Robert Dole, referred to Carter as "Southern-fried McGovern." Ford also blasted Carter for his vagueness on issues. "He wanders, he wavers, he waffles and he wiggles," he said. "We will build on performance, not promises; experience, not expediency; real programs instead of mysterious plans to be revealed in some dim and distant future."[24]

On Labor Day, Carter began his campaign in Warm Springs, Georgia—Franklin Roosevelt's summer retreat. The choice was not accidental. For decades, Democrats had opened their campaigns in Detroit's Cadillac Square to demonstrate their support for working people. Carter wanted to make a symbolic break with the past, show his allegiance to the South while also identifying himself with FDR. Like much of Carter's message, his themes were contradictory. While comparing himself to Roosevelt and his opponent to Hoover, he went on to emphasize the themes of fiscal responsibility and the need to fight inflation. "We should decentralize power," he said. "When there is a choice between government responsibility and private responsibility, we should always go with private responsibility. . . . When there is a choice between welfare and work, let's go to work."[25]

Numerous blunders during the first few weeks distracted attention from Carter's campaign themes. On just the second day of the campaign, Carter made a strained comparison between a small discretion by FBI head Clarence Kelley and the sins of Watergate. Despite his strong denunciations, Carter waffled when asked if he would have fired the FBI director. Carter's actions raised questions about the sincerity of his message of love and the depth of his judgment. He contributed to what Hamilton Jordan later called "the weirdo factor" by admitting, in a controversial *Playboy* interview, "I've looked on a lot of women with lust. I've committed adultery in my heart many times." Also, in the first of a series of three crucial debates, Carter listed Lyndon Johnson with Richard Nixon as a President who had lied to the American people. At the same time, Ford, executing a clever "Rose Garden Strategy," which forced public scrutiny on his opponent, kept hitting the right notes. "Jimmy Carter will say anything, anywhere to become President," he declared. Ford's attacks, combined with Carter's blunders, helped to close the gap. By October 1 the race was a dead heat, with each candidate polling 43 percent.[26]

Mondale believed Carter's gaffes were distracting public attention from what he believed should be the main emphasis of the campaign—the nation's economic difficulties. "The overriding fact of this campaign," Mondale's chief political strategist wrote, "is that there are more Democrats prepared to vote than there are Republicans. If we can persuade people to vote on a partisan basis, we are going to win. The way to do that, in my judgment, is to stress as strongly as possible those issues which reveal the traditional differences between the two parties and primary among them, of course, is the economy."[27]

Following through on this advice, Mondale never missed an opportunity to mention unemployment and other recession-related issues. His standard stump speech criticized the Republicans as parsimonious, cold-blooded enemies of the working class, and inveighed against the "insensitivity and heartlessness" of the Ford administration. He challenged Democrats not to be fooled by Ford's campaign pledges to deal with employment and housing. The President's conversion, he said, reminded him of something his father had told him. "During my career I've heard many deathbed conversions," Mondale remembered. "The trouble is, they sometimes get well. And they almost always forget." As the audience chuckled, Mondale moved into the heart of his message. "Mr. Republican President," Mondale shouted, "it's too late for you to be converted. We know your record. Where have you been when we needed jobs? Where have you been when we wanted you to fight inflation? Where have you been when we needed housing for our families? You haven't been around," Mondale concluded, frequently to thunderous applause.[28]

Watergate and the recession allowed Mondale to campaign on a traditional Democratic agenda. He reassured workers and ethnics that the Democratic party had abandoned its pretense of radicalism. "We have no radical schemes in mind for America in 1976," Mondale told a Wisconsin audience, "We simply want to return to some old fashioned things that have been forgotten—things like full employment . . . stronger families . . . decent education and government that doesn't lie." When asked his opinion on programs for desegregation of housing and schools in Northern cities, he gave vague answers. At one point, he sarcastically told the reporter who had brought up the question: "You want to know how many blacks I want to move into Polish neighborhoods."[29]

In some ways the campaign foreshadowed the discord that would characterize the Carter White House. When Carter, in a blatant appeal to middle-class ethnics, criticized the Supreme Court's role in expanding the civil rights of criminals, Mondale announced his support of the Supreme Court. While Carter claimed inflation was the key economic issue of the campaign, Mondale maintained that unemployment should be the first priority of a Democratic administration. In city after city he claimed that "counting discouraged workers, there are now more people out of work than the entire population of Ohio." To a largely working-class audience in Barberton, a suburb of Akron, he declared: "Any Administration that can't promise jobs shouldn't be in office."[30]

When the League of Women Voters approached him about debating Dole, Mondale readily agreed. Not only would it give him needed national exposure, but also he hoped that Dole, who had a penchant for "shooting from the hip," could be enticed into saying something stupid. They met on October 15 in Houston's Alley Theater for the first vice-presidential debate in history. Dole started on the offensive. Mondale, he said, "wants to spend your money and tax and tax and spend and spend." He was so completely under labor's thumb, Dole charged in his best jibe of the evening, that AFL-CIO President George Meany "was probably Senator Mondale's makeup man." But Dole's sarcasm also hurt him when he referred to World War II, and every other conflict in this century, as "Democrat wars." Not realizing that portraying the war against Hitler as a partisan cause had angered many voters, Dole continued. "I figured up the other day if we added up the killed and wounded in Democrat wars in this century, it would be about 1.6 million Americans, enough to fill the city of Detroit." Mondale, recognizing that his opponent had given him the break he needed, retorted: "I think Senator Dole has richly earned his reputation as a hatchet man tonight. Does he really mean to suggest that there was a partisan difference over our involvement . . . to fight Nazi Germany?"[31]

The debate boosted Mondale's spirits and his image. Viewing the Mondale/Dole contrast as a real plus for the campaign, Carter ran television ads everywhere except the South. As the screen flashed pictures of both men, an authoritative voice asked: "What kind of men are they? When you know that four of the last six vice presidents have wound up as presidents, who would you like to see a heartbeat away from the presidency?" More important than the reaction from the Carter camp was the public response. After the debates, crowds grew bigger and more enthusiastic. "Mondale is making it a lot easier for many Humphrey Democrats, a lot of liberal ideologues and the Udall types to come over to Carter," said Wisconsin Congressman David Obey. An NBC News poll following the debate showed 51 percent of respondents favoring Mondale as Vice President while only 33 percent considered Dole more helpful to his presidential candidate. Even in the South, where Mondale's liberal record had been expected to be an albatross, he outrated Dole, 48 percent to 37 percent. "Democrat Walter F. Mondale has emerged from the semi-anonymity that is the customary fate of vice presidential nominees and is drawing large and responsive crowds that exude an enthusiasm that Jimmy Carter rarely evokes," wrote a Washington *Post* correspondent. Mondale, another Washington *Post* reporter observed, "has combined a native wit and an easygoing manner with his 12 years of Washington experience to emerge as Carter's No. 1 asset in this campaign."[32]

Despite Mondale's impressive performance, prospects for the election outcome remained worrisome. In the middle of October, Carter led Ford 47–41 percent, with 2 percent for Eugene McCarthy, and 10 percent undecided. Caddell's private polls were more sobering, indicating "serious slides in all the big states." But just as the election appeared to be slipping away, Ford suffered a number of costly self-imposed reverses. During the second of three debates, Ford defiantly declared "there is no Soviet domination of Eastern Europe, and there never will be under Ford administration." Reporters hounded Ford for days asking for a clarification. At the same time, the *Wall Street Journal* reported irregularities in the President's personal and campaign finances. For a man trying to overcome the Watergate burden, even minor transgressions could become major political problems. Bad economic news for September—inflation jumped to an 11 percent annual rate while unemployment stood at an uncomfortable 7.8 percent—did not help Ford make the argument that he was best qualified to manage the economy.

Still, polls for the final days of the campaign indicated the race was too close to call. In Illinois, the Chicago *Sun-Times* poll indicated Carter's lead had shrunk to one percentage point; in New York, the Daily *News* showed Carter slipping from a 9 percent advantage to 6 percent. On October 30, a Harris-ABC poll showed the race dead even nationally—Carter with 45 percent and Ford with 44 percent with a 3 percent margin of error.[33]

In the final days, Carter and Mondale campaigned hard in the large electoral vote states (New York, Pennsylvania, Ohio, Illinois, and California). Realizing voter turnout would be the difference between winning and losing in key states, Carter depended heavily on the get-out-the-vote effectiveness of labor unions and big-city Democratic organizations—the very establishment groups he had shunned during the primaries. Mondale targeted a few states—Illinois, New Jersey, Ohio, Pennsylvania, New York and Wisconsin—which held 147 of the 270 electoral votes and the largest number of blue collar, ethnic, and urban voters.

On election night, Mondale sat in the Leamington Hotel in Minneapolis. As the night went on, the results trickled in, but the race was too close to call. Finally at 2 A.M., when Mississippi voted Democratic, Mondale and Carter were declared the winners. Mondale was sitting with a few close advisors in a private suite when he heard the results. "I was supposed to be excited," he recalled, "but I was too exhausted."[34]

They had won one of the closest elections in history. In the popular vote, a margin of less than 2 percent separated the candidates—Carter won 40.8 million votes to Ford's 39.1 million. In the electoral college, too, the outcome was sobering: 297 for Carter, 241 for Ford. It was the narrowest electoral victory since 1916, when Woodrow Wilson had defeated Charles Evans Hughes by twenty-three electoral votes. Observers noted that Carter and Mondale had succeeded in reassembling the New Deal coalition. While that certainly had been Mondale's hope, these contemporary analyses underestimated important changes transforming the New Deal coalition. The New Deal had built its electoral support on the white South, Catholics, blacks, Jews, and other urban ethnics, low-income voters, and union members. In 1976, the Carter/Mondale ticket did not score well with either white Southerners or Catholics. It did well among three traditional groups: blacks, Jews, and union members. While they retained support from part of the old coalition, it was nontraditional groups that made the margin of difference—white Protestants, educated white-collar workers, and rural voters.[35]

In a perceptive post-election analysis, Patrick Caddell argued that the Democratic party "can no longer depend on a coalition of economic division" to guarantee victory. Forty years of sustained economic growth, he argued, had created more "haves" than "have-nots." "In short," he concluded, "the old language of American politics really doesn't affect these voters." Middle class and financially more secure, most American voters were concerned with cultural and social issues. The challenge of the new administration was to retain the allegiance of those parts of the old coalition concerned with economic self-interest while also attracting new voters who were conservative on economic issues but fairly liberal on social issues. The administration, he suggested, had a great opportunity to update the New Deal and build a stable coalition for the rest of the century. The question confronting the administration, and the Democratic party, was whether these very different groups could work together as part of a harmonious coalition. They would not have to wait long for the answer.[36]

Mondale assumed the vice presidency at a critical point in the history of the office. The position's vague duties and the mediocre talent it had attracted made many scholars question its usefulness. "There is no escape," the historian Arthur Schlesinger, Jr. wrote in 1974, "from the conclusion that the vice presidency is not only a meaningless but a hopeless office." Schlesinger was not alone in that assessment. The Founding Fathers had created the office as an afterthought. For most of its history the office had been the object of public ridicule. John Adams, the nation's first vice president, described his position as "wholly insignificant." Benjamin Franklin said the vice president should always be addressed as "Your Superfluous Excellency." It was so insignificant to Daniel Webster that he turned down the vice presidential nomination in 1848. "I do not propose," he said, "to be buried until I am dead." The ridicule persisted into the twentieth century. Thomas Riley Marshall, vice president under Woodrow Wilson, pungently commented on the office's obscurity. "Once there were two brothers. One ran away to sea; the other was elected Vice President. And nothing was ever heard of either of them again." As recently as 1960, John Nance Garner, who had served two terms as Roosevelt's vice president, advised his fellow Texan, Lyndon B. Johnson: "The vice presidency isn't worth a pitcher of warm spit."[37]

Much of the problem stemmed from the vice president's ill-defined responsibilities. As Schlesinger commented sardonically: "The Vice President has only one serious thing to do: that is, to wait around for the president to die." Schlesinger was not far from the mark. The vice president's sole constitutional duty, other than to succeed the president, was to preside over the Senate. The vice president was not even a full member of the executive branch. The vice president could not propose legislation or sign it into law, veto bills, appoint executive officials or take over any of the significant duties of the president. Not until Kennedy became President was a Vice President even given space in the Executive Office Building.

The recent past had witnessed only marginal change in the vice president's role. Franklin Roosevelt had reestablished the idea of attendance at Cabinet meetings. In 1949, Truman had convinced Congress to make the vice president a statutory member of the National Security Council. These changes had little effect on the vice president's substantive role. As vice president, Nixon had spent much of his time traveling around the world on promotional tours and serving as Eisenhower's "hit man." In 1960, when asked by a reporter what major decisions his vice president had participated, Eisenhower responded: "If you give me a week, I might think of one. I don't remember." Neither Johnson nor Humphrey had contributed significantly to the office while Agnew's fierce partisanship had attracted considerable attention but had added nothing to the office's stature or power.

This history weighed on Mondale's mind when, in December, he met with the President-elect at Blair House, Carter's transition residence, to discuss their plans for the vice-presidency. Mondale presented him with a detailed memorandum outlining the role he wanted to play in the new administration. Careful research, along with conversations with Humphrey and Nelson Rockefeller, who had been vice president in the Ford Administration, convinced Mondale that the vice president's role had been "characterized by ambiguity, disappointment and even antagonism." Realizing that "my personal and political success is totally tied to yours," Mondale informed Carter that he hoped to break the cycle of frustration that had characterized the office. Mondale contended that the vice president's primary role should be as general advisor to the president. Too often, he argued, presidents had failed because they had ignored independent voices. As the only other member of the administration with broad responsibility unrestricted by loyalty to a department or agency, the vice president was in the position to provide such independent analysis. In order to fulfill this function as general advisor, the vice president needed access to the same information as the president, especially the daily briefings from the CIA and other intelligence agencies; a close relationship with other members of the executive branch; participation in meetings of key groups; an experienced staff member on both the National Security Council and the Domestic Policy Council; and finally, close and frequent access to the president.[38]

Carter, who felt fear of political competition had prevented previous presidents from taking full advantage of the vice presidency,
had no such concerns about Mondale and no hesitation about permitting him to play an active role in his administration. He agreed that
Mondale should receive the same intelligence reports as the president,
attend Cabinet meetings, National Security Council briefings, and
Economic Policy Group discussions. Carter offered a standing invitation for him to attend all of the president's political meetings. They
also agreed to schedule a regular Monday lunch where they could
discuss in private important business. "What was unique about their
relationship was that it was across the board," recalled Stuart Eizenstat. "Carter saw Mondale as his most senior advisor. No one else
had that breadth of relationship with the president."[39]

As evidence of his faith in Mondale and his desire to make the vice
presidency an important institution, Carter signed an executive order
making Mondale second in the chain of command for the control of
nuclear weapons. Since 1958, when Congress passed the National
Security Reorganization Act, the Secretary of State had served as the
deputy commander-in-chief. On the evening before the inaugural,
following a celebration at the Kennedy Center, Carter and Mondale
attended a classified briefing by the Joint Chiefs of Staff. As he
listened to the scenarios for nuclear war and contemplated the possibility of sending the orders that could kill millions of people, Mondale realized, perhaps for the first time, the awesome power of the
office he was about to assume. In the event of a nuclear attack in
which the President was incapacitated, Mondale would have two-to-
three minutes to decide whether to launch a lethal counter strike.
Over the next four years the constant presence of a military aide
carrying the Black Bag—the locked briefcase that contained the codes
needed to unleash the nation's nuclear arsenal—served as a sobering
reminder of that responsibility.

After agreeing to their ground-breaking institutional relationship,
they turned to the more mundane questions of where Mondale's
office would be located and how to organize their respective staffs.
Mondale wanted to be "in the loop" with an office in the West Wing
of the White House rather than in the Executive Office Building
where most vice presidents had spent their time. "The White House
operates not by structure but by osmosis," Mike Berman recalled.
"Most of the business is done by floating in and out of each other's
offices, bumping into people in the hall, dealing in the White House
restaurant. If you are out of the loop, it is very hard to be part of the

process." Mondale did not select the office that was traditionally held by the chief-of-staff because he did not want to get at odds with the President's own staff. "He felt that his clout within the administration would be stronger if he did not appear to be usurping power from the president's staff," recalled a White House staff member. Instead, he chose a small office just down the hall.[40]

In assembling his staff, Mondale depended on three talented men who had worked with him through most of his Senate career. He asked Dick Moe to serve as his chief-of-staff, while Jim Johnson became executive assistant to the Vice President, and Mike Berman assumed the position of counsel and deputy chief of staff. All three had grown up in fairly comfortable middle-class families and were raised in the post-Humphrey era of Minnesota politics. Johnson, who had been an antiwar activist, had gained his political experience while working for Eugene McCarthy in 1968. Educated at the University of Minnesota and Princeton's Woodrow Wilson School, he combined intellectual rigor with keen political skills. Dick Moe, a former DFL state chairman, had made his mark in 1966 by leading a daring though unsuccessful campaign against an incumbent governor. Despite differences that would emerge much later, both men shared Mondale's philosophy and temperament. A peek behind their composed and staid manner revealed a fervor for partisan competition and a passion for liberal values. Mike Berman was the advisor who, in background and style, was most different from Mondale. His casual dress and idiosyncratic manner stood in sharp contrast to the more formal personality of Mondale and his other confidants. He was also the staff member who, especially in the early years, dared to give Mondale critical advice. The Senator dubbed him "the mortician" because of his steady supply of critically perceptive comments.

Along with organizing his personal staff, Mondale lobbied to get loyal staff members placed in sensitive positions in the Executive Branch. "During the transition it was obvious that he had a detailed knowledge of how the bureaucracy worked and how he was going to have an influence on it," Stu Eizenstat commented later. By having people loyal to him in critical positions, Mondale hoped to prevent the President's staff from ever undermining his influence. "He got his people into key positions in the administration," boasted a Mondale staffer. Carter appointed David Aaron, who had served as Mondale's chief foreign policy advisor, as deputy national security advisor. Bert Carp, a close Senate aide, earned an appointment as domestic policy deputy. In perhaps the most dramatic demonstration of his desire to integrate the vice president into the administration, Carter asked Moe, Mondale's chief-of-staff, to also serve on the President's senior staff.[41]

Not surprisingly, Carter also surrounded himself with many of the people he felt most comfortable with. Hamilton Jordan, a brilliant political analyst who had masterminded his election, became his closest aide. Jody Powell, who had joined Carter in 1969 while a graduate student at Emory University, filled the press secretary position. Carter appointed two other long-time friends, Frank Moore and Robert Lipshutz, as chief congressional liaison and legal advisor to the president, respectively. Bert Lance, a close Carter friend and Georgia state highway commissioner, joined the administration as head of the Office of Management and Budget. As Domestic Policy Advisor the President appointed Stuart Eizenstat, a former speech writer for Lyndon Johnson and, later, an advisor to Hubert Humphrey during his unsuccessful 1968 presidential campaign.

With their respective staffs assembled, they began making hard decisions for Cabinet posts. Over the next six weeks, Mondale made sixteen trips to Plains to discuss appointments. These days spent together were important for both Mondale and Carter because it was the first time they had a chance to get to know each other well. A genuine friendship emerged. In making his Cabinet appointments, Carter placed a high priority on competence but he placed less emphasis on experience. Having run for office as an outsider, Carter wanted to bring fresh faces to Washington. "I think my inclination would be to go toward a new generation of leaders," he told the *National Journal* before his nomination. Mondale tried to convince Carter he needed to get "establishment" types into important positions if the government was going to work. For all major appointments Mondale solicited substantive advice from academics, Democratic "wise men," and political figures. Mondale spent days on the phone talking with old Democratic hands like Harry McPherson, Bill Moyers, Clark Clifford, and John Gardner; big-city mayors Tom Bradley of Los Angeles and Bill Green of Philadelphia; Capitol Hill heavyweights such as Muskie, Humphrey, Kennedy, Tip O'Neill, Russell Long, and Abe Ribicoff; and labor leaders such as George Meany, Leonard Woodcock, and I. W. Abel.[42]

The transition team held most of its meetings at Miss Lillian's Pond House in Plains. According to one participant, the sessions were "vintage Carter." During one marathon gathering, Carter discussed potential appointments with Mondale and a small number of leading

Democrats. After sitting in steel chairs for more than three hours without food or drink, many of the guests began showing signs of fatigue and hunger. All felt an urgent need to use a bathroom. But Carter persisted, methodically pushing through all of the points on his agenda without a break. Finally, well past noon, the meeting ended. While most of the participants scrambled for the nearest bathroom, Mondale approached a Carter aide and offered a few observations about the President-elect. "I learned three things about your friend Carter today," he said. "First, he has a cast-iron rear end. Second, he has a bladder the size of a football. And third, his idea of a party is a half glass of Scotch."[43]

For most positions, Mondale and the president worked together, drawing up a list of candidates, narrowing the options, and finally agreeing on their choice. The only domestic appointment Mondale was not consulted about was Attorney General. The President had already decided to nominate his close friend Griffin Bell. Perhaps knowing Mondale would object, Carter never told his vice president. Bell was a controversial figure. He held membership in a club that excluded Jews and blacks, had supported President Nixon's nomination of Judge Carswell to the Supreme Court, and had ruled Julian Bond could be expelled from the Georgia legislature for opposing the Vietnam War. "We were certainly aware," Johnson reflected, "that in the person of Griffin Bell and others there was an orientation toward the country and the Democratic Party which was very different from ours."[44]

Differences also emerged concerning foreign policy appointments. Both readily agreed on the appointment of Harold Brown as Secretary of Defense. Brown, a close Mondale friend, had a wide range of government experience in the Defense Department under Kennedy, as Secretary of the Air Force under Johnson, and as a member of President Nixon's SALT I negotiating team. As with the Attorney Generalship, Carter allowed for little discussion concerning the two key foreign policy appointments: Secretary of State and National Security Advisor. He had planned all along to appoint Cyrus Vance and Zbigniew Brzezinski. Mondale figured as much when, just two weeks after the convention, he traveled to Carter's home in Plains and Vance answered the door. "Carter had made up his mind before the election that he was going to appoint Brzezinski and Vance," Mondale recalled. "There was no consultation about those two."[45]

Though both men were critical of Kissinger's "balance-of-power" diplomacy and supportive of Carter's attempts to propose a new post-Vietnam framework for American foreign policy, they possessed profound differences in temperament and outlook. Brzezinski, a Roman Catholic, the son of a Polish diplomat who settled in Canada following World War II, had worked with Carter on the Trilateral Commission and as an advisor during the campaign. Deeply skeptical of Soviet intentions and convinced of the incompatibility of communism and capitalism, Brzezinski extolled the virtues of military power. Vance, a self-effacing Wall Street lawyer with a reputation as a low-key negotiator, was uncomfortable with grand designs or ideological distinctions and convinced of the need for compromise and negotiation. "Vance's philosophy was that of the traditional diplomatist," wrote the historian Gaddis Smith, "who, in an imperfect world where good and evil are forever mingled seeks to reduce the level of conflict and to discover areas of mutual interest through quiet bargaining with adversaries." [46]

Mondale had serious reservations about both men. He believed Vance lacked a geopolitical framework for interpreting world events. With a lawyer's penchant for detail, Vance, he thought, had too little sense of the interrelationship between world events. Mondale's greatest problem with Brzezinski concerned his personality, not his competence. Brzezinski, Mondale acknowledged, possessed a clear, compelling but simplistic framework. He feared, though, that Brzezinski's penchant for self-promotion would prevent him from being an effective team player. He also foresaw real potential for clashes between the quiet, self-effacing Secretary of State and the aggressive, sometimes strident, and always image-conscious National Security Advisor. [47]

On the eve of assuming the vice presidency, Mondale hoped that Democrats would unite behind Carter's leadership, but despite his optimism, many critical questions remained unanswered. Would the congressional Democrats join forces with the new president in pursuit of a common agenda? For the previous two years, despite large majorities, Democrats had been unable to agree on a common platform. How would Carter forge consensus within a party seriously divided by ideological and generational concerns? Carter had won election by exploiting Republican weakness and by making vague, sometimes contradictory, promises to the various Democratic factions. Could Carter translate his electoral success into effective governance? Finally, could Walter Mondale transform the vice presidency into a useful vehicle for continuing his efforts to bridge the gaps within the party? The answers to these questions would determine the success or failure of the administration and shape the future of the modern Democratic Party.

10

Democratic Dilemma

A brisk Arctic wind swept across the Capitol portico. The city below glistened with ice under a brilliant sun as a sea of spectators lined Pennsylvania Avenue. Standing on the temporary platform on the east steps of the Capitol, Mondale placed his left hand on the tattered family Bible which his wife held securely with both hands. The Bible, a family heirloom which recorded his parents' wedding and his birth, was open to the 23rd Psalm which began "The Lord is my shepherd . . ." At 11:58 A.M., two minutes before the inaugural oath was administered to Jimmy Carter, Mondale lifted his right hand as House Speaker Thomas P. (Tip) O'Neill administered the oath of office. Just a few feet away stood his children Teddy, Eleanor, and William. Although he had practiced the oath for days, Mondale feared he would forget the words. "I was sure I was going to blow it," he recalled. He did not. At the stroke of noon on January 20, 1977, Walter F. Mondale, who had begun his political career thirty years earlier in the local clubs of the Minnesota Democratic-Farmer-Labor Party, became Vice President of the United States.

The vice presidency represented a drastic change in Mondale's lifestyle. Before Carter chose him as his running mate, most people knew Mondale as the "other" senator from Minnesota. He lived in a modest home in Cleveland Park and drove to his Capitol Hill office in a battered 1969 station wagon. His salary jumped from $44,600 to $75,000. "Financially," Mondale quipped, "the job has been a help. As far as I can tell, I'm the only one who took the job because I needed the money."

In addition to pulling down a higher salary, Mondale enjoyed the opulence of the refurbished Naval Observatory mansion. Situated in upper Northwest Washington, the Victorian house, with its gabled roof, twenty rooms, twelve-foot ceilings, and twelve acres of land, was designated in 1974 as the official residence for the nation's second family. No longer would his family have to perform routine household chores. One of six stewards was always on hand to tend to those needs. Where once he relied upon his Oldsmobile to get him to work, he now commanded the road. Each time he ventured onto the streets of Washington he had two armored limousines from which to choose, and an entourage of Secret Service men to ensure safe passage.

The perks had their price, and for Mondale the most costly was the formality that attended even his most casual movements. "Everything is more formal now," Joan told a reporter in 1977. "You just don't take a trip to Boston, for example. It has to be advanced. You have to be briefed. More attention is paid to details." Even while ice fishing in Minnesota Mondale attracted attention. "There were Secret Service, at least 50 cameramen, and people asking me to sign autographs," he said describing a recent trip. "There I was at 2 P.M. holding a reception on the ice." In the past friends or neighbors would stop by the Mondale house without notice. Now the armed guards who patrolled the premises required all guests to provide advance notice of each visit.[1]

Mondale realized the President expected him not only to carry out his official responsibilities but also to serve as the administration's link to the established Democratic Party. Claiming they had played a key role in Carter's election, the party's major constituency groups wasted little time making their demands known. After eight years of Republican rule, the constituency groups believed undernourished social programs were starved for social spending. "Black people have a claim on Jimmy Carter—a strong one," wrote Vernon Jordan, executive director of the National Urban League. In addition to seeking Cabinet appointments, blacks demanded a massive attack on unemployment, increased aid to urban areas, welfare reform, and national health insurance. Labor concurred with these demands and added a few of its own, such as a raise in the minimum wage and quotas on foreign imports.[2]

These groups believed that a Democratic president could work with liberal leaders in the House and Senate to ensure Congressional approval of their ambitious social agenda. But much had changed since the last time Democrats controlled both the White House and Congress. Debates over the Vietnam War and civil rights had fractured the majority party. "If this were France," grumbled Tip O'Neill, "the Democratic Party would be five parties." The decline of partisanship and the end of the seniority system destroyed the chain of command a president used to whip his party in shape. "You know," remarked freshman congressman Richard Gephardt, "there is nothing the leadership can offer me, really nothing." Other institutional changes compounded the problem. Carter's three predecessors had engaged in constitutional clashes with the Congress, provoking a realignment in the relationship between the executive and legislative branches.[3]

The liberal groups' unrealistic expectations and Congress' resistance to executive blandishment promised trouble for any new Democratic president, but they were especially bothersome for Carter, whose cultural and ideological differences separated him from the traditional party power brokers. Carter did not speak the traditionalists' language or share their values. The self-serving perspective of well-organized interest groups clashed with Carter's Christian sense of self-sacrifice. "I owe the special interests nothing, I owe the people everything," he had said during the campaign. Carter also had little appreciation for Congress as an institution and none for its members' sensitivity and egos. Like many Southern politicians of the 1970s, Carter believed the party's key constituency groups, especially labor and northern liberals, no longer commanded public support. Successful governing, the President reasoned, required reaching out to the growing army of independent voters who held no allegiance to traditional party ideology. Fiscal realities reinforced his instinctive conservatism. Inheriting a $66 billion deficit, Carter had, in Eizenstat's words, "little financial room" to satisfy "the new-program demands of many of the groups which helped elect" him.[4]

Although Carter had campaigned in the general election as a liberal, he governed as a conservative. He proposed to balance his commitment to increased social spending with a determination to reduce the federal deficit. In keeping his campaign promise to attack unemployment and end the recession, the President proposed a two-year, $30 billion economic stimulus bill, including a modest $8 billion for public works and $11 billion in tax rebates. The bill provided far more than the Ford Administration had proposed, but it totalled only half of what labor leaders and many liberals requested. A few months later, Carter increased farm price supports far less than the farm belt demanded and he denied labor its requested increase in the minimum wage. He also canceled his promised tax rebate, claiming changed economic conditions made the proposal inflationary. "In reviewing economic policy this spring," George McGovern said, "it sometimes seems difficult to remember who won last fall."[5]

Relations with Congress also got off to a slow start. Congressional leaders felt overwhelmed by Carter's long list of legislation. Along with his economic stimulus bill, Carter had, within his first hundred days, submitted complicated legislation concerning government reorganization, food stamp revision, and election reform. The former governor paid little attention to Congress' newfound desire to be an equal branch of government. As part of his new austerity program, he cut funding for nineteen "unnecessary" and "expensive" water projects without consulting Congress. In February, Carter hastily announced he would propose a national energy policy within ninety days. Pressed by his self-imposed deadline, he drafted a major bill without consulting key congressional leaders.[6]

Mondale, a skilled politician who was sensitive to the changes within the party and sympathetic to Carter's attempts to broaden the coalition, hoped to use his position in the White House to guarantee that the old constituency groups were properly represented and use his prestige within the party to convince liberals of the President's noble intentions. Mondale was puzzled by Carter's insensitivity to some of the more subtle aspects of Washington politics. He could not understand why Carter insisted on alienating those groups, especially farmers and labor, who were essential to the administration's political success. "While Carter agreed with me in principle," Mondale recalled, "when he sat down with his slide-rule, he came up with programs that had little appeal to these groups. That bothered me." Mondale told the President that for the previous eight years Republicans, following the advice of the business community, had produced the worst downturn since the Depression. A Democratic president needed to listen to his constituencies and prove to them his concern for their interests.[7]

Mondale confronted a fundamental problem that became the central question which liberals and the Democratic Party needed to address in the mid-1970s: How does a party, whose coalition was forged during depression and sustained by decades of economic growth, face the threat posed by slower growth and rising inflation? It would be a difficult balancing act for even the most adroit politician because the party's two major factions were frequently hostile to each other's interests. Younger, independent voters tended to be economically conservative and socially liberal, with little sense of partisan feeling. They resented even the image of pandering to well-organized interest groups. Older voters remained wedded to the economic agenda of the New Deal and Great Society. Deeply partisan, they took pride in past accomplishments and jealously defended their organizational interests.

Mondale's old Senate colleagues pleaded with him to get the administration on track. "We no sooner got started and I was getting an earful from the Hill," Mondale remembered. They complained that the President's staff was arrogant and aloof; that it did not return phone calls and forgot to notify members of grants and appointments; that Carter did not use his discretionary power to benefit Democratic allies in Congress; and that the administration was slow replacing old Nixon-Ford appointees on the sub-cabinet level. Congressional Democrats felt little sense of common purpose with the President. The perception on Capitol Hill, commented the Vice President's congressional liaison Bill Smith, was "that the Administration in general and the President in particular are inept in dealing with the Congress. . . ." Though some of the problems reflected institutional changes, many were "the product of haphazard and uncoordinated Congressional liaison organization" which was "often unresponsive to Congressional demands."[8]

Mondale believed Carter and his Georgian advisors misunderstood Congress. Having campaigned as Washington outsiders, they tried to perpetuate that populist image in the White House. Wearing cowboy boots and forsaking ties worked well during the campaign, Mondale felt, but it did not impress Capitol Hill veterans. Meetings with the congressional leadership, which provided an opportunity for the President to exchange ideas with the key men on the Hill, proved a disaster. "I was baffled by the legislative meetings," Mondale recalled. As one of his new austerity measures, Carter served only sweet rolls rather than the customary full breakfast to congressional leaders. An irate Tip O'Neill, the corpulent House Speaker, grabbed Mondale after the first meeting and said: "I didn't get this way eating sweet rolls. I want a breakfast and I'm not coming back unless I get a meal!"[9]

Mondale hoped the gathering would offer a chance for give-and-take between the leadership and the President. Instead, Carter gave long monologues and appeared reluctant to engage the congressional leaders in a discussion. On one occasion Mondale presided over a session with powerful Senate committee chairmen. From his days on the Hill, Mondale knew that Senators rarely endorsed an administration proposal without first making suggestions. He sat patiently, planning to allow all of them to speak before requesting their support. Halfway through the meeting, Carter walked into the room. Mondale thought the President's presence would help his cause by showing administration concern and making it more difficult for the chairmen to oppose his policies. But rather than listening to the Senators finish their statements, Carter interrupted, lecturing them about their duty to support his programs. Mondale cringed, knowing that many delicate egos were hurt and political alliances damaged. "Carter's got the coldest political nose of any politician I ever met," Mondale said to an aide as they left the meeting. "All he had to do was sit there and listen."[10]

More than poor political instincts soured Carter's relations with Congress. Mondale felt that the President's desire to perform "good deeds," regardless of their political consequences, led him to squander his prestige on winless issues. During these early days of the administration, nothing bothered Mondale more than Carter's decision to cancel the water projects. Although he was correct in principle, Carter violated an unwritten Washington practice of pork-barrel politics and created an unnecessary confrontation with Congress. Mondale, who privately referred to the water projects decision as the "War on the West," recalled telling the President: "I know what you are trying to do. You are trying to create a government that will never waste a penny. We're in a democracy, and a little waste is inevitable. Someone's waste is another person's treasure." Carter resisted, and scribbled a note to Powell in late February: "Let press know we will hang tough on water projects." The Senate responded by voting, by a lopsided 65 to 24 margin, to add an amendment to the public works bill requiring continued spending for the water projects. Reluctantly, with Mondale's encouragement, Carter chose not to veto the bill and the money was restored.[11]

Mondale complained that a confused legislative agenda and poor policy coordination contributed to the President's problems with

Congress. Mondale felt that by pursuing an ambitious agenda the administration had diluted its limited political resources, frustrated Congress, and confused the public. He wanted Carter to focus his attention on the three issues by which Mondale believed the administration would be judged—energy, the economy, and SALT.[12] Hoping to make the White House more responsive to Congressional needs, Mondale also urged Carter to appoint Jordan as chief of staff. Jordan suggested instead that Mondale play a more active role in staff coordination. "Mondale has the ability, the intelligence and obviously the clout to deal with the problems I have described," he informed Carter. Mondale balked and Carter recognized such direct responsibility violated his earlier agreement not to give the Vice President direct staff responsibilities. Instead, the President asked Jordan to provide "overall political and policy coordination and communication among the White House staff." He refused to declare him chief of staff or abandon his "spokes on a wheel" concept of cabinet government. "This will in no way affect the direct access and relationship you have with me," he scribbled in a note to the cabinet.[13]

Almost daily, Mondale made suggestions for improving relations with his former colleagues on the Hill. He recommended that the President hold more frequent meetings with congressional leaders, establish informal contacts between the White House staff and Congress, cultivate leaders in both houses who could make the difference on close votes, and provide the Speaker with all the food he desired.[14]

Along with trying to improve congressional relations, Mondale served as a proponent for liberal principles within the White House. His first challenge concerned the administration's commitment to affirmative action. Alan Bakke, a 37-year-old white man, sued the University of California at Davis Medical School after it rejected his application for admission. He charged that the University had violated his rights by accepting less qualified minority applicants under a special admissions program reserving places in the class for disadvantaged minority students. Both the California trial court and the California Supreme Court agreed with Bakke. The university appealed to the U.S. Supreme Court.[15]

The case had enormous symbolic importance for the White House. The Congressional Black Caucus warned Carter they considered it of the "same significance as the Brown [v. Board of Education] decision." Eizenstat, agreeing with the Black Caucus, told the President, "It will be seen as a statement of this Administration's policy on an issue—affirmative action—which is an integral part of large numbers of Federal programs." But on September 1, Attorney General Griffin Bell drafted a "friend of the court" brief on behalf of the government which supported Bakke and concluded the Davis program was unconstitutional because it reserved a specific number of places in each class for disadvantaged minorities. Eizenstat informed the President the draft needed to "be substantially restructured and rewritten," because it did not state the administration's position in favor of affirmative action and against rigid quotas.[16]

Realizing Carter might be reluctant to overrule his testy Attorney General, Eizenstat asked the Vice President to get involved. Mondale went directly to the President and weighed in on Eizenstat's side. Supporting Bakke, he charged, would send "a political signal of the worst kind." "Why do we need this fight now?" he asked. "The administration was already battling with its liberal allies. Why provoke them more and why turn away from our campaign promise to support affirmative action?" Carter accepted the Vice President's advice and told Eizenstat to redraft the administration's position. Bell, who was fiercely protective of his department's prerogative, resented what he perceived as Mondale's politicization of a Justice Department issue. The Vice President, on the other hand, saw the Justice Department's handling of the whole incident as representative of the administration's most serious problems: an inability to understand the relationship between politics and policy.[17]

Carter forced Bell to accept Mondale and Eizenstat's recommendations. The final brief submitted to the Court removed the pro-Bakke language and condemned racial quotas only in passing. Instead, the brief argued that only one question needed to be addressed: "whether a state university admissions program may take race into account to remedy the effects of societal discriminations. We submit that it may." The most important principle involved in the case, the brief argued, is "that because the effects of racial discrimination are not easily eliminated, mere neutrality toward race often is inadequate to rectify what has gone before."

In addition to improving relations with blacks, Mondale was also working hard behind the scenes convincing Carter to shore up support with the labor community. Support for the Humphrey-Hawkins Full Employment Bill provided the Administration with an early test of its commitment. The bill set a full employment goal of keeping unemployment at or below 4 percent. Carter did not object to the bill's goals but he wanted leeway in meeting the deadline for full employment. "I've got to have some flexibility as president to consider inflation as well as unemployment," he told the Black Caucus. Not surprisingly, the business community strongly opposed the bill and, with the exception of organized labor and the very liberal faction of the Democratic Party, there existed little enthusiasm for the measure. Since liberals were willing to allow the President to change the target date for full employment, Mondale saw little risk in endorsing the legislation. Full employment was near the heart of all liberals and this bill provided the President with the opportunity to make a symbolic gesture of his support. With congressional approval almost certain, and with the bill stripped of any enforcement mechanism, Carter endorsed the legislation without embracing it. Not wanting to be closely associated with such a "liberal" bill, Carter chose not to participate in the ceremony honoring its passage.[18]

Passage of the legislation did nothing to improve the President's public standing. In July, Senate investigators accused Bert Lance, the flamboyant six-foot-four budget director, of accepting improper loans from a number of Georgia banks. Although fond of Lance, Mondale recognized a protracted public debate could cause irreparable political damage. "Bert, get out of here," he remembered telling Lance shortly after the story broke. "There is no medicine to take care of this. They're after you and they won't stop until they get you." Lance, convinced the "liberal" media were using him to attack Carter, believed he needed to stand firm. As the crisis dragged on through the summer, Mondale grew frustrated with the President's continued support of Lance. "A president's moral leadership is so precious that you can not spend a mere drop except for the highest calling," he told Carter. "When you get into personnel matters like this it is far better to cut your losses than to keep your friends." Mondale believed Carter raised troubling questions about his instincts as a president and politician by letting the crisis drag on. Many of the President's advisors though, resented Mondale's refusal publicly to defend Lance. The Vice President's allies in the media and Congress were leading the assault against their friend. A strong Mondale endorsement, they reasoned, would assure critics and save Lance.[19]

Day after painful day, more incriminating information surfaced. In September, Lance's picture appeared on the covers of *Time* and *Newsweek* and he was regularly the lead story on the evening news. The Comptroller of the Currency and the Internal Revenue Service both raised new and damaging questions about Lance's financial dealings. Picking up on those allegations, critics complained that Lance's questionable private banking practices were incompatible with his position as budget director. If those charges were not serious enough, a former Lance protégé already serving a jail term for embezzlement implicated Lance in a cover-up. Finally, on September 21, the President, in a moving, emotional performance accepted Lance's resignation with "regret and sorrow." While defending his beleaguered budget director, Carter stated Lance was his "most important friend in government" and only "across the board" advisor. He appointed another native Georgian, Deputy Director James McIntyre, to replace Lance.[20]

Carter's demonstration of support for Lance, combined with the Vice President's low-keyed public role in the affair, raised press doubts about Mondale's influence in the White House. For most of the year, the press had generated positive stories that focused on Mondale's considerable stature in the administration. In June, David Broder had concluded that "a close examination of Mondale's workweek leaves no doubt that there is more substance than ceremony in the schedule of the Vice President." Major stories in the New York *Times,* the Philadelphia *Inquirer,* and the Minneapolis *Tribune,* among others, confirmed Broder's conclusions. By October, however, many reporters were beginning to reassess their earlier views. "Suddenly," wrote *Newsweek,* "a sizable chunk of official and reportorial Washington was busily debating the abstruse question of Mondale's role and influence in the Carter Administration." Hedrick Smith and Jack Nelson, Washington bureau chiefs of the New York *Times* and the Los Angeles *Times* respectively, requested an interview with the President to discuss Mondale's role.[21]

Carter and Mondale feared these public doubts would undermine the Vice President's ability to represent the administration. "The incorrect perception of a weakened relationship will result in Mondale being less effective across the board on our behalf," Jordan wrote the President. "It is a potentially serious problem that merits your attention and action." Jody Powell seconded that opinion. "It is in your best interest to keep Mondale in a strong position to take the load off your shoulders," he advised Carter. "Fritz would appreciate your personal help tremendously. He is very concerned. He's not as scarred and calloused as the rest of us." In an uncharacteristic demonstration of support for his vice president, Carter telephoned reporters to reassure them of Mondale's influence in his administration.[22]

For Mondale, the decision to fire Lance came too late. Looking back, he felt the affair had started the slide from which the administration never recovered. The press, never close to Carter, became more critical after the Lance matter. "Rome isn't burning," said one Carter assistant, "but there's soot on the walls." Carter's approval rating dropped precipitously after the Lance resignation. "At just the time a new administration should begin hitting its stride," observed the *New Republic*, "Jimmy Carter's is slumping badly." Public confidence in the President hit a new low as he neared the anniversary of his inauguration. A New York *Times*-CBS poll showed that 50 percent of the American people considered themselves worse off than when Carter had taken office. Most disturbing to Mondale was evidence that much of the disapproval came from traditional Democratic mainstays—blacks, the elderly, and low-income groups. Carter seemed incapable of sustaining the image developed during the presidential campaign of an interesting and inspiring new leader. "If the Carter Administration were a television show it would have been canceled months ago," Russell Baker observed.[23]

As the year was coming to an end, it was obvious that Hubert Humphrey, Mondale's friend and mentor of nearly thirty years, was dying. The exuberance and energy of the Happy Warrior was being drained away by cancer. Knowing the end was near, Mondale convinced Carter to pay a tribute to Humphrey by flying the former Vice President to Washington for a final farewell. At Mondale's request, Carter gave Humphrey a chance to do all the things Johnson had denied him: to travel to Camp David, to sit in private sessions with the President, to have free access to the West Wing. He could not help but see the obvious contrast between his situation as vice president and Mondale's.

On December 22, 1977 Mondale and a few close friends escorted Humphrey back to Minnesota. "It was two old friends saying goodbye," recalled Penny Miller, the Vice President's secretary. On the flight back Humphrey was the life of the party. "There was so much more I had to teach you," he told Mondale, "but you're such a slow learner, I didn't get a chance to finish." Mondale, hiding his anguish, forced a painful laugh. At times, political differences and competition had caused minor tensions in their relationship. After returning to the Senate in 1970 as the "junior Senator" from Minnesota, Humphrey seemed at times resentful that Mondale had risen so quickly without ever having to engage in mortal political combat or to suffer agonizing defeat. Mondale, on the other hand, seemed puzzled by the unshakable bond that existed between Humphrey and the people of Minnesota. Although he worked harder cultivating support in the state and tending to its needs, Mondale never attained the stature that Humphrey enjoyed. But in recent years, as Mondale's star began to eclipse Humphrey's, their friendship had grown much deeper. "There was a special bond between them," Miller recalled. "The care and warmth between them was touching." [24]

On the evening of January 13, at the age of sixty-six, Hubert Humphrey, the symbol of a generation of American liberals, died of cancer. While thousands huddled in the cold outside, family and friends gathered for a memorial service in the Capitol Rotunda. "He taught us how to hope and how to love, how to win and how to lose," Mondale said in his hand-written eulogy. "He taught us how to live, and finally, he taught us how to die." Although lost in the moment's grief, Humphrey's death symbolically passed to Mondale the torch of American liberalism. As James Reston had commented earlier in the year: "Mondale now stands where Humphrey stood almost a generation ago as the leading candidate of his generation and his party for the Presidency." [25]

In 1968, the Vietnam war had confounded Humphrey's dreams of being president; in 1978, it appeared inflation could undermine Mondale's hopes. Carter and Mondale had campaigned and won election promising to stimulate the economy out of recession. After less than a year in office, however, Carter had shifted the focus of his attention to persistent inflation. The issue had its root in Lyndon Johnson's decision to fight the Vietnam War without raising taxes. An over-charged economy saw increases in consumer prices jump from 2 percent in 1965 to 6 percent in 1969. Nixon's wage and price controls only temporarily moderated the inflation rate. An election year loosening of fiscal and monetary policy combined with a worldwide oil price increase, a poor harvest, and a falling dollar created another surge of inflation in 1973–74. Since then inflation had held steady at 6 percent a year. In 1977, however, it showed signs of reviving. Consumer prices rose at 6.8 percent, two points higher than the administration had projected.

In January 1978, as part of his plan to attack surging inflation, Carter called on major companies and labor unions to give the administration prior notice of their wage and price plans. A few days later, the President presented a "lean and tight" budget for fiscal 1979 which included an overall spending boost of only 2 percent, the smallest increase in four years. While holding the limit on spending, the President proposed a $25 billion tax cut which swelled the deficit to $60.6 billion. [26]

Rising inflation combined with Carter's instinctive conservatism ended any hope liberals might have entertained about increased social spending. It also created a vexing political problem for the administration. "One of the dilemmas of a Democrat governing in the modern era," observed Stu Eizenstat, "is that you do have these constituency group expectations and yet you have the fiscal realities as well." Council of Economic Advisors Chairman Charles Schultze recalled that Carter "appreciated well before Fritz did that the 50 years in which the Democratic Party made its mark by building a whole batch of new social programs was coming to an end." Although elected with support from the old coalition of labor, blacks, and liberals, the President was unable to deliver the programs they demanded. According to Schultze, Mondale, like most liberals, never understood the new reality of fiscal restraint. "Carter was struggling with a problem he did not know how to solve while Fritz never recognized that the problem existed," Schultze argued. Mondale, he recalled, "personified one-half of the problem which Carter had to deal with."[27]

Schultze accurately recognized one part of Mondale's political strategy. Despite their declining political influence, Mondale believed the old interest groups had to serve as the foundation of any Democratic coalition. What Schultze did not understand was how Mondale's position on issues had evolved as he attempted to reconcile the old coalition with new fiscal realities. For most of his public career, an expanding economy had allowed him to support expanded social spending without advocating increased taxes. Incremental growth from a productive economy, he believed, would pay the cost of new social programs. Inflation threw a wrench into this approach. The emerging reality that government deficits contributed to inflation, which in turn decreased the real earning power of most workers, forced Mondale to reexamine his old approach. It would not be an easy transition. Mondale, according to a close aide, "was dragged kicking and screaming" to face up to the new realities. He came to the White House with a particular agenda and now he was being told it would all have to wait. "The old ideas still suited his agenda," recalled John Farmer, the Vice President's chief economic advisor. "He felt cheated."[28]

Mondale tried to develop a compromise position between his social vision and his recognition of new economic constraints. "We were at the turning point in the politics of the next decade," Mondale reflected years later. Declining growth rates created a zero-sum game where further expansion of the welfare state required shifting resources among groups. Mondale realized a growing economy was essential to fund increases in social programs. Liberals, he believed, needed temporarily to lower their expectations, fight inflation, and stabilize the economy. At the same time, he argued the administration could not callously turn its back on the aged, the needy, and the sick. "I tried to keep our constituency together by forcing them to confront the inflation issue and I fought within the administration to prevent unnecessary budget cuts," Mondale reminisced. "It was a tough job for an old progressive like me."[29]

As Vice President, Mondale tried to reconcile the politics of the Democratic coalition with the reality of fiscal responsibility. He believed a few billion dollars of additional social spending would not add substantially to the deficit but would make for much better relations with the traditional wing of the party. Mondale was frustrated by the fiscal restraints Carter's native conservatism placed on the administration. "The price of keeping your coalition together was so small in the context of the overall national budget. But Carter just would not understand this dynamic," Eizenstat complained. "Programs like WIC [Women, Infants and Children], Headstart, and Youth Employment had an importance beyond their sheer numbers. You could get a lot for a relatively small amount." While making the President aware of the coalition's political needs, Mondale hoped to explain Carter's economic policy to the Democratic constituencies. "I think it is important that I devote more time to strengthening our relationship with those constituencies and persuading them that our interests and theirs are inextricably tied together," he wrote the President in his first review of the vice-presidency.[30]

Mondale tackled the central problem facing the modern Democratic party. He brought formidable skills to bear on the problem, not the least of which were a sharp intellect and a deep commitment to the party. Most of all, the trust and respect earned during his dozen years in national politics allowed him to speak to all of the party's competing factions. Unfortunately for the party, and tragically for Mondale, Democrats were not prepared for unity in the 1970s. Still deeply divided over fundamental issues and uncertain of their mandate, many party leaders refused to heed Mondale's message of restraint.

If Mondale's mediation were to be successful, the President would have to provide considerably more leadership than he had in his first year in the White House. Carter had campaigned for office by brilliantly exploiting the cynicism and doubts that had emerged in the wake of Vietnam and Watergate. But his appeals were vague and ambiguous, resting more on a sense of public revulsion against the Washington establishment than on support for concrete proposals. Mondale believed that as Congress resisted much of his legislation, the media criticized him for being ineffective, and public opinion charted a steady decline in support, Carter lost confidence in his ability to communicate with the American people. Like others, Mondale noticed that the President had become sullen and reclusive, unwilling to fight publicly for his programs. "At some point during that first year," Mondale recalled, "Carter lost confidence in his ability to lead public opinion. He told me once that people no longer listened to what he had to say."[31]

In April 1978, Mondale wrote a long, thoughtful memorandum to the President spelling out his grievances and suggesting remedies.[32] "My most basic recommendation," he wrote, "is that you should dramatically increase the degree to which you emphasize the public education role of your presidency. In retrospect, I believe that this function has been seriously under-emphasized and that the Administration efforts have suffered as a result." Mondale felt Carter had failed to tell the nation where he was going and why it should follow. Because the President lacked a compelling political philosophy or well-grounded assumptions to guide his thought, his policies jumped between liberal and conservative. "I sense you are reluctant to define your own approach and philosophy regarding domestic issues," Mondale observed. "I have the impression that you intensely dislike being defined or 'labeled.' That may have some value, but I fear it also contributes to the feeling that people don't know you, they can't feel you, they don't know where you are going." The Vice President argued that by never establishing a sense of priorities for the administration, Carter had blurred the public's perception of his goals. "If there's one element of your Presidency that cries out for correction, in my judgment, that is it," Mondale stated.

Mondale believed Carter's training as an engineer compelled him to calculate rationally an exact answer to every problem with little sense of the political context in which issues needed to be examined. "Carter's anti-political attitudes used to drive me nuts because you couldn't get him to grapple with a political problem," the Vice President reminisced. "He thought politics was sinful." "The worst thing you could say to Carter if you wanted to do something was that it was politically the best thing to do." Mondale, on the other hand, enjoyed other politicians and relished the art of negotiation and compromise to build coalitions in support of legislation. "Mondale was always very oriented toward building coalitions, reaching agreement, finding common ground," recalled Jim Johnson. "Often Carter—especially in Congressional relations—struck him as making short-sighted decisions that would just make people mad, never be enacted into law, and just be counter-productive." Carter had a firm grasp of many issues and had good instincts, but he had no experience with the key Democratic constituency groups. Therefore his good ideas were frequently lost in the translation from conception to implementation. "I never understood how Carter's political mind worked," Mondale reflected. "He had been a loner for so many years that he was in many ways unpredictable, stubborn, often reclusive. He did not get out many times and fight for an issue. He had no confidence in his ability to do that. He wanted to lead the country through hard, gifted work. He wanted to persuade the country, like every good engineer does, with numbers and figures, not passion and eloquence."

Mondale suggested the President make a number of changes. First, he had to improve his speeches. "Most of your speeches tend to be descriptive and detailed demonstrations of what you know and the amount of work that went into a particular decision," Mondale wrote; "but at the same time they tend to be, for many listeners, fairly heavy and incomprehensible, lacking the eloquence and persuasiveness that a Presidential address should possess." Second, and far more important, the President had to resurrect his image as a strong and purposeful leader. Carter tried to lead the nation simply through hard work and careful management. The President spent "too much time poring over staff memos" in his office, and "not enough time in public giving speeches and appearing with people," Mondale wrote. "[W]hen we elect a President, we don't want a manager. We can hire them. We want a leader." Mondale felt the President was sheltered by his inexperienced Georgia advisors and needed to meet more often "with some of the wise and experienced people in this town and elsewhere, people who want nothing from you and who have no axes to grind." Carter needed to assert control over the administration by reorganizing the White House, disciplining disloyal Cabinet members, and designating Jordan as chief-of-staff.

Along with offering these suggested changes in Carter's style and the organization of the White House, Mondale made another plea for the President to reconsider his conservative economic policy. While recognizing that many people now considered themselves conservative, the Vice President claimed: "[I]f you ask people whether government should help provide more and better housing, education, health care, environmental protection and the rest, a very high percentage of the population still strongly supports government activity of that kind. . . . It is my hope that your Administration will demonstrate that we can have both jobs and price stability. If we can, we will have a decisive advantage over the Republican opposition which clearly favors trying to beat inflation at the expense of jobs, a position which I consider to be insensitive."

Carter thought carefully about Mondale's suggestions but in the end decided to reject most of them. "He listened to Fritz because he knew his attitude was dominant among Democrats and Congress," recalled Jordan. But Carter had a much different approach to politics than his vice president. "Mondale came to the vice presidency with a fairly set tradition and ideology. Carter did not have a unifying philosophy in the White House." The President conceived of himself as a pragmatic problem-solver, not a strong Democratic partisan and certainly not a defender of traditional liberal programs. Carter thought Mondale wanted him to be Hubert Humphrey by getting out and fighting for old liberal causes. "Mondale was asking something of Carter that it was not Carter's style or ability to do," reflected Jordan.[33]

Persistent inflation reinforced Carter's desire to continue a more fiscally conservative economic approach. In March 1978, the Council of Economic Advisors predicted inflation would continue at 7 percent for 1978 and most of 1979, while unemployment would continue to decline. At the same time, the Office of Management and Budget (OMB), in its spending guidelines for fiscal 1979, proposed major cuts in social services, including steep reductions in jobs programs, federal support for all human development programs (except Head Start), and Social Security benefits for those who retired early. Other cuts in programs dear to Mondale included over $530 million from HUD and nearly the same from Agriculture, including $150 million from the WIC program, and $1 billion from transportation. John Farmer, the Vice President's chief economic advisor, commented "that if the Administration is not to be perceived as retreating from our commitment to minority and disadvantaged youth in order to be 'fiscally responsible,' this decision cannot be allowed to stand in the fall."[34]

Mondale lobbied hard against the proposed reductions. "I spent a lot of time trying to keep domestic initiatives adequately funded and to prevent marginal cuts that would do nothing for the economy but would create a firestorm of resentment and opposition. We had lots of fights over these budget decisions," Mondale recalled. OMB director James McIntyre was the Vice President's chief adversary in small appeals sessions where the President decided on cuts in sensitive social programs. McIntyre, a soft-spoken Georgian, shared the President's commitment to governmental efficiency, his distaste for budget deficits, and his disdain for the special interest groups that made budget-cutting so difficult. He and Mondale spoke different languages. McIntyre was the technician, coldly calibrating the machinery of government to ensure against waste; Mondale was the political advocate, committed to the programs' objectives and keenly sensitive to their political significance.[35]

Although he participated in the entire budget process, Mondale saved most of his leverage for the final appeals process scheduled in the fall. This final meeting, held in the Oval Office with only McIntyre, the Vice President, and the President, revealed their different approaches to the budget and government programs. The President sat passively while Mondale and McIntyre debated the benefits of social spending. The Vice President, frequently emotional, his face flushed with anger as his fist pounded the table, argued the President gave OMB too much authority to impose its judgment on department and agency administrators who were much better equipped to decide their own needs. Since OMB had no political constituency, it was unable to understand the importance of some of the cuts it proposed. A Democratic president needed to "take care of its friends." "We made promises," Mondale argued, "now we needed to keep them." The President would get no credit from the business community by cutting the deficit by three to five billion dollars. He would, however, get lots of political credit from traditional Democrats if he supported their programs.[36]

McIntyre, forceful yet restrained, reminded the President he had also campaigned promising to balance the budget and to introduce fiscal prudence into the budget process. Three to five billion dollars might not sound like a lot of money in a trillion dollar budget, but over a period of years, it would add up. "Every penny we can save from spending cuts the deficit and makes the government more efficient and effective," he retorted. Like the Vice President, McIntyre recognized the reductions were largely symbolic and would not by themselves reduce inflation. Where Mondale wanted to send a signal of the administration's concern to the constituency groups, McIntyre hoped to demonstrate to the business community the administration's commitment to lowering the deficit and reining in inflation.[37]

These debates within the administration compounded public doubts about the President's ability to lead the nation. Changing economic conditions and the administration's indecisive response gave the impression the President had no coherent economic philosophy. In 1978, there was already speculation Carter would be a one-term president. While Republicans looked forward to the upcoming congressional elections, Democrats were gloomy. Despite a booming economy—the GNP grew over 7 percent in the first few months of 1978, unemployment had dropped below 6 percent, and four million new jobs were added to the workforce—inflation, surging forward at 11.3 percent, remained the dark cloud on the horizon. These figures undermined the President's voluntary controls as unions fought for double-digit wage increases to keep ahead of the rising cost of living. Polls now showed inflation had replaced unemployment as the nation's chief economic worry.[38]

Mondale worried that the President's zeal for fighting inflation would undermine the party's historic commitment to fight for the poor, the elderly, and blacks, but Carter's staff insisted he take tougher action even at the risk of offending traditional Democrats. "It is impossible to overestimate the importance of the inflation issue to your Presidency," Rafshoon wrote the President. "I endorse the toughest anti-inflation program (short of wage-price controls) among the options which will be given you." Many of the President's Georgia advisors resented Mondale's attempts to block further budget cuts. "We valued the contacts and experience that Mondale brought to the administration," recalled Jody Powell. "But at the same time we felt a general need to try and keep that perspective in check." Many felt they did not get the political benefits Mondale promised. "Everytime we added money to those constituency programs," recalled McIntyre, "the constituents were not satisfied. They always wanted more." Media advisor Gerald Rafshoon agreed: "We were giving them 90 percent of their agenda and all they talked about was the ten percent they were not getting."[39]

The debates intensified again in the fall as the administration debated its fiscal 1980 budget. Carter leaned toward a Treasury proposal that committed the administration to cutting the deficit below $30 billion. Liberals in the administration argued forcefully against that option. Labor Secretary Marshall called it a "dangerous symbol" because it risked increasing unemployment. Health, Education and Welfare Secretary Joseph Califano, a close Mondale ally, argued "the deflationary effect of spending reductions are negligible." Mondale and Eizenstat agreed the program's credibility required promising a tight budget for 1980, but they did not want Carter committing to an exact figure. Eizenstat wrote the President that pledging a definitive goal "will lock you into making decisions in the budget process which will be extraordinarily damaging to your Democratic constituency." Mondale suggested the President promise to "reduce the deficit to the low $30's," but avoid specifics.[40]

The Vice President was unpersuaded that cutting a few billion dollars from the deficit would have any impact on inflation. He was certain, however, that it would have a big impact on the Democratic party's perception of the President. The cuts would undermine his efforts to convince liberals the President understood their needs and would fight for their agenda. Mondale told Eizenstat he would have a difficult time defending the cuts. "Spent 30 minutes with Mrs. King who says she just can't keep defending him. There is open rebellion from liberals," Eizenstat's cryptic notes revealed. Mondale "feels Carter killing himself on $30 billion commitment. Says Califano is morose but will remain loyal. Says Vernon [Jordan] and [Benjamin] Hooks talk about going Republican. He says this is not what he campaigned for."[41]

The Vice President lost the debate. In October 1978, Carter unveiled a new anti-inflation plan designed to encourage greater wage-price stability and reduce Government spending. "I believe that we must firmly limit what the Government taxes and spends," Carter said. He requested labor and industry adhere to a set of voluntary guidelines designed to hold the line against inflation and, as Mondale feared, he promised to reduce the deficit below $30 billion in 1980. To encourage labor's support, Carter proposed a "real wage insurance" which provided a tax rebate if inflation exceeded 7 percent. Carter noted he had already used his veto to stop inflationary spending proposed by Congress and would not hesitate to do so again. "We must face a time of national austerity," he said. "Hard choices are necessary if we want to avoid consequences that are even worse."

Determined to lower the 1980 deficit below $30 billion, the administration now needed to identify programs for cutting. Much to Mondale's dismay, OMB suggested cutting adult employment programs, federally supported housing starts, direct aid to education, health prevention programs, and aid for cities. Mondale's advisors warned that the proposed cuts "will be portrayed as a major retreat in the Administration's commitment to the disadvantaged, minorities and the cities." [42]

Just as Mondale had predicted, the party's liberal wing erupted, creating an opportunity for Senator Edward Kennedy to galvanize those disillusioned with the administration. While Carter lectured the nation about fiscal restraint, Kennedy preached to liberals about progressive leadership. At the opening session of the party's December midterm conference in Memphis, Carter tried to ignore the liberal criticism of his austerity program and focus attention on past Republican sins. Despite an expensive film designed to extol his accomplishments and over 150 administration officials roaming the corridors seeking to convince wavering delegates of the administration's commitment to traditional Democratic programs, the President evoked only a tepid response from a half-filled convention hall. He received his only sustained applause when he accused the Republicans of giving the country "a tragic war abroad and bitter division at home; millions in unemployment lines and the highest inflation since the Civil War, break-ins and bugging and our nation's highest public trust betrayal." [43]

Liberals turned the conference into a grievance session with the President. They accused him of increasing defense spending while turning his back on labor, the cities, and the poor. Kennedy, in a ringing podium-pounding speech to a cheering crowd of 2,500, told the faithful to "sail against the wind" of public opinion and reject "drastic slashes" in domestic spending. "The party that tore itself apart over Vietnam in the 1960s cannot afford to tear itself apart today over budget cuts in basic social programs." [44]

Kennedy proved that he posed a serious substantive and stylistic challenge to Carter's leadership. The Massachusetts Senator made clear the political implications of his message by invoking the entire litany of Democratic interest groups that would be affected by the proposed budget cuts. He had clearly established himself as the spokesman of the Party's liberal faction. The contrast between the tepid applause that greeted the President's keynote address and the thunderous ovation that engulfed Kennedy could not have been more striking. Kennedy generated a spark of life which Carter, with all the accouterments of the presidency, could not produce. Yet Kennedy's support was not as deep as his applause indicated, for the Democratic divisions persisted. The older interest groups still exercised considerable influence within the party, but they no longer commanded a majority. They were also demoralized and lacking in creative think-ing. "There is a certain crisis of liberal leadership," commented Mi-chael Harrington. "We don't have any programs. We don't have the answers like we used to."[45]

By underscoring the schism within the party, the Memphis con-vention revealed the difficulty of Mondale's task. He felt the admin-istration could win the battle against inflation without clumsily cut-ting politically explosive social programs. "We had to give the people who elected us reason not to expect more money," he reflected. "We had to keep the spirit of compassion alive but not in a way that would contribute to inflation." He also empathized with Kennedy's message and instinctively identified with his cause. He hoped to bring the two sides together by increasing Carter's political awareness and lowering liberal expectations. "That is why these modest budget cuts meant so much to me. They were modest things but that helped me to talk to these people who were very close to me." As the liaison with the liberal community, Mondale had the task of convincing them Carter really did care about them. "I had to carry the debate and I didn't have any ammunition."[46]

Results from the previous month's mid-term elections had rein-forced Mondale's conviction that liberals needed to confront the infla-tion issue. Republicans, running on a platform of lower taxes and less spending, gained three Senate and twelve House seats. They did even better in state government, where they won six governorships and an impressive 298 state legislature seats. The most stunning blow for Mondale came in his home state of Minnesota, where tax-cutting Republicans won both Senate seats and the governorship by taking advantage of squabbling within the Democratic-Farmer-Labor Party.

Rather than defending specific Carter budget decisions, Mondale chose to lecture liberals on the importance of conquering inflation. He warned Democrats that if they "don't end the ever-increasing cost of living, we will be driven out of office as we were by the Vietnam War." He emphasized that without a growing economy all the other programs liberals supported would come under attack. He declared: "If we don't solve inflation, this society will suffer terribly. Every-thing we stand for will be eroded. Inflation can destroy everything we believe in. When we press for real income improvement, inflation burns up the increase; when we push for growth, our standard of living deteriorates; when we expand personal opportunity, inflation lays its damp hand on our dreams of a more prosperous future." If liberals did not beat inflation, he concluded, "it will mock all our efforts at social progress." The convention responded warmly to

Mondale's warning and voted down a proposal challenging the President's inflation program.[47]

By 1978, Mondale had matured, since his early Senate days, into a seasoned politician and an attractive public personality. As he approached his fiftieth birthday, he appeared more gracious and approachable than ever before. Mellowed by age and experience, he was less likely to lash out unexpectedly at those around him or make unreasonable demands on his staff. As his confidence grew, he narrowed, but never eliminated, the gap between his private and public behavior. Like the public Mondale, the private man usually conducted himself with a sense of dignity and usually a personal reserve that inspired the respect of those around him. There was a time when as an impulsive Attorney General and insecure junior Senator, he would root through staff files in search of careless work. Now, Mondale confidently delegated to his staff enormous responsibility without meddling in their affairs.

Unlike many figures in public life, Mondale seemed comfortable with himself. "Mondale, unlike all recent predecessors, does not have an uneasy relationship with himself," observed Joseph Kraft. "He knows who he is and where he came from, and has a sense of history and a sense of humor," remarked James Reston. An old Minnesota friend told the Chicago *Tribune* that Mondale was "one of the few politicians I've known who seems to get deeper the longer he goes along." Mondale's apparent lack of pretense made many wonder if he had the drive needed to run for president. "Fritz Mondale's career poses a fundamental question," wrote Martin Tolchin. "Does a basically decent man who is not possessed by inner demons have the stamina and drive to make it to the White House and become an effective President?"[48]

He had not completely discarded the insecurities that had plagued him early in his career. Mondale remained in many ways the small boy from Elmore trying to "make it" in the big city. He still viewed himself as the "outsider," a product of the rural Midwest, who was vying for influence in a provincial Eastern establishment. Easily bruised by criticism, he required reinforcement from friends about his ability and self-worth. He made constant reference to the contrast between his humble youth in rural Minnesota and his current status as a major national figure. Every time he walked into a plush presidential suite or rode in an long motorcade, he remarked about his roots. "Not bad for a kid from Elmore," he said on numerous occasions to those around him. Privately, he marveled about all the "famous" people he was meeting and the extraordinary places he had the opportunity to visit. "He has moved from his old simple middle-class house into the new Vice-Presidential residence—a Victorian monstrosity—without losing his sense of humor or proportion, or his sense of wonder about how it all happened," Reston commented.[49]

As his confidence increased, he displayed more frequently the dry wit which earlier he would reveal only in the company of close friends. While Mondale was traveling in Paris, a reporter asked him a detailed question in French at a news conference. Puzzled that his translator had momentarily abandoned him, the Vice President smiled and said: "I'm very glad you asked that question. I've wanted to talk about my program for child development but no one has asked me." There were a few chuckles, but the reporter persisted. Realizing his staff had left him on his own, Mondale decided to have fun. "The question then is how I can look so handsome and vital after such a long trip," he said, as the audience began laughing. On another occasion, when asked the difference between the Senate and the White House, Mondale quipped: "In the Senate, you have friends. In the executive, you interface." When a meeting to discuss executive–congressional relations with former Senate colleagues turned hostile, Mondale lightened the tone. "This isn't a caucus," he said gazing from behind a plume of blue cigar smoke. "Its an ambush." He occasionally referred to Carter as "Iron Ass Jimmy" because of his fondness for long meetings, and he dubbed National Security Advisor Zbigniew Brzezinski "Woody Woodpecker" because of his prominent facial features and his mound of red hair.

The enormous time demands did not prevent Mondale from spending as much time as possible with his family. Except for their annual family skiing and fishing vacation, for most of the previous twenty years the pressures of public life had provided Mondale few free moments with his children. Now, his oldest son Teddy was about to celebrate his twenty-first birthday, Eleanor was considering college, and his youngest, William, was finishing high school. Experiencing all the problems normally associated with young adulthood, compounded by the constant public attention, they required more fatherly direction and guidance than before. "He tries to spend an hour or so at bedtime a few nights a week, talking with the children in their rooms or reading with them," Joan said. Every few weeks, he sent the family stewards home early, put a grill on top of an old sawed-off oil barrel, and cooked hamburgers and hotdogs. He insisted on preparing the Thanksgiving day dinner. These small informal dinners provided the family with a few precious hours of privacy. He also invited his children to travel with him more often. Whether he was giving a political speech in Texas or negotiating delicate diplomatic issues with the Chinese, his children were never far from his side. One reporter noted that the Mondales appeared to be "a contented family with a husband, who, although often away, is deeply involved with his wife and children when he is home."[50]

Though always active in the arts, Joan now possessed the stature and influence to have an impact on administration policy. In 1977, she helped reactivate the Federal Council on the Arts and Humanities where she served as honorary chairperson. Using the Council as a bureaucratic base, she successfully lobbied the General Service Administration to increase funds spent for art in government buildings, helped establish a $20 million "liveable cities" project, and persuaded Labor Secretary Ray Marshall to expand job opportunities for unemployed artists. Sometimes referred to as "Joan of Art," she traveled regularly to art museums, craft shows, and exhibits hoping her presence would stimulate public interest in local artists. "This lady is not just a mouth," reported the Minneapolis *Tribune*. "She is muscle, and she is exercising a steadily increasing influence over federal policy on the arts."[51]

In most cases, her husband helped make these successes possible. Not only did the Vice President provide her with four of his staffing positions, he frequently lobbied on her behalf. On one occasion he called Budget Director McIntyre to plead for smaller spending cuts in the arts. "What's your reason?" McIntyre asked. "Because I wanna stay married," Mondale responded. Eventually McIntyre relented, and some funds were restored.

Not everyone appreciated Joan's high-profile role, however. Critics charged that her influence in shaping the administration's arts policy derived more from her husband's position than her accomplishments or skill. "The cancer of political interference has begun to undermine the credibility of the [arts and humanities] endowments," complained former National Endowment for the Arts chairman Michael Straight.[52]

For both Joan and Fritz, their new prominence required greater attention to style and appearance. Accepting the advice of friends, Joan wore more makeup than usual, made a few more visits to the hairdresser, and exercised greater care in choosing clothes. For Fritz, who always appeared impeccably neat in public, the vice presidency provided an excuse to add a few new off-the-rack suits to his dated collection. While in the Senate, Mondale had his hair cut by a local Washington barber. "The people in Minnesota like shitty haircuts," he told friends. Now, a hair stylist came directly to the Vice President's office. "He thinks he doesn't have time" to go to a barber, a friend remarked skeptically.

While most observers praised Mondale for restructuring the vice presidency, many questioned his effectiveness. Some critics suggested that he was a professional protégé; a man who lacked the independence to distinguish himself from the powerful men who made his success possible. Carter may have given Mondale unprecedented power in the White House but did the Vice President possess the fortitude to stand up to the President? "He floats like a butterfly," remarked one Washington observer, "but can he sting like a bee?" A liberal congressman complained to a Boston *Globe* reporter that Mondale had "sold out" his liberal friends by supporting Carter's conservative economic policies. "We thought at first that we'd be able to go to Mondale and gain his help in arguing our case on the inside," a prominent labor leader told *Newsday*. "But instead of being an advocate inside for his old friends, he's turned into an advocate for the administration to his old friends." Sources within the White House added weight to the doubts by suggesting that Mondale told "the President what he wants to hear." A Carter aide quipped that Mondale was afflicted "with the Minnesota Vice Presidential disease," which *Newsweek* translated as "a Hubertian overeagerness to please."[53]

In many ways, these doubts were an expression of general dissatisfaction with Carter's leadership. Inevitably, Mondale shared in the blame. Carter's declining support in the polls and Mondale's close relationship with those groups most disaffected with the President only compounded the problem. But they also revealed that Mondale suffered from a nagging image problem—a problem he never solved. Given the limitations of the office, Mondale had successfully balanced his commitment to liberal ideas with his loyalty to the President. For now, he could do little but educate critics about his role in the administration and hope that things turned around for the administration. "I don't think I can be an effective advisor to the President if I go out and give the public a report card every day about what I win and the President loses," Mondale told reporters. "My advice to him his personal, and I think he's got a right to expect it to be personal."[54]

These were fulfilling years for Mondale, but he had little time to enjoy the fruits of his success. For now, the burdens of power outweighed the sense of personal satisfaction. With inflation pressures increasing and liberal support eroding, Carter appeared destined to be a one-term president. Mondale may have helped forge a temporary truce with the party's left wing, but a permanent peace seemed an unlikely possibility.

11

In the Shadow of Vietnam

A few days after the inaugural ceremonies, Mondale packed his bags and headed on a whirlwind nine-day trip to Europe and Japan. The President scheduled the trip so soon after the inauguration to underscore his desire to consult with the allies on substantive issues. "It was," Mondale recalled, "the first big foreign policy assignment I ever had." The presidential send-off on the South lawn of the White House was the most visible sign of Mondale's key role in the Administration. "The leaders of other nations . . . recognize that Fritz indeed speaks for me," Carter said. "I doubt that this has ever been the case in the history of our nation with another vice president."[1]

Everywhere he traveled, Mondale assured traditional allies that the United States intended to pursue an activist foreign policy and underscored the theme of cooperation and consultation. "The security of each of our nations, and indeed the preservation of our democratic values, rests upon a strong Atlantic Alliance," he said in a brief statement on arriving in Brussels. In his first official meeting, Mondale reassured a worried NATO Council that the President's promised defense cuts would not affect America's commitment to Europe. "We cannot accept reductions in NATO defense capabilities except through negotiations with the Warsaw pact—negotiations fully securing allied interests and leading to a more stable military balance," he declared. The next day, Mondale met with West German Chancellor Helmut Schmidt for more than four hours trying unsuccessfully to convince him to speed his nation's economic growth and curb the export of nuclear technology to Brazil. Afterward, he made a two-hour symbolic visit to West Berlin to reaffirm America's commitment to preserve freedom in that divided city. "It's hard to imagine a symbol more dramatic than that of a failure of a system to succeed," he said while viewing the Berlin Wall for the first time. From Germany, the Vice President traveled to Rome where he met with Premier Giulio Andreotti about his ailing economy, and with Pope Paul VI to reaffirm Carter's pledge to end the arms race. Next stop was London, where Prime Minister James Callaghan warned him about continuing British economic trouble and the problems in Rhodesia. In Paris, Mondale informed the independent-minded French that the United States sought neither to dominate nor dictate to the allies, but instead looked for cooperation and consultation. The trip concluded in Japan where Mondale assured the government that "the administration does not intend to turn its back on Asia," despite Carter's promise to withdraw ground troops from South Korea.[2]

By handling many sensitive issues with skill and grace, Mondale emerged from his maiden diplomatic voyage as a forceful spokesman for the administration. "He never put a foot wrong," declared a surprised German official. "He said all the right things, and he said them eloquently." Bernard Weinraub of the New York Times declared that Mondale's trip had "healed some diplomatic cracks in Europe, calmed the fears of the Japanese and made the tacit, but unmistakable point that a new administration had attained power in the United States and that the private and secretive diplomacy of Henry A. Kissinger would no longer dominate foreign policy." David Broder, noting Mondale's inexperience in international diplomacy, said the trip was "the equivalent of teaching a youngster to swim by tossing him off the dock. But the boy from Elmore, Minn., has not drowned, in fact, he has managed rather well."[3]

Though he served as the administration's first emissary, Mondale did not play a major role in developing Carter's ambitious foreign policy agenda. He shared Carter's desire to create a new consensus for the nation built around arms control, close relations with traditional allies, and human rights. He agreed with the vision of America's role in the world the President had outlined in his May 1977, Notre Dame commencement address. With bitter memories of Vietnam and the intense divisions it engendered not far behind, Carter argued that American policy needed to be more sensitive to the rise of third world nationalism and to the indigenous origins of disputes. "We are now free of that inordinate fear of communism which once led us to embrace any dictator who joined us in our fear" he declared. Since he lacked experience in foreign policy and had greater interest in long-neglected domestic problems, Mondale planned to let Brzezinski and Vance develop a strategy appropriate to the new approach.[4]

His foreign policy activity may have lacked the sustained day-to-day involvement that characterized his interest in domestic politics, but the Vice President established himself as a link in the foreign policy apparatus. A full participant in the deliberations of the National Security Council, he also attended meetings of the Policy Review and Special Coordination Committees. He received the same daily intelligence briefing as the President, and reviewed the reports of the Secretaries of State and Defense, and the CIA Director. He also participated in the President's regular intelligence meetings and attended the Friday morning foreign policy breakfast with Vance and Brzezinski.[5]

From his vantage point, Mondale applauded as the administration took steps to demonstrate its differences with past policy. In the Middle East, believing the Kissinger process of shuttle diplomacy had outlived its usefulness, Carter called for a reconvening of the Geneva Conference to address the most difficult questions in the region: Israeli occupation of the Sinai and the Golan Heights, the future of the Palestinians, and the security of Israel. In his initial dealings with the Soviets he proposed a new and comprehensive strategic arms proposal that called for a steep reduction in arms production on both sides and a new agreement to "put the cap on the arms race." Despite considerable pressure to move forward, he stopped production of the new B-1 strategic bomber, and canceled deployment of the neutron bomb in West Germany. Fulfilling early campaign pledges, he called for cuts in defense spending, a limited withdrawal of American ground troops from South Korea, new diplomatic overtures to China, and closer economic ties with Western Europe. As a demonstration of his commitment to North-South issues and of America's desire to abandon colonialism, he also promised to negotiate and to place the Panama Canal Treaty before the Senate for ratification.[6]

As expected, the most dramatic new initiatives came in the area of human rights. In Africa, Carter placed his administration firmly on the side of black nationalists struggling for political justice. In Rhodesia, the administration sent a strong message to the internationally outlawed government of Ian Smith by convincing Congress to repeal the Byrd amendment. Adopted in 1971, the amendment had provided tacit moral encouragement to the white regime by allowing the United States to import chrome in violation of a United Nations ban. At the same time, the administration pressed South African Prime Minister John Vorster to grant independence to Namibia and to end its brutal policy of racial apartheid. In his first meeting with Soviet ambassador Anatoly Dobrynin, the President raised the issue of human rights and later responded personally to a letter from Soviet dissident and Nobel prize winner Andrei Sakharov. He also warned other nations, even close American allies, that the administration would consider suspending military and economic aid if human rights policies were not improved.[7]

On March 7, Carter announced to an editor's conference that he was placing his vice president in charge of the administration's African policy. Mondale, who had been surprised by the President's announcement, worried that getting tied down with responsibility for developing specific policies would limit his ability to serve as a general advisor to the President. For now, he accepted the challenge, but only until he had the opportunity to gracefully withdraw. Support for black nationalists struggling for freedom against a repressive white-minority government provided a compelling moral contrast that reminded Mondale of America's own struggle for racial equality. The following month, Mondale asked Carter if he could present the administration's case in a private meeting with South African Prime Minister Vorster. "I could help reduce suspicions of Zimbabwe Nationalists concerning our intentions, and reduce their objections to a U.S. role in the Rhodesian settlement process," his lunch notes set down. He believed that "neither the Nationalists, nor Vorster, or Smith appreciate the fundamental change in policy we have made toward [Southern Africa]. Putting them straight on our policy could be a major accomplishment of a meeting with Vorster." Eager to dramatize his new initiatives in Africa, Carter readily agreed.[8]

Over the next few weeks, Mondale immersed himself in the details of South African politics and history. Studying like a lawyer preparing for trial, Mondale met frequently with State Department experts and scholars, read widely on the history of the region, and studied detailed CIA-prepared psychological profiles of Vorster. State Department specialists who briefed Mondale for the talks were impressed by his relentless study for the meeting and his determination not to get bogged down in a South African negotiating style that emphasized hair-splitting, semantic traps. Mondale considered negotiating with the Prime Minister of South Africa as similar to exacting concessions from a stubborn mayor or a recalcitrant congressman. They were all politicians trying to deal with difficult situations, forced to choose between unattractive alternatives. Success, he thought, would require forceful, although quiet, diplomacy, conducted behind closed doors, not in public exchanges. Careful not to encourage a public confrontation, Mondale told reporters that he was approaching Vorster "in a constructive frame of mind. We hope for success." Despite his strategy, Mondale had no illusions about the difficulty of his task. Getting South African leaders to end apartheid, stop destabilizing other nations in the region, and comply with the United Nations resolution on Namibia, Mondale recalled, "was like trying to make Adolf Hitler a western liberal."[9]

On May 19, Mondale found himself sitting face-to-face with Vorster in a small room in the ornate Hofburg Palace in Vienna. The contrast between the two men was striking. On one side of the table sat the youthful champion of civil rights and energetic spokesman for the administration's new moral foreign policy. Sitting directly across from him was the dour, bulldog-visaged political patriarch of South Africa, who had once led a terrorist pro-Nazi group and who vigorously defended a policy of racial segregation.

Early in the meeting, Vorster challenged the Vice President's moral authority by suggesting Africa's racial record was similar in many respects to America's treatment of Indians. Mondale retorted that Americans had learned from their experience that attempts to exclude groups from mainstream society were bound to fail. If it did not change course, South Africa would learn that same painful lesson. Vorster proceeded to justify his apartheid policy by claiming that divisions in South Africa were not just between black and white but between and among numerous tribal and national groups. "The only way to look at your problem," Mondale countered, leaning slightly forward in his chair for emphasis, "is that you have four percent of the population running everybody else and you're going through all these definitions to try and avoid that reality. We can't accept that and we will not accept that."[10]

Having dismissed most of Vorster's self-serving justifications, Mondale assumed the offensive. He warned that future relations would depend on Pretoria's actions and attitudes toward political and racial change in southern Africa, including the beginning of a progressive transformation of Southern African society away from apartheid. He underscored that, in sharp contrast to previous American policy in the region, the new administration's approach was rooted in concern for human rights, not anti-communism. Mondale said the United States was prepared to work closely with South Africa in pursuit of better relations, but he made clear that failure to address injustices would force Carter to support mandatory sanctions.[11]

In a press conference held at the conclusion of his meetings, a South African reporter asked the Vice President if by "full participation" for blacks he was prescribing a "one man one vote" policy which was anathema to most whites. Mondale responded: "It's the same thing. Every citizen should have the right to vote and every vote should be equally weighted." Although an accurate reflection of the American position, the statement went further toward suggesting a specific solution to South Africa's political problems than the administration had wanted. Not surprisingly, Vorster responded angrily to the suggestion, and over the next few months used the comment to rally white support and frustrate attempts at reform.[12]

On his return to Washington, Mondale briefed the Cabinet on his meeting. He was not optimistic. "Vorster has our message," he said. "He may be more helpful than in the past on Rhodesia and Namibia. On Southern Africa, at least in the near future, we must be prepared for further tragedy, possibly on the anniversary of the Soweto riots, June 16." Mondale may have had little impact on Vorster, but his strong declaration of support for racial justice clarified the administration's position in the region and won praise from observers back home. The Washington *Post* noted that "[a]t times, Mondale's Air Force airliner seemed to be serving as an intercontinental version of a freedom riders' bus as it swept across Europe." Calling his effort a "tour de force," the *Post* claimed he had "set an assertive, liberal tone for American foreign policy, which stands in sharp contrast to the Carter Administration's more cautious approach to domestic problems."[13]

The favorable reviews of Mondale's initial foray into international diplomacy did not prevent critics from raising questions about the President's foreign policy. They charged that the administration showed little recognition of the complexity of international events or the relationship between power and morality. Many complained that the President seemed to be floundering in his own hyperactivity. An even greater threat resulted from conservative critics who charged that in his desire to address new issues, Carter had ignored the most fundamental challenge to American security: the growing power and aggression of the Soviet Union. The "most important reality facing us today," declared vanquished 1976 Republican presidential hopeful Ronald Reagan, "is that Western influence is declining while Soviet influence was expanding."[14]

Mondale strongly defended both the administration's active agenda and its human rights policy. Shortly after returning from Europe following his confrontation with Vorster, Mondale told the Cabinet of "the very real enthusiasm" that existed abroad "for the President's foreign policy initiatives." The allies realized that by "moving positively on so many fronts so early in his administration," Carter did not want "to subordinate or neglect any area requiring attention." In March, at a dinner honoring Senator Daniel Patrick Moynihan of New York, Mondale defiantly rejected "any definition of this country's national interest which fails to include a definition of our commitment to human rights." Three months later, he told the graduating class at the Naval Academy that supporting human rights was as important as maintaining defense capability. "We've survived for 200 years as a free people because we've had a strong defense and because we've never . . . lost our commitment to human rights."[15]

Only in the Middle East did Mondale express disagreement with administration policy. Carter, Brzezinski, and Vance believed if the United States were to play a constructive role in the region, it needed to convince both Israeli and Arab states that it would be a fair broker. Viewing Israel as the chief obstacle to a peace settlement, the administration was prepared publicly to criticize its ally. Carter insisted that Israel return to its 1967 borders with only "minor adjustments," endorsed the need for a Palestinian "homeland," abrogated Gerald Ford's promise to sell Israel sophisticated "concussion bombs," and excluded Israel from the list of allies given first choice on purchases of American weapons. Many Jewish leaders, already suspicious of Carter because of his southern heritage and Baptist fundamentalism, became convinced the administration did not have their best interests in mind.[16]

Like many liberal Democrats, Mondale had developed close ties with Jews in America and a deep appreciation for the Israeli perspective on the Middle East. Understanding the sensitive political nature of questions related to Israel, Mondale believed an effective approach needed first to gain the confidence of Jews in America. He felt Carter's remarks about supporting a Palestinian homeland, his desire to spell out in detail the sacrifices required by Israeli while making only vague references to Arab concessions, and his commitment to imposing an American solution on the region would only alienate already skeptical Jewish voters and make the peace process in the Middle East more difficult. On June 10, the Vice President complained to Eizenstat that Carter "has gone too public and hasn't brought along the Jewish community." He warned that the administration will "be in bad shape politically" if it alienated the Jewish community.[17]

Later that month, hoping to calm Jewish concerns about the administration's policy, Mondale planned a major speech at the Northern California World Affairs Club. The address, his briefing notes stated, provided "a good occasion for a public statement on our Middle East policy that can be helpful domestically." But after weeks of haggling with the State Department over language, Mondale found the final version of the speech fell short of his expectations. Despite the Vice President's strong objections, Carter insisted the speech simply clarify existing policy, and not, as Mondale hoped, announce new initiatives designed to placate Israel. In the end, it reiterated the administration's position that Israel's permanent borders should be "approximately the borders that existed prior to the war of 1967," called the Geneva Conference "crucial" to a Middle East settlement, and expressed support of "a Palestinian homeland or entity—preferably in association with Jordan."[18]

As Mondale feared, the address did little to calm Jewish anxiety. The New York *Times* called it "a reaffirmation of the basic American policy that had aroused Jewish and Israeli concerns." The paper quoted an anonymous Jewish leader who called the speech "warmed over Brzezinski." A few days later, New York Senator Jacob Javits attacked the Carter Middle East policy as "unrealistic," and gave a point-by-point rebuttal of the Vice President's remarks that included many of the points Mondale had hoped to make.[19]

Not even the election in May of right-wing Prime Minister Menachem Begin in Israel dampened Carter's enthusiasm for his peace initiative. Begin militantly defended Israel's claim to hold on to the land of Eretz Israel—including the West Bank and Gaza—and was fiercely committed to additional settlements in occupied territories. In October, undeterred by domestic political pressure or hardening Israeli attitudes, Carter announced the principles of the joint U.S.– Soviet Geneva Conference. The joint declaration called for a new Middle East peace conference that would ensure "the legitimate rights of the Palestinian people" and establish "normal peaceful relations" in the region. The PLO welcomed the declaration, saying it contained "positive indications toward a just settlement of the Middle East conflict." Jews in America exploded. Jewish groups picketed the White House and more than eight thousand telephone calls letters and telegrams poured in—most criticizing the decision. One Boston rabbi called the statement "an act of crucifixion against Israel and a second Munich."[20]

The communique outraged Mondale. "It was dynamite," he reflected. "I had no confidence that the Soviets had any intention of helping. It didn't accomplish what we needed which was face-to-face negotiations." Not only did he want the Soviets excluded from the process, he believed that the statement's provocative language would only strain already delicate relations with Israel. "The real problem here in my judgment is that we took the Jewish community completely by surprise with the communique and lacked any vehicle to explain it to them quickly," his lunch notes stated. Believing Carter's insensitivity to Jewish concerns led him to make such blunders, Mondale called for creating an informal Jewish advisory group to meet regularly with the President. "This will be far preferable, I think, to our recent habit of waiting for crises and then trying to put out the fire."[21]

While Mondale scrambled to extinguish the Middle East fires, the President decided to light another. In August 1977, the administration completed negotiations begun in 1965 for returning the Panama Canal. There were two treaties—one provided for mixed control of the canal until 1999, and the second defined American rights to defend the canal afterward. Following an elaborate signing ceremony, the treaty went to the Senate where a two-thirds majority was needed for ratification. A tricky diplomatic issue lay at the heart of the treaty, compounding the obstacles to approval. The Panamanian government wanted a settlement that would guarantee complete sovereignty and prevent American intervention, but Carter had to appease right-wing critics by asserting America's right to defend the canal during a crisis.[22]

With conservative groups using the treaties as a rallying cry for

American patriotism and national honor, Panama developed into a symbol far beyond its significance. During the 1976 Republican primaries, Reagan had won loud cheers by assailing the Canal negotiations. "We bought it, we paid for it, we built it and it is ours, and we intend to keep it," he asserted. In August, a poll showed 78 percent favored retaining the Canal, and only 8 percent for returning it to Panama. "Not since the Vietnam War labored to an end has any single foreign policy vote so starkly divided the nation or so stirred grass-roots activity to influence Congressional action," observed Hedrick Smith.[23]

Making full use of his close Senate contacts, Mondale helped coordinate the administration's lobbying effort. Most of his former colleagues warned the fight for acceptance would be long and difficult. "Nearly all of them point to grass roots opposition, some of which is extremely intense," his lunch notes stated: "They want to hear more, and they want the Administration to make a stronger case to the public." He was especially concerned about northern Democrats who had to stand for reelection in 1978. Many supported the treaty but feared a political backlash. He suggested the administration split conservative opinion by giving high profile to conservative supporters and "limit the opponents to the far-right crowd." The more the administration could "split up the opponents and try to isolate the Thurmond-Helms' crowd," he wrote the President, "the better our chances."[24]

By March, as the Senate moved closer to a vote, Mondale intensified his lobbying. Arizona Democrat Dennis DeConcini, who threatened to add a potentially lethal amendment giving American troops the right to intervene in Panama, presented the chief obstacle. Mondale, working closely with other administration leaders, eventually convinced DeConcini to attach his move as a nonbinding reservation rather than as an amendment. With DeConcini in line, Mondale was confident of victory. On the afternoon of March 16, he made a rare appearance in the Senate chamber to preside over the debate and possibly cast the tie-breaking vote. His vote proved unnecessary. After just an hour of debate, the Senate approved the Panama Canal neutrality treaty by a margin of one vote more than the required two-thirds, 68 to 32.

Mondale now turned his attention to the second treaty. Victory was by no means assured. Panamanians were angry about the De-Concini reservation. "This is not a day for celebration," said one Panamanian government leader. Reagan rallied opponents for a second fight, assuring the Conservative Political Action Conference that "the final outcome is not yet certain." Conservative predictions proved accurate. Three Senators who voted for the first treaty were withholding their support from the second, and their votes were critical.[25]

Over the next few weeks, Mondale spent at least one day a week on Capitol Hill trying to bring the wavering Senators back in the fold. He was at his creative best in dealing with California Republican S. I. Hayakawa. The 70-year old freshman Senator, who had voted against the first treaty declaring "We stole it fair and square," suggested he would switch his vote if given the opportunity to consult regularly with the President on foreign policy issues. Realizing that the Senator needed nothing more than some gentle ego-stroking, Mondale began planning an elaborate scheme. "Senator," he responded, "I think that makes a lot of sense. Lets call the President right now." After alerting the President to his charade, Mondale escorted Hayakawa to the Vice President's Capitol Hill office where they called the President. Playing his part perfectly, Carter told Hayakawa that he desperately needed his advice and thanked him for his selfless service to his country. Hayakawa repeated his demand: he would switch his vote only if they could set up a regular schedule of meetings, perhaps every two weeks, to discuss pressing diplomatic issues. While Mondale sat fighting to contain his laughter, Carter replied, "Let's not do that because I may need your advice more often." Flattered by the suggestion, Hayakawa readily agreed to vote for the treaty.[26]

On April 18, the Senate moved to vote on the second treaty. Mondale began the day early, visiting with wavering Senators. Later that afternoon, he once again assumed the chair of the President of the Senate, prepared to cast the deciding vote in case of a deadlock. After a few hours of heated debate, Mondale began recording the votes. By early evening it was clear that the administration had won another narrow victory—by the same 68–32 margin. Afterwards, an elated Carter declared: "This is a day of which Americans can always feel proud; for now we have reminded the world and ourselves of the things that we stand for as a nation."

The Panama victory represented a major accomplishment for the administration, but the costs were high. Mondale was satisfied that by successfully translating his years of service and personal connections in the Senate into votes for the administration, he had helped the President score an impressive legislative victory. But he also recognized that though Carter may have won the Capitol Hill battle, conservatives had scored a public relations coup. At a time of deep uncertainty about American power, the Canal had emerged as a reassuring symbol of America's glorious past. Effectively exploiting the public mood, conservatives painted Carter as weak and ineffective, unable to defend the national interest. Just one month after passage of the Panama Canal Treaties, thirty-eight Republican Senators boldly accused the administration of conducting a foreign policy "of incoherence, inconsistency and ineptitude." Carter had hoped the canal treaty would signal a new foreign policy consensus, instead it only widened the divisions inherited from Vietnam. "This was not a vote of confidence for Mr. Carter," wrote James Reston, "It was a suspended sentence."[27]

In 1978, criticism of Carter's foreign policy was mounting at home and abroad. More serious than the strong public backlash against the Panama Treaty was the general uneasiness that in foreign affairs, as in domestic policy, the administration seemed to have little sense of direction. During his first year in office the realities of international power politics forced the President to retreat or modify many of his bold foreign policy initiatives. Despite his tough stand against the sale of weapons overseas, he was forced to sell sophisticated aircraft to Iran and Saudi Arabia. He found it impossible to apply consistently his concern for human rights, especially in repressive countries in which the United States had vital strategic interests. The President committed himself to curbing the spread of nuclear weapons but precipitated a crisis in relations with Japan, West Germany, and Brazil by trying to pressure them into abandoning nuclear deals or projects. To many Western European and Japanese leaders, Carter's decision to cancel production of the B-1 bomber, and his waffling on the neutron bomb, made him appear indecisive.

In light of these problems, Mondale reconsidered his early optimism about administration strategy. Recognizing that an effective policy required a careful blending of strategic and moral considerations, Mondale believed the administration had failed to integrate its legitimate concern for human rights into a larger strategic framework. By creating tension among its allies without exacting any concessions from its enemies, the policy appeared insensitive to American strategic interests. "We did not candidly recognize there were times when our security interests had to be given more play," Mondale recalled. Also, by moving too quickly on many different fronts, Carter had confused the public, overwhelmed Congress, blurred his objectives, and invited partisan criticism. "[We] need to put it [foreign policy] into context of everything else we're doing and co-ordinate," the Vice President's November 1977 lunch notes recorded. "Too often we're having to backtrack after something becomes public and put out fires. Nearly everything has a domestic political consequence, and there's a need for direct political input early in the process."[28]

In the spring of 1978, in a long memo to the President, Mondale tried to spell out in more detail his problems with administration policy. He complained about the "inadequate strategic political thinking" that went into "the development of our foreign policy." Foreign policy initiatives, he felt, were not subjected to the same level of congressional and political scrutiny that domestic affairs enjoyed. "I have long sensed an attitude among the foreign policy advisors," he wrote in a veiled reference to Brzezinski, "that there is something suspect about looking at a foreign policy problem in the context of the political environment in which it must be fought. I couldn't disagree more profoundly with this attitude, and I think we must do everything possible to reverse it."[29]

As with domestic policy, Mondale felt that the President had become too immersed in the details of foreign policy and therefore lacked the distance to establish a broader vision of American strategic objectives. "I think you get too personally and too deeply involved in too many minor foreign issues," he wrote. Mondale believed that because Carter lacked a sense of priorities and a clear design for implementing his strategy, he frequently made decisions in a political vacuum. "A lot of these foreign policy things used to come shooting in on a memo to the President and it didn't seem to me there was any thought about whether they were domestically sellable."[30]

In many ways, Carter and Mondale's different approaches to foreign policy issues reflected contrasting views about the nature of presidential power. Seeing the office as a moral pulpit, Carter hoped to expose wrong and convince the nation to follow his leadership, regardless of short-term political risks. Mondale, always the practical politician, understood that a president's ability to exercise power related directly to his ability to sustain political support. "You had only so much power in the presidential bank and you could not throw it away. You had to have a strategic use of that power. The President did not feel that way," Mondale recalled nearly ten years later. "I tried to get the President thinking about sustaining domestic popularity so that he's strong enough to get selected things done. But Carter, the honest Baptist, always wanted to make his position clear, warts and all."[31]

With the administration divided and Carter unable to provide effective leadership, Mondale decided to assume more responsibility for articulating administration goals and shaping its policy. Other pressures were also pushing Mondale toward a more active foreign policy role. As stagflation limited the options in domestic policy, he turned to foreign policy as an outlet for his activist temperament. At home, political and fiscal restraints prevented Mondale from having an impact on those issues about which he cared most. But in the world of international diplomacy, a president had much greater room in which to maneuver, to negotiate deals and to advocate bold initiatives. Mondale, ever the astute politician, was hardly blind to the political advantages to be gained by bolstering his foreign policy credentials.

In May 1978, Mondale traveled to Southeast Asia on a twelve-day journey designed to reassert American presence despite the low profile Washington had maintained since Vietnam. While seeking to convince skeptical Asian leaders that the United States still had the desire and ability to act decisively in the region, he also needed to carry the administration's human rights message. It was not an easy mission. The biggest challenge of the trip came in the Philippines, where Mondale had to negotiate for the large American air force base at Clark Field and its naval base in Subic Bay, while also admonishing its American-supported dictator, Ferdinand Marcos, for ruling under martial law, suspending free elections, curtailing freedom of the press, and imprisoning political opponents.

The administration divided on the best approach for dealing with the temperamental Marcos. Patricia Derian, Assistant Secretary of State for Human Rights, argued that the bases, which brought dollars to the Philippines, could be used as a bargaining chip for release of political prisoners and a return to democracy. She wanted Mondale to send a clear signal of American dissatisfaction with the regime by deliberately avoiding the Philippines during his trip. The State Department, however, made clear it was more concerned about the strategic importance of the military installations than about Marcos' human rights violations. Mondale listened to both sides, but in the end agreed with the State Department. "I don't know what good not going would have done," he recalled.[32]

Pursuing a delicate balancing act, Mondale planned to make the trip but to keep human rights on the agenda. In a brief airport statement, he said: "When there are values and traditions which both our people cherish—freedom, individual liberty, human justice, democracy and national independence—I hope my visit can contribute to their greater fulfillment." The Vice President also insisted, over State Department objections, on meeting with opposition leaders. He did, however, back down from seeing Benigno Aquino, the most prominent of the jailed opponents of the regime, after Marcos made clear he would consider such a meeting a personal affront. In his private meeting with opposition leaders, Mondale stressed that both he and Carter were determined to press their campaign for human rights around the world. "When I meet with you, I hope that says something about where our Government is going and what it stands for. We are listening to all sides." For the moment, critics were impressed by Mondale's sincerity. "We got the feeling that the United States will do all it can to hasten the return of democracy to the Philippines," said one participant.[33]

In his private meetings with Marcos, Mondale continued to emphasize the importance of human rights. Though no record of the meeting exists, Mondale described his encounter with Marcos as "very direct, very sharp." "I went right after him," he reflected nearly ten years later. "I said we've got a very serious problem here. You've got martial law, you've got all these suspected human rights abuses. You've got a lot of your political leaders in jail when the only thing they've done is to be critical of your leadership. Good relations between the Philippines and us are impossible under these conditions. Human rights is a condition of a warm relationship."[34]

By most accounts, Mondale achieved at least one of his objectives. The Vice President and his close advisors were convinced his tough position on human rights placed Marcos on the defensive, making him more agreeable to American terms on Clark field and Subic Bay. "He worked Marcos over perfectly," recalled David Aaron. "He was both true to his ideals and mindful of American security interests." The impact on human rights, however, was less obvious. "Whatever Mondale might have said about human rights, and notwithstanding his perfunctory meetings with the opposition, his visit was seen by Marcos and Filipinos as an endorsement of the regime," commented a journalist.[35]

After leaving the Philippines, Mondale traveled to a crowded refugee camp in Bangkok where most of the refugees were Vietnamese supporters of the American-backed government in Saigon who had been forced to flee after the American withdrawal in 1975. Over the next three years, about three thousand per month had escaped communist persecution by making the short but dangerous trip to Malaysia. By the time the Vice President arrived in Bangkok, nearly seventy-six thousand refugees, many of them women and small children, were living in oppressive conditions in small, overcrowded camps with little food and poor sanitation. In what he called one of the "most moving experiences" of his journey, Mondale listened to terrifying accounts of mass murder in Communist Indochina. "The refugee problem is a product of the most pressing and tragic human rights problem in the world today," Mondale said as he surveyed the human wreckage. "I believe there is no more profound test of our government's commitment to human rights than the way we deal with these people." Pledging action, Mondale told Thai Prime Minister Kriangsak Chamanand that the United States would provide two million dollars in financial assistance and also admit up to twenty thousand refugees annually.[36]

Touched by his brief exposure, Mondale established himself as the point man in the administration efforts for dealing with the refugee problem. Over the next few months, while trying to funnel assistance to refugee camps in Malaysia, Mondale discovered that the tragedy had assumed frightening new dimensions as Vietnam began systematically expelling thousands of ethnic Chinese. Tens of thousands fled the country in a human flotilla searching for a new home. But Malaysia, already overburdened by crowded camps and limited resources, refused to provide sanctuary and instead forced the ships back to sea. Many died in the shark-infested waters as their small, unsafe boats disintegrated in the rough seas. Some estimated that by July 1979, nearly two hundred thousand "boat people" had already drowned.[37]

In the spring of 1979, with the American government either indifferent to or incapable of developing an effective response to this tragedy of global proportions, Assistant Secretary of State Richard Holbrooke turned to Mondale for help. "Short of the President, he was the only one who could pull the administration together," Holbrooke remembered.[38]

Over the next few months, Mondale worked behind the scenes to convince a reluctant State Department to condemn Vietnam's actions and to channel American resources into the area. "The Vietnamese were trying to sell the world on the theory that this was just poverty," he recalled years later. "I thought that was remarkable because they had been poor for five thousand years and never had boat people. It was doubly remarkable because the only people who were leaving were Chinese. It was a brutal, racist, vicious policy and had to be labeled as such." The State Department, however, took a strict legal position suggesting the United States had no right to tell Vietnam not to let the people go. "The issue here is not whether they are going to let them go," Mondale rejoined. "The issue is are they going to let them go in a safe and orderly manner or are they going to expel them." He turned to the Defense Department, suggesting the Sixth fleet be sent to rescue the boats at sea, but Defense officials objected to using the Navy for this kind of a rescue mission.[39]

After making little progress with either State or Defense, Mondale brought his case directly to the President. He argued that the boat people provided a test of the administration's commitment to human rights. "We cannot," he said, "lecture other nations on human rights and then refuse to save drowning women and children because it violates Navy procedure." Carter agreed and ordered the Sixth Fleet into the area to begin a massive boat lift.[40]

While pressing his own government to take a bolder position, Mondale helped organize a two-day international conference attended by representatives from sixty-five countries to focus world attention on the problem. The conference could not have chosen a more ironic setting for its meeting: Geneva's massive League of Nations Building, a mausoleum of failed hopes, it stood ominously as a monument to humanity's inability to prevent past tragedies. Heading the American delegation of 140 delegates, Mondale had less than forty-eight hours to solve a number of related issues. He could convince Malaysia to stop turning the refugees away only if he could provide assurances that other nations—Canada, Britain, France, and Australia—would provide permanent homes. "There can be no first asylum without final asylum," declared one Malaysian delegate. Finally, he needed to arouse world opinion against the Vietnamese and force them to abandon their cruel policy.[41]

Arriving in Geneva on July 19, Mondale spent the entire first day of the conference talking with delegations from all the relevant countries. Meeting privately with the representatives from the other delegations in the small conference rooms that honeycombed the ornate chamber, Mondale forcefully pleaded the American position. By the end of the day, his personal diplomacy began to reap benefits. The Philippine foreign minister announced that his country would open a temporary camp housing 50,000 new refugees. Representatives from other nations agreed to increase their quotas. Britain promised to accept 10,000, the French 5,000, and Canada 42,000. Even China pledged to resettle 10,000. Most significant of all, Malaysia declared a moratorium on pushing the refugees back into the sea. At the end of his first full day of negotiations, Mondale had already achieved more than anyone at the conference thought possible. As night fell, Mondale still had one important task to fulfill: arouse world opinion to condemn the vicious Vietnamese policy.[42]

The next day, in a moving speech which Vance called "one of the most significant acts of the Carter Administration," Mondale took aim against the Vietnamese. "Some tragedies defy the imagination," he said, "some misery so surpasses the grasp of reason that language itself breaks beneath the strain. Instead, we gasp for metaphors. Instead, we speak the inaudible dialect of the human heart." He compared their fate to that of the Jews forty years earlier, when the civilized world hid "in the cloak of legalisms." "Let us not re-enact their error," he pleaded. "Let us not be the heirs to their shame." Delegates dealing with such tragedy had little to cheer about that weekend. But Mondale's fiery speech brought them to their feet in the only sustained ovation of the conference. Forced on the defensive, Vietnam promised to stop unsanctioned departures of "boat people" for a "reasonable period."[43]

While playing a more active role in other areas, Mondale continued his involvement in the Middle East peace negotiations. Despite Egyptian leader Anwar Sadat's dramatic trip to Israel in November 1977, negotiations between the two nations remained stalled. Events conspired against a settlement. On March 11, Israel retaliated against a terrorist attack on an Israeli bus by launching a full-scale invasion of southern Lebanon. More than a thousand civilian lives were lost. An angry Carter ordered the United States to take the lead in the United Nations Security Council in condemning the invasion, demanding Israeli's withdrawal, and establishing a UN peacekeeping force. In May, the administration aggravated already strained Israeli relations when it pushed through the Senate the sale of sixty F-15 fighter planes to Saudi Arabia.[44]

It was under these difficult circumstances that Mondale proposed traveling to Israel. The ostensible purpose of the trip was to commemorate the thirtieth anniversary of Israeli statehood. The Washington *Post* commented that the journey promised "to be rich in symbolism but lacking in progress toward a settlement." But Mondale had different ideas. Along with discussing specific proposals designed to move the peace process forward, Mondale hoped to narrow the communications gap between Carter and Begin. Despite the President's sometimes provocative statements and his lack of sensitivity to Jewish opinion, Mondale had no doubts about Carter's genuine commitment to Israeli security. Somehow, he needed to convince Begin that he, too, should trust the President. While trying to bring Carter and Begin closer together, Mondale hoped to repair damage with the American Jewish community. As part of his effort, he asked the representatives of major Jewish groups to join him on his trip. "That was a very important symbolic statement," reflected Eizenstat. Making them a part of the administration's diplomatic team, Mondale believed, would indicate how deeply the administration valued Jewish opinion and provide him with the opportunity to plead Carter's case personally.[45]

To underscore the trip's significance, Prime Minister Begin and his entire Cabinet turned out to greet Mondale on his arrival at Ben-Gurion International Airport. "Your goodwill mission takes place at a time of anxiety and hope throughout the world," Begin said in his welcoming remarks. Mondale, though, remembered the reception line as "chilly." "Begin," he reflected, "gave a respectful yet cold speech welcoming me. Everywhere I was introduced I was lectured about how poorly things were between the two countries." Mondale, for his part, emphasized the "solid and unshakable commitment between Israel and the United States," and he used the forty-five minute ride to Jerusalem to "explain Carter" to the Israeli Prime Minister. "They could not understand each other," Mondale recalled. "I made a strong plea that he trust Carter. . . . I tried to interpret Carter to him," Mondale told Finlay Lewis. "I believe I made an impact on him because I think he was beginning to doubt us in our commitment to Israel."[46]

For his first public appearance Mondale chose a symbolic visit to the Wailing Wall. Because the United States had refused to recognize that section of Jerusalem captured during the 1967 war, the State Department insisted that Mondale could not visit the wall as an official American representative. But Jerusalem Mayor Teddy Kollek said he would boycott Mondale's visit if the Vice President refused an official escort. The politically savvy Mondale solved the problem by walking a legal tightrope: he would visit the wall as a private citizen and invited Mayor Kollek to serve as his official escort. The reasoning did not convince the State Department, but Mondale was more interested in sending a signal of concern to the Israelis than with pleasing legal experts at home.

The following day, in a speech at a state dinner in honor of the

Israeli Parliament, Mondale combined a strong reaffirmation of American support for Israel with a clear reminder of Israeli obligations to the peace process. The United States, he insisted, remained convinced that a peace agreement required Israel to withdraw from all Arab territories—the West Bank, the Golan Heights, and the Sinai-Gaza area—captured in the 1967 war. "We are convinced that without eventual withdrawal on all fronts, to boundaries agreed upon in negotiations and safeguarded by effective security arrangements, there can be no lasting peace," Mondale declared. While reassuring his hosts that "only Israel can be the final judge of its security needs," he insisted that "if there is to be peace, the implicit bargain of U.N. Resolution 242 must be fulfilled."[47]

Actually the speech went much further in pressuring Israel than Mondale had hoped. He had planned to make a general statement supporting the call for a negotiated solution without demanding that Israel withdraw from all the occupied territory. But as he boarded the plane carrying him to the Middle East, Carter sent a letter which insisted that his speech include a specific commitment from Israel to withdraw from all occupied land. Mondale was certain that Brzezinski had orchestrated the last-minute message to undermine his mission.

From Israel, Mondale flew to Egypt to meet with Sadat in the warm sunshine of the Egyptian leader's elegant beach house just east of Alexandria. As the two men strolled from the helicopters to a circle of wicker chairs, Sadat kidded Mondale about his grueling travel schedule, which would bring him back to Washington about 4 A.M. "You really should accept our hospitality and stay here tonight," Sadat said pointing toward his large mansion. "You know, under the martial law we have in this country, I could detain you." By the end of their brief meeting, Sadat had accepted Mondale's invitation to send his foreign minister to London—the first face-to-face political talks between Israel and Egypt in six months. "Let's hope this move will break the ice," Sadat said in a joint press conference with Mondale.[48]

The Vice President considered the trip a success, but not everyone shared his enthusiasm. Upon his return to Washington, he told Carter "there was substantially more flexibility privately from Begin and Sadat than anyone would ever suspect publicly." He was "especially convinced that Sadat was willing to go a long, long way to bring about a settlement." Yet Vance, who had opposed the trip all along, called it "unnecessary" and "not very helpful." In his memoirs,

Carter dismissed the effort, claiming Mondale had returned with "a very discouraging report" on his discussions with both Begin and Sadat. The President noted that both sides remained far apart on substantive issues, especially the future of the West Bank and the Gaza Strip.[49]

Vance and Carter had underestimated the impact of Mondale's trip. The Vice President's version of shuttle diplomacy did reap two rewards. First, he helped bridge the communication gap between Carter and Begin. The Israeli leader told a Mondale staff member that the Vice President's trip represented "a turning point for the better in previously strained U.S.-Israeli relations." Begin said "that he was deeply impressed by the Vice President's statement on the importance America attaches to good U.S.-Israeli relations made during their 45-minute ride from the airport to Jerusalem." The Jewish leaders who accompanied the Vice President also saw a noticeable change in Begin's attitude. "In Mondale, Begin saw someone who he knew had the best interests of Israel at heart," Eizenstat reflected. "I don't think he was ever sure [that] Carter did."[50]

Secondly, Mondale had helped to solidify Jewish support for the administration's position at home. Eizenstat noted at the time: "Mondale is a great and natural politician. Mondale really changes views of Jews on plane. Meets with them frequently. Meets them at end [of] tarp at bottom [of the] plane ramp and shakes hands." Many of the Jewish leaders found him a very reassuring presence during a difficult time in American–Israeli relations. Moved by the invitation to join his delegation, they concluded the trip more convinced of the Administration's sincerity. "To be there as an official member of the Vice President's delegation in the Jewish homeland, having him address the Knesset and giving expression to the American understanding of what Israel means to world Jewry was a moment unequaled in my public life," reflected Hyman Bookbinder.[51]

Believing that he had resurrected the stalled negotiations, Mondale wanted to make certain the State Department did not undo his efforts. In preparation for the Leeds Conference, Vance wrote a negotiating paper which according to Mondale contained "every buzz word" including a statement about "legitimate Palestinian rights." Mondale tried to get the version changed. "Vance out to blow every fuse," Eizenstat recorded Mondale as saying. The draft, the Vice President said, was the product of "Arabists in State Department." He complained to Carter about continued public statements on the Middle East that antagonized the Israelis. "We've got to get it off the public dialogue. If there's a public debate over this stuff, if we're exchanging papers that get into the press, we'll never get this thing settled."[52]

Realizing that it would be impossible to move the issue from the front pages, Mondale made another bold proposal: he suggested Carter appoint former Secretary of State Henry Kissinger as a special negotiator in the region. Mondale not only admired Kissinger's negotiating skills, but more important, he believed Kissinger would create bipartisan support for the Administration's policy and lessen the political fallout if there was failure. Appointing a special negotiator would also remove responsibility for Middle East policy from the State Department, which neither Mondale nor the Israelis trusted. The President seemed receptive to the idea, but Vance refused to relinquish responsibility to a third party. "I think it would have sent confusing signals if we had someone else negotiating," Vance reflected. "I felt the Middle East was something that the Secretary of State had to be involved in every day."[53]

With congressional elections just a few months away, Mondale cautioned Carter to proceed slowly with negotiations and to rebuild confidence with Jewish voters. Both Carter and Jordan disagreed, saying the only way the administration could win the confidence of Jews would be by achieving a settlement. The President suggested calling a summit in Washington to bring all three men together for face-to-face negotiations. Mondale forcefully opposed the idea. "I could see Carter getting those two leaders up there and the whole place blowing up," he later recalled. "I didn't feel like betting the whole government on something when we did not have the bird-in-hand at all." Fortunately, Carter decided "it would be best, win or lose, to go all out." In July, he rejected Mondale's cautious advice and invited Sadat and Begin to join him at Camp David later that fall.[54]

In September, as the three leaders assembled at the President's Maryland retreat, two basic problems needed to be addressed: the question of Israeli settlements on the Sinai and the resolution of claims to the West Bank and Gaza. The American position had been clearly stated—the solution had to be based on the principles of U.N. Resolution 242, stipulating Israeli withdrawal of occupied lands.[55]

According to the original plan, Mondale would not attend the summit but would instead serve as acting president in Carter's absence from the White House; but after just a few days of fruitless discussions, Carter asked Mondale to come to Camp David and help him in his dealings with Begin. Mondale recalled beseeching Begin to accept the conditions of the U.N. resolution by agreeing to withdraw from the Sinai. "Mr. Begin," Mondale pleaded, "this is not Judia and Samaria, this is not Jerusalem. We're on the brink of an historic breakthrough here. I know how painful this is but this is just land and buildings and brick. We can resettle these people. We should not let a couple of blocks of real estate stand in the way of this historic settlement."[56]

In the last three tense days, the participants finally reached a settlement. Although not the comprehensive solution Carter had originally wanted, the plan represented an important step. Despite Mondale's appeals, Begin made few concessions. While agreeing to a full withdrawal from the Sinai, he made no commitment to withdraw from the West Bank or Gaza and refused to address the sensitive Palestinian question in anything other than vague language. Perhaps realizing that both Carter and Sadat had invested too much in the process to allow the summit to end without reaching an agreement, Begin successfully extracted concessions by threatening to break off the talks at crucial moments. "For Begin," wrote William Quandt, "Sinai had been sacrificed, but Eretz Israel had been won."[57]

Mondale realized that the agreement left "unresolved ambiguities" that would continue to haunt the region. He was most concerned about Sadat, who had so bravely championed the cause of peace. He feared that Sadat had sacrificed too much and imperiled his situation at home. "When we left Camp David, I was certain Sadat was going to be killed and I was certain he knew it," Mondale recalled.[58]

Yet for all of its limitations, the Vice President believed the treaty marked a significant step toward peace in the region. It reconciled differences between ancient foes, provided for the security of Israel, and initiated a process for addressing other difficult issues. Mondale knew that he was witnessing a moment of great importance when, during the televised signing of the Accords, Begin and Sadat, the leaders of two historically hostile states, wrapped each other in a warm embrace. Sitting just a few feet away from the assembled heads-of-state in the East Room of the White House, Mondale nodded in vigorous assent as Carter, fatigued by thirteen days of intense negotiations, declared: "My hope is that the promise of this moment will be fulfilled." While recognizing that Carter's determination and skill had forged the final breakthrough, Mondale took great satisfaction in his own active role.

Unfortunately for the administration, the Camp David euphoria was short-lived. Mondale watched in dismay as a simmering public rift between Vance and Brzezinski over the appropriate American response to Soviet involvement in the Horn of Africa threatened to undermine the President's authority. The clash over Soviet activities in Africa reflected a more profound disagreement about the lessons of Vietnam. Brzezinski saw the Russians exploiting postwar American malaise by testing its will around the globe, probing for weak spots and moving actively to take strategic advantage. Treaties of friendship with Vietnam and Afghanistan; support for radical governments in Ethiopia and South Yemen; the sale of advanced MIG-23 fighter aircraft to Cuba—all were part of a larger Soviet plan to test American will in the aftermath of Vietnam. Where Brzezinski envisioned grand designs, Vance discerned local disputes. Rather than seeing the Soviets as a menace to global American interests, Vance observed a crumbling empire facing serious internal and external challenges.

Deep personal animosity exacerbated the tension between the two men. Brzezinski believed Vietnam had "traumatized" Vance by undermining his faith in American power and sapping him of the courage to confront Soviet aggression. "Cy would have been a great secretary of state in the 1880s when we did not have to deal with as many thugs in the world," Brzezinski reflected. He viewed Vance as an icon of a discredited WASP establishment. Whenever State Department spokesman Hodding Carter criticized him, Brzezinski assumed that Vance was orchestrating the attack. "Isn't that just like a WASP," he fumed at one point, "getting someone else to do his dirty work." Vance, in turn, looked upon Brzezinski as "a dyed-in-the-wool anti-communist," with a dangerous penchant for self-promotion who tried to impose a obsolete framework on complex international events.[59]

Instead of forcing reconciliation, Carter encouraged Brzezinski to continue speaking on behalf of the Administration. Never one to forego the opportunity for media exposure, Brzezinski made bold statements criticizing the Russians for violating the "code" of detente and calling the bloody fighting between Cambodia and Vietnam a "proxy war" between Russia and China. After months of politically costly delay, Carter moved to quiet public concern about his Soviet policy in a major address at the Naval Academy on June 7. Rather than easing public doubts, the speech raised more questions about who was making administration policy. The Washington *Post* commented that Carter gave "two speeches" that were "as dissimilar as the conflicting concepts of American–Soviet relations that embrace the opposing labels of Cold War vs. detente." In the end it was the President's stature that suffered. "The tussling is Jimmy Carter's fault," wrote Stephen Rosenfeld in the Washington *Post.* "He jumps around like a water spider on a June afternoon."[60]

The Brzezinski–Vance squabble and Carter's refusal to take charge of the situation frustrated Mondale, who repeatedly counseled the President to stifle the image-conscious Brzezinski. "[P]ress stories on rising tensions between the U.S. and USSR are getting out of hand," his breakfast notes for June 1 set down. "The time has come to calm the situation down publicly and put US–USSR relations back in their full and proper perspective." Realizing that Carter's speech had failed to calm the dispute, Mondale wanted the President to articulate a unified administration position on vital foreign policy issues. Privately, he complained that no one in the administration seemed to appreciate the grave political consequences that would result if the administration appeared unable to develop a unified strategy for dealing with the Soviets. The debate over the proper response to the Russian–Cuban intrusion in Africa, he feared, would revive old hawk–dove divisions among Democrats with neither side trusting Carter.[61]

Mondale believed Brzezinski deserved much of the blame for the problem. Their relationship, never warm, had turned decidedly colder during 1978. "Zbig tended to look at things from a strategic and foreign policy perspective leaving mostly to other people the question of the politics of getting things done," recalled NSC staff member Robert Hunter. "Mondale always thought in terms of the politics within which things happen." He respected Brzezinski's ability to discern broad historical patterns from seemingly unrelated events. But he believed most of his ideas were either impractical or dangerous. "He thought he wasn't tethered to the ground," recalled David Aaron. Moreover, Mondale believed that Brzezinski had overstepped his bounds—only the President and the Secretary of State could serve as the nation's foreign policy spokesmen. The NSC had to be a "loyal, quiet participant," he argued, "but not a public combatant." Most of all, Mondale felt that Brzezinski was insensitive to critical political considerations. "Politics is a bad word for Brzezinski," he said later. "The idea that a free people ought to have something to say about how they're represented and what they do around the world is considered a cheap idea. If you read the constitution you'll find that the founding fathers had a somewhat different point of view about the role of a free people." Brzezinski, Mondale concluded, "did not want to accept the additional discipline that was required to shape a policy that had public support."[62]

Brzezinski reciprocated the bad feeling. He complained that Mondale's penchant for oral briefings rather than intensive study created a "superficial grasp of affairs." He charged that Mondale lacked the vision and experience necessary to develop a dispassionate view of American interests and a strategy for protecting them. "In general, Carter rarely, if ever, thought of foreign policy in terms of domestic politics," he later wrote, "while Mondale rarely, if ever, thought of it otherwise."[63]

Mondale feared the internal bickering could doom the administration's chances of getting the Senate to ratify the SALT II treaty. After Moscow had rejected Carter's comprehensive proposal in March 1977, the two sides settled into the long and complicated process of finding common agreement. By 1978, despite progress on a number of important issues, the talks stalled on complex questions of weapons modernization, classification of the Soviet Backfire bomber, and development of American cruise missiles. At the same time, Russian military involvement in other parts of the world, especially Africa, led to a rising chorus of suggestions that the administration link the negotiations to broader changes in Soviet behavior.[64]

The administration appeared split on this crucial issue of linkage. Vance believed that Kremlin actions in Africa were not important enough to jeopardize the administration's top priority of passing a SALT II treaty. Brzezinski, however, wanted to use the promise of SALT as a constraint on Soviet actions. Like Vance, Mondale opposed efforts to link Russian behavior in Africa to an agreement on SALT II, but he also appreciated the political risks of appearing soft on the Russians—something, he complained, Vance never seemed to grasp. "In order for us to make the inevitable concessions in negotiations with the Soviet Union," he later explained, "we first had to be seen honestly by the American people, and by our allies as being tough."[65]

Mondale had been urging Carter to dispel public perceptions that the administration was "soft" on the Russians. If allowed to fester, that perception would erode confidence in SALT II and sap political support for other administration initiatives. In May 1978, hoping to set a stronger tone for the administration, Mondale delivered a tough anti-Soviet speech at the United Nations. In a broad review of U.S. arms control efforts, Mondale criticized Soviet activities in Africa and the Indian Ocean, accused Moscow of staging a "continuing buildup of unprecedented proportions in Europe," and attacked Soviet deployment of a mobile medium-ranged missile in Europe. Mondale believed that the speech served important strategic and political purposes. "We needed to make the point and keep making it because it was right, but secondly, the public had to know we were hardminded if they were going to give us the confidence to get [SALT II] done," he subsequently declared.[66]

In May 1979, after seven years of painstaking negotiations by three administrations, the United States and the Soviet Union reached agreement in principle on the SALT II treaty. In a breakfast meeting the following day, Carter made clear the importance he attached to the treaty. "I have only one life to live on this earth, as you have. I think the single most important achievement that could possibly take place for our nation during my lifetime is the ratification" of the treaty. The eighty-page, nineteen-article treaty went significantly beyond SALT I in setting both quantitative and qualitative limits on the superpower's nuclear arsenals. The agreement established ceilings on strategic launchers, reduced the existing levels of strategic weapons, constrained qualitative improvements in various weapons, and prescribed basic parity between the United States and the Soviet Union in numbers, but not the power, of strategic weapons.

Mondale knew that the debate over SALT II both in the Senate and in the nation would go far beyond the precise terms of the agreement and become a far-reaching discussion of the strategic balance and the Soviet threat. Soviet actions in the Third World, especially its involvement in the Horn of Africa, had contributed to a pervasive climate of mistrust which would influence attitudes toward SALT. Utah's Senator Jake Garn claimed the treaty was "so one-sided in favor of the Soviets" that it threatened the nation's security. In particular, conservatives charged, the treaty allowed the Russians to retain too many heavy, modern land-based ballistic missiles, failed to limit production of the Soviet Backfire bomber, and allowed the Soviets too many verification loopholes through which they could evade monitoring of their compliance with the agreement.[67]

Surveying the Senate, Mondale realized that a tough battle lay ahead. He estimated that approximately thirty conservatives would follow the lead of Washington Democrat Henry Jackson and not vote for SALT II under any circumstances. Oddly enough, the second greatest challenge came from liberals such as George McGovern who would vote against the treaty if the administration watered it down by giving in to hardliners. He believed this group had the support of about twenty Senators. Another slightly larger group led by Georgia Democrat Sam Nunn took just the opposite position. They would vote against the treaty unless defense expenditures were increased. Only about twenty-seven Senators would vote for the treaty under any circumstances. With thirty Senators opposed, the administration needed to win sixty-seven votes from the seventy Senators in the last three groups. Somehow they would need to keep the liberals opposed to increased defense expenditures in line while convincing more conservative Senators that the administration would substantially improve America's defense stature.[68]

Throughout the summer, Mondale worked as an integral part of the SALT task force designed to convince wavering Senators to support the agreement. While helping to plan administration strategy, Mondale met privately with individual Senators and established himself as their prime contact on SALT. The President hoped that the close friendships Mondale maintained in the Senate, and the reservoir of respect that still existed there for him, could win valuable votes. In some cases, the Vice President's congressional liaison believed that Mondale was the only person in the administration with the credibility to make a convincing case. Mondale was told with regard to Maryland's Paul Sarbanes: "You are probably the only one in the White House who can talk to him anymore." Similarly, he was informed about Oregon's liberal Republican Robert Packwood: "You are the one person in the Administration for whom he has the kind of respect that would cause him to listen to substantive arguments." The same kind of report came in on New York's eccentric Democrat Daniel Patrick Moynihan: "Your personal relationship and credibility with him could be crucial in keeping him from . . . making anti-Russian statements and otherwise gumming up the works."[69]

Mondale did not rely solely on his powers of personal persuasion to win over wavering Senators. In July, he embarked on an intensive SALT II roadshow, hoping to bring public pressure to bear on uncommitted Senators. The seven states he visited—California, Oregon, Kansas, Nebraska, South Dakota, Tennessee, and Pennsylvania—accounted for fourteen Senators uncommitted on SALT. His grueling schedule included seven major speeches to groups such as the World Affairs Council and the League of Women Voters, seven press conferences, four editorial conferences, twelve "exclusive" television interviews, a thirty-minute public affairs show on Portland television, and a public television excerpt of a meeting with reporters. "This is not based on trust," he told audiences. "This is based on our experience and our technical ability" to assure Soviet compliance. Speaking before packed audiences, Mondale argued that SALT should not be linked to other issues. "The stark reality is that neither of us can win an arms race in which there are no upper limits," he said in Portland. "It would be a futile search for temporary advantage. The more each side builds without restraint, the more each side is impoverished and the less secure each nation and the world become."[70]

Despite complaints from liberals, Carter believed he had to counter conservative criticism that the United States had allowed its nuclear forces to lag dangerously behind the Soviets. In June, he announced his decision to proceed with full-scale development of the MX missiles. Proponents argued that the MX would upgrade the land-leg of the nuclear triad by replacing the older and more vulnerable Minuteman ICBM's. Later that summer, again hoping to secure undecided conservatives, the President adopted an ambitious basing system for the new missile—an enormously complex mobile system, with two hundred missiles, each carrying ten nuclear warheads, deployed on circular roadways similar to racetracks. The two hundred racetracks and 4,600 launch sites would remove from public use 25 square miles of desert area in Utah and Nevada.[71]

Mondale rejected arguments that the United States lagged dangerously behind the Soviet Union and resisted Defense Department suggestions that the MX was crucial to American defense, but he understood the role that appearances played in both domestic and international diplomacy. Given Carter's opposition to the B-1 bomber and the neutron bomb, the administration needed to demonstrate its commitment to a stronger defense. He felt the administration could strengthen its nuclear capability and quiet critics by supporting cheaper and more effective submarine and air-launched missiles.

Though he supported the MX in principle, Mondale was stunned by the potential cost of the project and dismayed by the administration's poor handling of the politics of the decision. He had to fight for months to squeeze a few hundred million dollars out of the budget for education and now the administration planned to spend $33 billion on a new weapons system of limited value. Again, however, it was the lack of political planning that disturbed him most about the proposed massive tracking system. "Mr. President," he asked at an NSC meeting, "has anybody thought whether there is a chance of locating this system. What politician could say that I'm going to have a fifty mile race track down the center of his state and its going to be the target for all the bombs in the world." George Brown, a member of the Joint Chiefs of Staff and a strong proponent of the program, anticipated the question. "Yes," he retorted, "I have letters from governors who are willing to accept the system." Mondale realized that once environmental groups, public interest lawyers, and local citizen groups began making a political issue of using so much land for a massive weapons system, the governor would have a change of heart. "I guarantee you right now," he told Brown, "that when this program is announced, that governor will change his mind." For Mondale, it was another example of the administration's poor planning. "They came up with a plan that was a political impossibility and all we got was trouble," he reflected. "That was typical of the sort of thing that bothered me."[72]

Relations with the Soviets had also overshadowed administration debates concerning the normalization of relations with China. For most of 1978 Vance had urged caution, fearing precipitous action would threaten the Soviets and endanger the SALT negotiations. "Because of the Soviet's excessive fear of China," Vance told the President "any U.S. security cooperation with Peking would have serious repercussions on U.S.–Soviet relations." Brzezinski believed just the opposite: close American ties with China would scare the Russians into accommodation. He also resented the reverse linkage. He later reported his reasoning: "If we should make no linkage between SALT and Soviet misconduct—as Vance argued—then why should we let the Soviets link (negatively) SALT and better U.S.–Chinese relations?"[73]

Mondale recognized that normalization could precipitate a right-wing backlash, but he decided that appearing indecisive would be even more damaging. The administration needed a political victory, even at the cost of arousing the wrath of right-wing Republicans. Since most of the public would view normalization as a major diplomatic accomplishment, he believed it would blunt Republican charges of ineptness. Mondale had his own political future in mind as well, and he wanted to be identified with a foreign policy success that would bolster his foreign policy credentials. Along with the political and strategic considerations there existed a strong personal interest in China. Since his days as a boy when ministers from China would stay at his home in Elmore, Mondale had a fascination with the country.

Hoping to play a critical role in normalization, Mondale requested authorization to travel to China in the spring of 1978. "This is a mission that I personally want to undertake—it is of importance to your Asian policy and our new relations with the PRC, and it will also be of importance to me personally," his January lunch notes stated. But he was quickly outmaneuvered by Brzezinski, who managed to convince the President that he, not the Vice President, should make the trip. Relishing the opportunity to overshadow the Secretary of State, Brzezinski emphasized the two nations' shared antipathy toward the Soviet Union and suggested a broadening of the strategic relations between the two countries. His strong anti-Soviet statements raised Soviet anxieties and angered Vance but Brzezinski was now firmly in control of the administration's China policy. Upon his return, he moved quickly to resolve the remaining differences on the sensitive question of Taiwan, and push both countries toward signing an agreement. His efforts were rewarded in December 1978, when Carter signed an agreement to normalize relations with China beginning January 1, 1979.[74]

After signing the treaty, the question of how quickly to proceed toward normalization dominated discussion. Brzezinski continued to be bullish on the Chinese, but Vance, concerned about a Soviet backlash during sensitive SALT negotiations, continued to urge caution. He opposed giving the Chinese any benefits, especially the coveted "most-favored-nation" trading status, without providing the same to the Soviets. The internal bickering in the administration slowed the movement toward normalization, leaving the Chinese frustrated and somewhat bitter.[75]

Once again, Mondale asked the President if he could break the deadlock by making a high-profile trip to China. This time he made sure no one circumvented his efforts by skillfully presenting the trip in terms which both Vance and Brzezinski could approve. To Brzezinski he emphasized his support of a closer Sino-American relationship; to Vance he downplayed any strategic significance and presented himself as a counter-force to Brzezinski's preoccupation with beating up on the Russians.[76]

As he always did before an important foreign trip, Mondale established task forces to study and propose solutions on the major problems that would confront him. Setting up a small group which included David Aaron from the NSC and Richard Holbrooke from State, Mondale held regular meetings in the Roosevelt room in the White House. Most of the issues—export-import bank credit, hi-tech trade, telecommunications equipment, agreement on hydroelectric power—were not controversial but needed high level attention to get moving. With the President's authority, he forced the bureaucracy to respond to his requests. When OMB refused to support a proposal granting China a $2–3 billion credit line, Mondale convinced the President that OMB was being too cautious. When the Defense Department suggested it needed more time to study the termination of obsolete agreements with Taiwan, Mondale went to Harold Brown to complain about foot-dragging.[77]

The critical issue remained whether to grant China "most-favored-nation" status, making it eligible for cuts in tariffs to the same level as those applied to America's close trading partners. Vance remained the chief obstacle, but Mondale persuaded him that the initiative need not be presented as an anti-Soviet measure, as Brzezinski had suggested, but as part of developing closer cultural and economic relations with China. "It was a case of whether we would have a sterile, formal relationship or whether we could develop a broader, healthier relationship," the Vice President later explained. Convinced by Mondale's argument, Vance reluctantly agreed. "I will hold my nose and do it for you," he said.[78]

In August 1979, Mondale made his historic visit to China. Chinese Vice Premier Deng Xiaoping greeted the vice President, his wife, and daughter Eleanor at the Beijing airport for the start of the seven-day trip. Although he was the highest ranking U.S. official to have visited the Chinese capital since the opening of diplomatic relations, Mondale found the welcoming reception very proper. "There was no joy," he recalled. The Chinese had painted Beijing with signs announcing the arrival of another foreign dignitary, but made no mention that the American Vice President was in town. In a welcoming banquet in the Great Hall of the People, Deng reminded the Americans of their impatience: Relations would improve, he said, "so long as the two sides . . . deal with the concrete issues between China and the U.S. on a basis of equality and mutual benefit."[79]

The atmosphere changed dramatically the next day when in their private negotiation Mondale outlined the proposals he had personally shaken out of the bureaucracy: extension of up to $2 billion in credits, assistance in building a major hydroelectric plant, and most important, submission to Congress of legislation granting China most-favored-nation status. As he began listing the new initiatives, Mondale felt an easing of the tense and formal atmosphere in the room. "We started joking and having a good time," Mondale recalled. "It was like somebody threw a big switch," Chinese officials televised Mondale's speech at Beijing University—the first ever by a foreign leader. "No setting could be more symbolic of our relationship than this place of new beginnings," he told the audience. Mondale also took the obligatory swipe at the Soviets. "Despite the sometimes profound differences between our two systems, we are committed to joining with you to advance our many parallel strategic and bilateral interests. Thus any nation which seeks to weaken or isolate you in world affairs assumes a stance counter to American interests."[80]

The Chinese people responded warmly to his message. During a brief stay in the ancient Chinese capital of Xi'an, tens of thousands streamed into the streets in a outpouring of pro-American feeling. Reporters noted the contrast between the small, apathetic crowds that had greeted President Nixon and the hordes that swarmed around the Mondale motorcade. At one point, Mondale plunged into the crowd shaking hands and exchanging "ni hao" (hello), only to be rescued by attentive Secret Service Agents. "They almost walked over me," he recalled. On September 1, he opened the first U.S. consulate in China in thirty years, housed temporarily in a penthouse suite at a hotel in Canton.[81]

It was, by all accounts, an enormously productive trip that provided Carter with a coveted foreign policy triumph. "We were able to redefine the relationship," Mondale reflected. "American leaders had always gone to China and talked about the bear up north. They didn't like that too much because while they were concerned about the bear, they believed the importance lay not in our using them against the Soviet Union. They thought that diminished their importance. My trip established . . . that China was important in itself and that we hoped for better relationships." Mondale's effort at domestic diplomacy was even more successful. Despite their profound differences, both Vance and Brzezinski hailed the trip. Brzezinski termed it "a great success," while Vance called it "one of the most important and successful trips ever made by an American official to China."[82]

Mondale could point to a number of major foreign policy triumphs during Carter's first two-and-a-half years in office, but the administration found itself under siege from critics who complained about the general air of drift and uncertainty. Carter successfully pushed the Panama Canal Treaties through a reluctant Senate, negotiated a settlement in the Middle East, completed the negotiations for the SALT II treaty, and initiated an important strategic breakthrough with China. These victories did not, however, prevent Republicans from attempting to capitalize on Carter's foreign policy problems. Howard Baker, a potential Republican presidential candidate, predicted that foreign policy would be the leading issue in the campaign. "There's a growing view that America is an international patsy," he complained. Perennial conservative critic Ronald Reagan struck a similar note. "To the Communists and those others who are hostile to our country," he wrote in February 1979, "President Carter and his supporters in the Congress seem like Santa Claus. They have given the Panama Canal away, abandoned Taiwan to the Red Chinese, and they're negotiating a SALT II treaty that could very well make this nation NUMBER TWO." [83]

Memories of Vietnam haunted the Carter administration's attempts to construct a new framework for American foreign policy. With the party still divided over basic questions concerning America's role in the world, the proper use of force, and the nature of the superpower competition, Carter found it impossible to forge a consensus around a post-containment strategy. The President's naïveté and sometimes bumbling leadership compounded the problem. "His philosophy of repentance and reform was appropriate as criticism of past error," commented Gaddis Smith, "but it provided little guidance in dealing with new problems." Overwhelmed by strategic considerations, the administration's noble effort to balance power with morality created a haphazard and inconsistent policy. "Incoherence," observed Stanley Hoffmann, has "its roots deep in the Carter Administration's style of policymaking." While conservatives offered a comprehensible but simplistic view of the world that drew heavily on American national pride and past images of the Soviets, the administration never produced "a strategic rationale that brings the fragments together." [84]

Mondale believed the administration's inattention to the politics of national security left it vulnerable to demagogic appeals from the right. Many of the problems were beyond the administration's control: an aggressive Soviet leadership combined with a growing conservative movement at home would have created difficult problems for any administration. But many of the obstacles were self-imposed. The gap between the rhetoric and reality of the human rights policy, the public rift between Brzezinski and Vance, and the administration's inability to develop a consistent policy toward the Soviet Union all contributed to a public perception of weakness and ineptitude. "We looked like Christian pacifists," he recalled. He recognized that the Democratic party needed to develop a post-Vietnam foreign policy consensus that would be built around support for arms control, human rights, and moderate increases in defense spending. His experience in the Carter White House only confirmed his belief that an effective strategy for dealing with the Soviet Union and closer attention to the politics of foreign policy had to be at the heart of that new consensus.[85]

Despite the setbacks, these years marked an important evolution in Mondale's development as a national leader. He immersed himself in foreign policy issues, read diplomatic telegrams, attended NSC meetings, consulted with various experts, and made more than a dozen foreign trips. As a result he developed a more sophisticated view of complex international issues, learned how the bureaucracy worked, and received crucial diplomatic experience. Combined with his knowledge of the legislative process and his understanding of the political aspects of making foreign policy, Mondale emerged with a new confidence and skill in the art of international diplomacy. For now, however, painful domestic issues continued to occupy most of his attention.

12
Crisis

Despite Mondale's mediation, inflation was driving Carter and the liberals further apart. In January, the Labor Department reported that 1978 had ended with a 9 percent inflation rate, the third highest since 1945 and nearly three percentage points above administration predictions. The new figures only confirmed the President's desire to make inflation his number one domestic priority. He hoped to use his upcoming "State of the Union" Address to emphasize his renewed commitment to breaking the back of inflation. Searching for a phrase connecting him to the party's past, the President planned to announce a "New Foundation" for America. "We cannot afford to live beyond our means," a draft of the speech read, "to create programs we can neither manage or finance."

Mondale tried unsuccessfully to convince Carter to abandon the "new foundation" phrase and make the speech more optimistic. In a January 12 memo Mondale observed that the public was "still largely mystified" about the President's "personal work style and cast of mind," and complained that the new foundation theme did little to address these concerns. "Frankly," he wrote, "it is flat; there is no drive or life in it. It doesn't make people feel good about being Americans, and it fails to leave a sharp after-image in your listeners' minds." Mondale repeated his complaints a few days later at his lunch meeting with the President. He contended Carter paid too much attention "to the alleged sins of the past, and too many half-baked criticisms from the right are rehearsed." Mondale suggested the President "reaffirm the enduring values of the Democratic Party—compassion and pragmatism—that must guide us also in the future. You should reaffirm the strength and generosity of the American people and make them proud to be Americans." Rather than emphasizing what government cannot accomplish, Mondale suggested stressing "the historic role of government in getting people on their feet."[1]

Carter had a different idea. On January 22, a somber president lectured the nation about the need for fiscal restraint. In keeping with his theme, Carter submitted to Congress a "lean and austere" budget that reiterated his commitment to holding the deficit below $30 billion. It called for small cuts in many sensitive domestic programs: $600 million from Social Security, $400 million from school lunches, and $2.1 billion from social services. While clipping social programs, Carter announced a 3 percent increase in military spending. As he listened to the speech, Mondale thought about how dramatically the administration's priorities had shifted in just two years and how far it had moved from his original expectations. There were no initiatives to help the underprivileged; no attempts to make serious inroads against unemployment; no proposals for helping farmers, workers, or blacks. The administration that had come to office proposing a $50 tax rebate, suggesting revisions in the nation's welfare program, and providing a large program of public works, now declared inflation "our most serious domestic problem," withdrew the rebate plan, and scrapped designs for welfare.[2]

As Mondale expected, his old liberal friends exploded with rage. "I'm not going to allow people to go to bed hungry for an austerity program," thundered Tip O'Neill. "Human needs and national priorities have been sacrificed to political expediency," the Americans for Democratic Action, Mondale's former employer, cried. The liberal reaction frustrated Carter. Liberals simply did not appreciate, he complained, that modest reductions were necessary to prevent conservatives from using a sluggish economy as an excuse for exacting deeper cuts later. Mondale understood the President's need to demonstrate concern for inflation, but insisted that cuts in sensitive programs, no matter how modest, would only alienate potential allies without winning new friends.[3]

Compounding Carter's conundrum, a new crisis threatened to aggravate an already debilitating inflation. In late 1978, strikes and the departure of foreign technicians caused Iran's oil production to fall sharply. On December 27 exports ceased. The cutoff of Iranian oil presented the administration with a difficult policy choice. Should it enforce conservation by allowing domestic oil prices to rise to world levels, thus increasing inflationary pressures while also providing American oil companies with record profits? Or should it artificially hold the line, keeping the inflationary impact to a minimum but threatening continued dependence on uncertain Persian Gulf exports?

At first, the President called for voluntary energy conservation, but events in Iran, which encouraged other OPEC nations to increase dramatically their oil prices on the world market, forced the administration to act. Schultze, Energy Secretary James Schlesinger, and Treasury Secretary Blumenthal argued that immediate elimination of price controls offered the President "an opportunity to take complete charge of a major problem, which has been locked in political stalemate for eight years, and to resolve it in the national interest with a single, bold strike." Mondale, Eizenstat, McIntyre, and Fred Kahn, newly appointed Chairman of the Council of Wage and Price Stability, opposed the proposal because of its inflationary impact. They suggested a gradual decontrol of prices. Mondale was also concerned about the political consequences of a rapid rise in oil prices. With public confidence in the inflation program sagging, the President could not capitulate to the big oil companies. Mondale argued that between January and April of 1980, they would be running in primaries in oil-dependent states such as New Hampshire, Connecticut, Massachusetts, Vermont, Illinois, New York, Wisconsin, and Pennsylvania. "[W]e will not be seen as strong if we give in to all of the demands of the industry," he told Eizenstat.[4]

Carter sided with Mondale. In April, he presented Congress with a plan for gasoline rationing, and on national television he announced he would only gradually allow the price of domestic oil to rise to international levels. Furthermore, he proposed a windfall profits tax on the "huge and undeserved" profits that domestic oil companies would reap from decontrol. Despite his strong public appeal, Congress balked at the President's plan for emergency gasoline rationing. On May 10, the House crippled the President's energy program when it sent standby gasoline rationing to a humiliating defeat.

By far the most serious blows came from month after month of double-digit inflation. In the first three months of 1979 wholesale prices increased at an annual rate of 14.1 percent, while the GNP grew by only .4 percent. Polls showed overwhelming disapproval of Carter's handling of the economy. Mondale found himself forced on the defensive at Party events as loyal Democrats publicly questioned the President's leadership ability. On March 2, at a fund-raiser in Beverly Hills, disgruntled Democrats peppered the Vice President with questions about Carter's competence. Publicly, Mondale made light of the criticism, but privately he was deeply disturbed. He had not experienced such animosity since the 1968 campaign when anti-war activists had questioned Humphrey's commitment to peace in Vietnam. "You could feel public support evaporating," Mondale recalled. On the same day, a group calling themselves "Democrats for Change" purchased a full-page advertisement in the Los Angeles *Times,* which declared Senator Edward Kennedy "the leading choice among Democrats everywhere." If that were not enough, NAACP director Benjamin Hooks threatened that many blacks would vote against Carter in the Democratic primaries if he did not increase social spending for the poor.[5]

The spring of 1979 brought daily reminders of the painful economic choices Mondale confronted. The administration needed to curtail rising prices, but an aggressive inflation policy threatened to stifle economic growth and incite a recession. In April, the Commerce Department contributed to recession fears by recording a 3.3 percent drop in the index of leading economic indicators. Private economists predicted unemployment could rise to as high as 8 percent by year's end. The administration walked a political tightrope between inflation and recession. For now, the President's economic advisors believed inflation demanded their attention. Schultze recommended decreasing consumer spending by increased monetary restraint and selective controls over consumer credit. Mondale, however, did not want to deviate sharply from the current economic program. The alternatives, he charged, were not acceptable. Economic controls were impossible to enforce and would never pass Congress, while inciting a recession with monetary restraint violated every tenet of his political philosophy. Mondale recognized "boomy signs" in the economy, but suggested other signs indicated production and retail sales were beginning to slow down, thus making further action unnecessary. He wanted to weather the storm by controlling energy costs and publicizing violations of wage and price guidelines.[6]

With the administration in virtual paralysis, the specter of Ted Kennedy loomed large in Washington political circles. Kennedy for President groups were forming in key primary states, and in every poll Kennedy rated as the overwhelming favorite among Democrats, usually topping the President by two or three to one. Pat Caddell's private polls showed the Massachusetts Senator leading Carter among every ideological group—liberals, moderates, and conservatives. Even Democrats who expressed a favorable opinion of Carter gave their votes to Kennedy. In the polls, Carter lost every region of the country to the senator, even his native South.[7]

Emboldened by the poll results and dismayed by the administration's conservative course, Kennedy sharpened his policy differences with the President. In May, casting himself as the keeper of the party's flickering liberal flame, Kennedy proposed a sweeping $100 billion "womb-to-tomb" health insurance plan which would expand Federal health benefits for the needy and mandate private insurance for everyone else, regardless of age or income. Kennedy grabbed the limelight for his plan just weeks before Carter unveiled the administration's less comprehensive health care reforms. The Senator's actions infuriated Mondale who viewed his plan as fiscally irresponsible and politically impractical. Angry that his former colleague would stubbornly reject the administration's reforms in favor of his own quixotic plan, he also had no doubt of what motivated him. He expected Kennedy to use Carter's anticipated opposition to his grandiose proposal to justify his own candidacy.[8]

More immediately vexing to the President's political fortunes than the health insurance dispute was the gasoline shortage that plagued American consumers in early 1979. By May, gasoline lines in California ran as long as five hundred cars, and prices at the pump climbed above a dollar a gallon for the first time. "It's sort of like sex," explained one oil official. "Everybody's going to get all the gasoline they need, but they're damn sure not going to get all they want." In June, OPEC announced a 50 percent increase in oil prices. When New York's congressional delegation met with Mondale about the energy shortage, Mayor Ed Koch said, "I haven't seen a delegation this hot since the Vietnam War."[9]

Mondale's delicate balancing act was clearly failing. The President rejected much of his advice and the constituency groups appeared more interested in Kennedy's self-assured idealism than Mondale's melancholy message of restraint. These were difficult days for the Vice President. As early as January, he had suggested to his staff "a new relaxation theory," which involved withdrawing from key policy-making roles in the White House, making fewer public appearances on behalf of the administration, and scheduling more vacation time away from Washington. "There was a certain amount of fatalism in the idea," Mondale remembered. "I thought there was not much I could do to change things so why break my health trying." Friends noted that somber reflection and a downcast demeanor replaced Mondale's usual buoyant optimism and cheerful disposition. He spent less time in the office, frequently leaving the White House early in the afternoon for long tennis matches with Jim Johnson at the Vice President's mansion. Staff members found him detached and impassive. Eizenstat, after a long lunch with Mondale in June, described him as "very despondent," and "really heartbroken."[10]

Mondale's mood reflected his sense of futility within the administration. He experienced, in all its painful dimensions, the classic dilemma of a Vice President: How could he publicly defend policies that he vigorously opposed in private while still maintaining his own identity as an independent leader? Chief of staff Dick Moe argued that the Vice President had been so successful a team player the public no longer perceived him "to be on the cutting edge of any major issue." Mondale recognized the problem existed, but could think of no solution. A vice president could not assert his independence without alienating the president and forfeiting his influence within the administration. But there was a cost to be paid. Being forced to defend policies that ran counter to his public record blurred the public's perception of Mondale's philosophy. A Caddell poll in May 1979 showed nearly a quarter of all Americans did not know enough about Mondale to rate his job performance. Of those who felt they could comment, most found him honest, clean-cut, and sincere but very few could identify where he stood on substantive issues.[11]

Mondale's staff was also dissatisfied with the administration's direction and Mondale's role. Al Eisele, the Vice President's press secretary, noted after reading all of the staff year-end evaluations for 1978, "the only common denominator that emerges is the feeling that neither the Vice President nor any of us is very happy with the role he is now playing in this administration." Moe observed that Mondale was not "carving out a place as the progressive conscience of this administration"; Johnson saw "a basic divergence of basic political assumptions between WFM and the Carter White House"; Domestic Policy Advisor Gail Harrison worried that Mondale was having little impact in the development of administration policy; Congressional liaison William Smith believed Mondale had been ineffective in helping Carter to define a clear "political philosophy and overcome his image of ineptness and incompetence." Eisele concluded that "the 'most active and influential Vice President' story was getting old, that WFM's progressive image is being eroded and that he needs a more aggressive press strategy to avoid being eclipsed on the national—and Minnesota—scene." [12]

By the late spring of 1979, many of Mondale's early aspirations for the administration had disappeared. Mondale had hoped that by joining the ticket he could help ease the North-South tensions that had divided the party for over a century. That hope had faded. Now he concluded that the two geographical regions of the party were no longer separated by questions of racial equality but by subtle differences of political style and philosophy. Mondale realized Carter and his Georgia advisors represented a different political tradition from his, and it would take more than friendship and hard work to bridge the gap between them. But Carter was only part of the problem. Fiscal restraint and political realities prevented Mondale from focusing executive power on those issues—unemployment, civil rights, education, poverty—to which he had devoted his political life.

Mondale also worried about his own future. He knew he would be held responsible for the administration's record. He feared that rather than serving as a stepping stone to the presidency, the vice presidency would be the final resting ground of his public career. "Mondale could see his own political future going down the tubes without the capacity to do much about it because he was not the president," recalled Eizenstat. [13]

For weeks in the late spring Mondale agonized over his predicament. Despite all of his differences with the administration, he had established a close friendship and a strong bond of loyalty with the President. He was a deeply troubled man. Trapped between devotion to the President and commitment to liberal values, he searched for a way out. Mondale's conflict with Carter transcended policy matters. He, like many Washington insiders, believed the President and many of his advisors were politically inept, incapable of understanding the inner workings of Congress, and unable to project a clear and compelling image to the public. It would be impossible for a vice president to announce such strong disagreement and still retain the president's confidence. Circumstances compelled him to choose: loyalty to the president or political independence?

Reluctantly, Mondale began to think that only by resigning could he shock the administration out of its complacency and salvage his own political future. In long, agonizing sessions with his top staff people, Mondale discussed three options: resigning immediately, refusing to run on the ticket with Carter in 1980, or running and winning reelection and then resigning before the beginning of a new term. Mondale spent most of a warm spring afternoon sitting on the lawn of the vice presidential mansion listing the advantages and disadvantages of leaving office. An immediate resignation appeared the least attractive option. Resignation would only add fuel to persistent rumors he lacked the stomach for tough situations and probably destroy the President's chances of reelection in 1980. Removing himself from the ticket after the 1980 campaign would force him to campaign on the administration's record—something he hoped to avoid.

For Mondale the most attractive way out of his dilemma was to announce at the Democratic Convention that for personal reasons he would not seek nomination as Carter's running mate. By withdrawing at the convention Mondale could have the best of both worlds. By citing personal reasons, he could separate himself from Carter without appearing to insult the President and, at the same time, he would eliminate the need to campaign on the administration's record.

Ironically, Mondale, who helped pioneer a more influential and effective vice presidency, could not escape its curse. Other vice presidents had faced similar frustrations. Lyndon Johnson had faithfully performed his tasks but felt powerless as Kennedy's legislative team bungled one piece of legislation after another. Franklin Roosevelt's first vice president, John Nance Garner, was so disillusioned with the later New Deal program, that he placed his own name in nomination at the 1940 Democratic Convention. Only one vice president, however, had actually resigned from office because of disagreement with the president. In 1832, John C. Calhoun differed with President Andrew Jackson on the burning issue of states rights. Believing the individual state, as a "sovereign body," superseded the authority of the national government, Calhoun opposed Jackson's attempt to enforce the tariff. Shortly after his native South Carolina declared the federal tariff acts to be void and not "binding upon this State or its citizens," Calhoun resigned.

Unlike Calhoun, Mondale did not have a nullification crisis to justify his resignation. On May 27, realizing he needed to sort through his doubts and make a decision, Mondale left Washington for an unscheduled vacation. After a brief stop to deliver a commencement address at the University of Wisconsin, the Vice President returned to Minnesota where, as he had many times before, he sought refuge in the quiet splendor of the state's northern lakes. It was the most difficult hour of his career. He realized how much he longed for the political independence he had once exercised in the Senate and how much he relished older battles against conservatives foes of civil rights and poverty programs. At moments he regretted ever having agreed to become vice president. His hopes focused now on the presidency but it appeared that his years in the White House would make that dream impossible. Isolated deep in the Minnesota woods he used his special communications gear to seek the counsel of close friends. He spoke often with Joan, who had watched helplessly as her husband's spirits plunged over the previous months and who feared for the future. "I'll be better if you quit," she told him on Tuesday, May 29.[14]

No matter how much he lamented his predicament, he could not bring himself to resign. In part his decision grew from instinctive caution, a fear of dramatic initiatives whose consequences he could not carefully gauge. In part, it grew from his intense sense of loyalty, especially to those who had helped advance his career. Twenty years earlier he had kept silent despite his strong reservations about the war out of fear of embarrassing Humphrey. Today, Mondale remained silent, despite his disagreements with Carter, for fear of undermining the administration. Finally, his faith that he could help turn things around and play an even more dominant role in the administration led him to remain in office.

On Sunday, June 2, he returned to Washington with renewed enthusiasm. He called Moe, Berman, and Johnson together for an early breakfast meeting the following day. "I am ready to begin again," he announced, pulling from his briefcase a legal pad full of ideas and projects he wanted them to begin working on.

When he returned, Mondale found another potential confrontation with Griffin Bell awaiting him. This time the question was whether the government could continue to use the Comprehensive Employment and Training Act (CETA) to aid disadvantaged persons in sectarian schools. For years, the government had channeled CETA funds to religious schools that worked with the disadvantaged. Now, the Justice Department ruled that funding teaching or counseling positions was "precluded under recent decisions of the Supreme Court." The decision raised tempers in Congress, especially from Representatives with large Catholic constituencies in New York and Chicago.

Bell's decision infuriated the Vice President. Over the objections of his own staff, Mondale intervened, telling the President the ruling would extract a high political cost. At his June 19 lunch meeting, he warned that Bell's decision would lead "to deep and permanent problems with key leadership of Catholics, Jews, and other religious groups who will not understand our failure to at least try to defend them in court." Carter agreed and once again overruled his sensitive Attorney General. In a blustery five-page letter, Bell reminded the President he had been directed "to establish an independent Department of Justice, a neutral zone in the government where decisions will be made on the merits free of political interference or influence."[15]

Mondale feared the internal squabbling with Bell would distract Carter's attention from the problem that demanded immediate action—the energy crisis. Instead of accepting Mondale's advice and assuming a highly visible profile on the energy problem, Carter traveled to Europe to sign a strategic arms treaty with the Russians. From there he went to Asia, for a summit meeting with Asian and European leaders. While he was away, his political support unraveled further. Over the Fourth of July weekend, 90 percent of all gas stations in the New York City area were closed; 80 percent in Pennsylvania; 50 percent in Rhode Island. Mondale found the White House overcome with despair. He feared Carter's inability to handle the energy crisis would deny him the party's nomination. While Carter toasted the success of his SALT treaty in Europe, a domestic crisis gripped the country. Believing the President needed to take decisive action, Mondale joined Eizenstat in pleading with him to skip his planned Hawaii vacation and return directly to Washington.[16]

When Carter accepted the advice and returned to Washington on July 1, Mondale suggested the President establish a visible schedule showing he was trying to solve the energy problem. "The overall image should be of you working with your advisors to make progress in these areas," he and Jordan wrote. But Carter had a different idea.

In a series of lengthy memoranda over the previous months, Patrick Caddell, the President's brilliant but eccentric pollster, had convinced Carter that the energy crisis was symptomatic of a deeper malady pervading American society. "America is a nation deep in crisis," he charged. "Psychological more than material, it is a crisis of confidence marked by a dwindling faith in the future." Assassination, the Vietnam War, Watergate, and now inflation, undermined traditional American hope in the future. "Fundamentally, Americans believed themselves exempt from the processes of history," Caddell wrote. "Sadly, events ended that myth." Caddell's solution required a new type of leadership. Adopting James MacGregor Burns's distinction between transactional and transforming leadership, Caddell argued that the time was ripe for Carter to "become the relevant, thriving center of national revival, a popular leader [of] enormous personal consequence for every America[n]."[17]

Mondale forcefully opposed Caddell's analysis, claiming that it "sounds too much like an old scold and a grouch." He suggested that instead "of scolding the public we should play to their better instincts." Americans had faced crises before and solved them and we could do it again by applying concrete solutions to real problems, he maintained. "In my judgment Americans will respond well over the short term if we give them a reason for hope over the long term. We can be candid and honest but we should be affirmative." Unpersuaded by Mondale's advice, the President cancelled his previously announced speech and decided to remain at the mountain retreat until he found an acceptable alternative.[18]

On July 5, Mondale flew to Camp David to meet with the President and his key staff members—Powell, Rafshoon, Caddell and Eizenstat. Caddell handed around a polling survey and a new memorandum which repeated his central theme: America was afflicted by self-doubt, its people no longer had the old patriotic spirit, they were too self-centered. Carter spoke next, expressing support for Caddell's ideas. "We're irrelevant and people don't listen to us," he said. There was a "sense of despair in [the] country" that would "not be helped by passing programs." He refused to give another speech that simply announced more of the same old programs. He wanted to address the deeper spiritual concerns of the American public. Media advisor Rafshoon agreed. "You've become part of the Washington system," he observed. "You were elected to kick ass and haven't."[19]

At that point Mondale was angry both with Carter's advisors for suggesting what he believed to be stupid ideas and especially with the President for seriously considering them. He thought about getting up and walking out in protest, but decided instead to stay and fight. "We said we needed a government as good as her people, now we discovered we need a people as good as their government," Mondale reflected nearly a decade later. "Everything in me told me that this was wrong. I was morose about it because I thought it would destroy Carter and me with him."

Realizing the President had just rushed home after a grueling summit, Mondale suggested that fatigue was affecting his thought. America's problem, he said, did not result from a psychological disorder that required analysis; it stemmed from economic grievances which cried out for solution. Caddell's social psychology nonsense was a "dry hole." The American people, he charged, were looking for leadership, not sermons based on questionable social theories. The President needed to demonstrate his leadership by getting tough with his staff and cabinet, and by spending more time on domestic affairs. He suggested the President make a series of trips in this country to Democratic forums such as the mayors' conference and the NAACP. Rather than hiding away on a mountain top, the President needed to propose specific solutions, galvanize public support, energize the party, and through his demonstration of leadership give people hope. To Carter's advisors who were captivated by the idea of "kicking ass in Washington," Mondale pointed out that they were Washington now. They had become the insiders, Mondale reminded them, and it was time they learned to use the system to their own advantage.[20]

Carter remained firm, convinced the people had "given up on us and turned us off." The "country [was] not bad off materially," he said, the problem was with its "spiritual and moral values." Specific programs that might arouse the Democratic constituencies were not as important to him as they were to Mondale. Another energy speech, he anticipated, "would be ignored or picked apart just like the others." Carter felt he needed "drama and mystery" to grab the public's attention.[21]

It was unusual for Mondale to persist in criticism of a proposed policy. His usual approach was to state his position clearly and forcefully and then trust the President to make the right choice. This situation was different. "I say that Pat's speech is too negative against the American people," the Vice President declared, his voice quivering with anger. "You can't castigate the American people or they will turn you off once and for all."[22]

Carter worried that Mondale's uncharacteristic emotional display revealed a deeper discontent with the President's leadership. Perhaps for the first time Carter sensed the depth of Mondale's disenchantment. He stopped the meeting and invited Mondale to walk with him around the Camp David perimeter. For the next thirty minutes the two men engaged in a frank exchange. Mondale warned Carter that giving a speech based on Caddell's mistaken ideas would be political suicide. Carter held firm and told Mondale he was considering a Cabinet shakeup—a step Mondale had long advocated—that would include dismissing the Vice President's close friend, Joe Califano. Mondale protested, claiming that firing a respected liberal figure would send the wrong signal to the group whose support they most needed. The meeting ended with Carter promising not to fire Califano without first consulting Mondale, who was scheduled to leave on an extended trip.[23]

In seeking the Vice President's counsel at a critical juncture, Carter demonstrated that even during difficult times he was capable of magnanimous acts. "When I think back, it is extraordinary the length Carter went to try and handle me with dignity. I will never forget his generosity," the Vice President reflected. That bond of friendship, however, could not overcome their profound disagreement on this issue. Although touched by the President's personal concern, Mondale still refused to support Caddell's ideas. If the President went ahead as planned with the speech, Mondale felt he had no choice but to resign. "You have to go out and sell the President's program because you are the President's spokesman," Mondale recalled. "Most of the time I could sell the program with enthusiasm. This was too much for me. I could not carry that load."[24]

Over the next eight days almost 150 people—old Washington experts, mayors, members of the House and Senate, governors, labor leaders, economists, businessmen, ministers, and county officials—were flown up to the mountain. Mondale and Eizenstat labored behind the scenes trying to develop an energy program and convince the President to incorporate it into his speech. The Vice President sent Carter a memorandum at Camp David pleading with him not to address the American people as "sinners in the hands of an angry God." On Friday, Mondale checked in again, with Eizenstat's support, insisting the President propose specific programs to address the energy crunch. Mondale wanted Carter to make his energy speech more positive and place less emphasis on restraint by the American people. He urged: "Put energy up front. Put windfall up front. Gives us a bold way out." He suggested the President make parallels to the Manhattan project by emphasizing America's massive resources, talented workforce and commitment to success.[25]

On Sunday evening, July 15, the President gave his much awaited speech. After an anecdotal beginning that discussed some of the advice he had received over the past few days, Carter described the "crisis of confidence" that "strikes at the very heart and soul and spirit of our national will." The changes, he declared, resulted from the assassinations of prominent leaders, the Vietnam War, and Watergate. The nation had two possible paths: the path of selfishness which "would be one of constant conflict between narrow interests ending in chaos and immobility," and the path of "common purpose and a restoration of American values," which would lead to real freedom. Much of this opening suggested that he was ignoring Mondale and reciting from the Caddell memo. But the next two-thirds of the speech showed he had been listening to Mondale. He outlined a bold new program to free the country from its "intolerable dependence" on OPEC oil. "Beginning this moment, this nation will never use more foreign oil than it did in 1977," he declared clenching his fist for added emphasis. The program contained an ambitious conservation effort, including gasoline-rationing and quotas on foreign imports. As Mondale had suggested, the President closed with a ringing Churchillian call: "Let us commit ourselves together to a rebirth of the American spirit. Working together with our common faith, we cannot fail."[26]

In a blizzard of speeches and briefings Carter won popular and political support for his program. Senator Daniel Patrick Moynihan of New York said: "The President's program is do-able and should be done." Tip O'Neill called the speech "one of the strongest and best he has made." On Monday, in tub-thumping speeches to county officials in Kansas City and communication workers in Detroit, Carter drew the loudest and longest cheers he had heard in months. His approval rating spurted eleven points in a New York *Times*-CBS poll to 37 percent—the first upturn since a survey the previous March. Mondale, who had left Washington for a five-day trip preaching the merits of SALT II, found "ebullience" outside the capital. "The speech itself was upbeat and the response was upbeat," he said.[27]

The joy was short-lived. Just before leaving Nashville, Mondale received a call from Jordan informing him the President had fired a number of Cabinet members, including Califano, Treasury Secretary Blumenthal, and Transportation Secretary Brock Adams. He had also accepted the resignations of Attorney General Griffin Bell and Energy Secretary James Schlesinger. When Mondale's plane landed in Philadelphia, he found fifty reporters screaming at him. "They were angry and scared," he recalled. "They thought that the government was falling apart." Later that night, Mondale flew to Geneva. "I was never happier to get out of the country. It went from sugar to shit right there."[28]

Mondale had always insisted the President take control of his Cabinet. He had, on occasion, recommended firing incompetent staff and Cabinet members. During their walk around Camp David, the President had informed Mondale he planned a Cabinet shakeup. Though not specific about who would stay and who would leave, Carter did promise not to fire Califano without first consulting the Vice President. In Mondale's absence, however, the President's close advisors argued that only by asking for all Cabinet resignations, including Califano's, would he convince the public he was serious about taking control of the government. Rafshoon said it would be "a clear signal that you mean to get tough and do business differently." Besides, he argued, "You'll feel good after you do it."[29]

Mondale called Eizenstat at home late on Sunday evening, July 21. Eizenstat described him as "very distressed about firings." Mondale said Carter had finally helped himself with the speech and then lost it all with the firings. He complained that Carter had promised to discuss Califano's situation with him after he returned from his SALT trip, "but [the] decision was made to fire Joe without consulting him," Eizenstat recorded. The Vice President said he "seriously questions [Carter's] judgment." Again he recalled his hope that his presence on the ticket would help heal the North-South split that had long afflicted the party. "Now," Eizenstat noted, "he's not so sure." Many of the President's Georgia advisors, Mondale complained, were "not plugged into America and its institutions," and some were "haters," intent on perpetuating the geographic divisions within the party.[30]

Within a week of the Cabinet purge, Carter's popularity dropped even lower then it had been before his heralded speech: one poll showed him down three points in only seven days, and three weeks later Lou Harris reported Carter's overall rating had dropped to 74–25 percent negative, the lowest for any president in modern times, lower even than Nixon's ratings on the day he resigned from office in disgrace. As Mondale predicted, many liberals took strong exception to Califano's firing. Kennedy noted "the extraordinary irony that in a time of energy and economic crisis, the resignation of Secretary Califano was the first to be accepted." Missouri's Senator Thomas Eagleton praised Califano as "far and away the best Secretary of H.E.W. in my experience."[31]

Mondale, in Philadelphia addressing the World Affairs Council, released a terse statement saying the staff changes Carter made would "strengthen our government." But Mondale's geographic distance from the White House and his unconvincing support of the firings did not escape the purview of a skeptical press. Martin Schram of the Washington *Post* asked why, "[d]uring the most important week in Carter's presidency," Mondale "was out on the circuit," far away from the White House and the immediate fallout. Raising once again the question of Mondale's "toughness," Schram speculated that a more outspoken vice president could have prevented the Cabinet debacle.[32]

Mondale could hardly be accused of being unassertive in this situation. His forceful dissent threatened to split the White House wide open. The Vice President and many of his advisors were disgruntled by the convoluted process that produced the July energy speech and viewed the firings as another example of the Carter people's political naïveté. Many of the President's advisors, on the other hand, resented Mondale's opposition during the entire Camp David meetings. Some began leaking critical stories about Mondale to the press. "Mondale is a clown," one anonymous Carter aide told *Time*. "He has difficulty comprehending the significance of important issues. He is certainly not presidential material." Reports even appeared that Carter was searching for a new vice presidential candidate to run with him in 1980.[33]

Mondale complained directly to the President about his staff's covert attacks. The President sternly warned his aides about public criticism of the Vice President and repeated his threat to fire anyone caught making disparaging statements. Again, the President intervened at a critical moment to maintain the new institutional relationship he had established with his vice president.

As the heat of summer yielded to the cool breeze of fall, sounds of discord filled the air. Democratic political leaders feared a Carter-Mondale ticket would meet with certain defeat in 1980. Many began searching for a candidate to oppose the President in the upcoming Democratic primary. They did not have to search for long.

13
Challenge and Defeat

For twenty years he cast a shadow over Democratic Party politics. As the last scion of America's most powerful political dynasty since the Adams family, he had assumed legendary proportions. People listened to his words but heard the voices of his slain brothers. By the fall of 1979, Ted Kennedy was faced with a decision that had plagued him every four years since the death of his brother Robert: whether to run for the presidency. Publicly, Kennedy declared he expected Carter to win the nomination and insisted he would support him. Privately, he thought of challenging the President in the upcoming Democratic primaries. National polls showed the Senator leading the President by a 3–1 margin. The polls did not reveal Kennedy's considerable liabilities. Questions persisted about his involvement in a 1969 driving accident at Chappaquiddick bridge in which a young woman lost her life. Kennedy's estrangement from his wife, who maintained a separate Boston residence while receiving treatment for alcoholism, compounded questions about his character and personal style. More important, rising inflation and declining productivity raised doubts about the wisdom of his commitment to traditional liberal economic theories.

There was certainly no love lost between Kennedy and Carter. Kennedy's scorn for Carter as a national leader, wrote Theodore White, was "the contempt of a master machinist for a plumber's helper." Carter and his Georgia advisors, on the other hand, did little to hide their disdain for Kennedy who they believed epitomized the arrogance of an old discredited liberal elite. They viewed the youngest Kennedy as a man of considerable style but little substance who could never fulfill the public expectations raised by his brothers. Carter was confident that the intense glare of a national political campaign would expose Kennedy for the charlatan that he was and perhaps end his mythical hold on the public imagination. In June, Carter told a congressional delegation that if Kennedy ran "I'll whip his ass." [1]

While Mondale agreed that Kennedy could not win in a general election, he feared more than Carter the consequence of a Kennedy primary challenge. Mondale believed that by allowing his personal animosity to interfere with sound political judgment, Carter was making the confrontation more likely. [2] Mondale hoped the President would steal Kennedy's thunder by winning over the constituencies most likely to support the Senator's candidacy. He wanted the administration to strengthen its political standing so Kennedy "will conclude that he either can't win the nomination or that he can only win it at such a cost that the nomination will be worthless to him." The Vice President proposed two strategies: First, the President needed to convince Kennedy "that the South would so deeply resent the nomination being taken away from the first Southern president in a century" it would never support him in the general election. Second, and more important, Mondale suggested the President make amends with the "traditional Democratic constituencies"—labor, blacks, Hispanics, women, liberals, and party regulars. "It should be our goal to see that that base is not available to anyone else by cementing relations with those groups to such an extent that, even if they aren't inclined to support us enthusiastically, at least they won't be inclined to oppose us." [3]

The President, on the other hand, believed that performing a "philosophical flip-flop" to prevent a Kennedy challenge would only further weaken the administration and make it vulnerable to attacks from the moderate center of the party where both the primary and general election were to be won. Carter's political advisors ignored

Mondale's suggestions to undermine support for Kennedy's candidacy by proposing more liberal social spending, and instead advised Carter to win over the general electorate by balancing the budget and fighting inflation. "Getting into good shape with the Kennedy constituency was not possible for Carter and it was not the right thing to do," recalled Jordan. "The more we cater to the Kennedy agenda," Carter's media advisor Gerry Rafshoon recalled advising the President, "the more we would be hurt with the general electorate." The key to preventing a confrontation, he reasoned, was to "pursue policies which would increase our overall public standing."[4]

Carter's attempts to improve his "public standing," however, were clearly failing. By October 1979, his support on Capitol Hill had eroded to all-time lows and many Democrats called for him to withdraw from the race. With inflation soaring into double-digits, newly appointed Federal Reserve Chairman Paul Volcker had applied the monetary brakes. With the prime rate reaching all-time highs, the economy began its inevitable slowdown. In October, the Dow Jones index of industrial stocks lost nearly one hundred points, auto sales dropped 23 percent compared to the previous year, while rising mortgage rates strangled the housing industry. Although many economists predicted a deep recession for 1980, the President told the nation he would continue his anti-inflation plan of balanced budgets and tight control of the money supply.

Reports of a Soviet combat brigade in Cuba compounded Carter's problems. Just before Labor Day, Senate Foreign Relations Committee Chairman Frank Church, hoping to improve his position against a right-wing opponent in Idaho, announced that if the brigade were not removed the Senate would refuse to accept the SALT agreement. "The President must make it clear that we draw the line at Russian penetration of the Western Hemisphere," Church thundered at an August 30 press conference. Despite evidence that the troops had been in Cuba since 1962, Church's statements transformed the incident into a bold Soviet challenge to American interests in the Caribbean. A frustrated Carter contributed to the confusion by first declaring the brigade "unacceptable" and then concluding "that the brigade issue is certainly no reason to return to the cold war."[5]

Throughout the affair, Mondale counseled caution. He thought Church's self-serving and irresponsible statements made the administration appear impotent, but that was no reason to overreact to the incident. Not everyone in the administration agreed with this assessment. An irate Brzezinski asked Eizenstat if Carter was a "gutless wonder." If not for his loyalty to the President, he would "take some drastic personal action." More important, by further undermining the President's leadership, the incident eroded support for the SALT treaty. "The arithmetic of ratification was becoming increasingly an exercise in subtraction," wrote Strobe Talbott. On November 9, the Senate Foreign Relations Committee approved the beleaguered treaty by a vote of nine to six—less than the two-thirds support that would be needed for ratification.[6]

In response to the President's deepening political problems, Kennedy inched closer to running. In September, he said both his mother and wife had given their blessings to his candidacy. A week later, he dropped his longstanding endorsement of the President. Draft Kennedy movements began building around the country. By early November, Kennedy had made it clear he was entering the contest for the Democratic nomination. The night before his planned announcement he called Mondale to inform him of his decision. "Ted," Mondale told his former colleague, "I'm sorry for you and I'm sorry for us and I'm sorry for the Democrats, because I've been through so many of these fights. As civil as you and I think this is going to be, it won't. We don't intend to leave voluntarily. You wouldn't. And the Republicans are going to benefit from this."[7]

Certain of his eventual triumph, Kennedy ignored Mondale's words. The next morning, November 7, before an enthusiastic crowd at Boston's historic Faneuil Hall, Kennedy confidently strolled to the stage to make the announcement that many people had waited a generation to hear: he would seek his party's nomination for the presidency of the United States. Like his brothers before him, Kennedy promised to provide the leadership and vision the nation needed. "The only thing that paralyzes us today is the myth that we cannot move," he declared.[8]

Once again, Mondale felt trapped between the party's feuding factions. "Kennedy and I had worked together for twenty years," Mondale recalled. "The task of having to turn on an old friend and have him turn on us and to tear the party apart was terrible." Despite long years of service together in the Senate, Mondale and Kennedy were not close friends. Differences in style and temperament separated the two men. Although they shared similar voting records, their liberalism was evolving in different directions. Mondale's liberalism had mellowed in an attempt to accommodate changing economic and political realities. He had spent most of the decade trying to build bridges between the old and new, forging compromises between the party's vying factions. Kennedy, because of his enormous stature and secure political fortunes, felt little need to adjust his political views. He tried to unite the party's disparate coalition through the sheer force of his personality. Yet with all their personal and philosophical differences, they still competed for the same constituency, and the Vice President realized a Kennedy candidacy would put him in the unenviable position of defending a conservative president against a liberal challenger.[9]

Ironically, while the threat of a possible Kennedy challenge had demoralized the White House, the reality of a Kennedy candidacy reinvigorated the administration and helped heal the divisions between Carter and Mondale. At just the point when the administration appeared ready to split wide open, the emergence of a powerful threat from within the party created a new sense of solidarity. Kennedy helped the contending factions in the White House to overcome deep differences on other issues by providing them with a common enemy.

Mondale worried that the administration's strategy of fighting inflation by inciting a recession would provide Kennedy with an ideal platform for rallying the traditional constituencies to his cause. Little did he know two crises abroad would dramatically shift the agenda. The first crisis occurred in Iran, which had been in chaos since a popular uprising had forced the Shah to flee the country in 1978. In January 1979, Muslim religious leader Ayatollah Khomeini had returned to Teheran after fifteen years of exile. Over the next few months, he had consolidated power by forcing the resignation of the civilian government, killing former officials of the Shah's government, assuming control of the military, and shutting down opposition newspapers. The Shah sought refuge in the United States but the administration, hoping to establish good relations with the new government, discouraged him from coming. In October, with the Shah gravely ill, the administration reconsidered its position.[10]

Carter wondered how the Iranians would react if the United States provided a sanctuary for the deposed Shah. Although the Iranian government assured the President it would protect Americans in Iran, Carter remained skeptical. "I remember Carter asking: 'Does somebody have an answer as to what we would do if the diplomats in our Embassy are taken hostage?' " Mondale recalled. When he and the other advisors said nothing, Carter responded: "I gather not. On that day we will all sit here with long, drawn, white faces and realize we have been had." On October 23, despite his reservations, Carter allowed the Shah to enter the country for emergency medical treatment. On November 4, charging that the United States used the medical excuse as part of a plot to grant the Shah a permanent political haven, a mob of militant students seized the American embassy in Teheran making hostages of sixty-three Americans.[11]

Over the next few weeks Americans watched horrifying scenes of frenzied Islamic "students" burning American flags, chanting anti-American slogans, and parading their prized hostages around the embassy compound. The Ayatollah threatened to put the hostages on trial and promised to blow up the compound if the United States attempted a military rescue. Mondale counseled the President to maintain a high public profile, to isolate the Iranians through diplomatic channels and to reserve the use of military force if the hostages were put on trial. Realizing his options were limited, Carter ordered two aircraft task forces into the area, won the support of both the United Nations Security Council and the World Court, and issued a series of strong public statements. "The consequences of harm to any single hostage will be extremely grave," he warned.[12]

The Iranian crisis precipitated a major reordering of Administration priorities. Carter had won election in 1976 promising to cut Pentagon waste, deemphasize U.S-Soviet competition, and refocus attention toward questions of world poverty and control of nuclear arms. Now all that had changed. The need to win conservative support for the SALT treaty, along with Carter's growing recognition of international realities, dictated a much different agenda. In December, he announced that he would ask Congress for an increase in defense spending of almost 5 percent for fiscal 1981.

Mondale reluctantly accepted the President's decision to boost Pentagon spending. The issue that needed to be addressed, he believed, was not spending, but leadership. An increase in the defense budget would not guarantee the safety of American installations in troubled parts of the world. If the President had established clearer priorities in foreign policy and been more aggressive in fighting for them, he would not have been in a situation where he needed to prove his toughness with a dramatic defense build-up. But given the current political climate, Mondale saw increased spending as a lesser of evils. Without it the image of Carter as weak and ineffective would be permanently ingrained in the public's mind, end any hopes of ratifying SALT, and destroy any chance of reelection. On the other hand, greater defense spending would bring calls for sacrificing social programs at just the time the administration was trying to fend off a serious challenge from the party's left.

As the American hostages entered their eighth week of captivity, another crisis developed. On Christmas Day, Soviet troops invaded neighboring Afghanistan, toppling that nation's bumbling puppet regime. The attack represented a bold military operation aimed at ending a tribal rebellion against the Marxist government. The invasion moved Soviet troops to within several hundred miles of the oil rich and politically unstable Persian Gulf. Vowing to punish the Soviets for their intervention, Carter recalled the American ambassador from Moscow, rallied world opinion against the Soviets, banned American athletes from participating in the summer Olympics in Moscow, and imposed a politically risky grain embargo. He also recognized that the Soviet invasion made moot the question of Senate ratification of a SALT agreement. After years of negotiation, a frustrated Carter reluctantly requested that the Senate suspend consideration of the SALT II treaty.[13]

The twin crises in Iran and Afghanistan were a doubled-edged sword for the administration. As the American people instinctively rallied around the President during a time of twin crisis, Carter watched his job approval rating double to 61 percent—the sharpest one-month leap in forty-one years of polling. Capitalizing on his sudden surge of popularity, Carter decided to play the role of national leader by standing above the partisan fray, refusing to campaign, reneging on a promise to debate Kennedy. In the long run, however, the crises raised troubling questions about the administration's erratic foreign policy and the President's capacity for leadership.

Mondale agreed with the administration's new anti-Soviet rhetoric, but disagreed with specific policies. Though demonstrating American outrage by withdrawing the ambassador and orchestrating an Olympic boycott were both good policy and shrewd politics, a Rose Garden strategy and a grain embargo, the Vice President argued, were empty gestures that would exact a heavy political price. Mondale suggested that the President could deal his challenger a knockout blow by debating him in Iowa. By giving Kennedy the dialogue he demanded, the President would allow him to exit gracefully from the campaign. "I've always thought that if the President had been able to debate Kennedy in Iowa, it would have been over right there," Mondale recalled. Mondale also believed the Russians would circumvent the ban on American grain by purchasing supplies from other sources, but the administration would lose important political support in the farm belt. "There was a good argument that it wasn't going to work. There was even a stronger argument that it would make us weaker, not stronger, in the face of our adversary."[14]

The dramatic events abroad thwarted Kennedy's strategy of focusing public attention on the stagnant economy, but as Mondale feared, Kennedy pounced on both the Rose Garden strategy and the grain embargo. Ironically, Kennedy championed in public the same position that Mondale advocated so forcefully in private. "A grain embargo won't work and it's unfair to farmers," Kennedy charged. "The Soviet troops won't leave Afghanistan and the American farmer will pay the price for an ineffective foreign policy." Taunting the President for his refusal to debate, the Senator maintained that "the presidency can never be above the fray, isolated from the actions and passions of the time. A president cannot afford to posture as the high priest of patriotism." The Senator had to walk a fine line between clarifying his differences with the President and appearing strident or unpatriotic. He did not always succeed. The public exploded with anger after he criticized the Shah during a television interview in San Francisco.[15]

With Carter isolated in the White House, Mondale became the administration's chief stand-in on the campaign trail. Three days a week, Mondale met with Iowa Democrats in preparation for that state's highly publicized January 21 caucus. His role became so pronounced that an NBC reporter called him "Carter's secret weapon." Refusing to act the role of "heavy" in the campaign, Mondale never criticized Kennedy personally and he refused to discuss Chappaquiddick. Putting aside his private reservations, the Vice President vigorously defended both the grain embargo and the "Rose Garden" strategy. The embargo, he said, would have a "sharp, painful" impact on the Soviet Union leading to the "elimination of twenty percent of the animal and protein base in the Soviet diet." When questioned about the President's refusal to debate his opponent, Mondale insisted that the hostage crisis "demands his personal attention around the clock. We need that a lot more than we need one more political speech." At one point, Mondale accused Kennedy of forsaking national security and engaging in "the politics of the moment" by opposing the grain embargo. Support for the embargo, he declared, "was the patriotic route to take." Kennedy used the opportunity to call attention to his family's service to the country. "I don't think I or the members of my family need a lecture from Mr. Mondale or anyone else about patriotism," he retorted.[16]

As recently as October, Iowa polls had shown Kennedy with a thirty-four point lead over the President. That lead dissipated in the weeks following the Iranian hostage-taking and the Soviet invasion of Afghanistan. As he traveled through the state, Mondale felt voters warming toward the President and turning cold on Kennedy. On caucus night, in a dramatic change of political fortunes, Iowa Democrats chose the President over his challenger by 57 percent to 31 percent. The defeat tarnished Kennedy's image of invincibility and enhanced Carter's political stature.[17]

Mondale was shrewd enough to realize, however, that winning Iowa would not solve the administration's nagging problems. Fearing public attitudes would once again focus on the troubled economy, Mondale urged the President to develop an economic policy to counter Kennedy's call for wage and price controls. Carter and his advisors, however, were less concerned with presenting specific programs than with demonstrating American resolve abroad and identifying the President with the resurgent spirit of patriotism.

In January, while the Vice President campaigned in Iowa, the President considered a proposal to reinstitute registration for the draft. By the time Mondale returned from Iowa, the idea had developed considerable support within the White House. Mondale, however, made a desperate appeal to change the President's mind. In a long memorandum the Vice President complained registration "would undermine the unity you have fought to build and immediately engage the nation in a highly charged debate over the wisdom of our policies in Southwest Asia. It would drive families with sons at or near draft age toward the arguments of candidates who have questioned our foreign and defense policies for their own political purposes." That appeal, like so many, went unheeded. In late January, Carter asked for authority to revive draft registration and called for a 5 percent increase above inflation for the defense budget. The Soviets, he said, "must pay a concrete price for aggression."[18]

Despite Mondale's efforts, the party's battle lines were clearly drawn. Carter, tapping into the public's surging patriotism, assumed the stature of national leader making politically risky but necessary decisions to control inflation and defend American interests. Kennedy, tugging at the conscience of American liberals, admonished the party faithful "to sail against the wind" of public opinion and support rationing gasoline and freezing wages and profits. Primary results over the next month proved Kennedy was sailing against the direction of most Democrats. In March, Carter defeated Kennedy in his own backyard, New Hampshire. Rather than admitting defeat, the Senator sharpened his attacks, accusing the President of "sheer hypocrisy" for saying he had no time for campaigning while spending "hours upon hours" canvassing supporters by phone. He blamed Carter for creating a "war hysteria" to hide his foreign policy failures. The assault did little good. On March 11, Carter annihilated Kennedy in the Florida primary: 60.7 percent to 23.2 percent. The following week, Carter won Illinois by an even greater margin, 65 percent to 30 percent, collecting 138 delegates to Kennedy's woeful 14. With his decisive victory in Illinois, the President had amassed almost one-third of the delegates needed for the nomination.[19]

While Carter stayed at home in the White House, Mondale reluctantly carried the administration's message to the nation. In the first three months of the year, Mondale spent forty-nine days campaigning in twenty states. His schedule included more than 100 speeches, 75 receptions and 125 news conferences, interviews, and meetings with editorial boards. He received rave reviews for his performance. "He's the greatest surrogate in history," remarked one White House aide. "To a large degree, our political success has been due to him." Mondale's boundless energy and unpretentious speaking style impressed reporters who followed him on the campaign trail. "There's a special prize we will throw in the bag if you support President Carter," he told his audiences. "You get Walter F. Mondale for free."[20]

Mondale understood political circumstance and personal loyalty forced him to campaign for policies he privately opposed. No one who listened to the Vice President could have guessed that he harbored doubts. Despite his constant complaint that Carter had little appreciation for traditional Democratic constituencies, Mondale repeatedly invoked the memory of his mentor, Hubert Humphrey, to defend the President against Kennedy's charges that the administration had lost touch with its liberal tradition. "I know a progressive when I see one, and Jimmy Carter is a progressive in the Humphrey tradition," he repeated scores of times as part of his stump speech. He referred to Afghanistan as a dagger pointed at the lifeline of Western oil, and he equated support of administration actions in the Persian Gulf with national unity and loyalty. He also declared his support of Carter's efforts to balance the budget, cut revenue sharing, and decontrol oil prices.[21]

Mondale realized he alone could not carry the administration's message. Perhaps the most serious problem the administration faced was the public perception that Carter was weak and ineffectual. The President needed to show he was in command of the issues and had a realistic program for battling inflation while caring for the unemployed, and a strategy for winning release of the hostages without sacrificing American honor. Though publicly defending the President's Rose Garden strategy, privately Mondale pleaded with him to end his self-imposed isolation and assume the leadership role needed to convince the nation he was in control. In preparation for his April 7 lunch meeting, Mondale scribbled, "Carter must get out."[22]

By March, just as Mondale feared, public attention refocused on the slumping economy. Inflation skyrocketed to nearly 20 percent for the first two months of 1980. The budget deficit grew beyond administration predictions and on Wall Street the bond market nearly collapsed. As attention shifted away from the international crisis, pressure built for the President to act. Mondale persisted in his appeals for the President to adopt more liberal measures to counter Kennedy's appeal. Slowing down the decontrol of oil and rationing gasoline, he charged, could stop inflation and prevent Kennedy from exploiting the bad news for political advantage. He told Carter, "We'll be in trouble if this campaign turns to economics. EMK is talking freezes and controls and all we can say is it'll get better in 198[1] and to offer excuses. We are trying to hold down wages but not prices." Carter, however, rejected Mondale's advice and turned his attention to cutting the budget.[23]

Nothing roused Mondale to action faster than talk of budget cutting, especially in an election year. He suggested a "political look at the budget" to see how it would appeal "to mayors, the elderly, educators, labor, [and] minorities." Again, he urged that important domestic programs be salvaged, while others, especially education, be increased. "It is important to beef up the education programs . . . because they have merit, they are politically attractive and they add very little to the deficit." For labor, he suggested a small increase in public works. "Why let ourselves be drawn into an argument with them at this sensitive time, when a modest countercyclical program can be included without any impact on the budget deficit?" For minorities, he supported an ambitious $2 billion youth program. "We cannot afford to be perceived in the Black community as dragging our feet on the jobs component of this package." How, Mondale asked, can a Democratic president intentionally create a recession while also cutting social programs people needed for survival? In his mind, Republicans slashed budgets and created recessions; Democrats increased spending and produced jobs. Once again, he argued cutting a few billion dollars from the federal budget would have a negligible impact on inflation but a dramatic impact on the campaign.[24]

On March 14, Carter announced a new anti-inflation plan which promised to restore "discipline" to both government and American consumers. The plan involved shaving $13 billion in federal spending for 1980, including deep cuts in politically sensitive programs like CETA, child-health assistance, and food stamps. Not surprisingly, liberals condemned the new austerity measures. Kennedy, in his harshest attack to date, called it a "completely intolerable" policy that would harm the most vulnerable in society. Like Mondale, he complained that balancing the budget would have a negligible impact on inflation. Labor called his program an outrage. UAW President Douglas Fraser accused the President of reviving Herbert Hoover's economic policies.[25]

The Vice President not only thought Carter's budget cuts were bad policy, he also believed that announcing the decision just weeks before the crucial March 25 New York primary represented a serious political blunder. A Carter victory in New York, Mondale believed, could deal a fatal blow to Kennedy's candidacy. Now the President was giving Kennedy the potential opening he so desperately needed. The budget cuts decision was only one of a number of gaffes plaguing the administration in the weeks preceding the New York vote. On March 2, the United States supported a United Nations resolution denying Israel sovereignty over its capital city, Jerusalem, a vote that infuriated New York's large and politically powerful Jewish community.[26]

The budget cuts and the United Nations vote left Mondale discouraged and confused. Privately, he complained the administration was "hurting the poor, raising defense to the roof, dropping SALT, alienating the Jews and even moderate liberals." Mondale hoped Secretary of State Vance's testimony before the Senate Foreign Relations Committee, scheduled for March 21, would help calm the storm. He suggested the President instruct Vance to state the vote resulted from poor communications and did not reflect administration thinking. The President seemed agreeable, saying he expected the testimony would ease tensions with the Jewish community. But Vance resisted the pressure, refusing to condemn the vote. "What I said to the President was I would have to call it as I saw it," Vance reflected. "The vote was the right thing to do. If it had not come right before the primary no one would have made much of a fuss. But I believe that sound foreign policy comes before local politics."[27]

Agreeing in principle with Vance's position and frustrated with Mondale's persistent lobbying on behalf of the Jewish community, Carter consciously excluded his Vice President from a major administration decision. When Mondale called the President on the morning of Vance's Senate appearance, he found Carter evasive, refusing to reveal what instructions he had given the Secretary. Later that afternoon, instead of dismissing the resolution as the result of poor communications, Vance endorsed its basic thrust. He told angry Senators the United States had always opposed settlements as being "contrary to international law and an impediment to the successful conclusion of the Middle East [peace] process."[28]

Vance's statements stunned Mondale. He was even more shocked when he learned Carter had sent the Secretary a congratulatory note on his testimony. Mondale wondered if he was "getting set up" by the President. He told Eizenstat he was "beginning to wonder where the President is coming from." He complained that the United Nations vote and Vance's testimony had revived Kennedy's fledgling campaign and would cost them the primary. While he could not provide proof, Mondale suspected Brzezinski had something to do with the incident. Years later, Mondale still expressed bitterness. He said: "It was totally unnecessary, wrong, politically insane and suicidal. I don't know why it was done. It was the worst self-imposed accident of the whole campaign. Somebody wasn't leveling with me. There was a set of instructions floating around that were different from what I was being told."[29]

The administration's blunders precipitated a massive surge for Kennedy in the final days before the primary, resulting in smashing victories in New York and neighboring Connecticut. For the first time, Kennedy translated disapproval of Carter into votes for his candidacy. Suddenly, the race that only a week earlier appeared over, offered a stir of life. The victories guaranteed Kennedy would pursue the nomination until the June 3 finish. Arithmetic, however, still worked in the President's favor. Despite the twin losses, Carter continued to accumulate delegates. With a little less than two months until the final California primary, Carter could claim half of the 1,666 delegates needed for a first-ballot nomination.

Following the New York primary, Mondale found himself involved in intensive White House planning for a rescue mission in Iran. Mondale felt an attempt was necessary. None of the administration's efforts to date—breaking diplomatic ties with Teheran, expelling Iranian diplomats from the country, imposing a trade embargo on American goods bound for Iran, and freezing Iranian assets in the United States—had won release of the hostages. Only the Secretary of State stood in the way of a unanimous recommendation of military action. Vance argued that the administration had made substantial progress in gaining Allied support for sanctions and that a rescue attempt would cause hostage deaths and drive the Iranians into Soviet hands.[30]

Vance lobbied Mondale to oppose the mission. "I thought that Fritz would have both the position and the judgment to say this is a case with too many risks," Vance reflected. "I've been around that Defense Department most of my life and I'll guarantee you something will go wrong," he told the Vice President during a long, private walk around the Rose Garden. "It never works the way they say its going to work. There's a good chance a disaster could occur here and I hope you will give this serious consideration." Mondale had already made up his mind. Although the mission was dangerous, he thought the risk of doing nothing was still greater. Realizing he could neither stop the mission nor support it, Vance submitted his resignation. Mondale pleaded with him to stay. "This presidency is in horrible shape and your departure will be the worst signal possible," he said. "Can't you stay on for half a year and let us get out of this hole?" Vance refused the Vice President's appeal. "Fritz," he replied, "I know what you're talking about, but I made my decision and I've got to do it."[31]

In the days preceding the planned rescue mission, the administration searched for candidates to replace Vance. Mondale believed the President needed to find someone of stature to prevent the confirmation hearings from becoming an inquisition into the administration's foreign policy. He thought immediately of his old Senate colleague and Democratic stalwart Edmund Muskie. Muskie, who had national standing, was highly regarded in the Senate and was a moderate on foreign policy issues. Mondale also knew that Muskie would stand up to Brzezinski and not allow the combative National Security

Advisor to bully him the way he did Vance. With the President's permission he called Muskie to ask him if he were interested. After a long pause, Muskie agreed to accept the position.[32]

The President had less success with the Iranian rescue mission. On April 24, in the darkness and confusion of the night, one of the rescue helicopters collided with a transport plane killing eight servicemen and ending the mission. An immediate public uproar greeted news of the failure. The image of burning helicopters in the Iranian desert captured the sense of impotence many people felt about the administration's foreign policy. Some congressmen called for the President's resignation, while others demanded public hearings to investigate why the mission failed. Three days later, Carter announced Vance's resignation and Muskie's appointment. As Mondale had hoped, Congress and the media acclaimed Muskie's nomination, thus limiting the political fallout from the disaster. The President had dodged a potentially fatal bullet.[33]

On June 3, the primary season officially ended when the President's Ohio victory assured him of the delegates needed for a first-ballot nomination. Despite certain defeat, Kennedy promised to carry his fight to the convention floor. Most Democrats, however, were dissatisfied with the possibility of either a Kennedy or Carter candidacy in November. Kennedy had won many of the big industrial states, including New York, Pennsylvania, and New Jersey, but he showed little support outside the traditional Democratic strongholds. There were also ominous signs for the President. Throughout the primary season polls indicated most people voted for Carter not because they liked him, but to demonstrate support for the President in a time of crisis. Fewer than half of the Democrats who voted for Carter in the June 3 primaries said they would support him in a general election.

August was hot and steamy in New York as the Democrats assembled for their convention. Confronted with an embarrassing accusation that his brother Billy had accepted "payments" from the Libyan government, Carter dropped to new lows in opinion polls. An ABC-Louis Harris survey revealed the President's approval rating had fallen to an appalling 22 percent. From small-town sheriffs to senior senators, Democratic officeholders across the nation expressed fear a Carter-headed ticket would drag them down to defeat.[34]

Haunted by memories of the 1968 Democratic convention, which had crippled Humphrey's candidacy, Mondale joined other administration officials in promoting the campaign's theme of unity. The Vice President appeared on both the CBS and NBC morning news shows preaching the virtues of a united party. As in 1968, the Democrats confronted a spirited Republican party thirsty for victory. During the spring and early summer, while the Democrats feuded, the Republican opposition consolidated around Ronald Reagan. The former California Governor's message was as simple as it was compelling: love of country, fear of communism, and scorn of government. Telegenic features, combined with extensive experience in front of a camera, made Reagan a master craftsman of the new art of technological campaigning. Calling for a "new beginning" that included large reductions in personal taxes, cuts in unnecessary social spending, and massive increases in defense spending, Reagan promised to "renew the American spirit and sense of purpose." The party platform also rejected the Equal Rights Amendment, supported a constitutional ban on abortion, and advocated school prayer.[35]

Reagan tapped into the deep resentment many traditional Democrats felt toward their party. Aided by the remarkable growth in evangelical Christianity during the decade, the development of effective techniques for voter mobilization, and the establishment of a number of new conservative think tanks, this appeal to old values became an especially potent political message. Of course, Nixon had made similar appeals for the support of white southern Protestants, blue-collar ethnics, and Catholics. But the poor state of the economy allowed Reagan to make a further claim: Republicans were now not only the defenders of traditional American values, but also the party of new ideas and economic growth. Democratic flirtation with "radicalism" during the 1960s and economic mismanagement during the 1970s had allowed Reagan to capture the strategic center ground in American politics by identifying his party with traditional values, economic growth and an activist foreign policy.

The election picture was further clouded by the presence of a credible third-party candidate. John Anderson, a white-haired maverick Republican congressman from Illinois, helped Reagan's cause by announcing his candidacy as an independent "national unity" candidate for President. A liberal on social issues and a conservative on economics, Anderson had strong appeal to the same younger, educated, independent voters whom Carter had attracted in 1976. Democrats feared that without winning a single state, Anderson could siphon off enough support to tip the election to Reagan.[36]

Despite the serious challenge from both Reagan and Anderson,

Kennedy ignored pleas for reconciliation and persisted in his fight. He tried to free delegates from their obligation to particular candidates, and hoped Carter's delegates might be lured into supporting an "open convention" where he, or another liberal candidate, could be chosen. On Monday evening, delegates cast their votes on the rule change. Mondale and other administration officials worked the convention floor convincing Carter delegates to remain loyal. As expected, Carter's forces carried the vote by a safe margin. An hour later, from his suite in the Waldorf-Astoria, Kennedy withdrew from the fight.

The following night, in a stirring address to the convention, Kennedy provided the party with a forceful defense of liberal values. Calling "the commitment of the Democratic Party to economic justice" the "cause that brought me into the campaign and that sustained me for nine months across a hundred thousand miles," Kennedy admonished the delegates not to allow "the great purposes of the Democratic Party" to "become the bygone passages of history." For Kennedy, the speech was both a personal and political success. "No loser of a presidential nomination in modern times has dominated a political convention as did Edward Kennedy," asserted Robert Healy of the partisan Boston *Globe*. Following the address, an aroused convention voted in favor of Kennedy's liberal economic program with the exception of wage and price controls. Perhaps more important, the speech restored much of the Kennedy magic that seemed to have been lost during the long primary season. Though eloquently reminding Democrats of their historic mission, Kennedy did little to unite the party behind its nominee.[37]

Over the next two days, while delegates debated platform resolutions, Mondale refined his acceptance speech. After spending most of the previous year fighting political allies, he relished the opportunity to challenge Reagan and the Republicans. His first priority, as he told his speechwriting staff, was to expose Reagan as a radical who planned an assault "on all the fundamental progress made in social justice and human rights over the last fifty years—beginning with an unbelievable abandonment of the principle that women ought to have the same rights as the rest of Americans." If elected, he feared the Republicans "would repeal what Roosevelt and Truman and Kennedy and Johnson, and two generations of Americans have done to build a more just and a hopeful society." Mondale also realized that along with attacking Reagan he needed to articulate a Democratic alternative. "It can't be just a goddamn carp and strife, negative thing," he said. The speech needed to define a "vision" that could arouse the party for the fall campaign and reawaken a sense of national pride. "There's got to be a feeling," he insisted, "that this country can do it again."[38]

On the convention's final night, Mondale ascended the podium to address the delegates. Placing Carter firmly in the tradition of other great Democratic presidents, Mondale drew a clear distinction between the Democratic and Republican parties. "Last month in Detroit, another convention was held—isolated in a bubble of privilege from the city that hosted it. A comfortable convention, composed of America's wealthy, told us they symbolized the nation." The Democratic convention, in contrast, was "a mirror of all America—all of it, black and white, Asian and Hispanic, Native and immigrant, male and female, young and old, urban and rural, rich and poor." Employing the same rhetorical device Humphrey had used against Goldwater at the 1964 Convention, Mondale repeated Reagan's more outlandish statements and concluded with the question, "Who on earth would say something like that? Ronald Reagan did!" He sparked a responsive chord from the 20,000 people inside Madison Square Garden who joined along with the chant "Ronald Reagan did!"[39]

Mondale succeeded in ridiculing Reagan but he failed in his effort to provide a compelling Democratic message. The Washington *Post* editorialized that Mondale's "attempt to recapture the resonance of Hubert Humphrey's great and timely speech in Atlantic City 16 years ago" suggested that the Democrats "were so unconvinced of their own power to attract or persuade that they had decided to try to paint their opposition, in ever more terrifying hues and contours, as a monster." Of course it was not uncommon for vice presidential candidates to use the convention as a forum for attacking the opposition, and Mondale took full advantage of the opportunity. But it was noteworthy that the biting verbal thrusts that had filled Mondale's rhetoric during his early years in politics—the condemnation of economic monopoly and greed, the graphic recital of unmet social needs, the sermons about government's moral responsibility to address social injustice—were absent from this address, and from most of his other campaign speeches. For Mondale, the populist oratory of his youth had lost much of its relevance, but he had found no new language to take its place.[40]

Carter followed Mondale to the podium and attempted to provide his own vision for the Democratic future. It was a different Carter than voters had first seen four years earlier. His voice was drained of energy, the lines in his face deeper. Adopting a Truman give-em'-hell style, Carter gave a shouting stump speech. In a headlong assault on his rival, he depicted Ronald Reagan as a dweller in "a world of tinsel and make-believe" who would "launch an all-out nuclear arms race" and start "an attack on everything that we've done in the achievement of social justice and decency in the last 50 years." The nation, Carter cried, faced "a choice between two futures": a Democratic future of "security and justice and peace" and a Reagan future of "despair," "surrender," and "risk."[41]

Though forceful in their attacks on Reagan, neither Carter nor Mondale communicated a vision for the party. Instead, they tried to make Reagan's qualities of judgment and steadiness the central issues of the campaign. The unfortunate reality was that no single Democratic vision existed in 1980. Kennedy could still arouse the passion of the party's shrinking liberal wing with his inspiring defense of the New Deal, but he showed little sensitivity to those worried about expanding government and surging inflation. More than Kennedy, the Vice President realized inflation required liberals to adjust temporarily their agenda by refraining from new social programs until real growth could be restored. Unlike the President, Mondale had earned the respect of the constituency groups and understood their political needs. Unfortunately, Carter's stubbornness and the liberals' arrogance made futile any attempts at reconciliation. Unable to unite the party's warring factions, Mondale tried to impose a negative unity, hoping fear of Ronald Reagan would outweigh Democratic differences. As he would soon discover, the negative unity he strove so hard to achieve would be no match against an aroused Republican party.

Worn by the long primary season, Mondale turned his attention to the general election campaign. He knew it would be a painful uphill battle. Carter was in striking distance of Reagan in national polls—trailing by fourteen points in a Gallup Poll—but his electoral college situation was much worse. In three key states—New York, Massachusetts, and Texas, which together accounted for eighty-one electoral votes—Carter trailed by large margins. The heart of Carter's problem was Reagan's strength in the West and the erosion of Carter's base in the South. Reagan had a bedrock 118 votes from west of the Mississippi. With Republican states Indiana, Virginia, New Hampshire, and Vermont (all of which Carter had lost to Ford) added to his base, he could count on 150 of the 270 electoral votes needed for victory.[42]

Mondale's plan for winning the general election was nearly identical to the strategy used in every other Democratic campaign since 1932. "My premise has always been that there are more Democrats than Republicans, and if we can keep our own family relatively intact, chances are we'll win," he wrote. Success in November, Mondale reasoned, required a revival of the old coalition. "We must demonstrate that we care about unemployed auto workers, about drought-stricken farmers, about the elderly and others whom the Democratic Party has traditionally represented. We not only need to be perceived as caring about these people, but we also need to be perceived as doing something to help them through our policies." For the past fifty years, Mondale argued, Democrats had used the issue of unemployment to win the office from Republicans. This year was different. For "the first time in this century," a Democratic administration was running "for re-election in the midst of a serious recession created while it was in office." That situation provided Reagan with a perfect opportunity to argue he would be more effective in dealing with the recession. It was imperative, the Vice President asserted, "that we recapture the offensive on the jobs issue by demonstrating through our actions as well as our rhetoric genuine compassion for those who have lost their jobs and those whose jobs are threatened."[43]

The key to victory, he argued, was not to win back conservative Democrats who were likely to defect to Reagan but to rally liberal and minority voters. Convinced that Reagan would run better in the South than Ford had in 1976, Mondale believed the administration needed to offset those losses by winning more contests in the Midwest and Northeast. "In short," he concluded, "we must necessarily place a greater emphasis on a northern industrial strategy than we did last time, and that means appealing to traditional Democrats on traditional Democratic issues." He advised Carter to contrast the "Democratic approach of caring with the Republican approach of neglect, indifference and bias toward special interest." He urged the President to "make this a highly partisan campaign of Republicans vs. Democrats which appeals directly to our constituencies—Jews, labor, minorities, farmers, ethnics, women, environmentalists, etc."[44]

Mondale also feared Reagan's call for large tax cuts would force the administration into a defensive response. The President's economic advisors recommended a major tax cut carefully targeted to moderate-income taxpayers and business, and small spending increases for fiscal years 1981 and 1982. They divided on how much spending to approve. The Council of Economic Advisers and the Treasury Department favored a "low option" proposal that would increase spending $2.9 billion over two years. Mondale and Eizenstat supported a second option calling for an $8 billion spending increase. Mondale suggested that the "low option" would provide Kennedy supporters little reason to galvanize behind the President, whereas extended unemployment insurance, expanded economic development funding, job training, and aid to cities were all programs which, while necessary on their own merits, also had a direct political impact. In a July 12 conversation with the President, Mondale argued that an extra "2–3 billion [a year] can't have [a] negative impact on markets in [a] big budget. [We] need to show some decent concern for poor or [we will] lose [our] moral leadership." [45]

Later in the day, Mondale complained about the President's unwillingness to deal with the political realities of the budget. "Carter's got Baptist inclination not to do anything that'll help himself politically. If you say it's political he won't [exercise] leadership." Unless Carter began supporting more social spending, the Vice President said, he would be remembered as another Herbert Hoover. "We look heartless," he told Eizenstat. Though increasing savings and productivity was important, the President should not appease the business community, Mondale believed. He repeated what Humphrey had told Carter on another occasion: "The only way you can win the confidence of the business community," Humphrey said, "is to leave office." Mondale agreed with Humphrey's analysis. "[We] [c]an't go to these groups," he declared. "We look like two-timers and double-crossers." [46]

Reluctantly, Carter incorporated some of Mondale's suggestions into his August economic revival plan. He did not share Mondale's unflinching faith in the constituency groups but he realized he would need their help in a difficult campaign against Reagan. "Although [it] rubs me [the] wrong way," the President told his economic advisors, "we need to do it to keep from being savaged politically." The package included $27.6 billion in tax cuts for individuals and businesses, including a new refundable investment tax credit and about $3.6 billion in aid for economically distressed areas, research and development, and a bundle of energy conservation measures. "Our task is nothing less than to revitalize America's economy," Carter told a group gathered at the White House. "Increasing productivity is the foremost economic challenge of the 1980s." [47]

With his election-year economic program in place, Carter kicked off his campaign on Labor Day. Unable to articulate a unifying theme for the Democratic Party, the President launched into a strident attack against his opponent. In Atlanta, he suggested to a black audience that Reagan was a racist. Later, in Los Angeles, Carter raised the possibility of war if Reagan were elected. "Six weeks from now you will determine what kind of life you and your families will have . . . whether we have peace or war." New York *Times* columnist James Reston called Carter's campaign "vicious and personal," adding "even if he wins, it will be difficult for him to regain the support he needs to govern." Commented the Boston *Globe:* "The President seems bent on discarding his last ace, his reputation as a decent and compassionate man."[48]

While charges of "meanness" sidetracked Carter, the Vice President campaigned among the traditional Democratic constituencies. Between the Democratic Convention and election day, Mondale traveled over 30,000 miles and visited nearly thirty states. A typical day included fifteen hours of campaigning, meetings with labor and other interest groups, a speech at a high school, a press conference, and a pep talk to local campaign workers. His top objective was to bring Kennedy followers back into the fold. "Without him there's no way some of us would have gone for Carter," explained a former Kennedy delegate from Oregon. "We know we can trust him," said a Texas Hispanic leader. Ed Campbell, the Iowa Democratic chairman, introduced Mondale as "the great ecumenist of our party, our own Pope John." In his speeches Mondale portrayed the Democratic Party as the savior of the farmer, the worker, the small business owner, the student, the poor, and the handicapped. He spent most of his time in the urban-industrial corridor stretching from the Northeast to the upper Middle West. His speeches recited a long list of Carter's accomplishments. "After a few days of listening to him," a reporter noted, "it almost seems as if Hubert H. Humphrey has been President for the last four years."[49]

Mondale tried to undermine Reagan's appeal to traditional Democrats by hammering away at the theme that Reagan was "a negative, stale, classic anti-environment, anti-labor, anti-family farm program, anti-federal aid to education . . . right-wing Republican." In industrial cities he ridiculed Reagan's claim that when he was young there had been no racial problem. "Maybe he'd forgotten the days when he was a young boy in Illinois and there were race riots so bad that it caused the creation in his state of the first chapter of the NAACP. . . . Maybe he means the 50s and 60s, when Ronald Reagan fought us on the Civil Rights Act." He repeatedly tried to tie Reagan to his past. The Republican nominee, who had previously advocated making Social Security a voluntary system, campaigned stressing his fidelity to senior citizens, Mondale noted. "He must have had some stand-in or extra running around this country for the last 25 years," the Vice President said. "Either that or he just repealed 25 years of his political life." Reagan, he suggested, was a warmonger who proposed sending troops to North Korea, Ecuador, Pakistan, Angola, Rhodesia, and Cuba. "Every time a country gets the hiccups, he wants to send American forces there," Mondale declared.[50]

Despite the positive reviews Mondale received on the campaign trail, many Carter advisors were dissatisfied with his performance. Gerry Rafshoon wanted Mondale to attend fewer labor meetings and spend more time making television appearances. "It was like pulling teeth to get Mondale to do a television appearance on Sunday mornings," the media advisor recalled. "He didn't understand that it was more important to go on television and talk to the public about our programs, than it was to go to a labor convention, or a NOW convention, or to meet with Lane Kirkland or Andy Young." Mondale countered that selling yourself on television like laundry detergent was demeaning. Rafshoon responded it was no more demeaning than going "hat-in-hand" to labor leaders and asking for their support. Mondale disagreed: "These people are my friends," Rafshoon recalled Mondale saying. "I don't go hat-in-hand to them. We have a relationship."[51]

The exchange between Rafshoon and Mondale revealed two different generations of political style. From his early years in the Minnesota Farmer-Labor party, Mondale had learned the politics of social bonding by forging consensus among well-organized interest groups. Rafshoon understood better than Mondale the role of political advertising in a consumer society. He recognized most people voted as individuals, not as politically conscious members of well-defined interest groups. Mondale saw campaigning as a deliberative process where political candidates sought to build relationships with leaders of representative groups; Rafshoon, and the generation of media consultants he represented, believed dialogue was less important then projecting a carefully crafted image into the homes of every American.

Mondale and Rafshoon did agree on one thing: the media paid little attention to the Vice President. "I'd have to set my hair on fire to get on the news," Mondale remarked at one point. There was a reason for Mondale's problem. John Anderson's presence as a third-party candidate absorbed much of the news coverage that customarily went to vice presidents. Television correspondents assigned to the Mondale campaigned joked about their newly found anonymity. "Hello, you don't remember me," one correspondent said in a mock report, "I used to be on television every night—my face was my passport for hotels, restaurants and rental cars all over. . . . But then I was assigned to the Mondale campaign and now I need this [pulls out his American Express card] more than ever."[52]

Fortunately for the administration, the Republicans stumbled through the early weeks of the campaign as Reagan seemed determined to live up to his reputation as "a clutter bag of odd quotations, clippings, and misinformation." At a time when the Republican nominee needed to reassure the nation of his ability to handle delicate foreign policy issues, he opened old national wounds by referring to Vietnam as "a noble cause" in a speech to the Veterans of Foreign Wars in Chicago. While his vice-presidential running mate, George Bush, toured China hoping to demonstrate his expertise in foreign affairs, Reagan told reporters at home that he favored "official government relations" with Taiwan.[53]

By October, Carter and Mondale had closed the gap and the election appeared a dead heat. Everyone turned their attention to the lone debate between the two presidential candidates to be held a week before election day. On debating points, they were evenly matched. But in his closing remarks, Reagan focused public attention on Carter's responsibility for double-digit inflation, hostages in Iran, and Soviet troops in Afghanistan. "Are you better off than you were four years ago?" he asked. "Is America as respected throughout the world as it was?" Also, by mastering the symbols of presentation, Reagan effectively erased his image as a warmonger and emerged a clear winner. "Since he didn't walk out on stage and act like Dr. Strangelove," a Carter aide said, "it was a boost for him." Carter claimed victory; Mondale was less certain. He was impressed by Reagan's confidence and poise in defending himself against Carter's substantive jibes. "I had a very uneasy feeling," Mondale told reporters later.[54]

Early on the morning of November 4, Mondale cast his ballot in the small town of Afton, Minnesota. The election, he told reporters, was "as tight as any race could possibly be." Afterward, he held his traditional election-day breakfast with a few close friends and family. A few minutes later, Caddell called to tell him it "was over." The prediction proved accurate. The conservative Republican governor defeated Carter 50.7 percent to 41 percent in the popular vote. More convincingly, he won 489 electoral votes to the President's 49. He carried all but six states of the Union: Georgia and Minnesota, Carter's and Mondale's home states, plus Maryland, Rhode Island, West Virginia, and Hawaii, as well as the District of Columbia. The Republicans gained thirty-three House seats and twelve Senate seats, thereby winning a majority—their largest majority since 1928. John Anderson won only 5,719,437 votes or 6.6 percent.[55]

During his final weeks in office, Mondale reflected on his years as Vice President. He took great satisfaction in the personal relationship he had established with the President. Throughout four difficult years, they remained steadfastly loyal to one another. A genuine friendship emerged between the two men. At the last White House staff meeting, Carter said he "never had [a] closer relationship than with Fritz." The Vice President was, he said, "like a brother and a son." In an obvious reference to the tension that sometimes characterized their relationship, Carter warned his staff: "Don't do anything to hurt him." Mondale shared similar feelings for Carter. "Never before has a Vice President been so generously and so kindly treated by his President," Mondale wrote Carter a few days before leaving office. "On a personal level it was a spectacular relationship," he reflected. "His personal generosity toward me and my staff never wavered during the four years."[56]

That friendship cemented the groundbreaking institutional relationship they had established. Mondale considered the role he played in elevating the stature of the Vice President his most important contribution during his four years. It seems likely that the new role that Mondale pioneered will become a model for all future vice presidents. The two immediate successors to the office, George Bush and Dan Quayle, both adopted the Mondale approach. "My conclusion is that the Mondale model is a very good model," Bush told reporters in 1981. "I just think that from the beginning to the end he enjoyed the confidence of the President. He had access to him and could advise him and, when he had a difference, he presented it face to face but without a lot of people around, and thus he kept the confidence of the President." Before assuming office in 1989, Quayle sought Mondale's advice and expressed hope that President Bush would allow the Vice President to play a similar role in his administration.[57]

The President deserved much of the credit for that relationship's success. Defying precedent, he readily accepted Mondale's proposals for strengthening the vice presidency. He always solicited Mondale's opinion and carefully weighed his advice. At critical times in the relationship, the President intervened to silence critics and to reassure his vice president. For his part, Mondale, understanding a vice president's influence depended on his personal relationship with the president, labored to assure Carter of his loyalty. Though he concealed his differences with the President from other administration officials, he rarely refrained from confronting Carter with critical observations.

Assessing Mondale's influence on administration policy is more problematic. Many Carter advisors complained that Mondale's outdated political judgment undermined the administration's appeal to moderates. Former attorney general Griffin Bell contended that Mondale, who represented "the liberal bloc of the Democratic party," succeeded in shaping "administration policy to his way of thinking in important areas." The result was "the unclear, all-things-to-all-people voice that the public heard so often from the administration." The President's media advisor, Gerald Rafshoon, accepted Bell's critique. "Carter tended to overcompensate because he knew he did not have the support of the traditional Democrats," Rafshoon argued. "I felt that Mondale did not accommodate enough to our approach." OMB director James McIntyre suggested that if the President had rejected Mondale's pleas for more social spending and instead accepted his prudent fiscal advice, the administration could have held the line against inflation and avoided a costly election-year recession.[58]

These critics exaggerated Mondale's impact on the administration's economic policy. The Vice President's proximity to power did not always translate into influence. Carter, who came to office with a disdain for the party's entrenched leadership, was never receptive to Mondale's appeals for greater fidelity to the concerns of traditional Democratic organizations. "Fritz seemed to enjoy dealing with the special interest groups," Carter reflected. "He was much more interested in meeting their demands than I was. It was easier for me to ignore them or refuse their requests." Though he was more open to Mondale's advice on economic issues during the first eighteen months of the administration, Carter repeatedly rejected Mondale's calls for increased social spending once lowering inflation became his top economic priority. Despite the criticisms of many Carter advisors, it seems unlikely that Mondale's modest proposals, even if they had been accepted by the President, would have resulted in swelled deficits and higher inflation.[59]

Yet the differences between Mondale and Carter did reveal deep divisions within the Democratic Party and prevented the administration from speaking with a clear voice. Like many liberals, Mondale had mastered the inner workings of the Washington establishment but he seemed insensitive to the growing discontent of most voters, who felt alienated from the groups that claimed to represent them, frustrated with the institutions of government, and angry with many of its leaders. Carter, on the other hand, had an instinctive feel for the concerns of the average voter, but failed to master the mechanism of government. In part, the different perspectives reflected the individual strengths and weaknesses of each man. But they also highlighted the contradictory feelings of a nation struggling to reconcile its expansive expectations with limited resources. Voters who complained about government waste and cried for a balanced budget also pleaded for more federal aid for education and health care. This schism in the public mind, which was reflected in the contrasting styles of Carter and Mondale, made effective leadership in the late 1970s nearly impossible.

Ironically, Mondale's most notable accomplishments came in foreign policy. In the Middle East he played a sustained role in developing administration strategy and in building domestic support for new initiatives. His trip to Israel in 1978, especially his private discussions with Begin, represented an important step toward Carter's greatest foreign policy triumph—the signing of the Camp David Accords. He used the vice presidency as a moral pulpit, focusing public attention on the plight of the boat people and rallying international condemnation of Vietnam's brutal policy. In 1979, his negotiations with Chinese leaders helped ease tension between the two countries and establish a firmer foundation for Sino–American relations. Mondale had less success in dealing with the domestic political aspects of foreign policy. On Capitol Hill he served as a useful source of information and as an effective lobbyist. He played a significant part in the campaign to get Senate passage of the Panama Canal treaties. Yet, he had little impact on the two problems that eroded public support for Carter's foreign policy: the administration's confused approach toward the Soviet Union and his response to the hostage crisis in Iran.

A sluggish economy and the Iranian hostage crisis were the immediate causes of public dissatisfaction with Carter, but the discontent with the Democrats had roots deep beneath the surface of American politics. Rising oil prices, pent-up middle class anger only temporarily derailed by Watergate, and a blundering Soviet leadership created difficult, perhaps insurmountable, problems for the administration. Perhaps more important, the Carter administration reflected the failure of the New Deal coalition to adjust to a new age of limits. The economic means needed to fight inflation were incompatible with the political realities of the Democratic coalition. Dealing with inflation required imposing pain, through monetary policy that tightened the overall levers on the economy and precipitated a recession, or through budget cuts that refused tangible benefits to particular groups. A coalition nurtured on receiving the incremental benefits of a constantly expanding economy refused to accept the new politics of denial.

The compassionate populism, which had supplied a clear framework for Mondale's early years in politics, did not provide ready solutions to the morally ambiguous problems of the 1970s. Removing the vestiges of racial segregation, establishing a safety net for the poor and underprivileged, and exposing unfair business practices were striking enough in their simplicity to be both morally right and politically feasible. By the 1970s, however, enlarged minority group demands clashed with middle-class values and increased the political costs of addressing social problems. New issues such as busing and affirmative action were more complex, the solutions more costly, and the rights of conflicting groups less distinguishable. Inflation, which imposed a price on increased government spending, blurred beyond recognition the connection between morality and policies.

By 1980, the emergence of controversial social issues had eroded the party's class-based appeal, exacerbated cultural tensions within the coalition, and destroyed the sense of community that had bound together the disparate liberal coalition. Samuel Lubell had argued that, unlike past political realignments, the New Deal had depended on a sense of class-consciousness that transcended "not only regional distinctions but equally strong cultural differences." The future of the Roosevelt coalition, Lubell concluded, would depend on the Democrats' ability to foster "racial and religious tolerance among its own elements." But as the poor and working class withdrew from the political process, Democratic candidates were forced to turn to an increasingly middle and upper-middle class electorate. Polls showed many college-educated and financially secure voters were culturally more liberal and economically more conservative than working-class Democrats. As Democrats aligned themselves with the cause of social liberalism, Republicans skillfully exploited the cultural conservatism of the working class. "The politics of the 1930s and 1940s resembled a nineteenth century battlefield, with two opposing armies arrayed against each other in more or less close formation," observed the political scientist Anthony King. "[P]olitics today is an altogether messier affair, with large numbers of small detachments engaged over a vast territory, and with individuals and groups frequently changing sides."[60]

Racial tensions contributed to the fracturing of the liberal coalition. A quarter of a century ago the political scientist V.O. Key wrote that "in its grand outlines the politics of the South revolves around the position of the Negro." The statement remained true in 1980. Despite the massive mobilization of black voters since passage of the Voting Rights Act in 1965, the increase of white registration between 1960 and 1980 surpassed black by almost five to one. The mobilization of southern blacks and the defection of white southerners from the Democratic party dramatically transformed the demographic composition of the Democratic coalition in the south. Democratic presidential candidates between 1952 and 1960 never received more than one of fifteen of their southern votes from blacks. In 1980, Carter received about one in three of his southern votes from blacks. After 1968 Democrats lost regions of the South that had voted Democratic since Reconstruction. Before 1964, nearly 55 percent of all southern counties voted consistently Democratic in presidential elections. By 1980, that percentage had dropped to only 14 percent. The population shift from the Rust Belt to the Sun Belt compounded the problem by increasing the South's electoral power. In 1932, the Northeast and the Midwest accounted for 54 percent of the nation's electoral votes. By 1980, that percentage had reversed.[61]

A clear racial pattern also emerged outside the South. In the industrial Northeast and Midwest, the suburbs were white and Republican; the inner cities were increasingly black and Democratic. During the 1970s, many big industrial cities suffered serious population losses: St. Louis, Cleveland, Pittsburgh, and Detroit lost more than 20 percent of their population. Philadelphia, Chicago, and New York City saw population drop by more than 10 percent. The surrounding Republican suburbs were the major beneficiaries of this mass migration out of the city. Many middle-class whites fled the cities for the more prosperous suburbs, leaving behind decaying urban cores. New York City, for example, saw its white population drop by 30 percent since 1970. A similar pattern had developed in Boston, Los Angeles, Chicago, and Philadelphia.[62]

While many white voters resented their party's attempt to attract minority support, many blacks complained that the Democrats had taken their loyalty for granted. Faithful support had not prevented blacks from suffering a disproportionate share of economic pain during the recession. "When the economy sneezes, black people get pneumonia," said Vernon Jordan. By the end of Carter's term, the black unemployment rate stood at 14.7 percent—its highest level in five years and more than double that of whites. More than 30 percent of blacks had incomes below the poverty level. The median income of black families, which had risen from 55 percent of white income in 1960 to 61 percent in 1970, had fallen back to 59 percent in 1980.[63]

Many black leaders warned that their commitment to the Democrats was not unconditional. Gary, Indiana mayor Richard Hatcher captured the growing black cry for unity and independence when he told a civil rights conference that blacks needed to reject "the position we are in today—dependent in almost every facet of our lives on someone else, some nonblack person to assist us and allow us to survive." Black leaders pointed out that in the previous six presidential elections the most closely contested states had been in the South and the industrial Northeast. In all of these states, an effective program of voter registration was the key to unlocking black electoral power. In five southern states—Georgia, Texas, Virginia, and the Carolinas only 50 percent of voting age blacks were registered. In six southern states blacks represented 20 percent of the voting-age population. In many of those states the number of unregistered blacks exceeded Reagan's margin of victory in 1980.[64]

The decline of organized labor also frustrated Democratic attempts to sustain the New Deal agenda. In the 1950s, a third of the labor force was unionized. By 1980, it was one-fifth, and in the sun belt, only one-tenth. Not only had the percentage of the unionized work force declined, its membership had also become more middle class. After 1965, service workers and public employees made up a much larger share of membership. The manufacturing share of union membership plummeted from 51 percent in 1956 to 34 percent in 1980; half of the decline occurred between 1974 and 1978. The changing demographics of union membership exposed a serious gap between the views of many union leaders and the concerns of their members. "Labor unions talk about class struggles and oppression to people who can't tell Phil Murray from Arthur," observed one commentator. Many workers resented the inflationary impact of the spending, taxing, and regulatory progress advocated by many unions. A Los

Angeles *Times* poll showed that union members, by two to one, blamed unions more than business for inflation. "When union people become the suburban working class, their concerns change," said Congressman Mickey Edwards. "They are no longer concerned about social change. They're worried about inflation, the cost of groceries, and sending their kids to college. They now have the same interests as those people who were often the targets of the old labor leaders."[65]

The nature of campaigning presented a further challenge to Democratic candidates. Television had a dual impact on national campaigns. It nationalized issues by forcing candidates to articulate themes that could appeal to a broad spectrum of the electorate. This change proved difficult to a generation nurtured on union halls, interest-group conventions, and political rallies where the message was geared to a specific audience. At the same time, by making the relationship between the voter and the candidate more direct, the media had an individualizing effect on politics. Voters no longer depended on party functionaries or interest groups for information about candidates. Instead, they received information and made individual decisions while watching television in the privacy of their homes. Since the large constituency groups no longer exercised their role as intermediaries between politicians and the people, party affiliation, organizational strength, and prominent endorsements were less important than personal style and media presence.

By 1980, liberalism appeared fatigued by years of battle with reactionary conservatives and leftist critics, and exhausted from the demands of governance. The New Deal public philosophy appeared bankrupt: the class-based coalition had been disrupted by racial tension; economic growth—elusive in itself—did not ensure social stability; pluralism had not protected the rights of all citizens; and global anti-communism made little sense in a multi-polar world. Roosevelt had created a progressive community by appealing to groups that perceived of themselves as outside "the system." By 1980, many of those same groups had become the establishment.[66]

It was within this gloomy political environment that Mondale hoped to redefine liberalism's historic mission and reinvigorate the Democratic party. Not until the closing days of the Carter administration did Mondale provide a succinct statement of his new tempered liberalism. Delivered at the Woodrow Wilson Center in October 1980, the address established a firm philosophical foundation for Mondale's next campaign. Calling for a "redefinition of the tradition in American politics for which Hubert Humphrey stood," the Vice President warned that "progressives needed to adjust the liberal values of social justice and compassion to a new age of limited resources." That meant taking inflation as seriously as they had once considered unemployment. "Inflation hurts most the people living in the margins of society about whom progressives have always cared most," he said. In 1980, the Humphrey tradition needed to recognize that "our support of civilized, humane, effective anti-inflation policies is the best way to prevent the climate of generosity on which progressive programs depend from being killed."

Coping with inflation, he declared, was not the only imperative. Liberals needed to learn the proper lessons from Vietnam by making a clear distinction "between the legitimate use of power to protect legitimate American interests, and the indecent use of intervention in contradiction of American values." Progressives also had to show greater concern with implementing efficient, realistic, well-managed social programs without losing sight of the private competitive economic system. At the heart of Mondale's new liberalism was the recognition that liberals needed to pay closer attention to middle-class needs. "People do not cease to count once they leave the shadows of disadvantage and injustice," he concluded. "It is not illiberal for a middle-income family to want help with sending a child to college, or relief from confiscatory taxes; it is not inappropriate for progressives to advocate programs to help them."[67]

The Woodrow Wilson Center speech marked an important stage in the evolution of Mondale's thinking. For the first time he gave expression to the tacit assumptions that had guided many of his actions since 1974. In some ways the speech was incomplete. At a time when the nation's attention was fixed on a deepening recession at home and Soviet aggression abroad, Mondale could limit his discussion to economics and foreign policy. In time, however, a "redefinition" of the liberal tradition had to come to terms with the broader social, economic, and demographic changes that were transforming the party. Also, if his presidential ambitions were ever to be fulfilled, Mondale would have to move beyond academic treatise and present a concrete political message that would unite the party's competing factions behind his candidacy. Though rooted in the party's tradition for social justice, the message would also have to appeal to more conservative voters concerned about America's competitive position in the world economy, worried by the decline of traditional values, and troubled by the nation's declining military strength. Mondale had made an important step in defining his vision of the future, but now he faced an even more formidable task: to develop a political strategy appropriate for his new tempered liberalism.

Governor Rolvaag and Miles Lord look on as Mondale reads news
coverage of his appointment to the Senate in December 1964. (MHS)

The Minnesota Attorney General meets President Kennedy.   (MHS)

In a rare moment of family time, Mondale plays with his
daughter, Eleanor (1961). (MHS)

Joan and Fritz pictured along with their children, Eleanor, William,
and Ted, in this 1964 Christmas photo. (MHS)

The young and ambitious Senator ponders his future.   (MHS)

Posing for the folks back home during a public relations trip to South
Vietnam in 1966.   (MHS)

Vice President Humphrey presents Mondale with a cake celebrating
his thirty-ninth birthday.   (MHS)

A proud Mondale looks on as President Johnson signs the Fair Housing
Act of 1968.   (MHS)

A weary Senator listens to another round of committee testimony.
(Stanley Tretick)

A jubilant Mondale waves to the crowd during the Inauguration Day
parade, January 27, 1977.   (White House photo)

Relaxing with reporters on board Air Force II. (White House photo)

Mondale served as Carter's liaison with the civil rights community. Here he is pictured with Coretta King, Andrew Young, and "Daddy" King.

Despite the serious political differences that emerged during their four years in office, Mondale and Carter managed to maintain a healthy friendship.   (White House photo)

Mondale and Carter discussing issues during their regular Monday lunch meeting.   (White House photo)

Mondale dining with Imelda Marcos during a controversial trip to the
Philippines in May 1978.   (White House photo)

Mondale addresses a UN conference on refugees in Geneva.
(White House photo)

Since Carter refused to campaign while Americans were being held hostage in Iran, Mondale became the administration's chief spokesman during the Democratic primaries. Here he is pictured with challenger Senator Edward Kennedy.   (White House photo)

After working through the night, Mondale and Carter spend their final hours in the oval office monitoring the hostage crisis.
(White House photo)

Mondale and Carter discuss the latest hostage developments with
President-elect Ronald Reagan on inauguration day,
January 20, 1981.   (White House photo)

In small, intimate gatherings such as this one in Iowa, Mondale impressed people with his intelligence, compassion, and wit. Those qualities never translated to television (July 1983). (Robert Burgess)

A dispirited Mondale answers reporters' questions the
day after his defeat in the New Hampshire primary.
(Diana Walker/ Time Magazine)

"Fighting Fritz" displays boxing gloves following his primary victories in Alabama and Georgia.   (Diana Walker/ Time Magazine)

Mondale with his chief primary rivals, Senator Gary Hart and Jesse
Jackson, following a critical debate in New York.
(Diana Walker/ Time Magazine)

Mondale always felt most comfortable campaigning among struggling
workers, minorities, and other traditional Democratic groups.
(Diana Walker/ Time Magazine)

Mondale gives a triumphant "thumbs up" following his address to the
Democratic Convention in which he pledged to raise taxes if
elected President.   (Diana Walker/ Time Magazine)

Campaigning in Texas with his spirited running mate, Representative Geraldine Ferraro. (Bill Pierce/ Time Magazine)

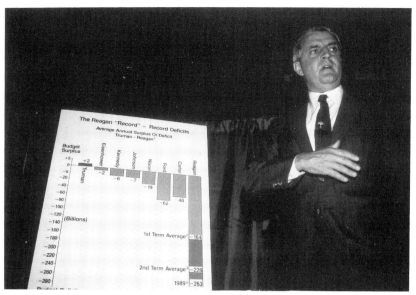

While Reagan campaigned by soundbites, Mondale lectured the nation
on the evils of deficit spending. Here he is shown with a chart
demonstrating the need for a fair tax increase.
(Diana Walker/ Time Magazine)

In the final days of the campaign large and enthusiastic crowds greeted
Mondale everywhere he traveled. (Diana Walker/ Time Magazine)

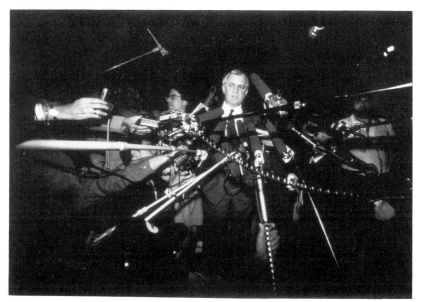

The omnipresent press crowds the candidate upon his arrival at a rally
in Seattle.   (Diana Walker/ Time Magazine)

Two pillars of American liberalism, Senator Edward Kennedy and Walter Mondale, attending a spirited public rally in Boston just days before the 1984 election.   (Diana Walker/ Time Magazine)

14

The Message

For many conservatives, the 1980 election represented the inevitable triumph of Richard Nixon's conservative majority. "Like a great soaking wet shaggy dog, the Silent Majority—banished from the house during the Watergate storms—romped back into the nation's parlor this week and shook itself vigorously," observed William Safire. While conservatives gloated over their victory, many Democrats viewed Reagan's triumph as a clear signal that the party should abandon its liberal heritage. "Basically, the New Deal died yesterday," Massachusetts Senator Paul Tsongas told reporters after the election. Ohio Democratic chairman Paul Tipps agreed with Tsongas' assessment. "The election tells me one thing," Tipps declared. "That is that any public figure who is a liberal Democrat has two choices: find another job or change his philosophy."[1]

There was good reason for liberals to despair. Every national poll revealed Republicans making major gains in public allegiance at the Democrats' expense. A New York *Times*-CBS poll in May showed the country becoming increasingly Republican and more conservative. In January 1980, 53 percent of those questioned identified themselves as Democrats, only 33 percent as Republicans. Four months into the Reagan presidency, the Democratic margin was 49 percent to 41 percent. The survey also showed growing support for the conservative view that "the Government has gone too far in regulating business and interfering with the free enterprise system." These same polls revealed a growing gap between black and white voters on economic issues, making even more difficult Democratic hopes of forging a bi-racial coalition.[2]

In May 1981, the President harnessed the emotional groundswell of sympathy generated by a failed assassination attempt into a significant legislative victory by forcing through Congress a budget resolution that called for deep cuts in many social programs and increased spending for the military. "The Great Society, built and consolidated over fifteen years, was shrunk to size in just 26 hours and 12 minutes of floor debate," observed Newsweek. In August, Congress passed Reagan's tax, plan which included a 25 percent reduction in tax rates over three years. Some observers favorably compared Reagan's success in enacting his conservative agenda to Roosevelt's achievement during the early days of the New Deal. "With a gift for political theater, Mr. Reagan has established his goals faster, communicated a greater sense of economic urgency and come forward with more comprehensive proposals than any new president since the first 100 days of Franklin D. Roosevelt," concluded one journalist.[3]

Critics charged that Reagan's tax policy favored the rich while his budget cuts hurt the poor, but congressional Democrats offered only token opposition. "Under the Reagan dispensation, shame is banished, greed enshrined, and the political supremacy of private wealth celebrated as frankly as it was in the Gilded Age," declared the New Republic. Despite the opposition of the liberal press and the Democratic party leadership, Reagan convinced many southern and conservative Democrats to support his radical program. Casting the debate in stark ideological language, Reagan forced Democrats either to support his popular program or to defend the "failed policies of the past." "I expected him to cut me off at the knee," said a frustrated House Speaker Tip O'Neill, "but he cut me off at the hip." While confident Republicans talked of realignment, humbled Democrats fretted about the 1982 congressional elections. Tip O'Neill told reporters: "1980 was not a realigning election, but 1982 may be."[4]

Emboldened by his legislative victories, Reagan challenged other cherished liberal programs. He appointed to the attorney general's office and to the Civil Rights Commission loyal conservatives who shared his hostility toward affirmative action. He cut funding for the civil rights division of the Justice Department and the Equal Employment Opportunity Commission. The Justice Department ceased preparing cases against segregation in schools or housing. Believing that meddlesome environmental regulations had hampered business, the Reagan administration delayed imposing penalties on chemical companies responsible for toxic waste dumps. James Watt, the controversial Secretary of the Interior, blocked additions to national parks and proposed that up to eighty million acres of federal lands be turned over to private developers by the year 2000. In a direct assault on organized labor, Reagan fired the twelve thousand striking professional Air Traffic Controllers, and loosened OSHA regulations governing the workplace.

Reagan's success left Democrats divided and confused. Many younger Democrats, first elected during the 1970s, appealed to independent, economically conservative voters who felt little kinship with the party's liberal past. Led by Colorado's Gary Hart, these self-identified "neoliberals" suggested Democrats needed to examine "market mechanisms, nonbureaucratic, nonprogrammatic methods" for addressing old problems. More conservative Democrats believed the party had become too closely identified with expanding welfare programs, vacillating world leadership, and the strident demands of numerous minority groups. They turned to Ohio Senator John Glenn, a former Marine fighter pilot who became the first American to orbit the earth. At the same time, many reformers argued Democrats needed to stop seeking greater middle-class support and instead build a class-based coalition among the poor and working class. Only when given an alternative and a voice within the party would these disaffected voters return to the party of Roosevelt. Civil rights activist Jesse Jackson gave voice to these concerns as he traveled the country mobilizing black voters. Senator Edward Kennedy remained the most articulate voice for maintaining the party's liberal direction. "I will never retreat on my fundamental commitment to old values of fairness, decency, equity and compassion," he said.[5]

Mondale removed himself from this heated internal debate by engaging in a "reeducation" program. "What I'm trying to do at first is resist simply responding negatively to this administration," Mondale told the Minneapolis *Tribune* shortly after leaving office. "I'm going to try to emphasize studying and learning again. I really want to spend some time in that area. I think the Reagan Administration is entitled to a good chance." Critics suggested that Mondale's "reeducation" program had more to do with political calculation than it did with intellectual exercise. William Henry of *Time* called it "a gesture so goofy on its face . . . that few people took it seriously enough even to mock it." A Baltimore *Sun* editorial called him "Walter Mitty Mondale" because of his lack of self-definition. He became the subject of ridicule in Gary Trudeau's *Doonesbury* comic strip. Duane, previously Carter's Secretary of Symbolism, told how "Mondale's people have given me complete carte blanche to create a new Walter Mondale." His job was to scrap Mondale's "old identification with liberalism and Jimmy Carter and giv[e] him a whole new political persona."[6]

The criticisms were not completely off the mark. The "reeducation" program conveniently removed Mondale from a heated public debate about Reagan's controversial policies. While many of his potential presidential rivals were forced to go on record either for or against Reagan's policies, Mondale planned to sit on the sidelines until the public delivered its verdict.

But the program also reflected Mondale's belief that both he and the party needed an intellectual boost. "I sensed late in my public career," he reflected, "that we were running out of new ideas." The constant demands of public office had allowed him little time for thoughtful reflection. Now, removed from national office for the first time in sixteen years, Mondale hoped to immerse himself in intellectual discussion, reinvigorate the party, and recapture the initiative from the Republicans.[7]

By 1980, the doubts and uncertainty that had characterized Mondale's first tentative quest for the presidency had dissipated. Four years in the White House had convinced him that he was prepared for the job. Mondale no longer feared the long, grueling days, the weeks away from his family, or the endless campaign stops. He was ready to make whatever sacrifices were necessary to achieve his goal. Before leaving the vice presidency, he told friends and political associates that he planned to seek the Democratic nomination for president in 1984. He discussed his plans with Joan and with his children. All enthusiastically supported the idea.

Mondale understood as well as anyone what questions a successful Democratic candidate needed to address. "How are we to develop our own policies toward a non or less inflationary approach which ensures substantial real economic growth?" he asked in a September memorandum. "What has experience and our efforts to achieve social justice over these many years taught us regarding the proper functions of the federal government?" Finally, he wondered if the party could develop positions on volatile "social issues" such as affirmative action, crime, abortion, gay rights, pornography, tuition tax credits, which would not leave "a mistaken impression that we do not care and are not sensitive to, do not identify with or place a high priority on working with people across this nation" who feel strongly about these issues. Identifying the critical issues represented an important step forward for Mondale and the party. Finding answers that were economically viable, morally justifiable, and politically feasible would be more difficult.[8]

Drawing on his long years of national service, Mondale attracted a host of former government officials and leading academics from universities around the country to help answer these questions. He created policy councils on economics, crime, and East-West relations which met biweekly from June through September. His economic policy group included former Council of Economic Advisers chairmen Charles Schultze and Walter Heller; former Congressional Budget Office head Alice Rivlin; former Federal Reserve Chairman G. William Miller; Nobel Laureates James Tobin of Yale and Robert Solow of the Massachusetts Institute of Technology (MIT); and a host of leading economists including Fred Bergsten of the Institute for International Economics and Lester Thurow of MIT. Sitting around a small seminar table in Mondale's office, they discussed issues ranging from the international effects of monetary policy to urban revitalization. Playing the role of inquisitive student, Mondale sat attentively taking notes and asking questions. "I finally understand how the Fed works," he said gleefully after one meeting.[9]

By the end of the year, Mondale had attended seventeen policy seminars on topics as diverse as law and order, monetary policy, and energy. The historian Barbara Tuchman, the journalist Elizabeth Drew, and speechwriter Marty Kaplan recommended books on topics ranging from ancient archaeology to modern economics. To strengthen his foreign policy credentials, Mondale made two trips to Europe, consulting with high government officials and NATO military commanders. In Israel he talked with Prime Minister Menachem Begin and Labor Party leader Shimon Peres. He also traveled to Japan, China, and South Korea.[10]

Along with his academic pursuits, Mondale attended to the more mundane matters of building an effective political organization. An untaxing position in the Washington law offices of Winston and

Strawn provided the time and money needed to run for President. Accepting a position as "of counsel," Mondale made himself available for special assignments and advice but had little involvement in the firm's day-to-day affairs. Despite his limited service, the firm paid a generous annual salary of $140,000. Combined with a $30,000 government pension, lucrative consulting fees from a number of private companies such as Control Data and Columbia Pictures, and dozens of honoraria, Mondale's income swelled to more than $400,000 in both 1981 and 1982.[11]

Realizing that the constituency groups still exercised considerable influence in key primary states, Mondale actively sought the endorsements from party leaders and elected officials, as well as from the representatives of major Jewish, minority, and liberal organizations. He devoted considerable attention to winning the support of the AFL-CIO, which planned to endorse a primary candidate for the first time in its history. Mondale also placed representatives on the Hunt Commission, another in a series of attempts to establish fair primary and convention procedures. By "front-loading" the calendar with early primaries and caucuses, tightly bunched in time and widely scattered geographically, the new rules favored established candidacies like his own and forestalled an outside challenger from winning the nomination before the national convention. According to the political analyst Alan Baron, Mondale was "better organized, at an earlier stage, than any other nonincumbent in history."[12]

Building on his twenty years in national politics and his experience in three presidential campaigns, Mondale recruited the finest talent from the Party's competing factions. Under the watchful eye of chairman Jim Johnson, Mondale reached out to many former Carter political operatives and disillusioned Kennedy aides. Bob Beckel, a combative former Carter congressional liaison and veteran of the failed 1980 effort, accepted appointment as campaign manager. Tom Donilan, also from the Carter White House, became a deputy campaign manager. Hoping to reach out to the Kennedy wing of the Party, Mondale asked John Reilly, who had been an advisor to both John and Robert Kennedy, to join the campaign as a senior advisor. Reilly agreed and brought with him many other seasoned Kennedy operatives. Paul Tully, who had played a major role in Kennedy's 1980 presidential campaign, accepted a position as Mondale's political director. Hoping to add a voice within the campaign that would speak for more independent voters, Mondale invited Bill Galston, a precocious political scientist from the University of Texas who had worked for John Anderson in 1980, to serve as his national issues director. Also from Texas he recruited Roy Spence as media advisor. Later in the campaign he would add Richard Leone, an experienced New Jersey organizer and former state treasurer, to his national staff.

Joining the new faces were many people who had worked for Mondale during his term as vice president. Maxine Isaacs continued as press secretary, Mike Berman as treasurer, and Marty Kaplan as chief speechwriter. Dick Moe, the candidate's talented former chief-of-staff, directed the congressional delegate-gathering operation. Mondale's family also agreed to join in the effort. Joan had always played an active role in her husband's campaigns. Now she would be joined by their children—Ted, Eleanor, and William—who put their personal lives on hold for two years to support their father's presidential ambitions.

Mondale was not always comfortable with maintaining the low-profile role mandated by his "reeducation" program. He missed the constant media attention and feared that others, especially Ted Kennedy, were grabbing the spotlight. His staff constantly reminded him that having raised public expectations with his "reeducation" program, he could not go public until he had something new and interesting to say. "Every time you appear in the media with nothing new to say, every time you fail to sound like a challenger equal to Ronald Reagan or anyone else, every time you fall back into a defense of the past, you run the risk of diminishing your stature," his press secretary warned. Her advice frequently went unheeded.[13]

In speeches at Columbia's School of Business and the Lyndon Johnson School of Public Affairs, Mondale spoke of the lessons liberals had learned over the previous twenty years. He expressed support of tax cuts for business, defended the Federal Reserve's high interest rates, and stressed the need for economic growth. Despite record unemployment, there were no calls for public works projects, only modest suggestions that deficits be reduced and interest rates be allowed to fall. He did not criticize Reagan's decision to dismantle the Comprehensive Employment and Training Act, the chief federal jobs program of the Carter administration. "Some of the CETA jobs were desirable, some were not," he told reporters. "I'm not calling for the restoration of that." "Where we overregulated, we should cut back. Where we fueled inflation, we should restrain our deficit. Where we overtaxed, we should push for tax relief. Where government has been clumsy or expensive, we should make government better." His speeches, bristling with praise of the free enterprise system, lauded "free market incentives" and supported the decontrol of oil and gas prices.[14]

At other times, however, a more partisan Mondale appeared, lashing out at Reagan for hurting the poor and working class, and for caring about only the rich. In July 1981, before a spirited Urban League convention, Mondale claimed that sixteen years of social and economic progress for blacks was now under assault. "What worries me today is that just when America is hitting its moral stride, there are those who would stop our progress dead in its tracks," he said. He spoke passionately of his support for the Voting Rights Act and efforts to extend it. "We marched, we petitioned, and some of us died," he declared as five thousand enthusiastic delegates shouted their approval, "And those who died did not die so that sixteen years later we could repeal the sacred act they won." In the same month that he praised free enterprise at Columbia, he told a Democratic fund-raiser in Los Angeles that Reagan was adopting an unfair policy of shifting wealth from the working people to the rich through new taxing policies and following "an utterly radical and reckless course to devastate the soil and water of this country." While admitting that the Democrats had made mistakes, he quoted Roosevelt to prove that Democratic errors were "sins of the warm-hearted" while the Reagan Administration's mistakes were "sins of the cold-blooded . . . a government frozen in the ice of its own indifference."[15]

In January 1982, the reeducation program culminated in a seminar at the Wye Plantation on Maryland's Eastern Shore. In the presence of 125 advisors and political experts, Mondale opened the meeting by affirming the resurgence of the Democratic Party. "The emotional collapse is over," he declared. "The finances are improving, and there is a general sense emerging that we can be competitive again." The party's central problem, he told those in attendance, "is that we are viewed as stale, backward-looking and tied to the status-quo." Rather than attacking Reagan, Democrats needed to define alternatives. "We must begin one issue at a time to identify the elements of our long-range vision. The answers will not come overnight and they will not all be painless," he warned. "Yet, I am optimistic that we can begin to make progress." He made clear the direction he wanted the party to move. "In 1980 we lost the middle class. They thought we cared only about the very poor," he asserted. "We have to emphasize the importance of federal efforts to serve the middle class."[16]

Mondale believed that by reforging an alliance with the middle class, Democrats could weaken the Republican stranglehold on the

conservative South. He also expressed confidence that he could translate his loyal service to Carter into political support in the South. "If
I have [a] natural constituency," he speculated, it is "from Massachusetts to Minnesota; Missouri to Maryland then West and South are
looking at me but not in love with me. [I] need to change that if I am
to be [a] national candidate." Suggesting the South was "a sleeper for
us," Mondale hoped that by combining his natural support among
blacks and liberals with a "reasonable proportion of [the] white vote,"
he could "force Ronald Reagan to campaign nationally."[17]

The discussion at the Wye Plantation touched on the central question plaguing Mondale's nascent presidential campaign, and, indeed,
the Democratic Party in the 1980s: What message would attract white
middle class voters without alienating traditional constituencies? Over
the next few years Mondale and his staff searched in vain for an
answer to this question. In part, Mondale's commitment to reforging
the New Deal coalition hampered his ability to find a solution. Though
social and demographic changes had eroded the base of support that
had sustained the constituency groups through much of the postwar
era, Mondale continued to believe that labor, blacks and liberal organizations provided the backbone of a successful campaign and the
foundation for effective governance. Tied by bonds of loyalty, Mondale refused to engage in public disagreement with members of his
coalition. "Whatever his private thoughts may have been," Galston
recalled, "he viewed it as something between a breach of political
etiquette and a breach of political morality to come out in public
against the grain of some important value, idea or policy that some
traditional friend espoused." However much he recognized the need
to update the liberal agenda, Mondale stubbornly refused to change
the way he built support for his program. "The commitment to an
older style of doing business politically," reflected Galston, "created
very strict limits to the real possibilities of rethinking."[18]

But the "message" problem transcended Mondale's limitations and
raised the issue of whether, in the 1980s, a Democrat could build a
broad coalition that included the white middle class. Reagan's rhetoric
had enormous appeal to voters frustrated with government regulations, high taxes, enlarged welfare rolls, and preferential treatment
for minorities. How could a Democrat appeal to these concerns while
also defending the needs of those groups who had suffered most from
Reagan's budget cuts? What message could convey a faith in positive
government without raising fears of encroaching national power?
Perhaps the racial gap remained the most difficult to bridge. How

would Democrats convince blacks that the party had not abandoned them without antagonizing whites? How would it address explosive issues such as affirmative action? Pundits and politicians agreed that the party needed a new message, but no one offered realistic answers to these questions.

By early 1982, Reagan's troubles had deepened more than anyone had anticipated. Industrial production plunged, unemployment grew to post-depression highs, and the deficit ballooned. The Federal Reserve Board's policy of strict monetary policy proved devastating to the auto and steel industries. Car sales fell to their lowest level in twenty years. Housing starts hit a fifteen-year low. Businesses were going bankrupt at a pace 42 percent faster than in 1980. By the summer of 1982, the unemployment rate had soared to 9.8 percent, the highest since the depression. States with heavy industry were hit hardest and blue-collar workers, women who had recently entered the workforce, and minorities suffered most. The President's program received a further blow when Budget Director David Stockman called the tax cut a "Trojan horse" to induce Congress to lower tax rates on the wealthy.[19]

The recession eroded public support for many of Reagan's policies. "The claim of supply-side economics is that it can cure a sick economy through the healing power of greed," wrote the New Republic's TRB. Reagan added to the doubts with his disengaged style and embarrassing displays of inattention and ignorance. "If ignorance is bliss," wrote the Boston Globe's Curtis Wilkie, "the Reagan Administration is the embodiment of the politics of joy." Of most interest to Democrats were polls showing the President losing the support of blue-collar workers. By early 1982, his overall approval rating dropped to 46 percent while 51 percent hoped he would not seek a second term. A majority of the public believed he did not do enough about unemployment and "cares more about serving upper-income people" than any other group. The sharpest decline in support came from Democrats who had voted for him in 1980.[20]

The recession may have wounded Reagan, but it also injured Mondale. With Reagan apparently faltering, Mondale felt pressure to establish himself as a credible alternative. "Every day he treads water," observed David Garth, "he falls behind." The reeducation program ended before it had addressed the central problem plaguing Mondale's candidacy: How could he reconcile his constituency politics with his desire to appeal to independent voters? With Democrats eager to make gains in the upcoming congressional election, Mondale abandoned his lower-profile reeducation program and brought his mixed message around the nation in a flurry of speeches and appearances for congressional candidates. During 1982, he campaigned for Democrats in ninety-five congressional districts, seventeen Senate races, twenty-two gubernatorial contests, and appeared in numerous Party events in more than forty states. He helped raise $2.2 million directly for the Committee for the Future of America. "If you covet a glimpse of Mondale these days, do not look in the library," a sarcastic David Broder wrote; "try the airport, instead."[21]

Before conservative audiences in the South and West, Mondale emphasized the themes of economic growth, meeting the needs of the future, and a return to excellence in education and science. Everywhere he traveled, Mondale reminded voters that his campaign focused on the future, not the past. "I seek the presidency to sharpen our competitive edge," he repeated hundreds of times. "I want an America whose Government pushes exports, whose industries modernize equipment, and whose workers train for the future." Stressing that America needed to compete in foreign trade and make the next generation "the best trained, the best educated in history," he attacked the Administration for cutting loans to foreign companies buying American goods. Sometimes sounding uncharacteristically jingoistic, Mondale called on the Administration to "get tough" with nations that erect trade barriers to American products. "What are our kids supposed to do?" he asked. "Sweep up around Japanese computers and sell McDonald's hamburgers the rest of their lives?" He advocated import restrictions "for a limited time" to provide American industries a chance to modernize; proposed an energy tax to discourage consumption and reduce the transfer of American wealth to foreign oil-producing countries; favored a more competitive export bank policy linked with a "much firmer" free trade approach; expressed sympathy for "tax breaks targeted on productive investment," and spoke about the possibility of seeking capital investment write-offs and tax credits for businesses with little or no taxable income. He promoted a capital budget that would finance the rebuilding and expansion of railroads, bridges, highways, subways, and ports. He toughened his position on crime by opposing plea bargaining for those accused of violent crime and by advocating construction of new prisons.[22]

Before more traditionally Democratic audiences in the Northeast and Midwest, he emphasized fairness and old-fashioned economic populism. In February, 1982, during a campaign swing through Ohio, Michigan, Wisconsin, and Iowa, he ridiculed the Administration's tax bill claiming it made taxes for major corporations "something like the United Fund—you send just what you think you can afford." Reagan, he said, had forgotten about children, ordinary Americans, and basic "fairness" in his program. Excoriating Reagan for "the most misleading and irresponsible budget ever submitted by a President of the United States," Mondale promised to reduce military spending, repeal some of the corporate tax benefits, and urge the Federal Reserve to bring down interest rates. He assailed the administration for destroying "the governmental structure of fairness that a shared consensus of Americans had put in place over all these years." At times, Mondale fine-tuned his message into a penetrating populist appeal. "It's as though they've found a forgotten minority—the super rich," he shouted, his voice full of contempt. "It's as though the nation had been dedicated to a new concept—free the Fortune 500."[23]

Staff members who traveled with the candidate observed Mondale's discomfort as he struggled to present a new message without abandoning his older commitments. Traveling companion Larry Hansen noted after one trip that the former vice president "desperately wants to be viewed as serious, as being forward-looking, as having some vision, as understanding the imperatives imposed on America by a rapidly changing world," but found that many of his themes lacked specificity. "WFM's long-range economic prescription—while headed in the right direction, does not sound well developed," he wrote. Mondale "decries the harm caused by budgetary cuts in social programming, but admits we cannot afford to return to 1965 and that certain reductions in discretionary and entitlement programs may be necessary." He had no idea, however, which entitlement programs he could cut and what the political consequences would be. "Fortunately," Hansen wrote, "he has not been pushed by the press for specifics."[24]

Before traditionally Democratic audiences of union members, unemployed workers, senior citizens, and minorities, an impassioned populist rhetoric replaced impassive discourses on economic policy. Despite his intellectual desire to rethink liberalism, many of the "new" issues never grabbed Mondale viscerally. "It seemed to me the times Mondale was most comfortable," Hansen reflected, "was when he was in front of his own people—labor unions, black audiences, teachers, Jewish groups [where] the old message still resonated." Before business groups, Mondale "used the right words but they were shorn of any detail and they certainly seemed to be shorn of any kind of passion." A man raised in a tradition with a deep commitment to issues of social and economic justice could not get too excited by questions of competence and productivity.[25]

In November 1982, Mondale tried attracting public attention to his efforts by writing an article for the *New York Times Magazine*. The attempt fell far short of his expectations. Mondale had not only failed to develop a well-defined message, but also the *Times* accidentally published an early unpolished version of the article that had been written largely by a speechwriter. Claiming to reexamine "old priorities and shibboleths," Mondale came out against inflation and for social progress; against waste and in support of efficiency in government; in favor of a "strong military capability" but opposed to a bloated defense budget. Progressives, he insisted, "must be responsive to business needs without being subservient to them," and accept that "we have stumbled on the issue of crime." It was, Mondale admitted later, "a soft piece and it appeared not to have an edge to it."[26]

The upcoming Democratic midterm convention, scheduled to meet in Philadelphia on June 25, provided Mondale with his first big challenge of the campaign, for he would be sharing the podium with Edward Kennedy, his chief competitor for the nomination. The press would be watching closely, trying to pick a winner. Mondale's polls showed that he pulled better than Kennedy among independents, Democrats who voted for Reagan, higher-income voters, and Southerners—exactly the group Mondale hoped to attract. As David Garth said; "Right now, Mondale must be regarded as the Democratic candidate with more potential than Kennedy in the race." Kennedy, however, still had a loyal following within the party itself, which made him a formidable primary candidate.[27]

For most of the previous year, Mondale had successfully used focused messages in appealing to specific party constituencies. But the mid-term conference, by gathering all party elements under the glare of the national media, would require a unified theme, an articulation of the "Mondale message." Hoping to discover that message, Mondale, on June 6, sat down at his typewriter—a rare event in itself—and wrote a thirteen-page draft of his speech. He began by identifying the party with its past battles. "When the waves of immigrants came to our shores it was our party that received them and [made] them a part of America. When our farmers were exploited by railroads and the grain trade, it was our party that preserved family farming." He went on to talk about the Party's struggle on behalf of senior citizens, blacks, women, and labor. "But while proud of our past, we know we must [be] measured by our vision of the future." After listing the litany of Democratic concerns—the environment, trade policy, basic industry, nuclear freeze, rebuilding the nation's infrastructure, and campaign finance reform—Mondale moved on to stress the importance of economic growth and entrepreneurship. "Most new ideas, most jobs, most productivity, and most competition benefitting the consumer comes from small business," he declared. "American entrepreneurship is a unique American advantage. . . . The democratic party must . . . listen more carefully to small business and be their ally and supporter." [28]

Mondale hoped that by reaffirming his commitment to old values and demonstrating his concern for new issues he could appeal to independent voters and the constituency groups. His delicate balancing act failed to convince his advisors. Speechwriter Fred Martin and former Johnson aide Harry McPherson argued for a more traditional approach, claiming he sounded, in Martin's words, "like a trend-minded Atari Democrat with whom our party's main constituencies have nothing in common." The speech might "get a glowing column from David Broder, but big deal," he argued. "What you want is to win the applause of the delegates in the hall and to show the reporters that you did just that." Martin rewrote the draft, removing the rhetoric about new solutions and substituting a biting attack on Reagan and praise for the party's "timeless" values. [29]

While instinctively attracted to the tone of the speech, Mondale wondered whether after a two-year education program he could appear before the national media and repeat old Democratic dogma. He sent both drafts to Marty Kaplan for his suggestions. Kaplan expressed alarm at a draft that, while full of emotion and drama, could have been used as a stump speech in 1976. "After listening," he wrote, "I'd be hard-pressed to name a single fresh theme or idea which holds it together." Kaplan, in turn, wrote his own draft, which lauded free enterprise and stressed the importance of productivity and national strength. Underlying the speech was a theme of repentance. "For a while, my fellow Democrats, this Party failed to pin its hopes on a growing free enterprise economy. I ask you tonight: let us put that behind us." [30]

Confused by the conflicting advice and unsure of his new message, Mondale chose the old gospel. In a flawlessly delivered speech, interrupted twenty-seven times by applause, he scathingly denounced the foreign, domestic, and military policies of the Reagan administration. He charged that Reagan was creating "two Americas—one where the well-to-do get more and more, and one where the rest of us get less and less." "In Reagan's America's," he continued, "if you're sick, they make you pay more. If you're young, they call ketchup a vegetable [a reference to the condiment's having been declared a vegetable under the provisions of the school lunch program]. If you're poor, they fire your lawyer. If you're hungry, they make you wait in the cold for cheese." Mondale was greeted with loud applause when he noted that the Constitution called for the government to "provide for the common defense and the general welfare. It's not the common defense or the general welfare. It says both." "Fellow Democrats," he concluded, "Our task is nothing less than to end the icy indifference and reunite America. Let this party of the people win this election for the people in 1982."[31]

Attacks against Reagan aroused the partisans, but they failed to articulate a substantive Democratic alternative. United under a new slogan, "With Fairness to All," party delegates papered over the divisions between liberals and conservatives, neoliberals and New Dealers. They blasted Reagan on every issue but offered only a few proposals for change. The platform criticized Soviet expansion in Central America as "unacceptable" but called for a military cut-off if congressional standards on human rights and economic reforms were not met. They tried to steal the mantle of "fiscal responsibility" by raking Reagan over the coals for his enormous budget deficits. At the same time, they proposed massive new spending programs, including a $7.5 billion federal jobs program.[32]

By July, Mondale's staff expressed satisfaction with the campaign's progress, although they noted a couple of potential trouble areas. Press secretary Maxine Isaacs, concerned about Mondale's continuing discomfort on television (she suggested he was not "intimate" enough for the medium) and his sometimes stilted public speaking style, recommended that he begin speech and television coaching. Mondale, stiff and emotionless, conveyed little warmth or personality over the tube. It was a familiar theme—once the cameras turned on, Mondale turned cold. "You'd be surprised how many people commented, after *Face the Nation,* that the best part was after the sound went off and you and the panel sat back, relaxed and smiled," Isaacs observed. Mondale, as he had in the past, expressed interest. "O.K.— Let's go," he scribbled. Then, as always, he found excuses not to attend the practice sessions.[33]

Johnson and Galston identified a far more serious problem. Mondale's Philadelphia speech had boosted his standing with party professionals and the organized constituencies. Perhaps because of that success, though, he was experiencing serious problems with opinion makers and the public. Opinion makers, they informed Mondale, "tend to think of you as uninspired, with few fresh ideas and no clear vision of the future. And many see you as constitutionally incapable of saying no to single-issue constituencies." The public lacks "a clear sense of who you are and what you stand for." They emphasized again—but offered no solution to—the central problem he faced. The "day-to-day task of keeping organized constituencies happy will tempt you to make commitments that reinforce opinion-makers' perceptions of you as weak and fragment your profile into a blurred jumble of unrelated entanglements."[34]

In November, the mid-term election results indicated that the Democratic message, despite its contradictions and inconsistencies, was scoring with voters. Democrats used broad public dissatisfaction with the economy to win back many voters who had defected in 1980. Although Republicans retained control of the Senate, Democrats won twenty-six House seats, seven governorships, and six more state legislatures. Perhaps at no time since World War II, the New York *Times* reported, did the outcome of a mid-term election depend so heavily on a single issue: the public's reaction to the Administration's economic performance. Discontent over Reagan's handling of the economy played a major role in most Democratic gains in the industrial Midwest, Pennsylvania, West Virginia, and Texas. Reagan lost support among many traditionally Democratic groups, including union households, Catholic and Jewish voters, blacks, and Hispanics.[35]

Mondale received more good news a few weeks later. On December 1, at a crowded press conference, Kennedy removed himself from the race saying his "overriding obligation" to his children prevented him from being a candidate. Mondale, who inherited much of Kennedy's support, emerged the biggest beneficiary. Some polls showed Mondale's support among Democrats jumped as much as 15 points following Kennedy's withdrawal.[36]

The mid-term election results and Kennedy's withdrawal presented great short-term possibilities for Mondale but long-term risks. The election convinced many Democrats, including Mondale, that given the poor economic climate, the "old gospel" could reassemble the coalition. "The standard Democratic line was Reagan was Hoover and all we have to do is a credible recreation of FDR and we're off to the races," said Galston. At the same time, Kennedy's withdrawal gave Mondale the opportunity to snatch the endorsements of most of the major constituency groups, locking up the nomination early and turning his attention to the general election long before the Convention. Both calculations carried long-term risk. The midterm election would be a good indicator only if the recession continued—which it would not. The intensified desire to win the constituency groups would compound his trouble with independent voters and muddle his "new liberalism" message.[37]

For now, however, these events appeared to confirm Mondale's inevitable march toward the nomination. In January 1983 Mondale outshone his opponents at the California State Democratic convention. Hart's uninspiring speech failed to distinguish any of the new ideas upon which he based his candidacy. Glenn, according to one report, "held the audience's attention with a methodical style that made him sound like the star sophomore in an elocution school." Mondale, on the other hand, electrified the audience by describing "what I'd do—right now—if I were President." He would "chop those deficits down by scaling the defense budget to reality . . . slam a lid on hospital costs . . . reduce the scheduled tax cut for the wealthy." He promised to push for a federal holiday honoring Martin Luther King and to send SALT II to the Senate. "Right now, today," his voice boomed around the cavernous convention hall, "I would repropose the Equal Rights Amendment and I would pledge that I would get that thing ratified." The hall shook, as delegates rose to their feet in enthusiastic applause. "It was Mondale's Show," declared David Broder.[38]

Mondale began 1983 with every reason to feel confident. He had a paid staff of thirty-five workers in twenty-three states, thousands of volunteers, and a $10 million budget. "I'll bet he'll have the nomination sewed up early and will be the next President," one House Democrat said. None of the other candidates could match him on organization, money, or name recognition. "It is far too early to say that the rest of the Democratic field is playing 'Stop Mondale,' " wrote Morton Kondracke in the *New Republic,* "but the other candidates are definitely trying to catch him." Mondale, wrote David Broder, "has the capacity to make this Democratic marathon dull, if he continues to pass each test as well as he passed last summer's Philadelphia mini-convention and last weekend's Sacramento talent show."[39]

In the weeks leading up to the February 21 announcement of his candidacy, Mondale worked with his speechwriters, Fred Martin and Marty Kaplan, to develop a clear statement of what he hoped to accomplish. The announcement, they said, needed to define a guiding philosophy that would unite the coalition behind his candidacy. Mondale agreed, but insisted that the speech not attempt to re-create him. Fidelity to the past and concern for the constituency groups had to be included. "I've got to define myself again, remind them who I am, where I came from, what I believe," he said. The frustrated speechwriters spent hours trying unsuccessfully to elicit from Mondale the guiding message of his campaign. "It was obvious that we were an author in search of a play," recalled Martin. "We had a hell of a time putting down on paper what this campaign was going to be all about." Early drafts of the speech focused on the need for community and the recognition of shared responsibility, but Mondale found the idea too abstract for public consumption. "People don't want to hear about community," he insisted, "they want to know about jobs, health care, and more practical concerns." Unable to articulate a simple compelling message that both captured his vision of the future and satisfied the party's important constituency groups, Mondale focused his attention on specific issues.[40]

While there was nothing wrong with the desire to outline his substantive position on major issues, Mondale needed a theme that would make his candidacy more than the sum of its various parts. Realizing that the campaign's message could come only from the candidate himself, his speechwriters tried to extract from Mondale why he wanted to be president. In a series of taped conversations, Mondale again expressed his desire to end the arms race, improve education, deal equitably with the poor and elderly, and make America competitive in the world economy. When pressed to crystallize his purpose into a word or phrase Mondale declared, "I'm ready." He strongly believed that his extensive experience as Minnesota's attorney general, United States senator, and vice president had provided him with unequaled knowledge of government, understanding of the issues, and ability to get things done. Since Mondale considered his experience to be the defining characteristic of his campaign, his speechwriters gave it a prominent place in the speech. "The result," said Martin, "was 'I am ready,' preceded by a laundry list of issues, concerns, topics, cares, and wants of enormous length."[41]

On February 21, in the company of 330 friends and supporters, Mondale announced his candidacy from the ornate House chamber of the Minnesota capitol. He spoke confidently of his experience, saying: "I know myself: I am ready. I am ready to be President of the United States." The statement drew an outburst of applause from the partisan crowd. While declaring that improved education and economic growth would enable the United States to "lead the world again," Mondale touched on problems ranging from the nuclear freeze to urban crime. Contrasting himself with Reagan, he dismissed the notion that government itself was the greatest problem facing the country. "Human suffering, a faltering economy, a dangerous arms race, a divided America; these are the problems," he said. "Today there are American families sleeping in cars, searching for work, and tasting the grapes of wrath." His biggest applause came when he declared his determination to reduce the "mindless, wasteful madness" of the nuclear arms race and negotiate a mutual and verifiable nuclear freeze, and later when he called for an Equal Rights Amendment to the Constitution. Mondale said he wanted an America "where working people don't have to pay more so that the privileged can pay less." Looking to the future, he called for a policy to strengthen entrepreneurship and free enterprise, a commitment to the sciences and a trade policy that "insists that our trading partners open their markets as wide to us as we open ours to them."[42]

The announcement did not give Mondale the lift he expected. In the first few weeks of the campaign, reporters hounded him about his association with Carter. Mondale, linked to Carter's failed leadership just as Humphrey had been crippled by his association with Johnson's Vietnam policy, decided not to make the same mistake Humphrey had made. To put distance between himself and the former president he served, Mondale revealed that he had disagreed with a number of administration decisions—the "crisis of confidence speech," the grain embargo, the Rose Garden strategy. He never, however, revealed the depth of his disaffection with the administration or his thoughts about resigning.[43]

Mondale also found himself trapped in the politics of Chicago, where an old supporter, Richard Daley, was campaigning for mayor against a black candidate, Harold Washington. In the final week of the Democratic primary, Mondale followed through on a long-standing promise and endorsed Daley's candidacy. The move infuriated blacks who charged that the Democratic Party refused to respect them despite their loyal support. Mondale's calculated gamble backfired when Washington won the primary. The columnist Carl Rowan, expressing the sentiment of many black voters, declared: "Mondale has some explaining to do."[44]

Potential rivals, sensing Mondale's vulnerability despite his organizational advantage, announced their candidacies. In April, John Glenn declared his campaign would be based on the "small town" values of "excellence, honesty, fairness and compassion" he had learned as a boy. Emphasizing traditional values and strong leadership qualities, he hoped to attract independent voters and disaffected Democrats. Running second to Mondale in most opinion polls, Glenn possessed two qualities essential for a television age: broad name recognition and star quality. "The difference between the two candidates is clear whenever they appear together," commented a reporter from the New York *Times*. "People turn their heads to get a glimpse of Mr. Mondale, but they pull out their Instamatics when Senator Glenn comes into view."[45]

If Glenn faded, other contenders were prepared to take his place as Mondale's chief antagonist. In his February announcement, Gary Hart had called upon Democrats to "break the grip of narrow, negative agendas and special-interest government in Washington," and to begin "the passage we must make between two worlds—the world of our parents and the one we will leave to our children." Jesse Jackson planned to build a coalition of discontent among minorities, the poor, and elderly whom he felt had been abandoned by both parties. Alan Cranston, a 68-year-old California Senator, hoped to fill the vacuum left by Kennedy's withdrawal. He argued that the nuclear freeze was the most important issue in the campaign. Fritz Hollings, an imposing silver-haired Senator from South Carolina, and Rubin Askew, a former Florida governor, emphasized the importance of having a Southern candidate on the ticket.

More unsettling than the Carter connection, the Chicago imbroglio, or the Glenn challenge were the persistent charges that Mondale was a captive of the "special interests." Former Carter advisor Hamilton Jordan raised the issue in an article published in the *New Republic*. "The question is," Jordan declared, "Can he be tough with the special interests?" Numerous stories appeared in the national press about Mondale's subservience to organized labor. "If there can be a President who is able to inspire a purposeful cooperation among industry, labor, and government," wrote the *Atlantic's* Gregg Easterbrook, "Mondale might prove to be the one, but to succeed, he must be willing to say no to his supporters in organized labor, as Reagan should be willing to say no to the wealthy." Critics pointed out that he promised to expand Medicare and Medicaid, extend unemployment insurance, provide new job training, deliver more money for teachers salaries, and create jobs for rebuilding America's infrastructure. While Mondale estimated the total cost at $30 billion, many experts put it much higher. Reporters recalled how he had temporized during the Vietnam War, unwilling to alienate his friend Hubert Humphrey. Perhaps now, they hinted, the same lack of courage would make him unable to offend established interest groups.[46]

Most of these lingering doubts about Mondale's political fortitude were unjustified. Critics lamented the growing influence of special-interest groups, but the decline of party organization and the financial demands of mass media campaigns had made interest group government a fact of life in the nation's capital. Every presidential candidate, from both political parties, courted these groups. Most often, Mondale's loudest critics were Democratic rivals who discovered the evils of special interests only after failing to win their endorsements; or Republicans who, after feeding from the troughs of big business, accused their opponents of being pawns of labor. In fact, few politicians rewarded his supporters more generously than Ronald Reagan. But the President, by keeping the political bargaining behind closed doors and presenting to the public a carefully choreographed message that conveyed strength and independence, severed the link between politics and policy. Mondale, on the other hand, practiced the politics of coalition building in the full glare of the media, thus accentuating the connection between seeking votes and promising benefits. Mass media allowed modern candidates to bypass traditional power structures and appeal directly to the anti-establishment sentiments of most voters. But Mondale practiced the politics of social cohesion. Believing that most people looked to responsible community leaders for clues about how to vote, he courted interest groups, local officials, and civic leaders but avoided direct appeals to voters.

Though he had been in the public eye for over two decades, Mondale remained an enigma to many who observed him. "By his own choice," wrote David Harris, "he is at the same time a formidable enough commodity to be considered a political fixture, yet as a person so unknown as to be effectively indistinguishable from his circumstances." The veteran journalists Jack Germond and Jules Witcover noted that despite his considerable talents, "Mondale's image is still hazy, if not contradictory." He was, they wrote, "always smart, occasionally tough, sometimes funny." He possessed the "savvy that comes from experience inside both Congress and the White House," and presented himself as "a practiced politician who knows all the moves and doesn't make dumb mistakes."

While on paper Mondale appeared to be "the ideal presidential candidate for the Democratic party in 1984," some people perceived him as old and stale, unable to adjust to new times. "The problem for Mondale is the image they've had of Mondale being around so long and being frozen on the left," commented an Alabama party leader. At the same time, many on the left, who invariably pointed to his public defense of Carter's conservative economic policies, suggested that Mondale lacked the toughness to fight for liberal principles. "People say he doesn't stand for anything," remarked a Kennedy partisan. In either case, Mondale's attempt to forge a moderate coalition within the party failed to arouse enthusiasm among any particular group. "No one's terribly excited about Mondale," observed one Democrat. "No one really dislikes him, but no one gets terribly excited about his candidacy, either."[47]

In many ways, Mondale's cautious, sometimes phlegmatic, manner contributed to his lack of definition. Reporters covering Mondale observed, in the words of New York *Times* correspondent Bernard Weinraub, a "contradiction between the private man, who speaks with intensity and conviction of the needs of the poor and the plight of the elderly, and the public speaker whose natural reticence enhances his caution on the campaign trail." In private, Weinraub wrote, "Mr. Mondale can be irreverent, self-deprecating, witty, and engaging. But when he climbs off planes and faces television cameras to speak at rallies and in public forums, his voice turns reedy and his speeches ramble. He seems formal, even somewhat stiff." Reporters noted that in small groups Mondale displayed an easy manner and an infectious humor. David Harris, after traveling with the campaign, claimed that if Mondale won the nomination, he "will be the most quick-witted Democrat to head the ticket since John F. Kennedy." Elizabeth Drew, the *New Yorker's* perceptive political reporter, observed that Mondale's "public persona is an odd combination of the gregarious politician and the contained private man." In private, she wrote, "he conveys that he cares about what he is saying, that he is indignant about the inequities he is describing." Although lacking "flair," he demonstrates "that he has thought about the important questions" and "that he is the most knowledgeable and experienced of the candidates."[48]

Mondale's Norwegian heritage, his personal reserve, and his discomfort with the star qualities essential for media campaigns accentuated his image problem. "His dignity is very important to him," said Isaacs. "You won't see him in any funny hats." Before every public appearance, Mondale carefully combed his hair, straightened his tie, buttoned his grey suit jacket and removed his reading glasses. He refused to be photographed with a cigar in his mouth or a drink in his hand. "When he sees the camera go up, it's as if a mask slides over his face," commented New York photographer Alex Webb. "The man I've been talking to withdraws, and I'm left with the politician." The result, concluded Weinraub, was "a politician who resists revealing himself to the public."[49]

These potentially serious problems did not prevent the Mondale organization from assuming a public posture of supreme confidence, even arrogance. Mondale's pollster Peter Hart dismissed the special-interest charge. "We certainly have an understanding of what cuts and doesn't cut against the candidate, and we don't think this one cuts," he said. In April, Mondale scored a decisive victory at the Massachusetts State Democratic Convention. "The Mondale machine continues to roll," reported Morton Kondracke. The Gallup poll showed Mondale leading Glenn by a margin of 32 percent to 13 percent, and more important, beating all possible opponents in the key opening primary and caucus states. On April 15, Mondale filed his 1983 financial report with the Federal Election Commission showing that his $2.1 million raised and $1.4 million spent was double that of his nearest rival.

But the campaign stumbled in Wisconsin where Cranston won with 39 percent of the vote to Mondale's 36 percent. In May, a Los Angeles *Times* poll showed Glenn with a slight national lead over Mondale. The Wisconsin loss and the Los Angeles *Times* poll precipitated a serious debate within the organization about how to respond to the growing chorus of critics accusing Mondale of pandering to the "special interests."[50]

Many staff members believed the "special interest" charge was a symptom of a much deeper problem. "What started as a mere flutter in the wind," an aide wrote Mondale, "has now become a major cliche that is mentioned on virtually every public and private occasion at which your candidacy is discussed." For most of the summer, in a number of intense and sometimes emotional strategy sessions, the campaign staff debated how Mondale should respond to the charges. While they disagreed in emphasis and direction, a number of close advisors urged Mondale to make fundamental substantive and stylistic changes. Issues director Bill Galston and speechwriter Marty Kaplan spearheaded the group, but they could count on the support of media advisor Roy Spence, political director Paul Tully, and numerous outside advisors who offered their services to the campaign. They agreed that Mondale had failed on two levels. First, he had not succeeded in presenting a favorable public image. Internal polls continued to show that most voters considered him boring, uninspiring, and just another "hack." Spence wrote that Mondale projected the image of "a nice guy, a typical old fashioned Democratic politician, a politician whose heart is in the right place but has no real depth, no inner strength, no real backbone—a politician who is so tied to the old answers that he is not up to the job of leading a New America." Second, and even more serious, Mondale's message continued to be muddled. Kaplan warned that the only theme that emerged from his announcement address was "I'm ready." "But," he warned, "few people feel they know what it is that you're ready to do."[51]

These advisors worried that Mondale's visceral commitment to older Democratic battles was undermining his credibility as a spokesman for many middle-class concerns. They wanted Mondale to identify himself with the issues of economic growth and national strength, to distance himself from the specific demands of the party's interest groups, and to emphasize his vision of the future. Rather than outlining his differences with Reagan, they urged Mondale to "offer a different way of looking at the world." The "laundry list" of issues would no longer suffice; he had to present a compelling vision that would arouse partisans and convince independents that he offered the best hope for the future of the country. Establishing that credibility would also require demonstrating his own strength of character by convincing Americans "that you will draw lines and stand your ground, take stands and fight for them, and kick ass, if necessary, to get the job done."[52]

These advisors all agreed Mondale lacked a simple compelling message, which would provide "an evocation of basic American values and idealism; a celebration of American possibilities" that was necessary to arouse political passion. A campaign running on "competence and experience," did little to "make people want to stand up and march out of the hall and go to the trenches for the Mondale candidacy." Television required candidates to transcend group identification and tap basic values common to most Americans. It reveled in star qualities of independence and downplayed party organization or affiliation. Harry McPherson suggested that Mondale had spent too many years listening to experts who "have ideas about how to restructure government programs to make them more effective in solving problems," but have no idea how to "speak to the gut." Quoting from Lincoln, he suggested that Mondale "disenthrall" himself from experts and "speak in simple terms—and sometimes in critical, get-off-your-duff terms—to the average fellow. After he wins the election he can redesign the erector set."[53]

Many of the changes proposed were stylistic, requiring a change in the way Mondale presented himself to the public. Kaplan pleaded with Mondale to develop "the speech." "It's about 12 minutes long," he wrote. "It doesn't explain the misalignment of currencies, but it does explain to confused people how the world works, who WFM is, and what America will be like once he's in office." Spence suggested Mondale change his hair style, his shirt collars, his hand gestures, his voice, and even his smile in order to convey strength and conviction on television. Mondale, complained an aide, sounded too rational and intelligent when discussing solutions to problems. They proposed that rather than listing the relative merits of various proposals before choosing the best option, he should convey "a thoroughly grounded and important conviction" by declaring only one possible solution. Real leadership in the electronic age, they argued, needed to take such liberties with the truth.[54]

In August, Galston and Kaplan decided to combine many of these grievances with their own suggestions into a single, comprehensive alternative for the Mondale campaign. After weeks of discussions and meetings with other disaffected staff members and careful research into Mondale's background, they decided on a unifying theme for the campaign: undiluted populism. Mondale, they argued, should identify himself "with a tradition which pitted the individual and the small community against the large and impersonal forces of big business and big government." The modern Democratic party, they argued, had been most successful when it identified with the shared frustration of groups which felt outside the political mainstream. Roosevelt and Truman had successfully translated the economic discontent of a struggling working-class into a powerful electoral majority. By 1984, the political chemistry had changed. A populist appeal required tapping into alienation from impersonal institutions, whether those institutions were large corporations, oversized government, or self-serving labor groups. Mondale's long history in DFL politics had made him very comfortable with certain aspects of the populist message, but now he needed to recognize that his candidacy, and possibly the party's survival, depended on his willingness to oppose many groups that had previously supported him. "Many of the[se] groups had become very elitist and Washington-oriented. The leadership of many groups was comfortable, somewhat out of touch with its membership," Galston reflected. "The problem with populism in 1984, was that populism must oppose not just entrenched corporate power but entrenched government power and entrenched labor power."[55]

The authors suggested a number of stylistic changes to complement the new message. He had to keep to a bare minimum the number of events where he surrounded himself with other politicians. He had to be specific about what he would ask his supporters to sacrifice and it had to entail real suffering. "Will you ask labor to moderate wage demands so that industry can become competitive?" they asked. "Will you ask students and teachers to add a month to the school year? Will you tell contributors that their taxes were cut too much?" He had to take "unequivocal stands on tough issues." "In the public's mind, politicians make calculations, but leaders hold convictions—and to hell with who hollers." Mondale should not deliver a different speech tailored to each audience's interest, but deliver the same message to different audiences. "Whenever you emphasize the areas where you agree with an audience, and downplay or eliminate points of contention, you will be accused of lacking strength and leadership," they wrote. They urged him to avoid providing audiences with reasoned discourses on important issues and instead speak more generally about the importance of values. "The trap is to descend into the boiler room—to give a perfect engineer's account of problems and fixup," they suggested. "The trick is to soar—to transform the topic into a test of values, character, and vision."[56]

These debates revealed the anguish of a campaign searching for a compelling rationale for Mondale's candidacy and for a solution to the Democrats' dilemma. Kaplan and Galston understood that, in this century, the Democratic Party was most successful when it identified with the concerns of common citizens and branded the Republicans as the protectors of wealth and privilege. Many observers also believed that populism remained an essential ingredient in any recipe for revitalizing the Democratic Party. Mondale, who had been nurtured on the fiery populism of Harry Truman and Hubert Humphrey, seemed perfectly suited for the new strategy.

Despite its apparent attractiveness, however, the memorandum failed to solve Mondale's message problem. In their eagerness to create a unified theme for the campaign, the authors underestimated the tensions inherent within the populist tradition. Two contradictory impulses had shaped populist thought in America. Economic populists viewed typical Americans as people who, whether black or white, were poor and needed a strong government to protect their rights and provide for their welfare. Since 1968, cultural populists identified the common person with the white working class, which was angry about forced integration, incensed by affirmative action, and exasperated by rising taxes. How could a candidate tap into the anti-government fervor of the cultural populist and still protect those groups—especially the poor, elderly, and minorities—who depended on the state for survival? How could an economic populist use federal authority to assail the evils of big business without arousing fears of expanded national power? Most important, since race was the prism through which many whites viewed initiatives designed to help the poor, could a Democrat who hoped to win white-working-class votes favor an agenda that enlarged government services? These critical questions, which had haunted Democratic candidates since 1968, were left unanswered.

On September 2, 1983 Galston and Kaplan pleaded their case at a meeting with Mondale and his senior advisors. They immediately ran into opposition from the professional campaign people. "It was the single biggest internal division in that campaign," recalled Beckel. Many of the political professionals in the campaign shared Kaplan and Galston's desire to articulate a message that would appeal to the middle class. But like Mondale, years of experience in building coalitions made them reluctant to alienate a traditional ally in favor of a risky strategy. Also, since Mondale was the Democratic frontrunner, they saw little need for major changes. Uncomfortable themselves with media campaigns, they feared that attempts to "remake" Mondale for modern politics would divorce him from his heritage and rob him of the genuineness which they, and so many other people, found so attractive. "We had to take into account the product that we had, which was Fritz Mondale. A product of the Democratic-Farmer Labor movement in Minnesota. A guy who had learned politics by coalition-building, had all of his principal communication through

newspapers and public speaking," recalled Beckel. Johnson also opposed the changes. "I believed Mondale was not going to be either
Robert Redford or Ronald Reagan no matter what we did. He was
going to be Walter Mondale. He had a tradition; he came from the
Midwest and had a record of public service. We had to be very careful
to allow him to be an authentic version of who he was."[57]

The strongest, and most thoughtful objections to the new strategy
came not from Beckel or Johnson, but from Mondale. Years of
service in the Washington establishment had made Mondale uncomfortable with the populist message which would have required him
to disavow many institutions and groups of which he was a part.
Mondale wanted to play the role of healer, the leader who would
restore competence and civility to public life. The populist message
required creating false enemies, oversimplifying difficult issues, and
raising false expectations. Populism, he argued, had an evil and dangerous history in America. Over the years, he had seen men like
Joseph McCarthy and George Wallace destroy individuals by tapping
into the darker side of the populist impulse. He believed that building
a community of mutual trust and benefit provided a better alternative
to creating a false association based on fear. That concern, of course,
never prevented Mondale from brandishing a selective form of economic populism that pitted the wealthy and powerful against the
"common people." He saw a careful distinction between the two.
"The line is between legitimate grievances about institutions that
don't bend in ways to give people a fair chance on the one hand, and
dark, demagogue attacks against 'them'—undefined, sinister forces
that are pushing people around shamelessly and cruelly without any
concern," he reflected.[58]

Mondale's distrust of the populist message reflected a deeper problem. Like many other liberals of his generation who witnessed the
limited success of many Great Society programs and felt the wrath of
a middle-class backlash in the 1970s, Mondale had grown weary of
ideology. Part of the liberal predicament in the 1970s, he argued,
stemmed from the disillusion that resulted from the unfulfilled promises of the 1960s. Politicians, in their desire to win public approval,
exaggerated the possibilities of change by promising painless solutions and immediate results. He called this approach "dawnism."
Believing there were no simple solutions to many problems, Mondale
refused to arouse expectations beyond what government could deliver. Abandoning faith in macro-solutions to economic problems,
for example, he focused attention on how specific policies could affect

particular sectors of the economy: Easing monetary policy to bring inflation down; industry-government-labor cooperation to increase international competitiveness; rebuilding the nation's infrastructure; restoring some Reagan budget cuts; cancellation of the third year of Reagan's tax cut.

Mondale also balked at many of the stylistic devices that had become second nature to most politicians. Perhaps the last major political figure who resisted television, Mondale defiantly refused to subject himself to media coaching. "He had people riding him for ten years to do something about his television appearance," Johnson recalled. His response was always the same: "I'm not interested in the remake artists and what they have to say. If I have to be a movie star to be a good politician then I don't want to be a politician." He refused to review tapes of his performances or watch his own news coverage. He disliked doing intimate events that provided little substance but good pictures and instead insisted on speaking to large crowds. He refused to use a teleprompter and usually read verbatim from a prepared text. His answers to questions, though thoughtful and intelligent, lacked 15-second theme bites that could be shown on the evening news.[59]

Mondale's objections to simplistic ideological appeals and his reluctance to embrace some of the more offensive methods of modern media campaigns, were understandable—even admirable. But in the age of "the permanent campaign," where high-priced consultants replaced political parties and the manipulation of symbols and images substituted for substantive policy, Mondale could not afford the luxury of adhering to his principles if he expected to win. Many of the stylistic proposals had already been accepted as common practice by other candidates. If adopted, they could have blunted criticism that Mondale was captive to the "special interests." In mass media campaigns, where communication with the voters was frequently limited to 30-second snippets, candidates needed to distill their message down to its essence. Reagan had already proven himself a master of this new art of campaigning. In 1980, his value-laden rhetoric had defined the differences between the parties and shaped the political debate. The inability of Mondale and other Democrats to respond in kind confused the public's image of the party and its message.[60]

Mondale's unwillingness to embrace tax reform provided a case study of his own and the party's inability to sustain a populist agenda. The one substantive recommendation included as part of the populist strategy required Mondale to support sweeping reform of the tax code. Mondale had already made clear that he considered the budget deficit the most important long-term economic problem facing the country, and he realized that just to cut the Reagan deficit in half in his first term in office would require a tax increase at an annual rate of about $100 billion. But many aides suggested that rather than raising taxes, Mondale should advocate a bold tax reform scheme that would allow him to run on a program of tax equity. The Bradley-Gephardt bill, which simplified tax rates and lowered the maximum tax rate from 50 percent to 30 percent, seemed perfectly suited for the strategy. The public overwhelmingly supported the idea of a simplified tax structure and many people felt the issue would give Mondale the added benefit of demonstrating his strength by standing up against the powerful special interests which would lobby to retain their tax preferences. "The exploitable political opportunity inherent in this issue," wrote Eliot Cutler, "is the ability to demonstrate that you are willing to run in some cases against the 'special interests,' that you are willing to take a (controlled) chance on an issue."[61]

Mondale rejected the idea, in part, because the current Bradley-Gephardt plan was revenue neutral and he was convinced that addressing the deficit required raising money. Adding to his doubts, Mondale's experience on the Senate Finance Committee had convinced him that tax reform was a good idea in the abstract, but in reality was difficult to enact. "Everyone that gets hurt raises hell and everyone that gets benefited doesn't believe it," he reflected. "I was scarred by my years on the Finance Committee to believe this was not possible." Mondale also feared alienating wealthy campaign contributors who felt their interests would be adversely affected by tax reform. The proliferation of political action committees combined with the excessive costs of modern media campaigns forced Democratic and Republican candidates to seek support from similar sources. These changes proved a greater burden for Democrats who needed to win the favor of powerful financial groups whose agenda was at odds with most Democratic voters.[62]

The issue came to a head in April 1983, when Mondale was invited to address a meeting of the American Business Conference (ABC), a group composed of the heads of the one hundred fastest growing midsized companies in America. Seizing the opportunity to position Mondale at the forefront on issues of productivity and investment, Galston inserted into the speech a strong endorsement of Bradley-Gephardt: "Over the long run, we must move toward a reform like the Bradley-Gephardt personal tax proposal, with its goals of simplicity and equity." Mondale omitted the reference and instead gave a subdued endorsement of tax reform during a question-and-answer session while at the same time expressing his support for continuing tax preferences for entrepreneurial firms.[63]

Afterward, an angry Mondale complained that his policy advisors needed to be more aware of the political consequences of their ideas. "Are they trying to kill me?" he muttered to Johnson. Although he had successfully dodged specific endorsement of the tax reform message in his statement, Mondale worried that copies of the speech containing the explicit language would leak to the public. Worse yet, he feared that the campaign's leading financial contributors, to whom he was scheduled to speak later in the day, would obtain a copy. Moving quickly to end that threat, Johnson frantically ordered an aide to rush back to the ABC conference hall and destroy all copies of the speech.[64]

The next morning, after reading a Wall Street *Journal* headline declaring "Mondale Backs Plan for Major Overhaul of the System of Taxing Personal Income," Johnson summoned Galston into his office. Holding in his hands a list of tax preferences that Bradley-Gephardt would either reduce or eliminate, he declared: "I don't think we can do this." At Mondale's request, he recited for Galston the political consequences of alienating each group. Galston reluctantly accepted that Mondale had "reached the political judgment that the campaign could not afford" tax reform. In subsequent statements Mondale put increasing amounts of daylight between himself and the legislation.[65]

Rejecting the populist message and convinced the special-interest charge would fade after a few primary victories, Mondale decided not to alter his strategy. If anything, his loss in Wisconsin only intensified his desire to lock up the early endorsements and avoid a bloody primary battle. A number of key tests confronted him beginning with the Maine straw vote on October 1. Mondale had to reestablish the inevitability of his candidacy if the early knockout strategy was to work. He scored the victories he needed. In slightly more than twenty-four hours, Mondale gained the endorsements of both the 1.7-million member National Education Association and the 14-million member AFL-CIO while also scoring a major victory in Maine. "Mondale's triple victory seemed to confirm the prevailing wisdom that, sooner or later, his superbly organized campaign would outclass the competition," wrote *Time*. Later, he captured the endorsement of the National Organization for Women, won a straw poll at a party dinner in Iowa, and finished a stronger-than-expected second to favorite-son Rubin Askew in a straw poll at the Democratic state convention in Florida. As a result, Mondale ended the year rising rapidly in the national public-opinion polls while his opposition continued to flounder.[66]

As he looked forward to the opening of primary season Mondale had reason to feel confident. He enjoyed a large lead in the polls, commanded a powerful organization, and had instant name recognition. Less obvious was the fundamental contradiction that lay at the heart of his campaign. Already there were ominous signs of the problems that would inhibit his presidential campaign. Pollsters found that voters perceived him as soft on national security issues, as "shopworn," as part of the failed Carter Administration, and as "overly concerned with pleasing the special interests." Some of the focus group findings were just as discouraging. "Overall, the most graphic tendency demonstrated by the group is to find fault with Walter Mondale," commented one aide. Peter Hart suggested that Mondale's problems could be tied together into one theme: "Walter Mondale's answers to America's problems are a return to the failed policies of the past." It was only a matter of time before one of his opponents exploited these weaknesses.[67]

15

Hart Attack

In early February 1984, Mondale and the campaign's chief advisors gathered in the Winston and Strawn conference room to discuss strategy for the impending Iowa caucus. The atmosphere was relaxed, the mood confident. With the Glenn challenge fading and none of the other candidates even registering in the polls, everything seemed to be moving along as planned. Mondale, it appeared, would win the nomination early and begin reassembling the coalition for the fall confrontation with Reagan. As Mondale warned his staff about complacency, a flustered Bill Galston charged into the room. Galston had been at the campaign headquarters reading a UPI report of Gary Hart's latest speech, delivered at Council Bluffs, Iowa, which described Mondale as a candidate of the "establishment past . . . brokered by backroom politics and confirmed by a collective sense of resignation." Fearing Hart had found Mondale's Achilles heel, Galston raced the two miles to Winston and Strawn to warn the campaign staff of the potentially lethal new line of attack. "I think we're in trouble if this becomes the campaign," he declared.[1]

Mondale and the others in the room did not share his concern. They saw no reason to deviate from the strategy of ignoring Hart. The "special interest" theme was a last ditch attempt to save a dying candidacy, Mondale argued. Answering the charge would only give it more dignity than it deserved.

But the "special interest" issue would not fade away. Hart, under the close tutelage of Pat Caddell, began focusing his message and sharpening his attacks on Mondale. On February 12, in a Des Moines debate held just nine days before the Iowa caucus, Hart asked Mondale to name an issue on which he and organized labor disagreed. His debate preparation team had warned him in advance that Hart would ask the question and had urged him to use the opportunity to lay the issue to rest by highlighting his differences on a few key issues. But Mondale refused, saying he would not "trash" his friends to win election. At issue, he claimed, was not just political calculation, but personal integrity. Hart, who had always depended on strong union support in his Senate races and had sought the same labor endorsements in 1984, might be willing to turn on his followers to win an election, but for Mondale being "true" to yourself and your supporters transcended the acquisition of votes. When Hart asked the question in the debate, Mondale refused to name his differences, answering meekly that labor wanted "a candidate they can trust, not run."[2]

Instead of responding to Hart's thrusts, Mondale continued to ignore his Democratic rivals and concentrated his assault on Reagan. In a series of speeches in Iowa and around the country, he claimed the President's domestic programs had hurt the poor, the elderly, and children. Mondale told a luncheon crowd in Manchester: "The people of New Hampshire won't settle for government by staff, policy by default, management by alibi and leadership by amnesia." On the President's home turf of Sacramento, Mondale accused Reagan of "serving wealthy and powerful special interests" and opposing programs designed to help women, children, and the elderly. In response to Reagan's charge that Democratic candidates were trying to buy favors with special interests Mondale retorted: "Nobody has served the wealthy and powerful special interests with more devotion for more years than Mr. Reagan." At a news conference Mondale said Reagan led "the most special-interest-oriented Administration in American history. I enjoy and welcome the special interest issue because I am going to win it. It exposes the Administration for what it is."[3]

Increasingly, Mondale focused his attacks on foreign policy issues. In part, an improving economy had blunted Mondale's criticisms of Reagan's domestic policies and made a shift in emphasis necessary. By December 1983, the unemployment rate had dropped to 8.2 percent, the lowest since January 1982. But the change also stemmed from a sense that Reagan was vulnerable on issues of war and peace. Three years into his presidency, Reagan had still not quieted public concern about his understanding of complicated national security issues. His deeply ideological approach to the world, implacable hostility to the Soviet Union, and unyielding mistrust of arms control had led to a dramatic increase in tension between the Superpowers. Armed with his massive defense budget and surrounded by men who shared his distrust of the Soviet Union, Reagan had intentionally blocked progress on both intermediate-range and strategic arms reductions. He postponed indefinitely negotiations on a comprehensive test ban treaty which had been supported by every American president since Eisenhower. Rather than resuming discussion on limiting anti-satellite weapons, the President proposed a vast and expensive "Star Wars" defense system. By 1983, Reagan's lack of progress on arms control had created broad public support for a nuclear freeze. Reflecting an impatience both with the arms race and with traditional negotiations, the freeze movement called for a "mutual and verifiable" comprehensive halt to the production and deployment of all nuclear weapons.[4]

Seeing Soviet influence behind all regional conflicts, Reagan had committed American prestige and resources to local struggles in Central America and the Middle East. In 1982, Reagan transformed the ancient struggle of religious factions in Lebanon into a test of will between the Soviet Union and the United States. Demonstrating his resolve to stand firm against Soviet aggression, the President had sent 1,600 Marines to Beirut on a confused mission to preserve peace in that war-torn country. In October, a car bomb exploded outside a Marine barracks killing 239 and wounding at least 75 others. A similar logic guided his actions in Central America. Convinced the Soviets, working through Cuban proxies, were conspiring to uphold a puppet regime in Nicaragua and to overthrow a democratically elected government in El Salvador, Reagan had greatly expanded American military presence in the area. Two days after the Lebanon tragedy, the President "liberated" the tiny Caribbean island of Grenada with a massive American military invasion. Though a public relations coup at home, the invasion aroused indignation among European allies and complicated chances of finding a negotiated settlement in El Salvador and Nicaragua.

Mondale hoped to tap into public concern with Reagan's handling of foreign policy and defense issues by kicking off the new year with a major foreign policy address before the National Press Club. Assailing Reagan's "ad lib foreign policy," Mondale declared that after three years of Reagan leadership, "the Middle East and Central America are at war[,] . . . U.S.-Soviet relations are in crisis and the arms talks have collapsed." If elected President, he promised to be "a president who knows what he's doing" and "use America's strength to build a safer world." He accused Reagan of opposing "every effort by every president of both parties . . . for the past two generations" to reduce the threat of nuclear war. "In the past three years," he said, "we have not had one single advance. Instead, we have had an escalating arms race." He then proceeded to define the specific steps he would take to advance arms control, including annual summit meetings, negotiating a nuclear freeze, a universal test-ban treaty, and an updated SALT III treaty.[5]

Despite his confident tone, Mondale was trying to make the best of a bad situation. From the beginning his campaign had been premised on the idea that Reagan's economic program would fail. Poor economic conditions would then allow Mondale to appeal to Democrats along traditional economic lines. Foreign policy questions added a troublesome dimension to his challenge. In many key primary states, doves exercised considerable influence, but to win in November a Democratic candidate needed to appear strong on defense issues. Also, over the previous two years, Mondale had intentionally muted his criticisms of Reagan's foreign policy in the hope of keeping public attention focused on the economy. Now, just as the Democratic primaries were about to begin, he needed to straddle the line between hawk and dove by taking definitive positions on many controversial issues. In some cases, like Lebanon, he needed to reverse previous positions. In a December interview with the New York *Times,* he had expressed full support of the American mission in Lebanon. Just a few weeks later, however, he reversed himself, calling for a complete American withdrawal. On other issues he felt compelled by political realities to express enthusiastic support even though he harbored private doubts. Though he publicly favored the nuclear freeze, for example, Mondale privately doubted America's ability to monitor Soviet compliance with a ban on production and wondered if the freeze concept could be reconciled with the complexities of U.S.-Soviet nuclear competition. He considered the freeze a typical example of "bumper sticker" foreign policy, but it was still better than the Republican position of encouraging an unconditional arms race.[6]

These inconsistencies had little impact on voters in Iowa. Less than two weeks before the Iowa caucuses, Mondale held a commanding 50 percent of the vote in a field of seven. "Iowa," declared Peter Hart, "was won." Glenn, who campaigned hard in the state and spent the legal limit, barely showed up in opinion polls. The day before the caucus, a CBS News survey found Mondale holding "the most commanding lead ever recorded this early in a presidential nomination campaign by a nonincumbent." The predictions proved accurate. Mondale won 49 percent of the caucus vote, more than his seven competitors combined. Hart finished second, with 16 percent. "We got the gold and silver medals," declared Peter Hart. "Everybody else fought over the bronze." Mondale showed strength across the board, drawing 46 percent of the vote in the state's largest cities while also performing well in the state's smallest communities. Only in middle-class suburbs, where his support dropped to 34 percent, did he show weakness, and even there he outdistanced his nearest rival.[7]

Mondale went into New Hampshire looking for an early triumph. A big victory would all but guarantee him the nomination. But New Hampshire was never hospitable to Mondale's brand of politics. Independent and unpredictable, it was a state which liked insurgents—McCarthy in 1968, McGovern in 1972, and Carter in 1976. Stuck between 30 and 40 percent in his own polls, Mondale based his strategy on a multi-candidate race where he would receive the plurality.

The media, especially the major networks, demonstrated their extraordinary power to set the agenda, define expectations, and shape the results of modern political campaigns. Since everyone had expected a big Mondale win in Iowa, most of the news stories focused on Gary Hart's surprising second place finish. In the eight days following Iowa, Hart received all the favorable media. The networks fought each other to get him on the air, newspaper reporters flocked to his candidacy, and money began pouring in.

Hart's media magnetism served to highlight Mondale's unease in front of the camera. Television coverage of the two candidates revealed a basic difference in style. Hart was pictured wearing a lumberjack shirt and blue jeans chopping wood for the cameras. Mondale campaigned in his "full Norwegian" outfit—dark grey suit, a white or blue shirt, and muted tie. Hart embraced television. Campaigning by media markets, doing two or three local television markets a day, Hart used public events to create visually pleasing pictures for the national news. Mondale, who campaigned in as many media markets, refused to allow the rituals of mass media to influence his dialogue with local supporters. Appearing at rallies, civic organizations, union halls, and factory gates, he aroused his audiences but failed to create a compelling picture that would communicate that enthusiasm on television.[8]

Mondale's decidedly nontelegenic features proved a serious liability in the days after Iowa. Although trim and athletic, he frequently looked heftier on television. The camera accentuated his jowliness, focused attention on the pockets of fatigue which frequently surrounded his blue eyes, and highlighted the slightly beaked nose that protruded from his face. Television transformed him, according to some observers, "into a cruel caricature of a self-satisfied politician."[9]

Despite his media problems, Mondale had deadly ammunition available for use against Hart. He could have publicized Hart's support of an oil import fee which would have been political suicide in oil-dependent New Hampshire. Like most Washington insiders, Mondale knew of the Colorado Senator's penchant for attractive women and active socializing that contrasted with his cerebral public demeanor. But confident of victory and hoping to avoid an emotional clash that would make reconciliation difficult, Mondale decided to remain silent. As primary day approached, his unease increased— crowds remained small and unresponsive. He sensed something was wrong, but he continued to hope for the best. In the final two days of campaigning, internal polls confirmed Mondale's worst fears. The slow trickle to Hart had turned into a flood.[10]

On primary day, Mondale paid a price for his restraint. Hart captured 39 percent to 27 for Mondale, 12 for Glenn and 5 or less for the others. Hart swept every category of voter, except those sixty years old or older. A CBS-NY *Times* poll revealed that the age group thirty through forty-four, which constituted 40 percent of the electorate, had picked Hart over Mondale by 41 to 19 percent. Political professionals who had already declared the primaries over were shocked. Tip O'Neill said it was the "biggest upset in Democratic politics since [Eugene] McCarthy went up against Lyndon Johnson in 1968." Hart had found Mondale's weakness. "In the voting booth," concluded David Broder, "Mondale's claim that 'I am ready' proved far less appealing than Hart's claim that 'I am new.' "[11]

On election night, a stunned Mondale, whose three-year master plan had been destroyed in one day, told campaign workers he would continue the fight. "We have only begun this campaign, and I have only begun to fight. . . . I am ready to win this nomination. I'm ready to give this everything I've got." Two days later, Mondale assembled his campaign staff at his Winston and Strawn office to assess the damage. "It's a tidal wave," Peter Hart said. They were losing ground in Maine; Massachusetts was lost; and the South—except for Alabama—was crumbling. Many advisors now privately counseled that he withdraw. A few, however, argued that Hart could never live up to the heightened expectations he had created over the past few weeks. "Gary Hart will suffer the worst and cruelest reconsideration anyone has ever received," Leone foresaw. But Mondale faced a formidable test. Johnson told him he would have to win at least two of the southern states in the upcoming "Super Tuesday" primary to remain a viable candidate.[12]

As he contemplated his options in the dark days following New Hampshire, Mondale felt like a fighter who had stayed for one bout too many. Oddly, even his closest friends questioned whether he was capable of taking a good punch. The New Hampshire primary represented the first time in twenty-four years of public life that Mondale had run individually and lost an election. He had conveniently dismissed the 1980 campaign as a referendum on Carter's failed presidency, not as a reflection on his performance or his potential as a presidential candidate. Now many people, including close advisers, wondered if Mondale possessed the resiliency needed to bounce back from defeat. Many of the old self-doubts and insecurities reemerged as he worried about losing the respect he had worked so hard to earn. "He had this feeling that he had been rejected and people just did not want him," Leone recalled.[13]

At first, it appeared that the doubts would win. But as staff members drafted a concession speech and laid plans to return to Minneapolis to announce his withdrawal, two considerations nagged at Mondale's conscience. First, he feared that if he quit, his name would be a burden to his children. "I am very conscious of my legacy towards you," he told his son William shortly after the New Hampshire defeat. "I can't give you money but I can give you a good name." Perhaps most of all, Mondale believed in his mission to reunite the

Democratic Party by finding common ground between its vying factions. Old friends reinforced the commitment in the days following his defeat. "You are the natural bridge between the past and the future; between what our party has stood for, what it has accomplished, and where it must go," Thomas Eagleton wrote his old Senate friend. "Hart may turn on some of the young people with his 'new ideas,' but many Americans will understand what the future requires only when it is explained to them by someone with real roots in the past and the party's traditions." Mondale was not willing to allow one primary loss to wipe out ten years of hard work. He was not going to give up without a fight. "Let's take the son-of-a-bitch on," he said.[14]

Victory would not be easy. After New Hampshire, Mondale's campaign went into a tailspin. "Something happened after New Hampshire which I had not anticipated," he reflected years later. "Suddenly, after he beat me there was a tornado. In the South where I had been leading by fifty points, I now trailed by ten. I couldn't get my feet on the ground. It was like a huge tornado blowing me away." The Hunt Commission reforms which Mondale had supported in hopes of gaining a quick victory were now working against him. Not even Maine, a caucus state with heavy union membership, could stop the Hart juggernaut. "Somebody told me this morning that this is building character," Mondale told reporters after hearing that he had lost in Maine. "I think I've got more character already than I can use." The Maine defeat was matched by a four-to-one drubbing in Vermont to Hart and a nearly two-to-one loss in Wyoming. "How much longer do I have to take this?" Mondale asked.[15]

In many ways, Mondale saw the clash with Hart as reminiscent of Humphrey's battle against McCarthy in 1968. In his mind, Hart represented the worst qualities of the new politics that had gained strength in the party since 1968. During the 1960s the Vietnam War had provided a common cause for this diverse and contradictory movement to coalesce. "[T]he soul of the new politics," commented Jack Newfield, "was moral horror at the war in Vietnam." When the war ended, however, the movement had lost much of its ideological unity. Some leaders remained true to their radical instincts by advocating muted forms of democratic socialism. A much larger number, however, reflecting the middle-class concern over rising inflation in the 1970s, retained their social liberalism but became increasingly more conservative on economic issues. These "radicals" of the 1960s became the "New Class" Democrats of the 1970s, and neoliberals of the 1980s. Despite these ideological differences, heirs of the new politics tradition shared a similar style. Adapting the anti-establishment impulse of the New Left to conventional politics, they fashioned themselves as reformers challenging the "Old Guard."[16]

Not surprisingly, Hart's challenge to Mondale in 1984 was similar to the McCarthy and Kennedy campaigns against Humphrey in 1968. All three men used a strong anti-establishment message, made effective use of television, and laid claim to vague "new ideas" for solving vexing problems. Unlike the previous challengers, however, Hart had little sense of the party's historic mission of helping the poor and outcasts and had no ties to its established leadership. "He got elected by using the Democratic label," Mondale reflected bitterly, "but without really believing in anything."[17]

On specific issues, few substantive differences divided Mondale and Hart. They had nearly identical Senate voting records, and Hart had supported most of the Carter administration's domestic and foreign-policy initiatives. They both favored cooperation among government, business, and labor in formulating a national industrial strategy. They agreed that economic growth had to be the centerpiece of the platform and that special attention was needed to recruit middle-class voters. On foreign policy as well, their differences were shaded in grey. Both opposed the MX missile and the B-1B strategic bomber, while favoring deployment in Europe of Pershing II missiles, ground-launched cruise missiles, and modernization of America's nuclear arsenal until a nuclear freeze agreement with the Soviets was signed. Both called for modest increases in the defense budget. To be sure, they had minor differences. While Mondale called for additional NATO spending and more money for conventional weapons, Hart advocated a smaller American presence in European defense and was a strong advocate of military reform. He was also less willing to use military force in the Persian Gulf and Central America. But both agreed Reagan's policy was too militaristic.[18]

On an abstract level, however, their differences were profound. Although only nine years apart in age, they gazed at each other across a generational divide. "Mondale and Hart would look at the same audience and see two different realities," Johnson reflected. "Mondale would see people by age, ethnic group, occupational status and deduce political leanings. Hart would see alienation, anti-government, concern about the future and a need for generational change." Mondale's political consciousness had been forged during the class struggles of the 1930s and 1940s, when farmers and laborers had formed groups to protect their interests. Hart grew up in the relative affluence of the early 1960s when ideology was muted by a common sense of social progress. Where Mondale hoped to forge a Democratic community by binding together the leading public-interest groups, Hart hoped to appeal to individuals and form a consensus around specific issues.[19]

The Vietnam War served as an important dividing point between the two men. They disagreed about the lessons of Vietnam and the uses of American military power abroad. "A generation of leaders that gave us Vietnam has now given us Lebanon and Central America," Hart said. His views on foreign policy, he asserted, were "formed in the fires of discontent of the Vietnam years." Hart announced that he would remove all American troops from Central America and would not commit U.S. forces to the Persian Gulf to protect the oil lanes. "In the third world," he declared, "the real enemy is hunger, poverty and disease, not Communism." Mondale responded by arguing that Hart had learned the wrong lessons from Vietnam. Though Vietnam had taught him, too, about "the limits of American military power," he added, "It does not teach us that there's no role for the United States." Hart, he charged, had ignored "the excesses of the extreme left" and failed to understand that the "world is a tough, dangerous place."[20]

Although painful, the losses to Hart were liberating. With his eighteen-month advantage in fundraising and organization swept away, Mondale was forced in desperation to justify his candidacy. By defining his candidacy in generational terms, Hart had transformed their fight into a struggle for the soul of the Democratic Party. With renewed enthusiasm, Mondale turned South for the March 13 Super Tuesday primary where three southern states—Florida, Georgia, and Alabama—were holding primaries on the same day as two New England states—Massachusetts and Rhode Island—and four others—Washington, Nevada, Oklahoma, and Hawaii—had caucuses scheduled. Together, the nine states offered 511 of the 1,967 delegates needed to win the nomination at San Francisco. Hoping to salvage his candidacy, he launched an aggressive negative campaign to raise doubts about Hart's ability to handle an international crisis. The campaign exploited public unease about Hart's "steadiness" in a crisis by producing a highly successful "red telephone" commercial. It began ominously with the image of a blinking red phone while a somber voice warned of having an "unsure . . . unsteady . . . untested" President. The commercial forced people to probe deeper into Hart's character and background.[21]

Mondale scored the crowning blow at a debate in Atlanta. In a practice session, Beckel suggested that Mondale challenge Hart's claim to "new ideas" by using a phrase made popular by a new fast food commercial. The advertisement showed an elderly woman examining a hamburger at a competing store and asking: "Where's the beef?" At first Mondale expressed skepticism. After all, he hoped to contrast his substantive approach to Hart's shallow media-created candidacy. But he was also frustrated that the media seemed so consumed by images in politics that it ignored many of his more substantive proposals. As he sat during the debate listening to Hart again contrast the old and new, Mondale decided to give it a try. "You know," he said leaning forward in his seat for emphasis, "when I hear your ideas, I'm reminded of that ad, 'Where's the beef?' " Mondale had never seen the commercial but he delivered the line perfectly.[22]

While Mondale raised questions about the lack of substance in his opponents "new ideas," his staff tried unsuccessfully to adopt some of Hart's successful media techniques. Hoping to create visually pleasing pictures which would highlight his leadership and independence, Mondale stood before a majestic sailing ship in New York Harbor to give a hard-hitting speech about tackling the difficult trade deficit. Uncomfortable with the contrived setting, which isolated him from his supporters, Mondale reached out and grabbed every local New York politician in the audience to surround him while he spoke. Rather than highlighting his independence and leadership, the visual underscored his image as a party figure. "When he was done the picture was Walter Mondale among ten fat, balding, white politicians," recalled press secretary Maxine Isaacs.[23]

On another occasion Mondale was scheduled to stand on the steps of the Maine state house to speak about the importance of federal-state cooperation. The visual was intended to convey his forceful leadership, his experience and his concern for local issues. Again, Mondale called all of the local state politicians to stand with him. The picture showed a sea of faces with Mondale lost somewhere in the middle. "It looked like the Politburo," Johnson said. "He would be live on local television with one minute to get his message across and he would spend half the time thanking all of the local politicians for their help," recalled Johnson.[24]

Defining his candidacy in clear and forceful terms, Mondale outlined the differences between himself and Hart. "No one can teach you to have guts, no one can teach you to care," he said in a trembling voice throughout the South. "What you see is what you get. No new hair spray. No new perfume. No new slogans. I am who I am; the product of my history, my values, my experience, my commitment." With new emotional intensity he established himself as the defender of Democratic values. "We are about to decide whether we are a generous party and a caring nation or whether we're not," he told a crowd in Tampa. "We will determine whether we care about people and average working families who've always been at the core of the Democratic Party or we won't. We will decide whether we will be a party that follows the polls or is led by principle."

> Today there's a new argument in the land, a new idea about the Democratic Party and where it should go. This I believe is the essence of the battle we're in. If you fight for values that the party has always believed in, you're supposed to go on a guilt trip, but if you fight against them, you're supposed to applaud. If you fight for better schools, you're old. But if you fight for big oil, you're new. If you fight for civil rights, that's a special interest. But if you buckle to the hospital lobby, that's a new idea. If you defend Medicare, you're cautious, but you attack entitlements, you're courageous. If seniors want Social Security, that's the past, but AT&T wants to tack a big bill on your phone for the privilege of using long-distance lines, that's the future. If a worker wants a raise, that's greedy, but if a plant closes down, that's trendy. If you want big corporations to pay their share of taxes, you're old hat. If you want working families to pay more in taxes, that's high tech. I don't accept it.[25]

As the election results trickled in from the South on Super Tuesday it appeared that Mondale's attacks on Hart had not worked. Hart won primaries in Florida, Massachusetts and Rhode Island; and caucuses in Washington, Oklahoma, and Nevada. Mondale won only two of the nine events—Alabama and Georgia. The television networks, however, interpreted the results as a comeback for Mondale, and Hart, who just a few weeks earlier had no organization and little name recognition in the South, found himself explaining why he had lost two states.[26]

Mondale paid a heavy cost for his efforts to push Hart outside the Democratic mainstream. For the past three years, Mondale had tried to redefine his message so middle class voters would find him more attractive. Now he conceded the independent vote to Hart and worked desperately to rally the old coalition in the primaries. The new strategy, while effective against Hart, probably limited his already weak appeal to marginal Democrats. "We were very concerned prior to New Hampshire that Mondale was developing a focus and a consistency in his attacks that were taking a toll on the president," reflected Reagan's pollster Richard Wirthlin. After New Hampshire, the Mondale campaign needed to devote more time and resources to winning the primary, but more important, it had "to use those resources to go back to their hard-core base, to the so-called special interests, and they had to go back to more traditional Democratic themes." Party warfare, Wirthlin argued, prevented the Democrats from "building a consistent and unified claim that Mondale offered Americans more for the future than Ronald Reagan."[27]

Following the Super Tuesday "comeback," Mondale returned to familiar ground—Michigan, Illinois, and then the northern industrial states of New York and Pennsylvania. While Hart floundered, Mondale focused on economic worries, vowing to protect jobs from foreign competition, never to cut social security, and to restore cuts in programs to the poor. In the Michigan caucuses, Mondale had the active support of the United Auto Workers and the strong endorsement of Detroit's popular black mayor Coleman Young. Hart had only a small staff centered at the University of Michigan. In a state dominated by the auto industry, Mondale was on the right side of two critical issues: domestic-content legislation and the federal government's bailout of the Chrysler Corporation. Even with all of his advantages, Mondale was worried. "I was still traumatized by Maine, which was a caucus state," he told reporters. Despite a heavy turnout, which normally favored an insurgent, Mondale scored an impressive victory in Michigan, winning 49 percent of the vote to Hart's 31 percent, and gaining 79 of 136 delegates.[28]

Most of the media attention focused on Illinois where Hart appeared to be wilting under the intense pressure. A number of avoidable gaffes contributed to public unease about his character. Hart was forced to apologize publicly to Mondale after accusing him of running negative commercials that never materialized. A few days later, after he had promised not to get involved in local Chicago politics, his campaign ran a television commercial that linked Mondale to the controversial Cook County Democratic chairman Ed Vrdolyak. Realizing the mistake, Hart promised to remove the commercial but could not. "How can a man run the country if he can't run his own campaign?" Mondale asked.[29]

In his basic stump speech in Illinois, Mondale tried to capitalize on his midwestern roots, strong union support, and experience. "I know you and you know me. We must have a president who knows what he's doing, but we must also have a president who knows you, your needs and your values," he declared. His appeal worked in a state with a 9.5 percent unemployment rate where one-third of the voters said their family situation had worsened over the past year. On primary day, Mondale managed a sizable majority over Hart in Chicago, pulling heavily from the ethnic blue collar wards of the northwestern part of the city, and battled to a surprisingly even showing in the heavily populated suburbs. Hart continued to score with those who considered themselves independent, although by a smaller margin than in New Hampshire. Once again, when pressed, Mondale proved his mettle. Illinois was a "must win" state. "If Illinois had gone the other way," he recalled, "it would have been difficult for me to carry on." Finally, Mondale felt back in control. "I'd found ground again," he said.[30]

The campaign moved next to the critical state of New York where polls showed Mondale with a slight lead. At New York City's Hunter College Mondale contrasted his two-decade commitment to the problems of the poor and cities with Hart's record on these issues. "I am not an unknown person who has to come here and explain where I stand on those issues," Mondale said. "I have been with you every day, every minute, for over 20 years." Hart, he charged, "has not only shown little or no interest in those programs, on the question of housing, he has a very very bad record." While forcing Hart on the defensive, Mondale appealed to the economic worries of New Yorkers, vowing again to protect jobs from foreign competition, to maintain Social Security and to restore cuts in programs for the poor, and—in a state where almost one-third of Democratic primary voters were Jewish—to safeguard the state of Israel.[31]

For the first time during the campaign against Hart, foreign policy emerged as an important issue. Before the New York primary Hart suggested in a television ad that Mondale would send American troops to Central America. "Why do you run those ads that suggest that I'm out trying to kill kids when you know better?" Mondale asked in a bitter nationally televised debate. "I think you ought to pull those down tonight," Mondale declared as the two men glared at each other across a small table at Columbia University. Hart seemed surprised by the vehemence of Mondale's attack. Forced on the defensive, he spent most of his time defending his vote against a federal loan for Chrysler and had few opportunities to articulate his "new ideas" theme.[32]

As primary day approached many surveys suggested that Mondale was losing support. An ABC poll showed his once commanding lead of 18 points had dwindled to just 2 points by the morning that the polls opened. Mondale read about the poll while driving through a working-class neighborhood of Queens. Gazing out the window at a long row of small factories and new construction sites, Mondale seemed pensive and withdrawn. "How can I lose New York," he muttered in a barely audible voice. "These are the people I care about."

Mondale's gloom proved unjustified; his strategy worked better than anyone had expected. With independents prevented from voting in New York's closed primary, Mondale put together the traditional Democratic coalition: Jewish and Catholic voters, union households, Hispanic and low-income groups, to win by an impressive 17 point margin. For the first time he also won a majority of conservative Democrats who had voted for Reagan in 1980. "I intend," Mondale told his cheering supporters, "to be a people's President. I'll never forget what you did for me today."[33]

Mondale felt at home in these heavily industrial states. Passionate defenses of the welfare state replaced tedious lectures about plant investment and high technology. Emotional tours of shut-down steel factories with unemployed workers replaced sterile trips to high technology laboratories with dignified technicians. This was politics of the heart, the kind of politics and the types of issues he was comfortable with. However sincere his attempts to develop a new agenda, his heart was always on the side of expressing concern for the less fortunate.

In Pennsylvania, a state hard-hit by recession, he hammered hard on economic issues. Visiting depressed steel towns outside of Pittsburgh, he reminded voters that Hart had opposed federal loans to rescue Chrysler, which had plants throughout western Pennsylvania. "He preached a gospel of jobs, arms control, tax reform, environmental protection and compassion," commented one reporter following the campaign. Once again, Mondale's message scored a big victory, winning 47 percent of the vote to Hart's 34. "Something powerful is happening, and I can feel it," Mondale said. There was a growing desire for "a change in Washington and tonight we've added the keystone to the foundation we're building to beat Ronald Reagan in November."[34]

Yet troubling signs existed beneath the string of victories. Even many of Mondale's supporters expressed reservations about his candidacy. In an NBC News survey following the New York primary, fully half of the people who said they voted for Mondale said their support was "soft." In Pennsylvania, 40 percent of those who voted for him complained that he made too many promises to interest groups, and about 30 percent agreed that the programs he espoused were outdated. Half of his supporters said they wished Senator Edward Kennedy would enter the race. Mondale pulled together the traditional Democratic coalition, but he showed little strength in the suburbs among the independent middle-class voters whose support he would need in order to win in the fall.[35]

Confident he had quelled the Hart uprising, Mondale tried to steal the "future" theme from his fallen foe. On April 19, in a speech at the University of Cincinnati, Mondale turned his attention to loftier concerns. "Today," he said, "we are as close to the 21st century as we are to 1968. Change is inevitable. But change for the worse is not inevitable. We must make history, not just watch it." Campaigning in Cleveland, Mondale used the arms control issue to contrast his vision of the future with Reagan's support for Star Wars. "If Mr. Reagan is re-elected he will feel no pressure to stop the arms race. He will see nothing to prevent him from extending the arms race into outer space. If those follies are permitted, there may be no turning back, and there may be no 21st century." Abandoning the aggressive style he had used so effectively in New York and Pennsylvania, Mondale staged a number of unexciting events designed to broaden his appeal to Hart's voters. He stood on the banks of the Trinity River in Dallas to condemn Reagan's environmental policies, and he sat inattentively through a "future forum" in Austin designed to demonstrate his concern for high technology.[36]

Hart, however, was turning up the heat. He accused Mondale of accepting money from PACs through delegate selection committees. Although Mondale had not violated any law, the issue touched a sensitive nerve. "We've got to deal with this because it gets to integrity," Mondale said privately. Hart's speeches found their bite as he tied Mondale to the Carter administration's failures. "We lost with Mondale before," said one of his television commercials. "He had his chance. He got up to bat. He struck out. Now he wants another turn. You know, he hasn't been out to the field yet." On May 8, Hart won both Ohio and Indiana by a hair, renewing doubts about Mondale's electability.[37]

Hart was not the only candidate staging a comeback. As the other aspirants faded from contention, Jesse Jackson claimed to be the only alternative to Mondale and Hart. "One leans on Humphrey and the other leans on Kennedy, which is further back," he said. "Both of them are talking forward but walking backward." Drawing large and enthusiastic crowds with his powerful crusade for black pride, Jackson turned out the black vote in massive numbers, winning 79 percent in Illinois and 87 percent in Pennsylvania. In two months he established himself as the leading black political figure in America.[38]

Mondale's relationship with Jackson had been strained from the start. Mondale believed the Democrats needed a united party to recapture the White House, and that Jackson's candidacy only divided the coalition and made his job more difficult. "If he hadn't run I would have been nominated by the middle of February," Mondale reflected with some bitterness. Having fought on the side of civil rights his entire life, Mondale became incensed when Jackson suggested that he was not qualified to receive black support. "All the years that I've put in [the civil rights movement] and this guy comes along and has the gall to challenge my record," one aide remembered Mondale saying on a number of occasions.[39]

Although campaigning for the same party's nomination, Jackson and Mondale did not talk the same language. "I would sit in meetings with the two of them and you would almost have to interpret," recalled Beckel. "You felt like you were at the United Nations." Mondale was a politician deeply committed to the Democratic Party who used the skills of compromise and consensus to build coalitions; Jackson was a preacher committed to his own cause but not to a party, who used theatrical skills to arouse passion and sustain hope among a committed following. Jackson, a product of the television era, understood sound bites; Mondale never appreciated television or learned how to use it. Jackson was an insurgent willing to take extraordinary risks; Mondale was an establishment figure forced by temperament and conviction to be prudent and responsible.[40]

The campaign only increased tensions between the two men. Both were, after all, competing for the same constituency. Mondale desperately needed black votes in the general election and did not trust Jackson's attempt to serve as a broker for black support. Mondale was also very aware that overt appeals to black voters could alienate many in the white middle class whose support he had struggled so hard to win. Rather than working to ease these tensions, Jackson exacerbated them. "He inspires and he scares but he never neutralizes," Mondale recalled. Jackson was especially controversial among Jewish voters who were concentrated in states such as New York, New Jersey, Florida, and California which were rich in electoral votes. On February 13, the Washington *Post* revealed that Jackson occasionally referred to Jews as "Hymies" and to New York as "Hymietown." He also refused to dissociate himself from Reverend Louis Farrakhan, leader of the Chicago-based Nation of Islam, who issued apparent death threats against the *Post* reporter who wrote the story. When combined with his championing of a Palestinian homeland and public embrace of PLO leader Yasir Arafat, Jackson's behavior caused serious worry among Jews.[41]

There was considerable debate within the campaign about how to deal with Jackson. "Of all the mistakes of 1984, the handling of Jesse Jackson was arguably the worst," recalled Galston. Many advisors wanted Mondale to make his break with Jackson at the NAACP convention meeting later that summer. A small group of advisors drafted a speech charging that Jackson had not renounced anti-Semitism, refused to repudiate Farrakhan, and stood outside the Democratic mainstream. Mondale opposed the idea. "I tried to draw a line between my opposition to Farrakhan's statements and getting into an open war with the first serious black candidate in American history," he recalled. "Not because I had much affection for Jesse, but I knew of the tremendous emotional significance of this event on blacks and other Americans. So I tried to follow a line where my objections were clear but stopped short of World War III." For some staff members, Mondale's refusal to break with Jackson was another in a series of decisions made because of a misguided commitment to maintaining harmony at the expense of principle. "That was the last opportunity to draw a line that middle-America could discern as being significant," Galston reflected. "In the Jewish community and beyond Mondale did not have the guts to stand up. That perception would be fatal in the fall."[42]

Mondale's attempts to mediate his differences with Jackson may have contributed to the public perception that he was ineffectual, but it seems unlikely that a public clash with Jackson would have produced better results. Jackson had placed Mondale in a politically untenable position. While most blacks viewed Jackson as a charismatic figure who represented their hopes of social uplift, many white ethnics saw him as a threatening figure with radical intentions. Rather than trying to ease differences, Jackson's unquenchable thirst for respect and deep desire to exercise political independence inevitably led him to frustrate efforts at compromise. Under these circumstances, Mondale probably pursued the best strategy possible. He understood that a public confrontation with Jackson would alienate needed black support, focus unwanted media attention on an internal party debate, and destroy any possibility of piecing together a winning coalition. At the same time, he forcefully rejected Jackson's demands for increased social spending and made clear that, if elected, he would actively cultivate more moderate black support. For now, Jackson held the party and its nominee hostage to his own ambition.

As the primary season wound to a close, Mondale began flexing his organizational muscle by aggressively wooing delegates. "The day after Ohio," Johnson said, "I became totally preoccupied . . . with the importance of delegates." Mondale had accumulated 1,603 delegates and needed less than a third of those outstanding for a majority of 1,967. Hart was far behind with 866 and, despite his recent victories, had no chance of winning enough for the nomination. To add a sense of drama, Mondale announced he would win the nomination by 11:59 A.M. on June 6.[43]

He based his projection on winning a healthy share of delegates from the June 5 New Jersey and California primaries. Setting a frantic pace, Mondale campaigned for twenty-five consecutive hours, flying from California to New Jersey and back again. This desperate performance could have served as a metaphor for the long and difficult primary season. His efforts fell short of expectations. On election night, he won New Jersey by 15 percentage points, but lost media-orientated California by a small margin. He took all 117 delegates from New Jersey but only seventy-two of the 306 delegates in California, leaving him short of the number needed for the nomination.[44]

On the morning of June 6, Berman informed Mondale that he had still not won the nomination. "Son of a bitch," Mondale yelled as he rolled out of bed. "Will this never end?" Over the next few hours, Mondale and a small team of workers around the country called uncommitted delegates, hoping to sway enough to allow him to make his promised victory speech. With only a few minutes to spare before the 11:59 deadline, Mondale made the long-awaited announcement. "Yesterday the primary season came to a close," he said, "and I congratulate Gary Hart and Reverend Jackson for the campaigns they have run. But today I am pleased to claim victory. As of 11:59 this morning, over 2,008 delegates had pledged their support to me. The race for the majority is over."[45]

Mondale had attained his goal of winning the Democratic nomination for president, but fatigue prevented him from relishing the victory. Observers noted that Mondale had flown more miles, given more speeches, and slept in more hotels, than any other presidential candidate in history. The grueling campaign season had exacted a physical toll, and Mondale spent the following week resting at the Long Island estate of his friend Herbert Allen. Sheltered in the privacy of mountainous sand dunes and twelve-foot privet hedges, Mondale caught up on missed sleep, ate his treasured cheeseburgers, made phone calls to key supporters around the country, and played tennis with his sons, Ted and William. For the first time in years, there were no press conferences, photo opportunities, or speeches. At times, he sat alone for hours reflecting on the struggle for the nomination and contemplating his strategy for the Fall. Confident that he was ready and qualified to be president, Mondale accepted his underdog status and planned to wage a Harry-Truman-style-campaign that would prove the doubters wrong.

Mondale's primary showing did little to dispel suspicions about his candidacy. He won only eleven of twenty-nine primary contests. Of the five states he carried with at least 42 percent of the vote, all were in the industrial Northeast—New Jersey, New York, Pennsylvania, Maryland, and West Virginia. He defeated Hart by 700,000 in that region, but lost the rest of the nation by more than 250,000 votes. In Illinois, Indiana, and Ohio Mondale edged Hart by only 50,000 votes. In only two states outside the frostbelt, Tennessee and Wisconsin, did he win at least 40 percent of the vote. He lost all six primaries west of the Mississippi and all five in New England. Even in his native agricultural Midwest he lost Wisconsin and South Dakota. In nearly every state the same pattern emerged. Mondale won the cities, Hart won everywhere else. Exit poll revealed that Mondale had won a plurality of white voters in only three states—New York, Pennsylvania, and New Jersey. Mondale secured his party's nomination because he effectively translated votes into delegates. His 39 percent of the primary vote translated into 49 percent of the delegates. Hart, who won 36 percent of the vote, received 36 percent of the delegates, while Jackson won 18 percent of the vote but had to settle for only 10 percent of the delegates.[46]

Even though Mondale had declared himself the winner in the Democratic primaries, his rivals promised to fight to the convention. "The one thing that can be said about this nomination contest is that it is not over," Hart said following Mondale's victory announcement. He promised to "recruit uncommitted, unpledged delegates on the grounds that to win this election this fall, the Democratic Party must put forward new leadership and a new vision for this country." Jesse

Jackson, bitter about the number of delegates won and promising to challenge run-off elections, insisted that Mondale appoint key members of his staff to high campaign posts, give him influence over how the party was to spend voter-registration money, and grant him a say in party commissions that would study delegate selection rules for 1988. "You must expand the party before you heal it," he declared. "You must have party justice before you have party unity." [47]

While Mondale tried pulling his tattered party together from its long primary fight, Reagan bathed in the pageantry of an international summit and misty-eyed patriotic ceremonies. Within the span of a few days, first on the slopes of Arlington cemetery and then on the bluffs of Normandy, Reagan touched a national nerve with moving memorials to American war dead. "These are the boys of Pointe du Hoc," the President said in tribute to the U.S. Rangers who had scaled the sheer cliffs on D-Day, forty years before. "These are the champions who helped free a continent." So confident was he of the upcoming contest that when Walter Cronkite asked Reagan how he planned to campaign against the Democrats, the President responded: "Just tell them what we've done and what we're going to do and pretend they're not there." [48]

Mondale hoped to use the vice presidential selection process to establish that he was not the man in the portrait Hart and the others had painted. In a series of private discussions with John Reilly, Mondale made clear the twin goals for his vice presidential search. First, he was committed to opening the process to include minorities and women, who had been ignored in the past. "He did not want to consider five white males," Reilly recalled. Second, he wanted to do something bold that would prove he was a strong and decisive leader. With polls showing him losing ten points to Reagan in the few weeks since clinching the nomination, Mondale realized he needed to capture the public's attention with a dramatic initiative. "It was clear to me from the beginning that this was going to be a tough year and that politics as usual would probably fail to stir the enthusiasm we needed to make a campaign of it," he later said. Choosing a member of a minority or a woman as his running mate, he reasoned, would serve both purposes: it would be a statement of the Democratic party's commitment to equal opportunity and would provide much-needed public attention. [49]

Using the successful Carter approach as a model, he planned to invite leading contenders to his home in North Oaks for private interviews. In a classic demonstration of constituency politics, Mondale solicited representatives of all party factions. Los Angeles Mayor Tom Bradley and Philadelphia Mayor Wilson Goode represented blacks; New York Congresswoman Geraldine Ferraro, San Francisco Mayor Dianne Feinstein, and Kentucky Governor Martha Layne Collins symbolized concern for women; Mayor Henry Cisneros of San Antonio represented Hispanics; Senator Lloyd Bentsen of Texas, Governor Robert Graham of Florida, and Senator Dale Bumpers of Arkansas demonstrated the candidate's concern for the South.

The process provided Mondale with much-needed exposure, but it also demonstrated his blindness to public perceptions of his ties to special interest groups. The approach had worked successfully for a novice like Carter, but for a party regular like Mondale, who already knew most of the key players, it appeared insincere and cynical. "The Vice Presidential parade could have become a grand drama—a celebration of the diversity of America, of individual achievement, and of the opportunities for advancement historically created by the Democratic Party," reflected the *New Republic*. "Instead, the process devolved into a cartoonist's caricature of interest-group clamoring." Jackson ridiculed the process as a "P.R. parade of personalities" and suggested Hubert Humphrey was "the last significant politician from Minnesota." Hart complained Mondale was "pandering" to women and minorities. The national media poked fun at Mondale's attempt to include minorities in the process. A *Newsweek* cartoon stated: "Did you get a shot of me with the woman? Good! How about the black guy? Great! Okay, send in the Indian and after that the midget."[50]

Mondale could deal with the public criticism of his process. What he found more difficult to accept were the demands made by women's groups. When the NOW convention promised a floor fight at the Democratic Convention if he did not choose a woman, it immediately transformed what could have been a bold choice into another example of interest group concessions. "I think I'm a strong man and a decisive one," an irritated Mondale told a NOW representative. "But somehow the press always portrays me as someone who gives in to every demand. On the one most important thing I might do in my candidacy I'll be portrayed not as a man who was strong enough to make history but a man who gave in."

Hoping to limit public speculation, Mondale kept a long list of potential nominees and never developed a short list. He discussed candidates, weighed their respective strengths and weaknesses, without eliminating anyone. Clear preferences did emerge. His first choice was Tom Bradley, but his 66 years denied him the much needed appeal to younger voters. His second choice was Henry Cisneros, but his relative youth and inexperience made him risky. "If Tom Bradley had been 56 rather than 66, Mondale would have taken him," recalled Reilly. "If Cisneros had been 46 rather than 36, Mondale would have chosen him."[51]

With time running out, he sent Reilly on a secret mission to ask Gary Hart if he would be interested. Hart said yes, but only under certain conditions: that he be heavily involved in disarmament negotiations and that he not be forced to lobby for legislation he did not support. Mondale, reflecting on his own frustrations in the Carter White House, did not object to Hart's conditions. The more he thought about Hart, the more inclined he was to ask him to join the ticket. The primaries had demonstrated his appeal, and he could help attract the independent voters whom Mondale desperately needed. Also, polls showed Hart was the favorite choice. There was only one problem. Mondale worried about the continued press investigations into Hart's personal life. A damaging revelation about Hart's past could destroy the campaign. After a number of discreet inquiries, Mondale discovered that investigations of Hart's rumored sexual exploits and drug use, which had ended when he lost the nomination, would be reopened. Unwilling to take the chance, Mondale nixed Hart and began thinking about other possibilities.[52]

In the final days, Mondale turned his attention to Mayor Dianne Feinstein and Congresswoman Geraldine Ferraro. As he began drafting his acceptance speech, his attention turned more toward Ferraro. "He said that she and Cisneros, better than Feinstein, seemed to most accurately portray what this country is all about," said Reilly. The daughter of Italian immigrants, Ferraro had raised a family, taught in the New York public school system, and attended law school at night. In 1974, she became a prosecutor heading a special bureau for victims of violent crimes. Later, she ran for Congress as a law-and-order Democrat. Her slogan: "Finally, A Tough Democrat." Entering Congress in 1979 she worked hard on lowly assignments and carefully cultivated the Democratic leadership, especially House Speaker Tip O'Neill. In 1983, with O'Neill's support, she was appointed to the powerful House Budget Committee. A liberal, she represented an ethnic working-class district in Queens which had given her 73 percent of the vote in 1982. Though, like most liberals, she opposed the MX missile and favored the ERA, she delighted many conservatives with her support for tuition tax credits and a military draft.[53]

On July 9, Mondale sent Berman to Ferraro's Queens home to

perform a quick check of her finances. Arriving early in the morning, he spent a few hours talking with Ferraro and her husband John Zacarro before she left, insisting on keeping a hair cutting appointment. For the rest of the afternoon, Berman sorted through the family's complicated financial records. Time prevented Berman from getting written responses to the elaborate questionnaire prepared for the occasion. Instead, he walked them through the form orally. After getting assurances that the family finances were in order, Berman reported to Mondale that no major problems existed.[54]

Mondale worried whether Ferraro would be an effective campaigner, if she really understood the rigors of a vice presidential race. On July 10, he dispatched Reilly on a secret mission to visit Ferraro in San Francisco, where she was chairing the Democratic platform committee. Along with asking the "Eagleton question"—"Are there any skeletons in your closet that could embarrass the ticket"—Reilly explained that if she were chosen, Mondale would make all the key decisions about how her campaign would be run. "We will run your campaign," he told her. "We will set your schedule. We will provide you with staff. Your participation will be shaped by Mondale." Ferraro flippantly agreed to these conditions and dismissed suggestions that she was not prepared for a national campaign. Sensing she did not understand the depth of the commitment she was making, Reilly underscored the central point: "You must cooperate." Again, Ferraro, perhaps annoyed by Reilly's patronizing tone, downplayed potential problems. "Running for Congress in New York," she said, "you see just about everything." Her cockiness annoyed Reilly who was convinced she did not understand the intensity of a national campaign. "There's a certain thing that happens to people who run in New York," Reilly reflected. "They think they've seen everything and Paris too." Despite his reservations, Reilly informed Mondale that Ferraro had agreed to accept his full control of the campaign. "I told him I did not think she understood the spotlight but she could probably handle it," he recalled.[55] After both Reilly and Berman reported back, Mondale made his decision. "Well, I think we've spent enough time on this," he told Johnson and Reilly. "I've decided I want to ask Ferraro to run with me. Let's go with her."

Mondale hoped that Ferraro's ethnic roots would shake Reagan's hold on the middle-class. At the same time, by choosing a woman, he would demonstrate his strong leadership and defy the conventional view that he was incapable of bold gestures. Initial press reactions to the announcement confirmed his optimism. William Raspberry wrote that "in one masterful stroke," Mondale had "rescued his presidential campaign from its dull predictability, transformed himself from the play-it-safe Fritz to bold statesman—and maybe moved several giant steps closer to the White House."[56]

In the wave of enthusiasm that greeted the announcement, party optimists hoped Ferraro's selection would give Mondale a chance in states where he trailed Reagan. "It's going to change the terms of the fall election from the old North-South, left-right terms," predicted one party pundit, who added that it would emphasize demographic factors. "A lot of ethnic Catholic Democrats around the country will identify with her and her background," said Tony Coelho, chairman of the Democratic Congressional Campaign Committee. With polls showing women favoring Mondale over Reagan, the Ferraro nomination could help rally the millions of unregistered women voters. There was one serious flaw in this reasoning. Although many Americans applauded the selection of a woman for the ticket, Ferraro appealed most to voters already loyal to Mondale. A liberal from New York with little attraction in the South, Ferraro only intensified Reagan's support in the South and West and allowed him to challenge Mondale in traditionally Democratic states in the East.[57]

The selection also only temporarily silenced Mondale's primary rivals. With polls showing him performing 10 percentage points better than Mondale in match-ups with the president, Hart pressed delegates to abandon the nominee in favor of his candidacy. "I have the best chance by far of defeating Ronald Reagan next fall," he repeated on numerous occasions. A temperamental Jackson remained Mondale's biggest problem. In the days leading up to the Convention, he lashed out at Mondale, Jews, white women, and the media for not treating him as an equal candidate. He claimed to be a victim of "cultural racism" and promised to "play a trumpet with a clear sound" at the convention. Unable to find an effective way of dealing with Jackson, Mondale decided to blast him. "I'm tired of this. I'm tired of your playing to the press," he told Jackson in a heated phone conversation. After defending his vice presidential selection process, Mondale warned: "I'm going to return it to you as fast as you give it."[58]

Mondale's hasty attempt to substitute Bert Lance for Charles Manatt as Democratic National Committee Chairman did not help efforts to build confidence in his candidacy. Just as he hoped Ferraro could solidify support among women and minorities, Mondale believed Lance could improve his stature in the South. Unfortunately,

Lance was still a very controversial figure. His reputation as a wheeler-dealer and his forced resignation as Carter's OMB director in September 1977 raised considerable concern among many party regulars. Also, by making the decision before he had received the nomination, Mondale made himself vulnerable to charges of arrogance. The intense negative reaction shocked Mondale and after twenty-four hours of indecision he reversed himself, retaining Manatt as Committee Chairman and assigning Lance to a temporary position. The whole incident undermined the impression of strong leadership he had tried to cultivate with the Ferraro appointment. "Here's Mondale doing exactly what Carter would have done—a little bit of pressure and he's on another tangent," commented a gleeful Republican. "What kind of leadership is that?"[59]

The four thousand delegates who crammed into San Francisco's Moscone Convention center witnessed a convention packed with drama and passion. Los Angeles Mayor Tom Bradley sounded the unity plea in his welcoming remarks. "We are not here to beat up on each other," he said, "but to beat up on Ronald Reagan." Their task was actually greater. They had to do more than "beat up" on Reagan, they needed to present a compelling vision of their own. "The problem," wrote the New York *Times*' Adam Clymer, "is how to retain the allegiance of the voting blocs that the New Deal glued together while shaking off the image of the New Deal itself, and with it the implication that the party's vision is a half-century old." William Greider, writing in *Rolling Stone* Magazine, observed a party "trapped between two constituencies" and uncertain "where the future lies." "Should they," he asked, "concentrate on rebuilding the tattered base of support among working-class families, threatened farmers and the alienated underclass? Or should they cultivate their new and growing base in the suburbs?"[60]

Mondale worked hard to develop a platform that would reflect a new consensus within the party. The platform avoided specific endorsements of special interest groups and instead emphasized economic growth, prosperity, jobs, and opportunity as the party's central goals. Critical of Reagan's budget deficits, it observed that "a corrosive unfairness eats at the underpinnings of our society." The platform said little about welfare and instead spoke of providing the poor with "the greatest opportunity for self-sufficiency." For the first time it included a section called "Controlling Domestic Spending," which advocated "a balanced program for reducing Republican mega-deficits." The *Congressional Quarterly* called it the "most conservative platform in the last 50 years." "The party of big and bountiful government of Roosevelt and Johnson has drawn a plan for penny-wise, efficient government," commented the New York *Times*. "It just proves that Mondale is moderate, cautious . . . and fiscally prudent," said Walter Heller.[61]

On foreign policy, Mondale tried to forge agreement in a party still torn by the Vietnam War. The compromise he eventually molded was as different from the neo-isolationism of McGovern as it was from the *Pax Americana* envisioned by John F. Kennedy. Mondale realized the expansionist rhetoric of Truman and Kennedy had been rendered obsolete by new international realities: strategic parity with the Soviets, the emergence of new industrial powers, and the rise of third world nationalism. But Mondale also rejected the neo-isolationist views of many post-Vietnam Democrats who naïvely dismissed the importance of military force, the existence of U.S-Soviet competition, and the need to defend American interests abroad. During the primary season most of the opposition came from the left, with Hart and Jackson calling for cuts in military spending and a unilateral moratorium on American missile deployment in Western Europe. Mondale rejected these positions and insisted on modest increases in defense spending, improvement of conventional forces, and a strong affirmation of America's commitment to European and Israeli security. Even a number of compromises with Hart's planks did not prevent the platform from noting "the threat to world peace posed by the Soviet Union" and "the Soviet leadership's dangerous behavior internationally and the totalitarian nature of their regime."

The convention also displayed new faces and an oratorical flourish not seen in recent Democratic gatherings. In a moving keynote address, New York Governor Mario Cuomo used *A Tale of Two Cities,* Saint Francis of Assisi, and his own immigrant experience to highlight the theme of family which Mondale saw as a metaphor for showing how government could help the less fortunate. "We believe in a single fundamental idea," Cuomo told the audience, "the idea of family. Mutuality. The sharing of benefits and burdens." The following night Jackson stirred the convention hall with his revival message. "Our time has come," he thundered. "Our faith, hope and dreams have prevailed, . . . America, our time has come! We come from disgrace to amazing grace. Our time has come!" Hart sounded his familiar theme, criticizing "the policies of the comfortable past that do not answer the challenges of tomorrow." He also promised to "devote every waking hour and every ounce of energy to the defeat of Ronald Reagan."[62]

Following Hart's speech the convention nominated Mondale on the first ballot by a comfortable 224-vote margin. Immediately after New Jersey announced its decisive vote, Hart addressed the convention, and, in a unity gesture, moved that Mondale's nomination be made unanimous by acclamation. "There is a time to fight and a time to unite. Our party has made its choice and we must now speak with one voice," he declared. Jackson followed him to the podium and added his own call for unity. "We are entering a new phase in our struggle for change, " he said.[63]

The Convention's final night presented Mondale with the opportunity he needed to shape the political debate in a way more favorable to his candidacy. It began with the acceptance address of the first woman vice presidential nominee. As Ferraro strolled to the podium the band played the theme from "New York, New York" and the convention erupted into a spirited ovation. "My name is Geraldine Ferraro. I stand before you to proclaim tonight: America is a land where dreams can come true for all of us." Her selection, she declared, sent "a powerful signal to all Americans. There are no doors we cannot unlock. We will place no limits on achievement." The convention loved it. As he looked over the electrified hall, Mondale felt confident he had made the right choice. Ferraro had supplied the excitement and drama he needed.[64]

Mondale realized that Ferraro could not sustain the ticket; only he could provide hope and inspiration to gloomy party leaders. For six weeks, Mondale had worked over successive drafts of his acceptance speech. Again, he faced the same problem that had plagued him on previous occasions. With a prime-time television audience looking on, he needed to convince skeptical independent voters that he and the Democratic party understood their concerns. But he also needed to rally the party faithful to his cause. Once again, his speechwriters labored through successive drafts searching for a unifying theme.

While he may not have created a new thematic recipe for the speech, Mondale did know what ingredients he wanted included. First, he hoped to convince independents and wavering Democrats that their party was no longer captive to left-wing liberals insensitive to their demands. While admitting past mistakes, he planned to reaffirm the party's commitment to traditional values, economic growth, and national strength.[65]

Mondale refused, however, to allow the celebration of American values to camouflage the difficult problems that needed attention. Most pressing of all, he believed, was the growing federal deficit which had swelled to an estimated $184 billion for 1984. Reagan's success, he reasoned, was built on the quicksand of borrowed money and sustained by the illusion of prosperity. With annual deficit forecasts of $200 to $300 billion for years into the future, Mondale felt strongly that a serious candidate for president had to present a fair and realistic program for addressing the problem. The president's program, he felt, fell far short of that standard since no credible economists believed economic growth alone would absorb the deficit. Though he understood the political attractiveness of a spending freeze, he felt it was unfair to the poor who already had suffered from Reagan's budget cuts. Reluctantly, Mondale concluded that any proposal for addressing the deficit would have to include a tax increase.

Mondale understood as well as anyone that advocating a tax increase would provide Reagan with the opportunity to paint him as an old-style tax-and-spend Democrat. In the weeks preceding the convention, his staff debated the wisdom of proposing a tax increase. All saw the need for a dramatic initiative that would attract attention and accentuate Mondale's leadership qualities. A few questioned whether supporting higher taxes would serve that purpose. Despite the political peril, Mondale planned to call for a tax increase without a spending freeze. The added revenue was necessary, he said, and he was committed to adding $30 billion in domestic programs cut under Reagan. "If I can't do something about those people savaged by the Reagan Administration then there is no point in me being President," he said. "It's the only way I can run."[66]

On the convention's final night, in the most important moment of his long political career, Mondale confessed past sins and spoke of future progress. "Tonight, we come to you with a new realism," Mondale declared, "ready for the future and recapturing the best in our tradition. We know that America must have a strong defense and a sober view of the Soviets. We know that government must be as well-managed as it is well-meaning. We know that a healthy, growing private economy is the key to our future." The Party's platform, he assured wavering Democrats, contained "no defense cuts that weaken our security; no business taxes that weaken our economy; no laundry lists that raid our Treasury." After diffusing potential criticism, Mondale moved on to make his case against Reagan. Charging that the nation was "living on borrowed money and borrowed time," Mondale blasted Reagan for record deficits which "hike interest rates, clobber exports, stunt investment, kill jobs, undermine growth, cheat our kids and shrink our future." Realizing that critics would demand more than vague promises, Mondale proposed to cut the deficit by raising taxes. "Let's tell the truth," he declared in an announcement that caught many Democrats off guard, "Mr. Reagan will raise taxes, and so will I," Mondale declared. "He won't tell you, I just did."[67]

In many ways, the speech represented a bold departure for Mondale. It omitted the obligatory references to the litany of Democratic interest groups which he usually insisted on including. Mondale thanked people for welcoming him into their "homes and businesses," but not their union halls; he pledged to sustain a constant level of defense spending, but did not promise new social programs; he spoke of tougher standards for teachers and students, but did not promise higher salaries or more student aid; he quoted Abraham Lincoln, the first Republican president, but not FDR. Finally, unlike past party nominees, Mondale made sacrifice a central theme of his address. He refused to say, as most of his Democratic predecessors had, that the nation's fiscal problems could be solved solely by taxing the rich. Everyone, he said, would have to bear part of the burden.[68]

The immediate reaction to Mondale's speech was overwhelmingly positive. The delegates, who interrupted him sixty times by applause, responded warmly to Mondale's crisp, forcefully delivered message of restraint. David Broder said that Mondale had presented himself "as a tough, chastened political realist." The *New Republic* declared "Mr. Mondale performed impressively."[69]

Yet for all of his recognition of the failures of the past and his indictment of Reagan, Mondale's address did not define a clear positive message for the campaign. "It did not add up to a philosophical distinction of his candidacy," reflected Martin. It lacked a compelling theme that could galvanize voters and establish his differences with Reagan. Mondale found himself caught in the middle of his attempt to strike a balance between the party's competing constituencies. While speaking of the Democratic party's historic commitment to the poor, the sick, and the disabled, he also told voters who had voted for Reagan, "I heard you. And our party heard you." He proposed to restore several billion dollars of Reagan's budget cuts and increase taxes on wealthy families, but promised no new social spending, only small new taxes on business, and a slower pace of increased defense spending. By not linking a call for new taxes with a plea for equitable reform of the tax system, Mondale failed to distinguish himself from Reagan. He also did not challenge expensive entitlement programs, which many believed would also have to be included in any realistic program to balance the budget. While a dramatic improvement over previous speeches, his address did not make the bold gestures Mondale needed to establish his credibility with most voters. "In 1984 Walter Mondale had to be John Hancock," Galston reflected. "He needed to write his name so large the king could read it without his spectacles."[70]

The convention ended with the traditional show of unity on the convention platform. The delegates swayed to Jennifer Holliday's stirring rendition of The Battle Hymn of the Republic, waved twenty thousand American flags in a demonstration of patriotism, and cheered as a triumphant Mondale stood side-by-side with his historic choice for vice president. It was precisely the image Mondale had hoped to project. "This is the week the Democrats took the flag back," said Tip O'Neill. "The picture was the Democratic party's future opening doors," observed Richard Leone. "It gave the lie to the GOP line of attack on 'Carter-Mondale' not by defending any detail of the past administration—it simply made the association with Carter irrelevant." Surveys suggested that the convention was a dramatic success. A *Newsweek-Gallup* poll showed Mondale jumping from a nineteen-point deficit to a two-point lead in less than a month. "Something intensely human and emotional happened in this gathering of the warring Democratic tribes that is hard to define and harder to measure," James Reston wrote. "It was a revival meeting in more ways than one, vaguely religious at times, and defiantly, even mockingly, political."[71]

The central question remained: Could Mondale and Ferraro lure middle-class white voters back into the Democratic Party? Mondale left the convention more confident than ever, but not everyone shared his optimism. William Greider reported that while roaming around the convention floor he could not find a single person who felt Mondale could win in November. Many Hart delegates felt the party's celebration of its ethnic roots ignored the real issues facing the party. Pat Caddell said Mondale's nomination proved the party was "brain dead." Jesse Jackson quipped that selling Mondale to the nation was "not going to be like giving away Michael Jackson tickets." One Hart supporter summed up the feeling of many Democrats: "I've been to four Democratic conventions, and this one is totally fatalistic. I'll bet seventy-five percent of the delegates here don't think we have a prayer in November."[72]

16

The Last Campaign

Hoping to sustain the momentum generated by the successful convention, Mondale and his running mate continued to emphasize the themes of "hard work," "patriotism," and "the American Dream" in the ensuing campaign. After a brief stop at Mondale's boyhood home of Elmore, they traveled to Ferraro's home in Queens, New York where they received a rousing reception from local residents and prominent New York Democrats. Virtually ignoring his Republican opponent, Mondale told the partisan crowd that Ferraro represented his party's vision of the future. "We have one national message to take to the American people and it is this," Mondale said. "In the future the American dream that worked for Gerry Ferraro must be the birthright of every single American without discrimination."[1]

After New York the Democratic ticket headed South, where they hoped to put Reagan on the defensive with their reaffirmation of traditional values. Drawing unexpectedly large crowds in Mississippi and Texas, they spoke of their concern for law and order, strong defense, and a "new realism." While Ferraro flexed her crime-fighting credentials, Mondale reminded audiences of the lessons Democrats had learned. "We didn't tell the American people they were wrong" after losing the White House in 1980, he said. "Instead, we began asking you what our mistakes had been." Mondale emphasized the importance of facing difficult issues like the deficit and the need for new taxes. "This debt will kill our economy unless we cut it down," he asserted. "These deficits are murder to your economy, and no matter who's elected President, the budget must be squeezed and taxes will be raised." The "new realism" required conservatives to face the possibility of new taxes and liberals to recognize the limits of government power. "In 1984 it is realism to know government alone cannot solve all of our problems," he told a crowd in Austin, Texas. "Much of it depends on us and our selves."[2]

Following the brief trip South, Mondale invited Ferraro to his North Oaks home for the first comprehensive strategy session of the fall campaign. At Mondale's direction, Jim Johnson displayed two large charts outlining the candidate's schedules for August and September. He suggested that Ferraro attend a few foreign policy seminars and be prepared for her first solo campaign swing through California in three days. Annoyed that Mondale had set her schedule without consulting her and disturbed by what she perceived as the patronizing tone of Mondale's staff, Ferraro decided to take a stand. "I did not want to get walked over," she recalled. "I knew that the campaign was not going to be easy. I knew that I was going to have to spend a lot of time convincing people that I could do the job. I did not want to have to start off by convincing the staff. If they did not know by that time why I was picked, then we had a problem. I had to do something to assert myself."[3]

Ferraro certainly did assert herself. "Why is it in ink?" she snapped, pointing at the schedule. "Why isn't it in pencil?" At one point during the meeting she shouted: "If I were Lloyd Bentsen you would not be treating me this way." According to her account, Ferraro told Mondale she could not make the California trip because she needed to tend to pressing congressional business in Washington and required more time to prepare issues. Mondale and his staff recall the scene differently. "Ferraro's account is bullshit," declared Reilly. They claim she refused to campaign in California because she wanted to take a vacation at Fire Island—not, as she claimed, to deal with congressional matters.[4]

Mondale grew increasingly annoyed as the bickering continued, with Johnson, later joined by Dick Leone and Paul Tully, insisting she make the California trip. "We have a terrific opening," Leone told her. "We are on a roll and you are the most interesting person in American politics. We can dominate the media right on through the Republican convention." But Ferraro was just as adamant in refusing. "I told you that I'm not going until I'm ready," she repeated. "I know what's best, I've been through it before in New York." Watching the spectacle in disbelief, Mondale must have thought how Lyndon Johnson would have reacted if Humphrey had displayed similar obstinateness. Mondale thought, recalled one close friend, "Ferraro was thumbing her nose at him and the campaign." He had spent the past four years traveling six days a week, working fourteen-hour days, sacrificing vacations and precious time with his family in order to have the opportunity to represent his party in the presidential campaign. Now Ferraro, who had no experience running a national campaign, was complaining because she wanted to take a vacation! Mondale almost exploded when Ferraro compared herself to Bentsen. If Ferraro were a male politician, he told aides later, he would not have tolerated her behavior for two minutes. Finally, Mondale stood up and summarily ended the meeting. "I guess that ends the conversation for tonight," he said marching out of the room.[5]

Mondale had terminated the meeting for the evening, but the discussion continued into the next day. When Mondale awoke the next morning anxious aides informed him that Ferraro had become completely unglued and spent most of the night crying. The reports were so grim that at one point, Mondale worried that she might quit the ticket. "It looks like I might have to pick a new vice president," he said. By late morning, however, Ferraro had collected herself and asked for a few private minutes with Mondale. At that session, Ferraro repeated her demand of the previous night. "They're not used to dealing with a woman, but they're going to have to learn," she said. "To help them along, let me suggest that until they can get used to recognizing I'm a partner in this thing, they should pretend every time they talk to me or even look at me that I'm a grey-haired Southern gentleman, a senator from Texas." Hoping to avoid a clash with his running mate, Mondale apologized for his staff's behavior and gently suggested that she be more accommodating.[6]

The experience in North Oaks irreparably impaired Ferraro's relationship with Mondale, which remained strained throughout the campaign. "After the meeting at North Oaks," recalled Leone, "Mondale saw Gerry as another problem that had to be managed." Ferraro, for her part, felt that Mondale never accorded her the respect she deserved. Despite his apology following the North Oaks debacle, he never consulted her about campaign scheduling or strategy. "What ended-up happening," she reflected with some bitterness, "is that they still did what they damn-well pleased. But at least they pretended that we were here to stay." The most serious strains, however, emerged between Ferraro and Mondale's senior staff. She found them arrogant and condescending; they accused her of being ignorant of basic issues and unwilling to spend the time to learn. "Gerry didn't do her homework," Leone said. "She was facile and glib enough to be pretty good on her feet." [7]

While Mondale's staff prepared for the inevitable assault on Ferraro's qualifications, another firestorm began raging over her family's finances. At the July convention Ferraro had promised to make public her tax returns and those of her husband before the legally mandated August 20 deadline. On August 12, before leaving for a campaign trip to California, she casually informed reporters that her husband had decided not to release his records. "I have to say that I requested my husband to do that, and my husband feels, quite frankly, that his business interests would be affected," she told a reporter. Reminded of her convention promise, she retorted: "If you're married to an Italian man, you know what it's like." Ferraro, not realizing the potential impact of the announcement, dismissed the whole incident. Mondale knew better. [8]

For the next ten days, the Ferraro-Zaccaro family finances consumed the entire campaign. The Ethics in Government Act of 1978 required Presidential and Vice Presidential candidates and their spouses to disclose their sources of income and their financial liabilities. In her congressional filings, Ferraro had relied upon a narrow exemption in House rules which allowed for non-release if the spouse was independent, had no knowledge of the family business practice, and received no benefit from it. Berman, however, had made clear in his meeting with Ferraro that if selected, Mondale would expect her to release all of her tax returns, regardless of her past practice. Ferraro's attempt to distance herself from her husband's successful real estate business also did not satisfy a skeptical press. On the west coast Ferraro encountered large and enthusiastic crowds, but she could not escape constant interrogation. At one news conference, eighteen of twenty questions concerned her family finances. Industrious reporters showed that Ferraro had been closely involved in her husband's business. She had practiced law and based her reelection campaign in his Manhattan office, he and his business associates had played a key role in financing her first campaign for Congress in 1978, and they were joint owners of numerous properties.[9]

Just two days after Ferraro's announcement, a New York *Times* poll indicated that the campaign was in a much weaker position than Mondale had anticipated. The poll showed widespread support of the Ferraro selection and a generally favorable impression of the Convention, but persistent doubts about Mondale. Over half of all respondents criticized Mondale for making too many promises and for lacking the toughness and experience to be president. Mondale was not even able to capitalize on growing public concern about the deficit—his central issue. Those who considered the deficit the major issue favored Reagan 64 percent to 25 percent. The survey showed Reagan holding a lead of 49 percent to 34 percent, identical to the lead he had held in June. "Reagan is vulnerable on the issues," commented a Mondale advisor, "but we can't really focus on the issues where Reagan is weak until Mondale reaches the threshold of being perceived as a leader who is minimally capable of running the country."[10]

The problems with Ferraro only compounded Mondale's frustration. Publicly, he maintained a composed and supportive demeanor, calling Ferraro a number of times to express his support. Privately, he was both perplexed and infuriated. It was ironic that Mondale—who possessed little wealth and had always stayed far from scandal—would now have his presidential campaign scarred by charges of financial impropriety. Why, he wondered, had she not told Berman about these problems? In her eagerness to become the nominee, had Ferraro intentionally misled him about her family finances? Or, did many of the revelations about Zaccaro's business come as a surprise to her? Whatever the reason, Mondale was trapped. He could not let her stand alone for fear of appearing weak and defensive, but he could not defend her either since he did not know whether new damaging evidence would emerge.

On August 20, after dominating the news for days, Ferraro released both sets of tax returns. Reporters now raised questions about a $53,459 bill for back taxes and interest for 1978, an illegal loan for $130,000, and the $175,000 Zaccaro borrowed from an elderly woman's estate for which he was the court-appointed conservator. Hoping to put the entire matter to rest, Ferraro scheduled a nationally televised press conference in New York for August 21. "Gerry, just stay there until you wear them out," Mondale told her. She followed the advice. Appearing before more than 150 reporters, Ferraro admitted she had been "sloppy" in handling her tax returns, but insisted she had not violated any House rules by failing to disclose her husband's business interests in her annual financial disclosure statement. "At no time did I violate any trust placed in me by my constituents," she said.[11]

Mondale believed Ferraro's impressive performance had finally laid the tax issue to rest. In a hastily called press conference he told reporters that Ferraro had "passed a test of leadership." His embattled running mate had, he asserted, "conducted herself with great skill, [and] intelligence; she showed strength under challenging circumstances and I found her most persuasive and most impressive." His confident public statement to the contrary, Mondale realized the incident had damaged his campaign. It had distracted attention from the issues and prevented him from making his case against Reagan. The incident also removed much of the luster from the Ferraro candidacy. "Joan of Arc," commented Peter Hart, had been transformed into "just another politician."[12]

While the Democrats fretted over Ferraro's finances, the Republicans met in Dallas for their extravagant coronation of Ronald Reagan. On the convention eve the Commerce Department released figures which added proof to Republican claims that they were the party of prosperity: the GNP had grown by a dramatic 7.6 percent in the second quarter, while inflation had dropped to a modest 3.5 percent annual rate. Reagan accepted the nomination claiming his administration had brought "a springtime of hope for America." Focusing on his previous accomplishments and not his future agenda, Reagan dwelt on arousing patriotic feelings and attacking the Carter administration. Uncharacteristically defensive, he blamed Democrats for the nation's unprecedented budget deficit. "We would say they spend money like drunken sailors but that would be unfair to drunken sailors," Reagan said. Tracing the journey of the Olympic torch across America, Reagan told stories of patriotic singing and celebration. In an emotional presentation, Reagan said the Los Angeles Olympic games symbolized the "melting pot" of America. Reagan called the election "the clearest political choice of half a century" involving "two fundamentally different ways of governing—their Government of pessimism, fear and limits, or ours of hope, confidence and growth." It was an impressive performance. "Walt Whitman wrote that he could hear America singing," commented Richard Cohen. "In Reagan's text, you could both hear it and see it."[13]

Trying to build momentum following the flap over Ferraro's finances, Mondale combined pleas for fiscal responsibility with a biting populist message. In speeches across the country he spoke of the limits of government, the need for reduced spending, the value of hard work, and family and religious values. He charged that Reagan's tax cuts had favored the rich while the burden of his huge budget deficit would fall on the backs of average working-class Americans. "The idea behind Reaganomics is this: a rising tide lifts all yachts," Mondale told a cheering crowd in Springfield, Illinois. "There's nothing wrong about becoming rich. Moving up the ladder is what America is all about," he said. "But opportunity for us does not mean taking from people trying to climb up that ladder and giving it to people on top. That's what Reaganomics means." He repeated his accusation that Reagan had a secret plan to raise taxes and his claim that the average American would be better off under a Democratic tax increase than a Republican plan. "If Mr. Reagan wins," Mondale declared, "he will sock working people with the biggest tax hikes and the deepest budget cuts, just like he did before; and he'll leave his rich friends alone." [14]

Certain he had the better argument and convinced voters would see through Reagan's shallow appeals to patriotism, Mondale believed he needed to make his case as forcefully as possible by constantly contrasting his responsible approach to government with the Republican president's reckless disregard for the budget deficit, the threat of nuclear war, and social justice. As part of his effort, Mondale challenged Reagan to six debates on specific issues. The challenge represented more than the desperate tactics of a losing candidate. It reflected Mondale's deeply held belief that campaigning represented an exchange of substantive proposals. "It illustrated on Mondale's part his vision of the American people being a thoughtful jury considering a complex set of issues and policy which they had a sacred obligation to balance and weigh," Johnson recalled. Mondale viewed the electorate as "thoughtful people coming to thoughtful decisions based on public officials who honestly describe problems and honestly propose practical solutions." Feeling little need to debate, Reagan scoffed at the suggestion. Agreeing to one, maybe two debates, he said that six would "bore the pants off" the public. [15]

During the final week of August, Mondale assembled his coalition for the upcoming campaign. He brought to North Oaks mayors, governors, congressmen, and civic leaders to assign them roles in the campaign. He also hoped to use the time to heal his differences with Jesse Jackson and finally win his endorsement. Just a few weeks earlier they had engaged in a public debate. Jackson had told the Los Angeles *Times* that Mondale "had no coherent regional strategy or themes to attract black voters." When told of the comment, Mondale muttered in the presence of reporters: "It looks like I'm going to have to win this on my own." But realizing he needed black votes, Mondale asked Jackson and the other black leaders to provide a "united front" behind his candidacy. "I need you now and I can't let this thing go on much longer," he pleaded with Jackson. Enjoying the media attention and taking pleasure in watching Mondale squirm, Jackson teased reporters by expressing support but refusing explicitly to endorse his party's nominee. Jackson's arrogance infuriated Mondale. "It was very embarrassing," he recalled. "I didn't know what he was going to do and I tried to put the best face on it. I was irritated."[16]

The black leaders Mondale had assembled in St. Paul proved just as obstinate. They angrily insisted that the price of their endorsement would be Mondale's approval of a multi-billion-dollar jobs program. Recognizing that embracing such a program would sabotage his appeals for fiscal responsibility, Mondale refused to budge. "I'm not going to do it," Mondale said repeatedly. "I got nominated on this program. I'm going to stand for reduction of these deficits. The only way we're going to get hope for black America and the rest of America is to get these deficits down. You're the ones who are paying the big price, and I'm not going to do it." For over an hour, they persisted with Gary, Indiana Mayor Richard Hatcher leading the charge. Only a moving speech by former Atlanta Mayor Maynard Jackson saved Mondale from near catastrophe by convincing the group to issue a unanimous endorsement. The following day, Mondale pronounced himself ready. "This campaign is now ready to move. We have our coalition together. Our case is strong. The contrasts couldn't be more basic."[17]

Rarely has the contrast between two candidates been more striking. Mondale's recollections of growing up during the depression revolved around memories of community sharing and activist government. Although they never benefited directly from New Deal programs, the Mondale family had been filled with hope of a more prosperous future by Roosevelt's inspirational voice and innovative reforms. "There was suffering during the depression," Mondale reflected nearly a half-century later, "but there was a sense that someone cared. Roosevelt cared."[18]

Reagan's youth—he had been born almost twenty years before the depression—reflected the rugged individualism of a more confident era. Reagan selectively remembered from his past those events which confirmed his celebration of small-town life. Ironically, his recollection of self-help and personal sacrifice characterized Mondale's depression experience more than his own. Reagan's family never experienced the poverty Mondale had known. Both of Reagan's parents worked in New Deal relief administration jobs distributing federal funds. "He is the sincerest claimant to a heritage that never existed," wrote Garry Wills. "The perfection of the pretense lies in the fact that he does not know he is pretending."[19]

Mondale came to political maturity at a young age, learning the skills of the trade as a campaign worker for Hubert Humphrey in 1948. For him politics was the art of the possible, realized by building coalitions around substantive appeals. Mondale believed politics should be a rational process where facts made sense of social reality. Reagan came to politics late in life, only after a long, mostly successful career in film. Where Mondale mastered the art of building coalitions, Reagan acquired the skill of projecting images and values through mass media. In Reagan's campaigns discussing issues was secondary, taking a back seat to invoking themes, creating visual images, and communicating shared values. "With Reagan, facts don't determine the case," remarked the *New Republic's* Sydney Blumenthal. "Facts don't make his beliefs true. His beliefs give life to facts, which are parables tailored to have a moral."[20]

Reagan understood television's enormous impact on the presidency; Mondale had little use for mass media and even less understanding of its impact. Michael Deaver, a public relations expert who joined Reagan's team in 1966, summed up their approach: "Television elects Presidents," he said. One scholar observed that "no previous administration had devoted so many resources to managing the news or approached the task with so much calculation." Applying mass-marketing techniques to national electoral politics, they exploited the news media's commitment to objectivity. "The truth of the matter is that Ronald Reagan is the perfect candidate," said his campaign manager Edward Rollins. "He does whatever you want him to do. And he does it superbly well." Where Reagan appealed to values and underlying passions, Mondale spoke of programs and issues. Reagan understood that politics in a television age was performing art, not political science. "Reaganism is politics-as-evangelism, calling forth a majority with a hymn to general values," George Will wrote. "Mondalism is politics-as-masonry, building a majority brick by brick."[21]

Perhaps most important, Reagan presided over a resurgent Republican party confident that peace and prosperity guaranteed victory. With its coffers brimming with contributions from generous corporate PACs and its organization staffed by veterans of successful national campaigns, the Republicans were ready for battle. Mondale stood as the titular head of a demoralized and splintered party reluctant to accept him as its spokesman. Along with its deep generational and ideological differences, the party lagged far behind its opponent in funds and relied heavily upon a limited pool of successful presidential campaign veterans.

Mondale hoped to erase Reagan's lead by continuing his combative style, highlighting the real choices between himself and Reagan on issues, and portraying himself as a forceful leader. Most polls showed Reagan with a 10- to 15-point advantage, well below the Labor Day lead enjoyed by Richard Nixon in 1972 and Jimmy Carter in 1976. As part of his strategy, Mondale had decided to demonstrate his concern for middle America by delivering the campaign's inaugural speech in Merrill, Wisconsin. Most of his staff argued that opening the campaign in a small midwestern town rather than at a labor-sponsored event in New York or Detroit would help establish his independence, clarify his values, and illustrate his "new" program for America.

A number of events conspired to dilute Mondale's "new realism" message. First, AFL-CIO head Lane Kirkland convinced Mondale that his presence at the traditional New York City Labor Day Parade would provide a needed boost to organized labor. Appreciating the symbolic significance of having the Democratic Party's nominee for President demonstrate his support for working men and women, Mondale agreed to make a brief appearance. Second, and more important, Mondale was uncomfortable with the planned Merrill, Wisconsin speech but uncertain what to say in its place. The unfortunate reality was that as he launched his campaign as the Democratic Party's nominee for President, Mondale had still not found a clear and consistent theme for his candidacy. His staff had prepared a speech which, by addressing middle-class concerns about education, law and order, and economic growth, would continue the "new realism" theme established at the Convention. Mondale, according to one advisor, complained that the speech was "too directed toward a constituency he was not fully convinced was the way to go." Despite the favorable response to his convention speech and the obvious need to gain support from Independents and conservative Democrats, Mondale had only reluctantly accepted designating the "realism" theme the central message of his presidential campaign. Making tough choices that required sacrifice during a time of fiscal uncertainty had a definite cerebral appeal. But instinctively Mondale longed to capture his father's populism and his party's past by espousing "old Democratic values" of compassion for the poor, hostility toward big business, and faith in government.[22]

On September 1, aboard the plane flying from Minnesota to New York for the campaign kickoff, Mondale agonized over his predicament. The central question of his candidacy had still not been answered: How could he be faithful to the liberal tradition he represented while also appealing to the independent and moderate voters he needed for victory. Somewhere over the Midwest, Mondale turned to an unlikely source—a 106-page memo prepared by former Hart pollster Patrick Caddell. Mondale and Caddell had a stormy relationship dating back to their days in the Carter White House. Mondale believed Caddell a brilliant but troubled personality. Caddell believed Mondale to be an old-fashioned politician out of touch with new realities. By the beginning of 1982, though, mutual need had pushed both men to repair their damaged relationship. But their efforts at reconciliation came to a dramatic end in February 1982, when the Boston *Globe* published a story about Caddell which used an old Mondale quote describing him as "crazy." His ego bruised by the remark, Caddell not only broke off negotiations with Mondale, but also promised to do everything he could to destroy him. "Tell Mondale that he has awakened a sleeping giant and I am going to spend every minute of every day of every week trying to defeat him," an irate Caddell told a Mondale aide on the day the *Globe* article appeared. As the mastermind behind the Hart strategy, Caddell almost succeeded. Yet as much as he still distrusted him, Mondale recognized Caddell's genius and, over the fierce opposition of some of his staff, gradually turned to him for advice during the general campaign.

Caddell argued that moderate/conservative white males, offended by Reagan's deep cuts in social programs for the poor and angered by his obvious pandering to the rich, were susceptible to a traditional Democratic appeal as the party of compassion. Caddell suggested that, rather than making the central theme of his campaign "Who offers the best vision for the future," Mondale should ask voters,

"What kind of people are we?" Mondale perked up as he read Caddell's advice. However flawed it might have been, Mondale found in Caddell's analysis what he was looking for: a message that would allow him to be true to himself and politically effective.[23]

Before the plane landed in New York, Mondale had ordered his speechwriters to redraft the Merrill, Wisconsin speech to reflect Caddell's advice. His staff erupted. Over the Labor Day weekend, the candidate and his key advisors gathered at New York's Plaza Hotel for another series of intense debates about the campaign's message, its targeted audience, and its program for winning independent voters. "Every old wound was reopened," recalled one participant. Most of his staff, citing numerous private and public polls that contradicted Caddell's analysis, argued for keeping the "new realism" theme. Though Mondale entertained their suggestions, he had made up his mind that "old values" would be his theme. "That's really what these people want to hear," he said.[24]

The decisions to march in the Labor Day parade and to alter the Merrill speech blurred Mondale's Labor Day message. In order to arrive on schedule for the afternoon rally in Wisconsin, Mondale could attend only the first hour of the New York parade. Unfortunately, most bystanders did not show up until much later. Crowds one deep lined the silent New York streets. The Merrill speech, rather than establishing a clear theme for the campaign, combined elements of old Democratic values and "new realism." "The result," concluded Leone, "was a mixed message Labor Day week as we tried to appeal to . . . [independents and marginal Democrats] on old traditional grounds rather than appealing to them by saying the party had changed and learned." The day ended in Long Beach, California where, just as Mondale hit his stride, a man fainted in front of him. "We need a medic," Mondale said, "We need a medic right away." The medical appeal seemed appropriate for the campaign itself.[25]

While Mondale scrambled, Reagan took wings. Riding a wave of personal and organizational confidence, the President exhorted voters "to make America great again and let the eagle soar." Reagan dismissed the Democrats as "that pack of pessimists roaming the land." Reagan exuded self-assurance to mostly white crowds in sun-soaked California where he had begun his political career. At Republican rallies smothered with colorful balloons and patriotic music, the President repeated the evidence of a booming economy and a safer world. Crowds by the tens-of-thousands greeted the President. Joyous fans constantly interrupted with shouts of "Four more years!" The message on one sign captured the mood: "Reagan is USA." Not surprisingly, the three major networks highlighted Reagan's visual extravaganza and sun-washed patriotism built around simple, relentlessly repeated code words: "future," "opportunity," "hope." Correspondents covering the Mondale campaign spoke of the "puny" New York crowds, showed a microphone not working and commented on the lack of a unifying theme in his speeches.[26]

Over the next few weeks, as he tried to recover from the Labor Day debacle, Mondale hit the administration hard on the deficit issue. Using charts and statistics, he showed how he would raise $85 billion in taxes a year from corporations and families earning more than $25,000 a year, and outlined plans to reduce federal spending in fiscal 1989 by $105 billion below Reagan's budget. Even the partisan *Wall Street Journal* praised Mondale for his carefully reasoned policy proposals. "The Mondale campaign is a campaign of issues—clearly delineated, forcefully argued, sincerely presented," claimed the *Journal*. "Whether the topic is the government's huge budget deficits, taxes, Medicare, or civil rights, the candidate speaks forthrightly and in detail."[27]

Reagan's campaign of slick commercials, quick one-liners, and visually pleasing demonstrations of shared values seemed more in tune with the national mood. While Mondale lectured the nation on the inherent risks of budget deficits, the Reagan campaign unfolded what *Time* magazine called "the slickest, most ambitious political ad ever made." Studded with vignettes of American life—a smiling old couple, the sun rising over the horizon, a house under construction—the film featured highlights from Reagan's political career. Without mentioning issues or programs, the film announced: "America's back." Seeing little difference between commercial advertising and presidential campaigns, the President's handlers adopted methods previously reserved for selling cat food and soft drinks. "That is what we have done in the past with Pepsi, to elicit a sense of feeling," commented the film's creator. "It is a sense of optimism, a sense of patriotism." The press criticized Reagan for running a campaign without substance, but their attacks did little good. "Mr. Reagan is pointing the way toward the campaign techniques of the future," commented Howell Raines, "while Walter F. Mondale, the Democratic Party and the press appear to be re-enacting the rituals of elections past."[28]

Critics charged that Mondale's emphasis on substantive policy choices, combined with his natural reserve and phlegmatic manner, made him a perfect foil for Reagan's media politics. "One might think Mondale was running for Director of the Office of Management and Budget," quipped the journalist Robert Kuttner. Mondale's staff pleaded with him to give fewer substantive speeches and spend more time crafting cameo spots for the evening news. Mondale had always resisted that advice in the past, referring to these events as "picket fences and puppy dogs." "He knew politics as retail, not wholesale," recalled Reilly. But unable to make a dent in Reagan's commanding lead, he reluctantly agreed to try a few media events.[29]

To dramatize his concern for struggling unemployed workers, he met with a young couple in Philadelphia who had lost their jobs. His staff provided him with clear instructions: no new policy proposals, no speeches, just look concerned and let the camera roll. It seemed easy enough. "So I understand you lost your job," Mondale said sitting in the comfortable suburban living room. "Yea," the woman responded, "but I got a new one that's even better!" Mondale's heart sank. This was not, he mumbled afterward, the best way to undermine Reagan's credibility. Willing to give the new approach a decent trial, Mondale then traveled to a paper factory to be pictured talking with average workers about their problems. Because of poor planning, he missed the shift change. Instead of seeing a concerned Mondale in touch with the problems of average Americans, viewers saw the plant manager present Mondale with a roll of toilet paper.[30]

The most memorable moment came in Green Bay, Wisconsin where Mondale traveled one afternoon to talk with twenty high school football players about his concerns for young people and his sensitivity to "new" issues. By now Mondale was growing tired of these appearances and longed to arouse a partisan crowd. After just a few minutes of standing before the apathetic group talking about his vision of a "greater America," Mondale realized the kids did not know who he was or what he was talking about.[31]

After the football meeting, Reilly grabbed Mondale and pulled him into an assistant principal's office at the school. He kicked out all the other staff and locked the doors. Reilly was angry with Mondale for trying to mimic the manner of modern media campaigns. "You're ruining yourself," Reilly told Mondale. "You're trying to be something that you are not." Mondale did not need much convincing. The past few weeks had left him deeply shaken. "I've never seen a guy who was so down," Reilly recalled. As tears welled in his eyes, Mondale spoke of his fears and disappointments. He worried that if he performed poorly his name would be a burden for his children. "His fear was that he would go down in history as an inept mistake,"

Reilly recalled. "His children would have to live with that legacy. He would be a burden. He would let down the party, Hubert, and his family." Perhaps, Mondale admitted, the critics were right: maybe he was outdated. He had spent his entire life in politics but he could not master these media events or understand Reagan's enormous popularity.[32]

Most of all, he could not understand his inability to reach middle-class voters. He was well-rooted in Democratic soil. As a teenager too young to vote he had helped organize his home district for Harry Truman and Hubert Humphrey. As he traveled across the country he recalled those early days with a quiet nostalgia. For all of the changes he had experienced, his values had remained the same. "I had a deep sense that I was in the tradition of Roosevelt, Truman, and Kennedy. I remember the days when we had the country and trust and faith and we did a lot of good things for America. I wanted to do it again. I had been in it so deeply. I had been on the Truman train. I'd been with Kennedy. I had these things in me when I campaigned."[33]

Mondale felt trapped between two worlds. "He could not be Humphrey with a full heart but he could not be Gary Hart with a full heart either," Galston reflected. He was aware of that tension every day of the campaign but he never found a way to reconcile it. He believed the presidential campaign should demonstrate the wisdom and insight gathered from years of public service. In his case, however, his history was a burden. By 1984, television, not organization, provided the means of communication, and a whole new generation of political technocrats filled the void left by party bosses. Media markets replaced union halls and thirty-second "visuals" on the evening news substituted for substantive discussions in the evening paper. In addition, the agenda had changed forcing Mondale to address new social issues like abortion, gun control, and school prayer which an earlier generation of Democrats had never considered. Heightened racial divisions had divided the coalition. Many white southerners and urban ethnics, angry because of the Party's close identification with the civil rights movement, had fled the party. At the same time, blacks frustrated by limited progress and persistent injustice used their added weight within the party to demand greater fidelity to their agenda. Class appeals to struggling laborers and farmers lacked persuasiveness in a workforce that was increasingly service-oriented and nonunion.

Mondale tried to develop a substantive agenda appropriate to the changed environment. Circumstances required him to preach a more restrained, fiscally conservative message. But however appropriate Mondale's warnings about the deficit and pleas for a tax increase may have been, they placed him in a politically untenable position. For one thing, Mondale was simply not credible as a fiscal conservative. "Mondale conveyed government, as surely as if he carried the ghost of [FDR's advisor] Harry Hopkins on his shoulder," wrote the journalist Ronald Brownstein. "Fritz Mondale embracing a balanced budget," quipped Washington insiders, "is like Orson Welles embracing designer jeans." Also, by focusing on lowering the deficit Mondale was unable to present a more positive image of the role government should play. As Kaplan and Galston had argued the previous fall, a sweeping populist message might have touched a sensitive public nerve and aroused more support for Mondale's candidacy. But years of working as part of the establishment had soured Mondale on sweeping indictments of "the system." Despite his populist roots, it seems unlikely that Mondale would have been any more credible as a populist than he was as a fiscal conservative. "Mondale appeared as the candidate not of the broad populist coalition that benefits from activist government, but of the party insiders," observed Kuttner. "Though Mondale himself was a man of decency and moderately progressive instincts, his candidacy reeked of smoked-filled rooms." Mondale "was the embodiment of the establishment," commented Texas agriculture commissioner Jim Hightower. "There was no sense that this man was going to change the balance of power."[34]

For now, Reilly ignored these more serious problems and reassured Mondale that despite all the changes that had occurred over the past decade politics was still a contest of clashing values. "Your values are good and deserve to be heard," he declared. A pensive Mondale sat in silence for a few moments, then responded: "Yeah, I may lose this election, but at least I will say something in defeat."[35]

On September 14, he summoned his senior campaign aides to Tupelo, Mississippi where he informed them about the new strategy. "I'm not doing any more of this teacher stuff," he said. "I want to be put in situations where I can make my substantive case and where I can make it passionately—where I'm with supporters, not people I've got to convince to be for me. I want to run a campaign now." He insisted on dropping visual events, such as shaking hands outside factory gates and speaking with high school students. "The only thing I know to do is to go out and be myself and say what I think," he recalled saying. "To speak to Democrats and anybody else who will listen and hope that decency and whatever else I am comes across. It's too late for me to do this marketing stuff. I cannot do it."[36]

While Mondale spoke of the dire consequences of unrestrained deficits, Reagan evoked images that touched a deep chord of patriotism. The President stirred up animosity at the Soviets marching into Afghanistan and the Iranians holding fifty-two American hostages. He had a photo session with the Olympic team, held an anniversary celebration of the invasion of Grenada, and posed in front of a B-1 bomber. "The essence of the Ronald Reagan campaign," ABC reporter Sam Donaldson asserted, "is a never-ending string of spectacular picture stories created for television and designed to place the president in the midst of wildly cheering, patriotic Americans. . . . God, patriotism, and Ronald Reagan, that's the essence this campaign is trying to project." When pageantry did not work, Reagan resorted to ridicule. If Mondale's "program were a Broadway show," Reagan declared, "it would be 'Promises, Promises.' And if it were a book, you'd have to read it from the back to the front to get a happy ending." "They never have understood the economy," the President said of the Democrats. "They still think G.N.P. stands for Gross National Promises." Ridiculing Mondale's "new realism," Reagan said the leaders of the Democratic Party had gone "so far left, they've left America." He parodied Mondale's economic plank: "He's got an economic plan and it has two parts—one, raise taxes; two, raise them again." By late September, Mondale languished fifteen points behind in most polls.[37]

As he moved closer to defeat, Mondale reached deep within himself to justify his candidacy. His new emphasis came in sharp focus in a talk to students at George Washington University on September 25—possibly his best speech of the campaign. Earlier in the year, after Hart's victory in the New Hampshire primary, desperation had forced Mondale to define his candidacy. Now it was Reagan's commanding lead in the polls that again compelled Mondale to stop listing the issues that separated him from his opponent and again speak of the underlying values that guided his candidacy. Using a teleprompter for the first time in the campaign, Mondale contrasted the old Reagan with the new and compared his values of compassion and community with Reagan's concern for selfishness and greed. "This election is about our values," he said. "Today, millions of children live in poverty. . . . Today, there are Americans roaming the streets and sleeping on grates, bag women and broken men. . . . Today, our country is peddling guns around the world. . . . The Republicans say they're for family values. But families that are worth the word don't disown their weaker children."

> This election is not about jelly-beans and pen-pals. It is about toxic dumps that give cancer to our children. This election is not about country music and birthday cakes. It is about old people who can't pay for medicine. This election is not about the Olympic torch. It is about civil-rights laws that opened athletics to women and minorities who won those gold medals. This election is not about sending a teacher into space. It is about improving teaching and learning here on earth. This election is not about the size of my opponent's crowds. It is about the size of his deficit. . . . I won't permit this crowd to steal the future from our children without a fight. I won't let them put ice in our soul without a struggle. They have a right to ask for your vote. But I'll be damned if I'll let them take away our conscience.[38]

Mondale's only hope of closing the chasm separating himself from the President was to score in the debates scheduled for October 7 and 21. During his practice sessions Mondale seemed to discover for the first time that he could improve his performance. Rehearsing his answers in front of a video camera, he paused to watch and analyze his responses. "Should I look at the camera or should I look at the questioner?" he asked. After trying it both ways, he appreciated the importance of keeping his eyes focused on the camera. "That's so much better," he said. "I understand now." Relaxed, puffing occasionally on a large cigar, Mondale recognized that he needed to appear more animated, use effective hand gestures, modulate his voice, show emotion, and personalize his message. "That thing about trying to find personal answers is everything, I'm convinced," he said in an unguarded moment.[39]

While working on the basics, his debate preparation team planned a dramatic gesture that would highlight Mondale's "toughness" and put the President on the defensive. After carefully studying the camera positions, Caddell had found that if Mondale stepped out from behind the podium, turned toward the President, and confronted him directly, the cross-angles would provide a dramatic image of confrontation. Although at first reluctant to engage in such theater, Mondale acquiesced, practicing the crucial pivot-and-turn almost a dozen times.[40]

As they walked on to the stage for the first debate, held in the Kentucky Center for the Arts, Mondale was shocked by Reagan's appearance. As the two men stood toe-to-toe at center stage for the traditional opening handshake, Reagan seemed confused and unable to focus. "When I said hello to him I knew he wasn't going to make it," Mondale recalled. After opening the debate by praising the President for restoring the nation's confidence, Mondale said Reagan reminded him of what Will Rogers once said about Herbert Hoover: "It's not what he doesn't know that bothers me, its what he knows for sure that just ain't so." Appearing sharp and confident, Mondale attacked a plank in the Republican platform that called for the appointment of judges who opposed abortion. He said Jerry Falwell had laid claim to "two justices" on the Supreme Court. When the President noted he had once been a Democrat but had left when he saw the party moving in the wrong direction, Mondale countered that Reagan left the party in 1960 when Kennedy was running for president. In the most tense exchange of the night, Reagan, responding to a Mondale charge that he would raise taxes if reelected, repeated his famous 1980 line: "There you go again." Mondale, anticipating the line, shot back. "Remember the last time you said that?" as he executed his well-practiced pivot-and-turn. It was, he charged, when Carter accused him of trying to cut Medicare. Once in office he had proposed a $20 billion cut in the program. "When you say 'There you go again,' people remember this," Mondale said.[41]

During the exchange Mondale watched the President grow progressively weaker as the debate ran well beyond its 90-minute scheduled length. After over an hour in the hot lights, Reagan began sweating profusely, his hands gripping the podium to support his weight. As they prepared to give their closing statements, Mondale thought the President might faint. "It looked to me like he might not make it through the debate," he recalled. Reagan did not collapse, but his rambling unfocused summary revealed his exhaustion.[42]

At the end of the debate Mondale strolled into a small holding room off-stage where jubilant aides stood ready to congratulate him on his victory. When he walked into the room, he seemed to show little of the joy appropriate for the moment. "He had this look of concern and shock on his face," recalled Tom Donilon. "His first thoughts were about the President and the presidency rather than his own political triumph." Mondale seemed genuinely saddened by what he had witnessed. "The President's not all there. His eyes were wandering, he seemed shaky. The President is out to lunch," Mondale said.[43]

Reagan's poor performance provided Mondale with a rare glimmer of hope during an otherwise disheartening campaign. "I thought I had a shot on the one issue that cut through everything else—his capacity to govern," he said. For the next week the President's age became a central issue of the campaign. The President's personal physician admitted that Reagan had tired during the ninety-minute debate. The *Wall Street Journal* featured the headline: "New Question in Race: Is Oldest U.S. President Now Showing His Age?" The evening news replayed the 73-year-old President's most embarrassing moments—dozing off during an audience with the Pope, being coached by his wife in response to a simple questions about arms control. James Reston wondered whether Reagan could survive four more years in office. At his age, he wrote, "neither he nor anybody else can be sure about the next four years."[44]

In public, Mondale appeared upbeat, telling reporters that the enthusiasm of the crowds would soon be reflected in the polls. "It's like a huge switch was thrown," he told *Time*. "Enormous crowds, but not just that; the nature of the crowds too: Every time you shake hands, its like a pile-up on the goal line. Several hundred people trying to get at you. I've never experienced anything like that."

In private, however, it was a different story. His staff found him irritable, he complained for the first time about not sleeping well. His verbal assaults on staff members equaled those of his early Senate days. "I don't know what happened between the first and second debate," Beckel recalled, "but it was clear to me there had been significant deterioration in temperament and body."[45]

Part of the problem was physical. While the nation focused its attention on the President's well-being, it was Mondale who was experiencing health problems. Like millions of other Americans, he took daily medication for chronic high blood pressure. The rigors of campaigning, with its long days, poor diet, and lack of sleep, forced his physician to increase his daily dosage. For a brief period, the more potent medicine made him irritable and sluggish with a brief attention span and short temper.

Even more damaging than the physical problems was a self-imposed psychological burden. Mondale spent most of the fall fearing that if he lost by the landslide proportions many people predicted, history would view him as an inept candidate, unfit to lead his party and unqualified for the presidency. His impressive debate performance, he believed, had finally vindicated him. He might still lose the election, but the public would now view him as a qualified candidate who simply ran against an invincible opponent. By regaining his dignity as a public figure, he would not be, as he so often feared, a burden to his children. Now, as he prepared for the second debate, Mondale wanted to do nothing that would jeopardize his stature. He told friends that he felt as if he "just got out of jail" and had no intention of going back. With their candidate still trailing by twelve points in the polls, his staff advised him to take risks in the second debate. But Mondale, afraid of losing the stature he had gained in Louisville, opted for a more cautious approach.

Finally, he simply lacked a clear strategy to win. Despite his performance in the first debate, he lost ground in the polls. "We had run out of theoretical gas," Johnson recalled. Over the previous six weeks, Mondale had fired every weapon in his arsenal at the President but seemed incapable of penetrating his thick armor. Even after his faltering performance, the public still perceived Reagan as a more forceful and decisive leader than Mondale. As they discussed strategy for the debate, campaign advisors admitted they had little chance of winning. The election had turned into a referendum on Reagan. As long as the President seemed physically fit and managed to string together a few coherent sentences over the course of the evening, he would be declared the winner no matter what Mondale said. "In a kind of ironic way," Leone wrote in his notes, "the extent of his [Reagan's] failure in the first debate made the second debate an easier test than it might otherwise have been and we're suffering the consequences."[46]

The combined physical and psychological burden revealed itself as Mondale walked on stage for the foreign policy debate. Days of sleeplessness had created large brown bags under his eyes making him look old and tired. Reagan, by contrast, looked fit and excited. This time the President's handlers made sure their candidate appeared more relaxed and less burdened with facts. He noted a Mondale commercial showing him on the deck of the *Nimitz* watching F-14s take off. "If he had had his way when the *Nimitz* was being planned, he would have been deep in the water out there, because there wouldn't have been any *Nimitz* to stand on," he said. He also effectively deflected the age issue. When asked whether he was youthful enough to stand the strains of office, Reagan responded: "I will not make age an issue of this campaign. I am not going to exploit, for political purposes, my opponent's youth and inexperience."[47]

Mondale charged that Reagan had failed the test of presidential leadership by not limiting the CIA's activities in Central America, not protecting American Marines in Lebanon, and not mastering the questions of nuclear arms control. He said the nation had been "humiliated" by Reagan's policies in Lebanon and "embarrassed" by publication of a CIA pamphlet "giving instructions for hired assassins." "A President must not only assure that we're tough," Mondale declared. "[He] must also be wise and smart in the exercise of that power." In response to Reagan's attempts to paint him as soft on national defense Mondale countered: "Your definition of national strength is to throw money at the Defense Department. My definition . . . is to make certain that a dollar spent buys a dollar's worth of defense." Cuts in the MX missile and B-1 bomber, Mondale suggested, could be used to strengthen conventional forces in Europe. "I accept your commitment to peace, but I want you to accept my commitment to a strong national defense." Even Reagan's rambling closing statement about driving down the California coast did not hurt public impressions of his performance. Republican surveys showed Reagan opening up a lead of twenty points by the next night. "I knew when I walked off that platform after the second debate that the election was over," Mondale reflected.[48]

Resigned to the inevitability of defeat, Mondale hoped to write his own political epitaph in the last few weeks of the campaign. Abandoning his decade-long desire to establish a more tempered liberalism, he spoke instead of the moral causes which had attracted him to politics and had always aroused his passion. No longer feeling the need to forge consensus, Mondale chose to inspire the faithful. He felt a sense of exhilaration and liberation he had not felt in years. At last he was the "open field runner" who freely expressed his moral sense of right and wrong without carefully calculated appeals to political self-interest. In desperation he had refound his faith. He would end his public career the same way he had started it more than two decades earlier: as an unrepentant liberal.

As he campaigned across the country in the final days he spoke about values that transcended interest group needs. Rising at 5 A.M., traveling to three or four states a day, drawing large and enthusiastic crowds, Mondale returned to the basic liberal values with which he had begun his career. Before a small black church in Memphis he spoke of the world portrayed in Reagan's commercials. "Its all picket fences and puppy dogs," he said. "When was the last time you heard the word decency, the word justice, compassion at the White House? . . . No one's hurting. No one's alone. No one's hungry. No one's unemployed. No one gets old. Everybody's happy." Complaining about the four million children removed from the school lunch program, he called the Reagan Administration "an insult to American decency." They "can hear the faintest drum—but they can't hear the cry of a hungry child," he declared. He spoke of the disabled and the unemployed, "the mentally ill, the handicapped, the broken, the aimless, the dispirited, those sad women who walk the streets, those people who sleep over the grates." For them the administration showed no concern, no interest. "Just turned them out on the streets," he claimed. "Some of them died. Some of them committed suicide, all of them are in desperate shape."[49]

In order to contrast his vision of community responsibility with Reagan's celebration of rugged individualism, Mondale recited one of Reagan's favorite speeches—the "City Upon a Hill" sermon that John Winthrop delivered to his fellow Puritans aboard the *Arbella* in 1630—and turned it against him. "Winthrop said something else that Mr. Reagan has forgotten and that runs across his whole government, and it's the most fundamental issue at stake in this election," Mondale told audiences. "Reverend Winthrop said to be a city upon a hill, we must strengthen, defend, preserve and comfort one another. We must bear one another's burdens. We must look not on our own things, but also on the things of others. We must rejoice together, mourn together, labor and suffer together. We must be knit together by a bond of love. And so may it always be in America. Let's be a community, a family where we care for one another. Let us end this selfishness, this greed, this new championship of caring only for yourself. Let's pull America back together. Let's have new leadership. It's time for America to move on."[50]

A crowd waited for hours at Flint Northern High School in Michigan. They streamed down Philadelphia streets to hear him at a noon rally. They flocked to Ohio's Mahoning Valley and lined the streets of small midwestern farm towns for his 117-mile bus route. In Chicago, 75,000 attended a candlelight parade in the chilly night air. "I've been all over this country and there's something stirring," he said. "The people are listening, they see the issues, they're concerned, they're ready to vote and we're going to win this election." On the Boston Common, 60,000 listened to Mondale, Kennedy, and O'Neill relive liberal glories. "I come to you today as a people's Democrat, as a full-employment Democrat in the tradition of Roosevelt and Truman and Kennedy and Humphrey," he told the crowd. He attacked the administration as indifferent to the underprivileged. "If you're unemployed, it's too bad. If you're old, its tough luck. If you're sick, its bad luck. If you're black or Hispanic, you're out of luck. And if you're handicapped, you shouldn't be." More than 100,000 turned out in New York's garment district undeterred by grey skies and the threat of rain. Balloons and confetti fluttered from the windows, where thousands of workers waved and cheered. A union leader said it was the largest crowd in the garment district since John Kennedy had campaigned in 1960. The crowds were so large and enthusiastic that Tom Wicker asked: "Is there something wrong with all those polls so unanimously predicting disastrous defeat for Mr. Mondale on November 6?"[51]

Women listened to him with tears in their eyes. Men shouted "Give 'em hell, Fritz." People pressed through barricades to touch him. Others held their children high over their heads to get a glimpse. "I brought my daughter out to see Walter Mondale," a poor Hispanic man in rural Texas told the Washington *Post*. "He is the last of a dying breed. The breed that cares for people."[52]

With a week left in the campaign, Mondale was leading only in Minnesota and the District of Columbia, and within striking distance in ten other states—New York, Pennsylvania, Massachusetts, Wisconsin, West Virginia, Maryland, California, Ohio, Illinois, and Rhode Island. No matter how he added up the electoral votes, he fell far short of victory. "I can't believe it," he exclaimed, "I see those faces out there and they tell me one thing. And I come back here and find out everyone's been kicking the shit out of me."[53]

The end of his long campaign came about eight hours before he cast his ballot. His family stood behind him in an old hangar at the Minneapolis International Airport where thousands crowded to see him. Mondale, his face drawn and his voice hoarse, reflected on the campaign and his life in politics. "Tonight, I end what may be the longest campaign in American history," he said. "For thousands and thousands of miles, through long days and long weeks and long months—now long years—through all the debates, through all the campaigns and speeches, through all of the joys and heartaches, I could hear you, and I could also hear Hubert pushing me on." He had traveled the length and breadth of the nation, Mondale told the crowd, but "I never really left Minnesota because I've been talking to America about Minnesota values . . . All that I am and all that I believe flows from what I have learned from you. . . . You have trusted me all these years." Hiding the pain of knowing that his long career of public service was about to end, Mondale placed his experience in its proper perspective. "[Y]ou have given me, a small-town boy from Elmore, a chance to shape our country and to shape our times," he said, his voice raspy with exhaustion and emotion. "And you have given me a life that is very, very rare and marvelous."[54]

Mondale accepted his forthcoming defeat with grace and dignity. He would have it no other way. Mondale watched the early morning election results from his suite at the St. Paul Radisson Hotel. There was never much reason for optimism. Just before noon, Johnson informed him that only a few states, including Minnesota, would be close. "We are going to lose," he said, "and lose big." A few minutes later, Mondale gathered his family in the bedroom of his hotel suite. Sitting on the edge of his bed surrounded by Joan and his children, he thanked them for devoting two years of their life to his candidacy. Though sharing her husband's intense disappointment, Joan listened stolidly knowing the children would also be looking to her for comfort. Eleanor cried, but William and Ted were too numb with fatigue to show any emotion. "We didn't compromise what we believed in," he said in a soft voice. "We are going to lose and lose badly but we have no reason to feel badly. Let's go out there and be champions tonight. We have nothing to be ashamed of."[55]

Mondale sat stoically through the afternoon as the dimensions of his defeat took shape. The results were staggering. Reagan carried forty-nine states—all but Mondale's home state of Minnesota, which he lost by fewer than four thousand votes, and the District of Columbia. He won 98 percent of the electoral votes (525 to 13), and 59 percent of the popular vote. Reagan won more than 70 percent of the votes in four states, more than 60 percent in twenty-eight, and more than 53 percent in eleven. A closer analysis exposed a serious erosion of support among many traditionally Democratic groups. Mondale drew consistently strong support from only two areas: frostbelt cities and black majority counties of the South. Race played a critical role in shaping party affiliation. Nationally, more than a quarter of the votes for the Democratic ticket came from blacks, while in the South blacks constituted almost half of Democratic voters. In many northern cities, the coalition was splintered between minorities who voted for the Democratic ticket and white ethnics who voted Republican. Polls also indicated that Mondale's effort to exploit the gender gap had fallen short. Women preferred Reagan over Mondale by a margin of 8 percentage points, while men favored Reagan by a formidable 24 percentage points.

After the polls closed, Mondale traveled the short distance to the cavernous St. Paul Civic Center to address a small dispirited crowd of three thousand campaign workers. Composed and reserved, he accepted defeat, saying he was "at peace with the knowledge that I gave it everything I've got." To campaign workers who yelled "no" every time he acknowledged Reagan's victory, he said: "I know how you feel because I've been there myself. Do not despair. This fight didn't end tonight. It begins tonight." For just a moment, as he glanced at his close aides and friends gathered around the podium, the disappointment pierced Mondale's normally unflappable public demeanor. His face grew red and tears welled in his eyes. But he quickly regained his composure, and, with Joan at his side, walked briskly off the stage.[56]

17

Liberal Legacies

"In another age and time," the historian William Chafe has written, "Walter Mondale might have been a sure bet to win the presidency." His public career had moved steadily upward, leading almost inexorably to the nation's highest office. As Minnesota's attorney general at the tender age of thirty-two, he had converted a ceremonial office into a center for activist government. His twelve years in the United States Senate had produced three significant pieces of legislation: the Fair Warning Standards Act, the Fair Housing Act of 1968, and the filibuster reform act of 1975. He also had helped shape national policy in a number of other areas, including child care, education, welfare, civil rights, and intelligence reform. Perhaps he left his most lasting contribution on the vice presidency. Defying two hundred years of history, Mondale and Carter redefined the nature of the office and in the process set the standard by which all future vice presidents will be judged.[1]

By 1984, Mondale was ready to assume the presidency. He had shown a capacity for growth during his twenty years in national politics. Discarding some of his early optimism about the possibilities of change, Mondale had developed a sophisticated understanding of the complexities of public policy issues and the ambiguities of presidential leadership. Refusing to raise false hopes and committed to proposing honest solutions to difficult questions, he had developed a tempered liberalism appropriate for an age of fiscal restraint. Ignoring the obvious political risks, Mondale had proposed substantive solutions to America's most pressing problem—the ballooning budget deficit. The intellectual growth was matched by increased personal maturity. Over time, he emerged as a seasoned politician who had earned the trust and respect of those who knew him. Unspoiled by fame, he remained an unpretentious man who never lost sight of his roots.

Yet Mondale's hopes of winning the presidency remained unfulfilled. In some ways, the campaign exposed his limitations as a candidate. A commitment to an older style of constituency politics and a refusal to adjust to the demands of a modern media age muddled Mondale's new liberalism message and contributed to his defeat. "Mr. Mondale is one of the few major figures on the American scene," commented David Shribman, "whose political style and vocabulary fit comfortably in a world of Al Smith, Franklin Roosevelt and Harry Truman." Mondale failed to communicate a single compelling message that captured his vision of America. "What cost Mondale," commented William Raspberry, "was the perception that Reagan, while perhaps on the wrong side of a number of specific issues, generally stood for what most Americans stood for, while Mondale, though often on the right side of the specifics, didn't really stand for anything at all." Perhaps more important, while Mondale rethought many of his liberal ideas, he never developed a political strategy for reaching independent or middle-class voters. He ignored evidence that many people perceived him as a captive of the Washington establishment, unable to distinguish between the needs of his constituency groups and the concerns of most voters. "He moved his home to the St. Paul suburbs, but his heart stayed on the Potomac," wrote David Broder.[2]

Mondale also never developed an effective television style that was essential for success in the modern media age. In 1984, the major networks limited their coverage of important addresses to fifteen-second bites on the evening news. Though the compressed coverage proved ideal for Reagan's conversational style which substituted slogans for speeches and pictures for words, it baffled Mondale. "Modern politics today requires a mastery of television," Mondale confessed in a press conference following his defeat. "I've never really warmed up to television, and, in fairness to television, its never warmed up to me."[3]

It would be short-sighted, however, to blame Mondale for the dimensions of the Democratic defeat in 1984. Regardless of the outcome, Mondale ran a competent campaign based on fundamental Democratic principles of justice, fairness, and community. He had the imagination to select the nation's first woman vice presidential candidate of a major party, and he possessed the courage to offer painful solutions to difficult problems. Calling Mondale a "good and decent and strong-minded man," the Washington *Post* editorialized that he "made the best fight he could for his party," and left the campaign "with [his] honor and with his reputation enlarged."[4]

Mondale had the misfortune of running for president against an unbeatable opponent. A substantial majority of Americans liked the President personally and gave him high marks for leadership. Polls showed that most Americans had decided early to vote for Reagan regardless of who the Democrats nominated or what they said. Voters interviewed by the Los Angeles *Times* said 47 percent had decided who they would vote for before the first primaries in February, while another 21 percent had decided before September. The New York *Times,* noting that the President's final vote margin was almost exactly what his margin had been ten months earlier, suggested that "it's possible . . . that everything that happened in-between was just a digression."[5]

In 1984, voters found Reagan's celebrated gospel of individualism more appealing than the philosophy of shared responsibilities that guided the modern Democratic Party and inspired Mondale's campaign for president. Like his liberal ancestors Woodrow Wilson and Franklin Roosevelt, Mondale envisioned America as a national community bound by common standards and devoted to similar goals. "I had an old-fashioned idea that one of the key roles of the nomination was to pull together a community of Democrats, progressive and conservative, and create a family," he reflected. "A good deal of my life was spent trying to knit together this community." But, by 1984, the public had grown tired of Democratic pleas for national community. In late September, the Washington *Post*/ ABC News Poll showed even people who believed Reagan's policies unfair and would lead to nuclear war, voted for the President because they believed they would personally gain more under his administration. "People voted their own self-interest," wrote Richard Reeves, "and mass movement was the product of those millions of self-interests—a politics of individualism."[6]

The public rejected Mondale's chastened view of the future in favor of Reagan's vision of an idealized America. Mondale lectured the public about the painful choices imposed by an age of limited resources. Reagan reassured a public that stubbornly refused to recognize the new realities. Unprecedented deficits, a growing gap between rich and poor, uncertain energy sources, and increased international competition provided ample evidence of the nation's tenuous economic status. But, lulled into complacency by Reagan's beguiling prosperity, most Americans refused to accept Mondale's warnings of future costs or his calls for national sacrifice. "Reagan was promising them 'morning in America,' " Mondale told friends after the campaign, "and I was promising a root canal."

Mondale also had to contend with the declining fortunes of a demoralized and divided party. At no time in this century has a major party suffered the electoral landslides experienced by Democrats in the years after 1968. In 1984, Reagan carried as many states, forty-nine, as the Democratic nominee for president won in the five elections since 1968. In losing four of the five presidential contests, Democrats won only 43 percent of the popular vote and 113 electoral votes. During the Roosevelt years, Democrats had retained the allegiance of the South and West while pulling heavily from ethnics in the Northeast and Midwest. But in 1984, Mondale won only 28 percent of the white southern vote, and his 44 percent showing among Catholics was the lowest of any Democratic presidential candidate since 1924. With its strong base of support in the South and West, the Republicans developed a major advantage in the electoral college. As Patrick Caddell argued, since 1968, twenty-three states with a total of 202 electoral votes supported the Republican presidential nominee in every election. Add to that the number of states that voted Republican four of the past five elections, and the Grand Old Party could count on 354 electoral votes—far more than the 270 needed for election. Only the District of Columbia voted Democratic in each of the elections.[7]

By brilliantly exploiting working-class concerns about social issues, Republicans tapped into popular perceptions of the Democratic party as the home of arrogant minorities, overbearing feminists, haughty intellectuals, and various disdainful interest groups. These charges, which Alabama Governor George Wallace introduced during his 1968 campaign for president and Richard Nixon flaunted in his appeals to the "silent majority," unraveled the class coalition that Roosevelt had assembled in 1936. As one scholar noted, Reagan, like Wallace and Nixon, "persuaded millions of voters in the great middle—

including many well below the income median—to look not to the top but to the bottom for their class enemy." According to exit polls, Mondale carried only those voters who earned less than $10,000; Reagan won every other economic group, his margin of victory widening as income levels increased.[8]

Racial tensions have played an important role in this transformation. Many white voters interpreted Democratic appeals for fairness as a thinly disguised plea for black favoritism. In a massive voter survey following the 1984 campaign, the Democratic National Committee found that middle-class voters viewed "fairness" as "a code word for giveaway." In fact, the results of the forty-three focus-group sessions were so damning that Chairman Paul Kirk ordered all copies of the $200,000 survey destroyed. But a similar study of a working-class suburb of Detroit produced the same disturbing conclusion. "Appeals to fairness," the author of the poll observed, "are now defined in racial terms and have been stripped of any progressive content."[9]

Despite Mondale's attempt to find common ground between the party's competing factions, there simply was no single message or theme that could appeal to all of the party's major constituencies. It was easy to argue that the old coalition had outlived its usefulness; it was harder to identify what new political configuration should take its place. Any Democrat who hoped to patch together the older New Deal constituency with more independent middle-class voters, had to navigate an ideological obstacle course. The new message had to show compassion for the poor and outcast without appearing to be preoccupied with welfare. It required an emphasis on excellence and competitiveness without sounding heartless or mechanical. On foreign-policy issues, where the wounds of Vietnam had left deep scars in the party, a candidate needed to appear strong and anticommunist but appeal to the large neo-isolationist wing in the party. Most challenging of all, the message needed to convince blacks of the party's strong commitment to racial equality without antagonizing white ethnics and southerners agitated by Democratic support of busing and affirmative action.

An earlier generation of Democrats had created the modern welfare state by wielding the populist club against the barons of wealth and privilege, but over time, many of the programs and policies that owed their existence to populist sentiment had developed their own entrenched interest groups and indifferent bureaucracy. Just as important, years of service in the Washington establishment, and a strong sense of loyalty to the programs and institutions they had created, had made many Democrats uncomfortable with the populist message. Severed from their ideological roots, recent Democrats have campaigned not as reformers promising to change the system, but as technocrats determined to make it function more efficiently. Liberals had always used government to challenge the status quo and assault the special interests. In recent years, Republicans have identified government with the status quo, and defined their antigovernment cause as an attack on special privilege. In response, Democrats failed to present a larger conception of government that defended prerogatives in universal language that served all groups.

After his 1984 defeat, many people had suggested that Mondale follow in Humphrey's footsteps by returning to Minnesota to lay the groundwork for a Senate campaign in 1986. But Mondale had been so exhausted by the campaign and so dispirited by its outcome that he could not seriously consider running again for public office. For months he languished in depression, replaying crucial decisions, questioning every aspect of his candidacy and his character. He wondered how history would treat him. He feared that no one would recall his days as a dynamic Attorney General, successful Senator or pioneering vice president. He would always be remembered by his last campaign. History, he feared, would deem him a loser.

The sudden transition to private pursuits was not easy for a man who had spent most of his adult life in the public eye. "For thirty years politics had been my life. It was the source of all my emotions. Then suddenly it was gone," he reflected. "One day you walk out of the door and you've got 40 cameras and every network and 20 foreign reporters out there, and the next morning you walk out and not even the dog looks at you." [10]

Like his father who had once surmounted a much different form of adversity, Mondale bounced back from his defeat and began thinking again about politics. In September 1987, nearly three years after the election, he returned to Minneapolis. His move fueled rumors that he would seek his old Senate seat in 1990. Mondale remained coy about his intentions, telling reporters his first priority was to develop business for his new law firm of Dorsey and Whitney. His only direct involvement in politics would be to help the son of his old mentor, Attorney General Hubert Humphrey III, raise money for his 1988 challenge to Republican Senator David Durenberger. All along, he struggled with his own indecision about running. He did not find private law practice fulfilling, but he feared losing another campaign. Although he led in all opinion polls, and had the strong support of the state DFL, Mondale would have to face a formidable foe in the popular and well-financed Republican, Rudy Boschwitz. There were other doubts as well. He believed the Senate could be an unforgiving place for former members who failed in their quest for the presidency. "It's never the same when they come back," he told Finlay Lewis. Senate barons had treated Humphrey, Muskie, and Mc-Govern—all failed presidential hopefuls—with a calculated coolness reserved for those who had betrayed the club.[11]

The 1988 presidential campaign did little to encourage a return to public life. Democrats hoped that Massachusetts Governor Michael Dukakis could successfully execute the strategy that had failed in 1984: appealing to independent voters while retaining the allegiance of more traditional Democrats. His state's economic record gave Dukakis more credibility than Mondale to talk about promoting economic growth, his reputation for fiscal prudence made him less vulnerable to "big spender" charges, and his lack of experience in Washington allowed him to run as an outsider untainted by the Carter administration. But Dukakis, convinced Mondale's promise to raise taxes led directly to his defeat, refused to offer substantive solutions to the budget deficit. Throughout the campaign, he clung to the specious argument that vigorous enforcement of the existing tax laws could recover $100 billion, pay for new programs, and balance the budget. While Mondale had called for fiscal restraint and lower expectations, Dukakis promised "good jobs at good wages," clean air, child care, and increased federal support for education, but never suggested how the additional spending would affect the deficit. Dukakis lacked both a clear ideology and a substantive agenda. He exposed the fundamental flaw of his candidacy in his acceptance speech at the Democratic convention in Atlanta when he identified "competence, not ideology" as the campaign's central issue. Dukakis' attempt to celebrate his lack of ideological definition only highlighted the seriousness of the party's beleaguered state.[12]

While Dukakis searched for a theme to justify his candidacy, Republican nominee George Bush focused his attacks on divisive "wedge" issues. Planning his campaign around quick one-liners aimed at the daily sound-bite on the evening news, Bush hammered away at Dukakis for opposing organized prayer and compulsory recitation of the Pledge of Allegiance in the public schools. "The Pledge and the flag are little hammer taps directed just below the knee of the electorate," wrote Richard Cohen. "They are designed to elicit a reflexive reaction, to obscure rather than explain, to camouflage a lust for office with a drop cloth made of red, white and blue." Bush also skillfully exploited racial tensions better than any candidate since George Wallace. The election, wrote Thomas Edsall, "served to reveal the continuing, and increasingly complex, significance of race in American politics." Bush's most effective advertisement showed a black rapist, Willie Horton, furloughed from a Massachusetts prison. The spot featured a stark, black-and-white scene of inmates walking thorough a revolving door, as an ominous voice announced that Dukakis had allowed many prisoners to escape. "Now [Dukakis] says he wants to do for America what he's done for Massachusetts." "This is not racism in a sheet and a hood," wrote Tom Wicker. "It is race consciousness in a white as well as a blue collar." [13]

The reluctance of either candidate to engage in a meaningful discussion angered Mondale. Calling the campaign "a disgrace," he complained that Bush and Dukakis were ignoring the tough choices that needed to be made. "There is no substance," he fumed. "The candidates are hidden. You don't get to ask questions. The negatives have taken over and its mud every night. Cynicism is growing and people feel that their intelligence has been insulted." He resented the growing influence of political managers who knew nothing about the issues and had little sense of loyalty to party. "The same people who have skill in commercializing toothpaste are called on to hustle a candidate," he charged. [14]

The contrast between the 1948 and 1988 presidential campaign revealed how much the political debate had changed since Mondale's initial involvement in politics. In 1948, Truman campaigned as a fire-breathing economic populist who denounced the "gluttons of privilege" dominating the Republican party. In 1988, Bush campaigned as a cultural populist who told cheering audiences about the "wide chasm" on "the question of values between me and the liberal Governor." Truman, playing to fears of economic uncertainty, embraced the New Deal banner and reminded voters that the Republicans were "the party of Hoover boom and Hoover depression." Bush, tapping into concern that Democrats were soft on defense and out-of-touch with mainstream voters, wrapped himself in the American flag to imply that his opponent was unpatriotic. In 1948, Truman traveled the country by whistlestop, carrying his powerful populist message directly to the people. In 1988, Bush campaigned by sound-bites, seeking Nielson ratings, not crowds at the tracks. To make the role reversals complete, Dukakis played the role of Dewey, the arrogant and aloof GOP candidate in 1948, who promised efficient administration and passionless government.

On election day, despite some Democratic gains in the West, Bush won 426 electoral votes and continued the Republican dominance of presidential elections begun in 1968. In their annual meeting following the election, many Democratic leaders ignored the deeper problems facing the party and instead took solace from their gains in congressional and state offices. "This election was not a rejection of the Democratic Party, but of the campaign run by Dukakis," declared a Michigan party official. David Broder expressed puzzlement at the Democrats' reluctance to recognize that their party confronted serious questions. "It's the equivalent of getting to hire all the extras in the burning of Atlanta scenes for *Gone With the Wind,* while the Republicans get to play Scarlett and Rhett," he wrote. "If they were a baseball team," observed the journalist Mark Shields, "the Democrats would be the Boston Red Sox or the old Brooklyn Dodgers, never able to win the Big One. If they were a car rental company, they'd be Avis. If the Democrats were an Olympic entry, they would be the Jamaican bobsled team." Reflecting the party's inability to appeal on a more abstract level, one Democratic consultant said: "We do better the closer we get to people's garbage."[15]

Six months after the presidential election, Mondale held an early morning press conference to announce whether he would seek his old Senate seat. While professing his "love" of public life, he told of the joy of being a private citizen and his concern about "the appropriateness of yet another Senate campaign." Saying he had watched too many Senators stay too long, Mondale claimed he had always vowed "that I would never be among them." For these reasons, he told the packed press conference, "I have decided not to seek a return to the United States Senate." His opponent's wife cried in relief at the news.[16]

Mondale hopes that freedom from political pressures will help him to play the role of party senior statesman. He believes a successful Democratic message will require a weaving of different perspectives into a single theme. Neoliberals, he suggests, correctly point out that economic growth and competence are important considerations. But Mondale feels they lack a sense of advocacy, a recognition that politics is a real battleground between competing interests. As conservatives suggest, the party must appear tough on social issues. But, he insists, it cannot abandon its support of positive government. Mondale argues that Democrats hopeful of attracting middle-class voters will need to show they have not abandoned the party's tradition of fairness and concern for the poor. Programs to pay for problems cost money and the middle class will have to pay its share.

In an effort to stay involved in the public debate, Mondale played an active role in providing advice to emerging governments in Poland and Hungary. In 1989, as chair of the National Democratic Institute, Mondale joined his former adversary Tennessee Senator Howard Baker on a trip to Poland. Together they furnished the newly elected Polish government with guidance on the subtleties of democracy. Upon his return, Mondale and the others convinced the Bush administration to double its financial aid to Poland. A few months later, Mondale traveled to Hungary where he headed an international group which observed that country's first free post-War election. That same year, as part of his effort to encourage debate and discussion about public issues, the former vice president established the Mondale Policy Forum at the Hubert Humphrey Institute of Public Affairs. Through conferences and seminars on important issues, the Forum hopes "to educate men and women for public responsibility in a world of momentous changes."

The Forum reflected Mondale's belief that the party was in dire need of an infusion of new blood. Mondale remembered with fondness his early years in politics when liberal intellectuals dominated the public debate, providing Democrats with a constant source of new ideas. In Minnesota, a resurgent liberalism had swept Humphrey and Freeman into office and had given the DFL control of the state legislature. He believed Democrats needed to find new intellectual inspiration if they planned to stage another revival. Mondale also hoped the Forum would counterbalance what he saw as a dangerous threat to American democracy: the lack of substantive debate in political campaigns. According to Mondale, in this new "era of the marketer," academics and other knowledgeable people were being replaced by the "pollsters, the focus group managers, the computerized mail specialists, the negative-attack genius, and above all, the fundraisers."[17]

By 1991, polls indicated that the public shared Mondale's frustration with the political process. At a time when fledgling democracies around the world looked to the United States for inspiration, Americans seemed apathetic about their political institutions. "I get so embarrassed when I see elections in Central America where you can get shot by either the left or the right for voting, and yet they vote at twice the rate we do in this country," observed one congressman. Opinion surveys revealed deep pessimism about the economy, uncertainty about the future, and unprecedented cynicism about political leaders. A private study of the American democratic process cited voter apathy and ignorance as evidence of a disaffection that had "broad, perhaps dangerous implications for democracy in this country." Other analysis suggested that Americans felt overwhelmed and impotent when confronted by the remoteness of government institutions, the magnitude of their activity, and the complexity of the public debate. Though the problem had deep roots, many people believed that the nation was paying for the artificial boom of the 1980s. "Things were better five years ago, I reckon, but I guess that was the time that we spent and borrowed too much," a Virginia woman said. "Now, the future doesn't look too bright. We owe too much and we've gotten ourselves in a bad way."[18]

As the heady optimism of the 1980s turned to gloom in the 1990s, and as the nation's failure to narrow the ballooning deficit helped nudge the economy into recession, some commentators viewed Mondale in a different light. Many, including President Bush, began to appreciate the wisdom of Mondale's call for a tax increase during the 1984 campaign. In June 1990, President Bush reneged on his campaign pledge of "no new taxes" and agreed to include revenue increases as part of a overall plan for addressing the deficit. Rather than expressing bitterness or gloating in vindication, Mondale rallied to the president's side. Overlooking the President's specious explanation for his late conversion, Mondale applauded Bush for having "the courage to change his mind" and "to acknowledge the truth about our nation's troubled finances." *Washington Post* columnist Richard Cohen suggested that the change should alter Mondale's place in history. "Until recently," he wrote in 1987, Mondale "was an asterisk in history, the great political klutz who lunged at the Electoral College and almost missed entirely." Mondale was denied the presidency, he concluded. "Maybe he'll settle for Prophet in His Own Time."[19]

The Republican reversal on taxes provided Democrats with the chance to regain the confidence of the group that had abandoned them in the 1980s: the white middle class. During the 1980s, Republicans lured many voters into the Republican fold with appeals to traditional values and promises of economic growth. But prosperity eluded many middle class families forced to cope with soaring costs for housing, health care, and college tuition. The growing disparity between rich and poor, the enormous profits earned by the very wealthy, and the President's apparent indifference to a stubborn recession, intensified the perception that the Republicans were defenders of corporate greed and selfishness. Democrats, hoping to exploit the opportunity, rediscovered their populist roots, portraying themselves as the defenders of the sons and daughters of Franklin

Roosevelt's "forgotten man," who, though living in a small home in the suburbs, still struggles to make ends meet. Polls showing that the end of the Cold War was focusing public attention on unmet domestic needs, strengthened the Democrats' case. In November 1989, Louis Harris reported "a political shift in the wind against anti-government Republican conservatism equivalent to that against pro-government Democratic liberalism during the 1970s and 1980s."[20]

Numerous obstacles lay in the path of a Democratic resurgence. As a congressional party increasingly dependent on contributions from monied interests and concerned with local issues and constituent service, Democrats have failed to articulate a compelling national message that defines their differences with Republicans and establishes a clear agenda for the future. "They don't think in themes," observed a critic, "they think in amendments." After surveying voters in 1990, David Broder concluded that the "American people have only a vague and muddled impression of the Democratic message." The opposition of leading Democrats to the popular Gulf War revived bitter memories of Vietnam and exposed the party's weakness on issues of national security. The party also remains vulnerable to racial appeals. Support for affirmative action and quotas serve as powerful metaphors which convey the discontent of white voters who see the party serving the poor and minorities at their expense.[21]

Nearly a half-century ago, Democrats participated in a similar painful reevaluation. The rebirth of prosperity and the end of World War II had forced liberals to reexamine priorities and to rethink policies designed for another era. Though the specific questions confronting the party in the 1990s are different from those of the 1940s, the challenge remains the same: How can Democrats build a broad coalition in favor of more activist government? As a young foot soldier in Hubert Humphrey's army, Walter Mondale fought to establish a Vital Center within the Democratic Party. He spent much of his years in public life struggling to sustain the liberal spirit, adjusting its agenda to an age of limited resources, and defending its integrity against assaults from the left and right. He worked toward building a compromise between the party's past and its future. How that process will be resolved is still uncertain. But Mondale's experience clarifies the nature of the challenge confronting the Democrats. As Bob Beckel recalled: "We've got to go to new places, we must find new ideas, and we must rebuild the party. But we must never forget this movement was born of passion and mission."[22]

Notes

Preface

1. Burdett Loomis, *The New American Politician*, 9–10; William Schneider, "JFK's Children: The Class of '74," *Atlantic* (March 1989), 35–58.

2. E. J. Dionne, *Why Americans Hate Politics*, 11–12.

3. Thomas Byrne Edsall with Mary D. Edsall, "When the Official Subject Is Presidential Politics, Taxes, Welfare, Crime, Rights, or Values . . . the Real Subject is Race," *Atlantic* (May, 1991), 53.

4. Robert Kuttner, "Ron Brown's Party Line," *New York Times Magazine*, (December 3, 1989), 126.

5. See: Thomas Edsall, *The New Politics of Inequality;* and Robert Kuttner, *The Life of the Party.*

6. William Galston, "The Future of the Democratic Party," *Brookings Review*, (Winter 1985), 20.

1. A Father's Faith

1. The description that follows is based on general studies of Norwegian immigrant experiences. See: Theodore Blegen, *Land of Their Choice: The Immigrants Write Home and The Land Lies Open;* Ingris Semmingsen, *Norway to America;*

Carlton C. Qualey, "Pioneer Norwegian Settlement," *Minnesota History* (September 1931), 247–280; Carlton C. Qualey and Jon A Gjerde, "The Norwegians," in June Holmquist, ed., *They Chose Minnesota;* Jon Gjerde, *From Peasants to Farmers;* and the classic *Giants in the Earth,* by Ole Rolvaag. Material on the Mondale family experience is drawn from family papers held by Clarence Mondale. Lester and Maria Mondale have written a family history entitled *The Mundale-Mondale Clan (MP-MHS).* Also useful was a lengthy interview of Lester Mondale conducted in 1974 by members of Mondale's Senate staff. This material was supplemented by the author's interviews with surviving family members.

2. Lester Mondale interview.

3. Lester Mondale interview; Finlay Lewis, *Mondale,* 32–33.

4. Lester Mondale interview; Clarence Mondale interview.

5. Lester Mondale interview; Finlay Lewis, *Mondale,* 34–36.

6. Robert Cowan, "A Family History," (MP-MHS); Clarence Mondale interview.

7. "Church journal," (MP-MHS); Lester Mondale interview.

8. D. Jerome Tweton, *Depression: Minnesota in the Thirties;* Raymond L. Koch, "Politics and Relief in Minneapolis During the 1930s," *Minnesota History* (Winter 1968), 153–170.

9. Clarence and Lester Mondale interviews.

10. Jon Wefald, *A Voice of Protest,* 8–17; David Rodnick, *The Norwegians: A Study in National Culture,* 13–20; Clarence and Lester Mondale interviews. The Mondale quotations are taken from an undated "Letter to the Editor" signed "T.S. Mondale," which is part of the Clarence Mondale Papers. The letter probably dates between 1937–39.

11. Arthur Naftalin, "The Tradition of Protest and the Roots of the Farmer-Labor Party," *Minnesota History* (June 1956), 53; David Lebedoff, *The 21st Ballot.*

12. George Mayer, *The Political Career of Floyd B. Olson.*

13. Arthur Schlesinger, Jr.'s three volume series *The Age of Roosevelt* remains the best general work on the New Deal. It should be supplemented with: William Leuchtenburg, *Franklin D. Roosevelt and the New Deal;* Frank Freidel, *Franklin D. Roosevelt: Launching the New Deal;* and the articles edited by John Braeman, Robert H. Bremner, and David Brody in *The New Deal.* For specific studies of social welfare policies see: James T. Patterson, *America's Struggle Against Poverty;* Robert Bremner, "The New Deal and Social Welfare," in Harvard Sitkoff, ed., *Fifty Years Later: The New Deal Evaluated;* Robert S. McElvaine, *Down and Out in the Great Depression.* On Roosevelt's impact on the local level see, D. Jerome Tweton, *The New Deal at the Grass Roots.*

14. The Minnesota Historical Society contains books written by town residents that provide insight into Elmore during these years. See: Elmore History Book Committee, *Elmore, Minnesota; and Faribault County Bicentennial Committee, Faribault County.* The best journalistic accounts of Mondale's early years are: William Barry Furlong, "Mondale's Minnesota," *Horizon* (October 1977), 67–74; William Chapman, "Mondale Traces Political Stirrings to Elmore, Minn.," *Washington Post,* August 11, 1976; Bill Gardner, "Elmore Remembers 'Crazylegs'," *Pioneer Press,* February 20, 1983; David Harris, "Understanding Mondale," *New York Times Magazine* (June 19, 1983), 26–36, 41, 52–56; and Finlay Lewis, *Mondale.*

15. Morton and Walter Mondale interviews.

16. David Harris, "Understanding Mondale," *New York Times Magazine* (June 19, 1983), 29–30; Clarence and Walter Mondale interviews.

17. Morton Mondale interview.

18. *Pioneer Press,* February 20, 1983.

19. The original police report was sent to Mondale by a town official in 1968. See: Walt Vereide to Mondale, February 29, 1968 (MP-MHS).

20. Yahnke interview; Walter Mondale interview; Elmore High School transcript in author's possession.

21. Walter Mondale interview.

22. Eisele notes, Eisele Papers; Walter and Lester Mondale interviews; Finlay Lewis, *Mondale,* 42–43.

23. Finlay Lewis, *Mondale,* 44–45.

24. Walter Mondale interview. The Reverend Mondale quotations are from the few scattered writings that have survived. On March 11, 1944, while recovering from a heart attack, he wrote a long letter to Lester which reflected on his religious beliefs. He also frequently wrote short poems and notes. All of the material can be found in the Clarence Mondale files.

25. *Pioneer Press,* February 20, 1983.

26. Washington *Post,* August 11, 1976 and January 20, 1977; Elmore High School Yearbook, 1946.

27. Clarence Mondale interview; Yahnke interview; Des Moines *Register,* July 13, 1989; Washington *Post,* August 11, 1976; Finlay Lewis, *Mondale,* 15.

2. Political Baptism

1. Theodore Mitau, "America Comes of Age," *MAC Weekly* (April 16, 1948). For general works on liberal thought at the time see: Arthur Schlesinger Jr., *The Vital Center;* Richard Pells, *The Liberal Mind in a Conservative Age,* 147–161; John Patrick Diggins, *The Proud Decades,* 168–176; and Richard Fox, *Reinhold Niebuhr, An Intellectual Biography.*

2. Young interview.

3. Hauser interview; Young interview. A copy of Mondale's Macalester transcript is in the author's possession.

4. Hauser interview; Char interview; Young interview.

5. For studies on the issue of liberals, communists, and the Popular Front see: Steven Gillon, *Politics and Vision;* Alonzo Hamby, *Beyond the New Deal;* Mary McAuliffe, *Crisis on the Left;* Maurice Isserman, *Which Side Were You On?;* and John Earl Haynes, *Dubious Alliance.*

6. *MAC Weekly,* October 29, 1946; December 10, 1946.

7. Minneapolis *Tribune,* March 19, 1947.

8. *MAC Weekly,* April 18, 1947.

9. Warren interview; Kirby interview.

10. Hauser interview; Gallos interview; Freeman interview.

11. "Young-DFL Convention," November 9, 1947, Donald Fraser Papers (MHS), Box 2; *MAC Weekly,* November 22, 1947; John Earl Haynes, "Liberals, Communists and the Popular Front," 520–521.

12. Mondale interview.

13. Eisele interview with Mondale, Eisele Papers.

14. Freeman interview; Carl Solberg, *Humphrey*, 124–130; John Earl Haynes, "Liberals, Communists, and the Popular Front in Minnesota," 543–557; Al Eisele, *Almost to the Presidency*, 70.

15. Freeman interview; Carl Solberg, *Humphrey*, 126–127.

16. Richard Kirkendall, "Election of 1948," in Arthur Schlesinger, Jr. and Fred Israel, eds., *History of American Presidential Elections, 1789–1968*, 3099–3145. Alonzo Hamby, *Beyond the New Deal*, 257–258; Irwin Ross, *The Loneliest Campaign*, 171–229.

17. Mondale interview; St. Paul *Pioneer Press*, October 14, 1948; Minneapolis *Tribune*, October 13, 14, and 15, 1948.

18. Char interview.

19. *MAC Weekly*, October 10, 1948.

20. Michael Barone, *Our Country*, 221; New York *Herald-Tribune*, November 4, 1948.

21. Samuel Lubell, *The Future of American Politics*, 43–68; Irwin Ross, *The Loneliest Campaign*, 248.

22. Samuel Lubell, "Who Really Elected Truman?" *Saturday Evening Post* (January 22, 1949), 56.

23. Alan Brinkley, "The New Deal and the Idea of State," in Steve Fraser and Gary Gerstle, eds., *The Rise and Fall of the New Deal Order, 1930–1980*, 85–121; Ellis Hawley, *The New Deal and the Problem of Monoloply*; Arthur Schlesinger, *The Vital Center*.

24. William Leuchtenburg, *Franklin D. Roosevelt and the New Deal*, 327; Samuel Beer, "In Search of a New Public Philosophy," in Anthony King, ed., *The New American Political System*, 5–44; James Holt, "The New Deal and the American Anti-Statist Tradition," in John Braeman, Robert Bremner and David Brody, eds. *The New Deal: The National Level*, 27–49. On Vital Center liberalism see: Arthur Schlesinger, *The Vital Center*; Reinhold Niebuhr, *The Irony of American History*. For critiques of the Vital Center see: Richard Pells, *The Liberal Mind in a Conservative Age*, 147–161; Godfrey Hodgson, *America In Our Time*, 67–98.

3. Organizing for a New Generation

1. A copy of Mondale's Macalester transcript is in the author's possession.

2. Mondale, "Great Things SDA Could Accomplish," 1949, SDA Papers, series II, 299; Fritz to Mom, n.d. (MP-P); Mondale interview.

3. Finlay Lewis, *Mondale*, 36–37.

4. Mondale interview; Finlay Lewis, *Mondale*, 72.

5. Fritz to Mom, n.d. (MP-P); Mondale to Tucker, September 1949, SDA Papers, series II, #78.

6. "Notes on the 1949 Convention," ADA Papers, unprocessed collection at the Wisconsin State Historical Society. Alonzo Hamby, *Beyond the New Deal*, 311–352; and Robert J. Donovan, *Tumultuous Years*, 22–33.

7. Dinnerstein to Mondale, January 22, 1951 (MP-MHS).

8. Fritz to Clarence, n.d. (MP-MHS); Waters interview. Mondale's predic-

tion proved only partially correct. The Labour Party did win a slim majority in 1950, but in October 1951 the Conservatives, led again by Churchill, returned to power.

9. Chattanooga *Daily Times,* November 18–19, 1949; New York *Times,* November 18, 1949.

10. Fritz to Betsy and Manfred, n.d. (MP-MHS).

11. Humphrey to Heaney, May 16, 1949, Humphrey Papers, Box 88; Freeman to Humphrey, June 16, 1949, Freeman Papers, Box 1; Humphrey to Freeman, June 20, 1949, Freeman Papers, Box 4; Freeman to Humphrey, August 12, 1949, Freeman Papers, Box 4.

12. The Union *Advocate* and Labor *Review,* quotes are from Haynes, "Liberals, Communists, and the Popular Front In Minnesota," 805–812. For Freeman-Humphrey correspondence see: Freeman to Humphrey, June 16, 1949, Freeman Papers, Box 1; Freeman to Humphrey, August 12, 1949, Freeman Papers, Box 4.

13. Arvonne Fraser interview; Naftalin interview; Mondale interview.

14. Freeman Interview; Freeman, "Oral History," Freeman Papers (MHS), 1–15; John C. McDonald, "The 'Rebirth' of Orville Freeman," *Progressive* (November 1955), 29–30.

15. Mondale interview.

16. Mondale to Rodger, September 6, 1950, Freeman Papers, Box 1; Freeman to Humphrey, May 4, 1950, Freeman Papers, Box 1; Mondale interview.

17. Freeman to Humphrey, May 4, 1950, Freeman Papers, Box 1; Minneapolis *Tribune,* March 27, 1950; Minneapolis *Star,* April 2, 1950.

18. Mondale to Loeb, ADA Papers (WSHS), series III, 63.

19. A copy of Mondale's University of Minnesota transcript is in the author's possession.

20. Mondale interview; Mondale's army records, which are in the author's possession, confirm the dates of his enlistment.

21. Mom to Fritz, n.d. (MP-MHS).

22. Fritz to Clarence, September 1950 (MP-MHS).

23. Mondale to Pete and Ginni, September 1952 (MP-MHS).

24. His friend Tom Hughes, already assigned as an information officer at the Camp, bragged that he was responsible for keeping Fritz out of battle. "I've got it 'arranged,' here so he'll stay after basic if CIC doesn't pick him up," Hughes claimed in a letter to a friend. "Our office is full right now for enlisted men but I think we can put him in here by February and if not then some office job in this area." Mondale's army records indicate that Hughes' influence was not as great as he imagined. On November 5, 1952 Mondale was ordered to the Personnel Center in Seattle, Washington as the first step toward assignment overseas. During a routine medical examination on November 12, doctors discovered a large cyst which required surgery and disqualified him for combat. See: Tom Hughes to Arvonne Fraser, n.d. (Fraser papers), Box 1; Mondale letter to author, October 17, 1990. Mondale's army records, including medical reports, are in author's possession.

25. Years later, while serving on the Senate Budget Committee Mondale would recall his experience as reason for cutting the budget of these information programs. "Our biggest problem was getting on the golf links in the morning

because all the instructors were out there playing golf . . . It is incredible—it is simply incredible . . . the millions of dollars wasted just on that one post . . . We worked like heck to get a driver assigned to us to take us out to the golf course." See: Senate Budget Committee, Markup Sessions, 1975, Budget Committee Archive, Dirksen Building, Washington D.C.

26. Mondale to Don and Arvonne Fraser, n.d., D. Fraser Papers, correspondence 1950-51.

27. Fritz to Pete, Fall 1951 (MP-MHS); Fritz to Don and Arvonne, n.d. (Fraser Papers), Box 1; Fritz to Pete and Ginni, September 1952 (MP-MHS); Fritz to Frasers, n.d. (Fraser Papers), Box 1.

28. Mondale to Pete, Fall 1951 (MP).

29. Mondale to Freeman, n.d. (Freeman papers), Personal, 1953.

30. Mondale interview; Clarence Mondale interview; Finlay Lewis, *Mondale*, 77 .

31. Clarence Mondale interview.

32. A copy of Mondale's law school transcript is in the author's possession. Finlay Lewis, *Mondale*, 46-47.

33. Minnesota *Daily*, July 13, 1984; Finlay Lewis, *Mondale*, 80.

34. Mondale to Senator Harold W. Schultz, D. Fraser Papers, Box 5.

35. Under the auspices of the ADA, Keyserling and Nathan joined other leading liberals in writing *A Guide to Politics* 1954, edited by Quincy Howe and Arthur Schlesinger, Jr. Despite the appearance of consensus, liberals disagreed on many basic questions. For more on the questions that divided liberals in the 1950s, see: Steven M. Gillon, *Politics and Vision*, 123-130.

36. John H. Fenton, *Midwest Politics*, 75-77, 87-88; Theodore Mitau, *Minnesota Politics*. International Research Associates, Poll 1954 (MP).

37. Mondale interview; Arvonne Fraser to mom, n.d. Fraser papers, Box 1; DFL, "Minnesota Builds—Two Years of Achievement in State Government," 1956, Kubicek Papers.

38. Joan Mondale interview.

39. Joan Mondale interview.

40. A copy of Mondale's law school transcript is in the author's possession. Joan Mondale interview; Finlay Lewis, *Mondale*, 46.

41. Finlay Lewis, *Mondale*, 53.

42. Mondale interview.

43. Minneapolis *Tribune*, October 11, 1958; Freeman interview; Mondale interview; Finlay Lewis, *Mondale*, 54-55.

44. Minneapolis *Star*, October 15, 1958; Minneapolis *Tribune*, November 27, 1959.

45. Freeman interview.

46. Minneapolis *Tribune*, May 4, 1960; A. Fraser interview; Orville Freeman interview.

47. Minneapolis *Tribune*, May 5, 1960; St Paul *Pioneer Press*, May 5, 1960.

48. Minneapolis *Tribune*, June 6, 1960; June 17, 1960.

49. "Progress in Consumer Protection," n.d. (MP-MHS); "A Report on Activities of the Attorney General's Office," n.d. (MP-MHS); "Report on Consumer Protection to the Attorney General," n.d., State Attorney General Papers,

70.F.6.5B; Robert Albrecht to Mondale, August 9, 1962, State Attorney General Papers, 70.F6.5B; Mondale to Board of Directors, Sister Elizabeth Kenny Foundation, June 27, 1960 (MP-MHS).

50. Finlay Lewis, *Mondale*, 66–67.

51. Minneapolis *Star*, May 12, 1960.

52. Minneapolis *Tribune*, June 6, 1960.

53. Brainard *Daily Dispatch*, December 29, 1960.

4. The People's Lawyer

1. Brooks interview.

2. Finlay Lewis, *Mondale*, 101–102.

3. Joan Mondale interview.

4. Joan Mondale interview; Minneapolis *Tribune*, November 18, 1964.

5. Minneapolis *Star*, July 19 and October 14, 1960; Minneapolis *Tribune*, July 22, 1960; St Paul *Pioneer Press*, July 23, 1960; St Paul *Dispatch*, July 14 and 21, 1960.

6. Kennedy to Mondale, "State of Minnesota vs. Holland Furnace," November 14, 1963, State Attorney General Papers, Correspondence, 1962; Finlay Lewis, *Mondale*, 106. For newspaper coverage see: St. Paul Pioneer *Press*, December 29–30, 1961; Minneapolis *Star*, December 28, 1961; St. Paul *Dispatch*, December 28, 1961; Trimont *Progress*, January 4, 1962; Minneapolis *Tribune*, December 29, 1961; St. Cloud *Daily Times*, December 28, 1961.

7. Minneapolis *Star*, December 30, 1960.

8. Mondale, "Suggestions for Particular Programs to be Recommended at the First Meeting of the Consumers' Advisory Council," August 1, 1962 (MP-MHS); Mondale to Conoyer, December 12, 1962 (MP-MHS); "Philosophical Position on the Need and Functions of the President's Consumers' Advisory Council to be Submitted to the Council," n.d. (MP-MHS).

9. Mondale to Ervin, August 15, 1962 (MP-MHS); Ervin to Mondale, August 21, 1962 (MP-MHS); Anthony Lewis, *Gideon's Trumpet*, 145–147.

10. Lebedoff interview.

11. New Ulm *Daily Journal*, March 19, 1962; Fairmont *Daily Sentinel*, March 2, 1962; St. Paul *Dispatch*, October 29, 1962; Washington *Post*, August 29, 1962.

12. Byrne interview; Brooks interview.

13. Lebedoff interview; Mondale to Val Imm, February 7, 1963; Gaylord Saetre, Press Release, n.d. (MP-MHS).

14. Berman interview; Brooks interview.

15. Finlay Lewis, *Mondale*, 112–121.

16. St. Paul *Dispatch*, June 9, 1962; St. Paul *Pioneer Press*, June 3 and 10, 1962; Minneapolis *Tribune*, October 17, 1962.

17. *Fargo Forum*, November 29, 1962.

18. For general works on Kennedy and civil rights see: Allen Matusow, *The Unraveling of America*, 60–96; Arthur Schlesinger, Jr., *RFK and His Times*, 307–394; Carl Brauer, *John F. Kennedy and the Second Reconstruction;* and Hugh Davis Graham, *The Civil Rights Era*, 27–46.

19. Minneapolis *Spokesman,* August 29, 1963.

20. Mondale speech, undated and untitled (MP-MHS).

21. Berman interview.

22. Minneapolis *Tribune,* November 23 and 25, 1963.

23. Spannaus interview.

24. New York *Times,* August 20–22, 1964; Harvard Sitkoff, *The Struggle for Black Equality,* 179–86; Joseph Rauh, "Organizing Mississippi, 1964," in Milton Viorst, *Fire in the Streets,* 233–272.

25. "Brief Submitted by the MFDP for the Consideration of the Credentials Subcommittee of the DNC," Rauh Papers, Box 86; Anne Romaine interview of Joseph Rauh, Romaine Papers (WSHS); Josephs interview.

26. Harvard Sitkoff, *The Struggle for Black Equality,* 179–86; New York *Times,* August 23–24, 1964.

27. Mondale interview; Minneapolis *Tribune,* August 24, 1964; Finlay Lewis, *Mondale,* 125–130.

28. Romaine interview of Rauh, Romaine Papers (WSHS); Mondale interview.

29. Josephs notes, Josephs Papers (MHS), Box 1.

30. Wallace Roberts, "The Mondale Myth," *New Times* (January 25, 1974), 26–31; Clayborne Carson, *In Struggle,* 123–129.

31. Mondale interview.

32. Josephs interview; Attorney General news clippings, 1964 (MP-MHS); Ruth to Mondale, n.d. (MP-MHS).

33. The quotes that follow are taken from numerous undated, untitled Mondale speech drafts from his last year as Attorney General. About a dozen drafts exist, and while they repeat some material, each appears tailored to a different audience.

34. Minneapolis *Tribune,* November 18, 1964; St Paul *Pioneer Press,* November 18, 1964; Mondale to Rolvaag, September 17, 1964 (MP-MHS).

35. Duluth *Herald,* November 18, 1964; Minneapolis *Statesman,* November 18, 1964; St. Louis *Post-Dispatch,* November 18, 1964. Also, see the summary of editorial opinion from around the state in the Minneapolis *Tribune,* November 23, 1964.

5. Learning the Ropes

1. Joan Mondale interview.

2. Mondale interview; Scribner interview.

3. Joan Mondale interview.

4. Finlay Lewis, *Mondale,* 233; Doris Kearns Goodwin, "Second Lady," *Ladies Home Journal* (June 1977), 56–64, 144–46.

5. Byrne interview; Scribner interview; Finlay Lewis, *Mondale,* 153.

6. Eisele interview with Jerry Schaller (Eisele Papers); Finlay Lewis, *Mondale,* 154.

7. These stories are all told by Finlay Lewis in *Mondale,* 113.

8. *Congress and the Nation,* vol. II, 1965–68, 2–4; *Time* (July 30, 1965), 12; (October 29, 1965), 22; Eric Sevareid, "Walter Lippmann—1964," *New Republic* (April 25, 1964). For general accounts of the Great Society see: Allen Matusow,

The Unraveling of America; William E. Leuchtenburg, *In the Shadow of FDR,* 121–160; and Eric Goldman, *The Tragedy of Lyndon Johnson.*

9. Minneapolis *Tribune* (October 24, 1965); St. Paul Pioneer *Press* (October 31, 1965).

10. Clarence Mondale interview; New York *Times,* November 19, 1964; St. Paul Pioneer *Press* October 31, 1965; *Congressional Record,* 89th Congress, 1st Session (July 14, 1965), 16781.

11. For 1966 legislation see: *Congressional Record,* 89th Congress 2nd Session (April 5, 1966), 7581 (April 18, 1966), 8215–8217. For 1967 Mondale-Montoya Meat Inspection Bill, see: *Congressional Record,* 90th Congress, 1st Session (November 27, 1967), 33839, 33841–33843, 33860, 33861, 33863, 33866, 33871, 33878–33881; (November 28, 1967), 33961, 33966, 33970.

12. See: Allan Matusow, *The Unraveling of America,* 181–87; David J. Garrow, *Protest at Selma,* 36–39; Harvard Sitkoff, *The Struggle for Black Equality,* 188–97; Hugh Davis Graham, *The Civil Rights Era,* 153–76; Howell Raines, *My Soul Is Rested,* 187–226.

13. Speech text, "Civil Rights March," March 13, 1965 (MP-MHS); Minneapolis *Tribune,* March 14, 1965.

14. New York *Times,* March 16, 1965; Mondale interview.

15. St. Paul Pioneer *Press,* October 31, 1965.

16. Mondale interview; *Congressional Record,* 88th Congress, 1st Session (August 17, 1965), 20625–20626; (September 8, 1965), 23072.

17. For a few of the better works on Johnson's Vietnam policy see: George Herring, *America's Longest War;* Hubert Humphrey, *The Education of a Public Man,* 313–53; Larry Berman, *Planning a Tragedy;* Eric Goldman, *The Tragedy of Lyndon Johnson;* and Vaughn Davis Bornet, *The Presidency of Lyndon B. Johnson.*

18. George Herring, *America's Longest War,* 108–144.

19. Nelson interview.

20. Berman interview.

21. Mondale interview.

22. Minneapolis *Tribune,* March 2, 1965; *Congressional Record,* 89th Congress 1st Session (August 16, 1965), 20531–31.

23. Minneapolis *Tribune,* January 11, 1966; St. Paul *Dispatch,* January 11, 1966.

24. Thomas Powers, *Vietnam: The War at Home,* 164–195; Doris Kearns, *LBJ and the American Dream,* 309–17; Nancy Zaroulis and Gerald Sullivan, *Who Spoke Up?*

25. "The War President," *New Republic* (July 16, 1966), 5–6; Allan Matusow, *The Unraveling of America,* 206–207; Robert Sherill, "The Democratic Rebels in Congress," *Nation* (October 10, 1966), 341–346; *Newsweek* (August 22, 1966), 38; *Time* (October 7, 1966), 29–30.

26. Schaller to Mondale, October 1966 (MP-MHS); Minneapolis *Tribune,* February 12, 1966; Eisele interview of Schaller (Eisele Papers).

27. Berman interview; Eisele interview of Conlon (Eisele Papers).

28. Berman interview; Eisele interview of Conlon (Eisele Papers).

29. See the *Minnesota Poll* published in the Minneapolis *Tribune:* May 2, 1965; July 18, 1965; April 3, 1966; May 8, 1966; September 11, 1966; September 18, 1966; October 9, 1966. For general works on Minnesota politics and government

see: Theodore Blegen, *Minnesota: A History of the State;* John Fenton, *Midwest Politics;* William Hathaway, *Minnesota Political Parties and Politics;* G. Theodore Mitau, *Politics in Minnesota;* Nelson Lowery, *The Minnesota Community;* Neal Peirce, *The Great Plains States of America;* and Millard Gieske and Edward Brandt, *Perspectives on Minnesota Government and Politics.*

    30. Finlay Lewis, *Mondale,* 115–16.

    31. Minneapolis *Tribune,* October 9, 13, 17, and 29, 1966.

    32. *Congress and the Nation,* vol. II, 1965–68, 6–8; Walter Dean Burnham, "Death of the New Deal," *Commonweal* (December 9, 1966), 284–87; Douglas Kiker, "Vietnam Issue," *Atlantic* (November 1966), 4.

    33. These statistics are taken from Mike Berman's comparative anaylsis of the 1966 and 1972 Senate races. See: Berman to Senator, "Analysis of the 1972 election," n.d. (MP-MHS).

    34. Mondale interview.

6. The New Politics and the Old

    1. Allan Matusow, *The Unraveling of America,* 206–7; "The War President," *New Republic* (July 16, 1966), 5–6; *Newsweek* (August 22, 1967), 99.

    2. "A Message of Defeat," *Nation* (January 23, 1967), 99.

    3. Thomas Powers, *Vietnam: The War at Home,* 229–51; Zaroulis and Sullivan, *Who Spoke Up?* 119–48; *Time* (August 4, 1967), 12–15.

    4. See the Minnesota Poll published in the Minneapolis *Tribune:* January 29, 1967; February 5, 1967; May 21, 1967; June 25, 1967; August 23, 1967; September 10, 1967; October 4, 1967.

    5. "Memo to Minnesota," October 1967 (MP-MHS); *Congressional Record,* 90th Congress, 1st Session (August 30, 1967), 24730; (September 29, 1967), 27387–27388; (July 25, 1967), 20199–20201; Minneapolis *Tribune,* July 22, 1967.

    6. See: James T. Patterson, *America's Struggle Against Poverty;* Allen Matusow, *The Unraveling of America;* and Daniel Patrick Moynihan, *Maximum Feasible Misunderstanding.*

    7. Walter F. Mondale, "Reporting of the Social State of the Union, " *Trans-Action* (June 1968), 34–38.

    8. Byrne interview; Scribner interview.

    9. Finlay Lewis, *Mondale,* 130–39; Rowland Evans and Robert Novak, "Mondale and Harris: Humphrey's Establishment Radicals, " *Harpers* (October 1968), 88–95; *Congressional Record,* 90th Congress, 1st Session (August 30, 1967), 24562. Also see interviews with Scribner, Byrne, Berman, and Mondale.

    10. Audio cassette, Macalester College Speech, November 11, 1967 (MP-MHS); MAC *Weekly,* November 17, 1967; Minneapolis *Tribune,* November 12, 1967.

    11. Godfrey Hodgson, et. al. *American Melodrama,* 376; Jack Newfield, *Robert F. Kennedy: a Memoir,* 187; David Halberstam, "The Man Who Ran Against Lyndon Johnson," *Harper's* (December 1968), 47–66.

    12. David Halberstam, "McCarthy and the Divided Left," *Harpers* (March 1968), 32–44. Jack Newfield, *Robert F. Kennedy: a Memoir,* 188.

    13. Mondale interview; Finlay Lewis, *Mondale,* 165.

14. Walter Mondale interview; Joan Mondale interview; Berman interview; Finlay Lewis, *Mondale*, 130–39.

15. Minneapolis *Tribune*, February 7, 1968.

16. Arthur Schlesinger, Jr., *RFK and His Times*, 883–920.

17. Mondale interview; Berman interview.

18. Godfrey Hodgson, et.al., *American Melodrama*, 375.

19. Mondale interview; Allan Matusow, *The Unraveling of America*, 206–09.

20. Scribner interview; Finlay Lewis, *Mondale*, 162–174.

21. *Congressional Record*, 90th Congress, 2nd Session (February 6, 1968), 2274–2279.

22. *Congressional Record* (February 6, 1968), 2533; (February 15, 1968), 3134–3135.

23. For contemporary summary and analysis of the debate see: 1968 *Congressional Quarterly Almanac*, 152–168; Washington *Post*, February 16–March 8; *Newsweek* (March 4, 1968) 21–22.

24. New York *Times*, March 1, 1968; Washington *Post*, March 1, 1968.

25. Mondale interview; Scribner interview; Finlay Lewis, *Mondale*, 170–172.

26. *Congressional Record*, 90th Congress, 2nd Session (April 5, 1968), 9138; New York *Times*, April 11, 1968.

27. Hart to Mondale, April 11, 1968 (MP-MHS); Finlay Lewis, *Mondale*, 172–174; St. Paul *Pioneer Press*, May 26, 1967; Minneapolis *Tribune*, March 15, 1968 and April 12, 1968.

28. Lester to Fritz, March 22, 1968 (MP-MHS); Ruth to Mondale, February 27, 1968 (MP-MHS).

29. Rowland Evans and Robert Novak, "Mondale and Harris: Humphrey's Establishment Radicals," *Harpers* (October 1968), 88–95.

30. Mondale interview; Solberg, *Humphrey*, 331–332, 336.

31. Finlay Lewis, *Mondale*, 132–33; Al Eisele, *Almost to the Presidency*, 330–31; Carl Solberg, *Humphrey*, 336–37.

32. New York *Times*, June 5, 1968.

33. Berman to Mondale, n.d. (MP-MHS); *Congressional Record*, 90th Congress, 2nd Session, June 6, 1968, 16162.

34. Al Eisele, *Almost to the Presidency*, 333.

35. *Esquire*, November 1968; New York *Times*, July 23, 1968; Solberg, *Humphrey*, 339; Al Eisele, *Almost to the Presidency*, 334–36.

36. Rowland Evans and Robert Novak, "Mondale and Harris: Humphrey's Establishment Radicals," *Harpers* (October 1968), 88–95.

37. Mondale interview; Eisele interview of Mondale (Eisele Papers). Al Eisele, *Almost to the Presidency*, 336–38, 345–46; Solberg, *Humphrey*, 352–54.

38. David Farber, *Chicago '68;* Allan Matusow, *The Unraveling of America*, 411–22; Joan Mondale interview.

39. Carl Solberg, *Humphrey*, 347–354; Albert Eisele, *Almost to the Presidency*, 345–348; Mondale interview; Joan Mondale interview.

40. Godfrey Hodgson, et. al. *American Melodrama*, 583–85; David Farber, *Chicago '68*, 165–208; Allan Matusow, *The Unraveling of America*, 419–420; Theodore White, *The Making of the President, 1968*, 370–371.

41. Solberg, *Humphrey*, 366–367.

42. Theodore White, *The Making of the President, 1968*, 380.

43. Mondale interview; Solberg, *Humphrey*, 373.

44. Minneapolis *Tribune*, September 1, 1968.

45. Minneapolis *Tribune*, September 17, 1968.

46. Minneapolis *Tribune* September 17, 1968; St. Paul *Pioneer Press*, September 17, 1968.

47. Eisele interview of Schaller (Eisele Papers); Eisele interview of Conlin, Eisele Papers); Scribner interview.

48. St. Paul *Pioneer Press*, September 23, 1968.

49. Herbert Parmet, *Richard Nixon and His America*, 499–501, 524–28; Jonathan Reider, "The Rise of the Silent Majority," in Steve Fraser and Gary Gerstle, eds., *The Rise and Fall of the New Deal Order*, 258–263; Carl Solberg, *Humphrey*, 355–71; Allan Matusow, *The Unraveling of America*, 422–26.

50. Allan Matusow, *The Unraveling of America*, 422–426; Marshall Frady, *Wallace;* Jonathan Reider, "The Rise of the Silent Majority," in Steve Fraser and Gary Gerstle, *The Rise and Fall of the New Deal Order*, 243–268; Thomas Edsall, *Chain Reaction*, 10.

51. Minneapolis *Tribune*, October 27, 1968.

52. Minneapolis *Tribune*, November 7, 1968.

53. Eisele interview of Mondale; Mondale interview.

7. Questioning Liberalism

1. Mondale interview.

2. Audio tape of Macalester College Speech, St. Paul, October 15, 1969 (MP-MHS).

3. Minneapolis *Tribune*, October 17, 1969.

4. *Congressional Record*, 92nd Congress, 1st Session (January 27, 1971), 737; (June 16, 1971), 20213; (July 20, 1973), 25116. Testimony before the Senate Foreign Relations Committee, 92nd Congress, 1st session, April 20, 1971.

5. Robert Coles, "Mondale of Minnesota," *New Republic* (December 25, 1971), 21–23; Walter Mondale, "Think of These Children," *New Republic* (December 26, 1970), 15–17.

6. Minneapolis *Tribune*, November 23, 1969; Robert Coles, "Mondale of Minnesota," *New Republic;* (December 25, 1971), 21–23; Mondale interview.

7. Finlay Lewis, *Mondale,* 189.

8. Smith interview; Roger Morris, "Mondale's Mixed Reviews," *New Republic* (July 31, 1977), 17–19.

9. For a complete transcript of the public hearings see: U.S. Congress. Senate. 91st Congress, 1st and 2nd Sessions. Committee on Labor and Public Welfare—Subcommittee on Migratory Labor, "Migrant and Seasonal Farmworker Powerlessness" (20 vols), Washington, 1970.

10. U.S. Congress. Senate. 91st Congress, 1st Session, Subcommittee on Migratory Labor, "Migrant and Seasonal Farmworker Powerlessness," June 9, 1969.

11. *Congressional Record*, 91st Congress, 1st Session (September 12, 1969),

25249; (April 22, 1969), 9889; (May 5, 1969), 11328–11331; (November 4, 1969), 32820; New York *Times*, March 22, 1971, 18.

12. Elizabeth Drew, "Reporter's Notebook," *New Yorker* (May 19, 1973), 118–120. Mondale's December 9, 1970 address on the Senate floor was later published by the Select Committee on Equal Educational Opportunity. See "Justice for Children," Government Printing Office, 1972.

13. Mondale, "Think of These Children," *New Republic* (December 26, 1970), 15–17; Walter Mondale, "Justice for Children"; John Inglehart, "Congress Passes Major Child-Care Program Despite White House Veto Threat," *National Journal* (October 23, 1971), 2125–2130.

14. John Inglehart, "Congress Passes Major Child-Care . . . ," *National Journal* (October 23, 1971), 2125–2130; *Congressional Quarterly Almanac*, 1971, 504–518.

15. *Congressional Record*, 91st Congress, 1st Session (March 4, 1969), 5125–5128; (March 29, 1969), 7238; (September, 9, 1969), 24780–24783.

16. U.S. Congress, Senate, Committee on Appropriations. 92nd Congress, 1st Session, 1972.

17. CBS Capitol Cloakroom (DNC Papers, NA).

18. Herbert Parmet, *Richard Nixon and His America*, 594–619; Alonzo Hamby, *Liberalism and Its Challengers*, 325–331.

19. *Congressional Record*, 91st Congress, 2nd session (March 20, 1970), 8381–8384; 92nd Congress, 1st session (December 4, 1971), 44765–44767.

20. Herbert Parmet, *Richard Nixon and His America*, 595–597; *Time* (February 23, 1970), 14–17; (March 9, 1970), 9–16; (March 21, 1973), 12–13.

21. *Congressional Quarterly* (December 11, 1970), 2953–2957; *Congress and the Nation*, vol. III, 512–517; Also see: *Congressional Record*, 91st Congress, 2nd Session (February 5, 1970), 2546–2559; (February 10 1970), 3105–3107; (February 17, 1970), 3560–3565, 3576–3579, 3587–3591; (February 18, 1970), 3786–3789, 3791–3794; (March 24, 1970), 8890–8899; (April 1, 1970), 9999–10004.

22. *Congressional Record*, 91st Congress, 2nd Session (February 18, 1970), 3801–3806; (February 19, 1970), 4132–4134, 4136–4139; (February 28, 1970), 5387–5389, 5396–5398.

23. New York *Times*, February 10, 1970; Washington *Post*, February 10, 1970.

24. New York *Times*, February 19, 1970; Washington *Post*, February 19, 1970; *Time*, April 2, 1970.

25. Mondale interview.

26. The committee produced thirty-six volumes of testimony and more than a dozen special studies on a wide range of issues related to desegregation.

27. Minneapolis *Tribune*, June 11, 1970; June 21, 1969; July 3, 1970; July 14, 1970; July 19, 1970; July 20, 1970; September 1, 1970.

28. Mondale, "Busing in Perspective," *New Republic* (March 4, 1972), pp. 16–19; Washington *Post*, February 19, 1972; Minneapolis *Tribune*, February 19, 1972.

29. Los Angeles *Times*, March 1, 1972; New York *Times*, February 20, 1972.

30. Mondale interview; Smith interview.

31. Stewart Alsop, "The Big, Ugly Sleeper," *Newsweek* (October 18, 1971), 130. For the best account of one of the most heated busing debates, see: J. Anthony Lukas, *Common Ground*.

32. Berman to Senator, December 16, 1972 (MP-MHS).

33. Minnesota Poll published in the Minneapolis *Tribune,* March 3, 1968 and June 15, 1969; Richard Scammon and Ben Wattenberg, *The Real Majority,* 230–231; Carl Solberg, *Humphrey,* 418–419.

34. Oliver Quayle, "A Survey of the 1972 U.S. Senate Race in Minnesota," August 1972 (MP-MHS).

35. Mondale interview.

36. Richard Rogin, "Joe Kelly Has Reached His Boiling Point," in Murray Freedman, *Overcoming Middle-Class Rage;* Brendan Sexton, "Middle Class Workers and the New Politics," *Dissent* (May–June 1969), 231–38; Kevin Phillips, *The Emerging Republican Majority;* Richard Schier, "Can the Democrats Learn from Defeat?" *Intellect* (July–August, 1975), 13–16; John Stewart, *One Last Chance: The Democratic Party, 1974–76,* 3–36; Richard Scammon and Ben Wattenberg, *The Real Majority,* 21; Theodore White, *The Making of the President, 1972,* 149; *Time* (July 17, 1972), 10–16; *Newsweek* (July 24, 1972), 32–40.

37. Mondale interview.

38. Minneapolis *Tribune,* June 13, 1972, June 25, 1972; Minneapolis *Star* October 17, 1972.

39. St. Paul *Pioneer Press,* June 11, 1972.

40. Transcripts of Mondale-Hansen debates, October 16–18, 1972 (MP-MHS).

41. Berman to Mondale, n.d. (MP-MHS); Staff meeting notes, June 26 and July 15, 1972 (MP-MHS); Carp to Senator, "Personal Thoughts about the Final Report," n.d. (MP-MHS).

42. Washington *Post,* January 14, 1973.

43. Berman to Mondale, "Analysis of 1972 election," n.d. (MP-MHS).

44. Berman to Senator, January 10, 1973; Mondale notes, n.d. (MP-MHS).

45. Harry McPherson, *A Political Education,* 475–476.

8. Searching for Common Ground

1. New York *Times,* November 8 and 13, 1972.

2. Albert Eisele, "Walter Mondale: Has He Ever Been Tested?" *Atlantic* (December 1974), 82–86; TRB, "Is Mondale the One?" *New Republic* (October 13, 1973), 8; Walter Pincus, "The Talk of Mondale in '76," *New Republic* (November 18, 1972), 15–16; Robert Coles, "Mondale of Minnesota," *New Republic* (December 25, 1971), 21; Minneapolis *Tribune,* October 29, 1972.

3. Doris Kearns Goodwin, "Second Lady," *Ladies Home Journal* (June 1977), 56–64, 144–46; Joan Mondale interview.

4. Joan Mondale, *Politics in Art.*

5. Mondale interview; New York *Times,* July 19, 1984.

6. Engelberg interview.

7. Tom Watson, "Liberal, Pragmatic Mondale Follows Careful Path to Power and Lead in Democratic Race," *Congressional Quarterly* (October 8, 1983), 2077–2083; Nelson interview; Culver interview.

8. Washington *Post,* March 1, 1974; Minneapolis *Tribune,* February 18, 1973.

9. Albert Eisele, "Walter Mondale: Has He Ever Been Tested?" *Atlantic* (December 1974), 82–86.

10. Herbert Stein, *Presidential Economics*, 133–208; Charles Morris, *A Time of Passion*, 157–181.

11. For general works on Watergate see: Bob Woodward and Carl Bernstein, *The Final Days;* Theodore White, *Breach of Faith;* and J. Anthony Lukas, *Nightmare: The Underside of the Nixon Years.*

12. Peter Edelman, "Mondale Office Organization and Substantive Issue Development," (MP-MHS).

13. Mondale interview.

14. Aaron interview.

15. Aaron to Mondale, March 29, 1974 (MP-MHS); Washington *Post,* July 10, 1974; November 18, 1974; New York *Times,* November 12, 1974.

16. *Congressional Record,* 93rd Congress, 2nd session (June 7, 1974), 18253; 94th Congress, 2nd session (June 2, 1975), 16468–16470.

17. Speech to Oklahoma City Democrats, March 9, 1974; Bowling Green State Address, March 1974 (MP-MHS).

18. Johnson interview.

19. Berman interview; Moe interview.

20. Minneapolis *Tribune,* November 22, 1974; St. Paul *Pioneer Press,* November 22, 1974.

21. Everett Carll Ladd, "Liberalism Upside Down: The Inversion of the New Deal Order," *Political Science Quarterly,* 91 (Winter 1976–77), 577–601; Ladd, "The Democrats Have Their Own Two-Party System," *Fortune* (October 1977), 212–223.

22. William Schneider, "JFK's Children: The Class of '74," *Atlantic Monthly* (March 1989), 35–58; Thomas Edsall, *The New Politics of Inequality,* 23–66; Burdett Loomis, *The New American Politician.*

23. For studies of recent electoral changes see: Norman Nie, et. al., *The Changing American Voter;* Everett Carll Ladd and Charles D. Hadley, *Transformations of the American Party System;* Richard Jensen, "Party Coalitions and the Search for Modern Values: 1820–1970," in Seymour Martin Lipset, *Party Coalitions in the 1980s,* 55–86; Martin Wattenberg, *The Decline of American Political Parties;* Thomas Edsall, *The New Politics of Inequality,* 23–66, 141–178.

24. David Broder, *The Party's Over: The Failure of Politics in America;* Anthony King, "The American Polity in the late 1970s: Building Coalitions in the Sand," and Austin Ranney, "The Political Parties: Reform and Decline," in Anthony King, *The New American Political System,* 371–396, 213–248; Nelson Polsby, *The Consequences of Party Reform.* On television, see: Austin Ranney, *Channels of Power,* 64–122; Thomas Patterson, *The Mass Media Election,* 173–82.

25. *Congressional Quarterly Almanac,* 1974, 145–153.

26. Moe interview; Mondale interview. Daniel Balz, "When the Man from Louisiana's There, It's a Long, Long Road to Tax Reform," *National Journal* (May 22, 1976), 690–695; "A Whole in the Bucket," *New Republic* (April 10, 1976), 5–7.

27. "Tax Muddle," *New Republic* (June 26, 1976), 3–5; TRB, "Knitting Loopholes," *New Republic* (July 31, 1976), 3; Daniel Balz, "Long Has Won the Battle But Will He Win the War?" *National Journal* (August 14, 1976), 1140–43. New York *Times,* July 19–26, 1976.

28. Senate Budget Committee, Mark-up Sessions, April 9–11 and November 5, 12, 1975; March 30, April 1, 1976. Budget Committee Archives, Dirksen Office Building, Washington D.C. New York *Times,* April 10–12, 1975.

29. Hugh Davis Graham, *The Civil Rights Era,* 27–73; Finlay Lewis, *Mondale,* 165–68.

30. *Congressional Record,* 94th Congress, 1st Session (February 20, 1975), 3840–3860; (February 21, 1975), 4119–20.

31. *Congressional Record,* 94th Congress, 1st Session (March 6, 1975), 5518–5526; (March 7, 1975), 5647–5649. *Congressional Quarterly* (March 1, 1975), 448–461; (March 8, 1975), 502–504; Michael Malbin, "Compromise by Senate Eases anti-Filibuster Rule," *National Journal* (March 13, 1976), 397–400.

32. Loch K. Johnson, *A Season of Inquiry,* 105, 153, 156, 229–230, 242–243.

33. U.S. Senate. Select Committee to Study Governmental Operations with Respect to Intelligence Activities, 94th Congress, 1st Session, vol 6, "Federal Bureau of Investigation," November 18, 19, December 2,3,9,10, and 11, 1975.

9. Fritz and Grits

1. Paul Wieck, "Long-Shot Jimmy Carter," *New Republic* (April 12, 1975), 16.

2. See: Jimmy Carter, *A Government as Good as Its People;* Walter Dean Burnham, "Jimmy Carter and the Democratic Crisis," *New Republic* (July 3–10, 1976), 17–19; *Time* (March 8, 1976), 15–20; *Newsweek* (December 1, 1975), 41–42.

3. Peter Steinfels, "Four Jimmy Carters," *Commonweal* (August 13, 1976), 520; Tom Powers, "Covering Carter," *Commonweal* (July 30, 1976), 501–3; James R. Wagner, "Carter: Outsider at the Threshold of Power," *Congressional Quarterly Weekly Report* (July 24, 1976), 1977–88; Vermont Royster, "The Enigmatic Man," *Wall Street Journal,* September 8, 1976; Albert Hunt, "The Vagueness Behind the Smile," *Wall Street Journal,* May 13, 1976; *Time* (May 10, 1976), 21–24 and (May 31, 1976), 12–15.

4. TRB, "Leap of Faith," *New Republic* (May 8, 1976), 8; John Dennis, "Jimmy Carter's Fierce Campaign," *Nation* (May 17, 1975), 592–96; E. Brooks Holifield, "Three Strands of Jimmy Carter's Religion," *New Republic* (June 5, 1976), 15–17.

5. For the best contemporary accounts of Carter's campaign see: Martin Schram, *Running for President,* 2–221; James T. Wooten, *Dasher: The Roots and Running of Jimmy Carter;* Jules Witcover, *Marathon.*

6. Jimmy Carter, *Keeping Faith,* 35–37; Jordan interview.

7. Mondale interview.

8. Witcover, *Marathon,* 359–364; Jordan interview, Powell interview.

9. Governor Carter and Mondale Issue Book, n.d. (MP-MHS).

10. Jordan interview; Mondale interview.

11. Los Angeles *Times,* July 16, 1976; *U.S. News and World Report,* July 26, 1976; Washington *Post,* July 18, 1976; *Time* (July 26, 1976), 25–26.

12. *Time* (July 26, 1976), 16; New York *Times,* July 18, 1976; Washington *Post,* July 18, 1976; Alan Ehrenhalt, "Harmonious Democrats Rally Behind Carter,"

Congressional Quarterly (July 17, 1976), 1867–1876; Witcover, *Marathon,* 368–70; "Garden Party," *Nation* (July 17, 1976), 36; Richard Rovere, "Letter from the Garden," *New Yorker* (July 26, 1976), 64–66 .

13. Jimmy Carter, *Keeping Faith,* 37; Washington *Post,* July 15, 1976.

14. Jimmy Carter, *Keeping Faith,* 37; Moe interview.

15. Video recording of Carter-Mondale Press Conference, July 16, 1976 (MP-MHS).

16. *Time* (July 26, 1976), 8–15; New York *Times,* July 16, 18, 1976; Washington *Post,* July 16, 18, 1976; John Farmer interview.

17. For general accounts of Carter's style and philosophy see: William Lee Miller, *Yankee from Georgia: The Emergence of Jimmy Carter;* Elizabeth Drew, *American Journal: The Events of 1976;* Betty Glad, *Jimmy Carter;* Robert Coles, "Jimmy Carter: Agrarian Rebel," *New Republic* (June 26, 1976), 14–19; Garry Wills, "Plains Truth," *Atlantic* (June 1976), 49–54.

18. Aaron to Mondale, "Jimmy Carter's Foreign Policy Position and Your Own," n.d. (MP-MHS).

19. New York *Times,* July 16, 1976; Minneapolis *Tribune,* July 16, 1976.

20. Mondale Acceptance Speech, July 15, 1976 (MP-MHS).

21. Carter Acceptance Speech, July 15, 1976 (MP-MHS).

22. Caddell to Carter, September 11, 1976, Powell Papers (CL).

23. New York *Times,* July 18, 1976; Johnson interview.

24. Ken Bode, "Closing the Carter Gap," *New Republic* (September 4, 1976), 18–21; *Time* (September 13, 1976), 11–14; "Strategy: Exploiting Carter's Weaknesses," *National Journal* (August 28, 1976), 1200–1203; Witcover, *Marathon,* 530–542.

25. Witcover, *Marathon,* 545–46.

26. Witcover, *Marathon,* 546–570; *Time,* September 13, 1976 and October 11, 1976.

27. Moe to Mondale, September 10, 1976 (MP-MHS); Moe to Mondale, September 14, 1976 (MP-MHS).

28. Washington *Post,* September 3,7,8,9,17 and 24, 1976.

29. *U.S. News and World Report* (October 18, 1976), 29–30; Los Angeles *Times,* September 24 and October 11, 1976.

30. Los Angeles *Times,* September 24, 1976; *Time* (September 20, 1976), 20.

31. Witcover, *Marathon,* 612–15; Washington *Post,* October 16, 1976; New York *Times,* October 16, 1976.

32. Washington *Post,* October 19, 1976; *Time,* October 25, 1976.

33. Witcover, *Marathon,* 425–29.

34. Mondale interview.

35. Walter Dean Burnham, *The Current Crisis in American Politics,* 229–250; Norman Nie, et. al. *The Changing American Voter,* 357–388; "Carter Comes Through," *National Journal* (November 6, 1976), 1582–1606; Rhodes Cook, "Final Returns," *Congressional Quarterly* (December 18, 1976), 3332–36.

36. Caddell to Carter, December 21, 1976, Powell Papers (CL).

37. Arthur Schlesinger, Jr., "Is the Vice Presidency Necessary?" *Atlantic* (May 1974), 37–44. For other useful studies of the vice presidency see: Michael Dorman, *The Second Man;* Sol Barzman, *Madmen and Geniuses;* Michael Harwood, *In*

the Shadow of Presidents; Michael Turner, *The Vice President as Policy Maker;* Joel Goldstein, *The Modern American Vice Presidency;* Paul Light, *Vice-Presidential Power.*

38. Mondale interview; Moe to Mondale, November 30, 1976 (MP-MHS); Ted Van Dyk to Mondale, November 29, 1976 (MP-MHS); Mondale to Carter, "The Role of the Vice President in the Carter Administration," December 9, 1976 (MP-MHS).

39. Eizenstat interview; Mondale interview. Mondale's briefing notes for the Monday lunches with Carter and the Friday morning foreign policy breakfasts provided a valuable source for this study. The National Security Council provided the author with a security clearance to examine the notes, which are held at the National Archives in Washington, D.C. The lunch notes were prepared by chief-of-staff Richard Moe and listed items of particular concern to Mondale's staff. The Friday notes were prepared by Mondale's national security advisor Denis Clift. Neither Moe nor Clift solicited Mondale's advice before writing the notes. As a result the notes do not always reflect Mondale's position on particular issues or provide insight into the Vice President's discussions with Carter. The author has used the notes to characterize Mondale's point of view only when they have been cooberated by evidence from personal interviews and White House documents. The Monday meetings will be cited as "Lunch Notes," (MP-NA); the Friday discussions as "Breakfast Notes," (MP-NA).

40. Berman interview; Eizenstat interview; Mondale interview.

41. Eizenstat interview; Berman interview.

42. Mondale notes, n.d. (MP-MHS).

43. Bert Lance, *Truth of the Matter,* 82.

44. Mondale interview; Johnson interview.

45. Mondale interview.

46. Mondale interview; Gaddis Smith, *Morality, Reason and Power,* 41–42; Zbigniew Brzezinski, *Power and Principle,* 42–43.

47. Mondale interview; Johnson interview; Aaron interview.

10. Democratic Dilemma

1. Los Angeles *Times,* April 12, 1977.

2. *Newsweek* (November 22, 1976), 15; *Time* (November 22, 1976), 16–17.

3. Dom Bonafede, "Carter and Congress — It Seems that 'If Something Can go Wrong, it Will,' " *National Journal* (November 12, 1977), 1756–1761; Thomas Edsall, "Congress Turns Rightward," *Dissent* (Winter, 1978), 12; *Time* (January 23, 1978), 8–16. For the best single volume on Carter and Congress see: Charles O. Jones, *The Trusteeship Presidency: Jimmy Carter and the United States Congress.*

4. Eizenstat to President-Elect Carter, November 14, 1976, Powell Papers (CL) Box 4.

5. *Time* (May 16, 1977), 15–16; *U.S. News and World Report,* June 6, 1977, 53; Ken Bode, "The George and Jimmy Show," *New Republic* (May 21, 1977), 28–35; Adam Clymer, "Promises, Promises: Home to Roost in the White House," *Nation* (March 12, 1977), 295–98; "Liberals and Carter," *Progressive* (July 1977), 5–6; George McGovern, "Memo to the White House," *Harpers* (October 1977), 33–35; Washington *Post,* May 8, 1977.

6. Haynes Johnson, *In the Absence of Power*, 154–68; Jack Germond, "Congress and Carter: Who's in Charge," *New York Times Magazine* (January 30, 1977), 22; John Osborne, "Carter and Congress," *New Republic* (March 5, 1977), 15–17; Robert Shogan, *Promises to Keep*, 204–14; Bob Rankin, "Carter's Energy Plan: A Test of Leadership," *Congressional Quarterly Weekly Report* (April 23, 1977), 727–32.

7. Mondale interview.

8. Mondale interview; Smith to Mondale, March 21, 1977 (MP-MHS); Smith to Berman, July 25, 1977 (MP-MHS); Smith to Moe, February 16, 1978 (MP-MHS); Frank Moore, Dan Tate and Bill Cable to the President, n.d., Jordan Papers, Box 34 (CL); Mondale to President, February 14, 1977 (MP-MHS); "Senate Democratic Caucus—Notes," n.d. (MP-MHS).

9. Mondale interview.

10. Farmer interview.

11. Mondale interview; Carter to Powell, n.d., Powell Papers, Box 39 (CL).

12. In response Mondale initiated an agenda process that the President used to establish legislative priorities for the next three years. He asked the Secretaries of each department to submit to him their priorities for the following year grouped in four categories: presidential, White House, Cabinet official, and agency priority. Mondale helped synthesize the suggestions and presented the final proposal to the President. See: Mondale interview; Smith interview; Staff to Vice President, August 29, 1977 (MP-MHS); Moe and Harrison to Vice President, October 26, 1977 (MP-MHS); Vice President to Executive Committee Members, n.d. (MP-MHS); Mondale, "Lunch Notes," March 7, 1977 March 21, 1977, October 11, 1977 (MP-NA).

13. Powell to President, January 16, 1978, Powell Papers, Box 39 (CL); Jordan to Carter, n.d., Jordan Papers, Box 37 (CL); Carter to Senior Staff, January 24, 1978, Powell Papers, Box 39 (CL).

14. Mondale interview; Farmer interview; Smith interview; Mondale "Lunch Notes," February 24, 1978 (MP-NA). "Lunch Notes," July 22, 1977 (MP-NA).

15. McGeorge Bundy, "Issue Before the Court: Who Gets ahead in America?" *Atlantic* (November 1977), 41–50; Nathan Letwin, "Bakke's Brief," *New Republic* (October, 1977), 17–18; Paul Delany, "Bakke case: Testing the Liberal Alliance," *Nation* (November 12, 1977), 498–99; "Meritocracy and its Discontents: a Symposium," *New Republic* (October 15, 1977), 5–9.

16. Jordan to President, n.d., Eizenstat Papers (CL); Lipshutz and Eizenstat to President, September 6, 1977, Eizenstat Papers (CL); Eizenstat and Lipshutz to President and Vice President, September 10, 1977, Eizenstat Papers (CL); Eizenstat and Lipshutz to President and Vice President, September 16, 1977, Eizenstat Papers (CL); Mondale interview; Eizenstat interview.

17. Eizenstat interview; Mondale interview.

18. The bill's signing ceremony, scheduled just days before the mid-term congressional elections, became a subject of controversy between the Carter and Mondale staffs. Since Mondale was the leading force in the administration behind the bill, Rafshoon suggested that the Vice President preside at a ceremony celebrating the bill's signing and that the affair take place in Minnesota, not Washington. Drawing a clear line between the Mondale and Carter camps, Rafshoon

wrote "let them" show their support; "we" should keep our distance. Rafshoon sent the memo for the President's attention, but it also circulated through Mondale's office. The Vice President was furious with Rafshoon's attempt to divide the White House staff into rival camps of liberals and conservatives. After confronting Rafshoon about the problem he complined directly to the President. Mondale interview; Rafshoon interview; Eisele to Powell, September 7, 1977, Powell Papers, Box 47 (CL). On the legislation itself see: John Osborne, "Dealing for Jobs," *New Republic* (November 12, 1977), 6–7; "Guaranteed Jobs for Economists," *New Republic* (December 17, 1977), 5–6.

19. Mondale interview; Rafshoon interview; Moe interview.

20. William Safire, "Lancegate: Why Carter Stuck it Out," *New York Times Magazine* (October 16, 1977), 37–39; *Newsweek* (September 19, 1977) 24–6 and (October 3, 1977), 35; "Dumping Bert," *New Republic* (September 1977), 8.

21. Rafshoon interview; Powell to President, September 28, 1977, Powell Papers, Box 39 (CL); Jordan to President, September 29, 1977, Powell Papers, Box 39 (CL). For examples of positive Mondale stories see: New York *Times,* April 24, 1977; Philadelphia *Inquirer,* September 18, 1977; Washington *Post,* June 12, 1977; Brock Brower, "The Remaking of the Vice President," New York *Times Magazine,* June 5, 1977; Finlay Lewis, "Mondale: New Style, New Power," Minneapolis *Tribune Sunday Magazine,* July 10, 1977.

22. Powell to President, September 28, 1977, Powell Papers, Box 39 (CL); Jordan to President, September 29, 1977, Powell Papers, Box 39 (CL); *Newsweek* October 10, 1977.

23. "Administration Under Siege," *New Republic,* October 22, 1977, 5–6; *Time* (October 17, 1977), 8–9; "Bad Day all Around: Lance Affair," *Nation* (October 1, 1977), 290; Elizabeth Drew, "Reporter at Large," *New Yorker* (October 10, 1977), 156–62; Haynes Johnson, *In the Absence of Power,* 199–214.

24. Miller interview.

25. New York *Times,* February 1, 1978.

26. For a thoughtful discussion of the inflation problem see: Charles Schultze to President, March 14, 1978, Eizenstat Papers, Box 144 (CL).

27. Eizenstat interview; Schultze interview.

28. Farmer interview.

29. Mondale interview.

30. Eizenstat interview; Mondale interview; Mondale to President, September 6, 1977 (MP-MHS).

31. Mondale interview.

32. The analysis that follows is drawn primarily from Mondale's April 1978, memorandum to the President entitled "Observations on Your Presidency." It has been supplemented with interviews with Mondale and all of his key staff people.

33. Jordan interview.

34. Farmer to Vice President, May 12, 1978 (MP-MHS); Farmer to Vice president, June 5, 1978 (MP-MHS); Eizenstat interview; Farmer to Vice President, June 8, 1978 (MP-MHS).

35. Mondale interview.

36. Mondale interview; McIntyre interview.

37. McIntyre interview.

38. "When in Doubt, Dump on Carter," *New Republic* (April 29, 1978), 5–6; Patrick Buchanan, "Why Carter Must Go," *Rolling Stone* (June 15, 1978), 18; Marshal Frady, "Why He's Not the Best," New York *Review of Books* (May 18, 1978), 18–23; Tad Szulc, "Our Most Ineffectual Postwar President," *Saturday Review* (April 29, 1978), 10–15; *Time* (June 19, 1978), 28.

39. Powell interview; McIntyre interview; Rafshoon interview; Rafshoon to President, September 1, 1978, Powell Papers, Box 50 (CL).

40. Eizenstat and Ginsberg to President, September 29, 1978, Eizenstat Papers, Box 145 (CL); Eizenstat to President, October 2, 1978, Eizenstat Papers, Box 145 (CL); Eizenstat to President, October 19, 1978, Eizenstat Papers, Box 145 (CL); Secretary of Labor to President, September 18, 1978, Eizenstat Papers, Box 145 (CL); Eizenstat, Jordan, Wexler to President, September 9, 1978, Powell Papers, Box 50 (CL); Califano to Attorney General, September 18, 1978, Eizenstat Papers, Box 145 (CL); Schultze to President, September 26, 1978, Eizenstat Papers, Box 145 (CL); Mondale, "Lunch Notes," December 8, 1978 (MP-NA).

41. Eizenstat notes; Mondale interview.

42. Carp and Harrison to Vice President, December 1978 (MP-MHS).

43. Washington *Post,* December 10, 1978; New York *Times,* December 10, 1978.

44. Washington *Post,* December 11, 1978; Ken Bode, "Miniconvention," *New Republic* (December 23, 1978), 13–15.

45. Washington *Post,* December 10–11, 1978.

46. Mondale interview.

47. Washington *Post,* December 11, 1978; New York *Times,* December 11, 1978.

48. New York *Times,* May 6, 1977; Harry Kelly, "Any Office But the Oval One," Chicago *Tribune Magazine* (September 18, 1977), 26–27, 44,47–49; Martin Tolchin, "The Mondales: Making the Most of Being Number 2," New York *Times Magazine* (February 26, 1978), 15.

49. New York *Times,* February 1, 1978.

50. Doris Kearns Goodwin, "Second Lady," *Ladies Home Journal* (June 1977), 56–64, 144–146.

51. Joan Mondale interview; Finlay Lewis, *Mondale,* 230–240.

52. Finlay Lewis, *Mondale,* 235; Martin Tolchin, "The Mondales: Making the Most of Being Number 2," *New York Times Magazine* (February 26, 1978), 17; Mary Lynn Kotz, "Washington's 'Joan of Art,' " *ARTnews* (September 1978), 46–55.

53. St. Louis *Post-Dispatch,* July 1, 1977; Boston *Globe,* December 31, 1978; *Newsday,* December 3, 1978; *Newsweek* (October 10, 1977), 31.

54. Boston *Globe,* December 31, 1978.

11. In the Shadow of Vietnam

1. Mondale interview; New York *Times,* January 23, 1977.

2. Clift to Moe, July 14, 1977 (MP-MHS); "Vice President Mondale Visits Europe and Japan; Remarks and Addresses," *Department of State Bulletin* (Novem-

ber 7, 1977), 181–97; Washington *Post*, February 11, 1977; New York *Times*, January 25–31, 1977; Los Angeles *Times*, January 25–31, 1977.

3. New York *Times*, January 31 and February 1, 1977; Washington *Post*, February 2, 1977.

4. Address by President Jimmy Carter at the University of Notre Dame, May 22, 1977, reprinted in *Weekly Compilation of Presidential Documents*, 13 (May 30, 1977), 773–79.

5. Clift to Moe, November 14, 1978 (MP-MHS); Mondale interview; Johnson interview; Aaron interview.

6. Haynes Johnson, *In the Absence of Power*, 154–68; Robert Shogan, *Promises to Keep*, 215–24. For the best general works on Carter's foreign policy see: Gaddis Smith, *Morality, Reason and Power;* John Lewis Gaddis, *Strategies of Containment;* George Moffett, *The Limits of Victory.* Also of great value are the memoirs of administration members, especially Zbignew Brzezinski, *Power and Principle;* Jimmy Carter, *Keeping Faith;* and Cyrus Vance, *Hard Choices.*

7. Brzezinski, *Power and Principle*, 39–50; Vance, *Hard Choices*, 256–283. Stanley Karnow, "Carter and Human Rights," *Saturday Review* (April 2, 1977), 6–11; Norman Cousins, "Bribery and Human Rights," *Saturday Review* (April 2, 1977), 4; Sandy Vogelgesany, *American Dream, Global Nightmares.*

8. "Lunch Notes," April 22, 1977 (MP-NA).

9. Washington *Post*, May 16, 1977; Mondale interview.

10. Finlay Lewis, *Mondale*, 221–23; *Newsweek* (May 30, 1977), 16–17; *Time* (May 30, 1977), 34; "Vice President Mondale visits Europe and meets with South African Prime Minister Vorster," *Department of State Bulletin* (June 20, 1977), 659–66; Mondale interview.

11. *U.S. News and World Report* (May 30, 1977), 31; Lewis, 221–23; Mondale interview.

12. Mondale press Conference, May 20, 1977 (MP-MHS); Vance, *Hard Choices*, 265–66.

13. Cabinet Meeting Minutes, June 1977 (MP-MHS); Mondale Foreign Policy Breakfast Notes, June 5, 1977 (MP-NA). Hereafter cited as "Breakfast Notes." Washington *Post*, May 20, 1977.

14. Washington *Post*, February 15, 1977; March 27, 1977; New York *Times*, June 10, 1977; "Carter at Sea," *National Review* (April 1, 1977), 371.

15. Cabinet Meeting Minutes, June 1977 (MP-MHS); "Breakfast Notes," June 5, 1977 (MP-NA); Washington *Post*, March 25, July 9, and November 21, 1977.

16. William Quandt, *Camp David Peacemaking and Politics*, 30–62; Brzezinski, *Power and Principle*, 83–94; Vance, *Hard Choices*, 159–95; Jimmy Carter, *Keeping Faith*, 273–318; Steven Spiegel, "Carter and Israel," *Commentary* (July, 1977), 35–40; Morton Kondracke, "Jimmy and Menachem," *New Republic* (July 30, 1977), 13–15.

17. Eizenstat notes; Mondale interview.

18. "Lunch notes," June 10, 1977 (MP-NA); Mondale speech to the Northern California World Affairs Club, June 17, 1977 (MP-MHS).

19. Washington *Post*, June 18, 1977; New York *Times*, June 18, 1977.

20. New York *Times*, October 2–3, 1977; *Newsweek*, October 17, 1977.

21. Mondale interview; "Lunch notes," October 11, 1977 (MP-NA).

22. Ken Bode, "Carter and the Canal," *New Republic* (January 14, 1978), 8–10; Gaddis Smith, *Morality, Reason and Power, 109–113*.

23. Gaddis Smith, *Morality, Reason and Power*, 109–132; George Moffett, *The Limits of Victory*, 112–137; Jimmy Carter, *Keeping Faith*, 152–85; Vance, *Hard Choices*, 140–58; Washington *Post*, August 11, 1977; August 23, 1977.

24. Smith to Mondale, August 1977 (MP-MHS); Mondale to Carter, August 1977 (MP-MHS); "Lunch notes," August 19 and 27, 1977 (MP-MHS).

25. New York *Times*, March 18, 1977.

26. Mondale interview.

27. Jimmy Carter, *Keeping Faith*, 183–85; New York *Times*, April 21, 1978; Robert Shrum, "Narrow Passage of the Canal Treaty," *New Times* (May 15, 1978), 6–7; "Panama Fever; Senate Vote," *Nation* (April 8, 1978), 388; Ronald Steel, "Rough Passage," New York *Review of Books* (March 23, 1978), 10.

28. Aaron interview; Moe interview; Mondale interview; "Lunch notes," (MP-NA), November 11, 1978.

29. These comments were included in the Vice President's April memo entitled "Observations on Your Presidency."

30. Mondale interview.

31. Mondale interview.

32. Mondale interview; Holbrooke interview; Raymond Bonner, *Waltzing With a Dictator*, 230–231.

33. Walter F. Mondale, "America's Role in Southern Asia and the Pacific," *Department of State Bulletin* (July 1978), 22–25; Washington *Post*, May 3–5, 1978; New York *Times*, May 8, 1978.

34. Mondale interview; Aaron interview.

35. Mondale interview; Holbrooke interview; Bonner, *Waltzing With a Dictator*, 246.

36. "Damn the Refugees and Full Speed Ahead," *Commonweal* (September 1978), 49–50; *Newsweek* (April 17, 1978), 70; New York *Times*, May 5, 1978; Vance, *Hard Choices*, 125–26; "Emergency," *New Republic* (June 30, 1979), 5–8.

37. Thomas Powers, "Unwanted," *Commonweal* (June 27, 1979), 360–62.

38. Holbrooke interview.

39. Aaron interview; Mondale interview.

40. Mondale interview.

41. Los Angeles *Times*, July 19–21, 1979; Mondale interview; Holbrooke interview; Aaron interview.

42. Holbrooke interview; Los Angeles *Times*, July 21, 1979; Boston *Globe*, July 21, 1979; Washington *Post*, July 21–24, 1979.

43. Vance, *Hard Choices*, 126; Mondale Geneva Speech, July 21, 1979 (MP-MHS); Los Angeles *Times*, July 22, 1979.

44. Gaddis Smith, *Morality, Reason and Power*, 163–65; Jimmy Carter, *Keeping Faith*, 304–13; Zbignew Brzezinski, *Power and Principle*, 247–52.

45. Mondale interview; Eizenstat interview.

46. Mondale interview; Finlay Lewis, *Mondale*, 237–238.

47. Mondale Speech, July 1, 1978 (MP-MHS); *Newsweek* (July 10, 1978), 34.

48. *Time* (July 17, 1978), 20; *Newsweek* (July 17, 1978), 47–48; New York *Times*, July 3–4, 1978; Washington *Post*, July 4, 1978.

49. Mondale interview; Vance interview; Jimmy Carter, *Keeping Faith,* 315.

50. Clift to Moe, November 14, 1978 (MP-MHS); Eizenstat interview.

51. Eizenstat notes; Bookbinder interview; Eizenstat interview.

52. William Quandt, *Camp David Peacemaking and Politics,* 198–201; Eizenstat notes.

53. William Quandt, *Camp David Peacemaking and Politics,* 197; Eizenstat notes; Vance interview; Eizenstat interview.

54. Eizenstat notes; Mondale interview.

55. For the best accounts of the Camp David negotiations see: Jimmy Carter, *Keeping Faith,* 319–404; Vance, *Hard Choices,* 219–226; and William Quandt, *Camp David,* 206–258.

56. William Quandt, *Camp David,* 256; Mondale interview.

57. William Quandt, *Camp David,* 256.

58. Mondale interview.

59. Aaron interview; Brzezinski interview; Vance interview.

60. For contemporary accounts of the Brzezinski-Vance debate see: Marilyn Berger, "Vance and Brzezinski: Peaceful Coexistence or Guerrilla War?" New York *Times Magazine* (February 13, 1977), 19–25; Tad Szulc, "The Vance-Brzezinski Squabble," *Saturday Review* (July 8, 1978), 18–19; Washington *Post,* June 2,8, 1978; New York *Times,* April 17, 1978.

61. Hunter interview; Aaron interview; "Lunch notes," June 12, 1978 (MP-NA); "Breakfast notes," June 1, 1978 (MP-NA).

62. Hunter interview; Aaron interview; Mondale interview.

63. Brzezinski, *Power and Principle,* 33–35.

64. Vance, *Hard Choices,* 45–63; I.F. Stone, "Carter, Africa, and SALT," New York *Review of Books* (July 20, 1978), 22–27.

65. Vance, *Hard Choices,* 91–92; Zbignew Brzezinski, *Power and Principle,* 178–190; Mondale interview.

66. Washington *Post,* May 25, 1978; Mondale interview.

67. *Newsweek* (February 19, 1979), 32–3; (May 21, 1979), 36–50; *Time* (July 23, 1979), 32–3.

68. Smith to Mondale, August 13, 1979 (MP-MHS).

69. Smith to Mondale, June 4, 1979 (MP-MHS); Beckel and Smith to Mondale, May 8, 1979 (MP-MHS).

70. Washington *Post,* July 17, 1978; New York *Times,* July 19, 1979.

71. Brzezinski, *Power and Principle,* 333–34, 336–38; Strobe Talbott, *Endgame,* 158–61, 167–76.

72. Mondale interview.

73. Vance, *Hard Choices,* 78; Brzezinski, *Power and Principle,* 196.

74. Brzezinski, *Power and Principle,* 202–208; Vance, *Hard Choices,* 114–116; Moe/Clift to Mondale, December 18, 1978 (MP-MHS); "Lunch notes," January 10, 1979 (MP-NA).

75. Brzezinski, *Power and Principle,* 408–19.

76. Vance interview; Brzezinski interview; Brzezinski, *Power and Principle,* 416–18.

77. Holbrooke interview; Mondale interview; Aaron interview; "Breakfast notes," August 2, 16, 1979 (MP-NA).

78. Brzezinski, *Power and Principle*, 415–18; Gaddis Smith, *Morality, Reason and Power*, 91–94; Mondale interview.

79. Mondale interview; Aaron interview; Washington *Post*, August 26, 1979.

80. "Vice President Mondale Visit to East Asia; Remarks and Toasts," *Department of State Bulletin* (October 1979), 10–13; New York *Times*, August 28, 1979; Washington *Post*, August 28, 1979; Chang Hu, "What Is behind U.S. Vice President Mondale's Visit to Mainland China?" *Issues and Studies* (October 1979), 4–7.

81. *Newsweek* (September 10, 1979), 35; *Time* (September 10, 1979), 40; Washington *Post*, August 29 - September 1, 1979; Mondale interview.

82. Brzezinski, *Power and Principle*, 418–19; Vance, *Hard Choices*, 115; Mondale interview.

83. *Newsweek*, February 26, 1979.

84. Gaddis Smith, *Morality, Reason and Power*, 245; Stanley Hoffman, "View from Home: the Perils of Incoherence," *Foreign Affairs* (February 1979), 463–91; Thomas L. Hughes, "Carter and the Management of Contradiction," *Foreign Policy* (Summer 1978).

85. Mondale interview.

12. *Crisis*

1. Mondale to Carter, January 12, 1979 (MP-MHS); Mondale, "Lunch Notes," January 15, 1979 (MP-NA).

2. Washington *Post*, January 24, 1979; New York *Times*, January 24, 1979.

3. Washington *Post*, January 24–25, 1979; New York *Times*, January 25, 1979.

4. Eizenstat notes; Blumenthal to President, March 16, 1979 (MP-MHS); Farmer and Harrison to Mondale, March 17, 1979 (MP-MHS); Farmer to Vice President, June 2, 1979 (MP-MHS).

5. Los Angeles *Times*, March 3, 1979.

6. Mondale interview; Farmer to Mondale, March 7, 1979 (MP-MHS); Farmer to Mondale, May 8, 1979 (MP-MHS).

7. Robert Shrum, "Drafting of a President," *New Times* (July 30, 1979), 31–35; Richard Reeves, "Inevitability of Teddy," *Esquire* (February 13, 1979), 6; Caddell to President, June 11, 1979, Jordan Papers, Box 33 (CL); Cambridge Survey Research to Democratic National Committee, May 25, 1979, Jordan Papers, Box 33.

8. Mondale interview.

9. Theodore White, *America In Search of Itself*, 260–64.

10. Moe to Mondale, January 29, 1979 (MP-MHS); Mondale interview; Eizenstat notes.

11. Cambridge Survey Research to Democratic National Committee, May 25, 1979, Jordan papers, Box 33; Moe to Mondale, June 9, 1978 (MP-MHS).

12. Johnson interview; Berman interview; Moe interview; Eisele to staff, February 6, 1979 (MP-MHS).

13. Eizenstat interview; Mondale interview.

14. Joan Mondale interview; Joan Mondale diary.

15. Mondale interview; Mondale, "Lunch notes," June 19, 1979 (MP-NA); Griffin Bell, *Taking Care of the Law*, 24–27; Carp and Harrison to Mondale, May 7, 1979 (MP-MHS); Carp and Harrison to Vice President, June 8, 1979 (MP-MHS); Carp and Harrison to Vice President, June 14, 1979 (MP-MHS); Vice President to President, June 19, 1979 (MP-MHS).

16. Moe interview; Johnson interview; *Newsweek* (July 9, 1979), 29; Theodore White, *America In Search of Itself*, 260–64.

17. Caddell, "Of Crisis and Opportunity," April 23, 1979, Powell papers, Box 40 (CL); Jordan and Mondale to President, June 28, 1979, Jordan papers, Box 33 (CL).

18. Mondale to President, July 3, 1979 (MP-MHS).

19. The best contemporary account of the debates at Camp David is Elizabeth Drew's, "A Reporter at Large," *New Yorker* (August 27, 1979), 45–73; also Stuart Eizenstat took detailed notes of the discussions which are in the author's possession.

20. Eizenstat notes; Elizabeth Drew, "A Reporter at Large," *New Yorker* (August 27, 1979), 45–73.

21. Eizenstat notes.

22. Elizabeth Drew, "A Reporter at Large," *New Yorker* (August 27, 1979), 45–73; Mondale interview; Rafshoon interview; Eizenstat interview.

23. Mondale interview; Carter letter to author, July 1988.

24. Mondale interview.

25. Eizenstat notes; Theodore White, *America In Search of Itself*, 265–68; Jules Witcover and Jack Germond, *Blue Smoke and Mirrors*, 30–36; Haynes Johnson, *In the Absence of Power*, 313–14.

26. New York *Times*, July 16, 1979; Theodore White, *America In Search of Itself*, 268–69.

27. Washington *Post*, July 17, 1979; Witcover and Germond, *Blue Smoke and Mirrors*, 37.

28. Witcover and Germond, *Blue Smoke and Mirrors*, 38–41; Mondale interview.

29. Rafshoon to President, n.d., Jordan Papers, Box 33 (CL).

30. Eizenstat notes.

31. Haynes Johnson, *In the Absence of Power*, 313–15; Washington *Post*, July 20, 1979; New York *Times*, July 20, 1979; Los Angeles *Times*, July 20, 1979; *Time* (July 30, 1979), 10–11; Theodore White, *America In Search of Itself*, 269–70.

32. Washington *Post*, July 29, 1979.

33. Jordan interview; *Time* (September 17, 1979), 33.

13. Challenge and Defeat

1. Theodore White, *America In Search of Itself*, 270–75; Witcover and Germond, *Blue Smoke and Mirrors*, 48–52; Elizabeth Drew, *Portrait of an Election*, 49–87.

2. Mondale to Jordan, January 24, 1979 (MP-MHS) Mondale, "Lunch notes," July 31, 1979 (MP-NA).

3. Mondale to Jordan, August 1979 (MP-MHS); Mondale interview.

4. Jordan interview; Rafshoon interview; Witcover and Germond, *Blue Smoke and Mirrors*, 51–53.

5. Brzezinski, *Power and Principle*, 346–52; Jimmy Carter, *Keeping Faith*, 263–64; *Time* (October 15, 1979), 43–45.

6. Eizenstat notes; Strobe Talbott, *Endgame*, 285.

7. Mondale interview.

8. Washington *Post*, November 8, 1979.

9. Mondale interview.

10. Mondale interview; Brzezinski, *Power and Principle*, 473–75; Carter, *Keeping Faith*, 435–46, 448, 454–57.

11. Mondale interview.

12. Mondale interview; Witcover and Germond, *Blue Smoke and Mirrors*, 79–84; White, *America In Search of Itself*, 15–18.

13. Brzezinski, *Power and Principle*, 426–37; Carter, *Keeping Faith*, 471–76.

14. Mondale interview; Carter, *Keeping Faith*, 476; Brzezinski, *Power and Principle*, 430–32.

15. John Judas, "Ted Kennedy's Faltering Campaign," *The Progressive* (February 1980), 19–21; Witcover and Germond, *Blue Smoke and Mirrors*, 85–88; Jeff Greenfield, *The Real Campaign*, 54–72.

16. *Newsweek* (April 7, 1980), 27–28; Elizabeth Drew, *Portrait of an Election*, 86; Dom Bonafede, "Mondale, the President's Preacher, Spreads the Gospel of Jimmy Carter," *National Journal* (December 1, 1979), 2012–2016; New York *Times*, January 12–13, 1980.

17. Greenfield, *The Real Campaign*, 70–73.

18. Drew, *Portrait of an Election*, 131–34; Mondale to President, January 1980 (MP-MHS).

19. Witcover and Germond, *Blue Smoke and Mirrors*, 141–65; White, *America In Search of Itself*, 275–97.

20. "Press Release," March 21, 1980, Vice President's Press Office, Box 94 (CL); Al Eisele to Vice President, April 14, 1980 (MP-MHS). New York *Times*, February 1, 1980; Washington *Post*, February 17, 1980; *Newsweek*, April 7, 1980.

21. Drew, *Portrait of an Election*, 64–67; *Newsweek* (April 7, 1980); New York *Times*, February 1, 1980.

22. Eizenstat notes; Drew, *Portrait of an Election*, 64–67; "Lunch notes," February 11, 26, and April 7 (MP-NA).

23. Eizenstat notes; Mondale, "Lunch notes," February 11, 1980, February 26, 1980.

24. Vice President to President, December 1979 (MP-MHS); Mondale interview; Johnson interview; Eizenstat interview.

25. Washington *Post*, March 15, 1980; New York *Times*, March 15, 1980.

26. Witcover and Germond, *Blue Smoke and Mirrors*, 154–55; Jeff Greenfield, *The Real Campaign*, 126–27; Elizabeth Drew, *Portrait of an Election*, 142–45.

27. Vance interview; Mondale interview. Vance claims that Mondale also wanted him to publicly censure the American ambassador at the U.N. for the vote. Mondale denies making the suggestion.

28. Mondale interview; New York *Times*, March 22, 1980.

29. Eizenstat notes; Mondale interview.

30. Cyrus Vance, *Hard Choices*, 408–11; Carter, *Keeping Faith*, 513.

31. Vance interview; Mondale interview.

32. Mondale interview.

33. "Lunch notes," April 25, 1980 (MP-NA); Carter, *Keeping Faith*, 519–21; Drew, *Portrait of an Election*, 179–80.

34. *Newsweek* (August 4 and 11, 1980), 21–22; *Time* (August 11, 1980), 14–19.

35. Greenfield, *The Real Campaign*, 82–94, 152–74; Drew, *Portrait of an Election*, 108–121.

36. Witcover and Germond, *Blue Smoke and Mirrors*, 228–42; Drew, *Portrait of an Election*, 147–57; Greenfield, *The Real Campaign*, 95–109.

37. Boston *Globe*, August 13, 1980.

38. "Notes of Speechwriters Meeting with Mondale," July 16, 1980 (MP-MHS).

39. Mondale 1980 Convention Speech, August 14, 1980 (Kaplan Papers).

40. Washington *Post*, August 15, 1980.

41. Washington *Post*, August 15, 1980.

42. Washington *Post*, August 15, 1980.

43. Vice President to President, July 15, 1980 (MP-MHS).

44. Vice President to President, July 15, 1980 (MP-MHS); "Lunch notes," May 23, 1980 (MP-NA).

45. Eizenstat to President, August 23, 1980, Eizenstat Papers, Box 192 (CL); Eizenstat notes; Mondale, "Lunch notes," August 26, 1980.

46. Eizenstat notes; Mondale interview.

47. Eizenstat notes.

48. Boston *Globe*, September 24, 1980; New York *Times*, September 21, 1980; Greenfield, *The Real Campaign*, 282–86; Elizabeth Drew, *Portrait of an Election*, 306–07.

49. Washington *Post*, September 2, 5, 23 and October 22, 1980; *Wall Street Journal*, September 24, 1980; New York *Times*, September 4 and October 21, 1980.

50. "Campaign Stump Speech," Fall 1980, Kaplan Papers; *Newsweek*, October 27, 1980, 38–39.

51. Rafshoon interview.

52. Hamilton Jordan, *Crisis*, 322–323; Washington *Post*, September 30, 1980.

53. White, *America In Search of Itself*, 385–87.

54. Drew, *Portrait of an Election*, 321–26; Greenfield, *The Real Campaign*, 226–247.

55. Mondale interview; Johnson interview; Minneapolis *Tribune*, November 5, 1980.

56. Mondale to Carter, January 13, 1981 (MP-MHS); Eizenstat notes; Mondale interview.

57. New York *Times*, January 21, 1981.

58. Rafshoon interview; McIntyre interview; Griffin Bell, *Taking Care of the Law*, 23–24.

59. Jimmy Carter, letter to author, July 1989.

60. Warren E. Miller and Teresa E. Levitin, *Leadership and Change;* Everett Carll Ladd, *Transformation of the American Party System;* Anthony King, "The

American Polity in the Late 1970s: Building Coalitions in the Sand," in *The New American Political System*, 372.

61. Earl Black and Merle Black, *Politics and Society in the South*, 232-58; V. O. Key, *Southern Politics in State and Nation*; John Hammond, "Race and Electoral Mobilization: White Southerners, 1952-1968," *Politics Quarterly*, #41 (1977), 13-27. For a dissenting perspective see: Harold W. Stanley, *Voter Mobilization and the Politics of Race*.

62. Thomas Edsall, " 'Rings' of White Anger," *Washington Post* (November 3, 1988); Mike Mallowe, "Coming Apart," *Philadelphia Magazine* (September 1989), 97; Mike Mallowe, "A Campaign in Black and White," *Philadelphia Magazine* (May 1987), 88; Dianne M. Pinderhughes, *Race and Ethnicity in Chicago Politics*; Paul Kleppner, *Chicago Elects a Black Mayor*.

63. *Newsweek* (March 10, 1980), 40; David Kusnet, "Black Depression," *New Republic* (November 24, 1979), 15-18.

64. Andrew Kopkind, "Black Power in the Age of Jackson," *Nation* (November 26, 1983) 521; Mark Kramer, "Jesse Jackson's New Math," *New York* (October 24, 1983), 36-39; Paul Delaney, "Voting: The New Black Power," *New York Times Magazine* (November 27, 1983), 34-39; Tom Wicker, "Blacks and 1984," *New York Times*, May 27, 1983; Christopher Madison, "Mondale Walks Tightrope to Hold Black Support Without Risking Jewish Vote," *National Journal* (September 8, 1984), 1654-58.

65. "Labor's Changing Profile," *Nation's Business* (April 1979), 31-35; Peter Pestillo, "Can Unions Meet the Needs of a 'New' Work Force?" *Monthly Labor Review* (February 1979), 33-34; Sidney Lens, "Disorganized Labor," *Nation* (February 24, 1979), 206-209; New York *Times*, September 5, 1982; Sidney Lens, "The American Labor Movement: Out of Joint with the Times," *In These Times* (February 18-24, 1981), 12-13; San Francisco *Chronicle*,September 18, 1981, 8.

66. Washington *Post*, December 11, 1978.

67. Walter Mondale, "Woodrow Wilson Speech," October, 1980 (MP-MHS).

14. The Message

1. New York *Times*, November 6, 1980; Washington *Post*, November 5, 1980.

2. New York *Times*, August 28, 1981; Adam Clymer, "The G.O.P. Bid for Majority Control," *New York Times Magazine* (June 14, 1981), 110-115; *Newsweek* (August 18, 1980), 21.

3. *Newsweek* (May 18, 1981), 38; Steven R. Weisman, "Reagan's First 100 Days," *New York Times Magazine* (April 26, 1981), 23.

4. "The New Gilded Age," *New Republic* (August 15, 1981), 5-6; New York *Times*, June 14, July 1, July 5, 1981; Richard Cohen, "Democrats Trying to Get Act Together to Confront Reagan's Budget Policy," *National Journal* (December 12, 1981), 2198-2202.

5. Tom Wicker, "Democrats in Search of Ideas," *New York Times Magazine* (January 25, 1981), 30-42; Richard Cohen, "Democrats Trying to Get Act Together to Confront Reagan's Budget Policy," *National Journal* (December 12, 1981), 2198-2202; Daniel Seligman, "The Search for a Liberal Agenda," *Fortune*

(August 24, 1981), 60–66. For the best general books on the 1984 presidential campaign see: William Henry, *Visions of America;* Elizabeth Drew, *Campaign Journal;* Jack Germond and Jules Witcover, *Wake Us When It's Over;* and Peter Goldman and Tony Fuller, *The Quest for the Presidency.* For the best scholarly analysis see: Gerald Pomper, *The Election of 1984: Reports and Interpretations* and *The American Elections of 1984,* edited by Austin Ranney.

    6. Columbus Ohio *Dispatch,* November 8, 1981; Finlay Lewis, *Mondale,* 248; William Henry *Visions of America,* 61.

    7. Mondale interview.

    8. Mondale to Johnson, September 13, 1981 (MP-MHS).

    9. Johnson interview; Mondale interview.

    10. Vaughn to Johnson, December 9, 1981 (JP).

    11. "Summary of Income Tax Returns of Walter F. and Joan A. Mondale," May 6, 1983 (MP-MHS).

    12. Torricelli to Mondale, June 1981 (MP-MHS); Morton Kondracke, "The Marathon Commences," *New Republic* (July 18, 1981), 21.

    13. Isaacs to Mondale, "Visibility Strategy II," August 31, 1981 (JP).

    14. "LBJ School of Public Affairs," transcript, May 23, 1981 (MP-MHS); "Columbia School of Business," transcript, November 11, 1981 (MP-MHS).

    15. "National Urban League," transcript, July 23, 1981 (MP-MHS); Los Angeles *Times,* November 15, 1981.

    16. Johnson, "Memorandum to 1982 Strategy Session Participants/Wye Plantation," n.d. (JP).

    17. Wye Plantation Meeting Notes, January 3–5, 1982 (MP-MHS); "Talking Points for the Wye Plantation," January 3, 1982 (MP-MHS); Harrison to Johnson, "Survey of Domestic Policy discussion at Wye Plantation," January 11, 1982 (MP-MHS).

    18. Galston interview.

    19. *Newsweek,* April 5, 1982, 17–28; *Time,* December 28, 1981, 64–65; William Grieder, "The Education of David Stockman," *Atlantic* (December 1981), 27–40.

    20. TRB, "Greed and Envy," *New Republic* (February 27, 1982), 6; Washington *Post,* November 25, 1981.

    21. Washington *Post* (February 7, 1982).

    22. Raleigh *Times,* March 2, 1982; New York *Times,* November 2, 1982; Minneapolis *Tribune,* March 10, 1982.

    23. The National Conference on Social Welfare, Boston, Massachusetts, April 27, 1982, transcript (MP-MHS); NAACP Convention, Boston, Massachusetts, July 1, 1982, transcript (MP-MHS); Democratic National Committee, Detroit, Michigan, July 14, 1983, transcript (MP-MHS); Constitutional Convention of the United Steelworkers of America, Atlantic City, New Jersey, transcript, September 22, 1982 (MP-MHS).

    24. Hansen to staff, February 22, 1982 (MP-MHS).

    25. Hansen interview.

    26. Walter Mondale, "The Reeducation of Walter Mondale," *New York Times Magazine* (November 3, 1982); Mondale interview.

    27. Morton Kondracke, "Fritz on Fire," *New Republic* (February 7, 1983), 14–17.

28. Mondale draft, June 6–7, 1982 (Martin Papers).

29. Martin to Mondale, June 7, 1982 (Martin Papers); Martin draft, n.d. (Martin Papers); Martin to Kaplan, June 11, 1982 (Kaplan Papers).

30. Kaplan to Mondale, June 15, 1982 (Kaplan Papers); Kaplan draft, n.d. (Kaplan Papers).

31. Mondale Democratic midterm convention speech, June 1982 (Kaplan Papers).

32. Philadelphia *Inquirer*, June 30, 1982; Washington *Post*, June 30, 1982).

33. Isaacs to Mondale, March 19, 1982 (MP-MHS).

34. Galston and Johnson to Mondale, July 19, 1982 (MP-MHS).

35. New York *Times*, November 3, 1982; Washington *Post*, October 31 and November 3, 1982; "Change the Course," *New Republic* (November 22, 1982), 7–8.

36. Peter Goldman and Tony Fuller, *The Quest for the Presidency*, 68–70.

37. Galston interview.

38. California Democratic Convention, Sacramento, California, transcript (January 15, 1983) (MP-MHS); Morton Kondracke, "Fritz on Fire," *New Republic* (February 7, 1983), 14–17; Washington *Post*, January 19, 1983.

39. Dom Bonafede, "Mondale at End of the Beginning of the Long Road to the Oval Office," *National Journal* (January 22, 1983), 162–165; Washington *Post*, January 6, 1983; Morton Kondracke, "Fritz on Fire," *New Republic* (February 7, 1983), 14.

40. Kaplan interview; Martin interview. Copies of the thirteen drafts of the speech are in the Kaplan Papers.

41. Martin interview. For a transcript of Mondale's meeting with his speech-writting staff see Kaplan Papers.

42. Presidential Announcement Address, St. Paul, Minnesota, February 21, 1983 (MP-MHS).

43. Boston *Globe*, February 25, 1983.

44. Washington *Post*, January 31, 1983.

45. On Glenn and other potential challengers see: William Henry, *Visions of America*, 48–86; Elizabeth Drew, *Campaign Journal*, 27–39; Peter Goldman and Tony Fuller, *The Quest for the Presidency*, 59–122; Jack Germond and Jules Witcover, *Wake Us When Its Over*, 36–62; New York *Times*, October 14, 1983.

46. Hamilton Jordan, "Mondale's Choice," *New Republic* (June 6, 1983), 15–19; Gregg Easterbrook, "The Perpetual Campaign," *Atlantic* (January 1983), 27–38.

47. Jack Germond and Jules Witcover, "All the Mondale Questions," *Washingtonian* (February 1983), 85–89; David Harris, "Understanding Mondale," *New York Times Magazine* (June 19, 1983), 29.

48. Elizabeth Drew, "A Political Journal," *New Yorker* (November 21, 1983); David Harris, "Understanding Mondale," *New York Times Magazine* (June 19, 1983), 26–37, 52–56; Sidney Blumenthal, "Made In Minnesota," *New Republic* (August 6, 1984), 16–19; New York *Times*, July 19, 1984; *Newsweek* (July 23, 1984), 41.

49. David Harris, "Understanding Mondale," *New York Times Magazine* (June

19, 1983), 29; Anthony Schmitz, "Lessons from the Prairie," Minneapolis *City Pages* (October 31, 1984), 7; *Newsweek* (January 9, 1984), 29.

50. New York *Times*, February 16, 1984; Morton Kondracke, "The Fritz Blitz," *New Republic* (May 2, 1983), 13−15.

51. Spiegel to Mondale, May 31, 1983 (MP-MHS); Aronson to Kaplan, June 3, 1983 (MP-MHS); McPherson to Johnson, May 24, 1983 (MP-MHS); Spence to Mondale, n.d. (MP-MHS); Kaplan interview; Johnson interview.

52. Aronson to Mondale, February 12, 1983 (MP-MHS); Moe to Mondale, March 10, 1983 (Moe Papers); Galston interview.

53. Aronson to Kaplan, June 3, 1983 (Kaplan Papers); McPherson to Johnson, May 24, 1983 (MP-MHS).

54. Kaplan to Mondale, May 25, 1983 (MP-MHS); Spence to Beckel, September 23, 1983 (Kaplan Papers); Spence, "Mondale Message Strategy," August 19, 1983 (Kaplan Papers); Spence, "Some Observations on Your Campaign Substance and Delivery," May 11, 1983 (MP-MHS).

55. Campaign Staff to Mondale, September 2, 1983 (Galston Papers); Kaplan interview; Galston interview.

56. Campaign Staff to Mondale, September 2, 1983 (Galston Papers).

57. Beckel interview; Johnson interview.

58. Mondale interview.

59. Johnson interview.

60. Sidney Blumenthal, *The Permanent Campaign*, 1−10; John Kenneth White, *The New Politics of Old Values*, 1−7.

61. Cutler to Mondale, May 27, 1983 (MP-MHS).

62. Mondale interview. For background on the impact of PACs on the Democratic Party see Thomas Edsall, *The New Politics of Inequality* and Robert Kuttner, *The Life of the Party*.

63. Galston interview; Johnson interview; Mondale interview.

64. Johnson interview.

65. Johnson interview; Galston interview; Kaplan interview; *Wall Street Journal*, May 10, 1983.

66. *Time*, October 10, 1983; Germond and Witcover, *Wake Us When Its Over*, 54.

67. Hart to Johnson, December 16, 1983 (MP-MHS); Gersh to Beckel, October 24, 1983 (Kaplan Papers).

15. Hart Attack

1. Galston interview.

2. Galston to Mondale, February 22, 1984 (Kaplan Papers); Mondale interview.

3. New York *Times*, January 14, 1984; January 29, 1984, February 18, 1984.

4. Jeffrey Porro, "Reagan's Arms Control Policy," *International Review* (March 1984), 21−22; Leslie Gelb, "Is the Nuclear Threat Manageable?" *New York Times Magazine* (March 4, 1984), 26−29; Strobe Talbott, *Deadly Gambits;* Roy Bennett, "Reagan's Foreign Policy," in *What Reagan Is Doing to Us,* edited by Alan Gartner,

Colin Greer, and Frank Riessman. On the political impact of Reagan's foreign policy see: Germond and Witcover, *Wake Us When Its Over*, 91-95, 335-36, 474-75; Elizabeth Drew, *Campaign Journal*, 13-15, 46-48, 101-14.

5. Washington *Post*, January 4, 1984 and February 27, 1984; New York *Times*, January 4, 1984.

6. Aaron interview; Washington *Post*, January 1, 1984; New York *Times*, December 12, 1983; September 21, 1983.

7. *Christian Science Monitor*, February 22, 1984; William Henry, *Visions of America*, 109-10; Goldman and Fuller, *The Quest for the Presidency*, 98-138; Germond and Witcover, *Wake Us When Its Over*, 124-39; New York *Times*, February 26, 1984; *Time* (March 5, 1984), 8-10.

8. Germond and Witcover, *Wake Us When Its Over*, 155-68; Goldman and Fuller, *The Quest for the Presidency*, 81-83, 128-40; Henry, *Visions of America*, 118-20.

9. *Newsweek* (July 23, 1984), 38.

10. Mondale interview; Leone interview.

11. Washington *Post*, February 29, 1984 and March 5, 1984; New York *Times*, March 1, 1984 and March 13, 1984; *Time* (March 12, 1984), 16-19.

12. Johnson interview; Leone interview.

13. Leone interview.

14. Washington *Post*, July 8, 1984; Eagleton to Mondale, February 29, 1984 (Kaplan Papers); Leone interview; William Mondale interview.

15. *Time* (March 12, 1984), 16-19; (March 19, 1984), 16-18; Washington *Post*, March 5, 1984; Mondale interview; Germond and Witcover, *Wake Us When Its Over*, 172-74; Henry, *Visions of America*, 134-35; .

16. Randall Rothenberg, "The Neoliberal Club," *Esquire* (February 1982), 37-46; "Son of Liberalism," *Saturday Review* (October 27, 1979); Sidney Blumenthal, "Hart's Big Chill," *New Republic* (January 23, 1984), 17-22; Richard Cohen, "Strains Appear as 'New Breed' Democrats Move to Control Party in House," *National Journal* (June 25, 1983), 1328-31; John Judis, "Neoliberals: High-tech Politics for the '80s?" *Progressive* (October 1982), 27-32.

17. Mondale interview.

18. On Mondale-Hart differences on issues see: Michael Gordon, "Behind the Defense Rhetoric, Some Key Differences Between Hart, Mondale," *National Journal* (April 14, 1984) 704-708; Timothy Clark, " 'New Ideas' v. Old—The Hart-Mondale Dispute Is Written in Shades of Grey," *National Journal* (March 17, 1984), 510-12; Timothy Clark, "Digging a Grave," *National Journal* (October 29, 1983), 2278; TRB, "Neoliberals, Paleoliberals," *New Republic* (April 9, 1984), 6, 41. Gary Hart's book *A New Democracy* should be read with Arthur Schlesinger's review in the *New Republic* entitled, "Requiem for Neoliberalism" (June 6, 1983), 28-30.

19. Johnson interview. Also see David Broder, "The Crucial Difference," Boston *Globe* (March 26, 1984), 19; Michael Barone, "Two America's Voting," Washington *Post*, March 19, 1984), A19.

20. Los Angeles *Times*, April 8, 1984; Leslie Gelb, "The Democrats and Foreign Policy," *New York Times Magazine* (December 18, 1983), 50; New York *Times*, April 9, 1984.

21. Germond and Witcover, *Wake Us When Its Over,* 175–79; Henry, *Visions of America,* 135–38.

22. Mondale interview; Beckel interview.

23. Isaacs interview.

24. Johnson interview.

25. New York *Times,* March 11, 1984; Tampa Speech, Tampa, Florida (Kaplan Papers).

26. Germond and Witcover, *Wake Us When Its Over,* 194–205.

27. Peter Hart and Richard Wirthlin, "Moving Right Along? Campaign '84's Lessons for 1988," *Public Opinion* (December/January 1985), 8–11, 59–62.

28. Washington *Post,* March 18, 1984; New York *Times,* March 18, 1984; Germond and Witcover, *Wake Us When Its Over,* 205–22.

29. Washington *Post,* March 18, 1984; Germond and Witcover, *Wake Us When Its Over,* 222–23; Henry, *Visions of America,* 139–43; Goldman and Fuller, *The Quest for the Presidency,* 162–68.

30. Mondale's Illinois "Stump Speech," (Kaplan Papers); Chicago *Tribune,* March 21, 1984; New York *Times,* March 21, 1984; Washington *Post,* March 21, 1984; Mondale interview.

31. Henry, *Visions of America,* 144–49; Goldman and Fuller, *The Quest for the Presidency,* 170–75.

32. *Time* (April 9, 1984), 20–22; Washington *Post,* March 30, 1984; New York *Times,* March 29, 1984; Henry, *Visions of America,* 149–50.

33. Donilon interview; Boston *Globe,* April 5, 1984; New York *Times,* April 4, 1984; *Time* (April 16, 1984), 12–14.

34. Eliot Cutler, "The Dialogue in Pennsylvania," April 4, 1984 (Kaplan Papers); Philadelphia *Inquirer,* April 11, 1984; Boston *Globe,* April 11, 1984; New York *Times,* April 11, 1984; Henry, *Visions of America,* 151–52; Germond and Witcover, *Wake Us When Its Over,* 248–52.

35. Boston *Globe,* April 4, 1984.

36. New York *Times,* April 20, 1984; Germond and Witcover, *Wake Us When Its Over,* 308–09.

37. Washington *Post,* May 10, 1984; Goldman and Fuller, *The Quest for the Presidency,* 186–89; Germond and Witcover, *Wake Us When Its Over,* 270–76, 308–09.

38. Morton Kondracke, "The Jacksonian Persuasion," *New Republic* (April 30, 1984), 13–16.

39. Mondale interview.

40. Beckel interview; Mondale interview; Morton Kondracke, "The Jacksonian Persuasion," *New Republic* (April 30, 1984), 13–16.

41. Germond and Witcover, *Wake Us When Its Over,* 158–60; Henry, *Visions of America,* 125–26; Mondale interview.

42. Mondale interview; Galston interview.

43. Johnson interview.

44. New York *Times,* May 24, 1984; Washington *Post,* June 6, 1984; Henry, *Visions of America,* 155–57; Germond and Witcover, *Wake Us When Its Over,* 313–16.

45. Washington *Post,* June 7, 1984.

NOTES TO PAGES 352–363 · 437

46. "Mondale's Primary Weakness Bodes Ill for November Hopes," *Congressional Quarterly* (June 16, 1984), 1441–1444; Washington *Post,* March 19, 1984; *Newsweek,* June 18, 1984, 26–37; Germond and Witcover, *Wake Us When It's Over,* 345.

47. New York *Times,* June 7, 1984.

48. Washington *Post,* June 10, 1984; Germond and Witcover, *Wake Us When Its Over,* 86–100.

49. Reilly interview; Mondale interview.

50. New York *Times,* July 6, 1984; "Come to Order," *New Republic* (July 30, 1984), 7; Dom Bonafede, "In Choosing a Running Mate Mondale May Have Uncovered a Hornet's Nest," *National Journal* (July 14, 1984), 1349–1351.

51. Reilly interview.

52. Mondale interview.

53. Ferraro's autobiography, *Ferraro: My Story,* should be read in conjunction with Sidney Blumenthal, "Once Upon a Time In America," *New Republic* (January 6/13, 1986), 28–36.

54. Berman interview.

55. Reilly interview.

56. Washington *Post,* July 15, 1984.

57. "Ferraro: Transforming the Political Landscape," *Congressional Quarterly* (July 21, 1984), 1721–1723; Alan Ehrenhalt, "United Democrats Court a Wider Audience," *Congressional Quarterly* (July 21, 1984), 1719–20; New York *Times,* July 15, 1984; *Time,* June 4, 1984, 18–22; July 23, 1984, 12–16; *U.S. News and World Report* (July 23, 1984), 21–23.

58. Boston *Globe,* July 11–12, 1984.

59. Washington *Post,* July 15–17, 1984; Rhodes Cook, "Lance vs. Manatt: Mondale's First Misstep?" *Congressional Quarterly* (July 21, 1984), 1731.

60. William Greider, "The Party of the Working Class Has Turned its Back on the Poor," *Rolling Stone* (July 19/August 2, 1984), 11–14, 110.

61. New York *Times,* July 8, 22, 1984; Timothy B. Clark, "Promises, Promises: Will the Democrats Play to Every Interest in the Platform?" *National Journal* (May 26, 1984), 1324–28; "The Democratic Convention," *Congressional Quarterly Weekly Report* (July 21, 1984).

62. Washington *Post,* July 17–18, 1984; Boston *Globe,* July 17–18, 1984.

63. Washington *Post,* July 19, 1984; Boston *Globe,* July 19, 1984.

64. Ferraro Convention Speech, July 19, 1984 (MP-MHS); Mondale interview.

65. Martin interview.

66. Leone, untitled and undated notes on the 1984 campaign (Leone Papers); Leone interview; Mondale interview; Johnson interview; Galston interview.

67. Mondale Convention Speech, July 19, 1984 (Kaplan Papers).

68. *The Baron Report,* #209 (July 30, 1984).

69. Washington *Post,* July 20–21, 1984; "Mondale's manifesto," *New Republic* (August 13/20, 1984), 5–6.

70. Martin interview; Galston interview.

71. Leone, untitled and undated notes on the 1984 campaign (Leone Papers); Harrison Donnelly, "Democrats Launch the Mondale-Ferraro Team," *Congressional Quarterly* (July 21, 1984), 1729–38; New York *Times,* July 22, 1984; Wash-

ington *Post*, July 23, 1984; *Time* (July 30, 1984), 24–27; *Newsweek* (July 30, 1984), 18–27.

72. William Greider, "Give 'Em Hell, Fritz," *Rolling Stone* (August 30, 1984), 10–15, 46; Richard Reeves, "Whose Party is it, Anyway," *New York Times Magazine* (August 5, 1984), 14–16, 37; Dick Kirschten and Richard Cohen, "Critical Decisions Confront Mondale as he Gears Up for the Fall Campaign," *National Journal* (July 24, 1984), 1428–40.

16. The Last Campaign

1. New York *Times*, August 1, 1984.

2. New York *Times*, August 3, 1984; Washington *Post*, August 6, 1984; *Newsweek* (August 13, 1984), 36–37.

3. Johnson interview; Ferraro interview.

4. Geraldine Ferraro, *Ferraro: My Story*, 148–150; Ferraro interview; Mondale interview; Johnson interview; Reilly interview; Beckel interview; Leone interview.

5. Mondale interview; Leone interview; Johnson interview.

6. Ferraro interview; Mondale interview.

7. Ferraro interview; Leone interview; Mondale interview.

8. Martin interview; Germond and Witcover, *Wake Us When Its Over*, 419.

9. New York *Times*, August 15 and 16, 1984; Goldman and Fuller, *The Quest for the Presidency*, 275–87; William Henry, *Visions of America*, 200–06; Germond and Witcover, *Wake Us When Its Over*, 442–46.

10. New York *Times*, August 14, 1984.

11. Ferraro interview; Johnson interview; Mondale interview; New York *Times*, August 22, 1984; Washington *Post*, August 22, 1984.

12. New York *Times*, August 22, 1984; September 3, 1984; Washington *Post*, August 22, 1984.

13. Jane Mayer and Doyle McManus, *Landslide: The Unmaking of the President, 1984–88*, 15; *Time* (August 27, 1984), 8–9; (September 3, 1984), 28–32; Washington *Post*, August 26, 1984.

14. Washington *Post*, August 25, 1984.

15. Johnson interview; *Time* (September 24, 1984), 21–22.

16. Mondale interview; Germond and Witcover, *Wake Us When Its Over*, 448–50.

17. Germond and Witcover, *Wake Us When Its Over*, 450–54.

18. Mondale interview.

19. Garry Wills, *Reagan's America*, 111.

20. Sidney Blumenthal, "Reagan the Unassailable," *New Republic* (September 12, 1983), 12.

21. Sidney Blumenthal, "Marketing the President," *New York Times Magazine* (September 13, 1981), 43; Mark Hertsgaard, *On Bended Knee*, 1–31; Henry *Visions of America*, 31–34; Jane Mayer and Doyle McManus, *Landslide*, 7; George Will, *The New Season*, 101.

22. Mondale interview; Peter Hart interview; Reilly interview; Johnson interview; Kaplan interview; Galston interview.

23. Leone, untitled and undated notes on the 1984 campaign (Leone Papers); Kaplan interview; Galston interview; Johnson interview; Leone interview; Donilon interview.

24. Reilly interview; Kaplan interview; Johnson interview.

25. Richard Leone, untitled and undated notes on the 1984 campaign, Leone Papers; Kaplan interview; Johnson interview; Reilly interview; Boston *Globe,* September 5, 1984; *Wall Street Journal,* September 7, 1984.

26. New York *Times,* September 5, 1984; Germond and Witcover, *Wake Us When Its Over,* 458–64; Henry, *Visions of America,* 226; Boston *Globe,* September 5, 1984.

27. Albert Hunt, "The Campaign and the Issues," in Austin Ranney, *The American Elections of 1984,* 140; *Wall Street Journal,* October 3, 1984; *Time* (September 10, 1984), 11.

28. *Time* (September 24, 1984), 13; New York *Times,* September 9, 1984.

29. Reilly interview; Robert Kuttner, "Revenge of the Democratic Nerds," *New Republic* (October 22, 1984), 14; Ronald Brownstein, "Mondale Gets Advice and Dissent from the Democratic Party's Left," *National Journal* (October 16, 1984), 1861–64.

30. Mondale interview.

31. Mondale interview.

32. Reilly interview; Mondale interview.

33. Mondale interview.

34. Robert Kuttner, *The Life of the Party,* 25; Ronald Brownstein, "Same Old Message?" *National Journal* (April 23, 1988), 1057–60.

35. Reilly interview; Mondale interview.

36. Mondale interview; Johnson interview; Berman interview.

37. Washington *Post,* November 6, 1984; Germond and Witcover, *Wake Us When Its Over,* 459–62; Goldman and Fuller, *The Quest for the Presidency,* 245–69; Michael Robinson, "Where's the Beef? Media and Media Elites in 1984," in Austin Ranney, *The American Elections of 1984,* 182.

38. George Washington Speech, September 25, 1984 (Kaplan Papers); New York *Times,* September 26, 1984; Washington *Post,* September 26, 1984.

39. Mondale debate tapes (MP-MHS).

40. Rubenstein to Eizenstat, September 16, 1984 (Eizenstat Papers); Leone interview; Goldman and Fuller, *The Quest for the Presidency,* 300–317; Germond and Witcover, *Wake Us When Its Over,* 494–505.

41. Mondale interview; Mondale-Reagan debate tapes (MP-MHS); New York *Times,* October 8, 1984; Washington *Post,* October 8, 1984.

42. Mondale interview.

43. Donilon interview; Mondale interview.

44. *Wall Street Journal,* October 9, 1984; New York *Times,* October 14, 1984; Henry, *Visions of America,* 249–50.

45. *Time* (October 22, 1984), 24–28; Johnson interview; Beckel interview; Leone interview; Isaacs Interview.

46. Leone, untitled and undated notes on the 1984 campaign (Leone Papers); Johnson interview.

47. Mondale-Reagan debate, October 21, 1984 (MP-MHS); New York *Times*, October 22, 1984, Washington *Post*, October 22, 1984.

48. Mondale-Reagan debate, October 21, 1984 (MP-MHS); Germond and Witcover, *Wake Us When Its Over*, 533–38; New York *Times*, October 22, 1984; *Time* (October 29, 1984), 22–26; Mondale interview.

49. Washington *Post*, November 3 and 6, 1984; New York *Times*, November 5, 1984.

50. Washington *Post*, October 26, 1984; November 3, 1984.

51. New York *Times*, October 25, 1984; November 2 and 5, 1984; Boston *Globe*, November 4, 1984; *Newsweek* (November 12, 1984), 30–31.

52. Washington *Post*, November 6, 1984; New York *Times*, November 5, 1984.

53. New York *Times*, October 18, 1984; *Time* (November 5, 1984), 18–20.

54. Washington *Post*, November 6, 1984.

55. Joan Mondale interview; William Mondale interview.

56. Washington *Post*, November 7, 1984; Minneapolis *Tribune*, November 7, 1984.

17. Liberal Legacies

1. William Chafe, *The Unfinished Journey*, 473.

2. Washington *Post*, February 19, 1985; February 20, 1985; Los Angeles *Times*, October 31, 1984.

3. *Wall Street Journal*, November 5, 1984; New York *Times*, November 8, 1985.

4. Washington *Post*, November 7, 1984.

5. New York *Times*, November 7 and 8, 1984; Washington *Post*, November 8, 1984.

6. Mondale interview; New York *Times*, November 7, 1984; William A. Schambra, "Progressive Liberalism and American 'Community,' " *The Public Interest* (Summer 1985), 31–42; Richard Reeves, *The Reagan Detour*, 104.

7. William Schneider, "An Insiders' View of the Election," *Atlantic* (July 1988), 31; William Galston, "The Future of the Democratic Party," *The Brookings Review* (Winter, 1985), 20; Peter Goldman and Tom Mathews, *The Quest for the Presidency*, 44–45.

8. Ronald Brownstein, "The Political Stakes," *National Journal* (January 12, 1985), 102–106.

9. John B. Judis, "Black Donkey, White Elephant," *New Republic* (April 18, 1988), 25. The DNC survey consisted of two parts. The first section contained the results of 43 focus-group sessions in six cities; the second, a 5,500-person nationwide poll. Though the national survey is available in at the National Archives in Washington, DNC officials claim that all copies of the focus-group study have been destroyed. See: "Principal Findings of the 1985 DNC Public Opinion Survey," DNC Papers (NA), Box 88–62.

10. Minneapolis *Star Tribune*, October 4, 1987.

11. Lewis letter to author, August 1990.

12. Robert Kuttner, "Dukakonomics," *New Republic* (July 18–25, 1988), 16–

18; Fox Butterfield, "Dukakis," *New York Times Magazine* (May 8, 1988), 22–25; New York *Times*, October 13, 1988. For general discussions of the 1988 presidential campaign see: Sidney Blumenthal, *Pledging Allegiance;* Jack W. Germond and Jules Witcover, *Whose Broad Stripes and Bright Stars?;* and Peter Goldman and Tom Mathews, *The Quest for the Presidency*.

13. Washington *Post*, October 13, 1988; Thomas Byrne Edsall, "Race in Politics," *The New York Review of Books* (December 22, 1988), 23; New York *Times*, November 18, 1988; Fred Siegel, "Campaign Across Cultural Divides," *Commonweal* (March 11, 1988), 138–41.

14. Minneapolis *Star Tribune*, November 20, 1988.

15. Washington *Post*, November 23, 1988; William Schneider, "Tough Liberals Win, Weak Liberals Lose," *New Republic* (December 5, 1988), 11; Washington *Post*, March 25, 1991.

16. Minneapolis *Star Tribune*, May 27, 1989.

17. Mondale comments at a DFL-sponsored forum entitled, "Liberalism in the 1990s," May 31, 1990. (Video in author's possession.)

18. New York *Times*, July 3, 1990; Washington *Post*, October 30, 1987.

19. Washington *Post*, May 27, 1990; January 29, 1990; October 13, 1991.

20. Washington *Post*, January 29, 1990; November 11, 1990; January 28, 1990.

21. Washington *Post*, January 29, 1990; November 11, 1990; January 28, 1990.

22. Beckel interview.

Bibliography

Manuscript Sources

ADA Papers	Wisconsin Historical Society (WHS)
Attorney General Papers	Minnesota Historical Society
DFL Papers	Minnesota Historical Society
DNC Papers	National Archives (NA)
Eisele, Albert	Private
Eizenstat, Stuart	Carter Library (CL)
Eizenstat, Stuart	Private
Fraser, Arvonne	Minnesota Historical Society (MHS)
Fraser, Donald	Minnesota Historical Society (MHS)
Freeman, Orville	Minnesota Historical Society (MHS)
Galston, William	Private
Humphrey, Hubert	Minnesota Historical Society (MHS)
Johnson, James	Private
Jordan, Hamilton	Carter Library (CL)
Josephs, Jeri	Minnesota Historical Society (MHS)
Kaplan, Marty	Private
Kubicek, William	Private

Leone, Richard	Private
Martin, Fred	Private
Mitau, Theodore	Minnesota Historical Society (MHS)
Moe, Richard	Private
Mondale, Clarence	Private
Mondale, Joan	Private
Mondale, Walter F.	Minnesota Historical Society (MHS)
Mondale, Walter F.	Personal Papers (PP)
Mondale, Walter F.	National Archives (NA)
Powell, Jody	Carter Library (CL)
Rafshoon, Gerald	Carter Library (CL)
Rauh, Joseph	Library of Congress (LC)
Romaine Papers	Wisconsin Historical Society (WHS)
Senate Budget Committee	Dirksen Office Building
Wortman, Donald	Private

Interviews

Aaron, David. Greenwich, Connecticut, October 26, 1987; New York, New York, October 2, 1989.

Beckel, Robert. Washington, D.C. March 2, 1989.

Berman, Michael. Washington, D.C, November 11, 1986; July 31, 1987; January 13, 1988₀nuary 26, 1990.

Blatnik, John. Washington, D.C, May 17, 1989.

Bookbinder, Hyman. Washington, D.C, August 30, 1989.

Brooks, William. Minneapolis, Minnesota. August 29, 1988.

Brzezinski, Zbignew. Washington, D.C. December 5, 1989.

Byrne, Phil. St. Paul, Minnesota. October 27, 1988.

Carp, Bert. Washington, D.C. July 23, 1987.

Carter, Jimmy. Letter to author, July, 1988.

Char, Harry. Telephone interview. May 12, 1989.

Clift, Denis. Washington, D.C. June 26, 1987.

Culver, John. Washington, D.C, July 28, 1987.

Donilan, Thomas. Washington, D.C. November 21, 1989.

Duncan, Charles. Telephone interview. November 10, 1989.

Eizenstat, Stuart. Washington, D.C. January 25, 1987; July 23, 1987; January 6, 1989; August 30, 1989.

Engleberg, Steven. Washington, D.C., July 27, 1987.

Farmer, John. Telephone interview. September 19, 1988.

Ferraro, Geraldine. New Haven, Connecticut, March 27, 1990.

Fraser, Arvonne. Minneapolis, Minnesota. March 9, 1989; June 7, 1989.

Fraser, Donald. Minneapolis, Minnesota. October 28, 1988.

Free, James. Washington, D.C. January 4, 1989.

Freeman, Orville. Washington, D.C, November 23, 1988.

Gallos, John. Telephone interview. May 3, 1989.

Galston, William. College Park, Maryland. March 1, 1989.

Goff, Robert. Minneapolis, Minnesota. June 12, 1989.
Hansen, Larry. Telephone interview, October 17, 1989.
Harrison, Gail. Washington, D.C, July 23, 1987.
Hart, Peter. Washington, D.C. November 21, 1989.
Hauge, Melvin. Elmore, Minnesota. May 12, 1988.
Hauser, William. Telephone interview. May 9, 1989.
Heany, Gerald. Telephone interview, May 23, 1989.
Holbrooke, Richard. New York, New York, January 25, 1990.
Hunter, Robert. Washington, D.C. July 28, 1987.
Issacs, Maxine. Washington, D.C. July 21, 1987.
Johnson, James. Washington, D.C, July 21, 1987; January 15, 1988; January 20, 1989; May 18, 1989; January 26, 1990; July 23, 1990.
Johnson, Sid. Washington, D.C. August 3, 1987.
Jordan, Hamilton. Telephone interview, April 14, 1987.
Joseph, Geri. Minneapolis, Minnesota. June 8, 1989.
Kaplan, Marty. Los Angeles, California. September 18, 1989.
Kirby, James. Telephone interview, May 4, 1989.
Kubicek, William. Minneapolis, Minnesota. November 22, 1988.
Lebedoff, David. Minneapolis, Minnesota. August 29, 1988.
Leone, Richard. New York, New York. October 2, 1989.
MacIver, Dale. Washington, D.C. May 18, 1989.
Martin, Frederick. Washington, D.C, January 5, 1989; March 1–2, 1989
McIntyre, James. Washington, D.C. March 22, 1988.
Miller, Penny. Alexandria, Virginia, June 21, 1988.
Moe, Richard. Washington, D.C. July 3, 1987; May 6, 1988; January 4, 1989; January 26, 1990.
Mondale, Clarence. Washington, D.C. June 2, 1987; June 21, 1989.
Mondale, Joan. Minneapolis, Minnesota. March 9–10, 1989; June 7, 1989.
Mondale, Lester. Telephone interview, December 12, 1988.
Mondale, Morton. Washington, D.C. July 23, 1990.
Mondale, Walter F. Washington, D.C. November 25, 1986; Minneapolis, Minnesota, February 8–12, 1988; May 9–10, 1988; August 31, 1988; November 22, 1988; March 9, 1989; June 7, 1989; August 11, 1989; January 3–4, 1990.
Mondale, William. Minneapolis, Minnesota. March 10, 1989.
Naftalin, Arthur. Minneapolis, Minnesota. October 28, 1988.
Nelson, Gaylord. Washington, D.C, June 22, 1988.
Nickoloff, Robert. St. Paul, Minnesota, June 8, 1989.
Olson, Wayne. Minneapolis, Minnesota. June 12, 1989.
Orde, Gordon. Elmore, Minnesota. June 12, 1989.
Powell, Jody. Washington, D.C. January 13, 1988.
Rafshoon, Gerald. Washington, D.C, March 22, 1988.
Rauh, Joseph. Washington, D.C. November 25, 1986.
Reilly, John. Washington, D.C, January 6, 1989.
Sanders, Edward. Los Angeles, California. September 19, 1989.
Schultze, Charles. Washington, D.C. September 24, 1987.
Scribner, Dwayne. Minneapolis, Minnesota. November 11, 1987.

Smith, William. Washington, D.C. January 15, 1987; January 15, 1988.
Spannaus, Warren. Minneapolis, Minnesota. November 22, 1988.
Vance, Cyrus. New York, New York. November 27, 1989.
Warren, Robert. Telephone interview. May 3, 1989.
Waters, Catherine. Telephone interview. May 24, 1989.
Wortman, Donald. Telephone interview. May 11, 1989.
Yahnke, Fritz. Elmore, Minnesota. May 12, 1988.
Young, Stanley. Telephone interview. May 9, 1989.

Newspapers and Periodicals

Boston *Globe*, January 1977–November 1984.
Brainard *Daily Dispatch*, December 1960–November 1964.
Chattanooga *Daily Times*, November, 1949.
Chicago *Tribune*, March 21, 1981.
Christian Science Monitor, February 22, 1984.
Columbus Ohio *Dispatch*, November 8, 1981.
Congress and the Nation, 1965–1984.
Congressional Quarterly, November 1964–August 1988.
Congressional Quarterly Weekly Report, November 1964–August 1988.
Des Moines *Register*, July 13, 1989.
Fairmont *Daily Sentinel*, December 1960–November 1964.
Fargo *Forum*, December 1960–November 1964.
Los Angeles *Times*, March 1972; July 1976–November 1980.
MAC Weekly, September 1946–December 1948; November 1967; November 1983–November 1984.
Minneapolis *Spokesman*, December 1960–November 1964.
Minneapolis *Star-Tribune*, January 1946–March 1989.
Minneapolis *Statesman*, November 1960–November 1964.
Minnesota *Daily*, July 13, 1984.
New Ulm *Daily Journal*, December 1960–November 1964.
New Republic, January 1964–December 1988.
New York *Herald-Tribune*, November 4, 1948.
Newsweek, January 1964–December 1988.
Philadelphia *Inquirer*, June 1982; April 1984.
Raleigh *Times*, March 2, 1982.
St. Cloud *Daily Times*, December 1960–November 1964.
St. Louis *Post-Dispatch*, November 1964; July 1, 1977.
St. Paul *Dispatch*, December 1960–November 1966.
The Nation, January 1964–December 1988.
Time, January 1964–December 1988.
St. Paul *Pioneer Press*, January 1948–March 1989.
Trimont *Progress*, December 1960–November 1964.
U.S. News and World Report, January 1964–December 1988.
Wall Street *Journal*, January 1976–November 1980; November 1983–November 1984.
Washington *Post*, January 1964–December 1988.

Government Publications

U.S. Congress. *Congressional Record.* Washington: Government Printing Office, January 1964–May 1976.

U.S. Congress. Senate. 91st Congress, 1st and 2nd Sessions. Committee on Labor and Public Welfare. Subcommittee on Migratory labor. 20 volumes. Washington: Government Printing Office, 1970.

U.S. Congress. Senate. 92nd Congress. 1st and 2nd Session. Select Committee on Equal Education Opportunity. 36 volumes. Washington: Government Printing Office, 1972.

U.S. Congress. Senate. 94th Congress. 1st Session. Select Committee to Study Governmental Operations with Respect to Intelligence Activities. Washington: Government Printing Office, 1975.

U.S. Congress. Senate. 92nd Congress. 1st Session. Committee on Appropriations. Washington: Government Printing Office, 1972.

U.S. Department of Justice. Federal Bureau of Investigation. Freedom of Information Act Request. Walter F. Mondale. April 1987.

U.S. Department of State. *Bulletin.* Washington: Government Printing Office, 1977–1980.

U.S. Government. Office of the Federal Register, National Archives and Record Administration. *Weekly Complication of Presidential Documents.* Washington: Government Printing Office, 1977–1980.

Books and Articles

Aaron, Henry. *Politics and the Professors: The Great Society in Perspective.* Washington: Brookings, 1978.

Abramson, Paul, Aldrich, John H., and David W. Rohde. *Change and Continuity in the 1980 Elections.* Washington: Congressional Quarterly Press, 1983.

Agranoff, Robert. ed. *The New Style in Election Campaigns.* Boston: Holbrook Press, 1976.

Alexander, Herbert E. and Brian A. Haggerty. *Financing the 1984 Election.* Lexington, Massachusetts: Lexington Books, 1987.

Auerbach, Laura K. *Worthy to Be Remembered: A Political History of the Minnesota Democratic-Farmer-Labor Party, 1944–1984.* Minneapolis: Democratic-Farmer-Labor Party, 1984.

Balz, Dan. "Long Has Won the Battle But Will He Win the War?" *National Journal.* (August 14, 1976).

———"When the Man from Louisiania's There, It's a Long, Long Road to Tax Reform." *National Journal.* (May 22, 1976).

Barnett, Lawrence. *Gambling with History.* Garden City, New York: Doubleday, 1983.

Barone, Michael. *Our Country: The Shaping of America from Roosevelt to Reagan.* New York: Free Press, 1990.

Barone, Michael. ed. *The Baron Report.* (July 30, 1984).

Barzman, Sol. *Madmen and Geniuses: The Vice Presidents of the United States.* Chicago: Follett, 1974.

Bass, Jack and Walter DeVries. *The Transformation of Southern Politics*. New York: Basic Books, 1976.

Bazelon, David T. *Power in America: The Politics of the New Class*. New York: New American Library, 1967.

Bell, Daniel. *The Coming of the Post-Industrial Society*. New York: Basic Books, 1974.

―――*The End of Ideology*. New York: Free Press, 1960.

Bell, Griffin. *Taking Care of the Law*. New York: Morrow, 1982.

Berman, Larry. *Planning a Tragedy*. New York: Norton, 1982.

Berman, Ronald. *America in the Sixties*. New York: Free Press, 1968.

Berman, William C. *William Fulbright and the Vietnam War*. Kent, Ohio: Kent State University Press, 1988.

Bernstein, Carl and Bob Woodward. *All the President's Men*. New York: Simon and Schuster, 1974.

Black, Earl and Merle Black. *Politics and Society in the South*. Cambridge: Harvard University Press, 1987.

Blegen, Theodore C. *The Land Lies Open*. Minneapolis: University of Minnesota Press, 1949.

―――*Land of their Choice: The Immigrants Write Home*. Minneapolis: University of Minnesota Press, 1955.

Blood, Robert O. Jr. *Northern Breakthrough*. Belmont, California: Wadsworth Publishing Company, Inc., 1968.

Blumenthal, Sidney. *The Rise of the Counter-Establishment*. New York: Times Books, 1986.

Blumenthal, Sidney. *The Permanent Campaign*. Boston: Beacon Press, 1980.

Bolner, James, and Robert Stanley. *Busing: The Political and Judicial Process*. New York: Praeger, 1974.

Bonafede, Dom. "Carter and Congress—It Seems that 'If Something Can Go Wrong, It Will.' " *National Journal*. (November 12, 1977).

―――"In Choosing a Running Mate Mondale May Have Uncovered a Hornet's Nest." *National Journal*. (July 14, 1984).

―――"Mondale, the President's Preacher, Spreads the Gospel of Jimmy Carter." *National Journal*. (December 1, 1979).

―――"Mondale at End of the Beginning of the Long Road to the Oval Office." *National Journal*. (January 22, 1983).

Bonner, Raymond. *Waltzing with a Dictator*. New York: Times Books, 1987.

Bornet, Vaughan. *The Presidency of Lyndon B. Johnson*. Lawrence: University of Kansas Press, 1983.

Braeman, John, Robert H. Bremner, and David Brody. *The New Deal: The National level*. Columbus, Ohio: Ohio State University, 1975.

Braestrup. Peter. *The Big Story*. New Haven, Connecticut: Yale University Press, 1983.

Brauer, Carl. *John F. Kennedy and the Second Reconstruction*. New York: Columbia University Press, 1977.

Brenner, Lenni. *The Lesser Evil: The Democratic Party*. Secaucus, New Jersey: Lyle Stuart, 1988.

Brinkley, Alan. *Voices of Protest*. New York: Vintage Books, 1983.

Broder, David. *The Party's Over.* New York: Harper and Row, 1972.

Brodie, Fawn M. *Richard Nixon: The Shaping of his Character.* Cambridge: Harvard University Press, 1983.

Brownstein, Ronald. "Mondale Gets Advice and Dissent from the Democratic Party's Left." *National Journal.* (October 16, 1989).

———"Same Old Message." *National Journal.* (April 23, 1988).

———"The Political Stakes." *National Journal,* (January 12, 1985).

Brzezinski, Zbignew. *Power and Principle: Memoirs of the National Security Advisor, 1977–1981.* New York: Farrar Straus Giroux, 1985.

Buchanan, Patrick. "Why Carter Must Go." *Rolling Stone.* (June 15, 1979).

Bundy, McGeorge. "Issue Before the Court: Who Gets Ahead in America?" *Atlantic.* (November 1977).

Burner, David. *The Torch Is Passed: The Kennedy Brothers and American Liberalism.* New York: Atheneum, 1984.

Burnham, Walter Dean. *The Current Crisis in American Politics.* New York: Oxford University Press, 1982.

———*Critical Elections and the Mainsprings of American Politics.* New York: Norton, 1970.

———"Death of the New Deal." *Commonweal.* (December 9, 1966).

Califano, Joseph. *A Presidential Nation.* New York: Norton, 1975.

Calleo, David P. *The Imperious Economy.* Cambridge: Harvard University Press, 1982.

Cannon, Lou. *Reagan.* New York: G.P. Putnam's, 1982.

———*President Reagan: The Role of a Lifetime.* New York: Simon and Schuster, 1991.

Capps, Walter. *The Unfinished War: Vietnam and the American Conscience.* Boston: Beacon Press, 1982.

Carson, Clayborne. *In Struggle: SNCC and the Black Awakening of the 1960s.* Cambridge: Harvard University Press, 1981.

Carter, Jimmy. *A Government as Good as Its People.* New York: Simon and Schuster, 1977.

———*Kepping Faith: Memoirs of a President.* New York: Bantam, 1982.

Caute, David. *The Great Fear.* New York: Simon and Schuster, 1978.

———*The Year of the Barricades.* New York: Harper and Row, 1988.

Chafe, William H. *The Unfinished Journey: America Since World War II.* New York: Oxford University Press, 1985.

Chester, Lewis, and Godfrey Hodgson and Bruce Page. *An American Melodrama.* New York: Viking Press, 1969.

Clark, Timothy. " 'New Ideas' v. Old—The Hart-Mondale Disputes are Written in Shades of Grey." *National Journal.* (March 17, 1984).

Clark, Timothy. "Digging a Grave." *National Journal.* (October 29, 1983).

———"Promises, Promises: Will the Democrats Play to Every Interest in the Platform?" *National Journal.* (May 26, 1984).

Clecak, Peter. *America's Quest for the Ideal Self: Dissent and Fulfillment in the 60s and 70s.* New York: Oxford University Press, 1983.

Cohen, Richard. "Critical Decisions Confront Mondale as he Gears Up for the Fall Campaign." *National Journal* (July 24, 1984).

Cohen, Richard. "Democrats Trying to Get Act Together to Confront Reagan's Budget Policy." *National Journal.* (December 12, 1981).
———"Strains Appear as 'New Breed' Democrats Move to Control Party in House." *National Journal.* (June 25, 1983).
Conkin, Paul K. *Big Daddy from the Pedernales.* Boston: Twayne Publishers, 1986.
Converse, Philip E., Warren E. Miller, et.al. "Continuity and Change in American Politics: Parties and Issues in the 1968 Election." *American Political Science Review. (December 1969).*
Cook, Rhodes. "Final Returns." *Congressional Quarterly.* (December 18, 1976).
———"Lance vs. Manett: Mondale's First Misstep." *Congressional Quarterly.* (July 21, 1984).
Cousins, Norman. "Bribery and Human Rights." *Saturday Review.* (April 2, 1977).
Cummings, Richard. *The Pied Piper: Allard Lowenstein and the Liberal Dream.* New York: Grove press, 1985.
Dallek, Robert. *Ronald Reagan: The Politics of Symbolism.* Cambridge: Harvard University Press, 1984.
Dean, John. *Blind Ambition.* New York: Simon and Schuster, 1976.
Dietz, Terry. *Republicans and Vietnam, 1961–1968.* New York: Greenwood, 1986.
Diggins, John P. *The Proud Decades.* New York: Norton, 1988.
Dinkins, Robert J. *Campaigning in America: A History of Election Practices.* Westport, Connecticut: Greenwood Press, 1989.
Dionne, E. J., Jr. *Why Americans Hate Politics.* New York: Simon and Schuster, 1991.
Divine, Robert. "The Cold War and the Election of 1948." *Journal of American History.* (June 1972).
Donnelly, Harrison. "Democrats Launch the Mondale-Ferraro Team." *Congressional Quarterly.* (July 21, 1984).
Donovan, Robert J. *Conflict and Crisis: The Presidency of Harry S. Truman, 1945–48.* New York: Norton, 1977.
———*Tumultuous Years: The Presidency of Harry S. Truman, 1949–53.* New York, Norton, 1982.
Dorman, Michael. *The Second Man.* New York: Delacorte, 1968.
Drew, Elizabeth. *American Journal: The Events of 1976.* New York: Random House, 1977.
———*Campaign Journal: The Political Events of 1983–1984.* New York: Mac-Millian, 1985.
———*Washington Journal: The Events of 1973–74.* New York: Random House, 1975.
———"A Political Journal." *New Yorker.* (November 21, 1983).
———"A Reporter at Large." *New Yorker.* (August 27, 1979).
———"Reporter at Large." *New Yorker.* (October 10, 1977).
———"Reporter's Notebook." *New Yorker.* (May 19, 1973).
———*Portrait of an Election: The 1980 Presidential Campaign.* New York: Simon and Schuster, 1981.

Dutton, Frederick G. *Changing Sources of Power: American Politics in the 1970s.* New York: McGraw-Hill, 1971.

Easterbrook, Gregg. "The Perpetual Campaign." *Atlantic.* (January 1983).

Edsall, Thomas. "Congress Turns Rightward," *Dissent.* (Winter, 1978).

——*The New Politics of Inequality.* New York: Norton, 1984.

——"Race in Politics." *New York Review of Books.* (December 22, 1988).

Edsall, Thomas, and Mary O. Edsall. *Chain Reaction: The Impact of Race, Rights, and Taxes on American Politics.* New York: Norton, 1991.

Ehrenhalt, Alan. "Harmonious Democrats Rally Behind Carter." *Congressional Quarterly.* (July 17, 1976).

——"United Democrats Court a Wider Audience." *Congressional Quarterly.* (July 21, 1984).

——*The United States of Ambition.* New York: Times Books, 1991.

Eisele, Al. "Walter Mondale: Has He Ever Been Tested?" *Atlantic.* (December 1974).

——*Almost to the Presidency.* Blue Earth, Minnesota: Piper Press, 1972.

Erskine, Hazel G. "The Polls: Demonstrations and Race Riots." *Public Opinion Quarterly.* (Winter 1967–68).

Evans, Rowland and Robert Novak. "Mondale and Harris: Humphrey's Establishment Radicals." *Harpers.* (October 1968).

——*Lyndon B. Johnson: The Exercise of Power.* New York: New American Library, 1966.

Farber, David. *Chicago '68.* Chicago: University of Chicago Press, 1987.

Fawcett, Edward and Tony Thomas. *The American Condition.* New York: Harper and Row, 1982.

Fenton, John M. *Midwest Politics.* New York: Holt, Rinehart and Winston, 1966.

Ferguson, Thomas, and Joel Rogers. *Right Turn: The Decline of the Democrats and the Future of American Politics.* New York: Hill and Wang, 1986.

Ferraro, Geraldine. *Ferraro: My Story.* New York: Bantam, 1985.

Fox, Richard. *Reinhold Niebuhr: A Biography.* New York: Pantheon, 1986.

Frady, Marshall. *Wallace.* New York: World Publishing Company, 1968.

——"Gary, Indiana." *Harper's.* (August, 1969).

——"Why He's Not the Best." *New York Review of Books.* (May 18, 1978).

Fraser, Steve, and Gary Gerstle. eds. *The Rise and Fall of the New Deal Order, 1930–1980.* Princeton, New Jersey: Princeton University Press, 1989.

Freedman, Murray. ed. *Overcoming Middle-Class Rage.* New York: Westminster Press, 1971.

Freeland, Richard M. *The Truman Doctrine and the Origins of McCarthyism.* New York: Knopf, 1972.

Freidel, Frank. *Franklin D. Roosevelt: Launching the New Deal.* Boston: Little, Brown, 1973.

Furlong, William Barry. "Mondale's Minnesota." *Horizon.* (October 1977).

Gaddis, John. *Strategies of Containment.* New York: Oxford University Press, 1982.

——*The United States and the origins of the Cold War, 1941–47.* New York: Columbia University Press, 1972.

Galbraith, John Kenneth. *A Life In Our Times*. New York: Ballantine Books, 1981.

Galston, William. "The Future of the Democratic Party." *The Brookings Review*. (Winter, 1985).

Garrow, David J. *Bearing the Cross*. New York: William Morrow, 1986.

——*Protest at Selma*. New Haven: Yale University Press, 1978.

Gartner, Alan, Colin Greer and Frank Riessman. *What Reagan Is Doing to Us*. New York: Harper and Row, 1982.

Germond, Jack and Jules Witcover. "All the Mondale Questions." *Washingtonian*. (February 1983).

——*Wake Us When It's Over: Presidential Politics of 1984*. New York: Macmillan, 1985.

——*Whose Broad Stripes and Bright Stars?* New York: Warner, 1989.

——*Blue Smoke and Mirrors: How Reagan Won and Why Carter Lost the Election of 1980*. New York: Viking, 1981.

Gieske, Millard and Edward R. Brandt. eds. *Perspectives on Minnesota Government and Politics*. Dubuque, Iowa: Kendall/Hunt Publishing Company, 1977.

Gieske, Millard. *Minnesota Farmer-Laborism: The Third-Party Alternative*. Minneapolis: University of Minnesota Press, 1979.

Gilman, Rhoda R., and June Drenning Holmquist. *Selections from Minnesota History*. St. Paul: Minnesota Historical Society, 1965.

Gillon, Steven M. *Politics and Vision: The ADA and American Society*. New York: Oxford University Press, 1987.

Gitlin, Todd. *The Sixties: Years of Hope, Days of Rage*. New York: Random House, 1987.

——*The Whole World Is Watching*. Berkeley: University of California Press, 1980.

Gjerde, Jon. *From Peasants to Farmers*. New York: Cambridge University Press, 1985.

Glad, Betty. *Jimmy Carter*. New York: Norton, 1980.

Glazer, Nathan. "Blacks, Jews, and Intellectuals." *Commentary*. (April 1969).

——"The Limits of Social Policy." *Commentary*. (September 1971).

Goldbloom, Maurice J. "Is There a Backlash Vote?" *Commentary*. (August 1969).

Goldman, Eric. *The Crucial Decade—and After*. New York: Vintage Books, 1961.

——*The Tragedy of Lyndon Johnson*. New York: Knopf, 1969.

Goldman, Peter, and Tom Mathews. *The Quest for the Presidency: The 1988 Campaign*. New York: Touchstone, 1989.

Goldman, Peter, and Tony Fuller. *The Quest for the Presidency 1984*. New York: Bantam, 1985.

Goldstein, Joel. *The Modern American Vice Presidency*. Princeton, New Jersey: Princeton University Press, 1982.

Goodwin, Doris Kearns. "Second Lady." *Ladies Home Journal*. (June 1977).

Goodwin, Richard. *Remembering America: A Voice from the Sixties*. Boston: Little, Brown, 1988.

Goodwyn, Lawrence. *Democratic Promise: The Populist Movement in America*. New York: Oxford University Press, 1976.

Gordon, Michael. "Behind the Defense Rhetoric, Some Key Differencees between Hart, Mondale." *National Journal*. (April 14, 1984).

Graham, Hugh Davis. *The Civil Rights Era: Origins and Development of National Policy*. New York: Oxford University Press, 1990.

Greenfield, Jeff. *The Real Campaign*. New York: Summit Books, 1982.

Greenstone, J. David. *Labor in American Politics*. New York: Vintage Books, 1969.

Greider, William. "Give 'Em Hell, Fritz." *Rolling Stone*. (August 30, 1984).

———"The Party of the Working Class Has Turned Its Back on the Poor." *Rolling Stone*. (July 19/ August 2, 1984).

———"The Education of David Stockman." *Atlantic*. (December 1981).

Gunther, John. *Inside U.S.A.* New York: Harper and Brothers, 1947.

Hacker, Andrew. "Is There a New Republican Majority?" *Commentary*. (November 1969).

Halberstam, David. *The Best and the Brightest*. New York: Random House, 1969.

———*The Unfinished Odyssey of Robert Kennedy*. New York: Random House, 1969.

———"The Man Who Ran Against Lyndon Johnson." *Harpers*. (December 1968).

———"McCarthy and the Divided Left." *Harpers*. (March 1968).

Hallin, Daniel C. *The Uncensored War: The Media and Vietnam*. New York: Oxford University Press, 1986.

Halvdan, Kohy and Sigmund Skard. *The Voice of Norway*. New York: Columbia University Press, 1944.

Hamby, Alonzo. *Beyond the New Deal*. New York: Columbia University Press, 1973.

———*Liberalism and Its Challengers*. New York: Oxford University Press, 1985.

Hammond, John. "Race and Electoral Mobilization: White Southerners, 1952–1968." *Politics Quarterly*. (1977).

Hargrove, Erwin C. *Jimmy Carter as President: Leadership and the Politics of the Public Good*. Baton Rouge: Louisiana State University Press, 1988.

Harris, David. *Dreams Die Hard*. New York: St. Martin's, 1983.

Hart, Gary. *A New Democracy: A Democratic Vision for the 1980's and Beyond*. New York: Quill, 1983.

Hart, Peter and Richard Wirthlin. "Moving Right Along? Campaign '84's Lessons for 1988." *Public Opinion*. (December/January 1985).

Harwood, Michael. *In the Shadow of Presidents*. Philadelphia: Lippincott, 1966.

Harwood, Richard. ed. *The Pursuit of the Presidency 1980*. New York: G.P. Putnam's, 1980.

Hathaway, William. *Minnesota Political Parties and Politics: Essays and Readings*. Minneapolis: University of Minnesota Press, 1976.

Hawley, Ellis. *The New Deal and the Problem of Monopoly*. Princeton, New Jersey: Princeton University Press, 1974.

Haynes, John Earl. *Dubious Alliance: The Making of Minnesota's DFL Party*. Minneapolis: University of Minnesota Press, 1984.

Henry, William A. *Visions of America: How We Saw the 1984 Election*. Boston: Atlantic Monthly Press, 1985.

Herring, George. *America's Longest War*. New York: John Wiley, 1986.

Hertsgaard, Mark. *On Bended Knee: The Press and the Reagan Presidency.* New York: Farrar Straus Giroux, 1988.

Hicks, Granville. "Liberalism in the Fifties." *American Scholar.* (Summer 1956).

Hochschild, Jennifer L. *The New American Dilemma: Liberal Democracy and School Desegregation.* New Haven: Yale University Press, 1984.

Hodgson, Godfrey. *America In Our Time.* Garden City, New York: Doubleday, 1976.

Hoffer, Eric. *The True Believer.* New York: Perennial Library, 1951.

Hoffman, Stanley. "View from Home: the Perils of Incoherence." *Foreign Affairs.* (February 1979).

Howe, Louise Kapp. ed. *The White Majority.* (New York: Random House, 1970).

Howe, Qunicy and Arthur Schlesinger, Jr. eds. *Guide to Politics, 1954.* New York: Dial Press, 1954.

Hu, Chang. "What is Behind U.S. Vice President Mondale's Visit to Mainland China?" *Issues and Studies.* (October 1979).

Huckfeldt, Robert and Carol Weitzel Kohfeld. *Race and the Decline of Class in American Politics.* Urbana: University of Illinois Press, 1989.

Hughes, Thomas. "Carter and the Management of Contradiction." *Foreign Policy.* (Summer 1978).

Humphrey, Hubert H. *The Education of a Public Man.* Garden City, New York: Doubleday, 1976.

Huntington, Samuel P. *American Politics: The Promise of Disharmony.* Cambridge: Harvard University Press, 1981.

Inglehart, John. "Congress Passes Major Child-Care Program Despite White House Veto Threat." *National Journal.* (October 23, 1971).

Issel, William. *Social Change in the United States, 1945–1983.* New York: Schocken Books, 1985.

Isserman, Maurice. *Which Side Were You On?* Middletown, Connecticut: Wesleyan University Press, 1982.

Jaynes, Gerald D. and Robin M. Williams. eds. *A Common Destiny: Blacks and American Society.* Washington: National Academy Press, 1989.

Johnson, Haynes. *In the Absence of Power.* New York: Viking, 1980.

Johnson, Loch K. *A Season of Inquiry.* Lexington, Kentucky: University Press of Kentucky, 1985.

Jones, Charles O. *The Trusteeship Presidency: Jimmy Carter and the United States Congress.* Baton Rouge: Louisiana State University Press, 1988.

Jordan, Hamilton. *Crisis.* New York: Putnam, 1982.

Judis, John. "Neoliberals: high tech Politics for the 80's?" *Progressive.* (October 1982).

———"Ted Kennedy's Faltering Campaign." *Progressive.* (February 1980).

Karnow, Stanley. "Carter and Human Rights." *Saturday Review.* (April 2, 1977).

Kearns, Doris. *Lyndon Johnson and the American Dream.* New York: Harper and Row, 1976.

Kelly, Harry. "Any Office But the Oval One." *Chicago Tribune Magazine.* (September 18, 1977).

Key, V.O. *Southern Politics in State and Nation.* New York: Knopf, 1949.

Kiker, Douglas. "Vietnam Issue." *Atlantic.* (November 1966).

King, Andrew A., and Floyd D. Anderson. "Nixon, Agnew, and the 'Silent Majority': A Case Study in the Rhetoric of Polarization." *Western Speech*. 35 (Fall 1971).

King, Anthony. ed. *The New American Political System*. Washington: American Enterprise Institute, 1979.

Kirschter, Dick and Richard Cohen. "Critical Decisions Confront Mondale as he Gears Up for the Fall Campaign." *National Journal*. (July 24, 1984).

Kleppner, Paul. *Chicago Elects a Black Mayor*. Dekalb, Illinois: Northern Illinois University Press, 1985.

Klien, Joe. "Mount Losemore." *New York*. (November 7, 1988).

Koch, Raymond L. "Politics and Relief in Minnesota During the 1930s," *Minnesota History*. (Winter 1968).

Kotz, Mary Lynn. "Washington's Joan of Art." *ARTnews*. (September 1978).

Kramer, Mark. "Jesse Jackson's New Math." *New York*. (October 24, 1983).

Kuttner, Robert. *The Life of the Party: Democratic Prospects in 1988 and Beyond*. New York: Viking, 1987.

Ladd, Everett Carl. "Liberalism Upside Down: The Inversion of the New Deal Order." *Political Science Quarterly*. (Winter 1976–77).

——"The Democrats Have Their Own Two-Party System." *Fortune*. (October 1977).

——*American Political Parties: Social Change and Political Response*. New York: Norton, 1970.

——*Transformations of the American Party System*. New York: Norton, 1978.

——*Where Have All the Voters Gone?* New York: Norton, 1978.

Larsen, Karen. *A History of Norway*. Princeton: Princeton University Press, 1948.

Lasch, Christopher. *The Agony of the American Left*. New York: Knopf, 1969.

Lass, William E. *Minnesota: A History*. New York: Norton, 1983.

Lebedoff, David. *The 21st Ballot: A Political Party Struggle in Minnesota*. Minneapolis: University of Minnesota Press, 1969.

Lekachman, Robert. "Death of a Slogan—The Great Society 1967." *Commentary*. (January 1967).

Lens, Sidney. "The American Labor Movement: Out of Joint with the Times." *In These Times*. (February 18–24, 1981).

Leuchtenburg, William E. *Franklin D. Roosevelt and the New Deal*. New York: Harper and Row, 1963.

——*In the Shadow of FDR*. Ithaca: Cornell University Press, 1983.

Levitan, Sar A. ed. *Blue-Collar Workers: A Symposium on Middle America*. New York: McGraw-Hill, 1971.

Lewis, Anthony. *Gideon's Trumpet*. New York: Random House, 1964.

Lewis, David. *King: A Biography*. Urbana: University of Illinois Press, 1978.

Lewis, Finlay. *Mondale: Portrait of an American Politician*. New York: Harper and Row, 1984.

Light, Paul. *Vice Presidential Power*. Baltimore: Johns Hopkins University Press, 1984.

Lipset, Seymour Martin, ed. *Party Coalitions in the 1980s*. San Francisco: Institute for Contemporary Studies, 1981.

Lipset, Seymour, and William Schneider. *The Confidence Gap: Business, Labor, and Government in the Public Mind.* New York: Free Press, 1983.

Loomis, Burdett, *The New American Politician: Ambition, Entrepreneurship, and the Changing Face of Political Life.* New York: Basic Books, 1988.

Lowi, Theodore J. *The End of Liberalism.* New York: Norton, 1969.

Lowry, Nelson. *The Minnesota Community: Country and Town in Transition.* Minneapolis: University of Minnesota Press, 1960.

Lubell, Samuel. *The Future of American Poltics.* New York: Harper Colophon Books, 1965.

———"Who Really Elected Truman?" *Saturday Evening Post.* (January 22, 1949).

———*The Hidden Crisis in American Politics.* New York: Norton, 1971.

Lukas, J. Anthony. *Common Ground.* New York: Knopf, 1985.

———*Nightmare: The Underside of the Nixon Years.* New York: Viking Press, 1976.

Madison, Christopher. "Mondale Walks Tightrope to Hold Black Support Without Risking Jewish Vote." *National Journal.* (September 8, 1984).

Mailer, Norman. *Armies of the Night.* New York: Signet Books, 1968.

Malbin, Michael. "Compromise by Senate Eases anti-Filibuster Rule." *National Journal.* (March 13, 1976).

Mallowe, Mike. "A Campaign in Black and White." *Philadelphia Magazine.* (May 1987).

———"Coming Apart." *Philadelphia Magazine.* (September 1989).

Martin, John Fredrick. *Civil Rights and the Crisis of Liberalism: The Democratic Party, 1945–1976.* Boulder, Colorado: Westview Press, 1979.

Matusow, Allen. *The Unraveling of America.* New York: Harper and Row, 1984.

Mayer, George H. *The Political Career of Floyd B. Olson.* St. Paul: Minnesota Historical Society Press, 1987.

McAuliffe, Mary. *Crisis of the Left.* Amherst: University of Massachusetts Press, 1978.

McDonald, John C. "The 'Rebirth' of Orville Freeman." *Progressive.* (November 1955).

McElvaine, Robert S. *Down and Out in the Great Depression: Letters from the Forgotten Man.* Chapel Hill: University of North Carolina Press, 1983.

McGovern, George. "Memo to the White House." *Harpers.* (October 1977).

McPherson, Harry. *A Political Education: A Washington Memoir.* Boston: Houghton Mifflin Company, 1988.

Mayer, Jane and Doyle McManus. *Landslide: The Unmaking of the President, 1984–1988.* Boston: Houghton Mifflin Company, 1988.

Melloan, George, and Joan Melloan. *The Carter Economy.* New York: John Wiley, 1978.

Miller, Warren E., and Teresa E. Levitin. *Leadership and Change: Presidential Elections from 1952 to 1976.* Cambridge: Winthrop Publishers, 1976.

Miller, William Lee. *Yankee from Georgia: The Emergence of Jimmy Carter.* New York: Times Books, 1978.

Mitau, Theodore. *Minnesota Politics.* Minneapolis: University of Minnesota Press, 1960.

Moffett, George D. III. *The Limits of Victory: The Ratification of the Panama Canal Treaties*. Ithaca: Cornell University Press, 1985.

Mondale, Joan. *Politics in Art*. Minneapolis: Lerner, 1972.

Mondale, Walter F. *The Accountability of Power: Toward a Responsible Presidency*. New York: David McKay, 1975.

———"Reporting of the Social State of the Union." *Trans-Action*. (June 1968).

Moore, Jonathan., ed. *Campaign for President: The Manangers Look at '84*. Dover, Massachusetts: Auburn House, 1986.

Morris, Charles. *A Time of Passion: America, 1960–1980*. New York: Harper and Row, 1984.

Moynihan, Daniel P. *Maximum Feasible Misunderstanding*. New York: Free Press, 1969.

Naftalin, Arthur. "The Tradition of Protest and the Roots of the Farmer-Labor Party." *Minnesota History*. (June 1956).

Namorato, Michael. ed. *Have We Overcome? Race Relations Since Brown*. Jackson: University of Mississippi Press, 1979.

Natoli, Marie D. *American Prince, American Pauper: The Contemporary Vice Presidency in Perspective*. Westport, Connecticut: Greenwood Press, 1985.

Neuman, Russell W. *The Paradox of Mass Politics: Knowledge and Opinion in the American Electorate*. Cambridge: Harvard University Press, 1986.

Newfield, Jack. *A Prophetic Minority*. New York: New American Library, 1966.

———*Robert F. Kennedy: a Memoir*. New York: New American Library, 1988.

Nie, Norman H, Sidney Verba and John R. Petrocik. *The Changing American Voter*. Cambridge: Harvard University Press, 1976.

Niebuhr, Reinhold. *The Irony of American History*. New York: Scribners, 1952.

Novak, Michael. *The Rise of the Unmeltable Ethnics*. New York: Macmillian, 1972.

O'Neill, Tip. *Man of the House*. New York: Random House, 1987.

Orfield, Gary. *Must We Bus?* Washington: Brookings, 1978.

Oshinsky, David. *A Conspiracy So Immense*. New York: Free Press, 1983.

Parmet, Herbert. *JFK: The Presidency of John F. Kennedy*. New York: Dial Press, 1983.

———*The Democrats*. New York: Macmillian, 1976.

———*Richard Nixon and His America*. Boston: Little, Brown, 1990.

Patterson, James T. *America's Struggle Against Poverty, 1900–1985*. Cambridge: Harvard University Press, 1986.

Patterson, Thomas. *The Mass Media Election: How Americans Choose Their President*. New York: Praeger, 1980.

Pierce, Neal R. *The Great Plains States of America*. New York: Norton, 1972.

Pells, Richard. *The Liberal Mind in a Conservative Age*. New York: Harper and Row, 1985.

Pestillo, Peter. "Can Unions Meet the Needs of a 'new' Work Force?" *Monthly Labor Review*. (February 1979).

Phillips, Kevin P. *The Emerging Republican Majority*. New Rochelle, New York: Arlington House, 1969.

———*Post-Conservative America*. New York: Random House, 1982.

———*The Politics of the Rich and Poor*. New York: Random House 1990.

Pinderhughes, Dianne M. *Race and Ethnicity in Chicago Politics.* Urbana: University of Illinois Press, 1987.

Podhoretz, Norman. *The Present Danger.* New York: Simon and Schuster, 1982.

———"Between Nixon and the New Politics." *Commentary.* (September 1972).

Polsby, Nelson. *Consequences of Party Reform.* New York: Oxford University Press, 1983.

Polsby, Nelson and Aaron Wildavsky. *Presidential Elections: Strategies of American Electoral Politics.* New York: Charles Scribners, 1976.

Pomper, Gerald. *The Election of 1980: Reports and Interpretations.* Chatham, New Jersey: Chatham House Publishers, 1981.

Porro, Jeffrey. "Reagan's Arms Control Policy." *International Review.* (March 1984).

Powers, Thomas. *Vietnam: The War at Home.* Boston: G.K. Hall, 1984.

———"Unwanted." *Commonweal.* (June 27, 1979).

———"Covering Carter." *Commonweal.* (July 30, 1976).

Qualey, Carlton C. "Pioneer Norwegian Settlement." *Minnesota History.* (September 1931).

Qualey, Carlton C., and Jon A. Gjerde. "The Norwegians," in June Drenning Holmquist, ed. *They Chose Minnesota: A Survey of the State's Ethnic Groups.* St. Paul: Minnesota Historical Society Press, 1981.

Quandt, William. *Camp David Peacemaking and Politics.* Washington: Brookings, 1986.

Raines, Howell. *My Soul Is Rested.* New York: Putnam, 1977.

Rankin, Bob. "Carter's Energy Plan: A Test of Leadership." *Congressional Quarterly.* (April 23, 1977).

Ranney, Austin. *Channels of Power: The Impact of Television on American Politics.* New York: Basic Books, 1983.

Ranney, Austin. ed. *The American Elections of 1984.* Durnham, North Carolina: Duke University Press, 1985.

Reed, Adolph, Jr. *The Jesse Jackson Phenomenon.* New Haven: Yale University Press, 1986.

Reeves, Richard. *The Reagan Detour.* New York: Simon and Schuster, 1985.

———"Inevitability of Teddy." *Esquire.* (February 13, 1979).

Reichley, A. James. *Conservatives in an Age of Change.* Washington: Brookings, 1981.

Rieder, Jonathan. *Canarsie: The Jews and Italians of Brooklyn Against Liberalism.* Cambridge: Harvard University Press, 1985.

Roberts, Wallace. "The Mondale Myth." *New Times.* (January 25, 1974).

Rodnick, David. *The Norwegians: A Study in National Culture.* Washington: Public Affairs Press, 1955.

Rolvaag, Ole. *Giants in the Earth.* New York: Harper and Row, 1929.

Ross, Irwin. *The Loneliest Campaign.* New York: New American Library, 1968.

Rothenberg, Randall. *The Neo-Liberals: Creating the New American Politics.* New York: Simon and Schuster, 1984.

———"The Neoliberal Club." *Esquire.* (February 1982).

Rovere, Richard. "Letter from the Garden." *New Yorker.* (July 26, 1976).

Sabato, Larry J. *The Rise of Political Consultants.* New York: Basic Books, 1981.

Sandoz, Ellis, and Cecil V. Crabb, Jr. eds. *The Tide of Discontent: The 1980 Elections and their Meaning.* Washington: Congressional Quarterly Press, 1981.

Sandel, Michael J. *Liberalism and the Limits of Justice.* Cambridge, England: Cambridge University Press, 1982.

Scammon, Richard M., and Ben Wattenberg. *The Real Majority.* New York: Coward-McCann, 1970.

Schambra, William A. "Progressive Liberalism and American Community." *Public Interest.* (Summer 1985).

Schandler, Herbert Y. *The Unmaking of a President.* Princeton, New Jersey: Princeton University Press, 1977.

Schell, Jonathan. *The Time of Illusion.* New York: Vintage 1975.

Schier, Richard. "Can the Democrats Learn from Defeat?" *Intellect.* (July–August, 1975).

Schlesinger, Arthur M., Jr. "Is the Vice Presidency Necessary?" *Atlantic.* (May 1974).

————*The Cycles of American History* Boston: Houghton Mifflin, 1986.

————*The Coming of the New Deal.* Boston: Houghton Mifflin, 1958.

————*The Crisis of the Old Order.* Boston: Houghton Mifflin, 1956.

————*The Politics of Upheaval.* Boston: Houghton Mifflin, 1960.

————*Robert Kennedy and His Times.* Boston: Houghton Mifflin, 1978.

————*The Vital Center.* Boston: Houghton Mifflin, 1949.

Schlesinger, Arthur, Jr., and Fred Israel. *History of American Presidential Elections, 1789–1968.* New York: Chelsa House, 1971.

Schmitz, Anthony. "Lessons from the Prairie." *Minneapolis City Pages.* (October 31, 1984).

Schneider, William. "An Insider's View of the Election." *Atlantic.* (July 1988).

————"JFK's Children: The Class of '74." *Atlantic.* (March 1989).

Schrag, Peter. "The Forgotten Americans." *Harper's.* (August 1969).

Schram, Martin. *Running for President: A Journal of the Carter Campaign.* New York: Pocket Books, 1977.

Seligman, Daniel. "The Search for a Liberal Agenda." *Fortune.* (August 24, 1981).

Semmingsen, Ingrid. *Norway to America: A History of the Migration.* Minneapolis: University of Minnesota Press, 1978.

Sexton, Brendan. "Middle Class Workers and the New Politics." *Dissent.* (May-June 1969).

Sexton, Patricia, and Brendan Sexton. *Blue Collars and Hard Hats.* New York: Randon House, 1971.

Shields, Mark. *On the Campaign Trail.* Chapel Hill: Algonquin Books, 1985.

Shogan, Robert. *Promises to Keep: Carter's First 100 Days.* New York: Thomas Y. Crowell Company, 1977.

Shrum, Robert. "Drafting of a President." *New Times.* (July 30, 1979).

————"Narrow Passage of Canal Treaty." *New Times.* (May 15, 1978).

Siegel, Fred. "Campaign Across Cultural Divides." *Commonweal.* (March 11, 1988).

Sitkoff, Harvard. *The Struggle for Black Equality.* New York: Hill and Wang, 1981.

Sitkoff, Harvard, ed. *Fifty Years Later: The New Deal Evaluated.* Philadelphia: Temple University Press, 1985

Small, Melvin. *Johnson, Nixon, and the Doves*. New Brunswick, New Jersey: Rutgers University Press, 1988.

Smith, Gaddis. *Morality, Reason and Power*. New York: Hill and Wang, 1986.

Smith, Hedrick. *The Power Game: How Washington Works*. New York: Random House, 1988.

Solberg, Carl. *Humphrey: A Biography*. New York: Norton, 1984.

Spiegel, Steven. "Carter and Israel." *Commentary*. (July 1977).

Stanley, Harold W. *Voter Mobilization and the Politics of Race*. New York: Praeger, 1987.

Steel, Ronald. "Rough Passage." *New York Review of Books*. (March 23, 1978).

Stein, Herbert. *Presidential Economics*. New York: Simon and Schuster, 1984.

Sternsher, Bernard. "Liberalism in the Fifties: The Travail of Redefinition." *Antioch Review*. (Fall 1962).

Stewart, John. *One Last Chance: The Democratic Party, 1974–1976*. New York: Praeger, 1974.

Stienfels, Peter. "Four Jimmy Carters." *Commonweal*. (August 13, 1976).

——— *The Neoconservatives: The Men who are Changing America's Politics*. New York: Simon and Schuster, 1979.

Stone, Gregory, and Douglas Lowenstein, eds. *Lowenstein: Acts of Courage and Belief*. New York: Harcourt Brace Jovanovich, 1983.

Stone, I.F. "Carter, Africa, and SALT." *New York Review of Books*. (July 20, 1978).

Sundquist, James L. *Politics and Policy: The Eisenhower, Kennedy, and Johnson Years*. Washington: Brookings, 1968.

——— *Dynamics of the Party System*. Washington: Brookings, 1973.

Szulc, Tad. "Our Most Ineffectual Postwar President." *Saturdady Review*. (April 29, 1978).

——— "The Vance-Brzezinski Squabble." *Saturday Review*. (July 8, 1978).

Talbott, Strobe. *Deadly Gambits*. New York: Vintage Books, 1984.

——— *Endgame*. New York: Harper and Row, 1979.

Turner, Kathleen J. *Lyndon Johnson's Dual War*. Chicago: University of Chicago Press, 1985.

Turner, Michael. *The Vice President as Policy Maker: Rockefeller in the Ford White House*. Westport, Connecticut: Greenwood Press, 1982.

Tweton, D. Jerome. *Depression: Minnesota in the Thirties*. Fargo: North Dakota Institute for Regional Studies, 1981.

——— *The New Deal at the Grass Roots*. St. Paul, Minnesota: Minnesota Historical Society Press, 1988.

Tyler, Gus. "Johnson and the Intellectuals." *Midstream*. (August/September 1967).

Vance, Cyrus. *Hard Choices*. New York: Simon and Schuster, 1983.

Viorst, Milton. *Fire In the Streets: America in the 1960s*. New York: Simon and Schuster, 1979.

Vogelgesang, Sandy. *American Dream, Global Nightmares*. New York: Norton, 1980.

——— *The Long Dark Night of the Soul*. New York: Harper and Row, 1972.

Wagner, James R. "Carter: Outsider at the Threshold of Power." *Congressional Quarterly*. (July 24, 1976).

Watson, Tom. "Liberal, Pragmatic Mondale Follows Careful Path to Power and Lead in Democratic Race." *Congressional Quarterly*. (October 8, 1983).

Wattenberg, Martin B. *The Decline of American Political Parties, 1952–1988*. Cambridge: Harvard University Press, 1990.

Wefald, Jon. *A Voice of Protest: Norwegians in American Politics, 1890–1917*. Northfield, Minnesota: The Norwegian-American Historical Association, 1971.

White, John Kenneth. *The New Politics of Old Values*. Hanover: University Press of New England, 1988.

White, Theodore. *In Search of History*. New York: Harper and Row, 1978.

——*The Making of the President, 1972*. New York: Atheneum, 1973.

——*Breach of Faith*. New York: Atheneum, 1975.

——*The Making of the President, 1968*. New York: Atheneum, 1969.

Wicker, Tom. "George Wallace: A Gross and Simple Heart." *Harper's*. (April 1967).

Wilkinson, J. Harvey. *From Brown to Bakke: The Supreme Court and School Integration, 1954–1978*. New York: Oxford University Press, 1979.

Will, George. *The New Season: A Spectator's Guide to the 1988 Election*. New York: Simon and Schuster, 1987.

Wills, Garry. *Reagan's America: Innocents at Home*. Garden City, New York: Doubleday, 1987.

——*Nixon Agonistes*. New York: Mentor Books, 1971.

——*The Kennedy Imprisonment: A Meditation on Power*. New York: Pocket Books, 1982.

——"Plains Truth." *Atlantic*. (June 1976).

Witcover, Jules. *Marathon: The Pursuit of the Presidency, 1972–1976*. New York: Viking, 1977.

Woodward, Bob, and Carl Bernstein. *The Final Days*. New York: Simon and Schuster, 1976.

Woodward, C. Vann. *Orgins of the New South, 1877–1913*. Baton Rouge: Louisiana State University Press, 1951.

——*Tom Watson: Agrarian Rebel*. New York: Oxford University Press, 1938.

——*The Strange Career of Jim Crow*. New York: Oxford University Press, 1974.

Wooten, James T. *Dasher: The Roots and Running of Jimmy Carter*. New York: Summit Books, 1978.

Zaroulis, Nancy, and Gerald Sullivan. *Who Spoke Up?* Garden City, New York: Doubleday, 1984.

Unpublished Material

Haynes, John Earl. "Liberals, Communists, and the Popular Front in Minnesota: The Struggle to Control the Political Direction of the Labor Movement and Organized Liberalism, 1936–1950." 2 volumes. Ph.D dissertation. University of Minnesota, 1978.

Naftalin, Arthur A. "A History of the Farmer-Labor Party of Minnesota." Ph.D. Dissertation. University of Minnesota, 1948.

Index